UBIQUITOUS COMPUTING, COMPLEXITY, AND CULTURE

The ubiquitous nature of mobile and pervasive computing has begun to reshape and complicate our notions of space, time, and identity. In this collection, over thirty internationally recognized contributors reflect on ubiquitous computing's implications for the ways in which we interact with our environments, experience time, and develop identities individually and socially. Interviews with working media artists lend further perspectives on these cultural transformations. Drawing on cultural theory, new media art studies, human–computer interaction theory, and software studies, this cutting-edge book critically unpacks the complex ubiquity-effects confronting us every day.

Ulrik Ekman is Associate Professor at the Department of Arts and Cultural Studies, University of Copenhagen.

Jay David Bolter is the Wesley Chair of New Media at the Georgia Institute of Technology.

Lily Díaz is Professor of New Media at Aalto University, Finland.

Morten Søndergaard is Associate Professor and senior curator of Interactive Media Art at Aalborg University Copenhagen.

Maria Engberg is Assistant Professor at Malmö University, Department of Media Technology and Product Development, and an Affiliate Researcher at the Augmented Environments Lab at Georgia Institute of Technology.

UBIQUITOUS COMPUTING, COMPLEXITY, AND CULTURE

Edited by Ulrik Ekman, Jay David Bolter,
Lily Díaz, Morten Søndergaard, and
Maria Engberg

NEW YORK AND LONDON

First published 2016
by Routledge
711 Third Avenue, New York, NY 10017

and by Routledge
2 Park Square, Milton Park, Abingdon, Oxon OX14 4RN

Routledge is an imprint of the Taylor & Francis Group, an informa business

Library of Congress Cataloging in Publication Data
Ubiquitous computing, complexity and culture / edited by Ulrik Ekman, Jay
   David Bolter, Lily Diaz, Morten Søndergaard, and Maria Engberg.
   pages cm
   Includes bibliographical references and index.
   1. Technology and the arts. 2. Ubiquitous computing—Social aspects.
   3. Information technology—Social aspects. 4. Computers and civilization.
   I. Ekman, Ulrik, editor.
   NX180.T4U25 2016
   303.48′34—dc23
   2015021399

ISBN: 978-0-415-74382-2 (hbk)
ISBN: 978-1-315-78112-9 (ebk)

Typeset in Bembo
by Florence Production Ltd, Stoodleigh, Devon, UK

Printed and bound in the United States of America by Publishers Graphics,
LLC on sustainably sourced paper.

CONTENTS

ILLUSTRATIONS

Figures

Plates

Tables

CONTRIBUTORS

Matt Adams co-founded Blast Theory in 1991, an artists' group making interactive work. Blast Theory is renowned for its multidisciplinary approach using new technologies in theatre, games, and visual art. The group has collaborated with scientists at the Mixed Reality Lab at the University of Nottingham since 1997. Blast Theory has shown work at the Venice Biennale, Sundance Film Festival, and at Tate Britain. Commissioners include Channel 4, the BBC, and the Royal Opera House. The group has been nominated for four BAFTAs and won the Golden Nica at Prix Ars Electronica. Matt has curated at Tate Modern and at the ICA in London and has taught widely. He has lectured at Stanford University, the Royal College of Art, and the Sorbonne. He is a winner of the Maverick Award at the Game Developers Choice Awards. He was a Thinker in Residence for the South Australian Government. He was the Visiting Professor in Interactive Media at the Royal Central School of Speech and Drama from 2007 to 2014. He is an Honorary Fellow at the University of Exeter.

Jay David Bolter is the Wesley Chair of New Media at the Georgia Institute of Technology. He is the author of *Turing's Man: Western Culture in the Computer Age* (1984); *Writing Space: The Computer, Hypertext, and the History of Writing* (1991; second edition 2001); *Remediation* (1999), with Richard Grusin; and *Windows and Mirrors* (2003), with Diane Gromala. In addition to writing about new media, Bolter collaborates in the construction of new digital media forms. With Michael Joyce, he created Storyspace, a hypertext authoring system. Bolter is now a co-Director of the Augmented Environments Lab and works closely with Prof. Blair MacIntyre, Prof. Maria Engberg, and others on the use of augmented reality to create new media experiences for informal education and entertainment.

Wendy Hui Kyong Chun is Professor and Chair of Modern Culture and Media at Brown University. She has studied both Systems Design Engineering and English Literature, which she combines and mutates in her current work on digital media. She is author of *Control and Freedom: Power and Paranoia in the Age of Fiber Optics* (MIT Press, Cambridge, 2006), and *Programmed Visions: Software and Memory* (MIT Press, Cambridge, 2011). She is co-editor of numerous volumes including the new edition of *New Media, Old Media: A History and Theory Reader* (Routledge, New York, 2015). She has been a member of the Institute for Advanced

Study (Princeton), a fellow at the Radcliffe Institute for Advanced Study at Harvard, and a Wriston Fellow at Brown. She is the Wayne Morse Chair for Law and Politics (2015); she has also been a visiting professor at Leuphana University (Germany), and a visiting associate professor in the History of Science Department at Harvard. She is currently completing a monograph entitled *Habitual New Media* (forthcoming MIT 2016).

Sean Cubitt is Professor of Film and Television and co-Head of the Department of Media and Communications at Goldsmiths, University of London; Professorial Fellow of the University of Melbourne; and Honorary Professor of the University of Dundee. His publications include *Timeshift: On Video Culture; Videography: Video Media as Art and Culture; Digital Aesthetics; Simulation and Social Theory; The Cinema Effect; EcoMedia;* and his most recent book *The Practice of Light* (MIT 2014). He has recently co-edited *Rewind: British Video Art of the 1970s and 1980s, Relive: Media Art History, Ecocinema: Theory and Practice, Ecomedia: Key Issues* (Earthscan/Routledge 2015), and the open access anthology *Digital Light* (fibreculture 2015). He is the series editor for Leonardo Books at MIT Press. His current research is on media technologies, environmental impacts of digital media, and on media arts and their history.

Lily Díaz is Professor of New Media, Visualization, and Cultural Heritage at the Media Lab in Aalto University, Finland. She leads the Systems of Representation research group and has been principal investigator for research and development projects in areas such as visualization and information design; design and implementation of digital archives related to cultural heritage; and design of interfaces for virtual reality. Her art and design work with cultural heritage has been shown at diverse national and international venues. She is a frequent guest and collaborator in conferences and activities in the area of media design and information technology as related to cultural heritage.

Jon Dovey is Professor of Screen Media at the Faculty of Arts, Creative Industries, and Education at the University of the West of England, Bristol. In 2008, he launched the Digital Cultures Research Centre of which he was the Director until 2012. He was a Knowledge Transfer Fellow at Bristol's Pervasive Media Studio from 2010 to 2012, co-authoring the *Pervasive Media Cookbook* (http://pervasivemediacookbook.com/). In 2012, he became the Director of REACT (Research and Enterprise for Arts and Creative Technologies) one of four Hubs for the Creative Economy designed to support collaborations between research and creative economies. He is co-author of *Game Cultures* (Open University Press 2006) and *New Media—A Critical Introduction* (Routledge 2009).

Ulrik Ekman is Associate Professor at the Department of Arts and Cultural Studies, University of Copenhagen. Ekman's main research interests are in the fields of cybernetics and ICT, the network society, new media art, critical design and aesthetics, as well as recent cultural theory. Ekman is behind the publication of *Ubiquitous Computing, Complexity, and Culture* (Routledge, 2015), a comprehensive anthology treating the question whether and how the development of network societies with a third wave of computing may have emerge another kind of technocultural complexity. He is also the editor of *Throughout: Art and Culture Emerging with Ubiquitous Computing* (MIT Press 2013). Ekman's publications include research articles and chapters such as "Editorial: Interaction Designs for Ubicomp Cultures," *Fibreculture* 19; "Design as Topology: U-City," *Media Art and the Urban Environment* (Springer 2015); "Of the

Untouchability of Embodiment I: Rafael Lozano-Hemmer's Relational Architectures," *C-Theory* (2012); "Irreducible Vagueness: Augmented Worldmaking in Diller and Scofidio's *Blur Building*," *Postmodern Culture* 19.2; and "Of Transductive Speed—Stiegler," *Parallax* 13.4.

Hasan Elahi is an interdisciplinary artist whose work examines issues of surveillance, citizenship, migration, transport, and borders and frontiers. His work has been presented in numerous exhibitions at venues worldwide and he has spoken to a broad range of audiences on his work at the Tate Modern, Einstein Forum, the American Association of Artificial Intelligence, the International Association of Privacy Professionals, World Economic Forum, and at TED Global. His work is frequently in the media and has appeared on Al Jazeera and Fox News. He is currently Associate Professor of Art at University of Maryland, roughly equidistant from the headquarters of the CIA, the FBI, and the NSA.

Katie Ellis is Senior Research Fellow in the Internet Studies Department at Curtin University. She has worked with people with disabilities in the community, government, and in academia, and has published widely in the area of disability, television, and digital and networked media, extending across both issues of representation and active possibilities for social inclusion. She has published five books on the topic and is series editor of *Routledge Research in Disability and Media Studies*. Her current projects include co-editing *The Routledge Companion to Disability and Media* with Gerard Goggin and Beth Haller, and *Disability and Social Media: Global Perspectives* (Ashgate) with Mike Kent. She commenced a prestigious Australian Research Council Discovery Early Career Researcher Award studying disability and digital televisions in 2013.

Maria Engberg is Assistant Professor at Malmö University, Department of Media Technology and Product Development, and an Affiliate Researcher at the Augmented Environments Lab at Georgia Institute of Technology. Her research interests include digital aesthetics, locative media, and media studies. She was one of the project members of *ELMCIP*, an international network and knowledge database for electronic literature, and is currently a project member of two large-scale research projects: *City Fables*. Artistic and design research (2013–2016) and *Living Archives: Enhancing the role of the public archive by performing memory, open data access, and participatory design* (2013–2017). She is the author of several articles on digital aesthetics, literature, and locative media, including augmented and mixed reality, and is writing a book on locative media aesthetic practices. She combines her theoretical work with digital media practice. She designs mobile media experiences for augmented and mixed reality for cultural heritage and informal learning experiences. With Jay David Bolter, under the name Far&Near, she creates augmented reality mobile media narratives.

Gerard Goggin is Professor of Media and Communications, University of Sydney. He is an Australian Research Council Future Fellow, undertaking a project on disability and digital technology. Gerard's books include *Routledge Companion to Disability and Media* (2017; with Katie Ellis and Beth Haller) and *Disability and the Media* (2015; with Katie Ellis), and with Christopher Newell, *Disability in Australia* (2005) and *Digital Disability* (2003). He is also widely published on mobile media, including *Routledge Companion to Global Internet Histories* (2016; with Mark McLelland), *Locative Media* (2015; with Rowan Wilken), *Routledge Companion to Mobile Media* (2014), *Global Mobile Media* (2010), and *Cell Phone Culture* (2006).

Mark Hansen teaches in the Literature Program and in Media Arts and Sciences at Duke University. His work focuses on the experiential and nonrepresentational effects of technologies. Hansen is author of *Embodying Technesis: Technology Beyond Writing*, *New Philosophy for New Media*, and *Bodies in Code*, as well as numerous essays on cultural theory, contemporary literature, and media. He has co-edited *The Cambridge Companion to Merleau-Ponty*, *Emergence and Embodiment: New Essays on Second-Order Systems Theory*, and *Critical Terms for Media Studies*. His book, *Feed-Forward: the Future of Twenty-First-Century Media* was published by Chicago in 2015. His current projects include *Designing Consciousness*, *Logics of Futurity*, and *Topology of Sensibility: Towards a Speculative Phenomenology*.

N. Katherine Hayles is Professor of Literature at Duke University. Her latest book is *How We Think: Digital Media and Contemporary Technogenesis*. She is presently at work on a book entitled *Enlarging the Mind of the Humanities: The Cognitive Nonconscious*. Her book *How We Became Posthuman: Virtual Bodies in Cybernetics, Literature, and Informatics* won the Rene Wellek Prize for the Best Book in Literary Theory for 1998–1999, and her book *Writing Machines* won the Suzanne Langer Award for Outstanding Scholarship.

Mogens Jacobsen is an artist. Born in Rome, Italy, in 1959, he lives in Copenhagen. In the 1990s, Jacobsen embraced the Internet and was one of the pioneers of Danish net art. Since 2001, he has mainly been working with installations often with interactive or networked elements. He is also a founding member of the Danish art group Artnode.org. He is Lecturer at the People and Computational Things department at the IT University of Copenhagen.

Giulio Jacucci is Professor at the Department of Computer Science and director of the Network Society Programme at the Helsinki Institute for Information Technology (HIIT). He has been Professor at the Aalto University, Department of Design 2009–2010. His research field and competencies are in human–computer interaction including mobile interaction, mediated social interaction, multimodal and implicit interaction, haptics and tangible computing, mixed reality, and persuasive technologies. Prof Jacucci has coordinated BeAware FP7 EU ICT that created the award winning EnergyLife application and was featured in Euronews, and currently coordinates MindSee on "Symbiotic Mind Computer Interaction for Information Seeking." He is also the co-founder and member of the board of directors of MultiTaction.com MultiTouch Ltd., a leader in interactive modular displays.

John Johnston is Professor of English and Comparative Literature at Emory University, where he teaches Modern and Contemporary Theory, Literature, Science, and Technology, Media Theory, and Biopolitics. He is the author of three books: *Carnival of Repetition*, *Information Multiplicity*, and *The Allure of Machinic Life*, and the editor of *Literature, Media, Information Systems*, a collection of essays by media theorist Friedrich Kittler. He is currently working on a book about techno-thrillers, science, and politics.

Sarah Kember is Professor of New Technologies of Communication at Goldsmiths, University of London. Her recent publications include a novel *The Optical Effects of Lightning* (Wild Wolf Publishing 2011) and a monograph *Life After New Media: Mediation as a Vital Process* (MIT Press 2012). She co-edits the journals of *Photographies* and *Feminist Theory*. Her previous publications include *Virtual Anxiety: Photography, New Technologies and Subjectivity* (Manchester University Press 1998); *Cyberfeminism and Artificial Life* (Routledge 2003); and the co-edited volume *Inventive*

Life. Towards the New Vitalism (Sage 2006). Her current research includes a feminist critique of smart media (*iMedia: The Gendering of Objects, Environments and Smart Materials.* Palgrave forthcoming), and an affiliated novel, provisionally entitled *A Day In The Life Of Janet Smart.* Sarah is also co-PI of an RCUK-funded project on digital publishing and part of the Centre for Creativity, Regulation, Enterprise and Technology (CREATe).

Jonas Löwgren is Professor of interaction design and co-founder at the School of Arts and Communication (K3), Malmö University, Sweden. He specializes in collaborative media design, interactive visualization, and the design theory of the digital materials. Jonas has taught interaction design in university and in companies since the early 1990s and initiated the influential two-year master's program and the Ph.D. program in interaction design at Malmö University. He has published over sixty peer-reviewed academic papers and four books, including *Thoughtful Interaction Design* (with Erik Stolterman, published by MIT Press), and a vast range of general-interest and pedagogical material. His design portfolio comprises some fifty projects from explorative research and professional contexts.

Malcolm McCullough is the author of *Ambient Commons—Attention in the Age of Embodied Information*, a book on information environmentalism and the benefits of attention to surroundings, and Professor of Architecture at the University of Michigan, where he teaches design studios and courses in pervasive computing. A widely recognized scholar on digital media culture, his previous books include *Digital Ground—Architecture Pervasive Computing and Environmental Knowing* (2004) and *Abstracting Craft* (1996), and on the basis of these he has given nearly fifty invited talks, in over a dozen countries. McCullough previously served on design faculty at Carnegie Mellon, and for ten years at Harvard. He is currently researching a book on responsive surfaces in architecture.

Cameron McNall is the Principal of Electroland LLC, an architect by training. The scope of his work is wide and encompasses architecture, sculpture, film, sound, interactive design, and installation art. He holds a Master of Architecture from the Harvard University Graduate School of Design and a Bachelor of Arts in Design from UCLA. He has received awards across disciplines, including the Rome Prize in architecture, NEA Fellowships in Sculpture, and numerous awards in film including presentation in the Siggraph theater. He co-founded the interactive art and design firm Electroland in 2002. Electroland is a pioneer in the creation of immersive interactive experiences. In the astonishingly short period of twelve years many aspects of what were experimental art projects have become commonplace aspects of social media and Internet culture. Cameron McNall discusses several projects and how they may be understood in the context of a rapidly shifting technology landscape.

Erin Manning holds a University Research Chair in Relational Art and Philosophy in the Faculty of Fine Arts at Concordia University (Montreal, Canada). She is also the director of the SenseLab (www.senselab.ca), a laboratory that explores the intersections between art practice and philosophy through the matrix of the sensing body in movement. Her current art practice is centered on large-scale participatory installations that facilitate emergent collectivities. Current art projects are focused around the concept of *minor gestures* in relation to color, movement, and participation. Publications include *Always More Than One: Individuation's Dance* (Duke UP 2013), *Relationscapes: Movement, Art, Philosophy* (Cambridge, MA: MIT Press 2009) and, with Brian Massumi, *Thought in the Act: Passages in the Ecology of*

Experience (Minnesota UP). Her forthcoming book projects include a translation of Fernand Deligny's *Les détours de l'agir ou le moindre geste* (Duke UP forthcoming) and a monograph entitled *The Minor Gesture* (Duke UP forthcoming).

Irene Mavrommati is an Assistant Professor at the Hellenic Open University, School of Applied Arts. She cooperates with the Research Academic Computer Technology Institute as an interaction design researcher and research project coordinator. She has previously been with Philips Design, the Netherlands (1995–2000). She has extensive experience in design and research, focusing in AmI systems' interaction, has led several EU FET research projects, and was member of the Disappearing Computer steering group. She holds a Ph.D. in Interaction Design in Ubiquitous Computing Environments (Dept. of Products and Systems Design Engineering, University of the Aegean), an MA (RCA) in Interactive Multimedia, and MA and BA in Graphic Design. She participates in art exhibitions with interactive installations, as well as technology exhibitions with research demo prototypes; she has authored several book chapters and research articles, with a focus in interaction within Ubicomp environments.

Dietmar Offenhuber is Assistant Professor at Northeastern University in the departments of Public Policy and Urban Affairs and Art + Design, where he heads the MFA program in Information Design and Visualization. He holds a Ph.D. in Urban Planning from MIT, and degrees from the MIT Media Lab and UT Vienna. His research focuses on the role of data representations in urban governance and civic discourse. Dietmar published books on the subjects of Urban Data, Accountability Technologies, and Urban Informatics. His artistic work has been exhibited internationally in venues including the Centre Georges Pompidou, Sundance, and the Hong Kong International Film Festival. His awards include the first price in the NSF Visualization Challenge, the MIT DUSP Outstanding Dissertation Award, the Paper of the Year Award from the Journal of the American Planning Association, the Jury Award at the Melbourne International Animation Festival, the Art Directors Club Silver Award, and awards from File São Paulo, Ars Electronica, and Transmediale.

Simon Penny, Professor of Electronic Art and Design, University of California, Irvine, is a media artist, teacher, and theorist with a longstanding concern for embodied and situated aspects of artistic practice. He explores—in both artistic and scholarly work—the intersections of computational technologies with cultural practices whose first commitment is to the engineering of persuasive perceptual immediacy and affect. Most of his artwork has involved the development of custom sensing and robotic systems. His current scholarly research centers around theories of embodied cognition. Penny was founding director of the Arts Computation Engineering graduate program at UCI. He was visiting professor, Cognitive Systems and Interactive Media masters, University Pompeu Fabra Barcelona, 2006–2013, and Professor of Art and Robotics Carnegie Mellon, 1993–2000. Recent honors include Labex International Professor, Paris8, and ENSAD 2014. See simonpenny.net.

Patricia Pisters is Professor of film studies at the Department of Media Studies of the University of Amsterdam and director of the Amsterdam School of Cultural Analysis (ASCA). She is one of the founding editors of *Necsus: European Journal of Media Studies*. She is program director of the research group Neuraesthetics and Neurocultures, and co-director (with Josef Fruchtl) of the research group Film and Philosophy. Her publications include *The Matrix of*

Visual Culture: Working with Deleuze in Film Theory (Stanford University Press 2003) and *Mind the Screen* (Ed. with Jaap Kooijman and Wanda Strauven, Amsterdam University Press 2008). Her latest book is *The Neuro-Image: A Deleuzian Film-Philosophy of Digital Screen Culture* (Stanford University Press 2012). For articles, her blog, and other information, see www.patriciapisters.com.

Helen Pritchard is an artist and researcher whose work is interdisciplinary and brings together the fields of Computational Aesthetics, Software Studies, Geography, and Material Feminisms. Her practice is both one of writing and making and these two modes mutually inform each other in order to consider the impact of computational regimes. Central to her work is the consideration of the material and affective structures of computation and the entanglement of nonhuman animals with ubiquitous computing. Her practice sometimes emerges as workshops, collaborative events, and computational art. She is a Ph.D. candidate in Geography at Queen Mary University of London and a researcher in the Department of Sociology at Goldsmiths, University of London. This research was supported by the RCUK Grant EP/G037582/1.

Jane Prophet is a Professor in the School of Creative Media, City University, Hong Kong. She is a British visual artist who combines mixed media, light, and computation to make installations, panoramic photographs, and sculptures from mathematical data. She completed her Ph.D. at Warwick University and her BA Fine Art at Sheffield Hallam. Her research interests include landscape design and sustainability, biological systems, and artificial life. Feminist technoscience underpins her collaborative works with life scientists and her practice-based interdisciplinary research has been recognized with a current Social Sciences Prestigious Fellowship from the Hong Kong Research Council to work with neuroscientists on a series of MRI experiments to explore death and contemplation as well as an earlier UK National Endowment for Science, Technology, and the Arts for interdisciplinary research.

Maria Poulaki is a Lecturer in Film and Digital Media Arts at the University of Surrey, UK. Her research focuses on complex structures and processes in films and other media texts as well as in the mind-body responses to them. Among her current projects are a monograph on film theory and cognitive science, and edited volumes on narrative complexity and compact cinematics.

David Rokeby's early work *Very Nervous System* (1982–1991) was a pioneering work of interactive art, translating physical gestures into real-time interactive sound environments. It was presented at the Venice Biennale in 1986, and was awarded a Prix Ars Electronica Award of Distinction for Interactive Art in 1991. Several of his works have addressed issues of digital surveillance, including *Taken* (2002) and *Sorting Daemon* (2003). Other works engage in a critical examination of the differences between human and artificial intelligence. *The Giver of Names* (1991) and *n-cha(n)t* (2001) are artificial subjective entities, provoked by objects or spoken words in their immediate environment to formulate sentences and speak them aloud. He has exhibited and lectured extensively in the Americas, Europe, and Asia. His awards include a Governor General's Award in Visual and Media Arts (2002), a Prix Ars Electronica Golden Nica for Interactive Art (2002), and a British Academy of Film and Television Arts "BAFTA" award in Interactive Art (2000). He currently teaches in the New Media department at Ryerson University and is Adjunct Professor at OCAD University, both in Toronto.

Teri Rueb (Doctor of Design, Harvard) works at the intersection of interactive media, sound, land, and environmental art. She is Professor of Media Study at the University at Buffalo where she also holds an affiliate appointment in the Department of Architecture and Planning. She is Founder and Director of Open Air Institute, a platform for connecting field-based learning and collaborative partnerships at the intersection of media, ecology, and culture. She is the recipient of numerous awards including a Prix Ars Electronica Award of Distinction for her project "Core Sample." Her work has been presented internationally and funded by the Arnold Arboretum (Harvard), the metaLab (Harvard), the Banff Center for the Arts, Edith Russ Site for Media Art, Klangpol, LEF Foundation, Turbulence.org, Artslink, and La Panacee Centre Pour Culture Contemporaine. She is currently working on a new sound walk for the Fenway in Boston, commissioned by the Isabella Stewart Gardner Museum.

Yvonne Spielmann is Dean of Faculty of Fine Arts at Lasalle College of the Arts in Singapore. Her book publications include *Video, the Reflexive Medium* (MIT Press 2008, Japanese edition by Sangen-sha Press 2011), which was rewarded the 2009 Lewis Mumford Award for Outstanding Scholarship in the Ecology of Technics. *Hybrid Culture* was published in German by Suhrkamp Press in 2010, and in English from MIT Press in 2013. *Indonesian Contemporary Arts* published in German from Logos Press in 2015, English edition forthcoming.

Henriette Steiner is Associate Professor at the Section for Landscape Architecture and Planning at the University of Copenhagen in Denmark. She graduated with a Ph.D. from the Department of Architecture at the University of Cambridge in 2008, after which she worked for five years as a Research Associate at the Department of Architecture at the ETH Zurich in Switzerland. She is author of *The Emergence of a Modern City—Golden Age Copenhagen 1800–1850* (Ashgate 2014) and has co-edited several books of which the most recent are *Phenomenologies of the City—Studies in the History and Philosophy of Architecture* (Ashgate 2015) and *Invisibility Studies—Surveillance, Transparency and the Hidden in Contemporary Culture* (Peter Lang 2015).

Morten Søndergaard is Associate Professor and curator of Interactive Media Art at Aalborg University Copenhagen (DK). International coordinator of the ERASMUS master of excellence in Media Arts Cultures; Founder and General Chair, IMAC—Interactive Media Arts Conference; Co-founder and head of board, ISACS—International Sound Art Curating Conference Series; Member of curator board, DIAS Art Space, Copenhagen. (2010–2015) Head of research of the Unheard Avant-garde project at the LARM audio archive infrastructure. Contributing editor at LEA (2011) and board member at OCR (2013); (2013) Editor, Mediekultur, DK. (1999–2008) Curator / Deputy Director at the Museum of Contemporary Art in Roskilde; (2004–2008) Head of advisory board, Kulturnet Denmark, The Danish Ministry of Culture, DK; (2009–2012) Senior Curator at the re-new festival of digital arts—www. re-new.org—in Copenhagen; In 2010 he commissioned Stelarc's Internet Ear Project for the exhibition *Biotopia—Art in the Wet Zone* (2010–2011); Curator of The *Unheard Avant-garde in Scandinavia* section at the *Sound Art—Sound as Medium for Art* exhibition at ZKM, Karlsruhe, March 2012–January 2013. Has published widely on curating, art and science, sound- and media art in English and Danish.

Orkan Telhan is an interdisciplinary artist, designer, and researcher whose investigations focus on the design of interrogative objects, interfaces, and media, engaging with critical issues in social, cultural, and environmental responsibility. Telhan is Assistant Professor of Fine Arts—

Emerging Design Practices at University of Pennsylvania, School of Design. He holds a Ph.D. in Design and Computation from MIT's Department of Architecture. He was part of the Sociable Media Group at the MIT Media Laboratory and the Mobile Experience Lab at the MIT Design Laboratory. Telhan's work has been exhibited internationally in venues including the 13th Istanbul Biennial, 1st Istanbul Design Biennial, the Armory Show 2015 Special Projects, Ars Electronica, Museum of Contemporary Art Detroit, and the New Museum of Contemporary Art, New York.

Kristin Veel is a Postdoctoral Research Fellow at the Department of Arts and Cultural Studies, University of Copenhagen. She completed her Ph.D. at the University of Cambridge, German Department in 2008 and has since then focused her research interests on the impact of information and communication technology on the contemporary cultural imagination, with a particular interest in issues of information overload and surveillance, and the way in which these are negotiated in film, art, and literature. She has published a monograph *Narrative Negotiations: Information Structures in Literary Fiction* (Vandenhoeck and Ruprecht 2009) and is co-editor of collected volumes, *The Cultural Life of Crises and Catastrophes* (de Gruyter 2012) and *Invisibility Studies—Surveillance, Transparency and the Hidden in Contemporary Culture* (Peter Lang 2015).

Joanna Zylinska is a Professor of New Media and Communications at Goldsmiths, University of London. The author of five books—most recently, *Minimal Ethics for the Anthropocene* (Open Humanities Press 2014) and *Life after New Media: Mediation as a Vital Process* (with Sarah Kember; MIT Press 2012)—she is also a translator of Stanislaw Lem's major philosophical treatise, *Summa Technologiae* (University of Minnesota Press 2013). She is one of the editors of *Culture Machine*, an international open-access journal of culture and theory, and a curator of its sister project, *Photomediations Machine*. She combines her philosophical writings and curatorial work with photographic art practice.

FOREWORD

N. Katherine Hayles

Ubiquitous Computing, Complexity, and Culture offers a rich array of resources to understand and analyze the third wave of computation, as digital media move off the desktop and into mobile devices, environmental monitoring systems, surveillance technologies, and a host of other embedded and pervasive technologies. Combining interviews and summary overviews with longer essays on specific installations and technical forms, this compilation takes its place among a mere handful of other texts about ubiquitous computing aimed toward researchers in the humanities and cultural studies. It therefore provides an excellent foundation for further inquiries into the broader and deeper implications of the cultural transformations associated with the third wave of computation in developed societies, including North America, Europe, Great Britain, China, Japan, and South Korea, among others.

Specifically, from my point of view it catalyzes questions about the kinds of cognitions these systems employ and the evolutionary trajectories they are tracing. In *What Technology Wants*, Kelly (2011) writes about complex technological systems as if they had desires of their own, among which he instances pervasiveness, complexity, and diversity. Certainly these qualities are self-evidently on display in ubiquitous computing, but it is far too simple to attribute their exponential growth to the technologies in themselves. As Raymond Williams astutely observed, such evolutionary potentials operate within complex social milieu in which many factors operate and many outcomes are possible: "We have to think of determination not as a single force, or a single abstraction of forces, but as a process in which real determining factors—the distribution of power or of capital, social and physical inheritance, relations of scale and size between groups—set limits and exert pressures, but neither wholly control nor wholly predict the outcome of complex activity within or at these limits, and under or against these pressures" (Williams 2003, 133).

Nevertheless, there is a kernel of insight in Kelly's analysis, namely that some technologies have a stronger evolutionary potential than others to grow, transform, and become pervasive. In these terms, we can say that computational media occupy a unique position among the thousands invented, developed, and marketed since World War II. Computational media are not necessarily the most important to human flourishing; that honor may go to water treatment and sanitation facilities. Nor are they the most transformative; transportation networks or agriculture could vie for that position. Neither have they saved more lives; antibiotics and a host of medical technologies would surely come in first here. *Rather, the uniqueness of computational media derives from a single but stunning property, which bestows on them a stronger evolutionary potential than any other: their capacity for nonconscious cognition.* It is this capacity that enables them to pervade every other complex technological system now in operation, including water treatment plants, transportation networks, and medical facilities. In fact, I cannot think of a single contemporary complex technological system that does not include computational components essential to its operation. We may draw an analogy with the planetary dominance of *Homo sapiens.* Humans are not the biggest species, nor are they the fastest or strongest. In one aspect, however, they outstrip every other species competing with them in their ecological niche (for better *and* for worse): their capacity for conscious and nonconscious cognition.

Notice that the above assertion focuses not only on higher consciousness, which enables humans to engage in language, mathematics, music, and other kinds of abstract thought, and not only on core consciousness, which humans share with many other mammals; it also includes nonconscious cognition. The last three decades of research in neuroscience, cognitive science, and related fields have revealed a level of neuronal processing inaccessible to consciousness but nevertheless crucially important to conscious/unconscious processes. Antonio Damasio (2000, 100) calls this the proto-self; I name it the cognitive nonconscious. Among the functions it performs within human brains are recognizing patterns too complex for consciousness to discern, learning from these patterns and forming anticipations from them, and integrating somatic markers from bodily systems into coherent body representations. More importantly, the cognitive nonconscious keeps consciousness from being overwhelmed by the flood of information arriving every microsecond from external and internal sources. Without the operation of the cognitive nonconscious, consciousness would likely become psychotic within seconds, assaulted by waves of information too complex, intense, and fast for it to handle.

It is not a coincidence that many of these processes are also exactly the functions performed by (external) computational media. Please do not misunderstand me here; I am *not* saying that the brain operates like a computer, a framework known as the cognitivist paradigm that still remains dominant in some areas of cognitive science. Notwithstanding the profound differences in embodiment between biological brains and computational media, including the brain's capacity for plasticity and its ability to incorporate all kinds of objects into its extended cognitive network noted by Andy Clark, the cognitive nonconscious as it operates in computational media performs many of the same *functions* as the cognitive nonconscious within the human neural system. These include sophisticated pattern recognition, learning, and anticipating developments from these patterns, and integrating diverse signals into coherent representations, for example in satellite imaging programs. And of course, the social and cultural roles played by computational media, including ubiquitous, pervasive, and embedded systems, are to keep human consciousness from being overwhelmed by the terabytes of information flowing through the atmosphere and around the globe, which these systems simultaneously generate, analyze, store, and transmit.

Why has the integration of technical nonconscious cognition with human cognitive capabilities not been more widely recognized and analyzed within the humanities and the culture generally? We may find a clue in how popular cultural typically represents sophisticated computational systems. From *Colossus: The Forbin Project* (1970) through *The Terminator* (1980) and up to *Her* (2012) and *Ex Machina* (2015), sophisticated computational systems have been represented as possessing consciousness—this in spite of the fact that no computational system has ever been shown to possess (as distinct from simulating) consciousness. It is as though because we ourselves are conscious, we cannot conceive of a powerful cognizer that would *not* have consciousness. In the cultural imaginary, sophisticated cognition equals consciousness equals thought.

The first step to bringing the cognitive nonconscious of technical systems into view, then, is to make a strong distinction between thought, associated with the complex achievements of higher consciousness in humans, and cognition, a much broader and more pervasive capability. In my view, all biological lifeforms have some cognitive capability, however humble, a position also advocated in Maturana and Varela's classic work (1980), *Autopoiesis and Cognition: The Realization of the Living*. This move enables an end run around tired questions about whether machines can think; they may not think in a human sense, for reasons that Hubert Dreyfus (1972, 1992) articulated decades ago, but they certainly cognize. Moreover, as they become smaller, more powerful, more networked, and more pervasive in the environment, their influences and interactions with human consciousness/unconsciousness, nonconscious cognition, and affect become correspondingly more important and pervasive, even as they may also become more diffuse and difficult to locate precisely.

The challenge before us, as I see it, is to understand in specific and detailed ways how technical cognitive systems work, at what points and through what mechanisms they impact human neural and bodily systems—conscious, unconscious, nonconscious, and affective—and the complex interactions that emerge between human and technical agencies. This is, of course, a tall order, one that will require extensive engagements and intellectual resources. *Ubiquitous Computing, Complexity, and Culture* is an essential contribution to this ongoing and crucially important project.

References

Cameron, James. 1980. Director. *The Terminator*.

Clark, Andy. 2008. *Supersizing the Mind: Embodiment, Action, and Cognitive Extension*. Oxford: Oxford University Press.

Damasio, Antonio. 2000. *The Feeling of What Happens: Body and Emotion in the Making of Consciousness*. New York: Mariner Books.

Dreyfus, Hubert. 1972. *What Computers Can't Do: A Critique of Artificial Reason*. Cambridge, MA: MIT Press.

Dreyfuss, Hubert. 1992. *What Computers Still Can't Do: A Critique of Artificial Reason*. Cambridge, MA: MIT Press.

Garland, Alex. 2015. Director. *Ex Machina*.

Jonze, Spike. 2012. Director. *Her*. DVD.

Kelly, Kevin. 2011. *What Technology Wants*. New York: Penguin.

Maturana, Humberto R. and Francisco J. Varela. 1980. *Autopoiesis and Cognition: The Realization of the Living*. Dordrecht, The Netherlands: D. Reidel Publishing.

Sargent, Joseph. 1970. Director. *Colossus: The Forbin Project*.

Williams, Raymond, Ed. 2003. *Television: Technology and Cultural Form*, 3rd edition. London: Routledge.

INTRODUCTION

Complex Ubiquity-Effects

Ulrik Ekman

Prelude

- Three tourists stop in front of a boom coming down at the entrance to a nature reserve, reading on the little display on the boom that the maximum number of people permitted in the reserve has been reached at this point in time, this close to the breeding season.
- A series of digital signposts and the GPS in the car lead the driver and his family down a set of side streets due to road repair and construction.
- A media art installation embedded in the city square has dynamic and interactive video portraits appear on the ground in front of busy passers-by and makes them stop, play, and wonder how they were followed and picked out beforehand.
- Every once in a while, a 17-year-old son gets irritated at having to use the Internet on his mother's computer—because he is quite frequently asked to consider buying new candles, bathrobes, bras, and women's magazines.
- An academic who gets home after a long day at work only vaguely notices that the lighting in the smart home is subdued a bit, the vacuum cleaner stops, and a string quartet replaces the pop songs from yesterday.

When our environments or surrounds today operate and occasionally display or demonstrate somewhat unexpected intelligent attention to us as individuals and social groups, this tends to disturb us in a number of ways. A supposedly "natural" setting turns out to be nothing if not a highly artificial context or an information-intensive environment, and it appears attentively oriented towards us rather than being neutral or perfectly non-caring. Second, a set of temporal processes and their events impinge upon us rather than just being independently ongoing. What is more, their directedness towards us appears to come not from distant otherness but rather from intimate sameness, in the sense that these processes and events often have the character of anticipating what we intend in consciousness and in embodied practices. Then, we are also, and not least, disturbed by vestiges of autonomy, artificial intelligence, and artificial life: Environmental spacing and temporalization harbor an unexpected form of intelligently organized and organizing complexity, different but perhaps not necessarily altogether foreign to the ways in which we exist, think, and comfort ourselves.

This set of experientially and practically disturbing behaviors is often what we today encounter as the consequence of the fact that technical context-awareness with an anticipatory pre-understanding of humanly meaningful intention and action has been a central and explicitly declared goal for the development of the third wave of information technology during the last twenty years. The intensified development of the logic of network societies, since the mid-1990s and in the wake of mainframe computers and personal computers as the two first waves, is now increasingly evident, although by far the most of this technical development is embedded infrastructurally to our cultures, mostly invisibly and as the vast reservoir of our "technological unconscious" (Thrift 2004). However, both in everyday culture and in research and development, we now overtly engage more and more often with such behaviors, without necessarily knowing how to approach them. For instance, this is the case with respect to the personalities and spatio-temporal practices built into Garmin, Magellan, or TomTom GPS and navigation systems, browsers, and apps such as Google Now and Facebook with detailed relational database knowledge of one's individual profile, interests, and desires. It is also the case when intelligent buildings and smart environments respond and interact with inhabitants and passers-by, and when networks of sensors and actuators monitor and help control traffic. It is the case when tracking systems monitor movement and help "secure" behavior in public urban spaces. Certainly, we notice this when being reminded that more and more people relate via mobile phones or computational entities that house intelligent assistants such as Siri, Cortana, Braina, Echo, Hidi, Vlingo, S Voice, or Voice Mate.

This already hints at a very important set of developmental technocultural tendencies, which is still in need of sustained public debate and critical scrutiny. It already gestures at developments whose insides, directions, and values are largely unknown except to specialists, although they are well on their way to change physical environments, computing, networking, everyday cultural practices, and our forms of social and individual life, our modes of interaction, media and communication, perception, and sensation. This might already be sufficient to observe that it is a gradually more pressing concern to figure out how one is to analyze, evaluate, and perhaps contribute actively to the mutual development of human and technical context-awareness, temporal anticipation, and autonomous agency, which is on the move in and across the network societies in the second decade of the 2000s.

FIGURE 0.1 The virtual assistant Cortana for Microsoft mobile phones

As citizens and as researchers, we are unlikely to know already how to approach the current co-development of the cultural practices of human social and individual lives and larger technical trends at stake in these systemic behaviors, such as ubiquitous computing (ubicomp), pervasive computing, ambient intelligence, and the Internet of Things. We are perhaps only in the early stages of articulating the issues to be debated, a task made more demanding because cultural practices and forms of life are to a large extent habitual and tacit knowledge, and because the technologies may appear "ubiquitous," "pervasive," or "ambient" but most often do so inconspicuously and invisibly. For example, the key concepts and aims are still underdeveloped and in need of further articulation. It is not altogether clear what is meant by an information-technological system demonstrating "intelligent and meaningful human-oriented context-awareness." It is also not clear, even with access to essential parts of modern human and social science, how to think of "human context-awareness," nor how to specify the role of technics in relation to this. As is clear in Figure 0.2, however, these developments are ongoing, with some speed, and that quite some debate is called for as regards their reach, their aims, their implicit sets of values, their views of human life and culture, society, and technology.

This anthology proceeds, then, from a certain recognition of difficulties, epistemic lack, and disempowerment in order to begin bringing about at least small changes, whose ramifications can nonetheless be quite uncontrollable. This book takes off in a situation of some adversity, delay, and displacement. It seeks to alter a state in which we only know that the complexity of the evolving phenomenon under scrutiny seems unmanageable, and that recognition of the need for an orchestrated transdisciplinary effort is perhaps not enough because it remains uncertain that insights from the disciplines involved can gain a foothold.

As citizens and researchers, what kind of sociocultural theoretical approach would you mobilize in the face of an innovative developmental phenomenon like the new technical and human movements and relations appearing and disappearing as interactivity in a smart building with a vast set of networks of sensors and actuators (e.g., responsive architectures with emergent spatializing designs)? What kind of sociocultural theoretical approach would you suggest when encountering the technical and human movements and relations forthcoming and dwindling as interactivity in and around your national library, involving hundreds of thousands of human interactants on the move along with several million entities tagged with radio frequency

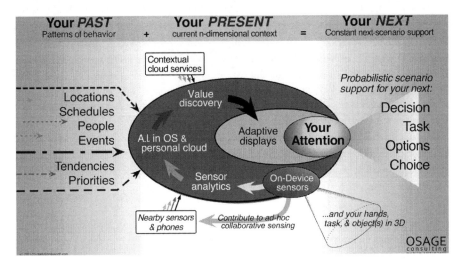

FIGURE 0.2 Context-awareness

Diagram courtesy of Clark Dodsworth, San Francisco: clark@dodsworth.com identifications (RFIDs)? What kind of sociocultural theoretical approach would you adopt in the face of the multiplicities of technical and human movements and relations coming together and withdrawing interactively in and around JFK, LAX, or Frankfurt Airport, including those of human individuals and social groupings, mobiles, heating, ventilation, and lighting systems, transport systems, security systems, and airplanes?

As a researcher in the human and social sciences concerned with finding or developing an adequate set of tools in sociocultural theory, one might find this is a tall order. One might have read, for instance, Gilbert Simondon and others on relational ontologies, Gilles Deleuze and Felix Guattari on assemblages, and Michel Serres on translation without a metalanguage. One might also have read Humberto Maturana and Francisco Varela on self-organization, and various kinds of science and technology studies (STS) or actor-network theory from early Bruno Latour onward. However, one then still is not necessarily convinced that one would have the right kind of tools to approach the kinds of "complexity" and "emergence" dynamically at play here.

As a researcher in hardware engineering, software development, or interaction design, would you be quite sure that your current studies of network topology, dynamic systems theory, along with certain recent sources treating of swarm intelligence, flocking, ant colonization, and Alife would be adequate to the kinds of complexity and emergence on the horizon for human-oriented ubicomp cultures?

Current Situations and Developments

We arguably find ourselves, as network society citizens and as researchers, in the process of engaging with a third wave of computation "throughout" or "all around," for example, in our practical lives, at work, at home, in leisure activities and games, in the media art at the museum, or in the everyday culture of the public sphere. One meets it, for example, via the frequent auditory signals and tactile vibrations from mobile phones, when drawing upon the services afforded by the massive development of wireless devices and overlapping networks (including WPAN, WLAN, and WMAN or WiMax). Likewise, one encounters it when engaging with the haptic interfaces and auditory culture of MP3 players (iPods), when partaking of the reading anywhere of e-books on networked iPads, Kindles, and other tablets, and when interacting with the RFID tagging of our libraries or supermarkets. We are in the enculturation of this third wave when getting upset by systemic locative and navigational practices, when witnessing the entry into our workplaces of interactive whiteboards, and during our increasingly frequent architectural encounters with smart buildings, sentient cities, and more expanded information-intensive environments. You meet it via the experience of augmented museum tours. As media artists working with surveillance art projects have also been demonstrating, as in Plates 1, 2, and 3, you encounter it not least in the rapid and extensive widening of effects from surveillance (CCTV, webcams, security video cameras, sensor networks, profiling and behavioral recognition, as well as biometrics and digital identity systems).

Considering all this alongside the rise of wearable computing, prosthetics, and implants, perhaps one can best appraise the more general contour of this actual development as a serpent-like and environmental recoiling in and around the life of the *anthropos* as such. One of the better examples is the integrative and embedding effort characteristic of pervasive healthcare—in the hospital and at the doctor's, of course, but certainly also throughout the milieux of the city and into the contexts of homes. On a much larger scale, one would want to consider the complexity of the orbiting satellites whose operationality underpins much of what goes on in ubicomp cultures in terms of networking, communication, and navigation (Plate 4).

One still has to acknowledge that both ubicomp and its enculturation call for further clarifications. For even now, more than twenty years after Mark Weiser's initial coinage of "ubiquitous computing" as a term (1988), and more than fifteen years after his seminal papers (Weiser 1991, 1993, 1994, 1997, 1999; Weiser and Brown 1995; Weiser, Gold and Brown 1999), there is not yet a general consensus as regards the definition of "ubicomp." In this book, the assumption is that the field of inquiry involves in particular a third epoch of computing (after the mainframe and the personal computer). This is taken to be one preoccupied with the question whether and how computing is, should be, or could be moving on from existing primarily as distinctly recognizable units so as to be multiplicitously and pervasively integrated into our living and working environments and perhaps altogether invisibly embedded in our life world and life form. In that case, a working definition of "ubiquitous computing" would be a sociocultural *and* technical thrust to integrate and/or embed computing pervasively, to have information processing thoroughly integrated with or embedded into everyday objects and activities, including those pertaining to human bodies and their bodily parts. Thus, if somebody is living with ubiquitous computing, it does not concern, or only marginally and momentarily concerns, engaging consciously with a single device or application for some definite purpose. Rather, it concerns engaging with multiple computational devices and systems simultaneously during more or less ordinary activities, without necessarily being aware of doing so. This is also to say that the models and practical implementations of ubiquitous computing addressed here largely adhere to something like Weiser's vision of a myriad of small, inexpensive, robust, networked information processing devices, perhaps mobile but certainly distributed at all scales throughout everyday life and culture, most often turned towards distinctly mundane, commonsensical, and commonplace ends. This sort of extensive distribution is referred to as a development of "out-of-the-box computing." This is due not least to Weiser's suggestive notion of a process of drawing computers out of their electronic shells so as to have the "virtuality" of computer-readable data and "all the different ways in which it can be altered, processed, and analyzed . . . brought into the physical world" (Weiser 1991, 98).

Technically speaking, the kinds and degrees of actualization of "embodied virtuality" as entire environments, processes of temporalization, and modes of technical and human individuation[1] are not least affected by the ideas and forces that shaped computing during the final years of the 1990s and the first decade of the new millennium. Ubicomp cultures have become more than a potential and a much more pressing factual concern in tandem with decreasing general hardware costs, reduction in power requirements, implementation of ubiquitous ad hoc networking (including high speed and/or wireless LAN and WAN), increasing development of mobile and distributed computing, widening of the ongoing deployment of embedded computation to include networked communications among units, deployment of materials for miniaturization and further specialization of sensors and actuators, increased portability of computational devices, thin and large new display technologies, pursuit of high-bandwidth interaction and innovative multimodal input techniques, presentation of group interfaces on organizational and sociocultural levels, as well as extensions of user-tailorability to include user innovation in more domains.

This anthology proceeds on the assumption that these advances are already having real effects, and that network societies and initiatives concerning a third wave of information technology are already well into co-developmental processes involving both expanded, more finely differentiated, intensive network cultures, and initiatives in ubiquitous computing, pervasive computing, ambient intelligence, tangible computing, and the Internet of things. Thus, the point of departure is the existence and continued emergence of cultures of ubiquitous computation. This also means that the precise character of a fuller actualization of the potential at stake is still an open question. In other words, it is taken for granted that the relation between the potential of ubicomp cultures and their actualization is today still undecided but also a matter of a very dynamic and energetic set of ongoing research projects and concrete technocultural developments, which call for quite some descriptive, analytical, and evaluative efforts. One must acknowledge that a fully developed, robust, pervasively distributed, relatively smart, context-aware, and innovatively ad-hoc networked ubiquitous computing has yet to emerge as a cultural and technical fact. This is the case whether the aim is invisibly embedded and "calm" infrastructural variants, overtly attention-getting and perhaps personalized ones, and/or some vaguely foregrounded or altogether peripherally present mixes. However, one must affirm, at the same time, that the actual technical developments as well as our everyday cultures and modes of interactivity (sociocultural, medial, communicational, psychological, and aesthetic) have already changed enough to warrant the recognition that in a number of ways we *are* individuating, socially and personally, in a ubicomp epoch and world.

Given that these developments have now been on their way for more than two decades, a number of research initiatives and their results can be drawn upon when undertaking work in this field. During these last two decades, we have had a number of conferences concerning the technics of ubiquitous and pervasive computing, many of which have resulted in the publication of conference proceedings, and these conferences now continue on a regular basis (Dourish and Friday 2006; Krumm 2007; Indulska 2008; LaMarca, Langheinrich and Truong 2007). Likewise, the interested reader will today be able to find at least a dozen books treating quite a few of the pertinent issues in the hardware engineering and the software or middleware development for ubicomp (e.g., Adelstein 2005; Cook and Das 2005; Szymanski and Yener 2007). In addition, the first more substantial and useful anthologies in computer science have now appeared (Symonds 2010, 2011). Nonetheless, a major part of the technical research issues is far from resolved. Device components, networks, as well as the different layers of protocols and applications remain in multiple strands of basic development rather than already being involved in undertaking a broader and higher level abstraction from a shared consensus or standard. Non-resolved computer science issues that are still common to most research projects at work on ubiquitous and pervasive computing include the sensation and collection of meaningful data on "human" activities; building models for real-world "human" activity; application of software agent technology, many of them only loosely integrated; appropriate unobtrusive interfaces; taking the right kind of care of security, privacy, ownership, and trust; appraising "human" factors and social impact; implementing, maintaining, and developing dynamic communications networks; managing the scales and heterogeneities of ad hoc networks in non-hierarchical ways; modeling collective failure modes; and appropriate consideration and design of energy consumption when many of the systems depend on batteries (Steventon and Wright 2006, 12; Crowcroft 2008).

In the human and social sciences, moreover, the field of research is characterized by a very noticeable delay in the development of cultural theoretical, sociological, psychological, and aesthetic approaches to ubicomp and its implications for our form of life. Some conferences have now been held, however, in Yokohama, New York, Weimar, London, and Copenhagen, mostly by culture and art organizations, a few by universities and research networks. In addition, an initial set of interesting book-length studies have begun to emerge. Malcolm McCullough and Adam Greenfield's individual studies provide a quite detailed account of what is at stake culturally and architecturally in the emergence of ubiquitous and pervasive computing, while drawing each in their own way on a sound, vocal skepticism so as to point towards a first set of critical evaluations (McCullough 2004, 2013; Greenfield 2006). The *Throughout* volume edited by Ulrik Ekman presents the first relatively comprehensive anthology with more than thirty expert researchers engaging in an explicit treatment of a considerable subset of the socio-cultural, ethico-political, media-specific, aesthetic, and philosophical aspects and implications of the contemporary development of ubiquitous computing (Ekman 2013).

This anthology makes extensive reference to the kinds of insights offered by these kinds of existing research. While doing so, it also insists on the infinite finitude of what is at stake in and for ubicomp cultures. It is generally assumed in this book that we have to deal with "ubiquity-effects," which may be exceedingly complex, but nonetheless *are* not ubiquitous in a strong, ontological, or metaphysical sense. The readers will thus find some insistence on engaging with "mere" ubiquity-effects, however complex. For, whether this takes place in cultural theoretical or technical discourses, the currently trendy terms of "ubiquity," "pervasiveness," and "ambience" most often come rather silently freighted with a notion of totalizing universality or even certain ontological and metaphysical remainders (altogether abstract idealizations and/or excessively essential or substantial extensions). Both the editors and the authors contributing to this book most often approach this as a call for ongoing rewriting and reconstruction, not least in the sense that remainders and implications of onto-theological and sovereign ideological notions must be questioned reasonably to be put under erasure in one or more ways. The book thus includes an effort towards a critique of the idea that ubicomp and its cultures are, should, or could be "ubiquitous"; that pervasive computing and its cultures are, should, or could be "pervasive"; that ambience and ambient intelligence are, should, or could be "all around"; or that the discourses, practices, creativity, and inventions involved extend, penetrate, and invade "throughout," or are at stake all over for everyone and at all times much as an omnipresence.

More specifically, this book delimits its scope by addressing in the main two unresolved questions among the great many awaiting further work in this field. First, given that ubicomp cultures are nothing if not increasingly mobile, increasingly dynamically energized, and increasingly engaged in intense and perhaps non-linear ad hoc networking, how is the *complexity* of what now confronts us as ubiquity-effects to be gauged or affirmed as a whole? Second, how can the demand in this field for a decidedly *transdisciplinary* mode of work and cooperation across the arts and sciences be met? The two sections below begin to flesh out what is at stake in these two core concerns of this anthology.

Complexity

The ubiquity-effects that generate the impressions that we are living on differently with ubicomp cultures are matters of mobility and modes of movement for very large numbers of entities and bodies. They dynamically energize the processes and relations in human sociocultural and technical systems on small, medium, and large environmental scales. They concern intense, ad hoc, and perhaps nonlinear kinds of networking and (dis)connectivity (as in Plate 5). In view of all this, there is quite some reason to assume that this implies complexity as a key problem.

This is today a highly important but underexplored and unresolved issue. Readers will find that the focus in this volume is on pursuing answers to the following problem statement, which is shared across all chapters and editorial texts:

> How is one to describe, analyze, synthesize, evaluate, reduce, or further the complexity of one or more of the current states and processes involving actualizations of ubiquity-effects?

This is a very broad and general generative problem concerning reality-effects and changes in our notions of reality. In this book, it is usually narrowed down slightly since each text contributed mainly enters into one of the three fields addressed: spatializing, temporalizing, and individuating operations and outcomes. Thus, the focal points are explorations of the potential or actual complexity of "ubiquity-effects" qua personal and social individuation, environmental and situative spacing, temporal anticipation and eventualization. In each case, such exploration traces the existing and still ongoing dispersals and relational movements in mixed realities involving ubicomp, whether this concerns processes of individuation with dynamics of anthropological, sociocultural, and technical networks, processes of human and technical context-awareness generative of situation, or the temporality of sociocultural and technical processes that let events unfold, with or without successful anticipation.

Perhaps the evocation of the human and technical myriads of on-off relations of interactivity with and within current mobile cultures is one of the easiest ways to illustrate that the problematics of cultures of ubiquitous information exist not as a totality or infinity but rather as so many matters of immanent complexity. In this actual but still emergent third wave of computing, its mobile devices and co-developing cultural practices might be one of the more obvious foci—not least the haptic culture emerging with mobile phones (gestured towards in Plate 6).

This because the multiplicitous everyday engagements among us, mobile phones, handhelds, and small tech make felt a culture of ubiquitous information qua the dynamics and energies of ad hoc network theories and practices—live as organized inorganicity, inorganically and organically live. Mobile computational entities and their cultural enfoldment are such good foci because they make felt the ways in which complexity arises from a vast number of distinguishable relational regimes and their associated state spaces, promising a defined system of interactivity for "ubiquity" (to come). It is not simple to say with respect to this interactivity whether and how human context-awareness will become technically other, whether and how technical context-awareness will become otherwise human. Probably, this interactivity will be concerned only very little with further developments of linear processing according to pre-established arrays or authority-weighted hierarchical trees of possibilities, just as it seems unlikely that it will come to involve thoroughly autonomous, self-adaptive, self-reproducing, or even mutant artificial life forms. If it will not be or become a matter of simplicity, however, this is because the mutual engagements in a wider ecology among machinic and human processes of interactivity are emergent—something which might be said to afford one kind of complexity to be explored in this book. Your cognitive synthesis of the cheetah figuration in Figure 0.3 would perhaps be one quite approachable example of a synchronic emergence, the coming to presence of a whole functional structure that is more and other than the large number of image parts involved and their properties.

The key wager here in this book, then, is that we need to revisit notions of complexity and emergence. This is so because the science of complexity is still an extremely young discipline. It is so because most of us are not yet particularly good at working through with these in mind, even though we have to—because only a few of us have the requisite methodologies—since these tend to go across physics, chemistry, biology, network topology, dynamic systems theory, and social or cultural theory. However, the renewed encounter with complexity and emergence solicited here is *also* a necessity because ubicomp cultures cannot but involve the movements, dynamics, more or less ad hoc relations, and modes of organization or self-organization pertaining to multiplicities of computational entities as well as humans.

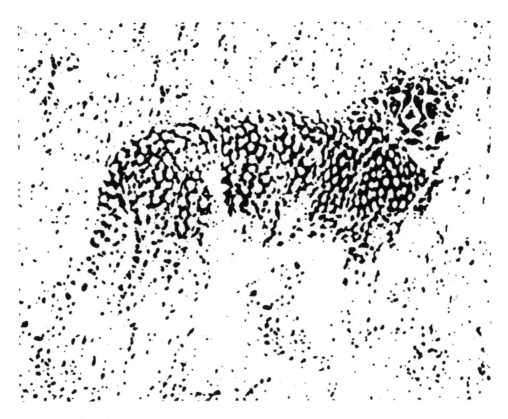

FIGURE 0.3 Cheetah emergent

The task at hand could also be given a first delineation or set of contours by looking at some of the qualities of a ubicomp system listed by Chalmers et al. (2006, 2):

> it will be *fluid*; its structure will *vary* in the short term and *evolve* in the long term; each non-human entity will be *purposive, vaguely or formally*; it will be partly *autonomous*—some of its interactions are determined by its purpose and its interactive experience rather than by invocation from a higher authority; it will be *reflective*—subsystems can report experiences to higher systems and perhaps humans to permit intervention or guidance.

From this approach it seems to follow that what takes place through interactivity in ubicomp cultures will not just involve complexity but will do so in a strong sense, that is, more or less irreducibly, and so interaction designs, humans, and technical systems are not only to be engaged with as dynamic but as evolving (and decaying or dying out). This is by no means the only kind of approach to complexity, however, as one might surmise by looking at Shin'ichi Konomi and George Roussos' treatment of the ways in which ubicomp technics are finding their way into large-scale real-world commercial information systems (rather than small-scale research simulations):

> The core enabler for ubiquitous computing is technology that makes the physical and digital worlds interlinked and thus intimately related. Every object in the world we live in has a digital representation that follows the situation of its real self and vice versa. This

unique linking of bits and atoms opens up numerous possibilities for new computing interactions, which are currently explored by ubiquitous computing research. One of the main implications of this interlinking is that people, places, and things acquire unique machine readable identities within systems of very large scale that must be accommodated within inflexible physical constraints and constantly changing usage context. To be sure, auto-identification capability opens up membership to ubiquitous computing systems for numerous entities and potentially results in massive increases to the number of constituent elements and system complexity. Understanding the issues raised by this increased complexity and exploring solutions can be hard to carry out in lab-based studies or case studies of limited scale. Such understanding often requires that experiments are carried out at scale, a fact that invariably implies high costs that are almost certainly prohibitive in a research context. Nor is it possible to identify and address such issues using large scale simulations, as these are limited by the simplified assumptions involved, and cannot take into account the emerging behaviors caused by real users.

(Konomi and Roussos, 508)

One observes that no matter which way one goes about it, one will have to draw upon notions of "complexity" and "emergence," neither of which is so far readily available in a clearly defined sense. While Konomi and Roussos also identify and acknowledge the question concerning complexity and emergence, their project does not embrace strong nor irreducible complexity but remains explicitly devoted to a version of reductionism—something allegedly necessary to meet the economico-practical limits and needs of the real (read: commercial) world. In fact, reductionism is both by far the most traditional response and a highly justifiable one, since otherwise most standards of scientific research and practical development are put in quite some doubt.

Hence, one can understand John Thackara's reaction in his book on designing in a complex world (Thackara 2005). In the name of a biomimicry of the lightness and seeming simplicity of natural phenomena and evolution, Thackara proposes that we reject and put aside the complexity of ubicomp cultures. He is quite plausible when criticizing some of the stronger claims made for ubicomp—that it will be seamlessly embedded in our environment, fully personalized, altogether self-adaptive, fully anticipatory of our needs, and deliver only information rich with contextually relevant meaning. However uncomfortable this is, it seems quite unlikely that the complexity of ubicomp cultures can be reduced away easily. This is what Thackara implicitly calls for when remarking on the claims made in this context: ". . . maybe I am missing something, but to me this translates as: Build systems that are too complicated to understand and then, after they are deployed, find ways to master their complexity. Hmmm" (2005, 204). He is no doubt right in his contemporary historical diagnosis: "Trillions of smart tags, sensors, smart materials, connected appliances, wearable computing, and body implants are now being unleashed upon the world all at once. It is by no means clear to what question they are an answer—or who is going to look after them, and how" (Thackara 2005, 198). He is also undoubtedly right that very few of us need to interact with an electronic toothbrush that harbors 3,000 lines of hard code. This does not entail, however, that one can avoid addressing interactions with the complexity of ubicomp culture as such, as complex.

Maybe there is a sound ethical insight and point to be found in Thackara's treatment. In that case, he appears to share that insight with Donald Norman who insists in his recent book on making a distinction between "complexity" and something "complicated" (Norman 2011). "Complexity" has to do with a state of the world, suggesting things with many intricate and interrelated parts, Norman argues. "Complicated" has to do with a state of mind, including not least the secondary meaning of that which is "confusing." Maybe the two authors could be brought to agree on Norman's suggestion that we forget about the complaints against complexity, only to complain against confusion, against whatever makes us feel helpless or powerless in the face of mysterious forces that take away control and understanding. On this view, something like bad interaction design for ubicomp cultures has no excuse, whereas good design can help tame the complexity, a complexity that is required but should be managed and be made understandable, according to Norman. This type of argument will not be helpful enough if complexity is irreducible and constitutive or if another kind of holism is required. Then it will not do to militate against complexity in the most traditional way, that is, by insisting on granting priority to some version of reductionism (in this case Norman's insistence upon reduction to the understandable). In other words, this will be insufficient in case an affirmative pursuit of the complexity of ubicomp cultures is called for. This will certainly be the case each time emergent traits are to be addressed, no matter how uncomfortable it might be to admit of non-decomposable contingency, non-linearity, and the unpredictable.

A more affirmative way to approximate a theoretical set of resources for dealing with complexity and emergence in this context can be found in a source as early as Warren Weaver's 1948 article on science and complexity. This text might be said to present several forward steps in that respect with its double distinction. It distinguishes first between "problems of simplicity" (largely concerned with two variables) and "problems of complexity." It then distinguishes between problems of "disorganized complexity" on the one hand (billions of variables as in physics and math, to be handled by probability theory and statistical mechanics), and, on the other, problems of "organized complexity" (the middle region concerning ways to deal simultaneously with a sizable number of factors that are interrelated into an organic whole). Perhaps Weaver's now classic article is particularly useful because it would allow us to see that most of our questions concerning the complexity of ubicomp culture and their interaction designs belong to such problems of "organized complexity," as are similar problems in biology, medicine, psychology, economics, and political science. Reduction to simply two variable problems is not possible, but it is also most often not a matter of applying a mathematics of averages to a huge number of factors. Not least, an approach via this middle kingdom of organized complexity might permit us to acknowledge the occurrence of emergence, that is, that which Weaver already pointed to when saying that members of diverse groups can work together to form a unit that is much greater than the mere sum of its parts (Weaver 1948, 542).[2]

Perhaps Herbert Simon's work on the sciences of the artificial can be said to function as a hinge for a number of the contributions and discussions in this book (Simon 1962). Simon's review of earlier twentieth century debates in the sciences concerning holism and reductionism as approaches to complexity provides a useful background or context for many of the exchanges in this book. Likewise, perhaps Simon's unapologetic pragmatism and his adherence to a version of reductionism can be said to function here as a general but initial focal point, just as its more specific character can be said to be under implicit or explicit scrutiny in many of the chapters in this book. In other words, this anthology may be read, as a more extended discussion whether the complexity of ubiquity-effects can be or should be approached via something like Simon's pragmatically oriented building of near-independent theories for each successive level of complexity, while also building bridging theories that show how each higher level can be accounted for in terms of the elements and relations of the next level below. Hence, it remains a subject of debate in this book whether one can or should adopt a pragmatic stance that:

- defines a complex system as one that is made up of a large number of parts that have many interactions and is weakly emergent in the sense that given the properties of the parts and the laws of their interaction it is not a trivial matter to infer the properties of the whole;
- affirms that complexity often takes the form of hierarchy in a broadly formalized sense (not necessarily with relations of authority (master/slave)), that is, a system composed of interrelated subsystems each of which is in turn hierarchic in structure until we reach some lowest level of elementary subsystem (Simon 1962, 183–185).

Since neither everyday discourses, nor existing research disciplines, nor the contributors to this anthology are in general agreement as to the definition of complexity, readers might in a first step wish to consider a significant subset of the more frequently cited issues that lead to the deployment of this concept:

- complex technical and/or human systemic behavior due to emergence and self-organization (Clarke and Hansen 2009)
- complex dynamics of technical and human metastabilities (Simondon 1964, 1989), multiplicities (Bergson 2004; Deleuze 1990, 1993), or networks of networks (Galloway and Thacker 2007; Barabási 2009)
- complex mechanisms such as artificial life forms, evolutionary or genetic software programming computational complexity (time-complexity, space-complexity) qua the amounts of resources needed for execution of algorithms
- self-adaptive interaction designs for ubicomp, pervasive computing, and ambient intelligence
- simulations of macro-tendencies arising from micro-movements as in the kinds of social complexity studied in computational sociology, with respect to mobile media and social media, for example
- the arrival of scale-free networks or small-world networks via the dynamics of computational networks such as the WWW, the Internet, mobile wireless networks, or current sensor-actuator networks
- environmental or ecosystemic complexity, in relation to sentient cities, smart buildings, or information-intensive mixed realities, for example, when these can be considered under the rubric of organized complexity (non-random, elements correlated, but number of elements, types of elements, and number of relations non-trivial)

The contributors to this book will demonstrate different approaches to the core issue of variants of complexity theory versus variants of scientific reductionism. However, the majority of the chapters can be read as an insistent voicing of a concern with complexities of ubicomp cultures whose spatial relations of movement, temporal intervals and events, and individuating relations of (dis)organization form comings together with emergent traits or concern bundles falling apart—more or less catastrophically. The wager hence appears to be that a great many kinds of ubiquity-effects may best be modeled or simulated as arising from complexity, in the form of a non-linear coming together and dispersal of diverse interactants and components. This necessarily means that such ubiquity-effects are to quite some degree unpredictable and uncontrollable, not least for cybernetics as a science of control. However, perhaps they are also positively emergent qua tendentially self-organizational (i.e., they are artificially "designing" qua letting local, momentary, and singular interactive dynamics eventually produce broader, more lasting, and more connective coordination and synergy). One will have to engage with existing ubiquity-effects and those to come to find out whether they are emergent in a *strong* and/or a *weak* sense. One will have to explore whether and how their spontaneous ordering of complex systems and patterns out of a multiplicity of relatively simple operations and interactions do and do not go beyond the qualities of their components.

Perhaps this remains at the heart of such ubiquity-effects: they must remain a complexly moving target, as points or as waves. In that case, this book might be read as affirming some kind of belief in a complexity of ubicomp cultures that cannot be strictly defined, only momentarily and locally placed as fluctuations somewhere between ordering of structures and dissipating into disorder (Nicolis and Prigogine 1989; Prigogine and Stengers 1984).

Transdisciplinarity

Ubiquity-effects imply a development of information-intensive environments and cultural engagements with complex situative mixed reality worlds. Such ubiquity-effects also entail the development of complicated technical events and mixed reality event-cultures, which involve humans. Moreover, ubiquity-effects can only involve mobility and relationality on the fly, informative ad hoc multiplicitous networkings, emergent architectures and designs, as well as complex modes of technical and cultural individuation. Considering the cultural and technical reach of this, it thus seems both obvious and difficult that any affirmatively holist, reductionist, or critical approach to the complexity of ubiquity-effects will have to draw upon a wide array of specialized disciplines. Research institutions such as the technical universities in Finland acknowledge this, for example. Group organizations within companies such as Microsoft, Intel, and Nokia affirm this. Mark Weiser and his Xerox Parc colleagues already remarked upon it when they solicited contributions from computer science, human–computer interaction (HCI), cultural anthropology, sociology, psychology, and cognitive science.

Thus, the complexity pertaining to the development of ubicomp cultures and their systems necessarily requires and draws upon thoroughly transdisciplinary modes of work and ongoing transdisciplinary exchanges. This is still today a partly unmet challenge. Hence, this book takes on one first and delimited but nevertheless significant subset of the challenges. It offers an exploration of the common grounds of expertise for contributors from four key disciplinary fields intimately involved in the development of ubiquity-effects: cultural theory, media art, interaction design and HCI, and software studies.

A first kind of transdisciplinary movement can thus be found in the relations and exchanges within each of the three parts of this book, for example, when contributors refer to other contributions and discuss insights within that part. Moreover, each contributor to the book not only unfolds a line of approach via her or his primary discipline (in theory, research, or in practice), but usually also provides an opening onto or moves through a set of relations to shared concerns in at least one other discipline at stake here. This can be a matter of openings and relations in a given part of the book, or it can involve one or both of the others parts as well.

Readers will therefore meet a quite considerable metastabilization, crystallization, or crosspollination of the chapters. One example would be when a researcher in interaction design working with interactivity in complex mixed reality situations with a certain technical context-awareness makes explicit how this might relate to certain current practices in contemporary media art and to cultural theoretical engagements with notions of affect, feeling, and emotion. It may also take the form of a software studies specialist scrutinizing the distribution of so many decentralized parallel algorithms for real-time processing of the events that afford complex ad hoc dynamic networking only to make explicit how this links up with questions concerning multiplicities and individuation in certain parts of cultural theory. Perhaps this happens when a media artist creating interactive mixed reality installations involving dynamic systems for tracking and projection forges links to related issues of surveillance and social media in cultural theory and notions of personalized interactivity immanent to the field of interaction design. Or it takes place as when a cultural theorist (deeply engaged with the question concerning the complexity of a dynamic relational ontology for individuation and its modes of movement) carves out a trajectory across media artists' and interaction designers' work on technical and human kinesthesia as well as software designers' programming of computational processes and structures on the move with people.

Thus, this book not least concerns an effort towards offering readers a set of transdisciplinary vectors, which might provide new insights via innovative experimentation and collaboration, cast a different sort of light on existing disciplinary approaches and questions, or involve more or less vibrant and resonating dissonances, conflicts, or oppositions. In other words, the transdisciplinary effort of this book goes toward the generation and dissemination of a multiplicity involving complex ubiquity-effects—traversed by four key disciplines to raise a question of another emergence that is not theirs.

This Book Emerges

The reader might wish to think of this book as a structural emergence (Protevi 2006), affording a reading experience of the functional structure arriving as a dynamic surplus out of its many interrelating components: 36 media artists and researchers, 28 chapters, 15 editorial texts, numerous connections among these, and hundreds of references plus key issues and concepts engaged with. It is obviously possible to approach such a reading experience in very many ways. One can start anywhere and move along the relational linkages of components in this book as a dynamic whole in process. It can be considered a whole with a permeable membrane to its environments, much like a cell in the flow of its becoming (Plate 7).

At some point in such reading travels, it will become apparent that emergent structuration here is to some extent determined by the insertion and maintenance of levels or strata. They comprise slightly longer and more general introductory editorial texts, four groupings of chapters, and shorter editorial texts accompanying such groups. Each group of chapters is concerned with one dynamic layer or set of relations in ubicomp culture, that is, those of cultural theory, media art, interaction design, and software studies. Naturally, the editorial choice of these layers is a forcing and gives only a subset (Badiou 2004, 2005, 2009). It is a reduction—in part made with a view to the (considerable but not infinite) expertise of the contributing researchers. However, it permits a first investigation of four key fields in which the question concerning the potential complexity of ubicomp culture is already both pressing and unresolved. Readers may want to consider these four layers as staying concerns, which reflect an engagement in research, and media art that gradually pushes towards the immanence of ubicomp culture, stopping short of any extended address of issues in such fields as coding and programming, hardware engineering, organic biology, chemistry, and physics.

This book as a synchronic emergence is also a matter of the way in which this book functions as three large book parts, which contribute significantly to its becoming a more complex structuration. All three parts of the book address the core research issue of the book: the potential complexity and reducibility of ubiquity-effects. In addition to contributing to this shared concern, or as a way of doing so, however, each part directs primary attention to one main field of questions: individuating, situating, and eventualizing, respectively.

Part I, its ten chapters by Mark B. Hansen, Erin Manning, Lily Diaz, Morten Søndergaard, David Rokeby, Teri Rueb, Simon Penny, Irene Mavrommati, Jonathan Dovey, Wendy Hui Kyong Chun, and its five editorial texts by Ulrik Ekman, Lily Diaz, Morten Søndergaard, and Jay David Bolter, addresses the question whether and then how human and technical individuations might be said to be complex in a situation and epoch with network societies and ubicomp. It seeks to address the ways in which current co-developments of the cultures of network societies and ubicomp technics are "individuating" (Simondon 1964, 1989, 1994).

Perhaps this is a matter of sketching how these processes have already delineated certain reducible, determinable, or coded modes of individuation, human and technical. Perhaps such address may take place as affirmations of emergent complexity in a strong, disorganized (Weaver 1948), or irreducible sense (Wolfram 1984), by insisting on non-linear and cross-cutting movements towards other ways of relating in and among individuals, social others, forms of life, and technics. It could be that individuating is seen as something to be approached as not altogether decomposable, but still mostly reducible to human and technical hierarchical architectures of processes and sub-processes, modules, and sub-modules (Simon 1962). Alternatively, some researchers and media artists might test their notion that individuations in today's network societies with ubicomp technics do demonstrate recognizable structurations and decomposable co-developments, but that, despite their obvious import, these are mainly delayed and displaced side effects of the dynamics at stake in disorganized or irreducible environmental complexity.

Across very many of the texts in this book part, the readers will find engagements with the questions concerning the increasing complexity of the current co-development of human and technical individuations. There is no evident agreement as to whether self-organization, agency, and adaptability are found in technical and human systems both, just as there is no altogether clear agreement whether the relation of co-development is symmetrical or asymmetrical, although a majority of the contributions appears to gesture towards granting anthropoid developments a privilege. Readers might find signs here that "we" have begun to live and develop with ubicomp technics whose individuations are now complex in ways that increasingly problematize notions that autonomy and intelligence only or primarily reside with humans. One might pick up signals here that it is increasingly problematic both to distinguish between *anthropos* and *techné* and to grasp their dynamic developmental relation. Moreover, it appears less and less certain that human development, technical development, and their co-development pose a question of organized complexity subject to reductionist approaches.

Part II, its eleven chapters by Yvonne Spielmann, Henriette Steiner and Kristin Veel, Malcolm McCullough, Sean Cubitt, Sarah Kember and Joanna Zylinska, Blast Theory, Electroland, Jane Prophet and Helen Pritchard, Mogens Jacobsen, Katie Ellis and Gerard Goggin, Dietmar Offenhuber and Orkan Telhan, and its four editorial texts, addresses the complex ways in which ubiquity-effects involve situating processes for both the technics of information-intensive environments qua mixed reality milieux with context-awareness and for the human travelers, visitors, or inhabitants with their types of context-awareness (Bolchini et al. 2007; Dourish 2004; Gellersen et al. 2002; Lukowicz et al. 2012; Schmidt et al. 1999).

Perhaps this goes on in the sense of affording clearly identifiable location, habitual dwelling with certain places and determinable responsive buildings, and spaces with an apparently meaningful architectural horizon. But perhaps it rather happens by displacing and making dynamic the notions of a situated and sensible point, line, and plane, whether in technical or human spacing or in their interaction. One good example of an effort to visualize some of the complexity of the dynamics of information-intensive environments with wired and not least wireless network relationalities can be found in Plate 8.

As in the first part of the book, there is no evident consensus or easy agreement among the contributors, now with respect to the status of the complexity of situating in network societies with ubicomp systems and devices.

The chapters include the taking of positions that insist on universal reductionism to something very much resembling a Cartesian spatiality when approaching the complexity of dynamic human and technical spacing of any given situation. But the reader will also find pragmatically heuristic reductionist takes that organize situative spacings but remain open to further complexification—as well as different kinds of pursuits of nonlinear and disorganized topological complexity whose dynamics just occasionally afford a situation of human and technics that can be registered or recognized as ordered, organized, and meaningful to us (Ekman 2015). Whether the contributors focus on the implications for cultural theory and experience, media art, or interaction design, this part of the book certainly does demonstrate, in various ways, that environmentality is becoming an increasingly complex issue on the side of human context-awareness, on the side of technical ubicomp context-awareness, and with respect to their ongoing meshes and dispersals.

As in the first book part, the encounter with the issue of technocultural complexity leads to a situation in which anthropocentric control and technical orchestration of the environment are to some extent on the verge of becoming crossed out. Likewise, technical ubicomp environments are to some extent on the verge of being granted the status of life, intelligence, or autonomy. Increasingly, "situating" appears questionable whether as determinable experiential contextualist meaning-production or as technically precise discrete mathematical location. Taken together, human and technical context-awarenesses more and more come to appear as complex dynamic membranes that constitute and deconstitute individual, social, biological, technical, and material atmospheres, ambiences, milieux, or ecologies. "Situating" is then the taking place of informative and transformative becomings, which concern a bi-directional transport of parts and relations from an external environment across a membrane, skin, or medium to an inner environment. As the reader will find in the chapters and editorial texts in this second part of the book, the inner technical and human cultural environments are increasingly recognized as complex, the exterior environments are increasingly approached as being of more or less irreducible situative complexity.

Part III, its six chapters by Maria Poulaki, Patricia Pisters, Hasan Elahi, Giulio Jacucci, Jonas Löwgren, and John Johnston, and its five editorial texts, enters into the temporalizing and event-specific traits of ubiquity-effects. This happens not only with regard to the real-time programming of technical context-awareness and mixed reality events. It also concerns the accompanying human event-culture for hyperdifferentiated network societies and their experience economies. That dimension can perhaps be visualized quite well via images of some of the interfaces to the programming in process control, which will coordinate among a number of events (Figure 0.4).

Examples that are more difficult would include diachronic emergence, or the kind of unpredictable and nonlinear temporal surprises suggestively visualized as the glitched tracing of dispersals and comings together of birds' trajectory flows in Plate 9.

Temporalizing and event-specific traits of ubiquity-effects notably include potential instances of human and technical co-emergence. These instances of diachronic emergence then appear as prior to structural and synchronic processual outcomes—the whole yields, processually or diachronically speaking, effects of self- and hetero-organization beyond the summation of its

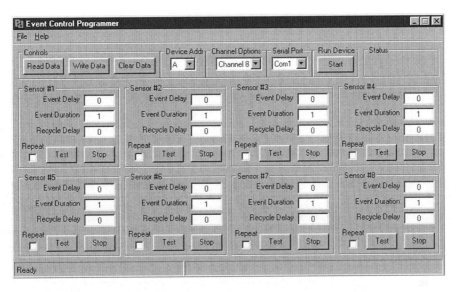

FIGURE 0.4 Event control interface

parts. For example, co-emergences go further than wholes because one is here cutting across complexifying eventualizations qua system changes, symbiogeneses, mutations, or different kinds of co-evolution.

Part III in effect inquires whether the events proper to the dynamics of contemporary network societies and their technics are reducible to a universal, linear, and homogenous time, or whether events rather concern more complex or even irreducibly complex temporalizations, heterogeneous and in the plural (Varela 1996, 185–216; Bohm 1986; Serres and Latour 1996). The readers will find, also here, that the contributors do not agree as to the reducibility of eventualizations (although the majority opt for quite identifiable reductionist stances that affirm one linear time, a universal container through which events pass). However, it is clear when one has read this book part that there is quite some consensus on at least two points. The event qua diachronic emergence is increasingly an issue that has to be addressed. The complexity of human and technical temporalizations along with their transversal interrelations of timescales as well as of both homogeneous and heterogeneous times is increasingly an issue that has to be addressed.

Insofar as this book is of complexity and emerges, readers may thus wish to consider in what senses it can or cannot be grasped as an individualized whole with parts (structural emergence as a potential problem). Moreover, readers may ask in what senses it can or cannot be grasped as one process on one time scale with one homogenous time of development (diachronic emergence as a potential problem). Not least, readers might inquire whether or not it can be grasped with recourse to a universalist scientific hierarchy of specialized disciplines and their ordering of time (transversal emergence as a potential problem).

Notes

1. In this book, "individuation" is generally used in a broad sense as the name of the processes whereby the undifferentiated tends to become individual, or the processes through which differentiated components become integrated into stable, if momentary wholes. It can thus be taken to refer broadly

to various kinds of generative or processual philosophical efforts, as in key parts of the work done by Bergson, Whitehead, James, the late Husserl, Deleuze, Bernard Stiegler, and Manuel De Landa. More specifically, however, it is used both here and elsewhere in this book with reference to Gilbert Simondon's developments of theories of individual, collective, and technical individuation. Here the individual or the collective subject is considered as an effect of individualization rather than a cause. Thus, the individual atom is replaced by the neverending ontogenetic process of individuation. Simondon also conceived of the pre-individual as the virtuality, reserve, or fund making actual individuation possible. Here individuation is an infinitely finite or always incomplete process, always leaving a pre-individual leftover, affording future individuations (Simondon 1964, 1989, 1992).

2. In this book, "emergence" is generally used in the sense found in significant parts of philosophy, systems theory, natural science, and art, i.e., it denotes a process whereby larger entities, patterns, and regularities arise through interactions among smaller or simpler entities that themselves do not exhibit the properties of the whole. In that general sense, emergence is central to theories of complex systems. More specifically, in this introduction I draw to some extent on the notion of "emergence" proposed by John Protevi in his work on Deleuze and complexity theory, including distinctions among synchronic, diachronic, and transversal emergence in homogeneous and heterogeneous variants (Protevi). Here "emergence" is defined as the diachronic construction of functional structures in complex systems that achieve a synchronic, diachronic, and transversal emergence in homogeneous and heterogeneous systems that achieve a synchronic focus of systematic behavior as they constrain the behavior of individual components. The debate concerning the ontological and/or the epistemic status of "emergence'" is unresolved and quite old at this point in time Readers may get a first overview of classical and more recent positions by consulting sources such as Bedau and Humpreys, Juarrero and Rubino.

References

Adelstein, Frank. 2005. *Fundamentals of Mobile and Pervasive Computing*. New York: McGraw-Hill.

Badiou, Alain. 2004. *Theoretical Writings*. London: Continuum.

Badiou, Alain. 2005. *Being and Event*. London: Continuum.

Badiou, Alain. 2009. *Logics of Worlds, Being and Event*. London: Continuum.

Barabási, Albert-László. 2002. *Linked: The New Science of Networks*. Cambridge, MA: Perseus.

Barabási, Albert-László. 2009. "Scale-Free Networks: A Decade and Beyond." *Science* 325 (5939): 412–413.

Bedau, Mark, and Paul Humphreys. 2008. *Emergence: Contemporary Readings in Philosophy and Science*. Cambridge, MA: MIT Press.

Bergson, Henri. 2004. *Matter and Memory*. Mineola, NY: Dover Publications.

Bergson, Henri, and Robin Durie. 1999. *Duration and Simultaneity: Bergson and the Einsteinian Universe*. 2nd ed. Manchester, UK: Clinamen Press.

Bohm, David. 1986. "Time, the Implicate Order, and Pre-Space." In *Physics and the Ultimate Significance of Time*, edited by David Ray Griffin, 176–208. Albany, NY: State University of New York Press.

Bolchini, Cristiana, Carlo A. Curino, Elisa Quintarelli, Fabio A. Schreiber, and Letizia Tanca. 2007. "A Data-Oriented Survey of Context Models." *SIGMOD Rec.* 36 (4): 19–26.

Chalmers, Dan, Matthew Chalmers, Jon Crowcroft, Marta Kwiatkowska, Robin Milner, Eamonn O'Neill, Tom Rodden, Vladimiro Sassone, and Morris Sloma. 2006. "Ubiquitous Computing: Experience, Design and Science." Accessed September 10, 2014. https://i2cs.cs.uiuc.edu/download/attachments/10456573/manifesto.pdf.

Clarke, Bruce, and Mark B. N. Hansen. 2009. *Emergence and Embodiment*. Durham, NC: Duke University Press.

Cook, Diane, and Sajal K. Das. 2005. *Smart Environments*. Hoboken, NJ: John Wiley.

Crowcroft, Jon. 2008. "Engineering Global Ubiquitous Systems." *Philosophical Transactions of the Royal Society A* 366: 3833–3834.

De Landa, Manuel. 2002. *Intensive Science and Virtual Philosophy*. London: Continuum.

De Landa, Manuel. 2006. *A New Philosophy of Society: Assemblage Theory and Social Complexity*. London: Continuum.

De Landa, Manuel. 2011. *Philosophy and Simulation*. London: Continuum.

Deleuze, Gilles. 1990. *The Logic of Sense*. New York: Columbia University Press.

Deleuze, Gilles. 1993. *Difference and Repetition*. New York: Columbia University Press.

Deleuze, Gilles, and Félix Guattari. 1987. *A Thousand Plateaus*. Minneapolis, MN: University of Minnesota Press.

Dourish, Paul. 2004. "What We Talk about When We Talk about Context." *Personal and Ubiquitous Computing* 8 (1): 19–31.

Dourish, Paul, and Adrian Friday, Eds. 2006. *Ubicomp 2006: Ubiquitous Computing: 8th International Conference: Proceedings*. Berlin: Springer.

Ekman, Ulrik, Ed. 2013. *Throughout: Art and Culture Emerging with Ubiquitous Computing*. Cambridge, MA: MIT Press.

Ekman, Ulrik. 2015. "Design as Topology: U-City." In *Media Art and the Urban Environment—Engendering Public Engagement with Urban Ecology*, edited by Frank Marchese. New York: Springer, in press.

Galloway, Alexander R., and Eugene Thacker. 2007. *The Exploit: A Theory of Networks*. Minneapolis, MN: University of Minnesota Press.

Gellersen, Hans W., Albrecht Schmidt, and Michael Beigl. 2002. "Multi-Sensor Context-Awareness in Mobile Devices and Smart Artifacts." *Mobile Networks and Applications* 7 (5): 341–351.

Greenfield, Adam. 2006. *Everyware: The Dawning Age of Ubiquitous Computing*. Berkeley, CA: New Riders.

Husserl, Edmund, and Rudolf Boehm. 1966. *Husserliana: Gesammelte Werke. Bd 10, Zur Phänomenologie Des Inneren Zeitbewusstseins*. Haag. Austria: Nijhoff.

Husserl, Edmund, and Reinhold Nikolaus Smid. 1993. *Husserliana: Gesammelte Werke. Bd 29, Die Krisis Der Europäischen Wissenschaften Und Die Transzendentale Phänomenologie*. Dordrecht, The Netherlands: Kluwer.

Husserl, Edmund, and Rochus Sowa. 2008. *Husserliana: Gesammelte Werke. Bd 39, Die Lebenswelt: Auslegungen Der Vorgegebenen Welt Und Ihrer Konstitution*. Dordrecht, The Netherlands: Springer.

Indulska, Jadwiga. 2008. *Pervasive 2008: Pervasive Computing, 6th International Conference: Proceedings* Berlin: Springer.

James, William. 2003. *Essays in Radical Empiricism*. Mineola, NY: Dover.

Juarrero, Alicia, and Carl A. Rubino. 2008. *Emergence, Complexity, and Self-Organization: Precursors and Prototypes, Exploring Complexity*. Goodyear, AZ: ISCE Pub.

Konomi, Shin'Ichi, and George Roussos. 2007. "Ubiquitous Computing in the Real World: Lessons Learnt from Large Scale RFID Deployments." *Personal Ubiquitous Computing* 11 (7): 507–521.

Krumm, John, Abowd, Gregory D., Seneviratne, Aruna, and Strang, Thomas, Eds. 2007. *Ubicomp 2007: Ubiquitous Computing: 9th International Conference: Proceedings*. Berlin: Springer.

LaMarca, Anthony, Marc Langheinrich, and Khai N. Truong. 2007. *Pervasive 2007: Pervasive Computing, 5th International Conference: Proceedings*. Berlin: Springer.

Latour, Bruno. 1996. *Aramis, or, the Love of Technology*. Cambridge, MA: Harvard University Press.

Latour, Bruno. 2005. *Reassembling the Social: An Introduction to Actor-Network-Theory*. Oxford: Oxford University Press.

Lukowicz, Paul, Alex "Sandy" Pentland, and Alois Ferscha. 2012. "From Context Awareness to Socially Aware Computing." *Pervasive Computing, IEEE* 11 (1): 32–41.

McCullough, Malcolm. 2004. *Digital Ground: Architecture, Pervasive Computing, and Environmental Knowing*. Cambridge, MA: MIT Press.

McCullough, Malcolm. 2013. *Ambient Commons: Attention in the Age of Embodied Information*. Cambridge, MA: MIT Press.

Maturana, Humberto R., and F. J. Varela. 1980. *Autopoiesis and Cognition*. Dordrecht, The Netherlands: D. Reidel.

Nicolis, Gregoire, and Ilya Prigogine. 1977. *Self-Organization in Nonequilibrium Systems*. New York: John Wiley.

Nicolis, Gregoire, and Ilya Prigogine 1989. *Exploring Complexity: An Introduction*. New York: W.H. Freeman.

Norman, Donald A. 2011. *Living with Complexity*. Cambridge, MA: MIT Press.

Prigogine, Ilya, and Isabelle Stengers. 1984. *Order out of Chaos*. Boulder, CO: New Science Library.

Prigogine, Ilya, and Isabelle Stengers. 1997. *The End of Certainty*. New York: Free Press.

Protevi, John. 2006. "Deleuze, Guattari and Emergence." *Paragraph* 29 (2): 19–39.

Schmidt, Albrecht, Michael Beigl, and Hans-W. Gellersen. 1999. "There Is More to Context than Location." *Computer & Graphics* 23 (6): 893–901.

Serres, Michel, Josué V. Harari, and David F. Bell. 1982. *Hermes—Literature, Science, Philosophy*. Baltimore, MD: Johns Hopkins University Press.

Serres, Michel, and Bruno Latour. 1995. *Conversations on Science, Culture, and Time*. Ann Arbor, MI: University of Michigan Press.

Simon, Herbert A. 1962. "The Architecture of Complexity." *Proceedings of the American Philosophical Society* 106 (6): 467–482.

Simondon, Gilbert. 1964. *L'individu et sa genèse physico-biologique*. Paris: Presses universitaires de France.

Simondon, Gilbert. 1989. *L'individuation psychique et collective*. Paris: Aubier.

Simondon, Gilbert. 1992. "The Genesis of the Individual." In *Incorporations*, edited by Jonathan Crary and Sanford Kwinter, 296–319. New York: Zone.

Steventon, Alan, and Steve Wright. 2006. *Intelligent Spaces*. London: Springer.

Stiegler, Bernard. 1994. "Temps et individuation technique, psychique, et collective dans l'oeuvre de Simondon." *Multitudes* 20 (6). Accessed August 27, 2009. http://multitudes.samizdat.net/Temps-et-individuation-technique.

Symonds, Judith, ed. 2010. *Ubiquitous and Pervasive Computing*. 3 vols. Hershey, PA: Information Science Reference.

Symonds, Judith. 2011. *Emerging Pervasive and Ubiquitous Aspects of Information Systems*. Hershey, PA: Information Science Reference.

Szymanski, Boles, and Bülent Yener. 2005. *Advances in Pervasive Computing and Networking*. New York: Springer.

Thackara, John. 2005. *In the Bubble: Designing in a Complex World*. Cambridge, MA: MIT Press.

Thrift, Nigel. 2004. "Remembering the Technological Unconscious by Foregrounding Knowledges of Position." *Environment and Planning D: Society and Space* 22 (1): 175–190.

Varela, Francisco J. 1996. *Embodied Mind*. Cambridge, MA: MIT Press.

Weaver, Warren. 1948. "Science and Complexity." *Scientific American* 36: 536–544.

Weiser, Mark. 1991. "The Computer for the Twenty-first Century." *Scientific American* 265 (3): 94–104.

Weiser, Mark. 1993. "Some Computer Science Issues in Computing." *Communications of the ACM* 36 (7): 75–84.

Weiser, Mark. 1994. "The World Is Not a Desktop." *Interactions* 1 (1):7–8.

Weiser, Mark. 1997. "It's Everywhere. It's Invisible. It's Ubicomp." *Training & Development* 51 (5): 34–34.

Weiser, Mark. 1999. How Computers Will Be Used Differently in the Next Twenty Years. In *IEEE Symposium on Security and Privacy*, 234–235.

Weiser, Mark, and John Seely Brown. 1995. "Designing Calm Technology." Accessed August 14, 2014. http://sandbox.xerox.com/hypertext/weiser/calmtech/calmtech.htm.

Weiser, Mark, and John Seely Brown. 1996. "The Coming Age of Calm Technology." Accessed August 15, 2014. http://nano.xerox.com/hypertext/weiser/acmfuture2endnote.htm.

Weiser, Mark, Rich Gold, and John Seely Brown. 1999. "The Origins of Ubiquitous Computing Research at Parc in the Late 1980s." *IBM Systems Journal* 38 (4): 693–696.

Whitehead, Alfred North. 1960. *Process and Reality, an Essay in Cosmology*. New York: Palgrave Macmillan.

Wolfram, Stephen. 1984. "Cellular Automata as Models of Complexity." *Nature* 311 (5985): 419–424.

PART I

Individuating

INDIVIDUATIONS

Ulrik Ekman

Does ubicomp culture mean that individuals and social groups develop and evolve differently, and are the whole of such individuations to be approached as a matter of complexity? Does ubicomp culture imply that computational entities, networks, software systems, interaction designs, and media become concretized differently, and must this as a whole be considered in terms of complexity? Is the term "ubicomp culture" to be understood as a short and somewhat artificial neologism in which hides some well-known distinction between the becoming of humans and the becoming of machines that will permit one to decompose each in some scientific manner, or does this term rather signal that that they remain intimately intertwined, co-emerge, and codevelop in a complex and perhaps non-decomposable sense?

This book section includes ten chapters engaging in depth with key aspects of such questions, moving towards a demonstration of the ways in which individuating with ubicomp culture might be considered complex, perhaps in ways permitting reduction, satisficing, or approximate solutions, or in some cases permitting only an acknowledgment of irreducible complexity in the face of problems that can only be worked on in one-to-one simulative correspondence.

The notion of "individuation" can here be read in a broadly metaphorical sense, as somewhat synonymous with psychological, subjective, and egological development, or grouped and social development, or organized, organic, and biological development, or technical, machinic, and algorithmic development. However, both this text and the entire anthology also include an invitation to reconsider this notion via an encounter with the way in which it is thought in the work of Gilbert Simondon.[1] This is tantamount to grasping an individual in a very general sense and as a relative reality: As an effect or a momentary result of an ontogenetic and relational process or operationality. An individual subjectivity-effect along with a collective sociality-effect are phases of concretization in a relational process of becoming. Such effects imply both a preindividual state and, after a phase of individuation, a remainder of a preindividual potential still to be actualized in coming individuations. Moreover, psychic and social individuations would here form only part of an ontogenetic process seeing to the development of a larger entity that involves the biological, the technical, and the environment or milieu.[2] Psychic and social individuations are partial and relative resolutions or concretizations appearing in a larger system that contains both a multiplicity of latent potentials and a distinct tension, a disparateness, or an incompatibility with itself.

More specifically as regards the key concerns of this book, this would entail a reconsideration of subjective and social becomings with ubicomp developments as a matter of complexification emerging from the processing and structuring of preindividual potentials. The complexity of individuated ubicomp culture is then a problem solution qua a phase in a transformative topological experiment. This transformative becoming concerns a complex transport of parts and relations from an external or extracultural environment across ubicomp technics as a membrane, skin, or medium to an inner-cultural environment for social and individual lives, and back, with a difference. Here technical and human cultural individuations are less distinct than being in transduction: The two terms are in co-emergent development and this is constituted by their relationality. Ubicomp technics would here be the process with which human individuals and social groups develop environmentally: The inner cultural milieux of an "I" and a "we" emerge with the ongoing maintenance of technics as a membrane to exterior milieux. Ubicomp technics become less as our other than as the envelope, curtain, or membrane for continuous bidirectional relational transports between environments exterior and interior to the developmental processes of human culture, network societies, social groups, and individual lives. The complexity at stake concerns what is concretized "inside" as an intricate cultural organization, "outside" as exteriorities of organized and disorganized complexity, and topologically as technics of selectivity (self-maintenance of individuation at and as a membrane that remains asymmetrical and polarized, permitting the centrifugal or centripetal transport of certain energies and bodies while opposing others). The synchronic emergence or processual structuration of a ubicomp culture is not solely a matter of integration and differentiation. It is also a matter of transduction understood as a prior dynamic, relational topology. A continuous technical or informative process generates numerous mediations—as a result of which interiorities and exteriorities arrive at the poles.

It is an open question whether living and developing with ubiquitous computing, individually and socially, is a relatively simple problem that can be reduced and solved by considering a few variables at play. It might be a problem of organized complexity with a moderate number of variables and relations that could be dealt with via computers and transdisciplinary research in the social and biological sciences. Perhaps it is rather a problem residing with disorganized complexity whose many variables will call on statistical tools and probability analysis.[3] However, it may remain a problem of irreducible complexity that admits only of direct simulation or trying.[4]

The contributions to this first of three large book sections making up this anthology address the issue of potentially complex technocultural individuating along four interconnected paths, each concerned with one dynamic layer or set of relations in ubicomp culture, that is, those of cultural theory, media art, interaction design, and software studies. Naturally, the choice of these paths is a forcing and gives only a subset; it is a reduction made in view of the (considerable but not infinite) expertise of the contributing researchers. It nonetheless permits a first investigation of four key fields in which the question concerning the potential complexity of ubicomp culture is already pressing and unresolved. Given that each of the three large book sections operates along these four paths, the reader may want to consider them as staying concerns that reflect an engagement that gradually pushes towards the immanence of ubicomp culture, stopping short of any extended address of issues in such fields as coding and programming, hardware engineering, organic biology, chemistry, and physics.

As Lily Diaz remarks in her interim text below, individuations with ubicomp culture pose thought-provoking questions to the ways in which *cultural theories* of individuation are to operate vis-á-vis the potential complexity of culture, technology, and the environment. The chapters by Mark B. Hansen, Erin Manning, Lily Diaz, and Morten Søndergaard present engagements with different parts of this, just as they indicate quite different approaches to be taken when considering the key issue of reductionism versus a more or less strong position in complexity theory.

For example, both Hansen and Diaz treat the way in which individuals and social groups currently live and develop with the billions of processors and software systems in context-aware and anticipatory ubiquitous computing and agree that it is far from obvious that the distinction between human and machine can be upheld in any strict or traditional sense. Here Hansen moves very far towards a strong position in complexity theory such as one might find it in the work of representatives from the hard sciences as well as in the social and human sciences.[5] He proposes the pursuit of a strong "objective" rethinking of the phenomenological tradition that will alter it so as to meet mediation, ubicomp technics, and the disorganized or even irreducible complexity of the appearance of the world at a quantum level (de)constitutive of any intentional subjective consciousness. Ubicomp technics, and relational databases in particular, thus proffer a dynamic and multiplicitous topological relationality in and of the sensible, which lets us as human subjectivities and socialities individuate with an expanded preindividual sensibility that operates prior to intentional consciousness and not necessarily in anthropocentric ways. Diaz, however, proposes that the complexity of ubicomp culture and surveillance systems is to be met by a nuanced reductionism, specifically the reductions of complexity in a systems theory (inspired by the work of Niklas Luhmann and Gregory Bateson). This, according to Diaz, will allow one to see that the complexity of human psychological and social systems and their development are of a different order from the complexity of ubicomp systems and their development. Quite contrary to Hansen, Diaz contends that the understanding of the world available through human observation is of a different order and type from the sensor-mediated form of observation and surveillance now to be found in the context-aware systems of ubicomp. Notably, media art projects and art systems permit of the generation of forms for the observations of observations, a kind of second-order move and reflexivity with a critical or "irritating" potential not to be found in ubicomp systems. In effect, where Hansen finds in ubicomp technics the very potential for expanded development of humans and their sensibility towards complexity, Diaz tends to find for the most part a reduction, a potential loss of human agency, quality of life, and critical reflexivity.

Morten Søndergaard's introduction to "Media Art" and the interviews with media artists, David Rokeby and Teri Rueb, in this section echo some of the concerns voiced by Diaz, especially as regards the perhaps special role played in the complexification of ubicomp culture by creative and critical potentials, not least those to be found in *media art*. When interviewed, Rokeby will also accord a certain privilege to human culture and in particular its media art projects. The interrelations and feedback loops between human interactants and computational systems in art projects such as *Very Nervous System* (1986–1990) and *The Giver of Names* (1991) can certainly be seen as precursors of more or less autonomous and intelligently human-oriented systems in ubiquitous and pervasive computing, perhaps not so much the billions of autonomous software agents calmly at work infrastructurally in networks as the more overt and personalized intelligent assistants we now begin to live with more continuously (e.g. GPS, Siri, Cortana, Google Now). His work on such art projects has led Rokeby to acknowledge that complexity and emergence are to be found on both sides and in their interactions. However, even if Rokeby grants the computational systems with which we now live something like behaviors resembling autonomy and demonstrating emergent effects from human and technical networkings, he will eventually insist on an anthropocentric privilege, both in principle and in his own media art projects. That is, when we consider a struggle between human and technical, complexity and control, and between valuing or protecting ourselves and celebrating the different capabilities of others (such as these technical systems), Rokeby will explore in detail the potentials for codevelopment but first and last rest with the human. Rokeby will perhaps grant that we evolve with our intelligent ubicomp environment and that this also enables certain transformative mirrorings of human complexity. However, he will not just trust technical emergence but insist on privileging a certain human freedom, human creativity, and a critical discussion of values over and above developments of technical control and autonomy.

Ever since Mark Weiser's first coinage in the first half of the 1990s of the terms "ubicomp" and "calm computing," (Weiser 1991) an important part of the research and development in the fields of human–computer interaction (HCI) and *interaction design* has been preoccupied with the issue of how to navigate between the freedom and the control of agency, across the situations and events involving ubicomp systems and human interactants. It is still a matter of some debate whether and how interaction designs for ubicomp culture are to tend towards the transparent and calm invisibility of an infrastructure for interactivity or towards a more personalized, attention-getting, even exciting unfolding, and mediatory laying bare of potential paths for technocultural interrelations and interactivities.[6] It is much less discussed and still far from clear, however, what complexities might be lurking in the arrival of multitudes of smart human-oriented interaction designs which are to foresee, enable, maintain, and adapt event-wise to the meaningful, intentional interactions of human in a given situation. Likewise, research is still much in the dark with respect to the kinds of complexity that could be said to be at stake in the novel organizations of humans, their practices, their environment, and their time when living on and individuating with such ubicomp interaction designs. Not least, we have seen very little research capable of following the fate of the potential complexities of what emerges from the ongoing dynamic *interrelations* of smart ubicomp interaction designs and the more implicit "interaction designs" embedded not in computational entities but in the embodied practices of ever so many parts of human everyday cultures.

In his more detailed interim text on interaction designs and individuation, Jay David Bolter remarks both on this unresolved state of affairs and on the ways in which such issues are broached in the chapter contributions by Simon Penny, Irene Mavromatti, and Jon Dovey. It is quite thought-provoking to observe, for example, the differences it makes to be working from within the disciplines of HCI and computer science, as Mavromatti, or from within the discipline of cultural and medial studies of pervasive computing, as Dovey. Neither Mavromatti nor Dovey focuses on the issue of free versus controlled agency so as to engage in more sustained ethico-political critiques, and they agree in a broad sense on finding in the emergence of complex ubicomp interaction designs, a certain set of affordances primarily to be approached as potentials for further human and technical development. They also agree that ubicomp and associated interaction designs display complexity. However, acknowledging the transdisciplinary character of ubicomp projects, Mavromatti remains primarily occupied with the interior workings of ubicomp as extended component-based systems with loose coupling of quite autonomous parts, that is, as systemic ecologies of artifacts, services, people, and infrastructure. Her effort is mainly a reductionist attempt to meet such complexity by delivering a common framework for design across system engineering, cognitive science, and sociocultural theory, and for interaction designs that will permit and promote end-user development.

In his work on emergent ambient literature, Jon Dovey does not so much go to work on the inside of such a system so as to generate technical potentials for human end-user individuation. Rather, Dovey remains situated as an individuation in process, asking whether and how literary experiences delivered through pervasive media systems produce events in the sense of new ways to live and perhaps understand one's moment in the complexity of the information flow of urban ubicomp culture. In the main, Dovey will mask the technical systemic complexity, but the approach towards ongoing becomings through the lived ambient esthetic experiences of individuals and socialities encountering locative narratives while on the move is not so much reductionist as a probability-based approximation to a disorganized complexity of human, urban, and data networks. In effect, Dovey advocates seeing encounters with ambient literature, whether as an interactant author or an interactant reader, as a departure from kinds of reductionism, as a take-off from the organized complexity of our worlds, individualities, and socialities so as to go further, exposed to disorganized complexity and contingency when interacting and living as intertwined with ubicomp systems.

When going through Ulrik Ekman's interim text on individuating with *software*, the reader cannot but be confronted by the realization that in ubicomp cultures our spaces and environments are also increasingly ones coded as context-aware mixed realities. One realizes that the events we live through are also ones tending towards being programmed and algorithmically anticipated. One realizes that our notions of memory, experience of the present, and future, as well as our notion of distinctions between individuations of the human and the machine are in transformation because multiple software processes continuously code, decode, recode, and overcode them. The dawning interest in cultural software studies is yet to yield more detailed results in terms of addressing the complexities of these transformations.

It is today far from clear how to approach the complexity of the dynamics of multitudes of humans deploying their context-awareness in a situation that is also a mesh with a dynamics of multitudes of more or less intelligent software agents and assistants with both internal technical and human-oriented context-awareness. Moreover, as Wendy Hui Kyong Chun's chapter contribution suggests, via an engagement with the complex interweaving of human and technical memory, human temporalization was never just human, and ubicomp technics tend to ask for a consideration of both an internal complication of memory and a more or less pervasive externalization of memory that feeds back in complex ways, not all positive or linear. Certainly today, relational databases, layers of software and applications along with firm or hardwired algorithmic processes must be acknowledged as a coded and coding complexification of the past, present, and coming times of individuation. Prior to evaluating this, for example, as an enabling condition of freeings of memory or as losses of heritage, tradition, and thoughtful appropriation with a difference, perhaps one would need first to consider how to approach the complexity of individuations with software.

Today, the individual and the social processes of semantic and discrete mathematical coding of selfies, self-presentations, self-surveillance, and self-documentation are perhaps the easiest and most concrete example of the way in which humans in network societies individuate with software, to the point of coding primary and secondary narcissism in external fashion. However, this is hardly ever studied in its complexity and as a software studies issue. Furthermore, the complexity of agile programming processes in software development, multitudes of software agents, and multitudes of operational intelligent assistant programs have not yet become subject to scrutiny, on their own and with respect to the transversal relations across human organisms, subjectivities, social groups, and networked computational entities. Cultural and technical software processes cross in and as individuations today—they constitute something like the liquid limit or soft membrane of organized technocultural complexity. Certainly, simple problems are not at stake. It is unclear how to think of the kinds of organized complexity at stake. The jury is still out as regards the implications and reach of coding for decentered and distributed individuations confronting disorganized or irreducible complexity.

Notes

1. The main references here are to Simondon, *L'individu et sa genèse physico-biologique* and *L'individuation psychique et collective*. However, consider also the excerpt translated into English, cf. Simondon, "The Genesis of the Individual."

2. To readers of Simondon's work on the mode of existence of technical objects, it will be familiar to have noted the kind of privilege that is granted in most places to human orchestration over and above technical individuations. See Simondon, *Du mode d'existence des objets techniques*. In this text I diverge on purpose by proposing a reconsideration of human cultural and technical co-development, a line of thought that is not necessarily anthropocentric. The complexity of ubicomp culture individuations might well be approached via a general phenomenology of machines, as Simondon's work would already suggest. However, this would then be a project to be pursued via a biological philosophy of technology that need not distinguish sharply or clearly hierarchically between technological and biological machinic beings but would rather see machinic constructions and dissipations across both, interior and exterior to human kinds of organism and organization. With both quantum computing and biotechnology in mind, it might be worthwhile revitalizing Simondon's thought on contemporary terms. Simultaneously, this would permit a critical and innovative rereading of the implications that Georges Canguilhem's lecture on "Machine et organisme" had for French thought after WWII, especially for André Leroi-Gourhan, Raymond Ruyer, and Simondon, but also, later, for Gilles Deleuze and early Jacques Derrida. I am indebted here to some of the insights offered in a lecture by Henning Schmidgen (2004).

3. When deploying the distinctions among simple problems, problems of organized complexity, and those of disorganized complexity, I am drawing upon the classical paper by Warren Weaver, "Science and Complexity" (1948).

4. For one good example of a computer scientist, entrepreneurial engineer, and physicist at work on irreducible complexity, consider the writings of Wolfram. Cf., Stephen Wolfram, "Approaches to Complexity Engineering," "Cellular Automata as Models of Complexity," and "Complex Systems Theory." Wolfram's work on fluid turbulence and cellular automata was an important factor in the rise of interest in complex systems.

5. The reader might wish to consider the kinds of introduction to complexity theory offered by some of the sources that have done much to broaden the interest in such approaches, often with a view to evolutionary biology, for example, Goodwin, Brian C. *How the Leopard Changed Its Spots: The Evolution of Complexity*; Kauffman, Stuart A. *The Origins of Order: Self-Organization and Selection in Evolution*. For an idea of the entry of complexity theoretical issues into the social and human sciences, consider the special issue edited by John Urry, cf., Urry, John. "The Complexity Turn." *Theory, Culture & Society* 22, no. 5 (October 1, 2005): 1–14. An excellent introduction to dynamical systems theory and complexity from a position in physics can be found in Nicolis, G., and I. Prigogine. *Exploring Complexity: An Introduction*. More recently, important work on the complexity of network relations and dynamics has been undertaken by Albert-László Barabási in "Scale-Free Networks: A Decade and Beyond." His earlier work does much to make apparent the broad significance of complex network dynamics in the kinds of network societies and everyday cultures with ubicomp under scrutiny in this book, cf., Barabási, *Linked*.

6. The developments in ubicomp, ambient intelligence, and pervasive computing, including mixed reality environments, augmentation, and mobility, have by now, with some delay, become solid parts of the work in HCI and interaction design. See, for example, the treatments in Jacko, Kuniavsky, and Sears. The debate concerning invisibility and visibility, embeddedness and explicit unfolding of interaction designs has spawned a number of accounts and arguments. For just two examples beyond the initial remarks by Weiser, see Adam Greenfield's argument in favor of a new ethics in this field and Yvonne Roger's call for approaches other than the one first presented by Weiser.

References

Barabási, Albert-László. 2003. *Linked: How Everything Is Connected to Everything Else and What It Means for Business, Science, and Everyday Life.* New York: Plume.

Barabási, Albert-László. 2009. "Scale-Free Networks: A Decade and Beyond." *Science* 325 (5939): 412–13.

Goodwin, Brian C. 1994. *How the Leopard Changed Its Spots: The Evolution of Complexity.* New York: C. Scribner's Sons.

Greenfield, Adam. 2008. "Some Guidelines for the Ethical Development of Ubiquitous Computing." *Philosophical Transactions of the Royal Society A* 366: 3823–31.

Jacko, Julie A. 2011. *Human-Computer Interaction Towards Mobile and Intelligent Interaction Environments 14th International Conference, HCI International 2011, Orlando, FL, USA, July 9–14, 2011, Proceedings Part III.* Berlin: Springer.

Jacko, Julie A. 2007. *Human-Computer Interaction. Part III. HCI Intelligent Multimodal Interaction Environments 12th International Conference, HCI International 2007, Beijing, China, July 22–27, 2007, Proceedings.* Berlin: Springer.

Kauffman, Stuart A. 1993. *The Origins of Order: Self-Organization and Selection in Evolution.* Oxford: Oxford University Press.

Kuniavsky, Mike. 2010. *Smart Things: Ubiquitous Computing User Experience Design.* Boston, MA: Morgan Kaufmann.

Nicolis, Gregoire, and Ilya Prigogine. 1989. *Exploring Complexity: An Introduction.* New York: W. H. Freeman.

Rogers, Yvonne. 2006. "Moving on from Weiser's Vision of Calm Computing: Engaging Ubicomp Experiences." In *Ubicomp 2006 Ubiquitous Computing 8th International Conference Proceedings*, edited by Paul Dourish and Adrian Friday, 404–21. Berlin: Springer.

Sears, Andrew, and Julie A. Jacko. 2008. *The Human-Computer Interaction Handbook: Fundamentals, Evolving Technologies, and Emerging Applications.* 2nd ed. New York: Lawrence Erlbaum Assoc.

Simondon, Gilbert. 1992. "The Genesis of the Individual." In *Incorporations*, edited by Jonathan Crary and Sanford Kwinter, 296–319. New York: Zone.

Simondon, Gilbert. 1964. *L'individu et sa Genèse Physico-Biologique.* Paris: Presses universitaires de France.

Simondon, Gilbert. 1989. *L'individuation Psychique et Collective.* Paris: Aubier.

Urry, John. 2005. "The Complexity Turn." *Theory, Culture & Society* 22 (5): 1–14.

Weaver, Warren. 1948. "Science and Complexity." *Scientific American* 36: 536–44.

Weiser, Mark. 1991. "The Computer for the Twenty-first Century." *Scientific American* 265 (3): 94–104.

Weiser, Mark, and John Seely Brown. "The Coming Age of Calm Technology." http://nano.xerox.com/hypertext/weiser/acmfuture2endnote.htm.

Wolfram, Stephen. 1984. "Cellular Automata as Models of Complexity." *Nature* 311 (5985): 419–24.

Wolfram, Stephen. "Complex Systems Theory." http://stephenwolfram.com/publications/academic/complex-systems-theory.pdf.

Wolfram, Stephen. 1986. "Approaches to Complexity Engineering." *Physica D* 2 (1–3): 385–99.

CULTURAL THEORY

Lily Díaz

One of the objectives in this volume for studying the individuation of complexity in culture through ubicomp is to examine the ways in which different formations (like an artifact, a behavior, or a discourse) emerge at certain historical junctures alongside concepts, visions, and even ways of being, and how these subsequently might come to be part of the order of things (or not). From an anthropological perspective, cultural theory has a rich history of documenting and studying such formations in different cultures.

The study of the Kula necklace exchange network among the native Trobrianders that began with Malinowski's fieldwork at the beginning of the twentieth century, for example, identified this practice and the seashell artifacts involved in it as a dynamic and important structuring component implicated in the spatio-temporal social organization of these communities. How you individuate, or who you are, and what is your place in the community, emerge during these public exchanges based on what necklaces you give as well as which ones you receive. It could be said that the Kula exchange "individuates" a social order for the Trobrianders, albeit one that may not be externalized in physical institutions such as the ones in our culture but rather, which is event-driven and emerges to exercise its power through performance (Malinowski 1922; Weiner 1976). More than collections of tangible and intangible items, culture can thus be seen as a driver of events and also as an event-driven force. As an anthropologist who has been doing cross-cultural research of navigation artifacts and techniques, Edwin Hutchins has noted how culture involves processes "by which our everyday cultural practices are enacted" (1995, 354) and these take place both inside and outside our minds and bodies.[1]

Culture is involved in our individuation into singular entities in society through our interaction with artifacts as well as through its organizing potentialities. In the case of the Kula exchange, materials, such as the types of shells used in the making, determine the identity of a necklace. Following the same recursive pattern, the necklace, either given or received, individuates both the giver and the recipient within a social order that is itself individuated through the performance.

As ubicomp technologies develop, spread, and become integrated into human activities, they individuate into diverse specificities such as tools used in particular contexts and activities. But context and infrastructure are not things that exist as if frozen in time. The category of social media tools, for example, is not something that was invented beforehand by one person, community, or corporation. It is something that is developing and individuating in a way that is contingent or at least dependent upon multiple historical and social conditions that vary. Because of this complexity, it is very difficult for designers and software developers to anticipate the gamut of possible uses of a given technology.

Individuation also occurs within and as a part of the realm of language, the first and most ubiquitous of human tools. As a human system of communication, language develops over time, individuating into multiplicities such as discourses and genres. The latter can in turn individuate and reify ideologies and practices. Sean Cubitt's chapter in this volume describes paradoxical aspects of the historical individuation of the notions of the "information environment." It also describes the ways in which this leads to subsequent individuation of other concepts, occluding their true nature. According to Cubitt, "environment" denotes that which it environs (or surrounds, encloses). In doing so, it simultaneously defines its own boundaries regarding what is internal as well as what is external to it. The organism cannot be part of it, since it is that which is surrounded. Confusion and paradox occur when discourses concerning these are treated as synonymous (Bateson 2000, 180). Cubitt uses this to elaborate a theory of environments as externalities from which the human is excluded. Information notions such as "the commons," "the radio spectrum," and "telecommunications" individuate historic- ally, as they are transformed and adapted to the contexts of colonial histories rife with political and economic conflict, and where subjects are already individuated into categories of the disenfranchised. From the "commons," a term initially used to denote the act of enclosure of the common land from which the poor were excluded, through its diverse iterations that include "the enclosure of skills traced by Marx" into its current use which denotes knowledge enclosed in databases to be commercialized "through intellectual property laws and . . . sold as a new [individuated] commodity to those from whom it was taken from" and as a term associated with the colonization of intellectual labor, we are confronted with a new, diffracted perspective of the information environment, one that reveals the northern, white, male, capitalistic orienta- tions of its individuating.

"All becoming is rife with tension," writes Erin Manning in her chapter in this volume, as she introduces us to the notion of the minor gesture. Standing as if she were at the edge of language, she proposes that it is not the artwork that is the minor gesture but rather "what activates it under precise conditions." In doing so, it also individuates the artfulness of the art object, just as it sees the emergence of the art institution and the artist who speaks its language. As a variability that is both durational and co-compository, there is allegedly no reduction of complexity in the examples that she presents. For example, in Song Dong's *Waste Not*, exhibited at the Sydney 2012 and Moscow 2013 Biennales, 10,000 objects gathered from the artist's mother's everyday life are displayed as multiplicities, gathered in the form of a flat, diagrammatic layout. "A core theme of *Waste Not* is the idea that people, everyday objects and personal stories are not only spiritually rich in thematic material but recognizable evidence of politics and history in family life" (Manning). Symryn Gill's *Pearls* (1999), on the other hand, enacts the transformation of an artwork that exists more than as an object, as part of a process of sharing. And in her own work, *Weather Patterns* (with Nathaniel Stern and Bryan Cera), Manning demonstrates how the artful is "not about form" or content, but rather about the capacity to be felt. The aim is to make the work relational, rather than simply interactive. "What is foregrounded is the quality of the object's material forces rather than its matter-form."

Following a desire to liberate the sensuous experience "from its default channeling through symbolic systems of signification . . . ," is Hansen's approach to the topology of sensibility. Hansen aims to guide us towards a new reading of phenomenology,[2] where topological culture individuates not as reduction but rather as a "direct response to worldly complexity." The material reality of an object "simply is that object" so there "operates an objective equivalence between the appearance of a being and its phenomenon."

As an example directly related to the key issue of this anthology, Hansen discusses the so-called "technological unconscious," which is structured through the "forging of topological relations by media machines" and which "necessarily implicates us in a sensibility that exceeds the processing capacities of our sense organs." Through this autonomy of topological culture it is possible to conceive of dimensions of human experience (as in ubicomp cultures), which are, their independence from consciousness notwithstanding, given in and as conscious time with technical mediations.

Notes

1. Hutchins' work is exemplary because of his comparisons between indigenous embodied methods for navigation that rely on tacit knowledge and methods that make use of highly codified knowledge embedded into an artifact, such as navigation charts.
2. According to Hansen, such expanded phenomenology must relax its grip on consciousness in order to focus on the world itself.

References

Bateson, Gregory. 2000 (1972). *Steps to An Ecology of the Mind*. Chicago, IL: University of Chicago Press..
Hutchins, Edwin. 1995. *Cognition in the Wild*. Cambridge, MA: MIT Press, 1995.
Malinowski, Bronislav. 1922. *Argonauts of the Western Pacific. An Account of Native Enterprise and Adventure in the Archipelagoes of Melanesian New Guinea*. London, UK: George Routledge and Sons Limited. Accessed on April 22, 2015, https://archive.org/details/argonautsofthewe032976mbp.
Weiner, Annette. 1976. *Women of Value, Men of Reknown*. Austin, TX: University of Texas Press.

TOPOLOGY OF SENSIBILITY[1]

Mark B. N. Hansen

Topological Rationality and the Necessity of Phenomenology

In concluding their introduction to a recent special issue of *Theory, Culture & Society*, Celia Lury, Luciana Parisi, and Tiziana Terranova note the particular paradox instituted by "the becoming-topological of culture" (Lury et al. 2012). On one hand, topological culture is said to generate an "immense extension of the reach of rationality . . . that precludes any contagion with sensuality, the visceral or feeling;" topological culture thus installs a "new formalism" that operates autonomously from the register of phenomenological experience and that cannot be "challenged by either the semiosis of language or a feeling body." By designating the topological mediation of contemporary culture as a "rationality" (here understood in a well-nigh Frankfurt school sense), Lury et al. (2012) mean to foreground the autonomy of its instrumental function: Simply put, the topological rationality of contemporary media culture operates as a formal logic unhampered by any merely human concerns.[2]

On the other hand, however, this same becoming-autonomous of topological culture is said to provide the impetus for a reinvention of sensuous experience that is rooted in a liberation of sensibility from its default channeling through symbolic systems of signification: ". . . insofar as the indices, meta-models, networks and experiments of topology are not detached from the material, from the body, language or the senses, but rather work in and through them, topo-logical rationality *participates in and renews the specificity of the material and the sensuous*. Topological rationality is thus . . . dynamic, soft and tractable, both precise and vague, able to operate the physical and sensual horizon of experience beyond and beneath the law-like symbolic system of signification" (Lury et al. 2012, 28; emphasis added).

This simultaneous embrace of topological culture's *autonomy* from human experience *and* of its potential to "renew the sensuous" basis of experience constitutes a paradox for our times. For how can we invest at one and the same time in topological culture's capacity to act in ways that do not involve humans at all *and* still maintain that such activity holds the promise to transform *our* sensuous and material lives?

As my way of intervening in current debates concerning topology and its role in cultural and media theory, I want to suggest that a "solution" to this paradox—if "solution" is indeed the correct term here—can be found in phenomenology, and more precisely, in the irreducibility of the domain of the phenomenal and the operation of appearance. As I see it, phenomenology—albeit in a much modified, "objective" mode—constitutes a complement to the becoming-topological of culture: Where the latter expands the operationality of culture beyond what can be accessed through human modes of cognition and presentational experience, phenomenology provides *perhaps the most viable* account of how the resulting expanded material domain—what I would call "worldly sensibility"[3]—can be made to reenter the fold of experience. Accordingly, I propose in what follows neither simply to demonstrate the viability of an objective phenomenology nor to show how this viability is itself the strict entailment of the becoming-topological of culture. Rather, I shall seek to reveal why the becoming-topological of culture effectively *requires an objective phenomenology or phenomenology of objective manifestation* as its complement.

Taking a cue from Matthew Fuller and Andrew Goffey as well as from Ulrik Ekman, all of whom adopt a critical perspective on Lury et al.'s (2012) enthusiastic embrace of the "topological turn" in cultural and media studies, let me specify my own investment in topology (Fuller and Goffey 2012; Ekman 2015). I am interested in topology above all because of its promise to inform a phenomenology capable of accounting for the asubjectal subjectivity that correlates to the objective operationality of today's culture. For me, as for all of the critics just named, this means first and foremost the objective operationality *of media culture*, that is, the capacity of today's media machines to generate appearances of worldly sensibility, to directly manifest the world independently of any synthetic operation of a subject or a consciousness. The impasse that an objective phenomenology faces can now be specified: How can we account for the qualitative experience of these direct manifestations of sensibility given that their subjectivity is a nonsubjectal one, a subjectivity that does not appear *to a subject* or a *consciousness*—in short, an asubjectal subjectivity (or superjectivity) of the world itself?

Without fully ratifying Lury et al.'s (2012) thesis regarding the "becoming topological" of culture and its characterization as a new "rationality," I would concur with them (and also with Fuller, Goffey, and Ekman) that today's media machines, be they databases or the devices driving virtual cities, are currently forging topological relations among elements of worldly sensibility that fall beneath the threshold of conscious awareness and attention. In this sense, they can be said to be implementing topology at the level of the concrete infrastructure of culture, what Nigel Thrift long ago termed the "technological unconscious" (Thrift 2004). Insofar as it is structured through the forging of topological relations by media machines, the world in which we live necessarily implicates us in a sensibility that exceeds the processing capacities of our sense organs. We can thus say that today's media topological world *itself* provides the impetus for the revitalization of phenomenology envisioned here: It literally demands a renewal of our understanding of sensibility. To make good on this demand, which is equally an opportunity, we need to develop the concrete modes in which culture is becoming topological into resources for a regrounding of phenomenology in worldly sensibility. Hence my focus on the operationality of relational databases.

Such a development effectively positions phenomenology as a complement to what Luciana Parisi has dubbed the "scientific study of culture."[4] More precisely, phenomenology constitutes that part of a scientific study of culture that is responsible for explaining the irreducible subjectivity of the objective manifestation of the world: An expanded, objective phenomenology becomes necessary *to account for the irreducible asubjectal subjectivity that characterizes the operationality of culture even as it resists taking form as a content of consciousness*. Insofar as it constitutes the *qualitative* dimension of the objective manifestation of the world, this asubjectal subjectivity is precisely what is "intended" (if we can repurpose this term) by the contemporary phenomenological gesture in its (technically) expanded field. This means that the renewal of the sensuous toward which Lury et al. (2012) gesture can only come to pass through this superjectal subjectivity that, for its part, necessarily correlates to any and every objective manifestation of the world.

If media topological culture can renew the sensuous, it is precisely and solely by confronting human experience with a dimension of sensibility and a mode of subjectivity—the sensibility of the objective and the subjectivity of the superjectal—that evades presentation in consciousness and that can best be manifested media-technically, or as I would prefer to put it, in a mode of "originary mediatedness."

Databases as Topological Machines

In order to bring a concrete dimension to our exploration of the autonomy of appearance—an exploration that is central for developing the nonanthropocentric objective phenomenology I am proposing here—let me begin by focusing directly on the sociotechnical "device" that is driving the "topological turn" in the material operationality of culture, namely the computational database. Such a focus is shared by three complementary yet divergent recent analyses that correlate mathematical analysis with cultural theory in ways that will prove to be directly relevant to the aims just enumerated.

The first of these is Adrian Mackenzie's "More Parts than Elements: How Databases Multiply," an exploration of the structure of relational databases via the excess of inclusion over belonging that informs French philosopher Alain Badiou's set-theoretical ontology (Badiou 2001). For Mackenzie, what is at stake in today's complex databases is the production of multiples, and specifically the possibility to "work on" or to "do" multiples, by which he means something like influencing the way in which multiples (data aggregations) are generated. Such work on or doing of multiples aims to produce new modes of inclusion and does so by exploiting the "excess that animates the multiple." "The lesson of the generic subset," concludes Mackenzie, "might be that more schemas, views, clusters, and tables also multiply the multiple in various ways" (Mackenzie 2012, 344).

Fuller and Goffey's discussion of relational databases in their essay, "Digital Infrastructures and the Machinery of Topological Abstraction," adopts an antithetical position by conceiving of the relational database as a "topological machine." By this, they mean a "device that intentionally or unintentionally engineers connections between things, generating continuities" (Fuller and Goffey 2012, 326). For Fuller and Goffey, the topological operation of databases contrasts with their more mundane function to enable "better logistical control of the entities" that they model. In their topological operation, databases function experimentally, in the sense we introduced above, to create new and unpredictable relations: "as topological machines, relational databases work through systems of relations to create, confirm or discover relations, and, as such, work to generate *new and potentially arbitrary* kinds of continuity as well as the properties of the figures thereby generated" (Fuller and Goffey 2012, 326; emphasis added).

As the title of her study, "The Governmental Topologies of Database Devices," makes clear, sociologist Evelyn Ruppert concurs with Fuller and Goffey in conceptualizing databases as devices. For Ruppert, this conceptualization is meant first and foremost to foreground the complexity of database operation, and specifically, the capacity of databases to intermingle the "performance of individuals and populations" in an "ensemble or system of relations" (Ruppert 2012, 120). Ruppert eschews the technicist focus typical of sociological approaches to database culture in favor of an "ontological framing" that "understands objects as already and always multiple and complex, and 'moves us from multiple interpretations of objects to thinking about multiple objects themselves' [citing John Law and Vicky Singleton]" (Ruppert 2012, 119). What results is a "topological analytics" that balances between the technological and subjective: "Rather than being technologically determined, these databases are bound up with a particular ontology of the subject and governing logic, and . . . there is not a determinist but a dynamic relationship between the two." Databases, Ruppert underscores, "do not simply add up data about subjects but materialize ontologically different subjects in relation to what they do. . . . joined-up databases materialize the 'individuality' of subjects in intensified, distributed, and fluctuating ways" (Ruppert 2012, 120).

With this conclusion, we return to the issue, first broached by Lury et al. (2012), of topological culture's promise to broker a more expansive anchoring of experience in worldly sensibility. For all the critics under discussion here, databases operate, in some way or other, with and on behavioral and environmental data that evade the scope of conscious thematization or attention. For Mackenzie, they operate on the multiple itself—meaning multiples that compose individuals and populations, as well as sets and sets of sets—such that the "status of the multiple" itself becomes "difficult to conceive apart from the technical processes of ordering, sorting, counting, and calculating" (Mackenzie 2012, 338). For Fuller and Goffey, the database extracts value from back end data by "drawing participants into, and/or implicating them within a system that draws on their activity in the production of socio-technically conditioned topological continua" (Fuller and Goffey 2012, 324). And for Ruppert (here following Bruno Latour), databases actualize the promise of the Tardean conception of the social by making it possible "to materialize a conception of population as a space of relations consisting of multiple aggregates of individuals with fixed metrics (biographies) along with complex and always varying ones (transactions, conduct)" (Ruppert 2012, 130).

By addressing and engaging worldly sensibility "directly," meaning, independently and prior to any "synthesis" into and by a properly subjective, intentional correlation or Kantian *Vorstellung*,[5] today's databases manifest the ontological operation of subindividual, asubjective—dare I say "superjective"—forces in ways that can transform experience. As the "direct" manifestation of such worldly forces, autonomously from their contributions to higher-order constellations or "societies" like human bodyminds or consciousnesses, topological actualizations of data must be understood to be what I shall call (with a nod to the Czech phenomenologist, Jan Patocka) "objective" appearances of the world itself *as it is* in some particular situation—indeed, they *are* the world itself *as it is* from that particular perspective or "data-point." Though they serve, in one sense, to give access to what remains outside the scope of our experience, these media-generated appearances themselves directly contribute to the sensibility of the world: They are in themselves acts of sensing, as I have underscored in *Feed-Forward*, and as such they do not simply mediate something else, but produce and manifest world sensibility as irreducibly—or we might well say, as *originarily*—mediated.

With this conclusion, we come back to the paradox of topological culture, namely, how a "topological" and "originary" mediatedness of sensibility (the above-introduced autonomy of appearance) that seems to operate entirely independently of human experience can at the same time promise to renew the latter's basis in sensibility, and thereby expand its scope. Rephrased in the wake of our invocation of relational databases, this promise can be specifically aligned with the capacity of databases to host pre-individual singularities (elements that operate at a level beneath the integrated individuation of an entity [Simondon 2005]), to wield them as worldly forces in their own right, and to bring them into the realm of manifestation as "objective appearances" of the world's being in particular situations.

Reconceptualizing Phenomenology

My proximate aim in this chapter is precisely to present an "objective" phenomenology (or phenomenology of "objective manifestation") that can be characterized by three fundamental commitments: 1) its eschewal of the traditional phenomenological reduction and privilege of intentional (human) consciousness in favor of the self-manifestation of the world, or what I would prefer to call "worldly sensibility"; 2) its celebration of the priority of appearance over ontology and its positioning of ontology (modes of existence) as an entailment of concrete appearances of the world (understood, following Czech phenomenologist Jan Patocka (1995), as the way the world *is*, the *being* of the world, in that particular situation); and 3) its foregrounding of technical mediation as a non anthropocentric and particularly capacious agent of appearance, such that acts of sensing performed by machines—an ever increasing source of sensibility—generate intentional or "quasi-intentional" appearances of the world (understood as just defined) that do not depend on consciousness or any other avatar of the subject.

In addition to presenting an objective phenomenology, I propose in what follows, and in response to the topic of this collective volume, to explore how such a phenomenology allows us to rethink two fundamental issues that directly concern the continuing relevance of phenomenology in a world where the temporal and spatial frameworks of human consciousness have become and continue to be ever increasingly marginalized. First, and most directly relevant to the concerns of this volume, is the relationship of phenomenology to complexity. Let me be blunt on this point: The objective phenomenology presented here seeks to embrace worldly sensibility in its complexity as a "direct" source for subjectivity, where "direct" has the specific meaning of "not filtered through intentional consciousness." As we shall see, this relationship entails a view of complexity that converges with Warren Weaver's category of "disorganized complexity" as well as Stephen Wolfram's concept of "computational equivalence," and it stipulates that the operationality of parallel computing in contemporary database culture and in much scientific experimentation gives unprecedented access to worldly complexity (Weaver 1948; Wolfram 1986). This, of course, does not mean that data driven searching and scientific experimentation operate without any reduction whatsoever, but rather that the reduction involved is imposed by the being of the phenomena at issue in conjunction with the apparatuses necessary to generate them (i.e., their appearing), *and not by the operational reference frame of any intentional consciousness or other avatar of the subject.*

In this respect, as we shall see, the paradigm for thinking the relationship of phenomenology to complexity is quantum theoretical, and specifically Bohrian. Most centrally, it reproduces the conjunction of epistemology and ontology that characterizes what I have elsewhere developed as a Bohrian phenomenology (Hansen, forthcoming), the crux of which is the autonomy of the phenomenon: Due to the absolute inaccessibility of the quantum entity, which strictly speaking *does not exist as such prior to the act of measurement*, it makes no sense to speak of the phenomenon or appearance as correlated to some independently existing entity or object that would furnish its ontological source. On the contrary, one can only speak of the originary phenomenon – the phenomenon, as it were, *in itself*, which (again following Patocka) is simply the world as it is from a particular perspective (through a particular experimental apparatus), and one must grant the phenomenon (or appearance) a certain autonomy, despite the fact that, prior to the act of measurement, it can only take the form of a determinate probability.

The point here is twofold: First that reduction as such is irreducible, and second, that there are different sorts and magnitudes of reductions. To simplify things for my purposes here, let me distinguish (in line with the notion of "objective" phenomenology) between "objective" and "subjective" reduction, where the latter means reduction in virtue of an intentional (human) consciousness or other avatar of the subject and the former means reduction in virtue of the phenomenon in itself, in conjunction with whatever measuring apparatus (or medium) is necessary to generate it (following Wolfgang Ernst [2013], I understand media in its most general operationality as measuring apparatus or device). This distinction between objective and subjective reduction will allow us to re-conceptualize the relationship of consciousness itself to worldly sensibility in its full complexity, and also—crucially—to dedifferentiate subjectivity from consciousness (or the subjectivity *of a subject*) and to anchor it instead in the appearances of worldly sensibility themselves ("asubjectal" or "superjective" subjectivity).

On such a view, consciousness properly constitutes a higher-order accomplishment—the composition of a "society" (in Whitehead's [1978] sense of the term[6]) out of elements of worldly sensibility that are themselves subjective—or alternatively, that are appearances *in themselves* of worldly sensibility; such an account describes a second-order "subjective" phenomenology (e.g. a phenomenology of consciousness) that arises from a first-order "objective" and technically-mediated phenomenology of worldly sensibility. As I have argued in *Feed-Forward*, the "asubjective phenomenology" proposed by Patocka furnishes an important resource here: Specifically, Patocka's brand of "objective" phenomenology situates appearance or manifestation as an objective achievement of the world itself (worldly sensibility), and not an accomplishment of consciousness processing data from the world. Taking off from where my earlier effort left off, I want to foreground what I now take to be the key insight at the heart of Patocka's project: The *inseparability of being and manifestation*, or—in terms perhaps more germane to topological culture—of operationality and phenomenality.

Nothing less is at stake in this inseparability than the anthropocentrism of phenomenology. By extending this inseparability to the activity of topological media—such that *every operation whatsoever would generate an appearance*—we are able to answer Renaud Barbaras's criticism of Patocka's asubjective phenomenology for its lingering anthropocentrism. According to Barbaras, what Patocka's brand of objective phenomenology cannot explain is why the world, in its act of manifesting itself as an "objective" appearance in every instance, necessarily manifests itself to a Dasein or human subject (Barbaras 2005, "Afterward"). For Barbaras, this conclusion—a necessary one given Patocka's methodology—contravenes the promise of Patocka's effort to rethink phenomenology as cosmology. For if the objective manifestation of the world (which is not a *representation of* the way the world objectively is, as it is for Husserl, but simply the way the world objectively is *in that specific phenomenal situation*) is in every case a manifestation that can be correlated with a subjective position, that *could be* an appearance to a human subject or consciousness, then the very promise of Patocka's asubjective reconceptualization of phenomenology comes to naught. If, by contrast, the objective manifestation of the world is an appearance generated through the operationality of topological media—if the access the latter grants to sensibility, its presentification of sensibility, is *the correlate of its* modulation of sensibility—then we are dealing with a logic of being and manifestation, operationality and phenomenality, that is not constrained by any correlation to an act of human consciousness or *Dasein*.

In line with this program for revitalizing phenomenology, we must oppose Lury et al.'s (2012) conviction that the autonomy of topological culture entails its *absolute non-relatedness* to human experience. Against this claim—all too resonant to my mind of speculative realism—I want to explore how the autonomy of topological culture rather calls into play a dimension of *human experience*—precisely its relation to and implication within worldly sensibility—that is itself opaque to *human modes of access*, and I want to suggest that it is precisely this dimension that accounts for the potential of topological culture to renew the sensuous basis for experience. More simply put, the autonomy of topological culture must not be understood as absolute non-relatedness: For while the autonomy claimed for topological operationality may mean that it is constituted without being calibrated to human sense ratios, *this doesn't in any way mean that it has no impact on human sensory experience*. Rather, we can say that topological operationality impacts human sensory experience *indirectly*, as I have argued in *Feed-Forward*, by first impacting worldly sensibility, the generalized and impersonal domain of sensibility from out of which human experience proper derives, and only subsequently coming to bear on whatever higher-order, human sensory and perceptual compositions that may arise from it. On this view, if the becoming-topological of culture holds the promise to renew the specificity of the material and the sensuous, it is precisely because of its exteriority with respect to the modes of sensing that have historically characterized the human. By composing the domain of worldly sensibility independently of any restriction to and without being channeled *through narrowly human modes* of sensing and cognizing, today's topological machines provide artifactual access to—and thus put humans into contact with—a domain of sensibility that exceeds what humans can process as "sensations." The central question this poses is how to account for the resulting extra-sensory contact with worldly sensibility: How, that is, can our subjective experience be influenced by something that we literally cannot directly sense? The answer, of course, has everything to do with the operationality of topological machines, and specifically, their capacity to mediate between sensibility and human sensing.

By topological machine, a term I borrow from Fuller and Goffey, I mean a machine capable of a bidirectional relationality that both permits the inclusion of elements exterior to its operational ontology and allows such inclusion to impact its ongoing dynamic development. As we shall see, it is precisely the dynamism and ontological flexibility afforded by topology, understood as topos-theoretical onto-experimentation that facilitates this opening to the exterior. For in the end, what is required in order for elements exterior to machinic operationality to transform that operationality is nothing less than a topological relationality, the forging of a continuity as a mode of connection. In their role as forgers of such continuity, digital devices *cum* topological machines have the power to reshape how humans sense themselves and their worlds by including within experience—or, we might say, by *introjecting into* experience—a domain of sensibility inaccessible to human sensory organs and by allowing that inclusion/introjection to impact the ongoing dynamics of human experience moving forward.

Let me be clear on what I mean here: I am not trying to suggest that today's topological machines—and exemplarily today's massive, aggregated relational databases—themselves have the power to generate radical novelty or to self-evolve. Rather, in attributing a certain autonomy to them, what I mean to underscore is the mode of their operationality in relation to human modes of experience, as well as the certain margin of indeterminacy that comes from their potential to forge relations that cannot be predicted in advance on the basis of their constituent elements. In a manner loosely analogous to the situation of quantum phenomena, as already mentioned, these relations do not strictly speaking exist prior to their genesis via technical operation, such that their status is probabilistic even if they are, as potential appearances, always already fully real (i.e., simply are the way the world really *is* in a particular situation). Accordingly, the power they grant to reshape sensibility stems from their capacity—as agents of sensibility—to operate "directly" on worldly sensibility and to generate worldly sensibility as a result of their operationality. The changes that they produce in the texture of sensibility form the catalyst, in a subsequent operation of composition, for changes in the sensibility informing human experience.

From Intrinsic to Pluralistic Ontology

In this and the next section, I shall develop further this objective and thoroughly technical phenomenology of manifestation with the aid of mathematical topology and specifically of topos theory as developed by Alexandre Grothendieck (Plotnitsky 2012; Zalamea 2013). My aim here is to explicate the non anthropocentric and objective aspects of the topology of sensibility. Then, in a final section I shall return to the concrete operationality of relational databases in order to reconsider how this topology of sensibility transforms the situation of subjectivity.

Taken as the catalyst for a phenomenology constructed on the basis of mathematics, the identity of appearance and being calls for a deployment of topos theory following the original, ontological inspiration that motivated Grothendieck to develop it (Plotnitsky 2012). Topos theory was intended to proffer a flexible and capacious procedure for generating a radically relative mathematics capable of including literally everything that there is, within the domain of mathematics proper, but also beyond its bounds. That is why Grothendieck sees in distinct topoi *distinct ontologies* and understands topos theory *as a plurality of possible ontologies*. In Arkady Plotnitsky's words, Grothendieck's topos-theoretical ontology is "that of the *multiple* of multiples-without-Ones: It is a multiplicity of possible ontologies, each of which may be governed by multiple possible logics" (Plotnitsky 2012, 352). By positioning appearance as the agent of a polymorphous and performative worldly sensibility, Grothendieck's topos-theoretical ontology provides a means for the complexity of the world to impact the latter's asubjective subjectivity and thereby to "count" for the ensuing phenomenology of sensibility, and indeed, to render it a topology of sensibility.

Far from constituting a logical supplement to set theory, as it does for Badiou, topos theory articulates a distinct theory of mathematical (and extra-mathematical) relationality. Its difference from set theory is decisive precisely because it liberates appearance from its *subordination to* ontology: In its wake, appearance need no longer be restricted to specifying the localization of the event's occurrence. By liberating appearance in this way, topos theory foregrounds the ineliminability of appearance as well as its inseparability from—its particular identity with—being. That is why, on Grothendieck's topos-theoretical ontology, being is not disjoined from appearance, as an inconsistent multiple that cannot appear as such; rather it is always necessarily coupled to appearance according to an open logic that refuses to limit in advance the configurations according to which being and appearance can be conjoined. On this score, not only is appearance case specific, but it holds the responsibility for assembling a relational nexus—indeed, a "society" in the full Whiteheadian sense of the term—that only subsequently, that is, as a result of the assembling itself, becomes unified within or under a particular ontology.

Whatever univocity of being there is on Grothendieck's topos-theoretical ontology is a provisional and contingent one, as Plotnitsky clearly discerns: "Grothendieck's topos-theoretical ontology is a kind of multi-universe. There may still be a *univocity* of being, which brings being and appearing together, and inscribes events, but only within each given ontology, amidst the plurivocity of such ontologies" (Plotnitsky 2012, 362). On this account, ontology—far from being the pre-instituted anchor for a multiplicity of possible appearances—is itself *a function of the play of appearances*, an accomplishment of the genesis of relational webs via the arrows and vectors that constitute topoi. In sum, Grothendieck's topos-theoretical ontology furnishes the basis for a multiple dynamic relational ontogenesis in which appearances, no longer subordinated to a pregiven, static ontology that they would serve to localize, themselves wield the power to create.

Ontology Comes Later

Having now revealed the particular priority claimed by appearance within topos-theoretical ontology, let us return to our main task of developing an objective, originarily (technically) mediated phenomenology, the first principle of which is the inseparability of being and appearance. What can topos theory contribute to such a project? Or, more precisely, what can the *ontological* understanding of topos theory contribute? And how does the resulting phenomenology contribute in turn to our understanding—and our mobilization—of our contemporary topological culture?

As the operator of the inseparability of being and appearance, the generalized relationality introduced by topos theory promises to fulfill the requirement we announced above: To provide a model for world manifestation where appearance simply is reality the way it is in a given situation *and* where the lingering anthropomorphism of Patocka's asubjective phenomenology (the requirement that such manifestation be, in every case, to a *Dasein*-like entity) can be abjured. On such a model, it is not the pre-installed correlation between reality and a subjective being capable of processing it that accounts for the equivalence of being and appearance. On the contrary, it is the world manifesting power of appearance itself—a power that operates independently of and prior to any correlation with any subjective entity—that accounts for this equivalence. In contrast to orthodox phenomenology, we must think appearance, without any neutralization whatsoever, as the actualization of a rich relational potentiality. Eschewing any phenomenological reduction, appearance directly engages worldly complexity: Indeed, what its ontological performativity manifests is nothing other than the asubjective subjectivity of sensibility, the superjective expression of worldly complexity. If such manifestation involves a "reduction"—of the potentiality of relationality as such—it is a reduction of potentiality to a particular objective situation, to a perspective on objective reality, and not the reduction *of the objective reality* of—and the *complexity* informing—the phenomenon.

As a special kind of category, and indeed a particular kind of topos that expands topology to objects with algebraic properties,[7] the topoi of topos theory operate as agents of a massively open-ended relationality, of a promiscuous sociality:

> From categorical or topos-theoretical perspective one starts with a certain, arbitrarily chosen space, *X*, potentially any space, without initially specifying it mathematically. Indeed, one can start with an object, say, a set of numbers, that is not spatial in any given sense and only becomes spatialized by virtue of its relations to other objects of the same kind, analogous to the relationships between conventional spatial objects. What would be specified, at first, are the relationships between spaces, such as categorical arrows, *Y X*, mapping one space by another space or multiplicity of other spaces. This procedure enables one to specify a given space not in terms of its intrinsic structure, say, as a set of points with relationships among them, but, in Yuri I. Manin's terms, "sociologically"—through its relationships with other spaces of the same category. An intrinsic structure—set-theoretical or other, say, topological, as the number of holes in a given space—is then derived from this "sociology."
>
> (Plotnitsky 2012, 357)

It is this radical sociological dimension of topos theory that accounts for its value for the cultural theorist. Conceived sociologically, topoi can be understood to operate as technologies for interrelating elements of the world following a procedure that is both immanent and radically external. Topoi enter into relations because of their formal homology with one another, but the scope of what can count as the content of such relations is literally unbounded.

That is why, as Plotnitsky underscores, topos theory explodes the alleged closure of mathematical thought and opens mathematics to the world in the most radical way: "Ontology—that which 'pronounces what is expressible about being qua being'—need not always be and *even cannot always be* mathematical, or only mathematical. Indeed, this is true even in mathematics itself: No matter how we try to configure it mathematically (via set theory, topos theory, or otherwise), any rigorously established mathematical ontology *always has a nonmathematical residue*" (Plotnitsky 2012, 352; emphasis added). Understood in this way, topos theoretical ontology constitutes a *radically extrinsic* and *pluralist* ontology that designates not a single form of being but an open set of modes of existence subject to what Plotnitsky calls translational or ontomathematical experimentation: "One can in principle think of practicing any given mathematics in any given ontological domain by thus experimenting *with the ontologies themselves*, since one changes a given ontology by this new practice as well, as again, Grothendieck did in the case of algebraic varieties" (Plotnitsky 2012, 363; emphasis added). With this conclusion, we encounter what may well turn out to be the fundamental principle of topos-theoretical phenomenology: *Ontology comes later.*

Relationality: Intrinsic or Extrinsic?

What remains for us to demonstrate is how objective appearances—the very agents of the objective phenomenology at issue here—are and must be coupled to subjective purposes (but not to subjective positions) in order for them to wield their ontological power to manifest the world as it is in a particular situation. What the brief introduction of topos theory introduces is a flexible procedure for constituting what, with Simondon, we can call "transductive" relations among heterogeneous elements, where the elements related are subsequent to the procedural operation of relationality (Simondon 2005). The transformational vectors central to topos theory take the place of "intentionality" in orthodox phenomenology and thus provide both a process for generating "objective" appearances that does not depend on subjective synthesis as well as an access to worldly sensibility as a heterogeneous and generative source of asubjectal subjectivity.

As a way of bringing my discussion to a conclusion, I want in this final section to return to the three discussions of databases (MacKenzie, Fuller and Goffey, Ruppert) introduced above in order to focus on two crucial issues that come to the fore when an objective, topological phenomenology is implemented by and through the operationality of relational databases. First is the crucial issue, that has already surfaced in our discussion of topos theory, of how to understand the latter's relationship to ontology: Is topos theory simply a specification of the logic of a unitary, set-theoretical ontology, as it is for Badiou and following him, for MacKenzie? Or, is it rather a transductive procedure that subordinates ontology to appearance, in a way that pluralizes, and in a sense, operationalizes ontology? Second is the equally crucial and related issue of how complexity enters into and is processed by technically implemented topos-theoretical modelling: Does such modelling follow a technicist logic that can be said simply to unfold potentialities contained in the databases at issue, and specifically in their often quite imperfect and seamless aggregation, as Fuller and Goffey maintain? Or does topological modelling in relational databases rather open a more complex relational field of potentiality—what we might call a plural and always transitory, pluralistic ontology of complexity—that is extrinsic in relation to the elements that constitute the databases at issue?

The three papers on relational databases yield a continuum of difference that allows, in relation to the above issues, two groupings. Fuller and Goffey's focus on the capacity for databases to generate unpredictable relations on the basis of imperfect aggregation introduces a more flexible and capacious account of how the technical can be articulated to the social than does MacKenzie's more formalist account of multiplying the multiple. And Ruppert's analysis of database operationality in terms of flexible and variable configurations of presence and absence (appearances), precisely because it translates topos theory's ontological pluralism and sensitivity to complexity into concrete terms, in turn provides an important sociological expansion—indeed a rendering-extrinsic—of Fuller and Goffey's restriction of ontology to the technical operationality of databases.

A. From Subduction to Topology

We could say that MacKenzie and Fuller and Goffey work with two different models of "inclusion," understood set-theoretically as opening up an excess in relation to the elements constituting a set. For MacKenzie, inclusion is combinational, meaning that, strictly speaking, it implements the excess of inclusion over belonging that is the core of Badiou's philosophical project; for Fuller and Goffey, by contrast, inclusion, while still marking an excess over belonging, is not really a mode of inclusion at all, since it occurs in the conflicts, ambiguity and not quite proximities that characterize today's imperfectly connected or "aggregated" databases. In sum, for MacKenzie the source for excess is intrinsic to the databases; whereas for Fuller and Goffey it is, in some sense, extrinsic to the elements constituting any set of databases. What hangs in the balance here is nothing less than the capacity of relational databases to operate as topological machines, that is, as machines capable of forging relations with "elements" of worldly sensibility that do not belong to them as their constitutive elements.

Mackenzie focuses on Google's *MapReduce* in order to concretize how the excess of inclusion over belonging—the very excess that informs Badiou's deployment of forcing—drives the development of database structure. Introduced in 2007 as a new programming technique and database infrastructure designed to expedite the processing of information, MapReduce operates by disaggregating (mapping) and reaggregating (reducing) large databases. According to Mackenzie, what MapReduce accomplishes is a rendering-dynamic of the database, a continuous reorganization of database structure: "The way in which multiples are made in databases is not just expansive (as in lateral aggregation). Data does not simply expand to predicate more and more actions, events, or phenomena. Modes of inclusion change alongside modes of belonging. . . . Indeed, while new kinds of elements may occasionally be added to a database schema, the repartitioning and selection of subsets seem far more important in trajectories through databases" (Mackenzie 2012, 348). It is precisely in these repartitionings and selections that Mackenzie locates the social extension of the set-theoretical ontology of relational databases; they work by "re-counting the situation," yielding openings for "new subjectifications," "new forms of value," and "new configurations of public-private space" (MacKenzie 2012, 346).

Notwithstanding its apparent promise to couple technicist ontology and social production, this shift to vertically aggregated data structuring—precisely because it remains dependent on the procedure of forcing[8]—can do no more than produce variant "logical" instantiations of a static technicist ontology via a process called "subduction": "The disaggregation and reaggregation we see in MapReduce subduct multiples. 'Subduction,' or forcing rather than completing multiples, seems to multiply them" (Mackenzie 2012, 348). However, subduction can only proffer new possibilities that are and can be nothing more than subsets of a fixed ontology, and that are, for this reason, formally equivalent. With this, we see that Mackenzie mistakes the multiplication of multiples for an opening of the new. This is because, despite the incompleteness that it would seem to insure, subduction can only draw on elements *intrinsic* to the database ontology to mark its break.

It is precisely in relation to the intrinsic-extrinsic divide that Fuller and Goffey's analysis of relational databases diverges most consequentially from Mackenzie's. For these critics, the operation of databases as topological machines marks a definitive departure from what has, up to now, been their typical, ordinary functioning. Specifically, the topological operation of databases yields a putting-into-contact of data with entities of all sorts, which is to say, with entities exterior to the set-theoretical ontology of whatever database is in question.[9] For Fuller and Goffey, this topological deviation results less from the topological operation of databases themselves than from the glitches and disconnections that are the result of the seamful, partial, and inconsistent aggregation characteristic of the current state of database consolidation in our world today.

With this focus on failures of connection, Fuller and Goffey's analysis allows us to distinguish two meanings of "topological" as it characterizes today's relational databases. First is the ordinary and intended operation of such databases to impose a data logic on the exteriorities that it brings into the sphere of its relationality. As Fuller and Goffey put it, topological machines "establish networks of relations—the points of intersection between data and *what that data links to and triggers*" (Fuller and Goffey 2012, 326; emphasis added). Such ordinary and intended *topological* operation of relational databases—and this is the crucial point here—is the expression of the ontology embodied by a given database, which is to say, of an instrumentalized ontology that is effectively imposed by the proprietary restrictions placed on access.

Not only does this suggest that the topological operation of databases does not *in itself* introduce ontological pluralization, but it points toward the empirical—the domain of appearance—as the source for any such pluralization. Here we come to another, second meaning of "topological": To designate the forging of relations *across* the seams, gaps, and divides that exist *between* distinct databases and the concrete modes of aggregation they instantiate. The resulting relations and the relational potentiality underlying them express the capacity of disparate elements to create/manifest complexity immanently, solely through their coming-into-contact and without requiring any center of indetermination or selectional principle. What results is a "description without a subject" (Badiou 2009) that, far from being a formal specification of a unitary ontology, is the concrete product of a complexity-generating sociological association.

Noting the "rather limited . . . possibilities for formally consistent working across databases," Fuller and Goffey conclude on this note of (minor) optimism: "Uncanny proximities are generated by separate sets of data that don't quite match, there is a calculated generation of conflicting qualities, and a systematic production of ambiguity as databases mesh slightly or fall grossly out of synch with each other and other scales of reality" (Fuller and Goffey 2012, 328). Though they do not say it in so many words, the payoff here is precisely an ontological pluralization of the sort promised by topos theory. Because it forges new relations that go *outside of the possible subsets that can be included* in any given database, this topological operation of databases necessarily privileges appearance over ontology, and effectively subordinates the selection of ontology to the dictates of appearance. With this conclusion, we can fully appreciate the stakes of our topos-theoretical intervention into database culture: For the promise that we have invested in topological culture—the promise of putting humans in contact with a broader scope of the sensibility informing experience—hinges on the potential for today's topological machines to forge relations *across* disparate aggregations of data and *outside* any particular intrinsic ontology that would dictate from the get-go what can be counted or included.

B. From Database Technicity to Social Complexity

In the contrast between Fuller and Goffey's just examined technicist expansion of database ontology and Ruppert's sociological expansion, it is precisely the scope of the ontology implicated in the topological operationality of relational databases that is at issue. Despite establishing the irreducibility of appearance as the crucial factor for selecting an operative ontology, whatever ontology is in question for Fuller and Goffey remains, in a quite narrow sense, a *database* ontology. That is why they must view the opening to the outside, the introduction of the unpredictable, as the exclusive function of contingent gaps between databases, rather than a more complex relational field that correlates such gaps with entities existing outside of databases and that ascribes an affirmative, complexifying power to the appearances generated by such a relational field.

It is, of course, just such correlation that lies at the very heart of Ruppert's analysis of New Labor social policy initiatives during the first decade of the twenty-first century. Applied to data, Ruppert's ontological framing of complexity—her embrace of the power of appearance to generate complexity—underscores the exo-referentiality that is constitutive of today's dynamic relational databases: "Data," Ruppert stresses, "is itself a materiality that can be assembled in multiple ways by folding in heterogeneous data from distributed sites" (Ruppert 2012, 125). This multiplicity, to say it again, does not stem from interpretation, but characterizes the different forms that a dynamic object necessarily assumes at different moments of its existence: the relational databases underwriting U.K. social policy governance constitute "assembling devices" that "do not assemble all data but do so selectively," in ways that create "unstable patterns of absence and presence" (Ruppert 2012, 125).[10]

With her flexible and pluralistic conception of the object, Ruppert's topological approach forcefully underscores the priority of appearance over ontology: "I adopted an ontological stance to argue that *different reals are enacted by different analytics*. It is a stance that understands *phenomena as already and always multiple and complex*, and does not deny other possibilities but positions these as questions of "ontological politics." All analytics order and enact the world in ways that make some elements and relations present while absenting others" (Ruppert 2012, 131; emphases added).

Ontological politics rooted in appearance versus unitary, intrinsic ontology divorced from appearance: With this divide, we can finally grasp the radical openness and contingency introduced by the topological approach. Beyond any expansion of database ontology via new modes of inclusion (Mackenzie 2012) or via opacities created by gaps between databases (Fuller and Goffey 2012), the topological ontology developed by Ruppert ascribes the dynamism of the database to *the continual modulation of the elements it potentially includes*. Crucially, because it obeys no pre-imposed restrictions—because it can literally encompass anything that data can "link to and trigger"—such modulation must be anchored by some specified aim.

With this conclusion, we can finally appreciate the specificity of the deployment of the term "topological" in concepts like "topological culture" and "topological machine": topological designates the bi-directional relationality that permits today's relational databases to include elements that are exterior to their operational ontologies *and* to allow such inclusion to impact their dynamic development in the future. To say that the appearances thereby generated are "objective" means that they are direct manifestations of worldly situations and are wholly independent from any processing through or synthesis by a subjective agent like a human consciousness. This objectivity of appearances *does not, however, mean that they are without any subjective dimension.*

It is precisely the probabilistic dimension of objective appearances that accounts for their subjectivity. For what the capacity to operate directly at the subindividual level of sensibility facilitates is a measuring of the power, the non-subjectal yet subjective—or better *superjective*—power, of elements of sensibility independently from and prior to their participation in macro-assemblages or "societies" (of which human bodyminds or consciousnesses would be one kind). Far from becoming subjective only by way of their inclusion in or synthesis by macroassemblages, these objective appearances are subjective *in themselves and in their own right*. And because the subindividual "units" of sensibility do not obtain coherence in relation to human experience until they become components of such macro-assemblages (or societies), their subjective-superjective power can only be expressed in probabilistic terms, as a measure of their likelihood to impact experience at the macro level.

We could thus say that the probability calculus takes the place of synthesis in orthodox phenomenology: It expresses the elementary subjectivity that constitutes an irreducible part of any "objective" appearance of the world. As Ulrik Ekman astutely observes, the liberation of subjectivity (or superjective subjectivity) from any figure of the subject at issue here calls for a phenomenology of "disorganized complexity" (Weaver 1948). Because it aspires to grasp the manifestation of the world in all its complexity—as the product of the immanent relationality of elements and without reducing it to what can appear to a subject/consciousness (or any avatar of selectivity)—such a phenomenology can only express the ontological core of appearance in probabilistic terms, or as I have put it in *Feed-Forward*, as real potentialities that are themselves composed of actualities, as real potentialities that do not lose their potentiality when and just because they become actual.

Returning one final time to the paradox at the core of my argument here, we can now understand how topological operationality, despite operating autonomously from human experience, can renew and expand the latter's basis in sensibility. It can do so precisely because, as implemented through the operationality of topological machines, it is able to access the primordial asubjectal subjectivity of sensibility, to enfold (or include) it in its operation in ways that are consequential for that operation, and to express divergent appearances (ways the world is from particular viewpoints or according to particular configurations of presence and absence) as distinct probabilities that do not refer to states of affairs separate from them but that are fully real expressions – that express the "real potentiality" – of the subjective-superjective power of worldly sensibility in all its concrete complexity.

Notes

1. I want to thank Ulrik Ekman for his generous and helpful comments and acknowledge how much they have helped me refine the argument presented here.
2. To the extent that the objective phenomenology developed here refutes the disjunction of the topological operationality of culture from human experience, while certainly recognizing its disjunction from presentation to and as content of (human) consciousness, my argument takes issue with its characterization as "topological rationality."
3. I introduce this concept in Hansen, *Feed-Forward: On the Future of Twenty-First-Century Media*. (Chicago, IL: University of Chicago Press, 2015).
4. The point for Parisi—one that is shared by an emerging group of theorists— is that topology, meaning the mathematics of topology as it is implemented in the technological infrastructure of our culture, actually and accurately describes its concrete operation. What is at stake here is nothing less than a new understanding of structure that looks to topology not as metaphor but as mathematical description. "This non-standard geometry," explains Parisi in a related interview, "crucially sustains that structures are not determined by points and by the distance between points. Instead points are determined by the vectorial forces that conjoin or not at the formation of a point. A structure itself is determined by the tendencies and the direction of vectorial forces as they mark a trajectory. If structural analysis has been central to the definition of culture, we propose that algebraic topology articulates an idea of structure in terms of continual transformation of forces and not in terms of specific points on a grid. It is important therefore to offer *a scientific study of culture* rather than an understanding of culture through scientific lenses" (Dawes, unpaginated).
5. When I use the term "direct" in what follows, I do not mean "unmediated" as such, for there is no such possibility where experience is concerned; rather I mean "direct" in the specific sense announced at the outset of this paper: "not filtered through intentional consciousness."
6. For Whitehead, a "society" designates an experiential entity of any sort, from an atom to a mass movement or historical transition. A society can be distinguished from a "nexus" (a "natural" grouping of actual entities) because of two factors: its members share a common end or purpose and they brought together by their differentiation from an environment that has a role in their ongoing operationality.
7. The basic unit of topos theory, the topos, is a special kind of category: a "category of spaces (with arrows) over a given space" (Plotnitsky, 358). A category is a "multiplicity . . . of mathematical objects . . . conforming to a given concept" together with their "morphisms" (or "arrows"), i.e., "those mappings between these objects that preserve the structures defined by this concept" (Plotnitsky, 356).
8. For Badiou, forcing names the operation that produces something new—an event of truth—from an existing situation. It is "a radical and systematic transformation of a situation by means of a series of actions acting upon, or proceeding from, the *real* of the situation—that which, prior to the activity of forcing, subsists in the situation as an invisible, unoccupiable, or 'impossible' site" (Entry on Forcing).
9. Fuller and Goffey concur with Mackenzie that databases can be described by set theoretical logic, but they hold such description to be impoverished: "On the face of it, most databases are best understood as describing sets, operating through the working methods of predicate logic. They allow the selection, differentiation, union, analysis and possible projection of the attributes of a relation, opening up a set of possibilities, configuring a field of action, facilitating a decision, in the absence of any direct consideration of the state or states of the referents to which the data 'belongs'" (327).

10. In developing her topological approach to the relationality of data, Ruppert draws on Law and Singleton's understanding of the object (the "fire object") as a flexible and contingent "presence" that "implies a set of absences" "An object is a presence. It is present, here and now. But, whatever the form of its presence, this also implies a set of absences. The present object implies realities that are *necessarily* absent, that *cannot* be brought to presence; that are othered. . . . we cannot understand objects unless we . . . think of them as sets of present dynamics generated in, and generative of, realities that are necessarily absent. Such objects are transformative, but the transformations are not the gentle flows discussed above in fluid objects . . . [Rather,] they take the form of jumps and discontinuities. In this way of thinking, constant objects are energetic, entities or processes that juxtapose, distinguish, make and transform absences and presences. They are made in disjunction" (Law and Singleton, 342–344).

References

Badiou, Alain. 2001. *Being and Event*, tr. O. Feltham. London and New York: Continuum.

Badiou, Alain. 2006. *Briefings on Existence: A Short Treatise on Transitory Ontology*, tr. N. Madarasz. Albany, NY: State University of New York.

Badiou, Alain. 2009. *Logics of Worlds: Being and Event 2*, tr. A. Toscano. London and New York: Continuum.

Barbaras, Renaud. 2005. *Desire and Distance: Introduction to a Phenomenology of Perception*, tr. P. Milan. Stanford, CA: Stanford University Press.

Dawes, Simon. 2013. "Interview with Celia Lury, Luciana Parisi and Tiziana Terranova on Topologies." *http://theoryculturesociety.org/interview-with-celia-lury-luciana-parisi-and-tiziana-terranova-on-topologies*, January 15, accessed October 10, 2014.

Ekman, Ulrik. 2015. "Design as Topology: U-City." Chap. 9 in *Media Art and the Urban Environment—Engendering Public Engagement with Urban Ecology*, edited by Frank Marchese. New York: Springer, in press.

Entry on "Forcing." To appear in the *Badiou Dictionary, Form and Formalism Blog. http://formandformalism.blogspot.fr/2011/03/badiou-dictionary-entries.html*, accessed January 24, 2015.

Ernst, Wolfgang. 2013. *Gleichursprünglichkeit. Zeitwesen und Zeitgegebenheit technischer Medien*. Berlin: Kulturverlag Kadmos.

Fuller, Matthew, and Andrew Goffey. 2012. "Digital Infrastructures and the Machinery of Topological Abstraction." *Theory, Culture & Society* 29 (4/5): 311–333.

Hansen, Mark B. N. 2015. *Feed-Forward: On the Future of Twenty-First-Century Media*. Chicago, IL: University of Chicago Press.

Hansen, Mark B. N. forthcoming. "The Physicality of the Medium." *ELH*.

Husserl, Edmund. 2010. *The Idea of Phenomenology*, tr. L. Hardy. Dordrecht, Netherlands: Kluwer.

Law, John, and Vicky Singleton. 2005. "Object Lessons." *Organization* 12 (3): 331–355.

Lury, Celia, Luciana Parisi, and Tiziana Terranova. 2012. "Introduction: The Becoming Topological of Culture." *Theory, Culture & Society* 29 (4/5): 3–35.

Mackenzie, Adrian. 2012. "More Parts than Elements: How Databases Multiply." *Environment and Planning D: Society and Space* 30: 335–350.

Patocka, Jan. 1995. *Papiers phénoménologiques*, tr. E. Abrams. Grenoble, France: Éditions Jérôme Millon.

Plotnitsky, Arkady. 2012. "Experimenting with Ontologies: Sets, Spaces, and Topoi with Badiou and Grothendieck." *Environment and Planning D: Society and Space* 30: 351–368.

Ruppert, Evelyn. 2012. "The Governmental Topologies of Database Devices." *Theory, Culture & Society* 29 (4/5): 116–136.

Simon, Herbert. (1962) 2005. "The Architecture of Complexity." *E:CO* 7 (3–4): 138–154.

Simondon, Gilbert. 2005. *L'individuation à la lumière des notions de forme et d'information*. Grenoble, France: Éditions Jérôme Millon.

Thrift, Nigel. 2004. "Remembering the Technological Unconscious by Foregrounding Knowledges of Position." *Environment and Planning D: Society and Space* 22: 175–190.

Weaver, Warren. (1948) 2004. "Science and Complexity." *E:CO* 6 (3): 65–74.

Whitehead, Alfred North. 1978. *Process and Reality: An Essay on Cosmology*, Corrected Edition. New York: The Free Press.

Wolfram, Stephen. 1986. "Approaches to Complexity Engineering." *Physics* 22D: 385–399.

Zalamea, Fernando. 2013. *Synthetic Philosophy of Contemporary Mathematics*. London: Urbanomic/Sequence Press.

WEATHER PATTERNS, OR HOW MINOR GESTURES ENTERTAIN THE ENVIRONMENT

Erin Manning

Weather Pattern

> The movements of the sun on a terrace in the late afternoon.
> The smell of red in the fall.
> The weight of closed skies in a dark, February winter.
> The moodiness of shadows on fresh snow.
> The light after the rain.

Minor Gesture

A weather pattern makes experience felt. Each weather pattern comes to experience differently and it is the how of this difference that makes it a weather pattern. The propeller of difference within the weather pattern can be thought of as a minor gesture. The minor gesture opens the field of experience to its differential, to the ways in which it subtly differentiates from itself. In the example of the tuning of the season to fall, which, in Canada, comes with the shift in leaves from green to red to yellow, with the smell of earth as the grass begins to dry out and the leaves fall on it and are stepped on, with the shift in light from the fullness of an immersive light to the becoming-angled light of winter, from the sense of warmth on skin to the layers of cotton and wool and silk and leather on skin, from the sense of ground felt with bare feet in sandals to the enclosure of boots, threshold sensations cannot be located in the objects themselves (the leaves, the sun, the earth) but in the complex variations of their seasonal unfolding, in the effects created at the interstice of one and the other, in the ways they co-compose with the memories of fall and winter, and, for the environment itself, with the complex habits of hibernation, seeding, growing that comes with any change of season. And also, in the more-than-human realm, the way houses begin to close themselves in for the coming winter altering the feel of public space, the way the air inside and outside are cut off from one another through closed doors and windows changing the quality of the inside, the way the streets open themselves up to a different kind of traffic, the way the earth prepares itself for the coming cold and the animals and worms and plants respond to the shifting rhythms. A lot is happening here that cannot be perceived as such, but makes a difference to how the complex ecology is experienced. Minor gestures that tune fall to winter are everywhere present, if difficult to pinpoint.

A minor gesture, aligned to the concept of the minor that Deleuze and Guattari develop both in their work on Kafka and in *A Thousand Plateaus*, is a gesture that tweaks the field of the experiential to make its qualitative operations felt, a gesture, in the field of the artful—the operation that makes experience felt rather than simply the object or effect delineated from that experience—that opens experience to its limit. The minor gesture is a gesture that emerges from within the field itself, not from its maker, a gesture that leads the field of experience to make felt the fissures otherwise too imperceptible or subtle to ascertain.

A minor gesture cannot be known as such. In the field of art, the artwork, the object-in-itself, or even the effect created by an ephemeral composition is not a minor gesture. The minor gesture is what activates it under precise conditions, what makes the attunements of an emerging ecology felt, what makes the work work. It is what tunes the work to its processual force, to what Deleuze and Guattari call "material forces" as opposed to "matter form" referring to how material is already imbued with force as opposed to the hylomorphic tendencies that come with the stabilization of matter on one side and form on the other (Deleuze and Guattari 1987, 95). A minor gesture introduces a kind of continuous variability into the work's process, a variability that is durational, that is as virtual as it is actual, a variability that co-composes across the measured time of the object and the a measure of event time. The minor gesture makes time felt, in the event. The time of the red leaf is felt not as a specific time measure. It is not simply a feeling of "oh, this is what happens in September." Rather it is a direct feeling of variability, a direct experience of the rhythm of time tuning to its difference, this made active and palpable by how this red (leaf), this (fall) smell, this (October) slant of sun moves the feeling of summer into the feeling of fall. The minor gesture: Not the leaf, not the color or the month or even the season, but the internal variability, the active differential, that tunes this particular ecology to the felt experience of time shifting. This is event time.

Artfulness

The minor and the major are not opposed. They are variabilities in differential co-composition. Speaking of minor literatures, Deleuze and Guattari write: "Minor languages are characterized not by overload and poverty in relation to a standard or major language, but by a sobriety and variation that are like a minor treatment of the standard language, a becoming-minor of the major language . . . Minor languages do not exist in themselves: They exist only in relation to a major language and are also investments of that language for the purpose of making it minor" (Deleuze and Guattari 1987, 104–105).

In the context of artistic practice, one major language is the contemporary art institution. The intercession into this major language via the minor gesture can take many forms. One way to think of the minor gesture in this context is to wonder at how the object operates a transduction in its passage from the everyday into the gallery setting. How does the becoming-artful of the object, occur? Consider, for instance, the work of Beijing-based artist Song Dong, entitled *Waste Not* (2005). This work is described in the following way:

> *Waste Not* [is] comprised of over 10,000 items ranging from pots and basins to blankets, bottle caps, toothpaste tubes, and stuffed animals collected by the artist's mother over the course of more than five decades. [. . .] *Waste Not* follows the Chinese concept of *wu jin qi yong* or "waste not," as a prerequisite for survival. The project evolved out of

a family necessity and the artist's mother's grief after the death of her husband. [. . .] The centerpiece of the installation is the architectural armature of the building where the artist was born. A core theme of *Waste Not* is the idea that people, everyday objects, and personal stories are not only spiritually rich in thematic material but recognizable evidence of the impact of politics and history on family life.[1]

Having exhibited in proximity to Song Dong's work twice, both at the Sydney and the Moscow Biennales (2012, 2013 respectively), and having had my work next to Song Dong's in the second of these biennales, I have had ample opportunity to explore, in his work, how the everyday object participates in a kind of ritual shift through its entering into the contemporary art exhibition. I say ritual because it seems to me that in work that transduces the everyday object, there is calling forth of a transitory magic[2] or occult quality that allows the object to carry within itself more than its everyday use-value. The flower pot, the shoe, the button, the blanket, the towel, the cooking pot, the hair-tie, and the plastic bag, each of these moves from its connection to use-value in the everyday to take on the aura, as Benjamin might say, of another kind of newly invented value. If this value is limited to the prestige value of the art market, I would say that the transduction does not successfully occur. It is when the value is truly invented in the passing from one site to another, and when this value continues to metamorphose in the field of variation the old-new object creates, that the object begins to carry within itself the potential for variation. We could even say that if this happens, the object-variation becomes a minor gesture.

In the case of Song Dong, the serial nature of the work is one thing that stages the potentiality of this minor gesture. As is often the case in contemporary art, repetition is key. But repetition alone is not enough. Variation-in-difference is necessary: The object must be capable of more than its initial transduction from the everyday into the gallery. It must continue to vary and its variation must be serial, in the sense that each object-variation is alive with the incipient memory and the imperceptible traces of its passage from one site to another, the sites that are not only physical, but also conceptual, sites of memory, of anticipation, and of attunement. Across the series, a tension appears that makes felt the complexity not of number but of multiplicity as a variation on itself. "Minor authors are foreigners in their own tongue. If they are bastards, if they experience themselves as bastards, it is due not to a mixing or intermingling of languages but rather to a subtraction and variation of their own language achieved by stretching tensors through it" (Deleuze and Guattari 1987, 105). All becoming, as Deleuze and Guattari say, is minoritarian, and all becoming is rife with the tension that comes with variation. There is no minor gesture that is and remains completely what it is. A minor gesture is a living variation.

Australian-based artist Simryn Gill's work is another strong example of the minor gesture. Take her work, *Pearls* (1999) (Plate 10). This work is based on the gift. The gift, as Gill activates the concept through *Pearls*, involves much more than a simple exchange: Gill asks us for a book that we are moved to give her. While it seems clear that the book should hold meaning for us, Gill does not make this a spoken demand. She simply invites a friend, an acquaintance, a fellow artist, to give her a book. This book is then carefully and meticulously torn and pasted to create a string of pearls, which the original owner of the book receives as a gift. Gill keeps the spine. The exchange may seem simple—an object into an object. But try to give away a book, to be ripped, that has followed you, stayed with you, that includes margin notes, that has made you think in ways you couldn't otherwise, that you've returned to either in fact or in spirit over the years. This is not an easy task. For two years I've wondered about giving up my first copy of *Le petit prince* with my childhood drawings in the margins and still haven't been able to let go of it. Gill knows that the exchange is complex. She is aware that what is moving across is not simply a book for a necklace. What is moving is at once book and the force of memory as it is awakened and created anew in the act of considering the giving-over. The object will not return. What will return will be variation itself.

Proposing variation not on the object per se but on the very quality of its potentializing materiality is what is at stake in *Pearls*. With the passage from one to the other, what is foregrounded is the quality of the object's material forces rather than its matter form. Like a shaman in a ritual process, Gill is aware of the power of the act of taking that which cannot be returned in the same way as it was given. This is the work of *Pearls*. What Gill does with the act of variation is make felt the inevitable transformation that always occurs in the sharing. What is given is the belief in the care of the very transformation that is already at the heart of the object. The Benjaminian aura is given and given back, transformed, this in the realm, as Benjamin would say, of both voluntary and involuntary recollection.

> Where there is experience in the strict sense of the word, certain contents of the individual past combine with material of the collective past. The rituals with their ceremonies, their festivals [. . .] [keep] producing the amalgamation of these two elements of memory over and over again. They [trigger] recollection at certain times and [remain] handles of memory for a lifetime. In this way, voluntary and involuntary recollections lose their mutual exclusiveness.
>
> (Benjamin 1973, 113)

Simryn Gill works with the ethos of care this passage of the aura entails, careful and caring in the act of taking care of the book's variation in transformation. The minor gesture here is the activation of a relational field that includes the book and the beads but also exceeds both of them, opening them up to the vectorization of their incipient tendencies, tendencies that now include, with the memories of the past in the present, the labor of the words and pages coming-into-variation as beads and the felt weight of that labor in the form of the necklace.

It is interesting to note that in *A Thousand Plateaus* one of the few mentions of "minor art" is related to jewelry. Deleuze and Guattari (1987, 401) write:

> Jewelry has undergone so many secondary adaptations that we no longer have a clear understanding of what it is. But something lights up in our mind when we are told that metalworking was the "barbarian," or nomad, art par excellence, and when we see these masterpieces of minor art. These fibulas, these gold or silver plaques, these pieces of jewelry, are attached to small movable objects; they are not only easy to transport, but pertain to the object only as object in motion. These plaques constitute traits of expression of pure speed, carried on objects that are themselves mobile and moving. The relation between them is not that of form-matter but of motif-support, where the earth is no longer anything more than ground (soil), where there is no longer even any ground at all because the support is as mobile as the motif. [. . .] Regardless of the effort or toil they imply, they are of the order of free action, related to pure mobility, and not of the order of work with its conditions of gravity, resistance, and expenditure.

The pearls are jewels in this sense: Their value is in the transduction they embolden. They are mobile both in their ability to signify and in their ability to be decorative. In so doing, they open the field of contemporary art to its uneasy outside, to that uncertain interstice between art and craft, between what is displayed and what is worn, between what is seen and what is felt. The aura they carryover is subtle, an aura that would probably be neutralized should the beads simply be hung on the gallery wall in multiples as contemporary art is, wont to do. For these beads are for wearing, for moving, for becoming with the multiplicity that is occasioned in the taking-on that is the act of fashioning the body. This fashioning, this living, must be felt as part of their variation-on-potential.

Minor gestures trouble institutional frameworks in the same way they trouble existing forms of value. This is their potential: They open the artistic process beyond the matter form of its object, beyond the prestige value that comes with all of the artistic conclusions[3] that surround us. The minor gesture is the felt experience of potential, the force that makes felt how a process is never about an individual, but about the ecology it calls forth.

When speaking of minor literature, Deleuze and Guattari begin with the proposition that what characterizes minor literatures is that "everything in them is political" (Deleuze and Guattari 1986, 17). What they mean by this is that the minor gesture is always already a collective expression, collective in the sense that it acts on the behalf of the ecology which gives rise to it. Against the major tendency of mastery, the minor gesture is the carefully crafted technique which pulls the potential at the heart of a process into a mobile field replete of force-imbued-material that is capable of making felt not only what the process can do but how the ecology of which it is part resonates through and across it. Always alive with a certain quality of transduction, the process clinched by a minor gesture is one that makes the threshold between process and object/effect felt.

Entertaining the Environment

In 2006, I began work on a piece entitled *Weather Patterns: Entertaining the Environment*. The piece, which is still evolving, was less about creating a finished work than about putting into a play a proposition: How to work with different technologies to activate a field of relation that, while it included the human, did not depend on the human. I hadn't coined the concept of a minor gesture then, but now I can see that it was indeed the question of the minor gesture that was at work: What would a work be like that seeks to open up the question of interaction toward a more-than-human perspective, a work that is interested in making felt something akin to the reddening of time that makes felt the fullness of a summer tending to autumn? How would a work work whose main concern was how the field of relation itself touched the limit of the sensible? What would a work be that was capable of awakening and keeping alive the intensive variability of the minor gesture?

This is not to dismiss the human's role in the field of artistic participation, but to recognize that the weather pattern cannot fully express itself in or via the human. Weather patterns move across in a field of relation activated in the realm of the more-than-human, in the ecology of experience generated by the variational field itself. What would a work feel like whose mandate it was not to entertain us, but to entertain the already entertaining environment? To attend to this question is to open up the issue not only of where the human is situated in the process of emergent fielding activated by a weather pattern, but to inquire into the very limits of interactivity; for there remains a tendency, within the very concept of interaction, to place the human in the center as the arbiter of process. To conceive of a work that resisted the tendency of placing the human at the center would necessitate a focus directed toward the environment's *own* capacity to make felt the complex ecologies at work. Given the centrality of human participation in my other artistic projects, it seemed to me that such an inquiry would not only open up the question of how an artwork can create the conditions for a participation generated as much by the environment itself as by human engagement, but would also provide a stronger sense of how, even when the participatory component of a work is led by human intervention, much more than human agency is at work. Like the weather, which opens up experience without situating the human as the arbitrator of the act, what I wanted to explore was whether interactivity could itself become environmental, more-than-human.

Weather Patterns began with a textile collection entitled *Volumetrics* (Plate 11). Conceived in relation to my other textile collection, *Folds to Infinity*, 2000 pieces of fabric cut in ways that intuitively produce what I have called "Slow Clothes," *Volumetrics* is a series of large 60 rectangular black pieces of fabric, each of which has rare earth magnets sewn into its surface. These magnets, as in the *Folds to Infinity* collection, encourage connection across pieces as well as enabling intuitive practices of folding (a folding that often occurs despite the participant). In addition to the magnets, elastic cord is woven through button holes with toggles to stop the cord. With the magnets, this allows for the creation of complex shapes. Snaps and zippers are also sewn into several of the pieces as well as a few buttons. All of these connective propositions work together as an invitation for a hands-on participation that can lead to the creation of both garments and architectures.

Initially conceived as a way to open the *Folds to Infinity* collection to a more volumetric composition (the fabrics used in *Folds to Infinity* are often diaphanous and so tend to lie flatter), *Volumetrics* was exhibited in its first iteration as a textile proposition in relation to *Folds to Infinity*. What I soon found, however, was that *Volumetrics* was incapable of doing the complex work I had come to expect from the *Folds to Infinity* collection. In the context of a participatory proposition, *Folds to Infinity*, in its iterations both as *Slow Clothes* and as *Stitching Time* (Plate 12), did not only elicit hands-on participation: It was also at times capable of creating a weather pattern—a modulated field of relation in excess of hands-on contact. It did so in different ways— sometimes through the field effect created by color and light, an effect that made felt the shifting affective tonality of the environment, sometimes through its operations as a choreographic object capable of tuning movement to shifting spacetimes of composition.[4] *Volumetrics* on the other hand read more as a stable object, its black volumes deadening participation (see Plate 13). Perhaps it was its blackness, perhaps it was the large size of the individual pieces or their weight, or perhaps it was how the pieces read in the context of contemporary art's interest in the minimal (often untouchable) object, for the black volumes do on their own give off a sense of elusiveness that the *Folds to Infinity* collection does not. Whatever the reason, it was noteworthy that on the few occasions when the two collections were exhibited together, the black volumes tended to be left untouched. This led to the slow incubation of the question of how to generate a weather pattern with *Volumetrics*, one that included the human but didn't depend on human participation (Plate 14).

Weather Patterns is a work in progress precisely because such events that are ecological at their core and resonant in excess of human participation are extremely difficult to actualize. The past five years (2009-2014) have been a time of continuous experimentation in this regard. The first stage involved sewing conductive fabric into a third of the pieces and connecting the conductive fabric to wireless proximity sensors also sewn into the fabric. This made the fabric responsive to its environment without needing to be directly handled. The idea was that movement in the proximity of the conductive fabric would generate a data stream that could be transduced into sound, activating an emergent soundscape in conversation with the incipient mobility of the environment itself. With the collaboration of artists Nathaniel Stern, Bryan Cera, Mazi Javidiani, and Andrew Goodman, this allowed us to extend the notion of participation beyond human tactile exploration of the fabric to how field effects (air movements, electromagnetic current) would tune the environment. The performance of the work would be its capacity to field subtle changes generated by the work over time. In the next iteration, fifty analog speakers were connected to a MAX MSP patch and distributed in the space, activated in relay. In a third iteration, light and movement sensors were placed in the environment, complicating the conditions through which the sound data was transduced. Tiny computer fans were also mobilized, though never successfully connected to the system. Nonetheless, they provided a complexity to the field through the background sound and air their movements produced. A future proposition would be to link the air current to the responsive environment.

The mobilization of *Weather Patterns* over a series of gallery exhibitions first in Milwaukee (with Nathaniel Stern and Bryan Cera) and then in Melbourne (with Andrew Goodman) allowed us to experience how data—as that produced not only by human movement but by all movement—might enable an experience of a quality of emergence in the environment that was otherwise imperceptible. This is what I am calling "entertaining the environment," with the idea of entertainment linked strongly to Whitehead's notion of "presentational immediacy," the experience of qualitatively felt effects in a relational field.

When artwork entertains the environment, the proposition is that there is awareness in the field of relation to how the environment is attuned and attuning to the gestures active within its ecology. From these two exhibitions, a number of questions emerged: How do we make felt, for the human participant, a minor gesture that is largely imperceptible? What does such work do if it cannot be readily be experienced as such by the human? How do we create the conditions for such time-based events that demand the slowness of participation?

When a minor gesture opens the way for an experiential variation on the object, what emerges is artful. Artfulness is the processual force of what art can do. It takes seriously the how of the object's variability, taking as art's measure not how it fits within the matrix of what is currently on exhibition in art circles, but how a process's minor gestures generate the more-than of art-as-object or effect.

The artful is not about a form, or a content—it is the capacity to make felt, in the event-time of a work's composition, how an object is already a field of relation, a differential variability. The artful, alive with minor gestures, is therefore always already collective in the sense that the how of its process cannot be limited to an individual subject. The artful is not generated by the individual, but by the making felt of how an ecology becomes expressive, tuning that making-expressive toward the generation of an aesthetic opening on experience, aesthetic in its original definition of making sensible, making felt.

Weather Patterns is in progress because it fails more often than it succeeds. Glimpses of the artful have been generated in each of the exhibitions of the work, but as an artistic experience, it remains tentative. This is also what keeps it alive. For the tentative is replete with tendency, open to vectors that activate the differential out of which the minor gesture can be crafted. Amplifying tendency in the spirit of the tentative, what is most interesting to me about *Weather Patterns* as it has evolved is its capacity to allow the question of process to linger. What has become key to the work is not so much the outcome (though how the work individuates is key to how it continues to resolve its conditions of emergence), but what kinds of minor gestures are generated in the process. This is why, in 2012, I decided to begin to send the work (as a proposition-on-variation more than as an object or a set of objects) to different artists—including, so far, choreographer Megan Bridge, sound artist Peter Price, and architect Samantha Spurr. Creating in a crowd, all of us taking as points of departure our own differing approaches to making a work work, makes even more apparent the inherent variability in the process of creating a weather pattern.

I outline this messy and nonlinear process of making a work to suggest that many of us who ask questions to art that include the technological are in fact engaged in the making or the thinking of weather patterns and their minor gestures—works that trouble, complicate, nuance, embolden, how experience is felt both for the human and beyond the human in the more-than-human realm, the realm that connects, that composes with the human, but is not limited to it. These works, it seems to me, take as their governing mandate the problematization of the interactive gesture itself, asking how it might be possible to make felt threshold transitions occasioned not only by the human participant, but by the wider environmental ecology, hence making the move from interaction to relation. How to make felt the relational field that is embodied in the shifting of light, the rhythm of tone, how to make felt the field effect of color? How to move the participant beyond the act of volition to the experiential realm both nonsensuous (alive in the fielding of involuntary memory) and sensuous (transducing into the now of event time)?

Weather Pattern

A weather pattern is brought into experience through a minor gesture. When the artwork exceeds its status as an object, when the work becomes relational rather than simply interactive, when there really is a sense that what is at stake is more-than the sum of the artwork's parts, a minor gesture has been generated. This minor gesture, present in each of the fields of action the work emboldens, is not the work as such. It is how the work works. Here, where entertainment exceeds human-centered narratives of consumption so aligned with capitalism, something else is at stake. Entertainment is distributed across the ecology of experience. The major language of matter form, the object, the gallery itself, is tampered with, and what emerges is the force of a gesture that opens art to the artful.[5]

Weather patterns are serial processes. Their beginnings and ends are difficult to ascertain. They are less directional than ecological. Their effects are distributed. None of these qualities make them ideal for the scene of contemporary art, a scene too often constrained by the bounds of what is already recognizable, of what is already imaginable.[6] Weather patterns, like the minor gestures that inform them, invent both modes of thought and modes of perception. In this sense, they are what Deleuze and Guattari call "collective assemblages of enunciation" (Deleuze and Guattari 1986, 18). They are field expressions that intensify experience without reducing it to a single point in time or space. They are not metaphors, but metamorphoses, active transducers of the everyday in the everyday.

When a technological process is used to activate a weather pattern, what is necessary, it seems to me, is a sense of how the technological can operate as a minor gesture. How can technology activate a field effect without making the field effect about the technology itself? How can technology be used to make mobile the sense of time in the event, the time of the event? How can technology be mobilized to open the event to both its individuation and its transduction? How can technology activate the aura of the ritual event, the aura, as Michael Taussig writes that opens the event to its involuntary memory: "It is involuntary memory which composes, no less than it is composed by, correspondences, and provides the home for aura" (Taussig 1995, 381). How can technology get beyond "mechanical reproduction" to activate the artful that is process-in-variation?

Weather patterns are present everywhere in our everyday. Some of these presentnesses are artful, and some not. Those that are artful are ones that make felt the intensity of material forces. Not all art is relegated to the human realm, and not all art is artful. The artful makes felt the art of time, the event-time of the threshold, of the weather pattern. The artful is more-than-human. It is ecological at heart, multiple, serial. Minor gestures couple the artful and art, "wresting from one's own language a minor literature," a minor art (Deleuze and Guattari 1986, 19). And here, in the midst of the variation, in the differential, the environment is entertained.

Notes

1. http://ybca.org/song-dong
2. This would connect to how objects are mobilized in most indigenous ritual practices. See, for instance, my discussion of how paintings are used within Australian Aboriginal ritual practices in *Relationscapes*.
3. Leo Kamen, art dealer and ex-owner of the Leo Kamen Gallery in Toronto, speaking of artistic practice, suggests that much art that sells within the contemporary art market is based on conclusions rather than processes. We like conclusions, it seems, but whether conclusions are artful is an open question.
4. For a more detailed exploration of the workings of *Slow Clothes* and *Stitching* Time in the context of more-than human participation, see my work on mobile architecture in *Always More Than One* as well as my piece entitled "Artfulness" in *The Nonhuman Turn* edited by Richard Grusin.
5. I foreground the gallery as a setting for contemporary art throughout not because I think the artful necessarily lives in the gallery setting. In fact, the artful and the gallery have a history of contention. Nonetheless it remains the case that for most artists, the gallery remains a site of experimentation and exhibition, and therefore the question of what the contemporary art gallery can mobilize in the name of the artful is important.
6. Curator Catherine de Zegher is an exception in this regard. Her exhibitions are alive with minor gestures, activated both through the works themselves and in their emergent relations. de Zegher's curatorial technique of choosing artists not based on flashy magazines or fame, but by travelling to their places of work and engaging with them one on one to bring out the relational force of their work is what enables the rare expression of the minor gesture within the setting of the contemporary art gallery. de Zegher's careful attendance to the choreography of exhibition is also key to this process as it allows artists to compose in relation to each other's work, sensitive to the openings created in their physical and conceptual proximity.

References

Benjamin, Walter. 1973. *Some Motifs in Baudelaire in Charles Baudelaire: A Lyric Poet in the Era of High Capitalism*. London: New Left Books.

Deleuze, Gilles, and Felix Guattari. 1987. *A Thousand Plateaus*. Trans. Brian Massumi. Minneapolis, MN: Minnesota University Press.

Deleuze, Gilles, and Felix Guattari. 1986. *Kafka: Toward a Minor Literature*. Trans. Dana Polan. Minneapolis, MN: Minnesota University Press.

Manning, Erin. 2009. *Relationscapes: Movement, Art, Philosophy, Technologies of Lived Abstraction*. Cambridge, MA: MIT Press.

Manning, Erin. 2013. *Always More Than One: Individuation's Dance*. Durham, NC: Duke University Press.

Manning, Erin. 2015. "Artfulness." In *The Nonhuman Turn, Twenty-first Century Studies*, edited by Richard A. Grusin, 45–80. Minneapolis, MN: University of Minnesota Press.

Taussig, Michael. 1995. "The Sun Gives Without Receiving." *Comparative Studies in Society and History* 37 (2): 368–398.

PEEKABOO, I SEE YOU!

About Observation, Surveillance, and Human Agency in the Age of Ubicomp

Lily Díaz

Introduction

An increased deployment of ubiquitous computing and surveillance systems continues to transform the world, blurring the boundaries between the human and the machine. Though ubicomp and surveillance systems can lead to quantitative augmentation and reach in complexity, this does not necessarily translate into qualitative improvements to human life. At stake is the issue of human agency and how these technologies influence our ability to act in the world. In this essay, I examine the relationship between complexity, observation, and human agency in the context of ubicomp and surveillance systems, from the perspective of Niklas Luhmann's systems theory. I contend that the understanding of the world available through human observation is of a different order and type from the sensor-mediated form of observation of computers. At the end of the essay, I present *Quotidian Record*, an interactive art installation by Brian House that makes use of surveillance practices to highlight the ubiquity of these practices in our everyday life. My aim is to ponder on the different perspectives that art systems can give us about the impact of information communications technology in human life as well as show an example of how complexity and reflexivity (Hayles 1999, 8)[1] are used by artists in the creation of art.

Until recently, human computer interaction was mostly limited to basic interplays with video recordings on a screen. For a large sector of the world's population, media remained mostly an analog thing, and anchored to the real and material as equivalent. However, ubiquitous computing (ubicomp) has changed this so that computing devices have become omnipresent in the world around us. Through the realization of digital infrastructures that cover the world, more and more computer-based communication artifacts are being used as part of everyday human activities. These developments are transforming the very core of human culture, since our doing in the world is connected to our thinking and feeling, and this in turn guides our doing.

The initially simple network has become a complex structure extending beyond the perceptual capacity of humans who now require sophisticated hardware and software to analyze and maintain it. Teleography's Submarine Cable map shows how it flows underneath the oceans and into the continental landmasses via underwater cable systems.[2] As a mist of waves pulsing down from a sky-borne mesh of transcontinental satellite systems, it observes us (Kurgan, 26, 39–54).[3] It is a digital membrane that is not autonomous. According to Castells, a managerial layer of human overseers formed into organizations channels its operations influencing its processes as it continues to spread, superseding itself, with layer upon layer of ever growing complexity (Castells 1996). As Ekman notes: "Ubicomp is already a movement within the interior milieu (of individuals and their memories, of social cultures and their past, as well as of current techniques with databases and rather capacious devices) . . ." (Ekman 2013, 217).

Complexity is a difficult term to approach. Systems scientist Jean Louis Le Moigne noted that, "a complex system is by definition built by the observer who is interested in it" (Le Moigne 1999, 24). Le Moigne's etymological investigation into the roots of term "complexity" reveals the meaning as situated in the act of bringing together, making connections, and creating entanglement and augmentation:

> The latin root is *Plexus*: interlaced, which generates *Complexus*, tangled, connected, embraced, entrained, and *Perplexus*: confused, muddled (*Perplexitas*: ambiguity), multiplex describes multiplicity. The etymological root reveals that the opposite of complex is not simple but implex (from *implexus*) [as in entwining] or that which characterizes a unit of action that is indecomposable, irreducible, and therefore unique.
>
> (Le Moigne 1999, 24–25)

As an epistemological tool, complexity moved into the foreground in the twentieth century through the study of living systems as open, complex entities. Sociologist Niklas Luhmann, who viewed the world as the ultimate complexity, developed a theory to describe complexity in systems. According to Luhmann, a system comes into being through observation that detects and marks (or indicates) a distinction on one side but not the other (Luhmann 2000, 37–39).[4] However, observation yields more than difference, since "it . . . reproduces itself through time with the help of indications that are themselves bound by distinctions" (38). Luhmann proposed that:

> Complexity is not an operation, it is not something that the system does or that occurs within it, but it is a concept of observation and description (including self-observation and self-description).
>
> (Luhmann 1999, 136; cited by Neves)

According to Neves, as an observation tool, complexity can be "applied to all possible states, if the observer is able to divide the unit of a multiplicity into elements and relations" (Neves 2006). It can be argued thus, that Luhmann's approach does not simply aim to reduce complexity through analysis but working at multiple levels, seeks to fathom how different forms of communication operate among humans.

Luhmann's theory can be used to examine systems in science, politics, and even art. In the case of the latter, my interests are grounded in the domain's ability to build bridges to other knowledge fields, and on the potential agency of the artist for generating new systems. In his work seminal work on *Art as Social System* for example, he proposed that communication occurs, when "several observers select a certain distinction so that, as their operations become attuned to one another, they generate a shared space or common ground" (Luhmann 2000, 55). As a creator of art, the artist's labor is twofold. She or he operates both as an observer of the work as it is being produced, and as an observer who in anticipation beholds how the work will be perceived. Observation not only guides the initial conceptualization but also repeats itself in the production of the work. This occurs primarily through the body, which the artist uses as an observation device and to bring complexity into the work of art:

[The artist] . . . He must rely on bodily intuition, teasing out the distinctions that matter, and in so doing, he must differentiate unconsciously . . . The artist's genius is primarily his body.

(Ibid, 38)

But the artist does not create the artwork alone but with the audience. Together they bring about the work of art "as a 'nontrivial machine' that reconstructs itself as a different machine in each operation" (Luhmann 2000, 39). He argues that because it generates observations of observations, the work of art also generates new forms of communications.

Luhmann regards agency as something that is created by humans within the social system (Gershon 2005). In art, it is the artist's body that operates as nexus element and site of agency. This social origin of agency through the interaction of collective and individual modes of observation shows how human understanding of the world is of a different type and order of complexity from the computer's sensor-mediated form of observation. It can be argued that in the machine the processes of mapping between knowledge domains by necessity involve projection, reduction, transformation, and translation. When carried on from a mathematical base, these operations usually lead to a reduction of complexity—and with this a diminishing of agency—that is instrumental in accommodating the human into the way of the machine. In reflecting on why these distinctions matter, I return to Ekman's thoughts of how [ubicomp is indeed] ". . . in the process of gaining a foothold in the exterior milieu (animals, vegetation, landscape, locations, spaces, geography, climate)" (Ekman 2013, 280). Since communications are an integral part of our ecosystem and vital to our subsistence as a species in planet Earth, we should consider carefully how much control we give to other systems (machines) that can facilitate, divert, and even block our information flows.

Throughout the essay, I ponder about the first- and second-order observations in ubicomp systems. Forms of first- and second-order observation are described in the discussions about ubicomp and surveillance systems, as are the notions of "self-observation" and "hetero-observation." First-order observation is direct and realized as perception from the location where the observer is situated. Second-order observation is based on the first-order observations of others and *recognizes a distinction between living entities and objects* (Luhmann 2000, 55). The instrument of observation is the form itself, for only via self-observation and hetero-observation one can regard oneself as observing as well as others observing (62). "Self-observation" is an observation expressed from within the system as when "somebody who observes himself, refers to himself and states something about himself" (Luhmann 2013, 60–61). "Hetero-observation" is an observation from outside the system that relates this entity to other entities outside itself. Luhmann's theory uses these notions to describe the role of observation as a structuring form used by humans when processing information. Observation, in Luhmann's view, is intentional behavior. In art systems this intentionality pre-supposes an opportunity for the observer(s) to participate in the communication. This "opportunity" is manifest already in the form or way in which the individual work of art presents itself. A theater play, for example, affords different communication parameters from a sculpture or an interactive installation. Also, the author of the work is in a position to control, direct, and even mislead (if he or she so desires) the observations generated by his or her work (Luhmann 2000, 77).

Calm Computing or Jungle of Observation Devices?

Ubiquity means omnipresence, the quality of existing or being everywhere.[5] Ubicomp technologies emerged partly as a response to the disenchantment with virtual reality and the agenda of building "worlds" inside the computer (Reeves 2012). During the mid-1990s, Chief Senior Scientist, Marc Weiser, coined the term ubiquitous computing to describe the new computing paradigm he was developing with his team at Xerox PARC (Palo Alto Research Center Incorporated). Weiser noted how the most profound technologies are those that disappear as they weave themselves, into everyday activities so that they become naturalized, or undistinguishable, from life itself (Bowkers and Leigh-Star 1999, 294–5).[6] To assist humans in their activities, he aimed to develop a vision that included context aware computing devices (Weiser 1991, 78–89).[7] This vision would be realized through "embodied virtuality".[8] Today, this vision is partly real, since "[u]bicomp artifacts . . . know where they are, what other items are around as well as maintain a record of what happened to them in the past" (Friedewald and Raable 2011, 55).

Weiser foresaw that these developments would not only help to overcome the problem of information overload but also, could promote a new type of calm and quiet computing. Despite the continued promises of new tools to provide comforts for the home, to improve in energy efficiency and safety in transportation, and to increase work productivity,[9] one could argue that fifteen years after its inception, the technological developments associated with ubicomp are, neither. Those concerned with global environmental pollution, for example, might balk at the ABI research report that states how over one billion image-capturing devices were built into the mobile phones and tablets created in 2012 (ABI Research). And nowadays, phenomena such as cyberbullying, cyberstalking, cyberfraud, identity theft, phishing, trolling, and others, are starting to be regarded as natural byproducts of life lived online and on camera. Furthermore, ubicomp experts themselves have noted how given the complexity emerging from the interconnected dependence between devices, applications, and human activities, it might not be possible anymore to maintain control of one's life and memories (Friedewald and Raabe 2011). Our reality seems to be that of a world fast becoming a jungle of observation devices and where conflict simmers underneath the surface.

Human Agency Begins through Observation

Observation, or drawing our attentiveness to the world around us in a systematic manner, is as basic an operation and need to humans as breathing, drinking water, or even thinking. To this extent we endlessly conjecture how our notion of reality is guaranteed by our own observations. We incur in this behavior when we engage in the simple activities that lay the foundations of human logical and intuitive comprehension (Luhmann 2000, 37).[10] Though our observations are limited by the extent of our sensory perception, the latter is also influenced by our human way of life in culture (Vygotsky 1978, 51).[11]

A good example is the game of Peekaboo that is played with small children, usually babies that are 6–12 months old. In the game, the older player will hide either herself or an object from the sight of the child and then reveal it suddenly while at the same time saying: "Peekaboo! I see you!" Aside the fact that it is just plain fun, the game is also about observation. It has a clear and repetitive structure (or schema) that emphasizes presence and absence: As people and objects move in and out of the child's field of vision, s/he observes and notices basic distinction that converge into patterns of perception grounded in human experience (Mandler 2010). The child learns to recognize that some things move on their own (people, animals) while others have to be moved (toys, furniture).

Mandler suggests that the first vestiges of human agency might be found here (Mandler 2010, 30).[12] As we grow, our skill as observers increases and widens to include multiple channels of perception. Further on, via engagements with other living beings and artifacts, our bodies also become progressively woven into the tapestry of the social and the cultural (Gell 1998, 20).[13] Through these we develop a perception of ourselves as independent, self-propelled entities who create and make use of complex artifacts to augment our understanding and action in the world.

Language and communications are among the most complex artifacts (or systems) that we employ as tools in our observations (Bateson 2000, 177–193).[14] A word such as "home" can be used to indicate the dwelling site of a "family" (or consanguineal human kinship unit). But "home" can also be represented as GPS location coordinates, it can be drawn as a diagram in the plans for a new structure, or described through the oral histories that tell the stories of the community, or even depicted in the form of photographs printed on the pages of an interior decoration magazine. Complexity here reveals an entanglement of diverse systems spawning space and time, and how these are gathered and enacted via activities and artifacts in human culture. It is very difficult for computer systems to approximate this realm. This is partly because of the heterogeneity that exists across human domains of knowledge and practice. Then there is the basic distinction between the mathematical substrate of computers and that one of humans that is based on experience (Sheth 2010).[15]

Human agency itself is about embodied and intentional behavior that impacts the world (Stern 2013, 22).[16] However, in its actualization and expression it also finds itself entrained with society through our use of artifacts (Sayed et al. 2010).[17] In their seminal 1997 paper on "tangible bits," Ishii and Ulmer observed this complexity when they stated how "our ancestors developed a variety of specialized artifacts to measure the passage of time . . . to predict the movements of the planets, draw the geometric shapes, and to compute." Interaction with these devices gathered within different "orders" of understanding that opened up access to experiences of space and time, as well as to *an understanding* of how these two should be experienced (Hookway 2014, 17; my italics).

However, not all observations are equal. As Paul Rabinow notes, the world of possibility remains latent for first-order observers, since it is only through second-order observations that possibilities are revealed that

> the second-order observer . . . can comprehend more extended realms of selectivity and identify contingencies where the first-order observer believes he is following a necessary path or acting entirely naturally. Simplifying matters somewhat, one might say that only the second-order observer notices that the first-order observer reduces complexity.
>
> (Rabinow 2008, 62)

And it is only through second-order observation that we can discern the blind spots established through the arbitrariness of first-order observations (Ibid., 64). Ubiquitous computing systems that employ surveillance, such as those using localization GPS, for example, efficiently handle (as first-order observations) multiple signals received from different satellite stations. These systems deploy inside-out sensors and methods such as time of flight (TOF) differences (calculated in the time it takes to receive data packets) and lateration (measurement of distances between known locations), to obtain first- and second-order observations (Morville 2005, 73).[18] These methods are used to determine the distance between satellites thus allowing for calculation of a mobile device's position. From a Luhmannian perspective, can the operations comparing time of signal emission and reception, be regarded as instances of a system's self-observation? The answer is no, since the basic distinction that precludes artificial systems from carrying self-observation still holds. The lack of mechanisms for recognizing individual receivers also indicates an absence of hetero-observation. Experts fittingly regard this as an instance of the system's blind spot (Hightower and Borriello 2001, 59).

Surveillance Systems and Ubicomp in Society

"Adding eyes and ears to our digital nervous system" is how Morville described the new interfaces being developed to handle the oceans of data pouring into cyberspace through global sensory networks (86). Surveillance as in "the careful watching of someone or something . . ." is indeed a form of observation. But the term itself gathers more. In its extension, surveillance implies attentive, vigilant, constant observation in order to obtain information. In its intension, the term evokes deterrence, prevention, or the inhibiting of action. Using Luhmann's terms, first-order and second-order observations coalesce, and synchronize in the interest of surveillance. However, they do not do so on their own but rather, are molded by other constraining forces in society, such as the political, or even the economic systems. Perhaps this is why surveillance seems to be a constant theme in situations involving the restriction of human agency. Michel Foucault's panopticon inquiry amply describes historical narratives that have supported the imposition of regimes of order to effectively inhibit human agency. These included the construction of spaces, practices, and processes for rendering humans into self-surveillant subjects (Foucault).[19] Our era of the networked Information Society, with the fluid spaces (Bauman and Lyon 2013) of non-places for disenfranchisement of "others" (border zones, refugee camps, places of rendition) continue this tradition (Bauman and Lyon 2013, 107).[20]

Surveillance is considered to be a central and problematic dimension of modernity, since it is a key provider of the data fuel that "powers" ubiquitous computing applications. Endemic to social media (Bauman and Lyon 2013), contemporary surveillance is partly about the gathering and processing of personal data for the purpose of influencing and managing the behavior of those whose information is collected (Lyon 2001). In this manner it is clearly implicated in the co-opting of human agency. Ajana describes the situation as an epistemic "informationization" and hybridization of control and monitoring facilitated by the spread of digital technologies and their use in the objects and activities of everyday life (Ajana).[21]

Ours has quickly become the consumer-based liquid modern society that Bauman foreshadowed where the notion of privacy and how we draw our boundaries regarding ourselves, our families, and our communities is constantly eroded. Notions such as "data at rest" and "data on the fly" are used to open legal loopholes and facilitate the syphoning of private information by military agencies as it travels from one location to another (Gellman, Soltani, and Peterson 2013). A recent article about Google Glass in The Economist shows how a critical difference of contemporary surveillance is in the overarching and systematic coverage, as well as in the close range approach (at the surface and sometimes even beyond the skin). Also, new systems of surveillance have emerged that operate at the intersection of what Abowd and Mynatt labeled as "context-awareness" and "automated capture and access" (Abowd and Mynatt 2000, 30).[22] In these systems identifier signals emitted by "outside-in" devices are collected by sensing infrastructures. As first-order observations these signals are then aggregated into data structures that are automatically passed on to the application interface layer for further processing.[23] From the perspective of Luhmann's systems theory among the questions that emerge are whether the data resulting through these aggregation processes really fulfill the criteria of simultaneously generating and marking distinction, and whether the observations performed through these aggregation processes qualify as second-order observations. Based on recent experiences reported in the media, the answer is no.

WikiLeaks and the Snowden (Wikepedia) affair showed us how, on a global scale, so-called "ban-optical" technologies (Bauman and Lyon 2013, 60–66)[24] regulate access and guard entrance into physical and virtual spaces (e.g., the nation, the work, the marketplace). Intangible and insidious, they are used as gambits of exclusion for those deemed as "undesirable." At the local level to (re) produce law and order, "synoptical" devices carry on "surveillance without surveillors" (ibid., 73).[25] The recent report published by PEN America that describes how ". . . levels of self-censorship reported by writers living in democratic countries are approaching the levels reported by writers living in authoritarian or semi-democratic countries" is a case in point of the success of these new types of systems.[26]

That the economic and political institutions of society play a role in this state of affairs is evident from the fact that it is through their infrastructures that surveillance systems seep into the very crevices of our existence. Turow and Draper give examples of this works in innovative Internet-based advertising and marketing strategies and methods that use cookies and web beacons to divert data emerging from basic interactions such as accessing a commercial website, clicking on a GPS-enabled device screen, or answering an email. For example, in March 2014, CBS 60 Minutes reported how clicking on a website such as The New York Times can mean that more than a dozen third parties "are on the page that are essentially tracking your movements" (Bellamy Foster and McChesney 2014). The data is further processed, analyzed, and aggregated with other data and output again as "data-doubles," or proxies that can be used in other tasks such as maintaining security or increasing profitmaking activities (Bauman and Lyon 2013, 8).[27]

According to Bauman, this process features a segmentation and "adiaphorization" of human agency that in the name of efficiency enables a disabling of moral resistance and critical thinking. Using Hanna Arendt's terms, there is a "floating" of responsibility to block direct attribution and disable possible moral evaluation of criminal behavior (Ibid., 88). Ethical questions are suspended in lieu of purported necessities, such as "the economy," or "the need to do business." The reverse of agency is in effect, if we consider this latter as something that is anchored to our bodies. This situation is further exacerbated by the naïve acquiescence of millions of subjects lured into so-called "visibility traps" peddled in the networked spaces of social media applications: "All the world is a stage!" declares a dramaturge in Facebook, quoting Shakespeare. In a world saturated by social media, we have become both subject and object of observation. It is the content of our lives and the experiences that are the sellable commodities.

In the bourgeoning atmosphere of simultaneous distancing and automation, it can be argued that the goodwill which initially attracted people to join social media platforms, thus spawning multiple industries and new ways of making a living, runs the risk of drying up into an "acreocracy" (Bateman 1876).[28] As Penny notes in this volume, even in fields such as healthcare, where so-called big data stands to support a host of medical discoveries, there are already documented incidents of the misuse of observation and data gathering through surveillance systems.

There Is No Simple Solution in Sight

The situation however, is not a clearcut case of "good guys versus bad guys." Ubicomp technologies can also play an important role in providing accessibility where physical challenges exist: As is described by Ellis and Goggins in this volume, aside from its ability to record everything in sight (The Economist), Glass' interface can also provide a more "natural" interaction that makes use of voice commands with head movements and is hands free.

There are also examples in which technologies and practices associated with surveillance have been used as deterrents to human rights violations. VIEVU, a Seattle company that sells wearable cameras to police forces for example, has argued that surveillance devices can be used as protection in documenting tasks involving legal liabilities.[29] Experimental data from Rialto, California, has been cited as evidence (Carroll 2013)[30] and President Barack Obama's recent call for the use of body cameras to strengthen community policing seems to support this argument.[31]

The issue of accountability through vigilance is one that can be used in the prevention of crimes against humanity from being committed. From this perspective, the Satellite Sentinel Project makes use of ubiquitous computing and surveillance systems to monitor and hopefully prevent the incidence of genocide in Sudan.[32] Along a similar and positive track, the ARTiVIS DIY Forest surveillance kit producers argue that, given the ubiquitous presence of surveillance, it might be wiser to try to harness it for the public good:

> The kit aims to repurposes surveillance technology to bring people and their communities together to protect their forests . . . Resulting video streams and collected data are expected to be uploaded and then become part of the online platform network for crowd-sourced surveillance and artistic manipulation purposes (ARTiVIS).[33]

And then there are the cases of mass entertainment, such as in sports events bearing costs that ascend into the millions and where Ubicomp technologies are used both as surveillance technique for crowd control (Friedewald and Raabe 2011, 59), as a way of creating new heightened experiences for the audience[34] and to efficiently sell products to a captive audience. In earlier days the question was "Can you see me?" Today the question might be "Did you see me?" What we see through our eyes, hear with our ears, and even the impact of our voices, our touch and our breathing can be recorded and tended back for display (and marketing) through a digital layer. More and more our agency in the world seems to exist in the form of an electronic replay of digital representations.

The current state of affairs is a conundrum. Though we are beginning to see initiatives in so-called location privacy-oriented technologies that seek to find ways to factor in human aspects such as identity and privacy, a large part of the problem has social and political implications (Krumm 2009). It behooves us to remember Bauman and Lyons' words of caution regarding how our interpretations of machines and technology are notoriously known for reversing the human sequence of actions following purposes (110). Considering the current situation, perhaps art systems can offer us different perspectives that more clearly reveal the different parameters and options and even allow us to envision potential outcomes. After all, according to Luhmann, art is an invitation to observe and communicate in an unusual manner and "creating a work of art . . . amounts to creating specific forms for an observation of observations" (2000, 69).

"Someone Has This Type of Data of You"

This is what Brian House said when explaining his motivation for creating *Quotidian Record*,[35] an interactive installation that was featured as part of the Ars Electronica 2013 *Total Recall, The Evolution of Memory* exhibition:

> I was interested in using some of the same methodology and type of data that is used in surveillance but have it be an aesthetic outcome. This kind of data exists of everybody, but people do not have it.
>
> (Lily Díaz, Interview with Brian House, August 5, 2014)

Developed during the year 2011, *Quotidian Record* has also been described by its maker as an acoustic autobiography, realized as a limited edition vinyl record.

A creative technologist, House characterizes his art practice as one that traverses alternative geographies, experimental music, and critical data practices. He also attributes the working methods used in this piece to the influence of American minimalist composers so that ". . . you set up an initial set of conditions . . . a mapping arrangement or strategy, and then you let it play out." Thus, the melodies in *Quotidian Record* were composed using data gathered by the artist who during one year tracked all his movements from one place to another.

To collect the data House used an iPhone and Open Paths, a secure server, and location-tracking software he had created. The data gathering process included automatic data collection (first-order observations) via an iPhone device. Initially in the form of longitude and latitude coordinates, the data was further analyzed and organized into categories such as "significant places." This process used self-observation carried on by House himself in order to map out the relationship of the artist with the most frequently visited places tracked by the system.

Shown in Plate 15, these sites, or "clusters of location" as House calls them, corresponded to meaningful real world places, such as "Home," "Work," or "Studio." To compose the melodies, House assigned these frequently visited significant places with notes on the music scale. It could be argued that House made use of hetero-observations during the early stage of research to link the "clusters of location" to other significant geographical units such as cities:

> Where are those clusters of location that I keep returning back to? I keep returning to this place over and over every night so that must be "Home." Places become organized in order of most to fewer visits. For each place I assign a harmonic interval and this is done by order. Cities are defined as a cluster of places within a ten-mile radius.
> (Lily Díaz, Interview with Brian House, August 5, 2014)

As the work progressed, these hetero-observations were superseded by reflexivity. These means that the initial rules used to encode the elements at the beginning were re-employed, at higher levels, in subsequent iterations. The sense of instrumentality however, was eventually discarded, in the interest of musical expression. As the author noted, "every city has its own different musical key and how these are" [were] "assigned is" [was] "an arbitrary decision" (House).

In its interaction and interface, the *Quotidian Record* installation makes use of the affordances provided by earlier media devices such as the analog vinyl disk format and a sound system with a turntable and speakers. Key elements in the installation include the vinyl record, shown in Plate 16, which gathers the music created by the artist, the turntable used when playing the available selection of melodies, and implicitly, the person who by playing the record engages in a tactile experience. Moving the turntable's arm to different spots on the disk's surface allows a person from the audience to "play" the system. This triggers a music performance in which we can experience the melodies recorded. Since the audience is possibly knowledgeable about these devices, it can also appreciate the *Quotidian Record* as being member of the class of Long Play (LP) vinyl record. From this membership, the artwork inherits a host of accumulated cultural understandings related to its making, distribution, and collecting (Luhmann 2000, 168).[36]

How the re-encoded data is saved as an LP vinyl and made available to the spectator for playing through an analog sound system's turntable also opens up the work for discussion among the audience about the relation of the work to the domain of media archeology. This further generates additional second-order observations. In Luhmann's terms, the installation both guides the audience's observation and communicates a difference about itself. Information design elements common to these recent history artifacts, such as the titles on the label section, on the recorded areas of the disk, and on the disk's slipcover also direct our attention to the fact that this is not a usual recording. There is no recording label or company advertised, and the work stands apart through the intentional observations of the artist who seeks and finds "something new in the old" (Zielinski).

As an artwork, *Quotidian Record* uses instruments and content firmly grounded on surveillance practices. Though the interaction is not open in the sense that the content is fixed, in the end the audience also participates. Through the work the artist allows those engaged with the piece to observe themselves as observers. They experience the observations and agency of another human observing himself. In the artist's own words: "I wanted to remind people that this [surveillance] exists for them too."

Towards a Critical Perspective of Ubicomp

For the past 100 years, the radical shifts in media propitiated deep fissures in the human communications and the environment. When Walter Benjamin remarked how "[e]very day the urge grows stronger to get hold of an object at very close range by way of its likeness, its reproduction," his warning was not only a critique to the destruction of earlier modes of cultural production but also a call for resistance to the use of art as a tool to promote the interests of a given political order. Five decades later it was the skillfully reconstructed female hand in the "Brilliance" TV advertising spot that showed the first ever filmed human motion capture simulation. A beckoning hand invited the viewer into the frame of vision whispering: "Come!" The spot, one of the most expensive advertising segments ever created, set a context and tone for one of the major debates of our times, namely that one of the relationship between the human and the machine. The growing inherence and potential regulation of the human body and agency through computing devices and surveillance systems belongs in this debate.

In this essay, I have tried to show how surveillance systems gather together a host of technological artifacts many of which, like computers, are now part of our everyday life. Using Niklas Luhmann's systems theory, I have tried to show how through the use of infrastructures, such as communication networks, these components are being clustered together into a separate (artificial) order with the implicit mandate to observe and follow. This intentionality is inherent in the systems that track us because they have been created to do so. The search for finer degrees of precision in observation is but a search for control of the human and the environment. Among the important questions that we have to continue asking, for what purpose and who really benefits?

Notes

1. According to Hayles, reflexivity is "the movement whereby that which has been used to generate a system is made, through a changed perspective, to become part of the system it generates."
2. Submarine Cable Map, *Teleography*, access date 25 March, 2015, www.telegeography.com/telecom-maps/submarine-cable-map/. The Map depicts 299 cables currently active or due to enter service by end of 2015.
3. Kurgan describes the basic stages of colonization of Earth's immediate atmosphere as a process initiated in the 60's and primarily driven by the United States military. Since then it has grown to include commercial interests as well as public agencies.
4. According to Luhmann, the other side is already structurally present, since it is co-presented along with the distinction.
5. Ubiquity, *Merriam-Webster Online Dictionary*, accessed 30 September, 2014, www.merriam-webster.com/dictionary/ubiquity.

6. The term "naturalization" of categories and objects describes the sense of familiarity that ensues when something becomes part of the everyday life. Bowker and Leigh argue it also leads to a certain type of forgetting.

7. For Weiser, context awareness referred to a synthesis of identity and location data.

8. Ibid., 80. Key components in embodied virtuality include distributed and mobile networks to connect all devices and allow for communication between all the elements.

9. P. C. Evans, M. Annunziata, "Industrial Internet: Pushing the Boundaries of Minds and Machines." The report argues for the use of ubiquitous computing to increase productivity and profitability in diverse industries.

10. According to Luhmann "Observation is a real, albeit prelogical mode of thinking."

11. According to Vygotsky, "humans personally influence their relations with their environment and through that environment personally change their behavior, subjugating it to their control."

12. Mandler, however, notes that a full understanding of intention however, appears at earliest in the second year of life.

13. Gell proposed that "Human agency is exercised within the material world." [since] "things with their 'thingly' causal properties are as essential to the exercise of agency as states of minds."

14. Bateson example shows the use of meta-communication or "communication about communication" to provide cues and propositions about type (classes) and to qualify and frame (order, associate). As a meta-communicative (framing) device, the term "home" for example, can evoke many dimensions in space and time.

15. Sheth argues for semantics-empowered convergence and integration to enable a new type of "computing for human experience, CHE."

16. Stern notes that human vision, for example, is "more than external data transmitted to our eyes: it is embodied."

17. The authors propose that agency is a sociocultural mediated capacity to act that is co-constructed with artifacts.

18. Triangulation can be performed by *lateration* that involves the use of multiple distance measurements between known points or by *angulation*, the measurement of angle or bearing relative to points with known separation.

19. Foucault's examples include, among others, the establishment of spaces in places to separate and exclude (leprosariums, mental asylums) and also comprises discourses to confine, re-purpose and create surplus from human labor (prisons, workhouses).

20. Among the examples that Bauman and Lyons provide of "othering" are marginal groups, minorities, or those who deviate from the norm.

21. Informationisation refers to the tangible effects of information technology deployment. For example the information devices are now with us always in specific locations as well as on the road.

22. Context-awareness relates to how sensors can "adapt their behavior based on the information sensed . . ."

23. As instruments of aggregation, profiles are used to establish new relations among the data.

24. Citing Bigo, Bauman and Lyon use the term ban-opticon to describe profiling technologies used to determine who is placed under surveillance.

25. Former objects of managerial discipline are now expected to self-discipline themselves. Users of social media produce their "database' transforming themselves into 'targeted categories'.

26. "Global Chilling: The Impact of Mass Surveillance on International Writers," *PEN America*, accessed 11 January, 2015, www.pen.org/sites/default/files/globalchilling_2015.pdf.

27. A "data double" is "made up with "personal data" only in the sense that it originated with a person's body."

28. Acreocracy, is a slang term that means in the interests of the landlord.

29. *VIEVU*, accessed 27 August, 2014, www.vievu.com.

30. R. Carroll, "California police use of body cameras cuts violence and complaints." *The Guardian*, Monday 4 November 2013, accessed 27 August, 2014, www.theguardian.com/world/2013/nov/04/california-police-body-cameras-cuts-violence-complaints-rialto.

31. "Fact Sheet: Strengthening Community Policing," *The White House, Office of the Press Secretary*, 01 December 2014, accessed 26 January, 2015, www.whitehouse.gov/the-press-office/2014/12/01/fact-sheet-strengthening-community-policing.

32. *Satellite Sentinel Project*, accessed 30 September, 2014, www.satsentinel.org.

33. "Keep an eye on your forest and share it with the world," *ArtiVIS*, accessed 9 May, 2014, http://diy.artivis.net.

34. "Enterasys Teams Up With Patriots on Wi-Fi Service for Fans," *Information Week Network Computing*, accessed 24 August, 2014, www.networkcomputing.com/wireless-infrastructure/enterasys-teams-up-with-patriots-on-wi-fi-service-for-fans/d/d-id/1233870?.
35. B. House, "Quotidian Record," *Brian House*, accessed 7 February, 2015, http://brianhouse.net/works/quotidian_record/.
36 Luhmann refers to "formal combinations of artworks" that "facilitate observation of observations" as the nexus between self-observation and hetero-observation.

References

Abowd, Gregory D., and Elizabeth D. Mynatt. 2000. "Charting Past, Present, and Future Research in Ubiquitous Computing." *ACM Transactions on Computer-Human Interaction* 7 (1): 29–58.

Bateman, John. 1876. *The Acreocracy of England, A List of All Owners of Three Thousand Acres and Upwards, With Their Possessions and Incomes, Arranged Under Their Various Counties, Also Their Colleges and Clubs.* Culled from "The Modern Domesday Book". London: B. M. Pickering. Electronic version at Internet Archive, accessed November 3, 2015, https://archive.org/details/acreocracyengla00bategoog.

Bateson, Gregory. (1977) 2000. *Steps towards and Ecology of the Mind.* Chicago, IL and London: University of Chicago Press.

Bauman, Zygmunt, and David Lyon. 2013. *Liquid Surveillance, A Conversation.* Cambridge, UK: Polity Press.

Bellamy Foster, John, and Robert W. McChesney. 2014. "Surveillance-Capitalism, Monopoly-Finance Capital, the Military-Industrial Complex, and the Digital Age." *Monthly Review* 66 (03, July-August): 1–31. Accessed March 29, 2015, http://monthlyreview.org/2014/07/01/surveillance-capitalism/.

Bowkers, Geoffrey, and Susan Leigh-Star. 1999. *Sorting Things Out, Classification and its Consequences.* Cambridge, MA: MIT Press.

Carroll, Rory. "California Police use of Body Cameras cuts Violence and Complaints." *The Guardian*, Monday November 4, 2013, accessed August 27, 2014, www.theguardian.com/world/2013/nov/04/california-police-body-cameras-cuts-violence-complaints-rialto.

Castells, Manuel. 1996. *The Rise of the Network Society.* Oxford, UK: Blackwell.

Ekman, Ulrik. 2013. "Of Intangible Speed: 'Ubiquity' as Transduction in Interactivity." In *Throughout, Art and Culture Emerging with Ubiquitous Computing*, 279–310. Cambridge, MA: MIT Press.

"Enterasys Teams Up With Patriots on Wi-Fi Service for Fans." *Information Week Network Computing*, accessed August 24, 2014, www.networkcomputing.com/wireless-infrastructure/enterasys-teams-up-with-patriots-on-wi-fi-service-for-fans/d/d-id/1233870?

Friedewald, Michael, and Oliver Raable. 2011. "Ubiquitous Computing: An Overview of Techology Impacts." *Telematics and Informatics* 28: 55–65.

"Fact Sheet: Strengthening Community Policing." *The White House, Office of the Press Secretary*, December 1, 2014, accessed January 26, 2015, www.whitehouse.gov/the-press-office/2014/12/01/fact-sheet-strengthening-community-policing.

Gell, Alfred. 1998. *Art and Agency, An Anthropological Theory.* Oxford: Oxford University Press.

Gellman, Barton, Ashkan Soltani and Andrea Peterson. 2013. *The Washington Post*, 4 November 2013, accessed November 3 2015, www.washingtonpost.com/news/the-switch/wp/2013/11/04/how-we-know-the-nsa-had-access-to-internal-google-and-yahoo-cloud-data/.

"Global Chilling: The Impact of Mass Surveillance on International Writers." *PEN America*, January 5, 2015, accessed January 11, 2015, www.pen.org/sites/default/files/globalchilling_2015.pdf.

Gershon, Ilana. 2005. "Seeing Like a System, Luhmann for Anthropologists." *Anthropological Theory* 5 (2): 99–116.

Hayles, Katherine. 1999. *How We Became Post Human, Virtual Bodies in Cybernetics, Literature, and Informatics.* Chicago, IL: University of Chicago Press.

Hightower, Jeffrey, and Gaetano Borriello. 2001. "Locations Systems for Ubiquitous Computing." *Computer* 34 (8): 57–66.

Hookway, Brandon. 2014. *Interface.* Cambridge, MA: The MIT Press.

House, Brian. "Quotidian Record." *Brian House*, accessed February 7, 2015, http://brianhouse.net/works/quotidian_record/.

"Keep an eye on your forest and share it with the world." *ArtiVIS*, accessed May 9, 2014, http://diy.artivis.net.

Krumm, John. 2009. "A Survey of Computational Location Privacy." *Pervasive Ubiquitous Computing* 13 (6): 391–399.

Kurgan, Laura. 2013. *Close up at a Distance: Mapping, Technology, and Politics.* Cambridge, MA: MIT Press.

Luhmann, Niklas. 2000. *Art as a Social System.* Translated by Eva M. Knodt. Stanford, CA: Stanford University Press.

Luhmann, Niklas. 2013. *Introduction to Systems Theory.* Malden, MA: Polity Press.

Luhmann, Niklas. 1995. "The Paradoxy of Observing Systems." *Cultural Critique,* No. 31, The Politics of Systems and Environments, Part II (Autumn): 37–55.

Le Moigne, Jean Louis. 1999. *La Modélisation des systèmes complexes.* Paris: Dunod.

Lyon, David. 2001. *Surveillance Society, Monitoring Everyday Life.* Buckingham, UK: Open University Press.

Mandler, Jean. 2010. "The Spatial Foundation of the Conceptual System." *Language and Cognition* 2(1): 21–44.

Morville, Peter. 2005. *Ambient Findability.* Sebastopol, CA: O'Reilly Media.

Neves, Clarissa Eckert, Neves, Baeta, and Neves, Fabrício Monteiro. 2006. "What Is Complex in the Complex World? Niklas Luhmann and the Theory of Social Systems." *Sociologias,* http://socialsciences. scielo.org/scielo.php?script=sci_arttext&pid=S1517–45222006000100004&lng=en&tlng=en.

"The People's Panopticon." 2013. *The Economist* (November) 16: 27–29.

Rabinow, Paul. 2008. *Marking Time, On the Anthropology of the Contemporary.* Princeton, NJ: Princeton University Press.

Reeves, Stuart. 2012. "Envisioning Ubiquitous Computing." In *CHI '12 Proceedings of the SIGCHI Conference on Human Factors in Computing Systems,* 1573–1582. New York: ACM Press.

Satellite Sentinel Project, accessed September 30, 2014, www.satsentinel.org.

Sayed, Sahil, Abhigyan Singh, Joanna Saad-Sulonen, and Lily Diaz. 2010. "Co-Construction as Complex Adaptive System." *The Journal of Community Informatics* 6 (2), accessed November 3, 2015, http://ci-journal.net/index.php/ciej/article/view/719.

Sheth, Amit. 2010. "Computing for Experience, Semantics-Empowered Sensors, Services, and Social Computing on the Ubiquitous Web." *IEEE Internet Computing* 14 (1): 88–91.

Stern, Nathaniel. 2013. *Interactive Art and Embodiment: The Implicit Body as Performance.* Canterbury, UK: Gylphi.

"The Making of *Brilliance.*" *YouTube,* Accessed March 29, 2015, http://youtube.com/watch?v=HZY5_ZzRdbk.

Turow, Joseph, and Nora Draper. 2012. "Advertising's New Surveillance Ecosystem." In *Routledge Handbook of Surveillance Studies,* edited by K. Ball, K. D. Haggerty, and D. Lyon, 133–140. New York: Routledge International Books.

Urquhart, Lachian. 2014. "Bridging the Gap Between Law & HCI: Designing Effective Regulation of Human Autonomy in Everyday Ubicomp Systems." In *Proceedings of Ubicomp 2014 Conference,* 355–360. New York: ACM Press. http://ubicomp.org/ubicomp2014/proceedings/ubicomp_adjunct/doctoral/p355-urquhart.pdf.

VIEVU, accessed August 27, 2014, http://vievu.com.

Vygotsky, Lev S. 1978. *Mind in Society, The Development of Higher Psychological Processes.* Cambridge, MA: Harvard University Press.

Weiser, Mark. 1991. "The Computer for the Twenty-first Century." *Scientific American* 265 (3):94–104.

Wikipedia. "Edward Snowden." Accessed November 3, 2015, https://en.wikipedia.org/wiki/Edward_Snowden.

Wilden, Anthony. 1972. *System and Structure, Essays in Communication and Exchange.* London: Tavistock.

Zielinski, Siegfried. 2006. *Deep Time of the Media, Towards and Archeology of Hearing and Seeing by Technical Means.* Cambridge, MA: MIT Press.

THE IMPLIED PRODUCER AND THE CITIZEN OF THE CULTURE OF UBIQUITOUS INFORMATION

Investigating Emergent Typologies of Critical Awareness

Morten Søndergaard

Introduction

The question raised in this chapter is inspired by the notion of the "citizens of the artwork" (Olmedo 2011)—what is the significance and impact on the audience unprepared for the technological interference into the everyday life and awareness by ubiquitous culture and art installations in public spaces? What constitutes these "unprepared" and maybe "unaware" citizens in the culture of ubiquitous information? What role does the citizen play in the creation of technologically defined and often "designed" environments? Furthermore, how could the position of the "ubiquitous" citizen be said to reflect back on the situation and constitution of the public space as an open and political space?

In the 1960s, the modern public space was described as a "citizen space" constituted by a "literary awareness"—a rational communicative conversation-based action of laws and various textualizations of discourses (Habermas 1962). Moreover, the public space was primarily thought of as a physical space facilitating the imagery of rational governance, more or less a face-to-face dialogue where different opinions were communicated. However, the very constitution of this "citizen space" has been changing rapidly since the 1960s—undergoing several transformations (the scale of which is outside the scope of this chapter to revisit historically). The "literary awareness"—and the very basis of the idea of a communicative (inter)action in public space—is partly and increasingly being replaced by a "media awareness" during the 1970s and 1980s; and, in the digital age, this process has transgressed even further into a new situation— perhaps best described as a "distributed awareness," which, in a first attempt at definition, means: Since the public space is being mediated on several platforms simultaneously, it is changing the mental configuration of the physical public space; but, more importantly in the context of this chapter, it is making the very space of the city (as the place for citizens), in which digital technology is everywhere, one of mental distraction and abstraction.

The citizen space always involves mediation to some degree—but with ubiquitous information technology everywhere boundaries between private and public are blurring, and the degree of mediation is intensifying, with an increasingly tight focus on the "users" of citizen-spaces. Thus, the citizen today is challenged by this competition for their attention, but also by the ever-decreasing time for true privacy. Privacy, and time for privacy, is rare—even to a degree that the very understanding of what is private is blurring. This may be witnessed in the attempt to create "nasty sound designs" in the United States to prevent certain (young) citizens to stay too long in public spaces (like car parks), thus, so the argument goes, preventing them from committing crimes. There is indeed a need for better, more egalitarian forms of "urban media designs" (Sterne 2005), which respect and understand the citizen and the challenges to awareness that a distributed mediated situation creates.

This chapter investigates emergent "typologies" in the distributed public spaces of the culture of ubiquitous information and asks the questions: What constitutes the awareness of this "ubiquitous" citizen (the citizen constantly interfering with and being interfered by abstract information-spaces of ubiquitous technology)? This question leads, I would argue, to another question: What practices and practitioners may be identified working with and in distributed public spaces?

The chapter traces one particular type of emergent hybrid practice: The frame-maker or, simply, the producer of technological and conceptual framings; instead of producing works of art, the hybrid artists in the culture of ubiquitous information are producing new domains. Thus, in the citizenship of ubiquitous culture, I will argue that the role as "producer" of platforms and domains is implied.

In the emergence of a critical awareness of the inter-citizen of distributed public spaces, an "implied producer" is operational. What follows will be an attempt to characterize and identify the "implied producer."

What follows draws on a number of projects from independent platforms emerging within the last fifteen years in order to further investigate the emergent typologies structuring the ubiquitous cultural landscape, from the hypothesis that 1) the "implied producer" emerges from an "abstract space" in-between the human and computer; 2) the "implied producer" is generating a "postphenomenological" focus on, what Don Ihde has termed "the technological embodied imagination" (Ihde 2009); and 3) the "implied producer" challenges the traditional cultural categories of the museum and the archive and introduces a new transdisciplinary space of participation.

Ubiquitous Participation?

The phenomenology of the culture of ubiquitous information—the very notion of *calling* it a "culture"—relies heavily on the paradox of, on the one hand, the engineering "idealism" of participation, where the audience is transformed into citizens with political and social responsibilities, and, on the other hand, the ability to transform the apparatus into a "cultural" medium—in this instance, to use the vernacular of Lefebvre, to facilitate a generative process of meaningful space production (Lefebvre 2008).

The generative process is deeply imbedded in the very idea of the "production of space" that constitutes the phenomenology of Lefebvre and which, in turn, is building upon the notion of active participation in constructing societal, cultural, or political "rational" coherence. For Lefebvre, it all comes down to our ability to impact real-life issues and situations—our ability to transform the basic elements that constitute our society: openness and production of spaces of dialogue. Two main lines of thought are dominant in theories of participation in social and artistic practices. One derives from a design-paradigm and is focused on the constructivist and commercial possibilities involved in participation—in design-methodology and creationist thinking. Another derives from a combination of art–history and performance/theatre studies and depends on a "performance-paradigm" of knowledge in a formulation of the theoretical understanding of participation–art as an art of the "audience turned citizen":

> Participation forecloses the traditional idea of spectatorship and suggests a new understanding of art without audiences, one in which everyone is a producer.
>
> (Lefebvre 2008, 241)

It seems reasonable to claim that the role of the producer, indeed the producer as an emergent typology inhabiting the theories of a culture of ubiquitous information is evident, even if it is mostly seen from the perspective of artistic production here. One of the consequences of this emergence of the producer as a replacement of the audience is that art, as a limited phenomenon and denoting specific genres, is replaced as well. Art, in this sense, is obsoleted in its traditional forms and formats and the entire scene is set for an ontological dance around the very notion of "art"—and how to navigate the emergent field of art production that follows the emergence of the implied producer.

The most recent theoretical discourses about participation have mainly taken two paths, which crudely could be described as issues concerning media with or without art. The first path is based on Umberto Eco (his essay about light art from 1959, "The Open Work") and Roland Barthes and has been focused on participation as an aesthetic and/or expanded work-category—a discourse also found in writings by Nicolas Bourriaud and Jacques Ranciere (Bourriaud, 1998; Ranciere, 2008). Here, however, the production is implicitly placed with the artist curator, thus identifying the discourse of most of "modern" and "contemporary" art curating in art galleries of the 00s and 10s—which I for that reason would term as the "traditional" discourse on participation seen from the art perspective.

The second path locates the issue of participation in the strategic and sociological transformation of media into the commercial–cultural domain. This domain without art might be judged as the domain where most of the social exchange is taking place, as writings by Jenkins would have it. This I would term the "commercial–cultural" discourse on participation seen from the media-without-art perspective.

What I am proposing is a different perspective on matters, a fresh analysis, as it were, of participation as a combined media-and-art practice. This perspective takes its starting point in participation as something practiced in everyday life.

> Far from suppressing criticism of everyday life, modern technical progress realizes it. This technicity replaces the criticism of life through . . . those activities which rise above the everyday, by the critique of everyday life from within: the critique . . . of the real by the possible and of one aspect of life by another.
>
> (Lefebvre 2008, xi)

Since Lefebvre's comment in the foreword of the second edition of *Critique of Everyday Life* (which originally came out in 1947), digital media have certainly realized a situation where technology repeatedly is pushing the limits of reality of everyday life to new frontiers. This, it seems to me, is the true ubiquity of technology: that the modalities of criticism (and critical thought) become transitory, fugitive, and invisible. This, however, does not mean that criticism in, what I choose to term as, the expanded cultural field of digital everyday life (short: expanded digital field) is extinct or just not important. On the contrary, the critical activity of philosophy, art, poetry, hermeneutics are very present, albeit ubiquitously. This means that cultural artefacts and for example works of art do not carry the same "implicit" authority anymore—it is not possible to assume an implicit reader of literature or an implicit visitor at an art museum that share the same fundamental cultural norms and values, and habits, of the author or curator. A circuit of cultural order has been broken—what has taken its place? What is the new role of the reader/visitor?

In "The Author as Producer," Walter Benjamin is calling for an active writer and an activation of the author into political and social questions and problems. What would ubiquitous culture look like to Benjamin? In the introduction to "The Author as (Digital) Producer," Krysa and Cox writes that social change does not simply result from resistance to the existing set of conditions but from adapting and transforming the technical apparatus itself (Krysa and Cox). Whereas Walter Benjamin in his essay "The Author as Producer," written in 1934, recommends that the "cultural producer" intervene in the production process in the manner of an engineer, to act as an engineer in the sense implied, is to use power productively to bring about change and for public utility. But what is the relevance for cultural production at this point in time—when activities of production, consumption, and circulation operate through complex global networks served by information technologies?

To call anything "culture" in the context of ubiquitous information technology, the generative process of producing space has to produce a "meaningful" public space that the citizen can relate to—an interpolated memory-space oscillating between the human and the computer. In the *Alter Bahnhof Video Walk* by Janet Cardiff and George Bures Miller at Documenta 13 (2012), this is exactly what is being offered. Viewers were given an iPod and headphones and asked to follow the prerecorded video through the old train station in Kassel. Cardiff and Bures Miller explain:

> The overlapping realities lead to a strange, perceptive confusion in the viewer's brain . . . when doing the walk the real sounds mix with the recorded adding another level of confusion as to what is real and what is fiction.
>
> (Cardiff and Bures Miller)

Fascinating as this walk in past–present may be (and the quality of the technology and quality of design invested in this were compelling), the *Alter Bahnhof Video Walk* seems to offer an "aesthetic" space rather than an actual citizen space: The confusion of fiction and reality is lovely, but it remains a purely artistic one (in the traditional sense: it is an artwork). What is addressed is a literary awareness, not a distributed one. What is emerging is a story of the Alter Bahnhof as a rite of passage, pointing out the layers of a very physical memory space and having technology facilitating, merely, this Bergsonian notion of durée. It is not possible for the audience to interact with the "new" space that emerges: Thus, *Alter Bahnhof Video Walk* does not constitute an Independent Platform. For that to happen, and for the implied producer to emerge, other strategies have to be applied.

A Walk in the Digital Wilderness . . .

In the Android app created by EcoArtTech called *Indeterminate Hikes+* (IH+), the app "transforms the mobile landscape into a series of sites of biocultural diversity and wild happenings." The idea is to re-appropriate "devices of rapid communication and consumerism" as "tools of environmental imagination, meditative wonder, and slow mobility." *Indeterminate*

Hikes+ typically plays out either as a tour guided by artists or as a self-guided tour equipped with a smartphone into which is downloaded the IH+ app.

"Sniffing out the wireless," "feel the rumble of combustion engines" (Plate 17), or "find a place to sit down. Ask passersby if they have seen a rabbit in the area" (Plate 18), enter into the awareness of the participants in the "tour-de-ubiquity," importing . . .

> the rhetoric of wilderness into virtually any place accessible by Google Maps, creates hikes, and encourages its hiker-participants to treat the locales they encounter as spaces worthy of the attention accorded to sublime landscapes, such as canyons and gorges. Thus the ecological wonder usually associated with "natural" spaces, such as national parks, is re-appropriated here to renew awareness of the often-disregarded spaces in our culture that also need attention, such as alleyways, highways, and garbage dumps. This project extends ecological awareness into mobile spaces, into the places humans actually live, democratizing conversations about environmental sustainability and ecological management that too often occur only in a scientific context.
>
> (Inderterminate Hikes 2012)

What IH+ does, I would claim, is to transform the space of ubiquitous information into a platform and activate the implied producer on that platform into a discourse of environment and "wild nature." This is a methodology, which is also moving beyond the concept of "cloud computing" and "big data" in a creative way.

Cloud computing is a concept for next generation Internet where data is organized in a different manner, than is the case in the current www setup. The speed and growth of the Internet means we are drifting away from taxonomy, and the search-oriented architecture gives us new possibilities in crowd sourcing and collaboration. IH+ is pointing towards a post-phenomenological situation by reinserting a technologically embodied imagination and perception into the abstract space of ubiquitous information, whereby a creative reinterpretation of awareness is triggered (Ihde 2009). An active technologically participating producer is indeed implied.

Thus, I will argue that we are faced with the question of formulating qualitatively new phenomena, concepts, and strategies in-between theory and practice. The construction of new domains is based on highly different competences unfolding in a hybrid space oscillating between atoms and bits.

One of the key features of this hybrid space is the fact that technologies, in the words of Mark Weiser, are disappearing, because "they weave themselves into the fabric of everyday life until they are indistinguishable from it." Furthermore, this development is often described as the ubiquity of computing everywhere—or ubiquitous computers that on the one hand is entering our world and becoming "as natural" as trees in the forest, as Weiser (1991, 104) has stated it:

> Computer access will penetrate all groups in society (. . .) ubiquitous computers will help overcome the problem of information overload. There is more information available at our fingertips during a walk in the woods than in any computer system, yet people find a walk among trees relaxing and computers frustrating. Machines that fit the human environment, instead of forcing humans to enter theirs, will make using a computer as refreshing as taking a walk in the woods.

On the other hand, this "hidden but always present" becomes a metaphor for the emergence of completely new parameters of reality and patterns of communication. Ubiquitous computers are the hidden texts, the unwritten parts of art in the expanded digital field. In the words of Lev Manovich: "What before was ephemeral, transient, unmappable, and invisible become permanent, mappable, and viewable" (Manovich 2009, 240).

Therefore, art and artists, as well as their users, viewers, and readers, receive a new role —". . . content, a cultural object, cultural production, and cultural consumption—are redefined . . ." [op.cit.]. Art is not representation, but participation in and production of real/ tangible connections and relations in an increasingly distributed and technologically motivated world. But what does that imply?

The Implied Reader Revisited

At this point, it would be useful to rewind the argument of the implied producer a little in order to understand better what pre-ubiquity cultural categories are active in the generative processes of awareness-production in a public space. When Wolfgang Iser wrote *The Implied Reader*, the relation of the human and the computer was not implied in his thoughts and patterns.

Iser wanted to take the critique of literature in the direction of the processes of communication that took place outside the text—and he explicitly saw this as a phenomenological project (Iser 1978, 276). In the case of the implied producer, however, the phenomenology is less clear—the complexity of the human/computer relationship, or interface, is changing the epistemological rules as well. But since Iser's focus was on the novel as a medium of communication, investigating the intricate patterns of the sender and the receiver as well as those of the intermediate "aesthetics" of the novel, the journey is not that far from the implicit reader to the user of "ubiquitous" computers as would be expected. Indeed, the question that is being discussed continuously, and will be discussed over and over again in years to come, is exactly that same intermediate role of the medium, and mediated communication taking place between humans, carried out in a still more sophisticated and intricate digital network of computers. In fact, I would argue that the same fundamental problematic, as those patterns that Wolfgang Iser points out with regards to literary communication, are involved in the framing and positioning of the user of the expanded art situation and a transforming framing of the art gallery.

Wolfgang Iser is focusing on the novel as a "new" medium and on the "meaning production" coinciding with "reader involvement" (Iser 1978, xi). The implied reader is an active reader set out on a journey to discover meaning in texts. Just as, according to Iser, it should be up to literary hermeneutics to map the topography of the no-man's land between text and theory, it should be our purpose to map the forms of production in the expanded aesthetic field of "ubiquitous culture."

Iser writes about the activity of accessing the unwritten part of a text as a process of creativity —a "game" of "gaps".

> The fact that completely different readers can be differently affected by the "reality" of a particular text is amble evidence of the degree to which literary texts transform reading into a creative process that is far above mere perception of what is written. The literary text activates our own faculties and enables us to recreate the world it represents. The product of this creative activity is what we might now call the virtual dimension of the text, which endows it with its reality. This virtual dimension is not the text itself, nor is it the imagination of the reader: it is the coming together of text and imagination.
>
> (Iser 1978, 279)

There is a hint of the implied producer in this formulation by Iser, since it presupposes the activity of the reader involving imagination as well as relating to (the construction of) reality (in the text). If we compare this to the notion introduced earlier of the abstract space by Lefebvre—which produces a "false" consciousness' that, in turn, generates a critical moment that may produce a "clearer" consciousness—then it would be possible to claim that the space(s) of ubiquitous information are akin to that of an abstract space producing a "false consciousness"?

What Is Implied in the Culture of Ubiquitous Information?

First of all, ubiquity itself is implying a number of things: the computer, a network, maybe a cloud of data. It also implies some kind of social or cultural impact of these technologies. Thus, this book claims that ubiquity implies the production of a cultural space where the status of phenomena or the processes of human understanding and investigation are based on hidden or undetectable information.

Second, it would follow from this claim that ubiquitous information technology constitutes a medium or a mediated framing of experience. It carries all the traditional characteristics of a medium. It is transparent, in the sense of Roland Barthes (writing about photography and the photographic "documentation" of reality): apparently untouched by "human hand" (Barthes 1980). As in the photograph, we perceive that which is reproduced and constructed as authentic because the traces of "the human hand" are invisible. Walter Benjamin even saw this transparency of the reproduction-medium as an apparatus that extends the reach of "the human hand" whereby it pervades reality in such a convincing way that it appears to be "without apparatus" (Benjamin 1934b). Therefore, I will claim that the culture of ubiquitous information is an apparatus implying the production of a "transparent" mediated space.

Third, the mediated space that the technology of ubiquitous information produces is complex and multifaceted. At one level, it is akin to the view of space based on the division Descartes established between *res cogitans* and *res extensia*. The Cartesian understanding of space is based on Euclidean geometry as extensions of lines and planes, which still, on one level, could be applied to the understanding of how the technology operates "behind the scene." After all, the space of ubiquitous information is a mathematical calculated space that is being made available to human experience. The "hand" behind it is "invisible" however the hand "at the front end" is very exposed—and not aware of being part of an enhanced mathematical space. In the thinking of Kant, of course, space and time are understood as *a priori* categories structuring all experience—and, again, in some ways, this is getting nearer to the actual set-up of a ubiquitous information-space since the mathematical "back-space" is, in fact, delivering a space experienced by and used by people. However, if we are going to understand what kind of space ubiquitous information technology is producing, its potential for culture and critical discourse, and its significance for the inter-citizen, then we need to analyze how real people with minds and bodies, and living real lives, are being implied into this space.

So, what replaces the literary hermeneutics in the expanded aesthetic field?

The Production of a Distributed Public Space

According to Lefebvre, the Cartesian space is an "abstract space" that alienates the role of the human being in the very same space: It excludes the "human hand."

To Lefebvre, abstract space becomes salient in explaining the complex gathering of many different and univocal "forces" and trends in a primarily "imaginary" space, as well as how this preconditions people's lives. This, according to Lefebvre, is a negative effect in the first instance:

> Abstract space is not defined only by the disappearance of trees, or by the receding of nature; nor merely by the great empty spaces of the state and the military—plazas that resemble parade grounds; nor even by commercial centres packed tight with commodities, money, and cars. It is not in fact defined on the bases of what is perceived. Its abstraction has nothing simple about it: it is not transparent and cannot be reduced either to logic or to a strategy. Coinciding neither with the abstraction of the sign, nor with that of the concept, it operates negatively [. . .] It has nothing of a "subject" about it, yet it acts like a subject in that it transports and maintains specific social relations, dissolves others, and stands opposed to yet others. It functions positively vis-à-vis its own implications: technology, applied sciences, and knowledge bound to power. Abstract space may even be described as at once, and inseparably, the locus, medium and tool of this "positivity".
>
> (Lefebvre 2008, 50)

Thus abstract space, in the first instance (and when it is habitually understood in Cartesian terms), is producing a "false consciousness": The human body and modes of perception, experience and lived life in a phenomenology constituting that which "generates illusions, and hence a tendency towards false consciousness, that is, consciousness of a space at once imaginary and real." However, and still according to Lefebvre, this peculiar framing of the abstract space produces a generative process from which, in turn, awareness is sharpened:

> Yet this space itself, and the practice that corresponds to it, give rise, by virtue of a critical moment, to a clearer consciousness. No science has as yet offered an account of this generative process, and this is as true of ecology as it is of history.
>
> (Lefebvre 2008, 411)

The question is, if a similar generative process may be located in the culture of ubiquitous information?

Performing Technological Embodiment

The *Augmented Reality Project* by the Danish media performance group, Boxiganga (a.k.a. Kjell Petersen and Karin Søndergaard), from 2000 works directly from the notion of producing social and embodied spaces based on "abstract" technologically created and controlled spaces. It is a project designed to investigate the invisible patterns of communication in a museum space. It is also an experimental research project concerning augmentation as a strategy within the paradigm of reactive media where the focus is on the experiences that take place on the edge of our senses, as they put it:

> In this project, visitors will come into contact with a series of staged and choreographed, high technology installations that can sense their presence. These "sensitive" sculptures are likened to pieces of furniture in a room. But the installations, each in its own way, don't only sense they also react. Thus they promote relationships through experiences that may take place at the edge of the senses.
>
> (Boxiganga 1998–2006)

This edge, the fusion of performing mind and technological body, is clearly visible in the practice and artistic strategy of Boxiganga. In 1998, they formulated the principles for an environment for exploring the use of the relation between humans and computers in an artistic/performative exploration of the museum space. Building from a tradition of Noh drama and "classic" performance art practice in the 1980s, the augmented reality project was shown at the first Electrohype in Bella Center, Copenhagen. Working with a network of Apple G3-computers, the basic principle was to place the computer and data processing in the background, thus achieving the illusion of reality in the "human-computer interaction." Art, the way Boxiganga sees it, is conceived as a network of open systems. And this is also where we find a significant parallel to Wolfgang Iser's project—that of the process of creativity. But Iser's intention is to point out the fact that we read as much as we do not read (the unwritten part of the texts are as important as the written part), which requires involvement and an activity by the reader to imagine the required amount of norms of reality that are represented, the "users" of the works by Boxiganga are asked to be "producers" of "relational patterns" of communication. And Boxiganga is supplying the framework for doing just that:

> We intend to develop relations-orientated multimedia works, which function in the social realm, in which we as people continually recreate and reinvent our existence—in relations between people. This is "relations technology" as opposed to functional or manifested technology; open systems in which content and relevance are directly dependent on involvement.
>
> (Boxiganga 1998–2006)

The Augmented Reality Project is organized into four complex, spatial constructions, of which I will mention here *I think You—You think Me*. Each construction, or augmented installation, plays with the notion of constructing the preconditions for how we experience actual phenomena and relations in physical space through hidden data processing.

> In our multimedia set-ups, the computer is relegated to a place where data is recorded, processed, and transmitted. We can then be concerned with multimedia in a context of Augmented Reality, with creating spatio—sensory, perceptive, and reactive constructs.
>
> (Boxiganga 1998–2006)

The reactive edge of human/computer experience is investigated in *I Think You—You Think Me*. Here, the reactions themselves are staged by two rather aggressive computer-generated personae—Robert and Roberta. They react to any person entering their stage (looking like a basketball court); first, by being mildly curious; but then, as you move closer to one of them, by showing more and more feelings of hostility—that is, the closer you get to Robert, the more aggressive he gets (at least, that is our conventional interpretation of their reactions).

These "faces" of digitally generated personas point towards the important notion that what is being augmented is their falseness: They create impressions of communication and emotion only based on calculated reactions based on a few "bodily" gestures. The human/computer relationship is not so much about the interface itself, but about how relations may occur and develop between digital and human phenomenological systems—how they react to each other from implicit patterns created by the media architecture in the space:

In fact, the basic function of the installations often requires that two visitors enter into a relationship and investigate an interpretation of the contents of that relationship. These installations then are situations for augmented relationships.

(Boxiganga 1998–2006)

Thus, the Augmented Reality Project highlights human–computer interaction *as being based on false consciousness*. But out of this consciousness emerges a new awareness—the generative process of which the Augmented Reality Project becomes the platform.

The culture of ubiquitous information, I will argue, is victim of the same negativity in that it is merely "there" as a medium for interaction, without being recognizable as a medium. It is transparent without documenting anything or without becoming an apparatus for the author-producer. It points towards an abstract user, which is an undefined and unrealized relation between the human and the computer.

Navigating the Spaces between Humans and Computers

The Swedish Biennale *Electrohype* may serve as a good example of how the process of technological imagination is producing abstract spaces of false consciousness, despite the work of excellent artists (operating within a "contemporary art" setting as best they can) and "good curatorial intentions" of introducing digital art into art galleries. In the 2008 edition, technology is being "hyped" in the modernistic gallery space of Malmö Konsthall. The interactive passage through the exhibition is stages like an adventure game with the artworks as the game site and you as the gamer. The curators point out the basic rules of the game, which have to be accepted by the audience: 1) Humans and computers are related, and 2) Technology enhances and transforms the human faculties of perception and understanding.

These rules, however, soon prove to be pointing us towards an abstract space of false awareness. The visitors are only seemingly producers of the game-field, since it is being controlled by the real producer—the abstract (but ubiquitous) Director of Malmö Konsthall, on whose orders and wishes of making an "technology-with-art" exhibition, the curators are acting. This creates a "false condition" for some of the works presented, which especially reveals itself in Bill Vorn's *Evil/Live 2* and Jessica Field's *Semiotic Investigation into Cybernetic Behaviour*.

Evil/Live 2 (Figure 6.1) consists of three large panels of electrical bulbs that each represents a life (light) that is created and dies (turned off). This visual movement of light is determined by an algorithm named "game of life," which, in the context of the exhibition, creates a meta-comment on the position you are in as visitor: You are playing a part, being a producer, in the "game of life." The digital algorithm of simulated reality is everywhere—but this ubiquitous evolution of digital life is being represented in Bill Vorn's installation, making the implicit producer visible and part of an electronic perception of the world. Evil/Live 2 points towards an alternative, albeit hazardous, new road: the impossibility of operating with "implicit producers" in the abstract spaces of the art gallery.

Jessica Field's *Semiotic Investigation into Cybernetic Behaviour* underlines the potential powerful dialectics of the "implied producer" situation, which activates the technologically embodied imagination by negating it satirically. Two robots, ALAN (Figure 6.3) and CLARA (Figure 6.4) are built from miscellaneous materials and media (new and old). Both are limited in the possibilities of "sensing" and "perceiving" the world, but not in the same way. ALAN can only "sense" movements and CLARA can only "sense" distance. They try to help each other (they are linked by a network) so that they may interpret what is happening around them

FIGURE 6.1 Bill Vorn Evil/Live2 detail. Video grab from video documentation by Morten
Søndergaard
Image courtesy of the author

FIGURE 6.2 Bill Vorn Evil/Live2. Video grab from video documentation by Morten Søndergaard
Image courtesy of the author

FIGURE 6.3 Jessica Field Semiotic Investigation into Cybernetic Behaviour. ALAN. Video grab
from video documentation by Morten Søndergaard

Image courtesy of the author

FIGURE 6.4 Jessica Field Semiotic Investigation into Cybernetic Behaviour. CLARA. Video grab
from video documentation by Morten Søndergaard

Image courtesy of the author

FIGURE 6.5 IH+ in Copenhagen, DK. Photo by Morten Søndergaard
Image courtesy of the author

when someone is approaching them. They are not very successful in finding out what is going on, or anything else for that matter, and their reactions border on the paranoid, giving us a sense of "a couple of poor robots alone in the world:" "is anyone there?" "Someone is moving close to us," etc. Like Boxiganga's *Robert and Roberta, Semiotic Investigation into Cybernetic Behaviour* points technology back at each of us, standing alone in front of the installation in the middle of a process of understanding. Their limits are our limits, in the sense that we know as little about them as they know about us.

What the cybernetic system is "afraid of" is the "users," and it exhibits some interesting anxieties about interacting with the extra-cybernetic world. But the very act and interpretation of anxiety may also be seen as a metaphor of the missing link or highly limited space of production between humans and computers: A cultural space of participation in which the semiotics of cybernetics is preventing any real interaction between the citizens of the machines and the citizens of the gallery space. Both are confined by abstract rules and regulations, caught in ubiquitous cultural codes without a hermeneutics of technological embodiment present.

However, as the examples of *Indeterminate Hikes* (Plate 19) and the *Augmented Reality Project* point out, the potential of a process of sharpened awareness is immanent. The difference lies in the ways in which the implied producer is being made operational as a citizen in a distributed public space. What are being produced, in fact, by *IH* and the *Augmented Reality Project* ARE exactly distributed public spaces. The practices of ArtLifeTech and Boxiganga demonstrate that the distributed public space is not simply THERE—it has to claimed and reclaimed again and again by independent platforms made operational by implied producers.

Concluding Remarks

In this chapter, I have argued that the independent platforms emerging in the culture of ubiquitous information works strategically behind the production of "false consciousness" by generating the potential for a process of sharpening awareness manifesting itself in a new typology: The implied producer.

I have approached the implied producer from three angles: 1) Wolfgang Iser's notion of the "implied reader," although hinting at the "hidden" text as essential, is not applicable to the hybrid spaces of the involvement of the physical body, the ability to augment reality outside the imagination, and—above all—the interactions between humans and computers which increasingly are becoming "invisible" and part of (and partly defining) the post-digital culture. 2) With a parallel to Wolfgang Iser's notion of the creative process and "game" of perceiving the unwritten text (and construct a reality), the analysis of *implied producers* led to a short outline of the new rules that are shaping cultural production. 3) The existence of the *implied producer*, in turn, transforms the function of the artist into a "platform-maker" rather than a producer of singular (and autonomous) "art-works," passing from the creative instigator of "indeterminate hikes" (using the title of my first example as a metaphor of what the implied producer produces) rather than "artefacts"—thus becoming the avant-gardist of everyday life in the culture of ubiquitous information.

References

Barthes, Roland. 1980. *La Chambre Claire*. Paris: Gallimard.
Benjamin, Walter. 1931–1934a. "The Work of Art in the Age of Mechanical Reproduction." In *Selected Writings* (2–1). London: Harvard University Press.
Benjamin, Walter. 1931–1934b. "Author as Producer." In *Selected Writings* (2–2). London: Harvard University Press.
Bishop, Claire. 2012. *Artificial Hells*. London: Verso Books.
Bourriaud, Nicolas. 1998. *Esthétique relationnelle*. S.l.: Les Presses du réel.
Boxiganga (Karin Søndergaard og Kjell Pedersen). Augmented Reality Project. 1998–2006. Accessed March 20, 2015. www.boxiganga.net.
Cox, Geoff, and Joasia Krysa. 2005. *Engineering Culture: On 'The Author As (Digital) Producer'*. Brooklyn, NY: Autonomedia.
Electrohype.se. 2012. Electrohype Exhibition 2012. Accessed June 10, 2012. http://electrohype.se.
Groys, Boris. 1998. *Logik der Sammlung—Am Ende des Musealen Zeitalters*. München/Wien, Germany: Karl Hanser Verlag.
Habermas, Jürgen. 1962. *Strukturwandel der Öffentlichkeit; Untersuchungen Zu Einer Kategorie der Bürgerlichen Gesellscahft*. Neuwied: H. Luchterhand.
Hansen, Mark B. 2001. *New Philosphy for New Media*. Chicago, IL: Chicago University Press.
Ihde, Don. 2009. *Postphenomenology and Technoscience*. Albany, NY: SUNY Press.
Indeterminate Hikes. 2012. Accessed October 14, 2013. http://ecoarttech.org/projects/indeterminate-hike.
Indeterminate Hikes Documentation. 2012. Accessed October 15, 2013. www.youtube.com/watch?v=sOkQE7m31Pw.
Iser, Wolfgang. 1978 (1974). *The Implied Reader*. London: Johns Hopkins Press.
Jacobsen, Mogens, and Morten Søndergaard. 2009. *Re-Actions—The Digital Archive Experience. Renegotiating the Competences of the (Art)Nuseum in the twenty-first century*. Aalborg. Denmark: Aalborg Universitets-forlag.
Lefebvre, Henry. 2008 (1958). *The Critique of Everyday Life*. Second edition. London: Verso.
Luhmann, Niclas. 2000. *Art as a Social System*. Stanford, CA: Stanford University Press.
Manovich, Lev. 2009. "The Practice of Everyday (Media) Life: From Mass Consumption to Mass Cultural Production?" *Critical Inquiry* 35 (2): 319–331.

Martin Lister, J. D. 2008. *NEW MEDIA: A Critical Introduction.* Second edition. New York: Routledge.

Olmedo, Maria Andueza. 2011. "A New Kind of Audience. The Citizen of the Work." In *Proceedings of The International Symposium on Soundscape "Keep an ear on".* Florence, May 20–22. www.paesaggio sonoro.it/keepanearon/abstract.php?id=185.

Rancière, Jacques. 2008. *Le Spectateur émancipé.* Paris: La Fabrique.

Sterne, Jonathan. 2005. "Urban Media and the Politics of Sound Space." *Open: Cahier on Art and the Public Domain* 9 (Fall): 6–15.

Weinberger, David. 2007. *Everything is Miscellaneous.* New York: Henry Holt & Company.

Weiser, Mark. 1991. "The Computer for the 21st Century." *Scientific American* 265, 3: 94–104.

Weiser, Mark. 1999. "The Computer for the Twenty-first Century." *ACM SIGMOBILE Mobile Computing and Communications Review*—Special issue dedicated to Mark Weiser (3–3): 3–11. http://dl.acm.org/10.1145/329124.329126.

MEDIA ART

Morten Søndergaard

"Media art" first developed as a "somewhat distinct" term in the 1960s under the influence of developments and experiments in global mass media and new mass communication technologies, which is most famously witnessed (and formulated in a popular form) in the writings and (in his day, radical) ideas of Marshal McLuhan (McLuhan 1964).

The term remains widely undefined (or it keeps being redefined) within the academic and theoretical world—and little consensus exists about the definition of media art. Some confusion stems from cultural differences: In English "media art" denotes art that is mostly screen based (like film and video), whereas in German "medienkunst" covers a wider area—the conceptual media-performative practices, notably as actions or installations, but also including (experiments with) sound, video, film, digital, and other media formats. In German, "medienkunst" also denotes the transformations of art practices under the influence of "new" technology and media, that is, digital media. In French the term "l'art media" is concerned with the "social issues" of art, the social constructions of media spaces and the way art may use those spaces to impact an audience (cf. "L'art Sociologique" (Forest 1977)).

These cultural differences are partly due to the fact that media art practice is a mixed domain. It has transformed art beyond recognition—and operated with great care across genres and art forms towards a consciousness of art-as-communication and investigation into the contexts and politics of human action. As a mixed domain, it implies a transformation of the aesthetic paradigms of art. Other elements than art is naturally part of the media art practices, and art is even transgressing beyond what is traditionally seen as art working into or simulating daily social or cultural (mass media/commercial) situations. As a mixed domain situation, media art is also inherently involved in a dialogue with the awareness of and users of media.

Claudia Giannetti (Giannetti 1998) suggests, in an article written for the seminal Media Art Net project[1] at ZKM curated by Dieter Daniels and Peter Weibel (Daniels 2003; Weibel 2004), that media art marks the liberation of art from art itself as well as a "reconstruction of the area" of art. According to Gianetti, media art practice constantly challenges the concepts and relations of art. Furthermore, media art constantly changes and renegotiates the concepts and relations of art to society and the public-at-large, as a consequence of being part of a "telecommunication-system."

> Contemporary art based on digital media and tools not only constantly questions its own status, but also queries the role of the artist, the position of the recipient in regard

to the work of art, the function of the work, the function of the machine, and—very importantly—the relationship obtaining among artist, work, and recipient. The frequency with which these questions arise, along with the diversity of perspectives possible and angles adopted, makes clear the futility of attempts—such as those by exponents of information or cybernetic aesthetics—to draw up universal definitions and/or rigid and homogeneous models for the ‹entirety› of contemporary art production, because the art triggers the continuous renewal and reformulation of these concepts and relationships.

(Giannetti 1998, 7)

According to Giannetti, then, media art constantly challenges the concepts and relations of art, as a consequence of being part of a "telecommunication system."

Performing the Modes of Complexity in Media Art

In the twenty-first century, at least four prominent attempts have been made to configure, or reconfigure, media art as a mixed domain in the epistemological "theatre" of global culture. Each attempt is part of an interconnected process accompanied by overlapping philosophical issues. I am suggesting to view media art as a practice, a truly transdisciplinary action-field which not only configures, but is reconfiguring a number of mixed domains operating with a combination of relations between science, art, technology, and society (what I term the SATS-relation complex). I am claiming that media art epistemology is framing existing trends as "domains" in a transforming action-field. This game of mixing domains, or "domain-game" (Søndergaard 2014) which media art as practice is framing, could be seen as a number of on-going reconfigurations of SATS-relations in the blending of domains into social and practice-specific paradigms. They are, as Law and Mol are suggesting, ". . . modes of relating that allow the simple to coexist with the complex, of aligning elements without necessarily turning them into a comprehensive system of a complete overview" (Law and Mol 16):

1. *The Contextualizing and Institutionalizing of Media Art as a New Paradigm.* Here, it may be possible to distinguish between two positions—a "realistic" position which claims that the optimal theoretical, artistic, or institutional (academic and political) configuration of media art does not exist yet (Zielinski 2013; Daniels and Naumann 2011). And an "idealistic" position which could be said to be epitomized by the CEO of ZKM, artist and theoretician of the media art field, Peter Weibel (Weibel 2004). According to Weibel, media art is a completely new configuration empowering the user and the artists in a different epistemological setup than those that already exist; and of which we have yet only glimpsed the true potential. Both positions, however, regard it as essential to work towards uncovering and constructing the field of media art, including its histories and specific technological framings. Oliver Grau (virtual art) at media art histories in Krems (Grau 2003) and Christiane Paul (Paul 2015) are also making important contributions to this configuration.

2. *Cultural Theory.* The theoretical study of media art as cultural phenomena is centered on the notion of "remediation" and media art as a reflection of a cultural theoretical epistemology (Bolter and Grusin 1999). This also marks out a positioning of predominantly media theorists who are looking to understand the expanded and expanding field of (new) media art. The media-phenomenological categories of immediacy and hybermediacy are placing the communicative situation of the psychological effects of media centre stage in the ongoing (de)construction of (an autonomous) art. This further transforms the theoretical

discussions of media art into what may be described as multilayered and richly diversified philosophical ventures into questions of representation and language (Manovich 2001), and subjectivity and experience (Hansen 2004). In each their very different ways, Manovich and Hansen investigate epistemologies of the deeply immersive culturality of media (art) ontologies emerging throughout the 2000s, and look at how they are being represented; or recycled into (self) representations.

3. *The "Design Perspective" on Media Art*. Media art is studied as design-based artefacts and pragmatic methodologies pointing towards an experience-based epistemology. Paul Dourish (Dourish 2001) decisively marked out a fundamental influence on and from design positions of the field of media art theory, and *Where the Action Is* may serve as a headline for a transforming understanding of interaction, and what that brings to (aesthetic) experience.

4. *The Politics of Media Art*. The relationships between art, audience, and society are completely transformed by media art. Thus, the question that Walter Benjamin posed (Benjamin and Schöttker 2002), whether intellectuals (artists, writers, etc.) may actually impact and change society (and still producing good art, texts, etc.) is intensified by media art. One element in this impact, of course, is Ubiquity and the construction of (our understanding of) memory (Chun, this volume), human knowledge, and culture inside/outside media (Hansen 2004; Cubitt, this volume), and the "holistic" countering of the neutralization of "big picture" issues of ubiquity.

The Mixed Domain of Media Art

If ubicomp reveals elephants in the server room (Simon Penny, this volume), then, as will be the argument in the following, media art reveals chimeras in the art domain.

Theoretically, the concept of media art remains unclear, and even, for some, bordering on the uncanny. Is it a metaphor? Is it a genre definition? Is the blend of media and art achieved on equal terms, or has one of them, that is, "art," the upper hand in the relation?

Some argue that "media art" is part of the wider domain of "contemporary art" which is blending formal elements from, or remixing the representational styles of, the field of technology and science (and thus belongs to the wider field of a cultural "art" history) (Paul 2008; Kwastek 2013); others that "media art," rather, is a new paradigm that implicates all other art disciplines and genres and the way we socially construct knowledge about society, politics, the global, etc. (Weibel 2004; Daniels 2003; Zielinski 2013)

However, it is not possible to give one decisive conceptual *definition* of media art. Theoretically, then, media art would appear to be a chimera—a fictional "monster" or a challenge to logical thinking and argument. Media art, it seems, eludes attempts to be included into disciplines such as art history or film and media science, and it does not fit into rigid periodical or stylistic framings.

Of course, this is partly due to the fact that it has proven difficult, if not impossible, to clearly categorize or even describe what media art *is*. The phenomena and artefacts being named "media art" are extremely varied and sometimes even contradictory. The lack of a definition of media art is, therefore, also indicative of a more prominent problem for theory: where should it begin? With art or media? With theory or practice? With science or technology . . . ? Do we start with (comparisons with) what is already recognized as "contemporary art"? Do we begin with history (and the archives)? Or is media art claiming a unique field of practice which yet has to be fully investigated and understood?

It seems evident, then, that the epistemological framing of media art is still being negotiated—and, partly, it seems, this points towards one shared feature of most media artistic productions: They instigate negotiations of epistemologies and the paradigms they configure. Thus, what in the first instance appear to be chimeras in the "art domain" are signs of complexity.

Media art is a mixed domain, which investigates and problematizes the epistemological contexts in which it is being produced. This is not least the case of media art produced in ubiquitous culture, and as the contributions of this volume are witnessing, then, on the one hand, media art practitioners are distancing themselves critically from technological and commercial cultural industries (affording naturalized interaction and usability); on the other, there are real efforts to implicate user-experiences in the production of complexities. It becomes a matter of finding alternative ways. And, as such, media art in ubiquitous culture inscribe itself into a genealogy of practices nudging art out of the art domain and into alternative, mixed domains of implied cultural significance framed and embodied by processes and temporalities of technology—and the individuation of users and producers of the field.

Note

1. The "www.medienkunstnetz.de" project hosted by ZKM (Zentrum für Kunst und Medientechnologie in Karlsruhe, Germany) aimed at providing free online resources for the study of Media Art.

References

Benjamin, Walter, and Detlev Schöttker. 2002. *Medienästhetische Schriften, Suhrkamp Taschenbuch Wissenschaft.* Frankfurt am Main, Germany: Suhrkamp.

Bolter, J. David, and Richard Grusin. 1999. *Remediation: Understanding New Media.* Cambridge, MA: MIT Press.

Daniels, Dieter. 2003. *Vom Readymade zum Cyberspace: Kunst/Medien Interferenzen, Materialien zur Moderne.* Ostfildern-Ruit, Germany: Hatje Cantz.

Daniels, Dieter and Naumann, Sandra (Eds.) 2011. *Audiovisuology Vol. 2. Essays: Histories and Theories of Audiovisual Media and Art.* Köln, Germany: Verlag Walther König.

Dourish, Paul. 2001. *Where the Action Is: the Foundations of Embodied Interaction.* Cambridge, MA: MIT Press.

Forest, Fred. 1977. *Art Sociologique.* Paris: Gallimard.

Gianetti, Claudia. 1998. "The Aesthetic Paradigms of Media Art." Medienkunstnetz.de. www.medien kunstnetz.de/themes/aesthetics_of_the_digital/aesthetic_paradigms/. (Accessed February 15, 2015).

Grau, Oliver. 2003. *Virtual Art: From Illusion to Immersion.* Cambridge, MA: MIT Press.

Hansen, Mark B. N. 2004. *New Philosophy for New Media.* Cambridge, MA: MIT Press.

Kwastek, Katja. 2013. *Aesthetics of Interaction in Digital Art.* Cambridge, MA: MIT Press.

Law, John, and Annemarie Mol. 2006. *Complexities: Social Studies of Knowledge Practices, Science and Cultural Theory.* Durham, NC: Duke University Press.

McLuhan, Marshall. 1964. *Understanding Media; the Extensions of Man.* New York: McGraw-Hill.

Manovich, Lev. 2001. *The Language of New Media.* Cambridge, MA: MIT Press.

Paul, Christiane. 2008. *New Media in the White Cube and Beyond: Curatorial Models for Digital Art.* Berkeley, CA: University of California Press.

Paul, Christiane. 2015. *Digital Art.* 3rd ed. New York: Thames & Hudson.

Søndergaard, Morten. 2014. "Redesigning the Way We Listen: Curating Responsive Sound Interfaces in Transdisciplinary Domains." *Proceedings of the 9th Audio Mostly: A Conference on Interaction With Sound,* Aalborg, Denmark.

Weibel, Peter. 2004. "New Protagonists and Alliances in Twenty-first Century Art." *Ars Electronica 2004—The 25 Anniversary of the Festival of Art, Technology and Society,* 38–46.

Zielinski, Siegfried. 2013. *[After the Media]: News from the Slow-fading Twentieth Century.* Minneapolis, MN: Univocal Pub.

COMPLEXITY AND REDUCTION— INTERVIEW WITH DAVID ROKEBY

Ulrik Ekman

This interview is the last in a series of four conducted in February 2014. All four interviews originated in David Rokeby's presentation for a conference in Copenhagen, Denmark, held by the Nordic research network "The Culture of Ubiquitous Information" supported by the NordForsk Research Organization.

Ulrik Ekman (UE): In the network societies which today are into their second phase, both an intensification and a widening of their network logics are being developed and installed. Media art finds itself situated in a context that includes the interactivity relating to the Internet, social media, and mobile media. However, it also includes situations and events relating to the pursuit of the goals of other major technocultural developments. Parts of ubiquitous computing, pervasive computing, ambient intelligence, and the Internet of Things are slowly but surely being deployed in the environment, allegedly in intelligent, human-oriented, and human-centered ways.

I know from other conversations that you regard this with some skepticism, finding here sources of beneficial and/or perilous complexification of human and technical context-awareness, including all that concerns the production and recognition of what makes sense for humans and machines in a given context. You call here for a well-balanced responsibility and a safeguarding of humanist concerns. In the wake of your insistence on the import of a certain critical distance to developments of more or less invisible machinic intelligence, it would be very interesting to hear you on your current position as compared with the remarks you have made much earlier.

In your text "Transforming Mirrors" (Rokeby 1991, 1995), you mention that developments of automata in the field of interactivity tend to mirror not so much individual interactors as human behavior itself. Here you draw upon Norman White's work on robotic processes which allegedly proceed with a kind of artificial sanity, something permitting a computational machinery to make sense of its environment or become context-aware. (White 1987) You make clear that self-replicating and self-sustaining machines or artificial life may remain a rather utopian ideal. However, you grant that the machinic behaviors at stake display synergy and emergence, and that self-organization of complexity can be traced here. Ubicomp, pervasive computing, and ambient intelligence projects frequently involve the programming of autonomous agents of various kinds, so they seem to share quite a bit with your model of automata.

Could you explain what you mean by emergence and complexity here, and then outline how one is to approach this as a human interactor?

David Rokeby (DR): In terms of automata, it is useful to draw on the example of the *Game of Life* created by John Conway (Gardener 1970). In this sort of automata, a complex array of behaviors (a large behavior space) is generated by a small number of simple rules. The automata occupies a grid (in the 1970s at the start, it was done on a chessboard or pad of graph paper and computed by hand). For each iteration, each square is examined in the context of its eight neighbors. A very small number of rules (I think four) determine the next state (occupied or unoccupied; 1 or 0) for each square based on ideas like loneliness, overcrowding, and birth. Very complicated but classifiable behaviors arise. But there is no simplified way to determine the next state. You must do the calculation for each square every time, and you must calculate every intervening step to determine any particular future state of the game.

This is very different from classical physics models where we can confidently calculate future positions of planets based on current conditions with straightforward equations. This is a classic example of a certain kind of complexity . . . an unpredictable but deterministic system relying on only a small number of rules. There are of course other definitions of complexity that do not rest on simple rules, but this kind receives a lot of attention because of the contrast between its simple definition and its complex behavior.

Examples of a kind of emergence can be found in the *Game of Life*. Certain layouts of entities in the game develop into coherent repeating patterns that will persist for a time, showing a kind of structural integrity in the manner of a stable social group or community. This is one kind of emergence. Some of these groups exhibit very complex dynamic behaviors and travel across the board, managing to survive many types of encounters with other unconnected entities. The most studied of these is probably the family of "gliders" and "glider guns." These coherent structures cannot be predicted by the rules or structure of the game and display coherent meta-behaviors. They have "emerged" rather than having been designed.

Another related kind of emergent behaviors is made up of stable artifacts of feedback loops. Consider the squeal of audio feedback you hear when someone places a microphone too close to a speaker. The feedback loop itself has started to resonate on its own, requiring no further input to continue, and it will remain until someone changes the nature of the feedback loop, either by moving the microphone, or turning down the amplifier, or applying a notch filter to deemphasize the frequency that the loop is resonating at. Much more complicated artifacts occur in more complex feedback loops. They are not a property of any of the individual elements, but can be a powerful feature of the system.

UE: How do complexity and emergence figure in your own work?

DR: When I was programming the behaviors of *Very Nervous System* (Rokeby, "Very Nervous System"), I eventually came to feel that I was tuning and modulating, bringing into focus these feedback loop-based artifacts. I would see glimpses of these phenomena during sessions of intense interaction with the installation. Then I would adjust parameters in the software to draw these emergent phenomena out . . . to make them more explicit. I discuss this in some detail in the text "Harmonics of Interaction" (Rokeby, "The Harmonics of Interaction").

An audio engineer at a concert uses banks of band-cut filters to remove any trace of these system resonances to keep the sound system as true to the sound source as possible in the complex acoustics of the physical concert space with all its surface reflections and reverberation. Composer and sound artist Alvin Lucier produced a famous piece in the late 1960s called "I am sitting in a room" in which he recorded himself reading a text starting with "I am sitting in a room," then playing it back into the same space and recording again, and repeating this over and over again until the sound of his voice was transformed into the sound of the space (Lucier). The voice was lost as the acoustics of the space reinforced itself to the point that it was all that remained.

When designing any kind of system involving feedback, including ambient intelligence systems, one needs to be aware of these emergent artifacts. One can choose to enhance them, to "turn up the McLuhan" you might say, emphasizing the message of the medium, or you can attempt to damp and filter them out until they dissipate. But the more complicated and heterogeneous the system, the more difficult it is to detect, identify, and study them.

UE: How should one approach them, then, in your opinion?

DR: It is important not to assume that all feedback artifacts are undesirable. Culture might be considered a complex artifact of social feedback. Likewise, ubicomp, pervasive computing, and ambient intelligence projects will foster unintended social behaviors in their inhabitants, both positive and negative, but directly attributable to the presence of the system.

Viral events on the Internet are a kind of temporary emergent phenomenon. The stimulus that generates a viral event is often undistinguishable from many similar things that seem to have no viral impact. But the community of *Twitter* users or *YouTube* watchers form a highly resonant system that, when stimulated in just the right way, causes a massive mutual reinforcement of interest in something that is on the surface, relatively undistinguished.

As *The Giver of Names* approached completion, I discovered that the piece was getting stuck, apparently falling into a state of obsession-like fixed interest in a certain set of ideas, from which it had a hard time escaping . . . (Rokeby, "The Giver of Names"). It felt like an example of something that might be described as artificial insanity. It is in fact something that can arise in any highly interconnected system. In this case, certain groups of ideas in the knowledge base of *The Giver of Names* referred back to each other in a dense cluster with more connections between the cluster nodes than there were connections reaching beyond the cluster. In terms of the Norbert Wiener definition of autonomy, this cluster of ideas had something resembling autonomy . . . Not autonomy per se, but a kind of self-reinforcement that made a network of things into a meta-entity.

In order to solve this problem, I had to create an algorithm that made the system bored of things it had thought about too much. I designed it so that too much mutual excitation in the cluster causes a kind of boredom to set in, decreasing the strength of connections in the cluster when they got "too hot" so that the locked-in behavior dissipated. This simple intervention caused an enormous improvement in the "balance" of the system's responses.

While I remain skeptical about the likelihood of the emergence of artificial consciousness, I do think that we need to consider our networks and complex systems in a similar manner to the way we think of neural structures. This in order to understand that they may start to exhibit behaviors that resemble and are as confounding as those found in human psychology. I do not mean that networks are becoming human . . . just that neural structures are the only structures we know that have a similar level of complexity and interconnectedness as networks. So, networks of tightly integrated devices may show some similar emergent behaviors.

UE: You often see interactivity as a mirroring feedback loop. To some extent you humanize Conway's *Game of Life* by way of an analogy, seeing there the ongoing formation of structures akin to social groups or communities. Also, in the case of Norman White's automata, mentioned in "Transforming Mirrors," you found a quest for human self-understanding, even though autonomous machinic agents with emergent traits were at play.

In this you keep to the well-known notion that technologies are extensions of ourselves, and presumably this would go for ubicomp *techné* as well. One might ask whether you are exaggerating the emphasis on human subjective self-reference in complex and emergentist processes of interactive individuation.

But then one notes at once that you also wish to stress that technics be approached as interfaces involving contact with the other and otherness, with ambiguity, with surprise beyond any strict control, and hence with another kind of contact involving an incorporation of complexity.

How do you see processes of human and technical co-individuation today, and what kind of approach do you deploy when trying to work with installations harboring tensions between interactivity as emergent complexification and interactivity as reductionist control?

DR: On a certain level, I think that the behavior of a crowd is less complicated than the behaviors of its constituent human participants. This may be more a result of a limited human ability to grasp the nuances of more complicated interactions between many individuals. It does not feel to me as though I am humanizing the *Game of Life*. I think I am gesturing in the other direction: that there is a quality of behavior in large social groupings that seems to mirror the kinds of aggregate behaviors we see in simple rules-based collections of interacting automata.

In Norman White's case, he is quite explicit about using the act of creating an autonomous machine as a mode of inquiry . . . a way of asking questions about himself. Not because he thinks he is similar to an autonomous machine, but that he thinks that the act of turning his own self-understanding into an autonomous creation that he can observe in action is a useful way to understand the strengths and inadequacies of this self-understanding. I felt very much the same way about *The Giver of Names*, and I am sure that in this I was influenced by Norman.

To anthropomorphize is a constant temptation when working with responsive machines and systems. But also, working with these systems is a great way to tame and temper this tendency. The sense of otherness or alienness became important to me through my work with *The Giver of Names*. It was something I had thought about previously in somewhat different terms before, but through *The Giver of Names*, it became clearer and more concrete.

It is also correct to a certain degree to see the human in the technical, because the technology does not arise out of a vacuum . . . We dream it up and punish ourselves with obsessive work to get it to function . . . We create technologies out of human need and human desire, and, being fundamentally narcissistic, we render exaggerated fragments of ourselves and our capabilities (and their absences) in the technologies we create. What is lovely is that, through this process, we can occasionally also end up with something that transcends the limits of our human viewpoint. Our best guesses about how to make machine intelligence tend to be borrowed from our understanding of our own intelligence. But some of the most exciting results have to do with things we are incapable of imagining

. . . The task there is to find a way to be sensitive to phenomena that lie outside the realm of well-established human values.

But this is simultaneously the most exciting promise and the most potentially dangerous (to us anthropocentric types). And we come to a universal contemporary struggle: How do we continue to value ourselves and give protection to those values while appreciating and celebrating the different abilities and achievements of "others?"

UE: In your own work, how do you approach this struggle—what happens to the tension between "othering" as emergent complexification and reductionist control to the "same?"

DR: The computer is carefully designed to offer an exceptionally detailed form of control. That makes me want to turn it upside down, and explore what it might be capable of at the other extreme.

I am to a significant degree a contrarian . . . or perhaps I am just obsessed with balance. I like to see if I can, in a sense, pervert the computer . . . to turn it against its natural characteristics . . . but productively, not nihilistically. But, truth be told, this is also about me, and the kind of balance I would like to engender in myself.

In my installations, I am trying to hold things in suspension, and sustain this state for as long as possible. The idea, which was born very early in the development of *Very Nervous System*, was to create a space in which to learn to be comfortable functioning in a space of continuously unfolding uncertainty. For me this is the maximally productive space.

We tend to zip through spaces and times of ambiguity and uncertainty as quickly as possible. To rest there is sometimes excruciating, but it is also a place of accelerated growth and learning. So I naturally gravitate towards a space where the boundaries are unclear, where strong and apparently opposing forces seem to bleed into each other. Human and technical, complexity and control . . . I prefer to see them as pairs of perpendicular dimensions rather than oppositions: X and Y rather than X and -X. As such, their tension is productive: X multiplied by Y.

Very Nervous System was designed to provide just enough verification of its interactivity to draw you into trusting that a relationship is there without fully understanding it, to hold you in the middle space, away from the clarity of these metaphorical X and Y axes. With *n-Cha(n)t* I pushed further towards emergent complexity, with much less affirming control . . . (Rokeby, "n-Cha(n)t") People got upset when the seven "entities" stopped paying attention to them and started focusing only on each other, which they would do when they were over-stimulated. In *Hand-held*, the balance has shifted back towards control (Rokeby, "Hand-Held"). *Hand-held* is essentially static, but invisible. In theory you can master the navigation of it in a way that you could never completely master *Very Nervous System*. But the strange play of presence and absence that are so much a part of that piece creates a different kind of "suspension" and ambiguity.

The best answer to your question is that there is no real trend to be found in my approach. I think of this space defined between control and emergence/autonomy as a palette. Each space within the continuum of the palette of interactive aesthetics has its place. Each expresses something different . . . allows one to comment on, unfold, unpack, reinforce, and destabilize different kinds of relationships. So it comes down to a question of broad literacy . . . know the entire domain of possibilities and use the most appropriate to the situation.

UE: This is an extraordinarily interesting laying bare of some of the deep motivations behind your work and the ways in which these manifest themselves in your installations. Your approach to the tension between complexification and reduction, emergence and control reminds me, among other things, of the crucial work by Gödel on undecidability and incompleteness. The space of uncertainty you refer to as maximally productive seems uncannily analogous to what generated modern computing in the first place. Both Alan Turing's work on the oracle-machine and Alonzo Church's work on the lambda calculus back in the first half of the 1930s could be seen as sorts of side-effects of staying engaged with such a space of undecidability. Interestingly, these engagements with the undecidable have generated some of the very strongest approaches to decision, control, and reduction that we currently live with.

DR: Yes, this field is ripe with paradox. One of my favorite metaphors is the Boltzmann machine, which you are no doubt aware of.[1] It directly addresses the importance of not falling onto local minima but prolonging, through a kind of tempering process, the resolution of the problem in order to give the best solution a chance to express itself. Sometimes I think this is the evolutionary advantage conferred by anger . . . We get "heated," a bit unpredictable, in the face of a roadblock, which sometimes shakes us or the system out of a rut. Anyway, the process of tempering results in a stronger, harder steel, which is also less fragile (some other hardening processes result in increased brittleness). The space of uncertainty leads to better results in the long run, but it does not mean in any way that the result is itself ambiguous or uncertain.

On the other hand, perhaps the paradox is a bit misleading. In the short-term implications Turing's work clearly leads to the computer and all the control that that implies. The longer term implications have not played out. One of our twenty-first century tasks is to understand what of us and our functioning can be understood in simple mechanical terms, and then to ponder what is left. It is very convenient and suitable for us to offload purely mechanical tasks to mechanical systems (I metaphorically include computers here) . . . This allows us to concentrate our energy on the things that we as humans excel at. One great fear is that at the end of this process, we might find that there is nothing "special" about us. My bigger fear is that we do a bad job in this process of off-loading . . . not bringing a sufficiently broad awareness to the task, and undervaluing things that we humans do, because they are invisible to us or the processes we use to assess them (which may tend to be "mechanical" in themselves and so specifically incapable of the task.)

Perhaps we need to consider the visible uses of the computer and its extensions as the most banal, obvious, and ultimately irrelevant use cases imaginable. These are the automatic and obvious uses, as we drive forward with our eyes fixated on the rearview mirror, as McLuhan would say. Perhaps the long-term (centuries long) implications are very different. It was this thought that gave me a bit of optimism in the late 1990s towards the end of the development of *The Giver of Names*. I saw how the precision and rigor, the absolute logic of the computer, allowed it to also function as a very particular kind of cognitive prosthesis . . . but only if we can avoid getting caught up in its purely logical agenda. We need to understand it as an extremely useful limit case, not as the complete story; to use it to help cast aspects of human-ness in relief, not in opposition, and not as something we can assume we can simulate, just because there are so many things that computers can simulate.

UE: It has struck me repeatedly during our conversation how consistent your remarks are with respect to directing focused awareness back unto the complexity of the human, not least as regards the many dimensions we do not recognize here.

This certainly has the virtue of wisdom—knowing at least some of the extent to which you do not know (yourself). It makes us aware of a human complexity we tend to forget we do not know.

However, this also brings along in the same movement certain kinds of reduction. Here human-oriented reduction also means a tendential reduction of technological autonomy and agency. This moreover entails that you tend to reduce away a more genuine coexistence and co-development of human and technological modes of individuation,[2] or transductions of these as Simondon would probably call it.[3]

This makes me hesitate, for is the interactivity around your installations then of the twenty-first century in which we find and increasingly live with ever so many autonomous and intelligent technical agents?

DR: It is certainly of the twentieth century (and the eighteenth and nineteenth with a bit of the twenty-first). Most of it was developed in the twentieth century. I spent almost forty years of my life there. I will praise balance here too. Broad frequency response . . . a balanced weighting of short-term, mid-term, and long-term considerations.

UE: One might say that this set of unique balances that you praise (and solicit) also raises the question of your position with respect to the tension between complexity and reduction in a more general vein.

It seems as if you have put aside the idea of advocating a positivistic reductionism. Your investment in a human-centered harmonics and tempering to balance makes me suspect that you also do not subscribe to a strong view of emergence and irreducible complexity, for example, complexity theory or chaos theory.

If this is not simply wrong, I am still left in doubt and wonder as to the more graded character of your position.

Would you suggest that emergence is either a misnomer or largely irrelevant, and that complexity can either be ignored or almost always be dealt with in terms of something complicated which is reducible, often in a few steps? Is it rather the case that you propose that we adopt a pragmatic and resolute reductionist stance even though emergence and complexity may be marginally impossible to avoid or reduce, in principle or in fact?

That would amount to saying that a complex system is made up of a large number of parts that have many interactions and is weakly emergent (given the properties of the parts and the laws of their interaction it is not a trivial matter to infer the properties of the whole.) Here complexity most often takes the form of hierarchy in a broadly formalized sense, that is, a system composed of interrelated subsystems each of which is in turn hierarchic in structure until we reach some lowest level of elementary subsystem.[4] Hence reduction almost always remains possible, but not always.

However, several of your remarks in this interview have also led me to think that you see this inversely, arguing that emergence and complexity always override part/whole and reductionist approaches but may be remedied or transcended, although not altogether. That is, synergetic emergences and internal collapses can be traced and analyzed but only belatedly and in deferred ways . . .

Could you elaborate on your position here?

DR: I once saw John Cage answering questions at my art school. One student asked a very long and involved question, and then Cage simply answered: "I feel very good about everything that you have said." You could say likewise that I feel good about everything that you say in this question.

I make a differentiation between a complexity that is generated by a surprisingly small set of rules on one hand, and complexity that is a function of pure randomness on the other (which is your irreducible complexity). In "Constructing Experience," I talk about my concern that we are building synthetic environments with too much of the rules- and algorithm-based complexity without understanding the importance of the massive complexity of complexly interrelated semi-autonomous systems (Rokeby, "The Construction of Experience"). In part, *n-Cha(n)t* is an exploration of automata with extremely complicated rule sets, and much of its beauty I ascribe to this tension. It is also interesting to think of emergence as sometimes an example of simplicity arising within a system of very complicated rules. What I dislike is homogeneity of approach. I like attacking a question from many angles, and reveling even in the fact that the various results are often deliciously contradictory. I think that people often think as though they are drawing in a drawing program with "snap-to-grid" enabled; that is to say, where established ideas have strong gravitational fields that waylay the trajectory of thought.

Reductionism is only a problem when it sees itself as an end. It is part of a process through which knowledge and understanding are developed. It seems that, as a species, we excel in capturing emergent behaviors and reducing them to rules and laws . . . (the whole process of the building up of society, the social contract, etc.). Once formalized, the once emergent behavior becomes stronger and fragile . . . both more and less stable. Competing emergent behaviors and competing rule systems fight it out. Some higher level emergent properties arise because of the lower level formalization.

In ancient Chinese philosophy, there is the distinction between "simple" and "easy." I only know this in translation so the nuances are perhaps lost on me, but I like to think that the simple is the reductive and the easy is the emergent. Perhaps in our context, simple refers to the simple rules that sometimes underlie complexity, and easy refers to the coherent higher-level behaviors that sometimes arise in a sea of complexity . . . (of course there is also the fact that we will come up with simplifying labels for complexities beyond our grasp . . . lossy versus lossless compression . . . but here I refer to the true emergence of a kind of structural coherence internal to the system, rather than a forced, reductive coherence in our minds).

My positions themselves are not stable; they are emergent and contextually dependent. They solidify when I am asked a question. Once thus formalized, they rattle around in my brain and persist or not. McLuhan was like this, much to the detriment of his academic standing. My job is to keep questions open against the natural gravity of reduction and formalization, not because I value the openness over the formalization, but because I feel that the general approach that our culture takes is out of balance and I need to lean against it a bit to do my part to correct it.

UE: If ubicomp cultures already in this early stage of their development include multitudes of computational entities that move, connect and disconnect on the fly, and form or deform technical infrastructures of a quasi-organic sort, this is different from but not that far from living agency. If this moreover includes multitudes of intelligent and autonomous agents in the application or software layer, this hints at the introduction of considerable technical autonomy and agency—different from but not necessarily that far from intelligent human autonomy.

Once one accepts this kind of context for interactivity one not only wishes to trace the relational unfolding of technical autonomy (automata in your vocabulary) with and against humans, and the relational unfolding of human autonomy with and against technics. One also wants to trace the relational unfolding of their co-individuation with and against a wider context or environment . . .

So, what happens to the oscillation between freedom and control in interactivity in general once you have both human and technical agents of complication and emergence?

How would this kind of scenery affect your work on concrete installations and their interaction designs?

DR: Well, it seems to me that you have two layers of relationship. One is the relationship between the individual human or artificial participant and the coherent structural limits that the environment itself defines. Another includes the social or quasi-social relations between like or different entities. Generally, coherent freedom/control oscillations in these social scenarios start in a fairly raw state where there is insufficient control against which to measure freedom. As multiple entities accumulated shared engagement time, a set of habits of engagement may evolve. These may formalize into agreed upon rules. As they evolve, they increase the efficiency of communication and coordination of activities, but they also begin to impinge tangibly on the freedom of individual entities. A healthy relationship involves a continuous renegotiation of terms of engagement . . . and this, at its best is perhaps another example of productive uncertainty. Control/structure must not be there for its own sake. A guitar string does not resonate until it is tight enough, but the aim of tightening the string is not tightness, but a balance between flex and tautness that allows (on one hand) and sustains (on the other) the oscillation.

In *Very Nervous System*, I was tuning the control/freedom ratio. I could have added some machine learning algorithms to allow the system to tune itself. My initial reason for not doing that was that I found so much of interest in the way a person's relationship to the system changed over time, that I did not want to muddy the exploration by having the installation change its behavior over time. If I were to allow it to participate in the tuning of the system, I would need to formulate a set of desirable attributes, or at least a mechanism by which the system (including the person) could hone a set of desirable attributes to provide a target to measure current behavior against. Simple targets like working to prolong the length of the period interaction are problematic. This is what a cat does when playing with a mouse . . . keep it just alive enough to stay fun. I also think of lab rats repeatedly pressing pleasure buttons and ignoring everything else until they die of starvation.

How do we establish, or evolve together with our intelligent environment, a set of worthy consensual goals that provide the basis for balance, trust, and long term survival? We cannot just trust emergence.

In terms of my approach to creating my installations in the midst of this sort of situation: it does not change. Optimal interaction requires simultaneous action, observation, and reflection—engagement on all levels. That is how I feel my way through the creative process, and that is what I hope the works themselves promote. This is how I hope some of us, in a position to nudge the direction of development, will proceed as we collectively develop, experience, and critique the evolving environment.

Notes

1. A Boltzmann machine is a type of stochastic recurrent neural network invented by Geoffrey Hinton and Terry Sejnowski in 1985. Boltzmann machines can be seen as the stochastic, generative counterpart of Hopfield nets. They were one of the first examples of a neural network capable of learning internal representations, and are able to represent and (given sufficient time) solve difficult combinatoric problems.

2. Gilles Deleuze provides an interesting quotation making clear how to approach Gilbert Simondon's notion of individuation: "Gilbert Simondon has shown recently that individuation presupposes a prior metastable state—in other words, the existence of a 'disparateness' such as at least two orders of magnitude or two scales of heterogeneous reality between which potentials are distributed. Such a

pre-individual state nevertheless does not lack singularities: The distinctive or singular points are defined by the existence and distribution of potentials. An 'objective' problematic field thus appears, determined by the distance between two heterogeneous orders. Individuation emerges like the act of solving such a problem, or—what amounts to the same thing—like the actualization of a potential and establishing of communication between disparates" (Deleuze 1993, 246).

3. The reference here is to "transduction" as thought by Simondon. Many readers of Simondon tend to agree on working with this notion in a short-hand version, defining it as a primary relationality constitutive of the two terms that it relates. Muriel Combes calls transduction the "mode of unity of being through its diverse phases, its multiple individuations" (Combes 1999, 15). Adrian Mackenzie explains: "For the process of transduction to occur, there must by some disparity, discontinuity, or mismatch within a domain; two different forms or potentials whose disparity can be modulated. Transduction is a process whereby a disparity or a difference is topologically and temporally restructured across some interface. It mediates different organizations of energy" (Mackenzie 2002, 25). A more detailed treatment of transduction as individuation in process by Simondon himself also exists in Simondon, Gilbert. *L'individu et sa genèse physico-biologique*, 18-22, and "The Genesis of the Individual," 315.

4. This is the kind of influential position taken by Herbert Simon in *The Sciences of the Artificial*.

References

Combes, Muriel. 1999. *Simondon individu et collectivité: pour une philosophie du transindividuel.* Paris: Presses Universitaires de France.

Deleuze, Gilles. 1993. *Difference and Repetition.* New York: Columbia University Press.

Gardner, Martin. 1970. "Mathematical Games: The Fantastic Combinations of John Conway's New Solitaire Game 'Life.'" *Scientific American* 223: 120–23.

Lucier, Alvin. "UbuWeb Sound—Alvin Lucier." http://ubu.com/sound/lucier.html

Mackenzie, Adrian. 2002. *Transductions: Bodies and Machines at Speed.* London: Continuum.

Rokeby, David. "The Construction of Experience." http://davidrokeby.com/experience.html.

Rokeby, David. "The Giver of Names." http://davidrokeby.com/gon.html.

Rokeby, David. "Hand-Held." http://davidrokeby.com/handheld.html.

Rokeby, David. "The Harmonics of Interaction." http://davidrokeby.com/harm.html.

Rokeby, David. "n-Cha(n)t." http://davidrokeby.com/nchant.html.

Rokeby, David. "Transforming Mirrors." http://davidrokeby.com/mirrors.html.

Rokeby, David. 1995. "Transforming Mirrors: Subjectivity and Control in Interactive Media." In *Critical Issues in Electronic Media*, edited by Simon Penny, 133–58. Albany, NY: State University of New York Press.

Rokeby, David. "Very Nervous System." http://davidrokeby.com/vns.html.

Simon, Herbert A. 1996. *The Sciences of the Artificial.* 3rd ed. Cambridge, MA: MIT Press.

Simondon, Gilbert. 1964. *L'individu et sa genèse physico-biologique.* Paris: Presses universitaires de France.

Simondon, Gilbert. 1992. "The Genesis of the Individual." In *Incorporations*, edited by Jonathan Crary and Sanford Kwinter, 296–319. New York: Zone.

White, Norman. 1987. "The Helpless Robot." http://year01.com/archive/helpless/statement.html

INTERFACE, BODIES, AND PROCESS—INTERVIEW WITH TERI RUEB

Jay David Bolter

Jay David Bolter (JDB): Our central theme is ubiquity and complexity in digital media culture. So you can see why we were so interested in having you participate in the project. I am particularly interested in your work because of your long experience with sound and sound-based installations.[1] Sound has been a neglected feature in mainstream work on augmented reality (AR) by computer scientists. But as AR and mixed reality (MR) are beginning to be applied on a large scale, which is now possible because of smart phones, sound is becoming an increasingly important feature. Your work is central for that reason, among many others. In discussing your work, we could begin with *Trace*, which I understand was your first GPS-based sound walk?

Teri Rueb (TR): Yes.

JDB: Why sound? Where did the interest come from for you in technologically mediated sound?

TR: There were several points of inspiration specifically for that work. The first of which was a reflection or meditation on loss. Originally trained as a sculptor, I was interested in an alternative mode of fashioning a kind of placeholder for loss, other than a tangible form such as a headstone. *Trace* was meant to be a kind of oral cemetery. I was also interested in working beyond the Western bias toward the visual—to think of sound as having the capacity to rejuvenate, to enliven, to enable a fully corporeal experience that was life-affirming. Instead of the contemplation of a visual or even physical form, as a reference to that which is absent, I wanted people to have a physical sensation that brought them to a sense of their own vitality. And that for me held a kind of therapeutic potential. I was also very interested in the long history of orality and peripatetic modes of rehearsing memory. I was looking at that time at song lines and seeing them as memorial forms, as recitations that are thought to revivify or conjure the dead. And I was also interested in the way in which oral forms of communication from song lines to peripatetic and rhapsodic forms bring listeners to an anchored sense of the here and now, because you have an obligation or imperative to deliver your words in a manner that is sensitive to the particular context and occasion of their delivery. That implies an intimate linking of audience and place. This linking is obviously still active in literate modes of communication, but in a different way, in which the body isn't often as actively engaged. And then very pragmatically because it was a mobile piece and I wanted that kinesthetic engagement through walking and feeling the contours of the land through the body, it didn't make sense to draw the eye to the screen, which would disconnect you from the flow, the kinesthetic or proprioceptive engagement with a place and a moment (Plate 20).

JDB: You were trained as a sculptor, but did you ever engage in any performance art or other forms that might have led you to the orality of these soundscapes?

TR: It is something that has been present since that first piece, and yet I have never explicitly written about my work as performative. I have been inspired by performance studies and particular performers, such as the Judson Dance Theatre or Yvonne Rainer's everyday movement. But before *Trace*, I had really never done anything that was performative in the sense of engaging my own body. I had, however, started making public art installations that involved an interactive component. They unfolded over time; they were event-based; they were ephemeral; and they engaged everyday audiences. I was conscious of a concern to engage audiences in non-traditional art spaces and also trying to bring people into a kind of physical interaction with the work. I was interested in interactivity of a kind that was linked to the past. It was not an interactivity that suddenly becomes possible simply because we have computer screens and mobile devices.

JDB: I'd like to move on to other pieces and use them as occasions to elaborate on themes you have raised in our discussion of *Trace*. You won the Ars Electronica prize in 2008 for *Core Sample*. What would you say are the similarities and differences between this work and the much earlier *Trace*?

TR: In *Core Sample* one of the most important differences is that I am composing the sound regions in a way that is tightly coupled to the contours of the landscape itself. (Plate 21). With *Trace* there were about twenty-four different sound regions, and they were quite far apart from each other, distributed along a network of hiking trails. So while there was certainly a concern for the arc of the trail as a structuring element, I wasn't thinking of the shape of those sound regions as being connected to the topography. With *Core Sample* I was. The first inspiration in looking at that site was this: It was an island that had been used in various ways in history from native American hunting and fishing, through colonial settlement grazing, and then more recently in the twentieth century to being used as a dump for the city of Boston. And the layering of the topography of the island itself reflected those moments in history. If you were to drill a core sample down through that island, those materials are present as an archaeological stratigraphy that speaks to that history. In order to bring people's consciousness to the intermix of the physical, social, and informational space of the island, I wanted to evoke a core sample. And the way I did that was to work with the various elevations that you would pass through as you went along the trail system that traverses the entire island. The island is structured with these two drumlins, two hill forms connected by what was originally a tiny isthmus, but through the piling up of trash over the years this has become a sixty-foot deep layer . . .

JDB: . . . In fact from classical archaeology we know that that is also the way that ancient cities evolved as the inhabitants built upon the garbage or rubble of previous occupations of the site. For example, the city of Troy had approximately nine layers. So in this sense Boston is reflecting a venerable archaeological tradition.

TR: In the process of researching this piece, I came into contact with the office of the city of Boston that identifies sites of archaeological significance as part of the process of approving new construction. It was remarkable to discover how many layers Boston itself has that have been marked and studied. The city of Boston as a whole is a remarkably engineered artifact of filling processes that took place over centuries. And indeed the piece

I did in Santa Fe took the question of archeology head on. I collaborated with a Navajo archaeologist and a ceramicist for that project, and the ceramicist's inspiration was to view the past as marked by the refuse of a culture, so he made thousands of slip cast crushed cans for the piece that we scattered across the landscape. It is fascinating on many levels to think both concretely and metaphorically about the material presence of a culture . . . Returning to *Core Sample*, as you move across those altitudes on the island, you hear sounds that correspond to that layer. Because these layers do not always constitute perfect vertical strata, there were nuances to the sound correspondences. It was in part creative interpretation, but it was also the result of research that I did in order to establish the position of the sound regions in dialogue with the topography. And that was new for me. The other shift in my thinking that is reflected in this work was the way in which the use of sound to express the topography beneath your feet could bring you into dialogue on different levels with a place. There is the explicit historical information that you glean from the sound overlay. There is also a pattern of rhythms and textures that hopefully bring you into a corporeal encounter with that place—as if you become part of the island itself. I didn't want to make a piece that makes people self-conscious about the environmental destruction at the site, which is admittedly a big part of the story that you are exposed to when you go to the island, which is presented as a success story of environmental reclamation. I think often those narratives have a didactic or moral dimension that I did not want to reinscribe. I wanted instead to bring people into an empathic encounter that places them in the system as players in an unfolding story. It is not that we are culprits, necessarily. At the other extreme, I don't think we are external to it, as the image of the steward places us in a potentially alienated relationship to the site. *Core Sample* was an exploration of the way in which a different kind of subjectivity could be teased out in formal relationship of sound to space.

JDB: If we think about the twin themes of ubiquity and complexity, I can see the immediate relevance of *Core Sample* for the theme of ubiquity in the sense that the visitor experiences these sound spaces everywhere, all around the island. But what about complexity? The work is composed of a complex layering of sounds that you as the artist have thought about very carefully. And the experience as a whole seems to be controlled, not chaotic or complex in that sense.

TR: The piece may strike you as controlled, but there are an incredible number of variables when you are working with GPS and site specificity. The scale and accuracy of GPS, at that time with those devices, was about three meters, which is very soft. The accuracy is also subject to environmental conditions, which causes variations on a day-to-day basis in some instances. There is also the variability of the weather and even the social conditions of the site and behavior of visitors. These can affect the path that you take through the soundscape. Finally there is the interplay between the recorded sound and the ambient sound. Serendipitous correspondences occur that often enhance the individual experience, for example, the recorded sound of thunderstorm on the exact spot you are standing may puzzle or alarm visitors who come on a cloudless day. For all these reasons, *Core Sample* is not so tightly controlled soundscape as it might seem.

JDB: I had forgotten about the importance of the ambient sound, for example, which clearly allows for the interaction between your planned sounds and the world in a way that you as the creator cannot entirely anticipate.

TR: Yes, and I make the sounds explicitly permeable to play against the ambient sounds. Many times visitors describe a doubt as to whether the sound is coming from inside or outside the headphones. They will take the headphones off for a second and realize that . . . no, the sound of a passing airplane is coming from the headphones and not from the sky. The sound is also spatialized so that it is swimming around you. And a lot of the composed sound includes ambient sound: there is a base layer of environmental sounds recorded on site that I set the composed sounds into. As field recordings from the place itself, these ambient sounds connect the soundscape to the place. That composition was also explicitly "thin." In fact, one visitor came back after the experience and said "we didn't hear anything." I thought maybe their device wasn't working. I checked it and in fact it was. That visitor was expecting a park service guide telling them "you're now standing at . . ."— in other words something quite explicit rather than the composed sounds that I had woven into the ambient sonic space, so that at certain moments you might indeed mistake what you are hearing for the given condition of the site.

JDB: I'm going to take this opportunity to ask about your relationship to the building of the technology of your various works. Do you work closely with a programmer?

TR: In the early days, with *Trace*, I was programming myself, and I had developed that prototype offsite initially in New York City. When I was there at the site itself, I had a research assistant who was doing a lot of the programming—scaling it up and making it robust for general audiences. Over the years, I was able to secure more funding so that I could work with teams, computer scientists for example. I worked with Zary Segall and a team of his students in making *Drift* in 2004. Around that time the University of Western England in Bristol was developing software originally called Mobile Bristol. This system was further developed by HP as a freeware called Mscape. It was robust and had a drag-and-drop WYSIWYG interface. For *Core Sample*, I was using that software. I could say that I did all the technical work on my own, but that is not entirely accurate because I was using that software which facilitated the work. Later HP disbanded their pervasive computing arm, which had developed MScape. The software has become AppFurnace, which is now fully commercial (Mscape was freeware). Now I'm making mobile apps, which are accessible to larger audiences. Even when I made *Trace*, I was saying that this sort of experience will be on your mobile phone shortly. The process took longer than I had anticipated, but now the tools are familiar and ubiquitous. Nevertheless, with the shift to mobile phones, it was like starting from scratch to get the full functionality working again on an iPhone, for example. I work with programmers now for the most part.

JDB: Let me ask you two questions that you have probably been asked often before. First, it seems inevitable to ask you about the relationship of your work to the Situationist *dérive*. Were the Situationists an influence for you?

TR: I'm certainly aware of and indebted to that history. And I feel in some ways aligned to the project of critiquing the spaces of the city as a top-down design with its formal and institutional imperatives, along with the social and political forces that shape and determine the urban fabric. For me, Lefebvre was also an early influence in thinking about space as a social product. I feel sympathetic to those political aims. And yet those aims are not a primary concern in my work. I think of my political interest in reframing the relationship of the body to spaces and the production of spaces as an expanded domain that enfolds sensation and affect. At this point I feel more aligned to an ethical aesthetic as articulated by Guattari. I think that his aesthetic accommodates a more complex and layered view of subjectivity and recognizes what I think is profound in these media: that they reorganize or reshape our consciousness at the corporeal level and at the discursive level—the full spectrum of what is implied in a post-human framework. The reorganization includes the psychoanalytic and the aesthetic, particularly in the sense of an aesthetic that always has a rhetorical imperative embedded in it. Our bodies and sensations are a reflection of and a domain of agency in the production of different subjectivities and spaces.

JDB: Your mention of agency leads me to ask: what is the relationship of technology to agency in your work? You suggest that you are interested in exploring the ways in which this technology reshapes our consciousness. How does that process work? Is it one in which the technology has agency?

TR: Not in the sense of a technological determinism. Rather, I locate that agency as a set of forces that might extend into the nonhuman and back again. It is not an agency that the technology itself holds. There is a kind of feedback loop.

JDB: Let me ask about one other possible influence. That would be the work of Janet Cardiff. Do you know her work and see her as an influence?

TR: I think she is doing something very different. I was first made aware of her work at the Banff Center when I was developing *Trace*. I don't explicitly remember the point at which I was alerted to her work. But I do remember being very excited at the thought of a genre in which narrative can be woven into an ambulatory experience. And on that level I see a relationship between my work and hers. But then our work parts company fairly quickly because I think that she is explicitly interested in narrative. While I have narrative elements in my work and some works that are explicitly exploring narrative, as is the case with *Itinerant*, ultimately narrative is not the driving force for me. I am concerned with the social and spatial conditions and the materialities that can be activated through these works that couple movement with a response from the system as much as the environment itself. That is a reflection of a different set of aesthetic concerns from those of Janet Cardiff.

JDB: We could talk about a whole set of your works, some of which you have already alluded to, such as *Itinerant* and *Drift*. Perhaps we should turn to *Grimpant*: The phenomenology of the experience of *Grimpant* seems very different from that of *Core Sample* or *Trace*. In this case the visitors are all together in a space.

TR: *Grimpant* is different in so many ways. I was collaborating with Alan Price. For this piece the original commission came to me from la Panacée in Montpellier, and I went there with the intention of making a sound walk, as an individual production, as I had many times in the past. My inspiration led me to a proposal that demanded the collaboration of someone with Alan's expertise, which is real-time responsive animation. *Grimpant* was seeking to explicitly interrogate the map or to put forward a kind of critical mapping agenda (Plates 20 and 21). I had also been influenced by one of my mentors at Harvard, who advised my doctoral work, Antoine Picon. He had written a fantastic treatise on the French architects and engineers in the Age of the Enlightenment, in which he made a claim about mapping strategies and modes of cartographic representation that were shifting at the early moment of the Enlightenment (Picon 1992). That was the critical context in which I was inspired. The experience of the work itself then became very visual. There is a sonic component as well. There are two elements: there is a projection in the gallery space, which is a dynamic map made up of layers of cartographic representation. These highlight historic and contemporary waterways and infrastructures of the city as well as human movement through the city and botanical growth. The human movement component has a connection to the present day in the form of a mobile app that people can use to move through the city and discover sounds that have been recorded *in situ* in response to various botanical forms in the city or sites of botanical significance that people identify. So they can go through the city and discover those geo-located recordings on site; they can also record their own reflections on site and upload them, or they can go to the gallery and see the entire collection of recordings represented as seeds on the map. Those seeds when activated will play back the sounds recorded out in the city. So there are two primary different mappings: One is a first-person subjective auditory engagement with the city, which is kinesthetic, and then the more conventional visual representation, which is dynamic and reflects the movement of people in the city currently and as an aggregation over time. So there is a friction between the first-person and third-person effect that mapping operations so often activate. *Grimpant* is thus a very different experience.

JDB: We haven't talked at all about *Elsewhere/Anderswo*. The piece dates from 2009, which makes it fairly recent. What is its place in your thinking about these issues?

TR: That piece makes me smile, because it was a little bit tongue-in-cheek. It was opposite in intention from *Core Sample*, where I was seeking to bring people into contact with the here and now. With *Elsewhere*, I found myself in Germany in a very unfamiliar environment: The city of Oldenburg and a small agricultural town, Neuenkirchen, near the Heath, the Heide. I had done projects in Germany before, but these places were unfamiliar, and I couldn't take the same approach as I had in done in *Core Sample*, which had an experimental documentary or oral history dimension to it. Unfortunately I don't speak German well enough to do an in-depth piece like *Core Sample*, interviewing people and doing oral history. So instead I was responding to hints or moments in the landscape, in the sites that were eventually identified, that seemed very familiar to me, like places I had grown up in the United States, but were at the same time not the same at all. That's a common feeling when we travel to places as outsiders or tourists: The desire to find your bearings by mapping to something familiar, anchoring to what you already have as a mental image of a place, or how you navigate and orient yourself socially, culturally, and physically. I was playing with that feeling, and I wanted to create patchwork or pastiche environments with very familiar and very iconic sonic references to place, which are layered in these environments—the botanical garden on the one hand, which is itself a pastiche, and then this little town, Neuenkirchen, which is on the surface an agricultural village, but is also a tourist zone that has been manicured and restored in order to give the impression of being an historic agricultural village. I was playing with that place—placing and displacing. The experiment was to make you a participant in an explicitly synthetic sound play. There is a strangeness too, because on the one hand you are in a botanical garden where you are passing from Alpine zone to desert zone in five footsteps. And then in the agricultural village the piece was structured along a bike path that circled the town and took you to various sites of large-scale outdoor sculptures, which dotted the landscape. Even on a farm or in the middle of a cornfield, you would see these enormous, Richard-Serra like sculptures.

JDB: You didn't see any buried Cadillacs?

TR: No, but there is an hilarious point as part of the outdoor collection that's called the Cemetery for Unwanted Sculptures, and it truly holds sculptures abandoned by artists, or shipped there to be abandoned. They are kind of half buried in the landscape. But *Elsewhere* was a lot of fun. Thankfully the Germans were generous enough to allow the lens of an American perspective on German pop culture, letting me freely play without taking offense. I hope. That was my sense of their response. But it was a bit risky, I think.

JDB: Another piece sited in Germany is *Drift*, which is a walk on the Wattensee. In your description you make explicit reference to ubiquity, suggesting (this is in 2004) that because of the ubiquity of GPS getting lost is itself an experience that is being lost. Do you feel that now ten years later this is even more the case? Do you have the sense that the ubiquity of media tracking and accompanying us has intensified? What does it mean to be lost in the digital age?

TR: A couple of ways to respond to that. On the one hand, yes, I've found myself succumbing to ubiquity. Not that I've been consciously resisting, but I never used GPS to navigate until about two years ago when I got my first iPhone. I liked to stumble along and follow my nose and feel a place through intuition or read a map. I do like to read physical maps. I like making that translation that you do yourself, reconciling the world with its representation. So there is that pragmatic response. Then there is also an effect that comes from relying more on the technology, on the GPS, and I do, I'm constantly referring to it now. I travel a lot and drive a lot—I love to drive and use my GPS on the iPhone—and I feel that maybe in some ways we are more lost, as the link that happens when you have to internalize the paper map that doesn't tell you where you are with a little electronic dot is lost. I don't think that it's just a matter of losing certain skills; I think we are losing a certain kind of consciousness and connection to place. But then maybe more importantly what does it mean to be lost in the digital age? I was in Africa last year in the bush with a friend who guides safaris. He is using GPS all the time, because for many of the places you go there is no road and you are driving for hours and hours going from one GPS coordinate to the next—ad hoc, making pathways through otherwise unmarked territory. At the same time where we were, there was no cellular reception; no phone call is going to go in or out to save you if you should get completely disoriented. So there was this extended time that I was without that kind of link. I was certainly in an unfamiliar place, so that it was not that I could claim that I felt more oriented for not using the technology. I had no idea where we were. I did know that I was connected to time in a way that was fundamentally different. The unfolding of time and your movement through the landscape . . . there was a much more fluid exchange of cues and connections even to the sunrise and the sunset and the stars that was only possible because of the setting aside of already preprocessed geospatial information that tells you where a Starbucks is in a city. I have to think more about that, but I really felt a new and profound sense of remoteness because of the radical absence of network connectivity in that place. Like no other remote place I've ever been.

JDB: As a final question, looking to the future, to what extent is your work influenced by the directions you see in the technology that you are using? One could fall back on a modernist notion of art and say that you been exploring the medium of location-based sound. But even without going that far, you clearly have a relationship to these technologies in which over the course of fifteen years now you understand their characteristics in profound ways. Do you see that process developing further? To put it another way, are you getting tired of creating location-based sound experiences or do you see more possibilities to develop there?

TR: I think of my practice more as trying to understand place, which is a complex thing—a spatial, social, physical, affective, discursive blend of forces that is always beyond full grasp. That's endlessly fascinating to me. But the travels that I have been doing recently—I was most recently in South Africa in an urban context— I feel the need to operate through a completely different mode to the problems and questions that are raised by trying to understand who we are in a moment of complex globalization processes. And so I am not sure what form that takes. I don't know whether it has explicitly to do with using technology to execute or instrumentalize an idea. But it certainly has to do with ways in which technologies have rewritten the scale and temporality of our everyday lives and subjectivities. I see myself in the future working collaboratively with larger groups, practitioners from vastly different fields. That's an intuition right now. It is a bit inchoate. I have commissions onboard now that are similar to works I have done in the past, and which are equally exciting to me even if they emerged prior to these recent travels that were profoundly altering.

Note

1   For all the media works of Teri Rueb discussed in this interview (including *Elsewhere, Core Sample, Grimpant, itinerant, Drift,* and *Trace*), see her website: http://terirueb.net/i_index.html.

References

Picon, Antoine. 1992. *French Architects and Engineers in the Age of Enlightenment.* Translated by Martin Thom. New York: Cambridge University Press.

INTERACTION DESIGN

Jay David Bolter

Interaction design can be understood as the combination of the perspectives and practices of the graphic and industrial design communities and the community of HCI (Human Computer Interaction). As such, the concept of interaction has never evolved far from the paradigm of an individual human subject in immediate procedural contact with a digital system. The media theorists and artists in this section take it as their task either to problematize that paradigm or to enlarge it (often through art) to include other forms of experience and other definitions of the subject.

Graphic and industrial design emerged as distinct practices at the beginning of the twentieth century, with the rise of the consumerism in economically advanced countries of Europe and North America. HCI is of course much younger, becoming a recognized discipline in computer science gradually in the 1970s and 1980s. It was only in the 1980s and 1990s that the perspectives of design and HCI could merge with the arrival of the desktop or personal computer (PC)—the PC and Apple Macintosh. These machines sold in the millions, at first largely to business users and creative professionals but then increasingly to consumers for home use. For the first time, computers became ubiquitous. The personal computer was also realizing Alan Kay's vision in becoming a medium of expression and communication, with the graphical user interface (Kay and Goldberg 1977). Earlier generations of users consisted of relatively small classes of programmers, engineers, or data entry employees, who were able and willing to work with minimal or demanding interfaces. The new groups of users needed well-designed interfaces for the everyday tasks of writing reports, sending emails, and eventually making and receiving graphics, video, and audio. The exponential success of the World Wide Web in the 1990s meant that businesses were now interested in advertising and selling over the Internet. In order to create compelling website, they turned to graphic designers, who had been composing print advertising since the beginning of the century.

At the same time, HCI was maturing as the academic study of the use of computer interfaces. Its roots lay in perceptual and industrial psychology and ergonomics, rather than the aesthetics of graphic and industrial design. The paradigm for HCI was individual- and task-oriented: The individual user engaged with a computer system to get work done. As HCI developed in the 1980s and 1990s, it came to understand this paradigm from the perspective of cognitive science. The user developed a *mental model* of how a computer system worked: that is, the configuration of its components and possible actions. The goal of good interface design was to bring the mental model into agreement with the actual function of the system. The test of this alignment between the user's mental model and the system was usability: A measure of how easily the user could perform the set of tasks of information retrieval and manipulation for which the system was originally designed. The HCI paradigm assumed that the best interface would be as simple and transparent as possible. Ideally the interface should disappear from the user's conscious interactions with the system. The user should focus entirely on the task (writing a document or email, working with a spreadsheet); she should not even be aware of the particular keyboard commands or mouse movements through which she shaped the text or made the calculations. Complexity was the enemy that could be conquered through good design, reduced to a series of simple, transparent views and interactions. HCI and in this respect the computer science community as a whole often extended the goal of transparency to the whole system. Influential computer scientists and HCI experts such as Don Norman (1998) and Mark Weiser (1991) have at various times suggested that the computer itself should disappear behind or into the design of our technological environment. Weiser himself was the original champion of ubiquitous computing, envisioning what is now called the Internet of Things as early as the late 1980s. In his version of ubiquity, computing devices are embedded all around the individual user, including refrigerators, thermostats, and other household appliances. They communicate with each other as well as the user seamlessly and often invisibly. The disappearing computer is a means of finessing the complexity of the ubiquity of the machines around us.

The modernist traditions of graphic and industrial design shared HCI's preferences for simplicity and, at least to some extent, transparency. For much of the twentieth century, the notions that form should follow function and that less is more were not mere clichés, but guiding principle in graphics, architecture, and product design. These principles were formative for the Apple Macintosh as well as its graphical interface. The design guidelines for applications for the Macintosh stressed the importance of transparency, predictability, and simplicity, requiring all third-party designers to use icons, menus, and windows in the same way. Steve Jobs himself acknowledged the influence of modernist product design (such as the work of Dieter Rams at Braun). Where HCI and the design traditions parted company was on the aesthetics of user interface design. Designers did not see a conflict between the beauty of a design and its utility, whereas HCI specialists often did.

In the 1990s, then, both HCI and the design disciplines assumed the interacting with a computer system should follow functionalist and modernist principles. Interaction design was a dialogue between an individual user and the computer system, and the goal was to reduce or hide complexity. In this model, however, the user was an idealized, autonomous figure— an individual who was herself not particularly complex. This model seemed plausible enough in the first decade of the Internet with the computer and communications software and hardware available at the time. This was the era of Web 1.0, in which users interacted predominantly with content and designs that were provided by (often) expert web designers. The tools that users had for making their own sites and media content were relatively hard to master. The conditions famously changed in the 2000s with the rise of sites and programs that facilitated user participation or indeed consisted almost entirely of user contributed content: Social networking sites, blogs, video sharing sites, and the rest. Despite the templates provided, Facebook or Wordpress blogs cannot possibly maintain the simplicity or (modernist) aesthetic quality of professionally authored sites. With the wealth of new forms and the explosion of contributors, ubiquity was at last achieved, at least in the industrially advanced nations. The number of people with Internet access is now in the billions, and the number of Facebook,

YouTube, or Instagram participants is not far beyond. In our current media culture, complexity can no longer be hidden. Interaction design must now take account of complexity not as a nuisance, but as integral to the process of interacting with networked systems.

Of equal significance is the development of new platforms for interaction: the smart phone, the tablet, and the smart watch. These new platforms permit forms of interaction that engage the user's body more directly than before as well as new forms of interaction among human users. Both traditional strands of interaction design (HCI and graphic and industrial design) have responded to these changed conditions by broadening their definitions of interaction. In *Where the Action Is* (2001), Paul Dourish offered social computing and embodied interaction as the two defining paradigms for HCI today. In her chapter in this section, Irene Mavrommati goes further in suggesting a number of theoretical foundations (including activity theory, distributed cognition, situated cognition, and actor-network theory) that could serve to broaden the field's concept of the "end-user."

The design community too has proposed various extensions and redefinitions under the rubric of "experience design": The emphasis is no longer on the user's mechanical interaction with the computer system, but rather on the experience that the system stages for the user. The aesthetics of the system is now understood by design theorists such as McCarthy and Wright in *Technology and Experience* (2004) as the whole range of the user's perceptual engagement with the digital as part of her lived world. The designer can no longer assume the relatively predictable and sensorily limited environment of the user's desk in which to stage the interaction, but must instead design for the complexity of the daily world. The complexity extends not only to the user's perceived environment, but even to the notion of the user as an individual, autonomous subject in the design. Social media suggests the value of designing for interactions among and between groups of users, and these interactions have the irreducible complexity of human culture. For the contributors to this section, however, even this broadening of the definition of the subject and of permissible experience may not suffice. For Mark Hansen, interaction design remains a manifestation of "topological culture," which Hansen believes needs the corrective of a new form of phenomenology, going beyond what Dourish suggested.

Meanwhile, media and digital art is exploring alternatives to the prevailing operational definition of the individual. For over a decade, Teri Rueb, interviewed in this section, has been creating sonic media works, such as *Trace* and *Core Sample*, that provide their participants with more nuanced relationships to history and place. Jonathan Dovey argues that the work of Rueb along with that of Janet Cardiff, Blast Theory, and Duncan Speakman call forth a new kind of "situated literary experience." Such art suggests strategies by which our media culture may ultimately subvert or circumvent the paradigm of interaction design altogether.

References

Dourish, P. 2001. *Where the Action Is: The Foundations of Embedded Interaction*. Cambridge, MA: MIT Press.

Kay, A., and A. Goldberg. 1977. "Personal Dynamic Media." *Computer* 10 (3): 31–41.

McCarthy, J., and P. Wright. 2004. *Technology as Experience*. Cambridge, MA: MIT Press.

Norman, D. A. 1998. *The Invisible Computer: Why Good Products Can Fail, The Personal Computer Is So Complex, and Information Appliances Are the Solution*. Cambridge, MA: MIT Press.

Weiser, M. 1991. "The Computer for the Twenty-first Century." *Scientific American* 265: 94–104.

THE ELEPHANTS IN THE (SERVER) ROOM: SUSTAINABILITY AND SURVEILLANCE IN THE ERA OF BIG DATA

Simon Penny

All Watched Over by Machines of Loving Grace

I like to think (and
the sooner the better!)
of a cybernetic meadow
where mammals and computers
live together in mutually
programming harmony
like pure water
touching clear sky.

I like to think
(right now, please!)
of a cybernetic forest
filled with pines and electronics
where deer stroll peacefully
past computers
as if they were flowers
with spinning blossoms.

I like to think
(it has to be!)
of a cybernetic ecology
where we are free of our labors
and joined back to nature,
returned to our mammal
brothers and sisters,
and all watched over
by machines of loving grace.

(Richard Brautigan, San Francisco, 1967)

Introduction

Brautigan's (1969) poem might be the root document of the San Francisco hippy techno-utopian movement, which spawned the Whole Earth Catalog and Apple Computer, which Theodor Rosak described in his essay From Satori to Silicon Valley (Roszak), and which was later dubbed "California Ideology" by Richard Barbrook and Andy Cameron. But what Brautigan et al. probably could not conceive of was the wholesale reconfiguration of society and economy which would necessarily attend the infiltration of computing into diverse aspects of life. Typical of that context—the era of the "giant brains"—is his portrayal of computers as coexisting but separate.

There are, as I have noted previously (Penny 2004) and as others have concurred (Ekman this volume), various conceptions of "ubicomp" (ubiquitous computing) which seem different enough to make the umbrella term of dubious usefulness. These include what we call Social Media, the Internet of Things, and Mobile Computing. Discourse around ubiquity (in the HCI community) has (understandably) tended to focus on immediate human experience with devices. The faceless aspect of ubiquity, the world of embedded microcontrollers, sometimes referred to as "the Internet of things" has largely evaded scrutiny in popular media and press, precisely because of its invisibility (though it has attracted the attention critical media-art interventionists for over two decades).[1]

The seemingly inexorable trend to ubiquity, we were told, would result in a calm technology that recedes from awareness, and abides in the background, seamlessly lubricating our interactions with the troublesome physical world, or at least the contemporary techno-social context (Weiser 1991). And this, somehow, would be better than the giant brains of the 1960s, the corporate mainframes of the 1970s, the PCs that chained us to the desk in the 1980s, or the Internet of the 1990s. But as John Thackara has noted:

> Trillions of smart tags, sensors, smart materials, connected appliances, wearable computing, and body implants are now being unleashed upon the world all at once. It is by no means clear to what question they are an answer—or who is going to look after them, and how.
>
> (Thackara 2006)

Pragmatic as Thackara is, his observation prompts us to reflect upon ideas of "progress," and the covert presence of a Victorian techno-utopianism in technological agendas, including ubicomp. A pithy summation of this syndrome is found in "An Interview with Satan" in which Satan explains:

> Technology is all about painstaking simplification, driven often by a desire for order and predictability, which produces complex—and unpredictable—effects. It's a kind of mania for short-cuts which leads to enormous and irreversible detours. Now this is my business in a nutshell . . . Imagine a world where every desire can be instantly frustrated, indeed where every desire can be guaranteed to arise precisely customized to the means for its dissatisfaction, where every expectation will be immediately, and yet unexpectedly thwarted . . . Technology cannot fail to bring about this world, since this would be a universe brought fully under control, consistent with the very nature of technology.
>
> (Dexter 1996)

The entirety of the phenomenon we call ubicomp is underpinned by network infrastructure, server farms, and Big Data. Like the cinema and the automobile, computing and digital communication has created entirely new industries and professional contexts. In the case of the automobile, the most obvious novelty was the emergence of automobile mass production itself. Further thought brings to mind the manufacturers of special parts—brake parts, engine parts, and the like. But beyond this horizon the automobile economy ramifies in all directions—mineral extraction and materials production, the oil industry, the rubber industry. The modern automobile has evolved symbiotically with the development of civil engineering and roadmaking and this in turn has had a huge effect on the shapes of our cities and towns. In the case of the cinema, the convergence in the second half of the nineteenth century, of several emerging technologies—photography, precision machining, chemical engineering, mass-produced optics, and electricity—to name the most obvious—led to the emergence of entirely new socio-economic phenomena, the most obvious being film studios and production facilities, with new career paths from cinematographer to producer to stuntman to "special effects." So it is with ubiquitous computing and it's complement, the Internet.

It is in the spirit of such holistic overviews that I here address ubiquitous computing and related matters. My goal in this paper is to draw attention to a range of "big picture" issues pertaining to infrastructure, energy and resource use, and socio-economic integration—centering on questions of sustainability and civil rights, touching upon some theoretical and historical issues where relevant.

Computing as Natural

"... computers, as if they were flowers ..."

The notion that computing is both natural and neutral no doubt serves the interests of those whose interests will be served by selling more digital appliances. We are increasingly naturalized to computing as a part of our environments and lifestyles. But ubiquitous computing did not just grow like a tree, integrated into the environment it was a product of. This is not to endorse some naïve notion of the natural, but to draw attention to the highly culturally specific and historically contingent nature of digital computing, as a class of computing, different from others (analog connectionist, and evolutionary computing), with no greater claim to legitimacy. Digital computing, as Jay Bolter argued long ago (Bolter 1984), is our paradigmatic technology—it is the technology that provides us with metaphors. In a decade or two, such ideas will seem as naïve as the "mechanism" of a previous epoch—that the universe and physiology could all be explained in terms of clockwork—gears and springs.

Babbage and Turing notwithstanding, Claude Shannon's deployment of George Boole's binary algebraic logic in analyzing electromechanical telephone switching networks is an originary moment in digital culture, because, in the process, he saw that electromagnetic relays could perform Boolean logical operations. Boole's work was classical Victorian scholarship, his major work being "Laws of Thought" (which, it is said, he pursued as a result of a mystical experience).

This is to say—there is nothing "God-given," which confirms that pixels, voxels, digital arithmetic, logic gates, or Boolean algebra are either natural correlates to physical reality, or optimal augmentations for the things people like, want, or need to do. The instrumenting of the world and the establishment of a global system of real-time communication and record keeping is undeniably real. But just as undeniably, it is an historically contingent human cultural effect.

We are of course naturalized to such ideas. Cognitivism tells us that the brain is a computer, Artificial Intelligence (AI) tells us that thinking is symbol manipulation. Modern genetics is full of the computer code analogy for DNA. Every year or so, there is a new claim that the universe is a giant Virtual Reality (VR) simulation. During the VR era of the 1990s, Ed Fredkin amused crowds with "twilight zone" stories that the universe was VR, or that the universe is a computer simulation, and as a result so are we, though we would be unable to know this. This was also the basic idea behind Rainer Werner Fassbinder's two-part Westdeutscher Rundfunk Köln (WDR) telemovie *World on a Wire* (1973).[2]

Fungal Technology

The mobile devices we use and are preoccupied with are the gritty salty detritus where the digital ocean laps against the shore of human temporality. The mobile phone in your hand (or the microcontroller in your car) is nothing but the materially immediate bud of a new global quasi-organism interconnected by a quasi-nervous system with optical, electronic, and radio-frequency dimensions and vast organs hidden from view.

We used to think of mushrooms the way we think of plants—as largely aerial manifestations with roots. Now we understand that fungi are vast underground organisms and the mushrooms are nothing but reproductive buds—manifestations of a Borg-like superorganism proliferating threadwise beneath our feet. In the Malheur National Forest in the Blue Mountains of Eastern Oregon, United States, a colony of *Armillaria Ostoyae* encompasses 10 km^2 (around 1000 acres). At this point it is regarded as the largest living organism in the world and is estimated to be at least 2400 years old, possibly nearly 9000.[3]

Critical theorists have rejoiced for a generation regarding the rhizomatic nature of the Internet topology. I cast the Internet/ubicomp scenario in this light merely to draw attention to the novel technosocial and geopolitical situation that has emerged in little more than twenty years. This fungal technology has grown rapidly, and while the scale of information transmission is well known, the contemporary landscape of resource use is as unprecedented as it is obscure. As the vast and ancient *Armillaria Ostoyae* of Oregon has exterminated acres of forest, so the ubicomp/social media/Internet complex has reconfigured the socio-economic ecosystem, leading to rapid growth in new profit centers (Amazon, Facebook, Google), and the collapse of long-established business models like department stores, newspapers, and the post office. This is not, of course, to endorse a simplistic technological determinism. Such changes are socio-economic systems, involving desire, wealth, and politics in complex feedback loops. There are ways in which contemporary ubicomp—like any new technology—feels novel and unprecedented. But it has grown out of and upon existing systems constructed largely by human actors immersed in and formed by cultural contexts. It is not my intention to imply some distopic sci-fi scenario but to explore and consider the implications, social and environmental, of this new symbiotic ecology of humans and representational machines.

We might well ask "is this phenomenon historically unique?" Has a substantial portion of the labor of humanity been so rapidly and embracingly marshalled around a technological complex in similar ways before? Printing and railway come to mind. Perhaps, more abstractly, precision mechanisms, from the clock to the lace making machine. As a techno-social revolution this would seem comparable, though it occurred over a substantially longer time period (see Mayr 1989). Or one may take Beniger's argument that the "information revolution" is just the most recent stage in the control revolution (Beniger 1989).

Symbiosis—Humans as Sensor and Effector Peripherals

Still, twenty-five years after the demise of Good Old Fashioned AI (GOFAI) (Haugeland 1985), one still hears excited conversation regarding the purported "singularity" (Kurzweil 2005) when computational "intelligence" exceeds human intelligence. Ergo, a generation after Dreyfus's phenomenological exegesis (in "What computers can't do"), the conception of intelligence which makes such a proposal even possible is thoroughly dependent on the idea that the requirements for thinking, or intelligent action in the world, are satisfied by the Physical Symbol System Hypothesis (Newell and Simon). In relation to the present discussion, it is important to recognize that however powerful localized or distributed digital computer systems are, they can only make meaningful interventions in the world by virtue of human interpretation of the world, and the accumulated history of such interpretation.

According to the Sense Map Plan Act paradigm of conventional AI, robots operate in the world via a serial von-Neumann process of input, processing, and output. This linear metaphor is based on the mechanistic models such as the industrial production line rather than biological, ecological, or enactive models. Internally, according to this model, perception is separate from action, separated by information processing, in a linear one-way process. The sensor and effector ends of the process are referred to, significantly, as "peripherals" and serve the function of transduction into and out of digital representations. This conception reproduces an enlightenment individual autonomy, and eschews consideration of community, inter-subjectivity, agency, feedback, adaptation, autopoiesis, or enactive conceptions of cognition.

The failure of GOFAI was rooted in the insurmountable difficulties in coordination of information systems with the real, lived physical world "out there." In hindsight, it should not have been a surprise that an automation of Victorian mathematical logic was neither necessary nor sufficient to equip a synthetic organism to cope in the world, but such was the hubris of the field. In this history we see AI cast not so much as futuristic but as anachronistic.

In an ironic twist, the techniques developed in AI for sophisticated data analysis, such as machine learning, data mining, and (so-called) knowledge engineering, have found a second life (as it were) on the Internet. The key to this success is that in the data world, the difficult translation of the real, lived physical world "out there" has already been done, mostly by humans who are unaware that they have been contributing to the construction of databases by tagging photos, entering text and generally providing metadata for the world.

Automating the interface with the world of electro-physical phenomena is one of the key characteristics of ubicomp, in its "embedded" manifestation. Seismic sensor nets autonomously collect the relatively simple data regarding the time and strength of geological vibrations (by converting them into voltages and then into numbers). But significantly, the realm of social and cultural understandings remains complex and locally specific and continues to evade automation. As with the Semi-Automatic Ground Environment (SAGE) system of the cold war, humans (still) do the work of subtle pattern recognition and processing of real world experiences into data for the machine learning algorithms to churn.[4] Every face identified in a photo, every place named on Google earth, every vacation photo uploaded, every character string decoded in reCAPTCHA,[5] every Facebook "like" enriches the databases. Crowdsourcing and social media mine human sensing. In a truly sci-fi scenario, we have become the symbiotic skin of the Internet, the membrane that converts the tangible to the virtual, the analog to the digital. The latter decades of the twentieth century were haunted by the spectre of sentient machines. That spectre has waned along with the fate of AI (see later in the text). With the growth of the Internet, worldwide web, and wireless communications, a different spectre haunts ubiquity. The emergence of a globally linked "datasphere" accessible to both machine and human agents (as presaged in sci-fi and media theory over the last three decades) is the phenomenon we might call Artificial Awareness (my neologism).

Infrastructure

The Cloud—Ubicomp's Virtual Reality

The terminology of the "cloud" encourages is to imagine dematerialized information floating around in an immaterial instantly accessible but placeless nowhere.
The "cloud" is this decade's version of "the virtual." While the metaphor of the "cloud" is poetic, "cloud computing" neatly obscures the gross material reality of today's communications infrastructure in the same way that "free" online services obscure the for-profit nature of the business.

Datacenters, or more colloquially, "server farms," now occupy huge tracts of land and consume vast amounts of power. In the city of London, more greenhouse gasses are generated due to computing (computers, servers, power consumption, and supporting infrastructure) than by all surface transport (trains, underground, cars, buses, taxis, etc.). Similarly it is said that the world's server farms consume more power than all civil aviation. As James Glanz noted in an article of mid 2012: "Worldwide, the digital warehouses use about 30 billion watts of electricity, roughly equivalent to the output of 30 nuclear power plants . . . Data centers in the United States account for one-quarter to one-third of that load . . ."[6] A significant proportion of the data transported over the Internet and stored in those server farms is junk—spam, records of clicktrails, and other automatically recorded metadata, or duplicated and outdated records. Glanz continued: "Stupendous amounts of data are set in motion each day as, with an innocuous click or tap, people download movies on iTunes, check credit card balances through Visa's website, send Yahoo email with files attached, buy products on Amazon, post on Twitter, or read newspapers online . . ." (Ibid.).

The Cloud is Full of Metal

The ubicomp/big data system consumes material resources and energy, and produces waste, at a prodigious rate. Substantial parts of national and local energy budgets are consumed by the information economy. Vast tonnages of copper and other metals hold it together, and the increasingly important global "rare earth" market is driven by the needs of digital technologies.[7] The constant updating of digital appliances is creating unprecedented pollution crises in countries least capable of dealing with the repercussions. This new socio-economic order consumes the labor of millions all over the world, from the computer science professor at Stanford to the programmer at Google to the cable guy who hooks up your modem, the salesperson at the Apple shop, the assembly workers in Shenzen and in the maquiladoras of northern Mexico, and the customer service representative in Bangladesh.[8]

Server Farms—the Internet's Landfill, Full of Data Trash

The notion that the Internet is clean and "green" is as bankrupt as the idea that computers would usher in the era of the paperless office. The environmental website planetsave.com summarizes:

If the Internet were a country, it would rank fifth in the world for amount of energy consumption and carbon dioxide emission. According to Greenpeace, the Internet consumes more power than Russia. . . . A large percentage of the data centers that house computer servers rely on non-renewable energy sources to power their cloud computing. In fact, according to Greenpeace, at least 10 major tech companies (which include Apple, Amazon, Facebook, and Twitter) depend on nuclear and coal-powered energy rather than renewable forms of energy such as solar and wind. Greenpeace estimates that, when functioning at full capacity, Google's eight server farms could use up to 476 megawatts of electricity, enough energy to power all of San Diego.[9]

Server farms continue to expand to support the illusory "cloud." Microsoft recently purchased 200 acres of industrial property from the Port of Quincy for $11 million:[10] "This new development will be the largest server farm in Quincy; the site is more than three times the size of the current property Microsoft owns there, which is the size of 10 football fields. The company is clearly building out its infrastructure in support of its cloud computing initiatives."[11] How much data (don't call it "information") is stored? In an National Public Radio (NPR) radio interview, a worker at a vast server in Nevada observed that the racks of servers they were looking at—standing on an area roughly 3m × 4m, the size of an average bedroom, could hold all the writing produced in the entire history of the human race. Meanwhile, the rows of server racks disappeared in all directions into the hazy distance—full of digital trivia generated in the last two decades (1990–2010). Nor are these sprawling data giants exclusively the territory of computing and communications corporations. Unsurprisingly perhaps, the U.S. National Security Agency (NSA) is a very active participant in big data collection and storage:

> The Utah Data Center, also known as the Intelligence Community Comprehensive National Cybersecurity Initiative Data Center, is a data storage facility for the United States Intelligence Community that is designed to store extremely large amounts of data . . . Its purpose is to support the Comprehensive National Cybersecurity Initiative (CNCI) . . . The megaproject was completed in late-2013 at a cost of US$1.5 billion despite ongoing controversy over the NSA's involvement in the practice of mass surveillance in the United States.[12]

The page goes on to report: "One report suggested that it will cost another $2 billion for hardware, software, and maintenance. The completed facility is expected to require 65 megawatts, costing about $40 million per year. The facility is expected to use 1.7 million gallons (6500 tons) of water per day."

The Friendly Face of Surveillance

Who Pays for Facebook?

I asked my students "who pays for Facebook?" Many of them looked at me quizzically, saying "its free." So I then asked them to reconcile that with the fact that Facebook is a multibillion dollar business, equivalent to Intel and Home Depot. Home Depot sells stuff. Intel sells a different kind of stuff. How can Facebook have expected revenue of around $8 billion this year? What does it sell, and to whom? Doubtless most of the readers of this essay will have a clearer understanding of the emerging phenomenon of Big Data Capitalism than my students, and of the ways that social media enterprises, ISPs and phone companies store, analyze, and aggregate user data, and merchandise it.

In the 1960s, it came as a surprise when it was revealed that department stores and similar businesses were no longer primarily in the business of selling goods but of market speculation. Storefront operations and product sales simply provided a revenue stream for investment. In social media, business is done in a wildly abstract way. Users partake of "free" services while (usually unknowingly) providing raw data to corporations in exchange. User Data is harvested and processed, packaged, and sold. That data includes names, ages, genders, hometown locations, languages, social connections (e.g., likes, friends, or followers), screen names, website addresses, IP addresses, interests, and professional history. Further intelligence is culled from tweets, posts, comments, likes, shares, uploads, downloads, and recommendations collected from Twitter, Facebook, LinkedIn, BlogSpot, WordPress, Myspace, YouTube, and other social media sites.

A recent post entitled "Big Data + Big Pharma = Big Money" reports on an obscure big data niche—"prescription drug information intermediaries." One of the players in this field, IMS Health Holdings Inc. of Danbury, Conn., earned nearly $2 billion in the first nine months of 2013. Intercontinental Marketing Services (IMS) says its collection includes "over 85 percent of the world's prescriptions by sales revenue," as well as comprehensive, anonymous medical records for 400 million patients, amounting to 45 billion healthcare transactions each year—10 petabytes worth of material—or about 10 million gigabytes, a figure roughly equal to all of the websites and online books, movies, music, and TV shows that have been stored by the nonprofit Internet Archive. "All of the top 100 global pharmaceutical and biotechnology companies are clients" of its products, the firm's prospectus says.[13] This is the landscape of data business—vast and highly profitable, but invisible—no goods, no warehouses, no advertising.

In 2010, it was revealed that Facebook had "outed" gay people via a combination of facial recognition and inference-based ad selection. In a recent post titled "Is Facebook outing gay users to advertisers," Adrian Chen notes ". . . this latest snafu underscores how nearly impossible it is for Facebook to both profit from your personal information and to guarantee it will never be shared without your permission . . ."[14] This is on the heels of a minor scandal where the Target retail chain, based on data analysis, was able to target women who were likely to be pregnant with special advertising. At least one family learned of their daughter's pregnancy this way.[15] Examples such as these reveal the complex legal and civil rights implications of this new and ambiguous territory, which is both free and charged, both public and private, both virtual and with real world effects. The emergence of social media has opened quasi-public virtual communications spaces, which have some of the qualities of good old fashioned public space (if such a thing ever existed) but offer wildly enhanced (telematic) capabilities, while at the same being private, controlled, actively surveilled, and generative of substantial profit.

On a personal and social level, ubiquity is forcing a reconfiguration of notions of privacy and of public space. Notions of self and of sociality underpin ideas of public and private. Hence the reconfiguration of these concepts implies both cognitive and cultural change. In order to better comprehend the transformation of "the private" and "the public," we must consider them together, and through the lens of ubiquity, which is the major vehicle via which these changes are occurring.

"Facebook 'Likes' Become Customized Walmart Ads"

Users pay phone companies and ISPs for service, but provide another revenue source which is skimmed off. In the United States, Verizon holds user data for 12 months, Sprint 24 months, Tmobile for 60 months, and AT&T for 84 months. Thus most users will have over a million pieces of information stored about them spanning over 40 months.[16] This kind of information is of course what fills the server farms, where it is constantly churned, remixed, analyzed, and sorted by sophisticated algorithms. Michael Rigley notes "Facebook likes become customized Walmart ads" (Ibid.).

Back in 1973, Richard Serra and Carlotta Fay Schoolman produced a short video called *Television Delivers People*, which noted "in commercial broadcasting the viewer pays for the privilege of having himself sold . . . It is the consumer who is consumed . . . You are delivered to the advertiser who is the customer."[17] The video notes that for every dollar spent by the broadcasting industry to deliver content (in 1973), the viewer paid $40 to receive it. The calculus in the Internet industry must be similar—consumers pay for hardware, software, connectivity, and subscriptions to online services in order to take advantage of free services. *Plus ca change* . . .

Two decades ago (in 1989), the fall of the Berlin wall was lauded in the west as the victory of democracy and free speech over state surveillance and repression, typified by the vilified Stasi of East Germany. Two decades after the collapse of the Soviet Union, Americans and others now partake in a system of surveillance arguably quite as invasive and far more efficient. Part of this system is called social media, and there is no small irony in the fact that we not only willingly partake in it but *pay* to do so.

Activist Politics of Big Data

Activists like the Electronic Frontier Foundation have mobilized around issues over several decades around the sociopolitical realities of big data, surveillance and the "digital commons," combined with an awareness of the waning of the concept of "public space" remind us that the landscape of the social has changes radically in the last twenty-five years, epitomized by the "always online" status of an increasing proportion of the population. The philosophical, political, and legal dimensions of this new condition continue to be debated. Meanwhile, corporate and state entities have colonized the new territory as if it was a legal *tabula rasa* and commercial data aggregation by operations such as Acxiom, Experian, Epsilon, and Choicepoint are just entering public awareness.[18] It is notable that interventionist artists and groups flagged these issues over two decades ago (Schultz 1993). During the 1990s, concerns tended to be grouped under the rubric of "surveillance" as in the work of Julia Scher, the Institute for Applied Autonomy, Trevor Paglen, Critical Art Ensemble, and others.

Databody

In 2003, media artists Brooke Singer, Beatriz Da Costa, and Jamison Schulte presented Swipe, a media intervention staged as a bar, where patrons were required to pay for drinks with a card and have their drivers licenses swiped. The (usually surprised) customer received a cash register receipt often 2–3 ft. long which included a printout of the data stored on the driver's license and in databases instantly accessible by that license swipe. This data included previous addresses, automobile and legal records. The exhibition blurb states:

Swipe addressed the gathering of data from drivers' licenses, a form of data-collection that businesses are practicing in the United States. Bars and convenience stores were the first to utilize license scanners in the name of age and ID verification. These businesses, however, admit they reap huge benefits from this practice beyond catching underage drinkers and smokers with fake IDs. With one swipe—that often occurs without notification or consent by the cardholder—a business acquires data that can be used to build a valuable consumer database free of charge. Post 9/11, other businesses, like hospitals and airports, are installing license readers in the name of security. And still other businesses are joining the rush to scan realizing the information contained on drivers' licenses is a potential gold mine. Detailed database records, of course, also benefit law enforcement officers who can now demand this information without judicial review in large part due to the U.S.A. Patriot Act.[19]

The accumulation of the *databody*—the digital representation of a person stored in databanks—has been a critical issue since the early 1990s, and came to a head politically with the scandal around the Total Information Awareness (TIA) program of the U.S. Information Awareness Office, which was briefly operational—from February until May 2003—before being renamed the Terrorism Information Awareness Program. In early 2013, at a private gathering in London, Google Exec, Larry Page, stated "anything you put in the cloud is there forever" (private communication). All the information we innocently put into the system is being watched, harvested, aggregated, and put to purposes we not only didn't authorize but mostly couldn't imagine.

Ubicomp For and Against the State

The advent of global ubiquity offers new repressive apparatus to the Nation State, and simultaneously challenges the coherence of the Nation State—a reality acknowledged by some states which control Internet communications. Nor is a clean separation between state and corporate operations possible. Consistent with the contemporary ethos of government subcontracting—with the likes of Haliburton and Blackwater—U.S. government agencies buy data and services from the likes of Acxiom and Epsilon. State surveillance is clearly not going away, as indicated by the ongoing revelations arising from the Wikileaks and Snowdon affairs. New revelations about such surveillance seem to occur every week. In October 2013, we have learned of the monitoring of the cell phones of German Chancellor Angela Merkel, Brazilian president Dilma Rousseff, French and Mexican politicians, and scores of others, seemingly for a decade or more.

In December 2013, new releases from the Snowdon files showed that in 2008, the NSA (and U.K. equivalent Government Communications Headquarters (GCHQ)) had been monitoring massively multiplayer online role-playing games (MMORPGs) such as World of Warcraft, Second Life, and Xbox Live. While there was no evidence of useful information being collected, it seems that so many operatives were deployed on those sites that there were calls from inside NSA for a "group" to prevent the agency's personnel from inadvertently spying on each other. This is reminiscent of reports of CIA and FBI infiltration of anti-Vietnam war activist groups in the 1970s. It was said that many such groups contained more state agents than actual activists.

In a not too surprising twist, it transpires that the CTO for San Francisco-based Linden Labs, Cory Ondrejka, "was a former Navy officer who had worked at the NSA with a top-secret security clearance."[20] In March 2014, it was revealed that the NSA had created false Facebook servers and had collected data on Facebook users. Founder Mark Zuckerberg was so disturbed by this he called President Obama and later wrote in a blog post: "I've been so confused and frustrated by the repeated reports of the behavior of the U.S. government. When our engineers work tirelessly to improve security, we imagine we're protecting you against criminals, not our own government." Yet curiously, the aforementioned Ondrejka is now (December 2013) the director of mobile engineering at Facebook.

In the early 1990s, when computer graphics and VR was all the rage, I was surprised, then not so surprised, to see that technical operatives moved between military work and entertainment industry work seamlessly, especially as the entertainment industry became interested in 3D simulation and the military became interested in shooter games as training simulators (Penny 2004). This observation led me to coin the phrase "military entertainment complex." In the same way, it is surprising, then not surprising that themes of cybersecurity, cyberwarfare, and cyberterrorism should be equally interesting to the NSA and to billion dollar corporations like Facebook.

Cyberwarfare has been a priority of the pentagon for years and no wonder. With appropriate hacks, control of power or communications infrastructures can bring a state to its knees without so much as a shot being fired. The capture of a CIA RQ-170 sentinel unmanned spy plane by Iran in December 2011 must have been deeply embarrassing. According to reports, it was captured by jamming satellite and land-based communications to the plane then issuing false GPS data to it. As a result the plane landed itself safely in Iran, thinking it was "home."

No doubt, if I was a technologically aware terrorist, gangster, or other ne-er-do-well, I would consider the use of these sophisticated quasi-anonymous social media systems for covert communications. Hakim Bey's formulation of the TAZ (Temporary Autonomous Zone) (Bey 1991) has had, and will continue to have, particular relevance in the rapidly changing technological landscape. And likewise, if I were a security operative, safeguarding communications for a state or a corporation, I would be thinking very carefully about the security of the systems I was responsible for.

Algorithms Take Command

The application of algorithmic automation across diverse aspects of human activity is one of the hallmarks of ubicomp. Most of these applications are relatively trivial or benign—the tracking of radio-frequency identification (RFID)-tagged goods, or the monitoring of oxygen levels in your car engine. But inevitably, when the stakes for wealth or power are high, control is taken "by whatever means necessary." So it is in the arcane world of algorithmic trading, also known as black box trading, which happens at such speeds that human oversight is not possible. In the May 6 "Flash Crash" of 2010, the U.S. stock market lost ten percent of its value in five minutes due to the activity of so called High Frequency Trading Algorithms (HFTs). The effect was so alarming and so complex that it took the staffs of the U.S. Commodity Futures Trading Commission (CFTC) and SEC months to piece together a rough picture of what had happened, which included so called "hot-potato" trading, where algorithms were selling and buying stocks to each other at high speed for miniscule profits.[21] As one might expect, an algorithmic arms race has emerged, with algorithms designed to detect and thwart, or profit from, the actions of other algorithms. Today, seventy percent of stock trading is algorithmic trading and trades take place in around seventy microseconds. To put the speed of these systems into perspective: an HFT can process more data in the time it takes for a human to click a mouse once than a human might read in their entire life.[22]

One of the more insidious effects of this algorithmic trading is that algorithms can act rapidly on financial announcements, reaping profits from changing values for investors while taking potential profits from slower moving actors, such as mutual funds. Such trading is known as "shadow trading," as it occurs far faster than the monitoring technology of stock markets can track. The NYSE has the capability to monitor trades only to ten milliseconds (1/100th of a second).[23] HFTs are performing operations in tens of microseconds, so an HFT might sneak in hundreds of trades before the watchdogs notice.

In the era of Big Data, useful information is generated less by sophisticated algorithms working on limited data than by relatively simple statistical processes working on almost unlimited data. Contemporary algorithmically derived knowledge and power is not so much about cleverness as about sheer speed and brute volume. People not only do not know but cannot know the decisions that are being made by such algorithms that directly and significantly affect the stock market, and thus play a substantial role in shaping our lives. As with the Flash Crash, the system is out of human control. By the time a human clicks a mouse (let alone the time it takes to realize something is going on), a billion more trades have occurred, which might have stabilized or further destabilized the situation. Any human reaction is already too late.

Some Conclusions

In the United States, at least in the popular view, the assumption of an uncomplicated identification between democratic freedom and "free enterprise" is axiomatic to political-economic discourse. In the academic ubicomp community, there seems to be a similar lacuna in the assumption that such "infrastructure" is politically neutral. How can it be neutral if it is designed by vested interests who put it in place for the specific goal of accumulating wealth and reinforcing their power? There seems to be an enduring underlying confusion between what developers and academics of liberal politics and general goodwill would like to see, or imagine as possible, and the stark reality of the technology as deployed, its purposes and results.

Ubiquity was built, and it was built by people with an interest, usually a financial interest. Ubiquity exists, largely because it makes money, or otherwise serves the interests of power. And in the process, it is something parasitic in the sense that it continues to suck energy and resources. Yes, there are the oft trotted-out poster children: smart green buildings, instrumented bridges, and sensor networks for seismic monitoring. But for every smart building there are ten autonomous weaponized drones, a hundred social media sites turning personal information into marketable data, a thousand miles of surveilled border, ten thousand RFID equipped commodities, and a hundred thousand online purchases.

Unlike many of my ubicomp researcher colleagues, I have the luxury that I am not beholden to corporate grants or institutions that are otherwise "in bed with" industry, so I am able to be explicit about issues on which they might be inclined to be reticent. Much research into aspects of ubicomp seems to proceed on the basis that these technologies are presumed to be ethically and politically neutral if not generally for the good. There is a taste of a rather irksome faux techno-utopianism in this.

Haven't we read enough techno-industrial history to learn that while visionaries and inventors are often motivated by a (sometimes foolishly deluded) belief in the redemptive potential of this or that technology, that such technological utopianism is short-lived, and these technological utopians are lauded only until the new technology turns a profit, at which point it's "business as usual?" It was this way for the locomotive, for the telegraph, for radio, and for the Internet. We've had a quarter century of liberatory technoutopian rhetoric from consumer digital technology corporations. Personally, I'm tired of being liberated by technology. It's too expensive and too much hard work.

In the same way that the term "ubiquitous computing" embraces several quite separate socio-technological phenomena, there are also diverging ontologies of ubiquity. According to one, data is a kind of glue that joins things and makes them work better. On the other hand is the panopticism of "total information awareness" in which people, individually and collectively, are managed, if not exploited, by data collecting and analysis—data-mining, and knowledge engineering: all the things AI has become. Third we are presented with the "HAL scenario," in which our fates are in the hands of uncontrollable algorithms.

I do not advocate a luddite or apocalyptic position, nor am I suggesting that digital communications corporations are by definition demonic, but it does seem that the field has tended to turn a blind eye to the fact that ubicomp would not exist if it were not enormously profitable and the motivation to continue to make such profits is a prime driver of technological development. In this it is, like all human culture, historically contingent. If ubicomp had developed in the Roman Empire, or the Vatican in the seventeenth century, or the Soviet state, it would be a qualitatively different phenomenon.

Ubicomp may be desirable or advantageous or alienating or exploitative or all these at the same time, but it exists and grows because it serves those who have the wherewithal to put it in place and so are poised to profit from it. Nor, of course could such profits be made unless the products did not conform to the desires of the market, albeit desires themselves largely formed by marketing (Television delivers you). How should we assess the "free labor" of millions who contribute, moderating fora, tagging photos, or contributing to open source code projects? (Terranova). Is that "data" fairly available to all, or is data-capital skimmed off? How do we distinguish, in a principled way, between data systems which are wholesomely integrated into larger socio-political systems, and those which are unethically parasitic upon them, or deployed for surveillance and control? Just as we've become acclimatized to the "information economy," the political economy of "big data" demands further accommodation. We can address emerging social problems as problems in the social domain, but as always, civil rights, legal adaptation, and governmental regulation play catch-up with changing technological contexts.

Notes

1. See, for instance, http://eyebeam.org/zapped-rfid-workbook
2. 1973, based on Daniel F. Galouye's 1964 American novel simulacron-3.
3. http://scientificamerican.com/article.cfm?id=strange-but-true-largest-organism-is-fungus. Accessed December 27, 2013.
4. The SAGE or Semi-Automatic Ground Environment was a cold war U.S. ur-project linking radar installations along the east coast of North America in the first large scale real-time network. Many key ideas developed for SAGE have had lasting impact on the development of computing and digital communications, such as time-sharing and the screen-keyboard-pointer interface.
5. reCAPTCHA is a free service used to protect your website from spam and abuse. reCAPTCHA, *GitHub*, https://github.com/google/recaptcha. Accessed September 5, 2015.
6. http://nytimes.com/2012/09/23/technology/data-centers-waste-vast-amounts-of-energy-belying-industry-image.html?_r=0. Accessed December 28, 2013.
7. Some of the rare earth metals (Lathanides) and other obscure metals such as Germanium, Iridium, Platinum, Tantalum are highly valuable and critical in electronics components, and present in very small quantities. Indium is used in touch screens. Nickel Metal Hydride batteries contain Lanthanum. Optical fiber contains Erbium. Tellurium is critical in solar cells (photovoltaics). Europium and Terbium

are used in compact fluorescent lamps. China supplies around ninety-five percent of the world market for most of these metals. Wiring is generally copper; hardware is often cadmium plated. Printed circuit boards contain high amounts of precious metals; about 20 wt percent copper, 0.04 wt percent gold, 0.15 wt percent silver, and 0.01 wt percent palladium. (Ref.—Recovery of Gold, Silver, Palladium, and Copper from Waste Printed Circuit Boards. Chehade, Ameer, Hisham, Naveena, Saeed, and Taleb. International Conference on Chemical, Civil and Environment engineering (ICCEE'2012) held in Dubai, March 24–25, 2012).

8. This paper is wide-ranging in several ways; however I am conscious of the fact that my examples are mostly from the United States. I do not mean to indicate anything by this except my comparative unfamiliarity with specifics in other countries.

9. http://planetsave.com/2011/10/27/how-much-energy-does-the-Internet-consume/. Accessed December 28, 2013.

10. http://wenatcheeworld.com/news/2013/dec/20/port-of-quincy-selling-land-for-microsoft-server-farm/. Accessed January 7, 2014.

11. http://datacenterknowledge.com/archives/2013/12/23/microsoft-expands-quincy-acquiring-200-acres/. Accessed December 28, 2013.

12. http://en.wikipedia.org/wiki/Utah_Data_Center. Accessed December 28, 2013.

13. http://propublica.org/article/big-data-big-pharma-big-money. Accessed 14 January, 2014.

14. http://gawker.com/5669316/is-facebook-outing-gay-users-to-advertisers http://cnn.com/2010/TECH/social.media/10/21/facebook.gay.ads/index.html. Accessed December 29, 2013.

15. http://forbes.com/sites/kashmirhill/2012/02/16/how-target-figured-out-a-teen-girl-was-pregnant-before-her-father-did/. Accessed January 7, 2014.

16. A stylish video by Michel Rigley summarizes some of the aspects of this new information economy. https://vimeo.com/34750078

17. The full video can be found at https://youtube.com/watch?v=nbvzbj4Nhtk and other sites.

18. See for instance Marwick, Alice E., "How Your Data Are Being Deeply Mined," in The New York Review of Books, January 9, 2014, http://nybooks.com/articles/archives/2014/jan/09/how-your-data-are-being-deeply-mined. Accessed December 31, 2013.

19. http://beallcenter.uci.edu/exhibitions/swipe-brooke-singer-beatriz-da-costa-and-jamie-schulte More information at http://turbulence.org/Works/swipe/main.html

20. http://technewscast.com/top-news/nsa-installed-spies-virtual-games/. December 9, 2013 11:31 pm.

21. See Report of the staffs of the CFTC and SEC to the Joint Advisory Committee on Emerging Regulatory Issues. September 30, 2010.

22. http://ted.com/talks/kevin_slavin_how_algorithms_shape_our_world.html. Accessed December 29, 2013.

23. "High Frequency Trading and the risk monitoring of automated trading." Fernandez Ferrandiz, Robert, Working paper of the Febelfin Academy, Brussels, March 2013, http://papers.ssrn.com/sol3/papers.cfm?abstract_id=2285407. Accessed December 31, 2013.

References

Beniger, James. 1989. *The Control Revolution: Technological and Economic Origins of the Information Society*. Cambridge, MA: Harvard University Press.

Bey, Hakim. 1991. *T.A.Z. the Temporary Autonomous Zone, Ontological Anarchy, Poetic Terrorism*. Brooklyn, NY: Autonomedia.

Bolter, David. 1984. *Turing's Man*. Chapel Hill, NC: University of North Carolina Press.

Brautigan, Richard. 1967. *Trout Fishing in America: A Novel*. New York: Dell.

Cisek, Paul. 1999. "Beyond the Computer Metaphor: Behaviour as Interaction." *Journal of Consciousness Studies* 6 (11–12): 125–142.

Dexter, Frank. 1996. "An Interview with Satan." In *FutureNatural: Nature, Science, Culture*, Eds. George Robertson, Melinda Mash, Lisa Tickner, Jon Bird, Tim Putnam, and Barry Curtis, 293–302. New York: Routledge.

Haugeland, John. 1985. *Artificial Intelligence: The Very Idea*. Cambridge, MA: MIT Press.

Kurzweil, Ray. 2005. *The Singularity Is Near: When Humans Transcend Biology*. New York: Viking.

Mayr, Otto. 1989. *Authority, Liberty, and Automatic Machinery in Early Modern Europe*. Baltimore, MD: The Johns Hopkins University Press.

Penny, Simon. 2004. "Representation, Enaction and the Ethics of Simulation." In *First Person*, Eds. Pat Harrigan and Noah Wardrip-Fruin, 71–82. Cambridge, MA: MIT Press.

Penny, Simon. 2013. "Trying to Be Calm: Ubiquity, Cognitivism and Embodiment." In *Throughout— Art and Culture Emerging with Ubiquitous Computing*, Ed. Ulrik Ekman, 263–277. Cambridge, MA: MIT Press.

Roszak, Theodore. *From Satori to Silicon Valley*. www-sul.stanford.edu/mac/primary/docs/satori/gathering. html.

Schultz, Jeffrey. 1993. "Virtu-Real Space: Information Technologies and the Politics of Consciousness." *Machine Culture*, SIGGRAPH93, Annual Conference Series, 159–63.

Terranova, Tiziana. *Free Labor: Producing Culture for the Digital Economy* www.electronicbookreview. com/thread/technocapitalism/voluntary.

Thackara, John. 2006. *In the Bubble—Designing in a Complex World*. Cambridge, MA: MIT Press.

Weiser, Mark. 1991. "The Computer for the 21st Century." *Scientific American* 265 (3): 94–104.

TOWARDS TRANSDISCIPLINARY DESIGN OF UBIQUITOUS COMPUTING SYSTEMS SUPPORTING END-USER DEVELOPMENT

Irene Mavrommati

Introduction

In the context of complexity and culture related to ubiquitous computing systems, the theme addressed by this volume, one has but to observe that culture and technology, ubiquitous in this case, have always been inter-tangled, in a relation that is seamless (when experienced), yet not at all straightforward when we attempt to analyze or comprehend its relationships. Our methods are tools themselves providing us structure in the way we grasp, conceptualize, and develop further our technological environment.

One defining element of ubiquitous technology has been from its very beginning transdisciplinarity (already mentioned by Weiser when he coined the very term "ubicomp" (Weiser 1991)). For each of the disciplines involved in developing ubicomp systems, this cooperation is done in parallel paths with each discipline mostly pursuing their own goals, often not sharing a broader common understanding of the implications or terms at play, with no common structure or language to help them take the discussion on further grounds. In an attempt to ease complexity and improve the level of this discussion, one important step is providing structure in the working methods for creating ubiquitous systems, so that the transdisciplinary teams involved can share common ground. With this in mind, a broad holistic framework is described in this chapter. It assumes two things: first that end-user development is a necessary element of ubicomp systems (and it has to be taken into account when developing such systems), and, second that ubiquitous computing systems are, in essence, component-based systems.

Ubiquitous computing (Ubicomp) environments are complex computing systems; they can also be understood as ecologies of artifacts, services, people, and infrastructure. Systems with such complexity can be approached as component-based ubicomp systems (Drossos et al. 2007; Gross and Marquandt 2007; Newman et al. 2002). Component-based systems are independent systems with loose coupling of interchangeable parts, which communicate via interfaces. This approach is better for scaling and is extensible, in terms of production, by many different manufacturers of ubiquitous computing technological modules.

This chapter outlines theoretical and methodological constructs, towards the definition of a framework for the design of component based ubicomp systems for the Internet of Things (IoT) that can potentially support end-user development (EUD). EUD in ubicomp environments is an area currently being researched; broader unifying theoretical foundations examining EUD in the context of IoT systems do not yet exist. A compilation and organization of underlying theories is attempted here, as well as concepts and methodologies from user experience design and system design, so as to build a framework for the overall design of artifact-based ubiquitous systems that support EUD. A broad perspective is adopted, attempting to bridge experience design and system engineering constructs with cognitive and sociocultural theories, in order to provide a common understanding to multi-disciplinary development teams that are involved in the creation of the underlying architecture of IoT systems.

Ubicomp technology will need to be deployed and used in an immense range of different contexts, for ubicomp systems to fit into the lifestyle of very different individuals, and to do so without requiring them to attend to this technology instead of their own daily pursuits. At the same time people's abilities in EUD are shifting, as younger generations become increasingly more adept into the setting up of applications and use of personal applets, home platforms, and several other computing devices. Ubiquitous computing applications must be able to adapt to varying and changing situations, to the specifics of different environments, to situations unforeseeable to application developers. One potential solution is to enable users to restructure their ambient computing applications (Drossos, Mavrommati, and Kameas 2007; Newman et al. 2002; Rodden and Benford 2003; Kameas and Mavrommati 2005). This solution has several benefits: (a) applications are adapted in the best possible way to users' own requirements; (b) applications can be incrementally improved by their very users; (c) users are able to design their own environments and interactive experiences in a proactive, creative way. EUD is therefore considered a valid approach for ambient computing environments that complements ambient intelligence.

It is assumed for ambient computing that it will turn out to be an infrastructure as seamless as electricity (Weiser 1991) or as networking is currently becoming. These usually work seamlessly, supporting human activities unobtrusively. Yet, one needs to also to have an idea as to how all the parts are connected when the system fails, so as to take the right remedial action. Selective transparency and the ability to expose the seams into the working of the ubicomp system, by providing end users with methods, models, and interface mechanisms, can help gaining a greater degree of understanding of, and handling of the ubiquitous environment.

Adding human and societal intelligence as a part of EUD enabled ubicomp systems is a way to explore emergent uses and potentially benefit from coupling the system's intelligence with the human intelligence. The system should therefore be considered from its early design in its total form, that includes people, societies, mental or physical tools, computing systems, agents and intelligent mechanisms, and the parameter of time and history, all as parts which evolve in a continuous interplay.

Overview of Framework

EUD in ubicomp environments is an area recently being researched; broader theoretical foundations or frameworks are not yet formulated. EUD, on the other hand, needs to have a focus in the application domain (Klann, Paterno, and Wulf 2006); AmI is believed to be such an area whereby research needs to provide approaches with practical relevance for this specific domain (Kameas and Mavrommati 2005).

Current EUD frameworks are either generic umbrella frameworks of all the application domains of EUD (i.e. Fischer and Giaccardi 2006), or concentrate in virtual and software environments, while AmI frameworks are concerned primarily with Service-Oriented

Architecture (SoA) aspects. Yet, a more appropriate perspective for understanding ubicomp systems is that of co-evolution and co-development between artifacts, applications, together with related EUD tools and people (the users), and as such it calls for a more holistic approach.

A first structure of underlying theories, as well as concepts and methodologies from user experience (UX) design and system design, towards a framework for the total design of Artifact-based ubicomp systems that support EUD, are presented in this paper.

The proposed structure (Figures 12.1, 12.2, and 12.3) consists of theories and methodologies trying to address a gap in theoretical foundations by defining a broad multidisciplinary framework. It is broad in that it tries to view the system in its totality, determining all its component parts, from the theoretical foundation, to user experience, to system design. There are mutual implications in the relationship of users, social structures, and AmI EUD systems as they function together in an iterative evolutionary cycle. Concepts described in this framework are interacting and interconnecting along the three different perspectives that are proposed: theory, experience/interaction design, and system design. The parts are interconnecting while key concepts in theory are echoed in design concepts, which, in turn, correspond to system design concepts and constructs. The social and cultural dynamics are addressed here as an inseparable part of ubicomp systems (with activity theory playing a key role as a theoretical foundation).

This framework is addressed to system developers, engineers, user experience designers, user interface and interaction designers, or social scientists. It aims to bridge gaps in the communication between members of those disciplines that collaboratively (but not always smoothly) are involved in the creation of AmI systems and applications, providing a unified overview, rather than disconnected views and frameworks separate for each discipline.

Theoretical Foundations

The theoretical foundations for artifact-based AmI systems that support EUD tasks are classified under four broad categories (Figure 12.2): *End-User Design*, *End-User Programming* (both these

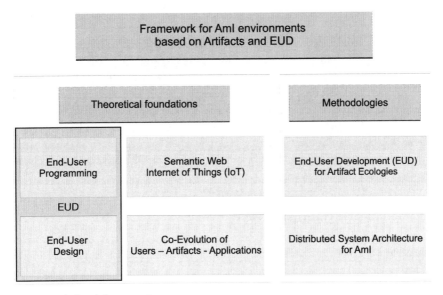

FIGURE 12.1 High-level framework

Image courtesy of the artist/author

form the bi-polar EUD methodologies), *Semantic Web/Internet of Things* (that loosely corresponds to the system design methodologies (Figure 12.3)), and *Co-evolution of Users, Artifacts, and Applications* (that relates to the evolution of the total system, and the perspective that is assumed in this chapter). An overall schema of the framework can be seen in Figure 12.1.

EUD Foundations: End-User Programming

Social Constructivism

Social constructivism refers to the individual making meaning of knowledge within a social context (Vygotsky 1978). It suggests that reality takes on meaning through the social process. Our lives are constantly being formed through the dialectical process of socialization. People's understanding of science follows a similar dialectic. The artifacts that people invent are continually shaped in order to be adapted to the continually evolving context of the human life and environment.

People and artifacts are interdependently shaped: people are shaped by their interactions with artifacts, tools, and machines (of physical or conceptual nature) and at the same time artifacts and tools evolve and change in response to the use that is made of them by communities of humans.

The theory of social constructivism applies the general ideas of constructivism to social settings. According to social constructivism, social groups create knowledge for one another and share it, sharing artifacts and meanings, subsequently creating a culture by collaboratively sharing constructs and artifacts. At the same time, immersion in a culture of shared meanings, concepts, artifacts, and tools assists in learning how to be a part of this cultural group. Social constructivism, in effect, extends constructivism theory by introducing the role of other actors and culture in human development.

Constructionism

Constructionism is an educational theory based on the idea that people learn effectively through making things (Papert 1986). It was inspired by Jean Piaget and his experiential/constructivist learning ideas. Constructionism argues that learning happens more effectively when people are active in making tangible objects in the real world (with these ideas connecting directly to experiential learning). Constructionism, according to Seymour Papert, is combining the following: "From constructivist theories of psychology we take a view of learning as a reconstruction rather than as a transmission of knowledge. Then we extend the idea of manipulative materials to the idea that learning is most effective when part of an activity the learner experiences as constructing a meaningful product."

EUD Foundations for End-User Design

Design Rationale

Design rationale is a theory based on the ecological approach of Gibson (Carroll and Rosson 2003). Ecological theory serves as a theoretical foundation to the social constructivism approach as well, influenced equally by activity theory and ecological psychology (Figure 12.2). Carroll has extensively argued for considering design rationale as theory and provided a related framework (Carroll 2000; Carroll and Rosson 2003). He argues for the value of capturing design rationale during the design process in order to understand and reflect upon system design.

Design rationale is the reasoning that leads to design decisions. Documenting design rationale is important for understanding the context behind design decisions and for validating design decisions. It helps those who are trying to interpret ambiguous design decisions or examples that don't fall clearly within a design principle, and to avoid going back and challenging/changing design decisions without knowing the reasons that led to them in the first place. A design rationale can also be an important tool in arriving to a design decision in the first place. The captured rationale should give advantages and disadvantages of a choice and include rejected alternatives (so that those alternatives don't keep popping up for reconsideration).

Design rationale in the context of this framework is considered as a foundation that can be applied not only to the design of systems (by teams of engineers and experience design specialists), but can also be used as a methodological foundation for end users to act as designers of their own applications. This theory's scenario based design methods can provide insight and inspiration for mechanisms supporting scenario based development as a means for end users to conceptualize and express application ideas.

Foundations for Semantic Web and Internet of Things

Distributed Cognition—DCog

Distributed cognition is a framework that involves the coordination between individuals, artifacts, and the environment, which was developed by Edwin Hutchins (1995). According to DCog, human cognition is distributed in the environment by placing reminders, knowledge, and facts onto objects and tools (internalized or externalized) within the surrounding environment that can be readily accessed so that this knowledge is retrieved. It emphasizes the social aspects of cognition, taking its influences by Activity Theory and the earlier work of Vygotsky.

According to Hollan, Hutchins, and Kirsch (2000): "Distributed Cognition views a system as a set of representations, and models the interchange of information between these representations. These representations can be either in the mental space of the participants or external representations available in the environment." Cognitive processes are distributed between different members of a social group and artifacts that are in use (internal or external). Cognition involves the coordination between the artifacts, processes, and people, and has a causal relationship through time, with earlier events impacting and transforming events that come later in time. Thus both EUD and the ubicomp system's active usage could be considered as user-mediated coordination.

Activity Theory: Understanding the Broader Picture

Activity theory is a broad philosophical framework that has influenced education, organizational design, and interaction design. It emphasizes social factors as shapers of interaction between agents and their environments. It originated in the 1920s from the work of Russian psychologist Lev Vygotsky, and his students and followers (his students Leontiev and Luria but also contemporary researchers such as Nardi, Bannon, Bodker, Norman, and Carroll have applied this theory in their research in collaborative systems and interaction design).

According to activity theory, consciousness is shaped by practice. People mediate their activity by artifacts; language and symbol systems are also considered by Vygotsky as tools for developing the human condition. Human activities are driven by certain needs for achieving certain purposes. This activity is usually mediated by one or more instruments or tools (the concept of mediation is central to the whole theory) (Bannon and Bødker 1991).

Activity theory consists of a set of basic principles that constitute a general conceptual system, which can be used as a foundation for more specific theories (Bannon 1997; Kaptelinin 1996; Kaptelinin and Nardi 1997). As Liam Bannon explains (at the activity theory online tutorial; Bannon 1997): "The basic principles of Activity Theory include object-orientedness, the dual concepts of internalization/externalization, tool mediation, hierarchical structure of activity, and continuous development. The principle of object-orientedness states that human beings live in a reality which is objective in a broad sense; the things which constitute this reality have not only the properties which are considered objective according to natural sciences but socially/culturally defined properties as well." Activity theory, as Bannon explains, separates internal from external activities. Mental processes are internal activities. Transformations between these two kinds of activities are mutual and are interrelated, in such a way that activities cannot be understood when analyzed in isolation (i.e., by separating the internal from the external ones). It is the general context of (both external and internal) activity that determines the cycle of transformation of external activities to internal (Bannon 1997).

Tool mediation is a central concept in activity theory. As Bannon (1997) and Kaptelinin and Nardi (1997) explain, tools shape the way human beings interact with reality. Bannon (1997) states that: "According to the internalization/externalization principle, shaping external activities ultimately results in shaping internal ones. Tools reflect the experiences of other people who have tried to solve similar problems earlier and invented or adapted and modified the tool in order to make it more efficient. This social accumulative experience is accumulated in the properties of tools (structure, shape, material, etc.) and in the knowledge of how the tool is used."

Tools are created and transformed during the development of the activity itself and are carriers of a particular culture—the historical remnants from that development. The use of tools is a means for the accumulation and transmission of social knowledge. It influences the nature, not only of external behavior, but also of the mental functioning of individuals. As noted by Bannon and Bødker (1991): "Artifacts are there for us when we are introduced into a certain activity, but they are also a product of our activity, and as such they are constantly changed through the activity. This "mediation" is essential in the ways in which we can understand artifacts through activity theory." Activity theory can be used as a conceptual framework addressing how human thinking could advance further via the use of (technological) tools. Having human activity in its focus, it has gained an international and multidisciplinary importance, and is especially influential in understanding Human Computer Interaction (Kaptelinin and Nardi 1997) and in the areas of computer-mediated communication and computer-supported collaborative environments.

Foundations for the Co-evolution of Users, Artifacts, and Applications

Situated Cognition and Gibson's Ecological Psychology

The typical approach on cognition treats the perception and motor systems as input and output of humans. Embodied Cognition on the other hand, considers the mind and body in continuous interaction as a single entity: knowledge happens via the body interacting with the world (Winkielmann, Niedenthal, and Obermann 2009).

Moreover, in the Situated Cognition approach, knowledge is determined by both the agent and the context. "Knowing is inseparable from doing" (Brown, Collins, and Duguid 1989), while "knowledge is situated in activity bound to social, cultural and physical contexts" (Greeno and Moore 1993). Gibson views on visual perception have influenced situated cognition theory (Greeno 1994). To Gibson, visual perception is not solely about input from the eyes providing the brain with symbolic representations, but more about people perceiving certain elements, by selectively viewing from a huge amount of information and identifying certain aspects of the environment, that change or remain stable. Such perceptions of the environment co-determine the possibilities for use of the environment or the artifact. This process of perception —driven by people's intentions—evolves in time, for persons and societies alike.

Situated cognition is influenced from ecological psychology's perception-action cycle (Gibson 1986). A key principle of the ecological perspective, adopted by the situated cognition approach, is the notion of affordances, a popular design conceptual construct, originally introduced by Gibson (1977), describing the *relationship between objects and tasks that can be performed with them*. Gibson (1986) defined the term as properties that present possibilities for action that are directly perceptible by people to act upon. He focused on the affordances of physical objects and suggested that affordances were directly perceived instead of mediated by mental representations such as mental models. Affordances are seen by Gibson as "preconditions for activity," not determining behavior per se, but increasing the chances of certain actions to happen.

Objects can "afford" certain types of actions to be done with them, as a result of their physical shape, their material, and the cues and cultural knowledge of usage. Don Norman (1990) further

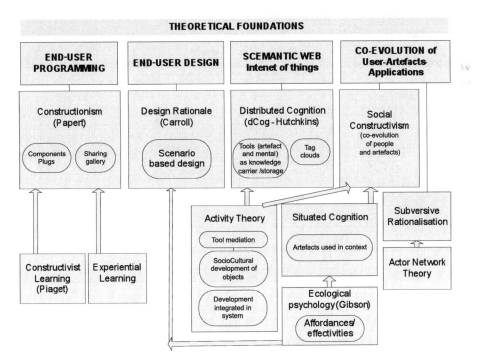

FIGURE 12.2 Theoretical foundations view
Image courtesy of the artist/author

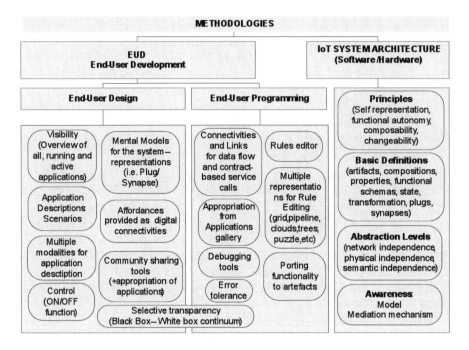

FIGURE 12.3 Methodologies detailed view.
Image courtesy of the artist/author

elaborated on the concept of affordances by introducing *perceived affordances*, in parallel with the actual properties of the object. To Norman, affordances stem from properties and signify *how the thing can possibly be used*. With perceived affordances, he emphasizes "the agent's perception of an object's utility as opposed to focusing on the object itself."

Technology "hidden affordances," introduced by Bill Gaver (1991), was the further elaboration of the concept, signifying functions of interactive systems that are not always directly and immediately perceived. Gaver has addressed technology affordances (apparent as well as hidden) in the context of interactive systems design, considering them as "properties of the world defined with respect to people's interactions with it."

Subsequent to *affordances*, the term *effectivities* has been introduced by Gibson, signifying the abilities of the person itself that determine what he/she could do, and the interaction taking place as a result. It is effectivities and affordances together, working simultaneously, that determine action and perception (Gibson 1986; Greeno 1994). Which affordances are picked up and used is determined by the person interacting within the environment and perceiving it based on his/her effectivities.

Subversive Rationalization

Subversive rationalization, introduced by Andrew Feenberg (1992), describes the constructivist nature of technology. Subversive rationalization suggests that technologies evolve and change through being adopted, used over time, and adapted by people. Technology transformation is seen as an eventual result that is guided by social, democratic, and human values. So, technology is shaped as a result of adaptation to the cultural logic of the people who use it (and is not solely defined by the technology designers). This view bears similarities to the perspective of Lev Vygotsky that was described earlier.

Actor–Network Theory

Actor–network theory is a "material-semiotic" method, in that it maps material (involving things) and semiotic (involving concepts) relations. It is assumed that many relations are of dual nature, both material and semiotic.

Actor-network theory tries to explain how material–semiotic networks come together to act as a whole, looking at explicit strategies for relating different elements together into a network so that they form an apparently coherent whole (for example, an establishment that consists of networked operations between its agents and artifacts, can act as a system itself, such as for example a store or a bank). Actor-networks' structure is seen as constantly in the re-making and thus their nature is transient. It has a constructivist approach, avoiding simplistic explanations of events (such as for example explaining a successful event by saying it is "true" and the others are "false").

Methodologies for Ubicomp Systems Supporting EUD

Methodologies for the end users to be able to configure ubicomp systems based on artifacts are separated in methods, guidelines, tools, and interface elements that enable EUD, and in methods that enable the *system mechanisms* that support EUD (such as specific architectural styles, and the related principles and mechanisms, ontologies, and system schemas that it uses). Methods described here relate to the corresponding areas of the theoretical foundations that were outlined above.

End-User Development for Artifact Ecologies

EUD is defined as having two distinctive facets in this framework:

End-User Design: Signifies access, control, and the ability of customization of ubiquitous applications. It draws its influence from the experience and interaction design perspective.
End-User Programming: The software systems' design and implementation perspective of EUD. Possibilities are provided to completely alter applications or create new ones, by giving end users syntactic tools (such as a rules editor).
In the context of AmI applications, end-user design is at one side of the spectrum, while at the other side is end-user programming.

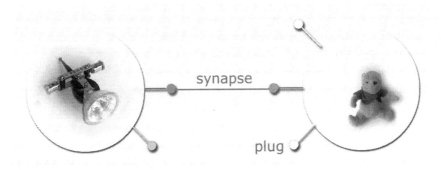

FIGURE 12.4 Programming publish–subscribe concepts provided for end users for an AmI EUD tool
Image courtesy of the artist/author

End-User Design

This term is used in order to refer to a significant step beyond the classic end-user customization, whereby the user becomes a designer, envisioning, planning, designing, and adapting his/her own ambient experience, empowered by shared knowledge facilitated via public application galleries. End-user design includes overview of active and running applications, manipulation functions such as the on/off switch (universal and per application), the customization and adaptation of given applications. It also includes the configuration of settings (by selecting options) in order to customize a given AmI application. This can be the most frequently used part, the easier to comprehend and manipulate by end users, and is defining the surface elements of the manifestation of the application rather than its core functionality. This concept also involves tools and mechanisms that support collaborative sharing for applications that can be semi-automatically adapted to another environment.

Multimodal interfaces can act complementarily in systems that support end-user design. Text-based scenarios and techniques from scenario-based development can help with application descriptions by end users. A cascading degree of complexity, from the interfaces of the end user design functions to more detailed end-user programming (e.g. rules editing), is suggested (Figures 12.4, 12.5, and 12.6).

FIGURE 12.5 Users involved in defining Ambient Intelligence Applications
Image courtesy of the artist/author

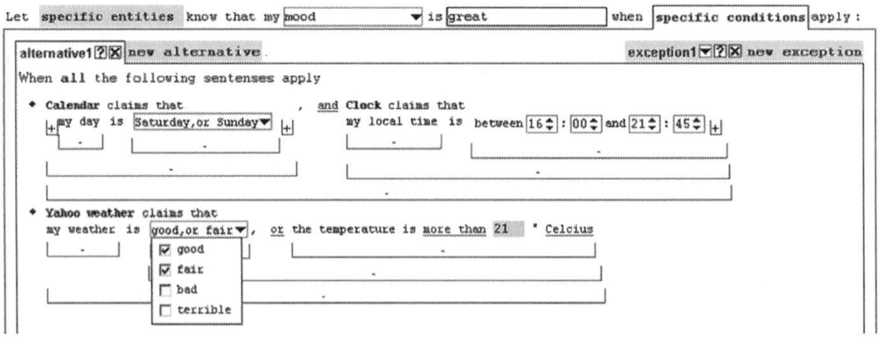

FIGURE 12.6 An expression editor employed to let the user set up an awareness application in an AmI Environment.
Image courtesy of G. Metaxas, Amelie System

Mental tools for reasoning on the end-user design of AmI applications can be provided (i.e., by visual representations or promoting mental models of the system that correspond to the functional models). Such mental constructs (Figure 12.4) assist users in gaining an understanding of the configurable components of the system, and the way they can be associated; it is an enabler to reason and assign functionality. Where mental models are not in place, easy and self-explanatory interfaces are needed; nevertheless due to the complexity involved in end-user development, and the subsequent difficulty to cater for all necessary functions with easy to use interfaces, we stress the need for straightforward and robust mental models that are very useful in the early days of this domain.

End-User Programming

A cascading view of editing complexity can start from the overview provided by end-user design and range to the manipulation of the specific connection rules and programming syntax. Multiple visuals for syntax methods can be tested for rule editing (i.e., Pipeline view, bubbles view, tree structure, grid; Figure 12.6). Provision of syntax can be coupled by automation or semi-automation techniques for rule editing.

Distributed IoT System Architecture

Artifacts get augmented by producing descriptions of their properties (what the object is), abilities (what the object knows how to do), and services (what the object can offer to others) accessible to users in the digital space, and by participating in broader group-compositions. They can enhance their functionality—they can be adaptive and context aware, or provide augmented or alternative use. Methods for collections of artifacts should be in place so that they can be configured to synergize their functions. Artifacts can thus publicize their abilities in digital space; they also acquire extra capabilities, which, during the formation of IoT applications, can be combined with capabilities of other augmented objects or adapted to the context of operation. These new characteristics of augmented objects need to be indicated to people.

The architectural framework of Gadgetware Architectural Style (GAS), described by Drossos, Goumopoulos, and Kameas (2007), is addressing the AmI/Ubicomp hardware and software required for end user-mediated coordination via EUD, and is extended in Goumopolous and Kameas (2009) to include sharing of awareness information in pervasive computing systems. This technological supporting framework is one that can allow for the end users to act as designers and developers, and as such is adopted as a concrete methodological framework regarding the software and hardware system design of AmI systems focused on EUD. Key elements that are adopted as related methodologies for system design are outlined below.

End-User Programming: Basic Definitions

The basic definitions adopted from GAS (Drossos et al. 2007) pertaining to the software and hardware ubiquitous system design are:

Artifacts: Tangible objects that can express their properties digitally. Artifacts can be augmented with sensors, actuators, processing, networking, etc., or a computational device that already has embedded some of the required hardware components. Software applications running on computational devices are also considered to be artifacts. Artifacts can be simple or composite, from a single sensor to an augmented building, from tagged objects to systems and infrastructure elements (i.e., sound system, central heating, etc.)

Properties: Representations of the physical characteristics, capabilities, and services provided by artifacts. Some properties are artifact-specific (such as the physical characteristics), while others may be not (i.e., services). Properties can be modeled as functions (either evaluating an artifact's state variable into a single value or triggering a reaction to an actuator artifact). Emergent properties are those that result from artifact compositions. All properties of an artifact are encapsulated in a property-schema that can be sent on request to other artifacts or tools (e.g., during artifact discovery).

Plugs: The digital constructs representing artifact properties. Plugs are defined by their direction and data type and are distinguished into Input plugs, Output plugs, and Input/Output Plugs. Plugs in this approach have a certain data type that can be semantically primitive (e.g., integer, Boolean, etc., relating to the syntactic level of programming), or semantically rich (e.g., image, sound, etc.—in general, services that can be used as output content streamable from actuator devices). Plugs are the constructs that make visible the artifacts' properties, capabilities, and services to people, agents, and other artifacts.

Synapses: Associations between two compatible plugs. When a property of a source artifact changes (a state transition of the source artifact causing change of value), the new value is propagated through the synapse to the target artifact, resulting in state transition at the target artifact(s). Synapses relate the functional schemas between artifacts, enabling the functional / context changes.

Artifact compositions: A collection of two or more artifacts' properties that can be combined (composed) for a meaningful purpose. AmI applications can usually be handled as service compositions. The act of composing artifacts into certain applications can be assisted by end user tools.

Functional schemas: An artifact is modeled in terms of a functional schema. Functions in a functional schema can be simple or complex according to what is required to define the property. Functional schemas can range from sensor readings to rule-based formulae (with multiple properties), to first-order logic (quantifying over sets of artifacts and properties).

State: A concept useful for reasoning about how things may change (there is no hidden internal state). The values for all property functions of an artifact at a given time are the state of the artifact.

Transformation: A transition from one state to another. Transformations are the results of internal events (such as the change in the state of a sensor) or they may result from changes in the artifact's functional context, happening via the synapses of the artifact.

Artifacts as Components

Publish-Subscribe methods can be accessible and understood by end users, when using concepts from the theory of affordances and effectivities (Gaver 1991; Gibson 1977). In this context, creation of applications is achieved by interconnecting affordances available in the environment, and accessing those at the artifacts' level, either physically or virtually so as to enable easier comprehension of the system's threads when needed to be unveiled by end users.

The approach taken as a starting point is that ubicomp environments consist of components that can be accessed as augmented artifacts, which use publish-subscribe methods for their communication. In the approach of Kameas and Mavrommati (2005), Mavrommati et al. (2004), and Drossos et al. (2007), augmented artifacts can be associated by people using the model of *Plugs* and *Synapses* occurring between them.

Plugs represent connectable "capabilities" (both physical/sensory and digital service). An artifact has physical properties, as a result of its tangible self, while it offers services, resulting from its digital self. They are software classes that make visible the artifacts' capabilities to people and to other artifacts. They can correspond to artifact affordances relating to the embedded sensors the artifact may have (e.g., containment, surface, pressure, temperature, etc.) or to services they may provide (light, sound, etc.).

A synapse (link) is an association between two compatible plugs. This is an invisible link explicitly created to achieve a particular working of the two capabilities together. Synapses can be formed by the intelligent environment but can also be accessed by external overview software in devices, acting as editors. Such an editor can be used to review artifacts and their collections and associate those (Mavrommati et al. 2004). By using the proposed abstractions of connectable Plugs and Synapses, one can combine the augmented objects and build new types of applications (functional groups of artifacts' associations) by connecting their connectable capabilities in synaptic associations, and then describing the properties of these associations.

Introduction of the idea of affordances (stemming from objects' physical disposition, sensors and perceived use) enriches the plug-synapse construct. Such affordances have the potential that they can be used via an ontology, which provides a second level of semantic interpretation of the physical characteristics. Thus the system abstractions of capability (i.e., "Plugs") and the ontology relate to the affordances that stem from the physical characteristics and perceived use of the object.

According to Norman (1990), affordances "refer to the perceived and actual properties of the thing, primarily those fundamental properties that determine just how the thing could possibly be used." Up to now, the ways that an object could be used and the tasks it could participate in have usually been determined by these physical affordances, that are, in turn, determined by its shape, material, and physical properties. By giving to the physical objects the possibility to act as components of an augmented environment, and to interconnect to form ubicomp applications, the objects acquire in fact new affordances, which are given to them via the augmented environment. The ways that we can use an object are a direct consequence of the anticipated uses "embedded" in its physical properties. This association is in fact bi-directional: each object is suitable for certain tasks, but it is also their physical properties that constrain the tasks it can be used for. These new characteristics of augmented objects need to be somehow indicated to people. One way to do this is via a special purpose software mechanism that can run in several interface modalities and devices. Such a mechanism/tool can be generally referred to as "Editor" (Figure 12.5).

Principles

Drossos et al. (2007) describe a conceptual framework for the system architecture of AmI systems that can be accessible to end users. The underlying principles, relating to artifacts are:

Self-representation: The artifact's physical properties (that are closely associated with the artifact itself) are available through digital representations.

Functional autonomy: Artifacts function independently—without pre-requiring other artifacts in order to function.

Composability: Artifacts can be used as building blocks of larger and more complex systems.
Changeability: Artifacts that have access to digital storage can change the digital services they offer (and thus change themselves).

The ways that an artifact can be used is usually determined by its affordances that stem from certain aspects of its characteristics (physical or digital). Affordances describe the perceived and actual properties of an artifact, that determine how the users will handle it and the tasks they will perform with it, depending on their own effectivities like experience and skill, or any disabilities they may have. Artifacts get augmented by producing descriptions of their properties, abilities, and services in the digital space, and by participating in broader group-compositions, they can enhance their functionality—they can be adaptive and context aware, or provide augmented or alternative functionality. Methods for collections of artifacts should be in place so that they can be configured to synergize in their functions.

Abstraction Levels

Three abstraction rules are established by the proposed system architecture, as in Drossos et al. (2007):

Network independence: The Plug/Synapse model is independent of the underlying protocols needed for example to route messages or to discover resources in realization of an application.
Physical independence: The services offered by an artifact are decoupled from the artifact itself. They are independent and can evolve, whereas its physical characteristics cannot be altered. Thus the creation of artifact compositions does not always require the continuous presence of an artifact.
Semantic independence: The description of applications (compositions of artifacts) is based on the types of the plugs that are associated, but is independent of how the plugs are realized within the artifacts.

Conclusions

In this chapter we described concepts, methodologies, and their relationships towards a framework for ubiquitous systems that foster end user-mediated coordination via EUD. We suggest that researchers should consider EUD as an inseparable element of ubiquitous computing systems, in the sense that ambient systems can provide the principle elements that enable people to perceive and handle ubiquitous applications. Affordances provide the implied use (affordances being the relationship that develops between objects and the tasks that can be performed with them) (Gibson 1977), which may or may not be realized; nevertheless the elements that can afford and effect it should be present in the ubiquitous system.

End-user tools, structures, and mechanisms are mediators for the development and co-evolution between ubiquitous artifacts, applications, environments, and people. EUD possibility can be affected by relevant system design that has included EUD elements and mental models for the user—which should be available to people even when the system is relying on agents and automations for realizing its ubiquitous functionality.

It is important to consider the system with a number of co-dependencies that it includes, from the different perspectives involved. An important split is to distinguish between end-user design (the more creative "designerly" aspects of humans, but also the ones that are based on more intuition and direct physical involvement, by subsequent observation and manipulation) and end-user programming (that pertains the more systematic, analytical, and syntactic mental tasks, which are facilitated by different abstractions and syntaxes, as seen fit per case of different users). The full functionality that is possible from the part of end-user programming may not be used by all users, or for complex applications cases, due to the cognitive load and the programming complexity involved. Nevertheless the possibility should be there, present and accessible to end users, whose culture and knowledge will co-evolve with ubiquitous systems in the future.

The perspective to be adopted in ubiquitous systems is that of co-evolution and co-development between people, EUD tools, and systems—primarily drawing from activity theory and ecological psychology. The ubiquitous system, its end-user tools, and people's perspectives on them are developing together and are cross-influenced in an iterative cycle, in the context of sociocultural developments. The conceptual and methodological framework developed in this direction should therefore be broader and multidisciplinary in its scope. This framework addresses the relationships between three broader perspectives: those of a) understanding human cognition, b) defining a wider spectrum of interaction-concepts and methods for people to access the EUD ubiquitous system, and c) understanding the system design of the ubiquitous system and how it can be constructed.

Expansion on the proposed framework structure and the concepts that it provides, and investigation into the issues that still remain open can provide valuable insight and guidance to the broader foundations of ubicomp systems of the future, used by people and augmented human environments. Ubiquitous computing researchers need to develop umbrella frameworks, which can serve as the basis of integration of more detailed sub-frameworks (theoretical and methodological) from each of the three perspectives, while items that remain open can be addressed and outcomes of future research can be added.

References

Bannon, L. 1997. *Activity Theory*. http://irit.fr/ACTIVITES/GRIC/cotcos/pjs/TheoreticalApproaches/Actvity/ActivitypaperBannon.htm.

Bannon, L., and S. Bødker. 1991. "Beyond the Interface: Encountering Artifacts in Use." In *Designing Interaction: Psychology at the Human-Computer Interface*, edited by J. M. Carroll, 227–253. New York: Cambridge University Press.

Brown, J. S., A. Collins, and P. Duguid. 1989. "Situated Cognition and the Culture of Learning." *Educational Researcher* 18 (1): 32–42.

Carroll, J. 2000. *Making Use: Scenario Based Design of Human Computer Interactions*. Cambridge, MA: MIT Press.

Carroll, J., and M. B. Rosson. 2003. "Design Rationale as Theory." In *HCI Models, Theories, and Frameworks: Toward a Multidisciplinary Science*, edited by J. M. Carroll, 432–460. Burlington, MA: Morgan Kaufmann.

Drossos, N., C. Goumopoulos, and A. Kameas. 2007. "A Conceptual Model and the Supporting Middleware for Composing Ubiquitous Computing Applications." *Journal of Ubiquitous Computing and Intelligence*, special issue on Ubiquitous Intelligence in Real Worlds. 1: 1–13.

Feenberg, A. 1992. "Subversive Rationalization: Technology, Power, and Democracy." *Inquiry* 35 (3): 301–322.

Fischer, G., and E. Giaccardi. 2006. "Meta-design: A Framework for the Future of End-User Development." In *End User Development*, edited by H. Lieberman, F. Paternò and V. Wulf, 427–457. Berlin: Springer.

Gaver, W. 1991. "Technology Affordances." In *Proceedings of CHI 1991*, 79–84. New York: ACM Press.

Gibson, J. 1986. *The Ecological Approach to Visual Perception*. New York: Lawrence Erlbaum Associates.

Gibson, J. J. 1977. "The Theory of Affordances." In *Perceiving, Acting, and Knowing: Toward an Ecological Psychology*, edited by R. Shaw and J. Bransford, 67–82. Hillsdale, NJ: Lawrence Erlbaum.

Greeno, J. G., and J. L. Moore. 1993. "Situativity and Symbols: Response to Vera and Simon." *Cognitive Science* 17: 49–60.

Greeno, J. G. 1994. "Gibson's Affordances." *Psychological Review* 101 (2): 336–342.

Gross, T., and N. Marquardt. 2007. "Collaboration Bus: An Editor for the Easy Configuration of Ubiquitous Computing Environments." *15th Euromicro International Conference on Parallel, Distributed and Network-Based Processing (PDP'07)*, 307–314. Available at: http://nicolaimarquardt.com/research-documents/CollaborationBus_TechnicalReport.pd.

Hollan, J., E. Hutchins, and D. Kirsh. 2000. "Distributed Cognition: Toward a New Foundation for Human-Computer Interaction Research." *ACM Transactions on Computer–Human Interaction* 7 (2): 174–196.

Hutchins, E. 1995. *Cognition in the Wild*. Cambridge, MA: MIT Press.

Kameas, A., and I. Mavrommati. 2005. "Configuring the E-gadgets." *Communications of the ACM* (CACM), special issue section on The Disappearing Computer. 48 (3): 69.

Kaptelinin, V. 1996. "Activity Theory: Implications for Human-Computer Interaction." In *Context and Consciousness: Activity Theory and Human-Computer Interaction*, edited by B. Nardi. Cambridge, MA: MIT Press. Excerpt online at: http://quasar.ualberta.ca/edpy597mappin/readings/m15_kaptelin.htm.

Kaptelinin, V., and B. Nardi. 1997. "Activity Theory: Basic Concepts and Applications." In *CHI '97 Extended Abstracts on Human Factors in Computing Systems: Looking to the Future*, 158–159. New York: ACM.

Klann, M., F. Paterno, and W. Wulf. 2006. "Future Perspectives in EUD." In *End User Development*, edited by H. Lieberman, F. Paternò, and V. Wulf, 475–486. Berlin: Springer.

Mavrommati, I., A. Kameas, and P. Markopoulos. 2004. "An Editing Tool that Manages the Devices Associations." *Personal and Ubiquitous Computing* 8 (3–4): 255–263.

Newman, M., J. Sedivy, C. M. Neuwirth, W. K. Edwards, J. I. Hong, S. Izadi, K. Marcelo, and T. F. Smith. 2002. "Designing for Serendipity: Supporting End-User Configuration of Ubiquitous Computing Environments." *ACM SIGCHI DIS2002*, 147–156. New York: ACM.

Norman, D. A. 1990. *The Psychology of Everyday Things*. New York: Doubleday.

Papert, S. 1986. *Constructionism: A New Opportunity for Elementary Science Education. A Proposal to the National Science Foundation*. Cambridge, MA: MIT.

Rodden, T., and S. Benford. 2003. "The Evolution of Buildings and Implications for the Design of Ubiquitous Domestic Environments." In *Proceedings of the CHI 2003*. Florida, USA.

Vygotsky, L. S. 1978. *Mind in Society: The Development of Higher Psychological Processes*. Cambridge, MA: Harvard University Press.

Weiser, M. 1991. "The Computer for the Twenty-first Century." *Scientific American* 265 (3): 94–104.

Winkielman, P., P. M. Niedenthal, and L. M. Oberman. 2009. "Embodied Perspective on Emotion-Cognition Interactions." In *Mirror Neuron Systems*, edited by J. A. Pineda, 235–257. New York: Humana Press.

AMBIENT LITERATURE: WRITING PROBABILITY

Jonathan Dovey

> The living embodies the ambiguous record of the change of the world in which it unfolds.
> This is the narration of the living.
>
> (Nadin 2013, 46)

In Media Res

A cool autumn evening in late September 2009, I am standing leaning on a bicycle in the busy centre of my hometown, Bristol, as dusk falls and the evening lights switch on. I am listening through headphones to an audio recording of a father and son discussing their location. The recording was made by them a day or two before and linked to this location. I have "discovered" it by cycling about looking for the flags that come up on the handheld screen attached to the handlebars of the bike. The recording is inconsequential chitchat, yet I become overwhelmed with a huge sadness, shedding tears. There in the midst of the evening commuter bustle, isolated in headphones I find myself accessing grief I did not know I had. At the time my own father was, I realized, dying, while my own son was flying the nest.

This moment was produced by Blast Theory's piece, *Rider Spoke*, in which participants are given a bicycle with a pair of headphones and a Global Positioning System (GPS) device. The soundtrack invites riders to find a special place in the city, asks us to decide who we want to be in this experience, to rename ourselves. We are then prompted to recall memories: "Remember a time where you last held hands, go there, record and locate a memory for other riders to discover. Cycling through the streets your focus is outward, looking for good places to hide, speculating about the hiding places of others, becoming completely immersed into this overlaid world as the voices of strangers draw you into a new and unknown place" (Arnolofini). The voice in *Rider Spoke* is a carefully written invitation to participate, a call to action that orchestrates a gentle Rogerian questioning. The probing questions, the moment of isolation within the urban, the experience of eavesdropping on the confessions of others, all produce an encounter that has the potential to open up the participant to new insights and experiences.

Living Inside the Web

Data flow now complements human traffic and the flow of goods in and around our cities. These systems are large scale, city wide, national, and global; they are dynamic, responding to what people do; they integrate embodied and imaginary experiences, material, and mediating objects. In short, they begin to become complex systems, which increase our opportunities for new forms of reading and listening experience.

This chapter explores what might happen when data aspires to literary form. It asks how can situated literary experiences delivered through pervasive media systems produce moments where the individual reader or listener is repositioned and offered new ways to experience and understand their moment within the complexity of the urban informatic flow?

This chapter draws on my research in a working community of creative technologists working with pervasive media platforms since 2002 (Dovey and Fleuriot 2012). In particular, its insights are indebted to the work of the artist Duncan Speakman (and his company, Circumstance). As well as drawing on the literature of pervasive and ubiquitous arts and on literary sources, the second half of this chapter is based on a research interview with Speakman and his collaborator, Tom Abba. Their approaches have significantly influenced my conclusions. The chapter locates itself within a field of work on "locative narrative" (Hight 2010), building on McCullough's work in urban information systems to consider the situated and the ambient as co-constituting particular aesthetic experiences (McCullough, *Ambient Commons*). It turns to examples of conventional psycho geographic literature of place (WG Sebald and Teju Cole) to consider what kinds of literary forms are being remediated in pervasive media systems, before turning to the particular case of *These Pages Fall Like Ash* produced by Circumstance in 2013. I then draw on the work of Bateson and Nadin to argue that what I am proposing as the field of ambient literature is an example of designing for probability, as a response to the disorganized complexity of human, urban, and data networks. (Bateson 1972; Nadin 2013) Ambient aesthetics here are understood as grounded in emergence, potential, and ambiguity as a means to produce encounters between humans and the complex systems to which they are subject.

Post Locative But Still Situated

We are entering a new phase of pervasive computing, where its daily presence becomes banal. For most citizens this might mean a taken-for-granted reliance on Geographic Information System (GIS) systems in the form of Satnav in vehicles or Google maps on handheld devices. Rowen Wilken argues that since the advent of Google Maps open Application Program Interface (API) and the iPhone in the 2005–2009 period, the promise of the locative has been delivered: "Both developments . . . have had a profound impact in fostering the democratization of and opening of access to, geolocation services and associated infrastructure" (Wilken 2012). These services and infrastructures include the invisible systems of tracking, sensing, and actuating technologies that constitute urban traffic flows, global flight control, military defense systems, and many types of supply chain including for instance food and medicine. Here locative systems are also part of bigger ubiquitous computing and IoT systems. However these infrastructures are dominated by the computer sciences' definition of context, that is to say how a device knows where it is, its direction of travel, temperature, etc. As Ulrik Ekman observes: "The developers and users of ubicomp have so far tended to grant a certain primacy to the physical environment and a rather empirical notion of 'context.' This focus still in the main ignores or parenthesizes the human users and their context awareness" (Ekman 2013, 42). Although the examples I want to discuss in this chapter are concerned with space and place, they are hard to tie down under the "locative" banner. Here I build on previous work (Dovey and Fleuriot 2012), which argued that artists and artisanal projects in the field of ubiquitous computing made use of a very wide range of sensor/actuator technologies to deliver media experiences. These assemblages used GPS but also Quick Response (QR) codes, Radio Frequency Identification (RFID), accelerometers, cameras, and movement sensors as input channels. The number of possible touch points between user, system, and meaning is proliferating. In his discussion of the definition of the "ambient" Ulrik Schmidt observes: ". . . ambience is the distinctive *effect* characterized by an *intensification of being surrounded*" (Schmidt 2013, 176; author's italics). One response to the complexity of the information systems we increasingly inhabit might be a renewed insistence on the importance of using them for meaningful experiences:

> . . . urban computing isn't simply about the city. It's also part of the city, and its meaning and consequences arise not simply as informational accounts of urban space (directories, maps, listings, and so on) but as sites for new sorts of individual and collective meaning-making. In a word, urban computing is situated rather than dislocated. Framing the city as a source of experience rather than a source of trouble raises the design question: How are information technologies implicated in the aesthetics of everyday practice?
>
> (Bassoli et al. 2007)

The distinction above between situated and dislocated is central to my argument.

However I want rather to look at some of the history and practice of situated literary practice that offer us "new sorts of individual and collective meaning making" (Bassoli et al. 2007, 44).

Attention and Ambience

This repositioning is part of a creative and critical approach to the politics of attention. The world of information overload and attention scarcity produces distraction as social malaise and attention as its answer: "In an era of changing planetary circumstances, personal attention to immediate surroundings seems like a manageable first step toward some huge cultural shift." (McCullough 2013, 13)

In his consideration of this manageable first step, McCullough (2013) turns to the category of the ambient as a way to start to think about the modality of information in the urban environment. Here ambient begins to take on more of a sense of the situated, where something akin to an atmosphere is brought into focus, rather than existing merely as background as in "ambient music" or "ambient light." Schmidt's analysis of the ambient argues by contrast that while "there is a close relation between ambience and ubiquity in the sense that ambient fields are experienced as 'total fields' all over and ubiquitous," the ambient event should unfold in a way that preserves background and foreground in constant balance, in a decentered "flat" field (Schmidt 2013, 177). Here the idea that ambient experience can "close in on itself as a distinguished moment and potentially become a focal point, a climax, within a longer span of time" is understood as a problem, a failure of the ambient aesthetic (Ibid. 178). The evidence I want to explore here however argues *precisely the opposite*, that the creative direction of the mise-en-scène of the everyday should be exactly concerned with producing moments of attention that focus the subject in their surroundings. Rather I want to explore what McCullough states is his key question: ". . . do increasingly situated information technologies illuminate the world, or do they just eclipse it?" (McCullough, 20). I want to argue for a poetics alert to embodiment, textuality, sonics, and technology that enhances awareness and understanding of the intrinsic phenomena of the world that we share.

Ambient Literature

There is already some research emerging from locative media studies (Gordon and de Souza e Silva 2011) that combines with narrative and literary theory to produce the research field for situated literary experience (Farman 2014). De Souza e Silva and Sutko argued as long ago as 2008 that mobiles can be used to connect people with their environments not immerse them in the device itself at the expense of their embodied presence, in relation to Alternate Reality Game (ARG) and Pervasive Gaming (de Souza e Silva and Sutko 2008). Jeremy Hight coined the term "locative narrative" to describe the way material and virtual reading could be combined to produce literatures that are "experientially driven literally and figuratively as a person moves through space on Earth" (Hight 2010). What is missing, however, is a more specific attention to the literary in these accounts. "Content" may be understood as data, media, narrative, but is rarely understood as story, poetry, or drama, the genres that have the self-conscious force of the literary. Indeed the role of the writer that has been under represented as "content" has become the word for the meaning making functions of digital delivery platforms. This is significant because it has to do with how newly emergent forms become adopted. Writers, poets, and dramatists could be forgiven for not recognizing themselves in a field dominated by instrumental information systems designed to manage environments to maximum efficiency. So far, the field of locative narrative has been constructed as an experimental space beyond the mainstream of cultural experience, circulating around the gallery, media art, and heritage circuits. The publishing industries are only now beginning to become alert to how these forms might scale.

My interest at this point is aesthetic rather than sociological; I am interested in what moves us rather than what informs us. Many of the most powerful mediated experiences I have had in the past fifteen years have been delivered using situated text and music; I have been terrified, delighted, and disturbed. I have danced with strangers, stood crying alone in the middle of town, and re-inscribed my city with a lattice of associative memories. Understanding these experiences requires an engagement with form; with the emerging techniques that give writing, composition, and dramaturgy their place in making sense of the complexity of urban experience. In considering for instance the specific qualities of a Janet Cardiff and Georges Bures Miller Audio Walk, Teri Rueb's work, some of the work of Blast Theory (e.g., *Uncle Roy all Around You* and *Rider Spoke*) and, most significant for me, the development of Duncan Speakman's work, I argue that we can identify techniques, rhetoric, and effects that could constitute a poetics of urban informatics.

Situating Literatures

Before returning to some of the text/audio experiences mentioned earlier, I want to establish them as part of a literary rather than techno social history. This tactical repositioning is intended to emphasize not technological novelty but continuity with the literary forms of place, which might offer some original resources for understanding the modes of attention afforded by the kinds of situated literary practices referred to above.

The first objection that might be raised to the idea of the "situated literary experience" is that all literary experiences have always been situated, while the reader's attention and imagination might be absorbed in the world of the book the reader's body will be stubbornly in the world. While the visual sense is fully engaged with the page, there is always the "risk" of auditory distraction, hence the design and social construction of the library as a space designed to minimize distraction and maximize concentration. This mode of absorbed concentration has become a dominant frame for understanding the book. In his writing on "Private Reading," Alberto Manguel devotes several pages to the solitary pleasures of reading in bed, where the immersive attention conditions of the library are reproduced in a different form (Manguel 1996). However, he also acknowledges,

> ... there is no doubt that the act of reading in time requires a corresponding act of reading in place, and the relationship between the two acts is inextricable. There are books I read in armchairs, and there are books I read at desks; there are books I read in subways, on streetcars, and on buses.
>
> (Manguel 1996, 151)

The development of travel, urbanity, and mobility through the nineteenth and early twentieth centuries produced a mobile reading market supplied in the U.K. for instance by the WH Smith bookstall chain (1792) and later by the Penguin imprint for the easily affordable but literary, pocket sized paperback (1935). Texts and reading practices have been an increasingly dense feature of urban life for the past three hundred years. The "solitary reading" paradigm of the private collection or university library is actually a comparatively minor part of the history of reading. Coffee houses, newspapers, handbills, fly posters, letters, and signage have all been part of the daily experience of the city.

In this context, we can start to rethink the idea of the situated literary experience. Reading (or listening to literary performance) has always been "situated" in the sense that it is an embodied practice, habituated to a very fluid range of tools and contexts. In an essay called *You Are There*, Anne Fadiman wrote about the pleasures of reading literary fiction and travel literature in situ: "The consummate You-Are-There experience requires us to see *exactly* what the author described, so that all we need to do to cross the eidetic threshold is to squint a little" (Fadiman 1998). We have extended this range in the past thirty years, first with the Walkman (and the potential not only for mobile music but also for literary text to be delivered on the move), and now with portable screens (plus audio) extending this range of tools once more. Experiences of text interweave themselves into our daily lives with a bewildering promiscuity. Despite the dominance of the solitary reading model, the city has always been a text-mediated experience. Since 2012, these literary modes have been available in the seamless continuity of Amazon's Whisper sync Kindle service that makes it possible for the user to switch between text reading and voice narration in over 45,000 titles that have now been recorded.

Psychogeographic Tropes

Before we turn to a specific example of a technologically enabled situated literature, I want to spend a short time looking elsewhere, over the fence as it were, at the literary field of place-based writing. These examples serve to emphasize that reading and writing the complexity of city has been a key figure of modernism with a history of poetics available for Ambient Literary practices. The research literature arising from the first wave of locative media commonly claimed the experience as the technological embodiment of the flâneur (Barber 2014), with the potential to afford a Situationist derive (Levine 2014), frequently understood as a tactic in a de Certeau inspired reclamation of space (Koefoed Hansen 2014). In thinking about what modalities of writing have seemed most successful in my own experience of place-based work, I want to turn to some complementary examples from the literature of psychogeography. I draw on passages from two examples, WG Sebald's *Austerlitz* and Teju Cole's *Open City*.

Austerlitz is an account of the wandering life of Jacques Austerlitz, a disconsolate, disconnected academic met by chance in Belgium by the unnamed narrator who reports the biography as told to him in fragmented encounters over half a century. At the dramatic heart of the novel is a passage that describes how Austerlitz, descending into breakdown, is losing himself in long nocturnal walks across London. He is a lost soul, randomly crisscrossing the city in vast aimless loops troubled by incorporeal images. He recounts how he was repeatedly drawn back to Liverpool St Station, to the chaotic flow of bodies in its "eternal dusk." He finds himself gripped by the "wrenching vortex of the past;" the station imbued with is history, as marshland, as Priory and as site of the original Bedlam:

> I often wondered if the pain and suffering accumulated on this site had ever ebbed away, or whether thy might not still, as I sometimes thought when I felt a cold breath of air on my forehead, be sensed as we pass through them on our way through the station.
>
> (Sebald 2001, 183)

One morning he finds himself guided by a cleaner to a long disused "Ladies Waiting Room" where a dark, hallucinatory experience unfolds: "I felt as if the room where I stood was expanding, going on for ever and ever in an improbably foreshortened perspective" (Sebald 2001, 191). He continues, ". . . the waiting room where I stood as if dazzled contained all the hours of my past life, all the suppressed and extinguished fears and wishes I had ever entertained . . ." (Sebald 2001, 192).

In fact what is happening is his recognition of a key repressed memory; the moment when as a four-year-old holocaust refugee in 1939 he meets his new adoptive parents for the first time, an episode that has been entirely forgotten for more than fifty years. The whole hallucinatory episode in the Station comes to a focus in Austerlitz's discovery:

> I became aware, through my dull bemusement, of the destructive effect on me of my desolation through all these past years, and a terrible weariness overcame me at the idea that I had never really been alive, or was only now being born, almost on the eve of my death.
>
> (Sebald 2001, 192)

This is a prototypical example of a kind of writing that is the literary complement to the developing range of ubiquity effects. It becomes a kind of urban phantasmagoria of place, with memories, hauntings, architectural, cultural, and social histories all focusing on Austerlitz's rediscovery of his own holocaust origins. His encounter with the material history of place brings him to a new sense of self. The literary technique produces from the chaotic swirl of the twentieth century and the complex "tides" of people in the city a focal point at which the narrator can be reborn.

Chapter 13 of Teju Cole's *Open City* achieves a different effect. A novel of peregrination and vagary, this section begins with the narrator, a Nigerian psychiatrist practicing in New York, experiencing what we might understand as a "glitch" in the system of urban life by forgetting his pin number at an ATM. He becomes obsessed and anxious at this "unsuspected fragility in myself," and later, after seeing his Wall Street accountant, goes down to Battery

Park hoping to find calm in his customary city explorations. Like Austerlitz he begins to recall the history of the area, how in the first half of the nineteenth century it had been at the epicentre of the nation's burgeoning capitalism, partly through the city's profits from slaving, which continued long after slaving became illegal after the Abolition of 1820. He recounts how the city accumulated great wealth from the building, outfitting, and insuring of slave ships and that these very profits were the foundation for City Bank, AT&T, and Con Edison—some of the biggest brands on Wall Street. He wanders past the Bowling Green remembering how it "had been used in the seventeenth century for the executions of paupers and slaves" (Cole 2011, 164). He recalls watching Chinese dancers and being drawn to the sound of musicians playing the erhu, (the two string Chinese violin): "The song, the clear day, and the elms; it could have been any day from the past fifteen hundred years" (Cole 2011, 16).

His mind then veers sharply to his underlying mood, dwelling on the recent suicide of one of his patients, an academic called only "V," for whom he feels guilt and responsibility. V studied the transatlantic slave trade; her obituary claimed that "she wrote of atrocity without flinching," and yet the narrator knows she paid the price. The music of the erhu seemed "to summon to my mind's eye the long ago spirits that V had been so concerned to honor in her work" (Cole 2011, 165).

Open City withholds resolution; no connections are offered between the day's events. We are left with the narrator's memory, "Of standing alone, in Wall Street, my memory gone, a pathetic old-young man padding about in the grip of some nervousness, while all around me the smart set made deals, talked on cell phones, and adjusted their cufflinks" (Cole 2011, 166). These apparently random events of a New York afternoon become a meditation on forgetting. The complexity of the city is here expressed through the flow of memories, individual and cultural, as well as its momentary impressions. The passage is a fictionalized act of remembrance that enacts the operation of cultural memory especially as an unending series of aporias and erasures.

Both these passages construct an intense sense of the subject in the city; we experience cosmopolitan spaces and rhythms through their perceptions. Both passages use circumstantial material detail to ground the prose; we are looking at the narrators' worlds through their eyes. Both passages use walking as the core action, a derive that produces temporary moments of coalescence where the swirl of narrators' attention settles into new meaning. A mise-en-scène is palpable, material details of place become the focal points that mark the character exposition. Through using history (holocaust and slave trade), the subject is placed in time as well as space, and we are reminded that the city is a dynamic constantly changing construction. When we move to thinking about situated literary experiences, these tropes are translated into platforms where the narrator becomes *you*. The use of locative and pervasive technique puts the reader/listener inside the flow of the urban system.

Leaving Space for the World to Happen

These Pages Fall Like Ash was advertised as a public shared reading experience, over a fixed time period for which 200 people bought £12.00 tickets. Two hundred copies of a book, with a wooden cover, were sent to the participants. The desirability of the physical text object was a key feature of the project design and one of its main marketing successes. The book also contained an envelope with a series of locations and dates. On arrival at a location, participants could connect to a Wi-Fi network that would release episodes of the story, made available in three chapters and five locations over eighteen days. Readers would be taken on a journey to different areas in the city discovering different content as they returned at different times, a spatialized serialization. This story is of a relationship between characters inhabiting the same places, but as it were, in different dimensions of time and space.

> The story is about a moment when two cities overlap. They exist in the same space and time, but they aren't aware of each other. It's a tale about two people who have become separated, one in each world, about their fading memory of each other and their struggle to reconnect. One of the cities is your own; you become part of a narrative as you travel from place to place. Your version of the story becomes about you and your place in your own city, about what you would hold on to about what you would fight to remember.
>
> (Abba and Speakman)

The wooden book contains two printed booklets, one of fragments pertaining to a city subject to endless flood and dissolution, an eco-fiction about the permanent "struggle against the pervasive force of a single element." The other is a book that invites the readers' own observations of historical detail in the actual city and offers prompts for experiential note taking of one's own:

> This book is yours
> and much of it is blank, waiting to be written
> You can think of it as a representation of
> the city you live in
> It can become a map, a guide, or just a notebook
> It can be a way to help you remember,
> A way to help you measure and record the
> Things you value, it can even be a way of creating a universe
> It may make suggestions, but it will not tell you
> What to put on the pages
> And it will not judge you when you do (3).

As far as a user guide goes, a brief comparison of the language here with a conventional user guide serves to underline what this techno literary address to complexity and emergence consists of. A conventional user guide (for a piece of software or equipment) is precisely aimed at giving the user a means to control the object through a series of instrumental instructions, if you perform this operation you can predictably assume the same result each time. This will remain true however complicated the software or equipment. Here however, the language is entirely conditional, an invitation to experience what emerges from the contingent circumstance of the users' moment. It is "Blank waiting," "You *can* think of it as a representation," "It *can* become a map," "It *can* be a way to help you remember," "It *may* make suggestions." Rather than the instrumental grid of a GIS mapping software reducing the complexity of street level experience to a series of markers here is an approach that while authored is open to what emerges afresh in every user experience.

The aim of *These Pages Fall Like Ash* was to investigate the relationships between the physical and geo located forms of the story. It is part of a series of works that Speakman has been producing for fifteen years that investigate place, mediation, and attention. In particular Speakman has developed a range of strategies for taking the forms of the sound walk and what

Hewlett Packard pioneered as the geo located "mediascape" and making them specific but portable, that is, working with any given urban setting without being tied to one location (Hull et al. 2004). His 2007 piece, for instance, "Always Something Somewhere Else," asks the user to find a tree, then a memorable stone, then water; these locations are then tagged and recalled by the GPS system so that the listener inscribes his or her own mapped narrative onto the city. More recently, the curated collection *Short Films for You* (2012) circulated in a handsome box containing a book, an MP3 player and pair of headphones. Each of the audio stories asked the user to find a location, for instance a railway station where we are asked to observe "a man drinking, reading a newspaper" before starting to listen to the story that unfolded with a generic "railway station" as its setting.

These Pages is typical of what I take to be a significant stage in the development of ubiquity effects, the struggle for a genuinely mixed reality. This is not a "game layer" nor an augmentation but a piece in which the physical book and the Wi-Fi texts are conceived as co-constitutive, just as the precise mix of "being in *this* world" and "imagining *a* world" produces the effect of a situated literary experience:

> the fiction is in a café in this other city. So it doesn't matter that that café in the other city isn't the same as the café you're in, it's just that it is a café. The same things happen, people go in there, they buy coffee, they sit down, and they hang out. You pick a café in your city, you say, "This is my café." It then keeps that as a GPS location and then the following episodes are released, but you have to go back to the café to read them. So it's still tied in terms of site, but you've chosen the sites and we release the episodes regularly but it forces you to go back. Then it asks you, "Now for the next chapter you need to find a vantage point."[1]

Once potential sites have been established that make the work repeatable in different cities, the authors then turn to giving those sites "traction" in the text. Here the writing techniques echo some of the work of Sebald and Cole examined above, where the attention of the reader moves back and forth between the inner world of the narrator and the external world of the city. Here particular details of location are picked out that direct the readers' attention to their surroundings connecting the narrated world of the page or soundtrack to the embodied world of the reader. Speakman and Abba describe discovering and planting "hooks" where there could be a reasonable expectation of a continuity of perceptual field between text and world:

> So what we keep talking about was this notion of leaving hooks in the text that stay with you when you look up from the page . . . One of the really clear examples for us when we were sketching it was we wrote a little piece about how the character in it . . . was with her kid and the kid was drawing and she was noticing the marks that the kid was making on the wall and she started looking at all the marks on the wall as she walked along, full stop. That's where you stop reading the text and that's where you walk to the next location. The idea was that each section would have a hook like this, so that then as you walk you'd start noticing this. . . . I think we had a lot of those in there, . . . we had lots of moments of that in all these pieces and that was, for me, the only way we could really deal with making the text situated.
>
> (Ibid.)

The city with its increasingly embedded urban informatics is a complex system. However complex systems are not random; they have ordered and predictable elements that produce emergent and unforeseen elements. Cities are places of common spaces, railway stations, ATMs, bus stops, hospitals, palaces, prisons, and universities. These common nodes in the network of any major city offer a way to think about the first problem of the "situated." How can the text be about a particular place yet also work away from that specific context? There is no future for a literature that is not portable, like the book. But these generic places, schools, town halls, markets, and malls offer a way for the text to have an ambient relation to the place of the reader as well as offering the space for the emergent experience that is at the heart of the potential for context-related cultural practices.

Speakman's approach to producing such moments of coalescence in the face of chaotic cities and their layered histories is to "frame" events in the textual equivalent of the wide shot. A long take with a locked off wide frame that insists the viewer takes in the full range of available information,

> With Circumstance stuff in general, we've always said . . . we try and leave space for the world to happen . . . we've always designed for emergent things, by saying, "*Well here's our frame and the frame is fixed and what you see, experience, hear, feel within that frame just becomes part of the work, whatever it is. It doesn't matter what it is.*"
>
> (Ibid.; my italics)

The way to deal with emergence is to offer a frame for the experience, a frame structured in time and narration that offers the potential for the user to have a particular kind of encounter with the world around her. In this sense, the frame authored by the artist is always a reductionist strategy for dealing with a complex reality. It says look at, listen to, experience *this particular* place in the urban landscape. However, this framing is not in the representational register of cinema where we are usually to understand how the specific pro filmic event has a symbolic relation to our shared world; here the framing is to offer the reader or listener a point of view from which to experience the life of the city unfolding.

It is becoming clear that the cultural forms of context aware systems demand a very broad approach to experience design. The transmedial narrative, the ARG, the pervasive game, and now, I propose, ambient literature, all need attention to the flow of the user experience (UX) in a way that goes beyond conventional "UX." These emerging forms all need real-world testing, iteration, and balancing between elements of text, technology, world, and user behavior. Testing explores the boundary between the work, the user and the world in order that the predictable elements of the overall system can be appropriately exploited and the unpredictable elements of the system can be appropriately managed.

Writing for Probability

In all three cases, Sebald, Cole, and Circumstance have used the resources of the city as a way of staging an encounter between the subject and his or her place in time and space. These encounters are narrated in such a way as to construct a momentary point of focus, a coming together of the multiple elements of urban experience that offers us a new perspective. The visual, sonic, social, and historic resources of the urban become the elements of a live and emergent mise-en-scène. In each case, there are specific techniques of narration, including hallucination, memory, history, the hidden city, hooks, and frames, which produce the particular kind of encounter that remake our place in the world. (There are also, it should be noted, differences between third and second person narration that are important ways to distinguish between the literary and the immersive and interactive.)

To consider this work systemically, we may imagine that there are (to be reductive) notably three systems in play that produce the encounter.

The city is a complex system, which has common settings, consistently occurring spaces and predictable behaviors. However, this system also produces an infinite number of emergent behaviors on a minute-by-minute basis, behaviors that are unpredictable in their specificity. A collision-causing wrong turn on an urban freeway can slow down and block traffic flow for a whole city, resulting in cancelled appointments, failed student examinations, postponed surgery, or missed marriages.

Second, we can consider the human subject experiencing the artwork as a complex system on its own. Appearing at the event through constituting networks of cultural capital and marketing, arriving in all kinds of physical states with running noses, drunk, or in love; each with hugely different memories, identities, tastes, and technicities. Each subject is a complex, conscious organism.

Third, the techno-assemblage of the delivery platform itself, in this case a physical book, with notebook and pencil as well as printed words on its pages; a tablet, phone, or laptop connecting to the locally built Wi-Fi mesh at each of the story's locations. The connected device itself is a complicated though not necessarily complex device. It is significant that Abba and Speakman chose locally constructed Wi-Fi meshes rather than other forms of connectivity that would have the potential to be connected to the Internet. They chose in this instance to isolate their platform from the complexity of the Internet. The "dead drops" tech platform for *These Pages Fall Like Ash* is secreted within the city, rather than an externally imposed system grid such as those produced by GPS systems that reduce the city to a set of coordinates.

The challenge for the artist working with ambience is to respond to these three dynamic systems in a way that produces a *meaningful* encounter that might take the form of a feeling, a perception, an understanding, perhaps a new awareness of self. While the encounter cannot be reduced to a prescription, I do want to argue that the ambient artist has the potential to orchestrate experiences of the subjects' time and place within these overlapping and interacting systems. Bateson argued that the human subject exists in a state of dynamic feedback produced by the interactions of the three systems of social, mental, and environmental ecologies (Bateson 1972, 440). For Bateson, the problem of human subjectivity was our inability to step outside of our own mental ecology to understand our systemic natures or impacts. Wisdom, he suggested, is understanding the impact one has on the systems that constitute us. The successful ambient artwork can afford us something of this experience, offering a sense of how we are part of complex dynamic systems. While these works may deploy the instrumental systems of urban informatics, they are anything but reductively instrumental experiences. The success of the ambient art encounter depends on time, change, and ambiguity.

All the systems that produce the encounter are dynamic: the city scene, the technocultural assemblage, the human subject—all these are always in flux. There is no ubiquitous computing system that could reduce this dynamism to a predictable set of "operations." A counter-strategy is developed by the ambient artist who choreographs a tentative encounter between systematic elements, which produces experience as form. Part of the pleasure in the form is that it is a response to dynamic systems, by its nature ephemeral. The experience is fleeting, contingent on the changing mise-en-scène. Whereas representational art forms have offered us an experience of stasis, events captured in time forever (and therefore out of time), the experiences at hand here puts the reader/listener into time, we become as parts of the flow and change of the dynamic systems.

What is the relationship between the three systems I have identified at play in *These Pages Fall Like Ash*? Are we to identify reducible hierarchical arrangements of components, so that the ambient artwork is to be understood as having structures that make it predictable rather than emergent? (Simon). Of the three systems I have identified the text platform, with its use of programmes that connect portable device to dead drop data units via Bluetooth or Wi-Fi, could clearly be read as a system of predictable communication and control routines. However, the text in the book invites unpredictable user participation. The narrative elements delivered to mobile reading devices are poetic rather than analytic or informational. We know from literary reception studies that such texts may produce a wide variety of interpretative outcomes and meanings for different readers. The computing platform may to some extent be hierarchical, but its meaning is ambiguous.

The city can be understood as a vast effort to achieve a system of organized complexity (Weaver 1948), characterized by patterns from many different constituent systems. Planners, infrastructure managers, property developers, educationalists, and public health administrators all work on data based methodologies that seek to make the city predictable, knowable, and manageable, increasingly in real time (de Waal 2011). However, as every city dweller knows, the urban systems that make the city possible also frequently fail, cities are overcrowded, polluted, shanty shaped, and dangerous environments where healthy survival depends not just on a grasp of the predictable power laws of urban living but on picaresque improvisation and invention in the interstices of urban processes.

Third, the human system, you and I as subjects produced in the encounter, could also be approached, biologically speaking, as hierarchically organized and predictable systems—from the micro cellular to the organ to body and brain. However, as Bateson helps us see, understanding the relation of the parts does not help us to understand consciousness. It is this aspect of the human subject as system that is privileged in the art works in play. The entire systemic arrangement privileges design that affords moments of consciousness that are unpredictable. Here a consideration of the relationship between the systemic elements in play brings us back to thinking about how meaning is made.

The successful work of ambient literature depends on ambiguity. The ambient register may be the counterpoint to "smart" systems, eschewing the imposition of instrumental operations of predictable and reproducible cause and effect on the complex systems of its constituent parts. Mihai Nadin's recent work argues for the importance of the human capabilities of anticipation as distinct from the computers' calculation of probability. He makes ambiguity a leading value in his argument against instrumental systems that assume complexity is reducible to a set of predictable operations: "Ambiguity, the signature of complexity, holds more information than does the well-defined cause-and-effect chain characteristic of the physical" (Nadin 2013, 43).

We may not know in the ambient art experience what exactly we are supposed to do, or what we are aiming for. Our instructions are frequently ambiguous and require active participation, perhaps at the risk of investment of self, and at the least in moving our bodies from one place to another. We want art that offers us a sense of discovery, and therefore has ambiguity and the potential to be lost as fundamental: "Discovery is never made at the end of a GPS record of returned data, but rather in defiance of it" (Nadin 2011, 48). What we see, read, or hear is likely to be uncertain in its intention and outcome. Did the artist know that effect would be produced when the sun went down on that building? Has everyone noticed that or is it just me? How could the designers have known that such a woman with such an umbrella would cross the square when the story was talking about just such a type of woman? These moments are temporary, ambiguous, and unpredictable in their meaning but, unlike the theatre or the gallery, they are part of the unscripted shared material world. They produce an encounter between the complexity of embodied experience and the complexity of the city stage: "The living embodies the ambiguous record of the change of the world in which it unfolds. This is the narration of the living" (Nadin 2011, 46).

This analysis advocates for an ambient literature taking off from the organized complexity of our worlds. The ambient literature author draws upon a program of limited reductionism only to go further. This does involve a dramaturgy that evokes a situation for the reader/listener by specifying *this* place at *this* time with *these* words on *this* platform, but it also notably opens into contingency. The experience is one of formation on a temporary stage shaped by the dynamic complexity of the systems that constitute its moment or event. An ambiguous and temporary encounter is produced, essaying the impossible, where the experience exploits emergent properties to produce a transcendence that collapses and disappears as quickly as it has formed. Ambient literature has the potential to enact the experience of living as part of complex systems.

Note

1. Duncan Speakman and Tom Abba of Circumstance in Interview with the author.

References

Abba, Tom, and Duncan Speakman. "These Pages Fall Like Ash." http://pagesfall.com.
Abba, Tom, and Duncan Speakman. 2013. *These Pages Fall Like Ash—The Book*. Bristol, UK: Circumstance.
Arnolfini. "Blast Theory: Rider Spoke." http://arnolfini.org.uk/whatson/blast-theory-rider-spoke
Bateson, Gregory. 1972. *Steps to an Ecology of Mind*. San Francisco, CA: Chandler.
Bassoli, Arianna, Johanna Brewer, Karen Martin, Paul Dourish, and Scott Mainwaring. 2007. "Underground Aesthetics: Rethinking Urban Computing." *Pervasive Computing, IEEE* 6 (3): 39–45.
Barber, John F. 2014. "Walking-Talking: Soundscapes, Flaneurs, and the Creation of Mobile Media Narratives." In *The Mobile Story: Narrative Practices with Locative Technologies*, edited by Jason Farman, 95–110. New York: Routledge.
Cardiff, Janet, and George Bures Miller. "Cardiffmiller." http://cardiffmiller.com/
Cole, Teju. 2011. *Open City: A Novel*. New York: Random House.
de Souza e Silva, Adriana, and Daniel M. Sutko. 2008. "Playing Life and Living Play: How Hybrid Reality Games Reframe Space, Play, and the Ordinary." *Critical Studies in Media Communication* 25 (5): 447–65.
de Waal, Martin. 2011. "The Ideas and Ideals in Urban Media." In *From Social Butterfly to Engaged Citizen: Urban Informatics, Social Media, Ubiquitous Computing, and Mobile Technology to Support Citizen Engagement*, edited by Marcus Foth, Laura Forlano, Christine Satchell, and Martin Gibbs, 5–20. Cambridge, MA: MIT Press.
Dovey, Jon, and Constance Fleuriot. 2012. "The Pervasive Media Cookbook: Cooking up; Communicating Pervasive Media." *Ubiquity: The Journal of Pervasive Media* 1 (2): 149–69.
Ekman, Ulrik, Ed. 2013. *Throughout: Art and Culture Emerging with Ubiquitous Computing*. Cambridge, MA: MIT Press.
Fadiman, Anne. 1998. *Ex Libris: Confessions of a Common Reader*. New York: Farrar, Straus and Giroux.
Farman, Jason. 2014. *The Mobile Story: Narrative Practices with Locative Technologies*. New York: Routledge.
Gordon, Eric, and Adriana de Souza e Silva. 2011. *Net Locality: Why Location Matters in a Networked World*. Chichester, West Sussex; Malden, MA: Wiley-Blackwell.
Greenfield, Adam. 2006. *Everyware: The Dawning Age of Ubiquitous Computing*. Berkeley, CA: New Riders.

Hight, Jeremy. 2010. "Locative Narrative, Literature and Form." In *Beyond the Screen: Transformations of Literary Structures, Interfaces and Genres*, edited by Jörgen Schäfer and Peter Gendolla, 303–309. New Brunswick, NJ: Transaction Publishers.

Hull, Richard, Ben Clayton, and Tom Melamed. 2004. "Rapid Authoring of Mediascapes." In *Ubicomp 2004: Ubiquitous Computing*, edited by Nigel Davies, Elizabeth D. Mynatt and Itiro Siio, 125–42. Berlin: Springer.

Koefed Hansen, Lone. 2014. "Paths of Movement: Negotiating Spatial Narratives through GPS Tracking." In *The Mobile Story: Narrative Practices with Locative Technologies*, edited by Jason Farman, 128–142. New York: Routledge.

Levine Paula. 2014. "On Common Ground: Here as There." In *The Mobile Story: Narrative Practices with Locative Technologies*, edited by Jason Farman, 143–158. New York: Routledge.

McCullough, Malcolm. 2004. *Digital Ground: Architecture, Pervasive Computing, and Environmental Knowing*. Cambridge, MA: MIT Press.

McCullough, Malcolm. 2013. *Ambient Commons: Attention in the Age of Embodied Information*. Cambridge, Massachusetts, MA: MIT Press.

Manguel, Alberto. 1996. *A History of Reading*. New York: Viking.

Mieville, China. 2010. *The City and the City*. New York: Random House.

Nadin, Mihai. 2013. "Antecapere Ergo Sum: What Price Knowledge?" *AI & SOCIETY* 28 (1): 39–50.

Rueb, Teri. "Teri.Rueb." http://terirueb.net/i_index.html

Schmidt, Ulrik. 2013. "Ambience and Ubiquity." In *Throughout: Art and Culture Emerging with Ubiquitous Computing*, edited by Ulrik Ekman, 175–187. Cambridge, MA: MIT Press.

Schäfer, Jörgen, and Peter Gendolla. 2010. *Beyond the Screen: Transformations of Literary Structures, Interfaces and Genres*. New Brunswick, NJ: Transaction Publishers.

Sebald, Winfried Georg. 2001. *Austerlitz*. New York: Random House.

Simon, Herbert A. 1962. "The Architecture of Complexity." *Proceedings of the American Philosophical Society* 106 (6): 467–82.

Tuters, Marc, and Kazys Varnelis. 2006. "Beyond Locative Media: Giving Shape to the Internet of Things." *Leonardo* 39 (4): 357–63.

Weaver, Warren. 1948. "Science and Complexity." *American Scientist* 36 (4): 536–44.

Wilken, Rowan. 2012. "Locative Media: From Specialized Preoccupation to Mainstream Fascination." *Convergence: The International Journal of Research into New Media Technologies* 18 (3): 243–47.

Wilken, Rowan. 2014. "Proximity and Alienation: Narratives of City, Self, and Other in the Locative Games of Blast Theory." In *The Mobile Story: Narrative Practices with Locative Technologies*, edited by Jason Farman, 175–191. New York: Routledge.

Wilken, Rowan, and Gerard Goggin. 2015. *Locative Media*. New York: Routledge.

SOFTWARE STUDIES

Ulrik Ekman

Increasingly, we individuate, are individuated by, and individuate with the software systems of contemporary network societies—not just the most visible parts of software behind new media, social media, and mobile media, but their personalizing, infrastructuralizing, and relational databased-generating variants in ubicomp culture.[1] Billions of states and processes of psychic and social individualizations are also unfolding along with a decentralized distribution into the practices of everyday cultures of billions of computational entities with software systems. These stay in position or move, connect and disconnect by cables or wirelessly (regularly, ad hoc, or non-linearly), and insist on individuation as a matter of technocultural transcoding. Individuation increasingly transduces cultural *and* technical software. Individuations of citizens of network societies involve and modulate across a mismatch between semantic social codings of norms and values *and* discrete digital codings of norms and values. Individuation with the codings, decodings, recodings, and overcodings proper to software is still a largely unrecognized ubiquity-effect. In spite of the recent efforts in software studies (Fuller 2008; Mackenzie 2006; Manovich 2013) we still have too few accounts of the ways in which we are unceasingly at work on becoming one and whole with cultural and technical software as our processual and relational environmental membranes.

However, it is not only that research tends not to articulate the ways in which the semantic and discrete mathematical codings of software as dynamic membranes constitute and deconstitute our individual and social atmosphere, ambience, milieu, or ecology. Today it also remains an unresolved matter how to approach a fact that is fast becoming difficult to ignore: Individuations with software cut across traditional distinctions of humans and technics, inside and outside, and they are complex. It is hard not to notice, but it is difficult to approach the fact that human individuals, social groupings, and software processes are very numerous and highly differentiated, that their interior and exterior networking relations imply non-simple interactivity, and that wholeness of individuation is emergent in the sense that it is far from trivial to figure out the properties of the whole even when the properties of the parts and the rules of their interactions are known.

For the most part, current research handles this via a divide and conquer strategy and via reductionism. Arguably, the actualization of human individuations and the concretizations of technical software developments are two different kinds of processes, and while they may *appear* complex and emergent, this is either a matter of a current lack of knowledge or largely irrelevant.

In either case one should proceed by approaching such matters as complicated rather than complex and emergent—and then relegate further epistemic work to the kinds of reduction offered by the relevant disciplines in the human, social, and natural sciences (in this case most likely psychology, sociology, anthropology, biology, and computer science). One may consider such approaches affirmed when observing that we almost always find meaningful the answers concerning human individuation presented via the modes of systematic reductions of complexity proper to these disciplines in the human and social sciences. Likewise, concretizations of software development for systems in ubicomp, ambient intelligence, pervasive computing, and the IoT almost always are adhering to the conventional top-down modular reductionist paradigms in software engineering and computer programming. Coded software systems and their processes are built hierarchically to achieve predicted goals by following strict plans that specify the details of each component part, their relations, and their overall behavior. Generally speaking, here the unity as well as the hierarchized specialization of the sciences is respected, and the approaches across the faculties share the assumption that reductions moving towards the simplest physical entity anchors knowledge.

However, a number of important insights that pertain to human individuation (including social systems and organizations) and concretization of ubicomp software disturb this mode of operation. Recognition of both human individuations and software development as distributed systems with types of decentralization granting more or less autonomy to a variety of agencies have tended to put pressure on the notions of hierarchy and an obviously unified path of reductionism. Something similar must be said with respect to the import of non-local causes for the becomings at stake, the import of two-way and many-to-many relationships, as well as the import of holism which systems theory, chaos theory, and complexity theory have done much to emphasize during the last half century. The wager here would then be that the processes of individuation in biological, psychological, and social systems as well as in the development of ubicomp software systems are so complex that their behaviors cannot be deduced from the properties of their elements and perhaps cannot be predicted no matter how much knowledge or data is made available. In the strong case, complexity theory would insist that reductive models are ontologically prevented from offering workable algorithms for prediction, that is, the behaviors of systems of human individuation, ubicomp software systems development, and the systems of their co-development *are* emergent, are to be regarded as computationally non-decomposable, or as being of irreducible complexity.

It may be tempting to dismiss this as theoretical hyperbole that either cannot be substantiated when the actual practical and empirical conditions are considered or can be considered of no more than marginal, "molecular," or rarefied far-from-equilibrium import. However, several factors in the research agenda for ubicomp culture and in the actual contemporary dynamics among individuals, social groupings, and ubicomp systems might well be said to put in doubt such dismissal.

For example, a given mixed reality situation such as a traffic intersection in the ubiquitous city Songdo in South Korea notably includes a number of context-aware systems, each with numerous computational entities and layers of software systems. These include a smart traffic control system, local and a city-wide surveillance systems, wireless and wired Internet systems for citizens, the infrastructural ubicomp systems implemented from the outset in every building and every street (e.g., city service systems, trash collection systems, AC, heating and lighting systems, etc.), and environmental monitoring systems with networks of sensors and actuators dealing with waterflow and tides, pollution levels in air and waterways. Citizens of Songdo thus live and individuate with numerous and partly overlapping software systems, and the call in ubicomp research for context-awareness to work with intelligent semantic inference relatively often means that functional order and structuration does not emerge because the problem of making sense is NP complete (nondeterministic polynomial time; i.e., no fast solution—member of the set of decision problems that can at best be solved in polynomial time on a non-deterministic Turing machine) or of irreducible complexity. For example, to demand of a traffic control system that it follows, predicts, and adapts to vehicular movement, that it produces semantic inferences as to the likely situated intent of human pedestrians, and that it makes sense of activities so as to take into account earlier and coming security issues for vehicles and humans—this brings about not a smooth and continuous traffic flow but congestion, a stop, and perhaps a long standstill—because such semantic inferences demand excessive computational power and time due to the complexity, which is disorganized if not irreducible.

However, individuating with the ubicomp culture of Songdo also does function, and in a complex fashion: It does involve productive synchronic emergence. Especially the mobile and ad hoc connective kinds of systems permit of the emergence on the fly of kinds of networked order out of the apparent chaos of humans in cars, buses, trains, and on foot and software systems in the environment, in the streets, in means of transportation, and in various handheld devices. As with mobs and swarms, it is not immediately clear that this kind of synchronically emergent structure can be analyzed as a focused systemic behavior produced by numerous parts interlinking upwards to a level of a more global whole. Nor is it clear that the properties of the whole of human and software systems constrain downward all the interactions of parts. It might be more productive to follow complexity theory to demonstrate that one or more attractors in the systemic phase space at stake are generating nonlinear negative feedback loops which constrain and enable patterned and structured behavior in a basin of attraction. This would then lead to further work on ways to think the coming into presence of such a structured functional network behavior. Notably, this might be thought as one actualization out of many potential ones modelled by the quasi-cause of a certain distribution of singularities in a manifold.[2]

This is already to acknowledge that studies of individuations with software in contemporary ubicomp culture are to take place beyond crude reductionism, and on the other side of the early influence of chaos theory. If insistence on emergence here implies a certain resistance to reductionism, this does not necessarily mean that one subscribes to the deconstruction of hierarchy that had early complexity theory work with notions of distributed flat systems, not least in organizational theory. One would perhaps instead agree with Herbert Simon's later reconsideration and his argument that complex systems have an architecture, and that structures, including hierarchical ones but not only these, constitute enabling conditions for complexity. (Simon 1962) Being complex, both human individuation and software developments would then always involve hierarchies. Looking at the standards and models for modern and current computer science (e.g., for computers, software, HCI, networks and protocols, databases), which are all explicitly layered and stratified top-down, one might find confirmation that computer scientists have long assumed and accepted that it is much more efficient for complex systems to be composed of subsystems that might in turn be composed of subsystems and so on down to the simplest system unit and process. One can turn to any number of existing ubicomp software systems and find confirmation that they are developed with a view to rather clear specifications of levels of code and the interfaces between such hierarchical levels. One could be tempted to say that human individuals and ubicomp systems coexist as two kinds of synchronic emergences forming a unity, each a complex hierarchal system with a great many levels of agents and sub-agencies, modular and sub-modular processes, whether this is a matter of subjects as organisms or organized software systems.

However, as complex systems, human individuation and ubicomp software development are not thoroughly hierarchical and fully decomposable in their ways of emerging. Simon of course knew only too well that complex systems do not just work with a neatly layered and statically structured or nested mode of organization but also involve development or evolution over time and a variety of cross-cutting connections that need not respect hierarchy. This introduces questions concerning diachronic emergence as well as transversal emergence, and both of these are likely to imply more complex work on complex systems.

The subject qua an organized individuation emerges as a unity on one level from sublevel emergences (cells, organs, somatic body . . .), just as it contributes to what appears on levels above (social body, populations . . .). Likewise, a software application on a computer emerges as an organization of higher level code from what goes on in an operating system, device drivers, Basic Input/Output System (BIOS) system software, just as it contributes to larger systems, for example, in networks of computers. However, the time scales at these levels are sometimes the same but most often not the same—the individual develops and dies faster than the group in a social body, the operating system and the database develops or halts more slowly than the application and the user interface. To an application, the operating system appears a structural systemic unit, whereas the application appears a process of events to the operating system that has a longer time scale. To the individual, the social and the biological inheritance appears most often as structural units, whereas the other way around an individuation appears mostly a processual evolutionary and social experiment among many. Consequently, one needs to consider a notion of diachronic emergence that allows for both a temporal homogeneity with potentially nonlinear feedback loops and a temporal heterogeneity that may not be linear just as it may not be approachable in reductionist fashion.

As John Johnston demonstrates elsewhere in this volume, our individual lives unfold in tandem with anticipatory computational algorithms for high frequency trading in futures on the financial markets, and nonlinear flash crashes may have both human and computational futures mutate or dissipate. The general ideal aim for ubicomp to be or become capable in a given situation of anticipating and then assisting human individuals or social groups in their ongoing everyday cultural activities and intended goals cannot but involve an artificial temporalizing intelligence qua an algorithmic approximation to what is to happen in the events of human temporalizations. One needs only to look to the increasing use of intelligent profiling on the Web or to the current efforts by Microsoft, Google, and others to develop the next paradigm for intelligent assistants in order to realize that control of diachronic technocultural emergence is on the agenda, and that this may be of irreducible complexity.

As Wendy Hui Kyong Chun begins to show in this section in her rereading of the heritage from Von Neumann and others, such diachronic emergences also concern individuation processes for human and technical memorization. Living on in ubicomp cultures includes individual, social, and biological memory but also, and increasingly, the manifold of technical memory developing via the dynamics of relational database cultures. According to Chun, ubicomp culture makes evident that memory is never simply personal or social but always also technical, and that this is not to be reduced to dead storage but must be approached rather in a more complex implicit, regenerative, and actively priming sense. Notably, technical and human memorizations retain and remain and repeat, but with a difference. The renewal or the freeing of memory implicit in the detour through habit and technicization has memories breach, leak, spread, more or less ubiquitously, and more generally problematizes the distinction between the times of the inside and the outside, system times and environmental times.

Ubicomp culture has not yet been studied seriously with a view to complexity and emergence. Generally speaking, even in existing research informed by complexity theory by far the most energy has been spent on theorizing and discussing phenomena of synchronic complexity—emergences of functional structures. After some of the initial debates, fueled not least by chaos theory, one can today observe a general willingness to work at the interstices of flat systems and hierarchies. Deleuze's work across consistencies and strata is a case in point, as is Manuel Delanda's early rethinking of some of this in terms of not only of meshworks and hierarchies but also interconnections of these. Diachronic emergence is treated far less but then usually with the generation of hierarchies over time in mind. Emergences from heterogeneous temporalizations are treated least, if at all. In general, studies of ubicomp culture are lagging behind in these matters, and since competent software studies are still relatively rare, this lag is especially grave with respect to an understanding of the complexity of individuation with software, both in terms of development and in terms of evolution or mutation.

On a first view, heterogeneous diachronic emergence tends to be reduced to an event flowing in homogeneous Euclidean time qua universal container, just as it tends to be reduced to structural synchrony qua the arrival of an analyzable functional systemic hierarchy. Simon's argument in favor of working with complex systems primarily via architectural hierarchies is perhaps a paradigmatic example. Simon was well aware that such complex systems included what he called "cross-cutting connections" that do not fit in with the hierarchy. But, in good pragmatic reductionist fashion, he opted for the hope that these are best approached as not too important for the structure and the development of the system. If one were to follow Simon when approaching individuations with software in ubicomp cultures, non-linearities in human individuations (such as negative feedback loops, dissipation, irreversibility, unstable or chaotic behavior, mutation) would tend to be bracketed, as would irregular, dysfunctional, generative and self-generative processes in software development. Moreover, this kind of parenthesizing of cross-cutting connections is most likely to prohibit any serious treatment of the interlinkage and joint processing of software and human individuation. It most likely means reinforcing the traditional distinctions between technology and culture, machine and man, software program and subjectivity, etc., so as to damp out the issues of their systemic co-structuration and their co-development or co-emergence.

Even without adopting a strong position in complexity theory, it is possible to suggest a path conducive to more nuanced treatments. A researcher such as Stephen Wolfram in effect turns Simon's main line of approach on its head, opting for going as far as possible towards meeting complexity in its disorganized variants, only then to try to suggest how still to do efficient and predictable work in "complexity engineering." Wolfram is quite willing to take on diachronic emergence, and to assume that the evolution of a great many systems probably remains of irreducible complexity (that is, computationally irreducible). This seems to many a scientifically problematic assumption since no general predictions can then be made as to the behavior of such systems. The systemic evolution admits of no short-cut predictive procedure, and only one-to-one or direct simulation can lead to "results." Since Wolfram is also an engineer, he is confronted on a daily basis with the demand for quite precise determination of the operations of each component of the system at stake. However, his approach is to relax this constraint in order to draw upon complex systems. He will aim at satisficing, or request just some general or approximate specification of the overall behavior of the system. This in effect means to design and to engineer systems that should have particular attractors in phase space, and Wolfram finds an interesting resource here in cellular automata that can go very far towards meeting complexity. However, given his need to respect the results required in engineering and software development, he will draw upon cellular automata in the sense of multiple scale modular systems, and he will in the main look, much like Simon, to hierarchical relations of the master/slave type among the modules emerging. Nonetheless, this approach is and stays much more open to complexity and emergence, and it notably engages with synchronic, diachronic, as well as cross-cutting emergence from contingency or randomness.

One might well consider the hypothesis that in ubicomp culture cross-cutting or transversal emergence is of key importance for individuations with software. If one does not have a notion of layers and layers of software processes operating and developing in synchronicity but also in asynchronicity (heterogeneous temporalizations) accompanied by a notion of layers and layers of individualizing and socializing processes with their kinds of synchronic and diachronic emergence, one is lacking the basic resources to work towards the complexity at stake. Moreover, if one does not have a notion of transversality, it remains impossible to engage with the ways in which the processes of human organisms, individuals, and social groupings intersect with processes of software, firmware, and hardware so as to engender types of self-organizing systemic behaviors, which do not admit of reduction to the sum of the parts, and which go across in ways that do not allow one to distinguish clearly between human and machine or grant primacy to one or the other.

Notes

1. Here, as elsewhere in this anthology, the notion of "individuation" is used both in general and more specific ways, more or less metaphorically. In this text, however, "individuation" is mostly thought in close alignment with the ways in which it appears in the work of Gilbert Simondon. In brief, it concerns the appearance or emergence of individuations qua stages of becoming through transduction in a metastable environment. Simondon offered a theory of individual and collective individuation, in which the individual subject is considered as an effect of individuation, rather than as a cause. Thus the individual is an effect of the never-ending process of individuation. Simondon also conceived of the pre-individual as the reserve making individuation itself possible. Individuation is an always incomplete process, always leaving a pre-individual leftover, itself making possible future individuations. Furthermore, individuation always creates both an individual and a collective subject. Cf., Simondon *L'individu et sa genèse physico-biologique;* Simondon *L'individuation psychique et collective.*
2. I am referring to Gilles Deleuze's concept of a quasi-cause as it appears in *Difference and Repetition.* My remarks here concerning synchronic emergence as well as what follows concerning diachronic and transversal emergence are indebted to the insights in Protevi's work on Deleuze, Guattari, and emergence. See also Protevi.

References

De Landa, Manuel. 1997. *A Thousand Years of Nonlinear History.* New York: Zone Books.

Deleuze, Gilles. 1993. *Difference and Repetition.* New York: Columbia University Press.

Deleuze, Gilles, and Félix Guattari. 1987. *A Thousand Plateaus.* Minneapolis, MN: University of Minnesota Press.

Fuller, Matthew. 2008. *Software Studies: A Lexicon.* Cambridge, MA: MIT Press.

Kitchin, Rob, and Martin Dodge. 2011. *Code/Space: Software and Everyday Life.* Cambridge, MA: MIT Press.

Mackenzie, Adrian. 2006. *Cutting Code: Software and Sociality.* New York: Peter Lang.

Manovich, Lev. 2013. *Software Takes Command.* New York: Bloomsbury Academic.

Protevi, John. 2006. "Deleuze, Guattari and Emergence." *Paragraph* 29 (2): 19–39.

Simon, Herbert A. 1962. "The Architecture of Complexity." *Proceedings of the American Philosophical Society* 106 (6): 467–82.

Simondon, Gilbert. 1964. *L'individu Et Sa Genèse Physico-Biologique.* Paris: Presses Universitaires de France.

Simondon, Gilbert. 1989. *L'individuation Psychique Et Collective.* Paris: Aubier.

Wolfram, Stephen. 1986. "Approaches to Complexity Engineering." *Phys. D* 2 (1–3): 385–399.

UBIQUITOUS MEMORY: I DO NOT REMEMBER, WE DO NOT FORGET

Wendy Hui Kyong Chun

Mark Weiser's influential vision of ubiquitous computing in the *Scientific American* article, "The Computer for the Twenty-first Century" stresses that, in order for computers to become ubiquitous, they need to "vanish into the background." Ubiquitous, that is, does not simply mean everywhere, but everywhere yet nowhere visible (etymologically, the term ubiquitous stems from the "Ubiquitarians," Lutherans who believed that Christ's corpus was present "everywhere at once").[1] This vanishing was to be central to the very success of ubicomp, defined by Weiser as the habitual embrace of computers. For ubicomp to work—for computers to become devices that enable new thoughts and more face to face communication—computers would have to move from devices that demanded a user's undivided attention to instruments that could be used without thinking. Curiously, to render computers peripheral, objects that were previously inert, from badges to boards, were to be animated. To be able to use machines unconsciously, machines needed to become more aware (in particular of their location) and to lose their "individualized identity or importance" (Weiser 1991, 99). Unindividuated computers had to remember—to capture and track users—so that users could forget and thus think and live.

This notion of technology needing to remember so that humans could forget (and eventually remember) has a long history. Vannevar Bush, outlining his vision of the memex (a never built analog machine that allegedly inspired the WWW), argued that the memex was to solve the problem of the ever-increasing yet increasingly unconsultable scientific archive by enabling more permanent and intuitive data traces and trails (Bush 1945). The memex was to make man's excursions more pleasurable by enabling him to "reacquire the privilege of forgetting the manifold things he does not need to have immediately at hand, with some assurance that he can find them again if they prove important" (Ibid., Section 8). Of course, this linkage of forgetting to inscription extends to the very concept and function of writing. In Plato's *Phaedrus*, Theuth offered the gift of writing to King Thamus as a way to "make the Egyptians wiser" and to "improve their memories." His invention, however, was rejected by the King as harmful, since it "will produce forgetfulness in the souls of those who have learned it" (Derrida 1981, 75, 102).

Intriguingly, Weiser himself draws parallels between ubicomp and writing, describing writing as "perhaps the first information technology," one that is also "ubiquitous in industrialized countries." He notes: "not only do books, magazines, and newspapers convey written information, but so do street signs, billboards, shop signs, and even graffiti. Candy wrappers are covered in writing" (Weiser 1991, 94). Constantly in the background, these "literacy technology" products transmit their information easily via inattentive glances. The goal, then, was to make computers as omnipresent and non-distracting as writing. Even more intriguingly, Weiser views writing as an information technology because it makes memory collective: "The ability to represent spoken language symbolically for long-term storage," he writes, "freed information from the limits of individual memory" (Ibid.). Writing both stores and disseminates memory.

To what extent, though, is memory something personal and intimate, which is then freed by writing? Similarly, does complexity arise from many different individual systems interacting, or rather than from processes of individuation? These questions are key to understanding the stakes of ubicomp and to answering the related questions: Is computation something personal, which is then made ubiquitous? And how is complexity fostered and managed by individuation? Perhaps bizarrely for us, living in an era of ever-proliferating smartphones and pads, Weiser disqualifies personal devices as forms of ubicomp. The personal computer, he insists, is "a misplaced idea" because such machines "cannot truly make computing an integral, invisible part of people's lives" (Ibid.). Personal devices are failures because they are personal, because they need to be carried from place to place. In contrast, pads were to be as ubiquitous and as non-individualized as "scrap paper" (Ibid.): they were to be peripheral and attached to locations rather than persons. Computers, he stresses, were to have multiple subjects, rather than subjects have multiple devices (Weiser and Brown 1996).

In this article, I respond to the questions outlined in the previous paragraph by emphasizing the extent to which memory, which underpins modern computing, is never simply personal. I thus chart a different history and present of ubiquitous computing, one that reveals the links between Jean Luc Nancy's work on writing as corpus and the corporeal underpinnings of ubiquity (again, omnipresent yet invisible divine body). Specifically, revisiting my analysis in *Programmed Visions: Software and Memory* of von Neumann's founding analogy between the human nervous system and computational devices, I argue that the embedding of memory within the machine— so central to the emergence of modern computing—also fundamentally changes memory by making memory storage (Chun 2000). To counter this containment of memory, which both localizes computers and inadvertently renders the world into "dead storage," I turn to recent work in neurobiology on implicit and explicit memory. This work reformulates memory as a series of constant actions that cannot be separated from acts of perception, thus challenging the notion that memory is content or storage. Indeed, in terms of implicit memory, there would seem to be no separate memory (organ) or nonporous boundary between animal and environment: Implicit memory—as a form of knowing without remembering—responds to environmental cues. To be clear, the point of this move to neurobiology and implicit memory is not to condemn von Neumann for being wrong or to celebrate neurobiology as inherently true. Given the influence and importance of von Neumann's work, who really cares if his postulations about human memory were correct? The point is to rethink the relationship between knowledge and remembering, repetition and habit, to make the world "live" once more, so that we refuse the deadening of the world brought about by memory as storage and realize the fundamentally collective nature of memory and writing.

Memory Machines (Again)

As I have argued in *Programmed Visions*, memory is a central category of new media. Memory underlies the emergence of the computer as we now know it: The move from calculator to computer depended on "regenerative memory."[2] Computers, however, did not simply borrow the term memory from biology; they also fundamentally changed the meaning of the term. We now do something once considered impossible: We store things in memory. We do not store memory traces; we store things in memory. This conflation of memory with storage is astounding, not only because of the volatility—the ephemerality—of much computer memory, but also because memory and storage are historically opposed. Memory stems from the same Sanskrit root for martyr and is related to the ancient Greek term for baneful, fastidious. Memory contains within it the act of repetition: It is an act of commemoration—a process of recollecting or remembering. In contrast, a store, according to the Oxford English Dictionary (OED), stems for the Old French term "to build, establish, furnish."[3] A store—like an archive—is both what is stored and its location. Stores look toward a future: We put something in storage in order to use it again; we buy things in stores in order to use them. This erasure of the difference between memory and storage thus erases the difference between the past and the future, positing digital media as an ever-increasing archive in which no piece of data is lost. Memory-as-storage hardens information—turning it from a measure of possibility into a "thing"—while also erasing the difference between instruction and data and the vicissitudes of execution.[4]

This hardening of memory can be traced to what we now consider the origin of modern computation: John von Neumann's mythic, controversial and incomplete "First Draft of the **E**lectronic **D**iscrete **V**ariable **A**utomatic **C**omputer (EDVAC)" (1945), which conceived of non-human computers as abstract, nervous memory machines. A key feature of this report is its abstractness: von Neumann outlines a "hypothetical element, which functions essentially like a vacuum tube–for example, like a triode with an appropriate associated RLC-circuit— but which can be discussed as an isolated entity, without going into detailed radio frequency electro-magnetic considerations" (von Neumann 1945, 9). According to von Neumann, this abstractness is necessary because, although treating the elements as real vacuum tubes would be ideal, introducing such technical specificities "would produce an involved and opaque situation in which the preliminary orientation which we are now attempting would be hardly possible" (Ibid.). Complexity stems from technical actualities. The vagaries of the machinery (vacuum tubes, etc.), which are not necessarily digital, but can be made to act digitally, threaten the clean schematic logic needed to design this clean, logical machine.[5]

This fateful abstraction, this erasure of the vicissitudes of electricity and magnetism, depends on an analogy to the human nervous system. Von Neumann specifies the major components of the EDVAC as corresponding to different neurons: "2.6 the three specific parts: CA [Central Arithmetic], CC [Central Control] (together C), and M [Memory] correspond to the associative neurons in the human nervous system. It remains to discuss the equivalents of the sensory or afferent and the motor or efferent neurons. These are the input and the output organs of the device . . ." (von Neumann 1945, 3). These neurons, however, are not simply borrowed from the human nervous system. They are the controversial, hypothetical neurons postulated by Warren McCulloch and Walter Pitts in their "A Logical Calculus of Ideas Immanent in Nervous Activity," a text McCulloch claims von Neumann saved from obscurity (McCulloch 1965) (von Neumann would later describe these neurons as "extremely amputated, simplified, idealized") (von Neumann 1966). Following McCulloch and Pitts, von Neumann ignores the more complicated aspects of neuron functioning: thresholds, temporal summation, relative inhibition, changes of the threshold by after-effects of stimulation beyond the synaptic delay, etc.[6] This analogy thus relies on and fosters an overlooking of the complications and specificities of both technical and biological components, reducing them to black boxes, in which timing and sequence can be ignored.

These idealized neurons, like software after them, were based on a conflation of stimulus with action, word with result. McCulloch and Pitts sought to create "a logical calculus of the ideas immanent in nervous activity" through a conflation of word with result, asserting that "the response of any neuron [is] factually equivalent to a proposition which proposed its adequate stimulus" (McCulloch 1965, 21). That is, a proposition (instruction/program) that proposed a result is functionally equivalent to its result (execution). This conflation grounds programming, in which process in time is reduced to process in space. As Edsger Dijkstra asserts in his famous "Go To Statement Considered Harmful," "the quality of programmers is a decreasing function of the density of go to statements in the programs they produce" because go tos go against the fundamental tenant of what Dijkstra considered to be good programming, namely the necessity to "shorten the conceptual gap between static program and dynamic process, to make the correspondence between the program (spread out in text space) and the process (spread out in time) as trivial as possible" (Dijkstra 352). That is, go tos make difficult the conflation of instruction with its product—the reduction of process to command, execution to legislation— which grounds the emergence of software as a concrete entity and commodity, which grounds programs as the "source" of computers' actions. Go tos make it difficult for the source program to act as a legible source, painfully revealing the work necessary to make the source code a viable source and the fact that source code is only source code after the fact.[7] This glossing over the vicissitudes of execution is also evident in von Neumann's discussion of memory.

Von Neumann's use of the term memory—his borrowing from biology—was not necessary. Prior to "The Draft," mechanisms designed to store numbers and functions necessary for computing were called storage devices or "the store," following Babbage's terminology. J. Presper Eckert's 1944 "Disclosure of Magnetic Calculating Machine" referred concretely to disks or tapes designed to store data. Further, computer storage as memory is no simple metaphor, since rather than explaining something unknown via something known, it does the opposite: It explains computer storage, which actually existed and was well-known, via human memory, which was unknown. It asserts the existence of a biological organ not known to exist—an assertion that would have profound consequences for how we would imagine the human mind.

Although von Neumann at first viewed memory as comprising afferent neurons, he soon changed his mind, based on his own experience with computers, in particular with the number of vacuum tubes needed to create the types of reverbatory circuits McCulloch and Pitts described. In a reverse move, he postulated human memory as something unknown but logically necessary, making clear that his first analogy was based on a leap of faith. In *The Computer and the Brain*, written ten years after "The Draft," von Neumann writes, "the presence of a memory— or, not improbably, of several memories—within the nervous system is a matter of surmise and postulation, but one that all our experience with artificial automata suggests and confirms." Von Neumann goes on to emphasize our ignorance regarding this memory:

> It is just as well to admit right at the start that all physical assertions about the nature, embodiment, and location of [human memory] are equally hypothetical. We do not know where in the physically viewed nervous system a memory resides; we do not know whether it is a separate organ or a collection of specific parts of other already known organs, etc. It may well be residing in a system of specific nerves, which would then have to be a rather large system. It may well have something to do with the genetic mechanism of the body. We are as ignorant of its nature and position as were the Greeks, who suspected the location of the mind in the diaphragm. The only thing we know is that it must be

a rather large-capacity memory, and that it is hard to see how a complicated automaton like the human nervous system could do without one.

(Neumann et al. 2000, 61)

This passage reveals how quickly the computer moved from a system modeled on ideal neurons to a concrete model for more complex biological phenomena. This statement, which seems to be so careful and qualified—we basically do not know what the memory is or where it resides—at the same time, asserts the existence of a memory organ or set of organs based on an analogy to computers: "The only thing we know is that it must be a rather large-capacity memory, and that it is hard to see how a complicated automaton like the human nervous system could do without one." This guess regarding capacity assumes that the brain functions digitally, that it stores information as bits, which are then processed by the brain, rather than functioning more continuously in a "field-based" manner.

Neurons as switching elements drive von Neumann's "logical" guess regarding memory capacity, as well as his confusion over its location:

> In the human organism, we know that the switching part is composed of nerve cells, and we know a certain amount about their functioning. As to the memory organs, we haven't the faintest idea where or what they are. We know that the memory requirements of the human organism are large, but on the basis of any experience that one has with the subject, it's not likely that the memory sits in the nervous system, and it's really very obscure what sort of thing it is . . . (Ibid. 39)

Digital switching devices, based on the reduction of all processes to true/false propositions, insatiably demand memory-less memory. As von Neumann explains in "The Draft," the need for memory increases as problems are broken down into long and complicated sequences of operations. Digital computation needs to store and have access to intermediate values, instructions, specific functions, initial conditions, and boundary conditions, etc. Prior to the EDVAC, these were stored in an outside the recording medium such as stacks of paper cards. The EDVAC was to increase the speed of calculation by putting some of those values inside the memory organ, making porous the boundaries of the machine. This incorporation marks the difference between human and machine computers, making memory, as Derrida has argued, "*a prosthesis of the inside*" (Derrida 1998, 19). This incorporation, however, was not simply sequestered in the "organ"; it also bled into the central arithmetic unit, which, like every unit in the system, needed to store numbers in order to work.

To contain or localize memory, von Neumann organized it hierarchically: There were to be many memory organs, defined by access time rather than content. For instance, in the 1946 *An Electronic Computing Instrument*, von Neumann et al. (2000) divide memory into two conceptual forms—numbers and orders, which can be stored in the same organ if instructions are reduced numbers—and into two types: primary and secondary. The primary memory consists of registers, made of flip-flops or trigger circuits, which need to be accessed quickly and ideally randomly. Primary memory, however, is very expensive and cumbersome. A secondary memory or storage medium supplements the first, holding values needed in blocks for a calculation. Besides being able to store information for periods of time, such a memory needs to be controllable automatically (without the help of a human), easily accessed by the machine, and preferably rewritable. Interestingly, the devices listed as possible secondary memories are other forms of media: teletype tapes, magnetic wire or tapes, movie film, or similar media.

(The primary media was also another medium—the Selectron was a vacuum tube similar to those used for television (Neumann 1966)). Von Neumann et al. (2000) also outline a third form of memory, "dead storage," which is an extension of secondary memory, since it is not initially integrated with the machine. Not surprisingly, input and output devices eventually become part of "dead storage." As he argues later in *The Computer and the Brain*, "the very last stage of any memory hierarchy is necessarily the outside world—that is, the outside world as far as the machine is concerned, that is, that part of it with which the machine can directly communicate, in other words the input and the output organs of the machine" (Von Neumann et al. 2000, 39). In this last step, the borders of the organism explode. *Rather than memory comprising an image of the world in the mind, memory comprises the whole world itself as it becomes "dead."*

This last step renders the world dead by conflating memory—which is traditionally and initially regenerative and degenerative—with other stable forms of "analog" media such as paper storage, a comparison that is still with us today at the level of both memory (files) and interface (pages and documents). This conflation both relied on and extended neurophysiological notions of memory as a trace or inscription, like the grooves of a gramophone. It was memory as something that never faded and that did not depend on repetition: memory that once inscribed lived forever as files.[8]

There Is No Memory (Organ)

Von Neumann's hypotheses about the computer and the brain, and McCulloch and Pitts' ideas about neurons and memory, were not without their critics. Karl Lashley, a psychologist who was also part of the Macy conferences, responded to von Neumann's difficulty in understanding the brain's neuronal capacity by arguing that the memory worked through the mass, non-localized action of neurons. He based this theory on his work with mice, who still remembered things, even after various parts of their brains had been removed: "The memory trace is the capacity of many neurons to work together in certain permutations" (quoted in McCulloch 1965, 102). Although Lashley's theory of mass action has since been disproved, its understanding of memory as distributed has been essential to rethinking memory as connection.

Indeed, contra the cybernetician's early speculations, memory does not seem to be a simple organ, nor the brain structured like a CPU that enacts numerical algorithms based on stored data and commands. In a fundamental way, memory does not seem separable from the operational apparatae of that complicated automaton, the human nervous system. Also, rather than simply acting digitally (in an all or none manner), neurons act in a far more complex and chemical manner: Intra-neuronal communication is mainly chemical rather than electrical, although, of course, these two cannot be entirely separated. Recent developments in neurobiology that have sought to understand the automatic nature of the nervous system, or, to use von Neumann's terms, the complex human automaton, arguably show there is no memory organ: There is no organ, separate from perception, that simply stores implicit memories.

This is a point made elliptically in Nobel Prize recipient Eric R. Kandel's book *In Search of Memory*, which combines autobiography, history, and science to relay advances in neurobiology to a lay public. As he explains, memory is now divided into explicit and implicit memory, where explicit memory is linked with consciousness—with the conscious recall of people, places, objects, facts, and events—and implicit memory—unconscious, procedural memory—underlies the classic habitual behavior and its mechanisms for change. Constant repetition can transform explicit memory into implicit memory (and vice versa). Implicit memory underlies habituation (the acclimation of organisms to certain types of signals), sensitization (the opposite of habituation, so thus enhanced alertness to usually noxious signals), and classical Pavlovian conditioning (the coupling of an innocuous with a noxious signal, so that an animal reacts to the benign signal as though it were a noxious one). Implicit memory is intimately tied to perceptual and motor skills, to unconscious, mechanical, reflexive actions that are constantly repeated, to humans as automata (a field that von Neumann would engage in more in his later years). Implicit memory refers, as K.B. McDermott argues, to manifestations of memory that occur in the absence of intentions to recollect (McDermott 2000, 231). *It is knowledge without knowing.* It is memory that is directly performed without knowledge or any awareness that we are drawing from memory (Kandel 2006, 132).

The classic distinction between these two types of memory, as Kandel explains, stems from the most famous case of anterograde amnesia, H.M. Patient H.M. (later revealed to be Henry Gustave Molaison) underwent surgery to cure his epilepsy in 1953. During this surgery, H.M.'s neurosurgeon, Dr. William Scoville, removed from both sides of his brain, the inner surface of his medial temporal lobes and hippocampus. After the surgery, H.M. could not make any new long-term explicit memories. He could remember things before the surgery and his short term working memory was functional, but he could not convert short term memories into long-term ones. So, although he would work with the neuroscientist Brenda Milner for many years, he would greet her as if meeting her for the first time each time.

He could however, as Milner discovered, still learn things, still acquire to new habits, albeit without conscious recall. She famously taught him how to draw each day and, even as he forgot ever drawing, he became a better drawer each day. H.M.'s case was thus key to disproving Lashley's notion that memories were not localized, but also to proving that there were two physically separate memory systems—implicit and explicit memory—and that there were two types of memory within these memories: short term and long-term. As Kandel puts it, Milner proved that Freud's notion of unconscious memory was correct: that most of our actions are unconscious (Ibid, 133).

But what is implicit memory? Kandel's experiments with aplysia, a type of snail they "trained" in various ways (classic habituation, sensitization, and classic conditioning), and whose neurons they cultured, have been key to understanding the neurobiological underpinnings of implicit memory. In these experiments, sensitization became the strengthening of a tie, habituation the weakening of one. (These experiments of course, assume that for aplysia, there is only implicit memory.)

Using cultured and isolated aplysia neurons, Kandel was able to show the following: In short term implicit memory, the connection—that is the amount of neurotransmitter glutamate—between the sensory and motor neuron is strengthened.[9] In long term memory, more ties—at a specific synapse—are created.[10] Importantly, the maintenance of this new connection does not happen at the nucleus, but rather at the axon terminal itself. The intense serotonin pulses convert the prion like protein CREB (a prion is a protein that can fold into two distinct shapes, one of which is dominant and the other recessive) into the dominant form. In the dominant form, the protein is self-perpetuating: It causes the recessive form to change its shape and become dominant and self-perpetuating as well. This dominant form activates the dormant messenger RNA, which regulates the synthesis at the new synaptic terminal and stabilizes the synapse.

The actions of prions make clear that one constantly repeats in order to remain the same. Hence the seeming permanence of memory, a seeming permanence that relies on a constant regeneration: a process that can be as destructive as constructive. Mad Cow Disease, caused by a prion, leads to mad humans, humans that can't remember, can't recall: The same mechanism lies at the heart of both the destruction and construction of long term memory.

In vertebrates, implicit memory is more complex and involves the amygdala: It involves changes to the very sensory system that initially perceived the event. In memory recall, the "same neurons that retrieve the memory of the stimulus are the same sensory and motor neurons that were activated in the first place."[11] Importantly, for every action, there are two pathways that are involved: one that is direct (implicit) and another that goes through the cortex (explicit). The basic idea is the same as in invertebrates: Training leads to a strengthening of the connections between the neurons. The difference between implicit and explicit memory Kandel views as the difference between bottom up (serotonin-based) changes and top down (dopamine) based responses, in which dopamine is central to the stabilization of "spatial map" in the hippocampus. Involuntary memory is sparked by the outside world; voluntary attention arises from the "internal need to process stimuli that are not automatically salient" (Ibid. 313). This would imply that habitual memory (to the extent that habit and memory can be separated) is provoked externally, whereas conscious recall is provided internally.[12]

There is a lot we still do not know about memory and especially the relation between explicit and implicit memory; and Kandel's text is not definitive. What MRIs really show and the specifics of the biological bases of mental illness are not known definitively (Roskies 2007, Coleman 2008). Regardless, this work poses the question: If memory is the strengthening and development of certain pathways—pathways that are not particular to memory but to sensory motor action and perception—is memory something separate, something that is stored? That is, what does memory have to do with memory? Does memory even exist? Although Kandel does not explicitly raise this question, others working on implicit memory do, arguing that implicit memory is a form of long-term priming that has more to do with pattern recognition and perception than with explicit memory. That is, implicit memory has little to do with meaning, with signification—with the recall of a signified from a signifier. Implicit memory—changes that persist (Kandel 2006, 160)—is learning. This kind of learning, further, cannot be localized to the brain. If memory, as E. Tulving has suggested "has to do with the after-effects of stimulation at one time that manifest themselves subsequently at another time" (Tulving 1983, 7), then memory itself—as Henry Roediger III has argued (Roediger 2003)—engages far more than the CNS: Our immune system, for instance, would seem to be also a memory system.

Rather than arguing whether memory exists and what is or is not memory, what is most needed is a change of perspective: One that acknowledges that memory is an action, an activation and difference in structure, making perhaps, memory not anything because it is everything. A change in perspective makes the questions not "what is memory?" and "where is memory stored?" but, rather, "what relations are central to habituation/training, which are evidence both of remembering and forgetting?" To what extent, that is, can we consider memory a habit of living that involves repetition as both living and dead repetition?[13] Kandel links memory to continuity: It is "essential for the continuity of experience. Without the binding force of memory experience would be splintered into as many fragments as there are moments in life" (Kandel 2006, 10). Without memory, or life as a consistent thing—ourselves as a being—disintegrates, but also, "when changes persist, the result is memory storage." The evidence of memory storage is what it allegedly enables: persistence.

Regenerating Memory

Memory is not storage. Memory is not something that simply remains: If any memory remains it is because it is constantly regenerated. The conflation of memory and storage is dangerous because it fosters a misleading ethos that forgets the collective care and effort—good and bad—that goes into any memory.

Memory as a collective act is evident in our daily experiences with computers, which do make their memory seem—against physics—permanent and ubiquitous. If things remain now it is not because digital memory is more robust than paper; the opposite is true. Silicon degrades far more quickly than paper; websites—even seemingly as solid and permanent as geocities—disappear. Clouds are clouds—mercurial mixtures of vapor, liquid, and solid. Despite this, digitization can be considered a form of "saving" because it preserves content through a process of "reformatting:" a reading, which is a writing elsewhere. All computers read by writing elsewhere, or, to use Nancy's terms, by exscribing: by copying and disseminating. Importantly, exscription has little to nothing to do with meaning, but everything to do with communicating (Nancy and Lydon 1990). For Nancy, exscription—a writing that uses meaning to strain against meaning, a writing that exposes the writer—is a cry, a plea, a response a "knowing nothing" that is nonetheless crucial to the experience of being as being with.[14]

The digital saves materials, against its physics, because it addresses another key archival issue: access. It saves by "communicating." From the Library of Congress' early attempt to digitize its collections, the *American Memory Pilot* (1990–1994), to Google's plan to digitize over ten million unique titles, its Book Search Program (announced in 2004), digitization has been trumpeted as a way for libraries finally to fulfill their mission: to accumulate and provide access to human knowledge. They provide access by making what was once seemingly singular or limited, rampantly reproducible, that is, ideally ubiquitous. This rapidly reproducing environment makes the real historical task of the archivist becomes clear: to decide which materials to discard. As Cornelia Vismann has argued (Vismann 2006), the key mission of the Chancellery—the act it gets its name from—was not the simple storing of official documents, but rather their official deletion: cancellation. And so, through the transformation of archiving to reformatting and rewriting (to exscribing), digital objects do seem to have an unnatural persistence. Things we considered or wanted to be ephemeral, things we think are private, are saved, and circulated all the time: from *facebook.com* profiles read by human resources officials to "revenge porn." The fear or trust in the digital as storage stems from constant and ubiquitous machinic and human acts of repetition. Through these acts of repetition, which are central to the very functioning of computers—things remain without remaining; by becoming dynamic they spread.

New media, that is, remain by leaking, ubiquitously. New media are not simply about leaks—they do not simply enable events such as WikiLeaks and whistleblowers such as Snowden—they are themselves leaky. New media work, technically and socially, by breaching—and thus bizarrely sustaining—the boundary between public and private, open and closed. At every level, our networked machines leak: our wireless devices broadcast our signals, which are read in, but not usually read by others. They work promiscuously by downloading all signals and then actively deleting what is not directly addressed to them. Our cell phones read in all signals in the area but can only (usually) decode their own. Every click can leave a trace; every friend—every password—can compromise trust. Our machines operate by repeatedly leaking: by repeatedly repeating, reading, writing, and erasing. They work by constantly exposing their would-be users. They are wonderfully creepy.

Networked computers are ubiquitous, that is, because their signals, which have little to do with meaning, are always touching us, because they are always communicating. In this sense—to return to Weiser's analogy—ubiquitous computing is writing. As Nancy argues, writing is touching, a "touching on the body" (Nancy and Rand 2008, 11): it is "a suspension of meaning which is fragile and repeated" (Nancy and Lydon 1990, 63). This touching is also a profound exposure—an exposure without which there could be no "us," no communication.

Intriguingly, the majority of our signals have nothing to do with the messages we'd like to send: from extensive headers to any package to the "handshakes" (can you read me?) necessary for Transmission Control Protocol (TCP) to work. DDOS (Distributed Denial of Service) attacks reveal the extent to which communications on a network is about anything but communicating meaning: it is about touching and repeating (touchingly repeating?). DDOS attacks work by machines and humans (knowingly or unknowingly) constantly refreshing or requesting a website. Although DDOS attacks are hostile, they are also indistinguishable from more benign actions such as "slashing" something. As the founder of Slashdot founder Rob Malda noted, slashdotting a site often translates to making it inoperable: A hug from a mob is indistinguishable from a DDOS attack (Mankelow 2012). Communication, ubiquitous communication, is a constant touching; a "hug" that can also threaten violence and that is also not fundamentally about meaning. DDOS attacks and other moments of communal action on a network reveal the extent to which community, however inoperable, has become a network weapon: They reveal that community has nothing to do with what we have in common, but rather actions—actions such as remembering, requesting with.

This remembering, this requesting with, links humans and machines. Memory and computers are also ubiquitous because habitual memory—a knowing that is no knowing at all—is provoked by the environment rather than the self. It is not only "recalled directly through performance without an awareness that we are drawing from memory" (Kandel 2006, 132), it is also a "property of the external world" (Ibid., 313). Human memory, like computer memory, thus fundamentally compromises the distinction between inside and outside. Memory in other words is always ubiquitous: penetrating everything and everywhere and also fundamentally collective and individuating because it is habitual.

To end where Weiser starts, and where another book (*Exhausting Obsolescence, or Updating to Remain the Same: Habitual New Media*) must begin, the habitual—a knowing which is no know at all—is key to orchestrating the ubiquitous. According to Weiser, computers as habitual, was an antidote to "computer addicts," who were chained to their screens: computers, used habitually, were to foster dialog and dynamic human communication. Although Weiser places the habitual in an inferior position, the habitual is central to orchestrating and negotiating mass action in the age of neoliberal empowerment and individualism. Habits are repetitious actions in each device and in humans that communicate: from distributed control protocol that mediates the signals of various devices to make sure that 3G networks work efficiently (that every signal makes it through). Through habits, technologies become second nature: autonomous yet intimate, individual yet collective. Through habits, we have arguably become our technologies: we click, stream, update, capture, upload, share, grind, link, verify, map, save, trash, and troll. Habits, such as friending, have been central to the transformation of our data trash into "Big Data:" largely verifiable masses of data traces.

Habits are strange, contradictory things. Habits are humanly-made nature: they are practices acquired through time, that are seemingly forgotten about as they move from the voluntary to the involuntary, the outer to the inner. As they do so, they penetrate and define a person: a habit was traditionally an outer garment, such as a nun's habit. More darkly, they take on a life of their own, independent of an individual's will (drug habits). William James called habits "the enormous fly-wheel of society, its most precious conservative agent. It alone is what keeps us all within the bounds of ordinance, and saves the children of fortune from the envious uprisings of the poor" (James 1890). Habit, that is, is ideology in action. At the same time, habits are viewed as central to individuality: they not only mark individual difference, they also give an individual the time s/he needs to attend to other things, to think, while, at the same time, marking an individual's lack of self-control, since habits are mainly automatic actions prompted by outside stimulus (Wood and Neal 2007). As Catherine Malabou has outlined in her preface to Félix Ravaisson's *Of Habit*, habits are usually understood in two ways: first, as mechanical repetition that erodes what is distinctively human; second, as fundamental to life, to how we persist (Malabou 2008).

However, ubiquitous technologies do not simply penetrate our everyday routines through habits, they also create new habits and, more fundamentally, change what habits do through their constant renewal—through their "newness." Importantly, "new" does not only mean wondrous and singular, but also "coming as a resumption or repetition of some previous act or thing; starting afresh, resurgent": "something restored after demolition, decay, disappearance."[15] This constant renewal changes the effects of habitual repetition. Habits traditionally "habituate": they help us to ignore the new and different in our environment, so we are unlikely to acquire new products (Verplanken and Wood 2006). However, habits now habituate us to change itself. New media habituate us to the acquisition of "new" habits by habituating us to the update: to repetition that deliberately alters. Through habits, the ubiquitous updates, revises, orchestrates, manages, and lives on.

Notes

1. OED reference.
2. The move from calculator to computer is also the move from mere machine to human-emulator: the term computer was first resisted by IBM because computers were initially human. To call a machine a computer was to imply job redundancy (Martin Campbell-Kelly and William Aspray, *Computer: A History of the Information Machine* (1996, 115)). John von Neumann, in his mythic and controversial 1945 *The First Draft Report of the EDVAC*, deliberately used the term "memory organ" rather than "store," also in use at the time, in order to parallel biological and computing components and to emphasize the ephemeral nature of vacuum tubes. (John von Neumann, *First Draft Report of the EDVAC*, section 6.1, Contract No. W–670–ORD–4926, between the USORD and the University of Pennsylvania. Accessed September 12, 2003) Vacuum tubes, unlike mechanical switches, can hold values precisely because their signals can degenerate—and thus regenerate.
3. OED reference for "store" and etymology of memory.
4. This odd conflation of memory with storage—which is perhaps not new but newly conflated, defines the difference between human and machine computers: machinic computers—computers as we now know them—incorporated within themselves the human computer and the pieces of paper (the instructions and data) humans read and wrote.
5. von Neumann describes this deferral as "only temporary"; however, Pres Eckert and John Mauchly, the original patent holders of stored program computing, would allege that von Neumann did not touch on the "true electromagnetic nature" of the devices because it was outside his purview: von Neumann, they contended, merely translated their concrete ideas into formal logic. (William Aspray, *John von Neumann and the origins of modern computing* (Cambridge, Mass: MIT Press, 1990, 42). In fact, rather than a temporary omission, abstractness was von Neumann's modus operandi, central to the "axiomatic" (blackboxing) method of his general theory of natural and artificial automata and in consonance with his game theory work.
6. He goes on to state "It is, however, convenient to consider occasionally neurons with fixed thresholds 2 and 3, that is, neurons which can be excited only by (simultaneous) stimuli on 2 or 3 excitatory synapses (and none on an inhibitory synapse). (cf. {6.4}) It is easily seen that these simplified neuron functions can be imitated by telegraph relays or by vacuum tubes. Although the nervous system is presumably asynchronous (for the synaptic delays), precise synaptic delays can be obtained by using synchronous setups" (John von Neumann, *First Draft Report of the EDVAC*, section 4.2)

7. The argument that source code is only source code after the fact draws from the first chapter of *Programmed Visions* (Wendy H.K. Chun, *Programmed Visions: Software and Memory*. Software studies. Cambridge, Mass: Massachusetts Institute of Technology Press, 2011). In it, I stress the fact that source code is historically posterior to object code—source code emerged with introduction of higher-level programming languages and early programmers debugged the "object" rather than the source code. Source code is not executable. For it to become so, it must be compiled or interpreted and this making executable of code is not a trivial action; the compilation of code is not the same translating a decimal number into a binary one. Rather, it involves instruction explosion and the translation of symbolic into real addresses; that is, a breakdown, using numerical methods, of the steps needed to perform what seems a simple arithmetic calculation. This is most clear in the use of numerical methods to turn integration—a function performed fluidly in analog computers—into a series of simpler arithmetical steps. Also, some programs may be executable, but not all compiled code within that program is executed; rather lines are read in as necessary. So, source code thus only becomes source after the fact.

8. Indeed, von Neumann, perhaps drawing from psychoanalytical arguments that memories never die (one of von Neumann's uncles introduced psychoanalysis to Hungary and von Neumann apparently loved to analyze jokes) or from his personal experience (he allegedly had a photographic memory and could recall conversations word-for-word), presents the following "negative" and not entirely "cogent" for memory as storage by comparing memory to a filing system:

   There is a good deal of evidence that memory is static, unerasable, resulting from an irreversible change. (This is of course the very opposite of a "reverberating," dynamic, erasable memory.) Isn't there some physical evidence for this? If this is correct, then no memory, once acquired, can be truly forgotten. Once a memory-storage place is occupied, it is occupied forever, the memory capacity that it represents is lost; it will never be possible to store anything else there. What appears as forgetting is then not true forgetting, but merely the removal of that particular memory-storage region from a condition of rapid and easy availability to one of lower availability. It is not like the destruction of a system of files, but rather like the removal of a filing cabinet into the cellar. Indeed, this process in many cases seems to be reversible. Various situations may bring the "filing cabinet" up from the "cellar" and make it rapidly and easily available again . . . (John von Neumann, *The Computer and the Brain*, 36)

   Von Neumann's "negative argument" relies on files and the human mind as the owner/manipulator of files. It also depicts the human brain as surprisingly non-plastic: easily used up and unerased, hence once more the need for great storage

9. This happens due to the transmission of serotonin, which leads to the production of cyclic Adenosine MonoPhosphate (AMP), which in turn frees the catalytic unit protein kinase A, which then enhances the release of the neurotransmitter.

10. This is because, repeated stimulation causes the kinases to move into the nucleus, leading to the expression of the CREB protein, which then generates new synapses.

11. As Eric Kandel puts it, if we remember anything of this book, it is because our brain has changed. See Eric Kandel, *In Search of Memory: The Emergence of a New Science of Mind*, 215.

12. This separation of voluntary from involuntary memory/emotions maps nicely onto theoretical ruminations on the relationship between affect + feelings (involuntary and voluntary emotions. Affects are involuntary and caused by factors other than the self, such as circulating signals. This arguably reveals why crises are so privileged now: moments when both are active)—moments when new pathways can be built.

13. Intriguingly, in describing explicit memory—in which we do not simply recall but rather experience an event once more—Kandel emphasizes creativity. The brain, he asserts, only stores a core memory. Upon recall, though, this core memory is "elaborated upon and reconstructed, with subtractions, additions, elaborations, and distortions" (Eric Kandel, *In Search of Memory: The Emergence of a New Science of Mind*, 281). That which persist, that which is recalled and that traumatizes—that we experience each time as though it were the first time, as though it just happened, memories that are persistent and will not leave us alone—are not simply missives from the past, but repetitions that are created each time.

14. Bataille's writing, Nancy continues, "uses the work of meaning to expose, to lay bare the unusable, unexploitable, unintelligible, and unfoundable being of being-in-the-world. That there is being, or some being or even beings, and in particular that there is us, our community (of writing-reading)" (Jean-Luc Nancy, "Exscription," 64).

15. OED citation for "new."

References

Aspray, William. 1990. *John von Neumann and the Origins of Modern Computing.* History of computing. Cambridge, MA: MIT Press.
Bush, Vannevar. 1945. "As We May Think." *The Atlantic*, July 1, 1945. http://theatlantic.com/magazine/archive/1945/07/as-we-may-think/303881/?single_page=true
Campbell-Kelly, Martin, and William Aspray. 1996. *Computer: A History of the Information Machine.* New York: BasicBooks.
Chun, Wendy H. K. 2000. *Programmed Visions: Software and Memory.* Software studies. Cambridge, MA: MIT Press.
Coleman, Gabriella E. 2008. "The Politics of Rationality: Psychiatric Survivors' Challenge to Psychiatry." In *Tactical Biopolitics: Art, Activism, and Technoscience*, edited by Beatriz Da Costa and Kavita Philip, 341–63. Cambridge, MA: MIT Press.
Derrida, Jacques. 1981. "Plato's Pharmacy." In *Dissemination*, edited by Jacques Derrida, 61–172. London: The Athlone Press.
Derrida, Jacques. 1998. *Archive Fever: A Freudian Impression.* Chicago, IL: University of Chicago Press.
Dijkstra, Edsger W. 2002. "Go-To Statement Considered Harmful." In *Software Pioneers: Contributions to Software Engineering; [contributions to Sd&m Conference Software Pioneers, old Bundestag, Bonn, Germany, 28/29 June 2001]*, edited by Manfred Broy and Ernst Denert, 351–55. Berlin: Springer.
Eckert, J. Presper. 1944. "Disclosure of Magnetic Calculating Machine." http://archive.computerhistory.org/resources/text/Knuth_Don_X4100/PDF_index/k-8-pdf/k-8-u2775-Mauchly-letter-plus.pdf.
James, William. (1890) 1996. *The Principles of Psychology.* Ann Arbor, MI: University of Michigan Library. http://psychclassics.asu.edu/James/Principles/prin4.htm
Kandel, Eric R. 2006. *In Search of Memory: The Emergence of a New Science of Mind.* New York: W. W. Norton & Co.
McCulloch, Warren S. 1965. *Embodiments of Mind.* Cambridge, MA: Massachusetts Institute of Technology Press.
McCulloch, Warren S. 1965. "What Is a Number, That a Man May Know It and a Man, that He May Know a Number?" *General Semantics Bulletin* 26/27: 7–18.
McDermott, K. B. 2000. "Implicit Memory." In *Encyclopedia of Psychology*, edited by Alan E. Kazdin, 231–34. New York: APA; Oxford University Press, 2000.
Malabou, Catherine. 2008. "Addiction and Grace Preface to Felix Ravaisson's Of Habit." In *Of habit*, edited by Félix Ravaisson, Clare Carlisle, and Mark Sinclaire, vii–xx. London, New York: Continuum.
Mankelow, Trent. 2012. "Quotes from Webstock 2012." Accessed June 01, 2012. http://optimalusability.com/2012/02/quotes-from-webstock-2012.
Nancy, Jean-Luc, and Katherine Lydon. 1990. "Exscription." *Yale French Studies* 78: 47–65. http://jstor.org/stable/2930115.
Nancy, Jean-Luc, and Richard Rand. 2008. *Corpus.* New York: Fordham University Press.
Roediger, Henry L. 2003. "Reconsidering Implicit Memory." In *Rethinking Implicit Memory*, edited by Jeffrey S. Bowers and Chad J. Marsolek, 3–18. New York: Oxford University Press.
Roskies, Adina L. 2007. "Are Neuroimages Like Photographs of the Brain?" *Philosophy of Science* 74: 860–72.
Tulving, Endel. 1983. *Elements of Episodic Memory.* Oxford: Clarendon Press.
Verplanken, Bas, and Wendy Wood. 2006. "Interventions to Break and Create Consumer Habits." *Journal of Public Policy & Marketing* 25 (1): 90–103.
Vismann, Cornelia. 2006. "Out of File, Out of Mind." In *New Media, Old Media: A History and Theory Reader*, edited by Wendy H. K. Chun and Thomas W. Keenan, 97–104. New York: Routledge.
von Neumann, John. 1945. "First Draft of a Report on the EDVAC." Section 6.1, Contract No. W–670–ORD–4926 between the USORD and the University of Pennsylvania. Accessed September 12, 2003.
von Neumann, John. 1966. *Theory of Self-Reproducing Automata: Papers of John von Neumann on Computers and Computer Theory.* Cambridge, MA: MIT Press.

von Neumann, John, Paul M. Churchland, and Patricia S. Churchland. 2000. *The Computer and the Brain.* 2nd ed. New Haven, CT: Yale University Press.

Weiser, Mark. 1991. "The Computer for the Twenty-first Century." *Scientific American* 265 (3): 94–104.

Weiser, Mark, and John S. Brown. 1996. "The Coming Age of Calm Technology." Accessed November 18, 2013. http://ubiq.com/hypertext/weiser/acmfuture2endnote.htm.

Wood, Wendy, and David T. Neal. 2007. "A New Look at Habits and the Habit-Goal Interface." *Psychological Review* 114 (4): 843–63.

PART II
Situating

SITUATING: CONTEXTUALITY AND CONTEXT-AWARENESS

Jay David Bolter

The volume proceeds from the obvious fact that, as our digital technologies multiply, there arises a culture of ubiquity. We come to expect that digital applications and platforms will strive to occupy every niche in our personal, social, and economic environment. Although the processes of proceduralization and digitization are the result of human decisions, they do sometimes seem to possess an inevitable momentum. As contributors to this volume have repeatedly noted, the vision of ubiquitous computing as well as the term itself came from Mark Weiser (1991), who worked as a chief scientist at Xerox PARC in the 1980s and 1990s. He proposed that computers would be integrated into our daily lives as controls for all sorts of everyday devices, such as refrigerators and thermostats. These devices would be networked to communicate with each other as well as us, working behind the scenes to anticipate our needs. The current fascination with building out the IoT could be seen as the continuation of Weiser's vision.

Weiser had already appreciated one important aspect of the way in which our society would incorporate the digital: that is, by situating it in our lived world. At the same time, he was responding to the dominant rhetoric of the 1990s, the rhetoric of cyberspace and Virtual Reality. In this early phase of the development of the World Wide Web, digital enthusiasts were promoting a vision of our digital future in which the computer offered us an escape from our situation, into a place that John Perry Barlow, for example, characterized in his "Declaration of the Independence of Cyberspace" as a realm of "mind" (Barlow 1996). In cyberspace, he and others argued, the limiting conditions of our lived social and cultural worlds could be overcome or simply ignored. In cyberspace we did not have bodies. Because video was still relatively difficult to deploy on the Internet, we did not typically see each other in our digital communications and interactions, so that markers of race, gender, and economic status could supposedly be erased. At the same time, Virtual Reality (VR) had (temporarily it turned out) eclipsed Artificial Intelligence as the paradigmatic myth of the digital. The expensive prototype VR systems of the day also offered a few lucky users the opportunity to escape their situation by entering into a visual world consisting entirely of computer graphics. Weiser understood his ubiquitous computing as the opposite of VR. While VR and by extension the desktop computer as the portal to cyberspace promised to take us into the computer, ubiquitous computing proposed to distribute computers throughout our everyday world. The computers become part of our world instead of the reverse.

As noted above, Weiser's vision seems to be coming true. We do have computing devices embedded in many of the devices with which we interact, and these devices are in some cases beginning to talk to one another. But Weiser was wrong in one important respect: he expected that all these computing elements would come to operate seamlessly and invisibly "behind our backs." He imagined that the desired goal was to have the digital disappear into our environment. It is curious in retrospect to assume that we would happily surround ourselves with smart refrigerators, toasters, and vacuum cleaners, but would not want to see or understand the computers that ran them. As it happened, by far the most culturally and economically important expressions of digital ubiquity today are media devices: smart phones, tablets, video screens, laptops, and even desktop computers (still), and on the near horizon forms of wearable computing such as smart watches. These are the devices with which we surround ourselves, and we invent more and more ways for them to connect to each other at the level of hardware, software, and communicative practices (e.g., social media). As Steve Jobs understood so well, we do not want our media devices to disappear: we want our phones and tablets to be visible emblems of our participation in media culture. The IoT may someday come to pass, but at present ubiquitous computing is actually ubiquitous media, and media platforms are very much a part of our situation.

Some of these media platforms, such as television monitors, are fixed, but become ubiquitous because we locate them in more and more places—in bars, restaurants, airports, and other public spaces as well as our homes. Many of these artifacts are portable and become part of our embodied world simply because we take them with us wherever we go. Portable and wearable media technology as a mass phenomenon is relatively recent, with the large-scale adaption of the smart phone coming in the first decade of the twenty-first century. But this technology is already being recognized and studied as part of human-computer interaction (HCI). Paul Dourish (2001) has specifically argued that "embodied interaction" along with social computing constitutes the new digital paradigm. It is true that smartphones and tablets and strapped-on smart watches become part of our physical situation. Many applications of Augmented and Mixed Reality for these devices are beginning to engage us proprioceptively, as we have to hold the phone in a particular orientation or manipulate it for the experience to work.

One of the important aspects of these artifacts is that they know and respond to is our location. GPS and cell-tower tracking make phones and tablets location aware, anchoring digital information from "cyberspace" at particular points in our environment. The phone can place information in the world, and, as we know well, it can report our location back to the Internet (and to the NSA). This reciprocal relationship, a key to whole set of applications, reconfigures our relationship to the digital. In "The Information Environment," speaking of network media cultural in general, Sean Cubitt suggests that we become alienated from information when it becomes part of our environment and requires elaborate techniques of navigation. But, if this process of alienation is true for information that resides in networked cyberspace, the locating of information (or digital created perceptual experiences) in the visual surround offers other, more hopeful possibilities. The displaying of information in the near space around us suggests that the information can function on a scale and at a pace to which we can literally relate (our bodily dimensions), and that the information pertains directly to our world. Much of what is inserted in an augmented environment is advertising for restaurants, hotels, and merchandise, it is true, and the goal of locating such information is to put the advertising message in front of us at precisely the moment when we are most likely to be willing to buy something. But location awareness can also be used to enhance our understanding or connection with our surroundings, as is the case with the work of the MR performance group, Blast Theory (whose interview is included in this section). For nearly two decades, Blast Theory has been exploring the artistic possibilities of mixed reality to mediate between subjects as well as with the environment. Here situating is both of a matter of interactive communication between individuals and procedural interactions with information in space.

Other artists who contribute chapters or are interviewed in this section also explore how new opportunities for interaction with digital information can be situated in our physical environment. Jane Prophet and Helen Pritchard write about Technosphere 2.0, a new mobile version of Prophet's original web-based work from the 1990s. The new version "lives" on interconnected mobile Android applications, allowing the user to 3D creatures, which are viewed through the screen of the phone and appear to occupy physical space. Prophet and Pritchard see these apps as "experiments through which we test hypotheses that mixed reality opens up the possibilities for more affective experiences." Their project is art that interrogates the technology of ubiquity without necessarily assuming an oppositional stance. In an interview in this section, Mogens Jacobsen claims that his art does not address ubiquity directly, but rather derives from his passion to free digital art from the controlling assumption that the art space was or should be restricted to the GUI and the desktop.

Other media theorists in this section are less attracted by the possibilities of ubiquitous and embodied computing than they are concerned about unintended social and cultural consequences. In "A Portrait of the Artist as a Smart City," Steiner and Veel examine the contemporary discourse surrounding the "smart city," in which technology is represented as saving the city from collapse because of the size and complexity of the information economy. They find this discourse to be naively optimistic, belonging to the modernist tradition of attempts to "improve the city by rendering it as a (complex) system." The paradox is that attempts to eliminate complexity call for greater complexity in the form of additional layers of technology in the urban fabric. In his contribution, Malcolm McCullough examines the issue of complexity and information overload, in terms not of the city as a whole, but of the individual (possibly urban) subject. His essay is a meditation on the concept of distraction in the contemporary digital ambiance. He concludes that "[t]he kinds of sensibility that attention to surroundings help to cultivate seem very necessary to productivity and well-being in an age of information superabundance and overconsumption." Through a close reading of several works by Japanese artists, Yvonne Spielmann argues that contemporary artistic practices not only contribute to a conceptual framework for understanding connectivity and complexity, but also "take a critical stance and pursue creative interventions into contemporary networked processes." In one of the most original contributions to this section, Ellis and Goggin look at the relationship of disability and locative media and argue that disability itself as a kind of cultural location, one that has a complex relationship to class, gender, and ethnicity. Finally, in "Media Always and Everywhere: A Cosmic Approach," Kember and Zylinska extend their critique to the notion of ubiquity itself. They question the assumption that the computational paradigm is in fact a "defining aspect of our lives in the early twenty-first century." They challenge us to imagine ubiquity in terms that are not technology centered—a challenge that leads them to a figuration they call "cosmic media."

Altogether, the interviews and chapters in this section indicate the variety of ways in which our "situation" can be understood in the context of ubiquitous and mobile digital media.

References

Barlow, John Perry. 1996. *A Declaration of the Independence of Cyberspace*. Electronic Frontier Foundation 1996 [cited April 3, 2015]. Available from https://projects.eff.org/~barlow/Declaration-Final.html.

Dourish, Paul. 2001. *Where the Action Is: The Foundations of Embedded Interaction*. Cambridge, MA: MIT Press.

Weiser, Mark. 1991. "The Computer for the Twenty-first Century." *Scientific American* 265: 94–104.

CULTURAL THEORY

Maria Engberg

To ask how cultural theory relates to situating or situation is to pose a tautological question. Cultural theory is always concerned with the situation or context of any phenomenon that it studies. The context may be examined along a variety of dimensions: historical, aesthetic, intertextual and semiotic, social, or economic. From the perspective of cultural theory, nothing is "context-free." Thus, from this perspective, the devices of ubiquitous computing are not only embedded in a matrix of other technologies, and they are not only in communication with each other over the Internet. They are also embedded in the history of earlier media forms (such as films, radio, and television). They are equally in communication with myriad assumptions about the nature of the human in a digital media culture, and her relationship to technologies.

Yvonne Spielmann's essay in this volume introduces non-Western perspectives and positions by "practicing another vision of mobile connectedness in mixed reality situations." The Japanese artists whose work Spielmann analyzes suggest a different aesthetic response to technological environments. Statements from the artists themselves (notably Fujihata) in the essay suggest that there is a degree of orientalism of Japanese media culture from Western point-of-view, resulting in that Japanese artists fill a position of "exotic Other" (Said 1978) in critical and curatorial practices worldwide. The observation notwithstanding, Spielmann asserts that Japanese artists' works exemplify principles that "construct novel network options closer to a decentralizing connectivity," placing them apart from Western modern conceptualizations of spatiality and visuality. However, the decentralized connectivity that the Japanese artists foreground resonates with artists elsewhere on the globe, evident in early works such as *Poietic Generator* (Auber 1986) and a concern that emerges in the artist interviews in this volume. Nevertheless, Spielmann's essay reminds us of the ease with which rhetoric of ubiquity in technoculture take on a global quality that is rarely questioned or qualified.

In Chapter 19 in this book, Henriette Steiner and Kristin Veel choose to interrogate the rhetoric of contemporary urban planning, the smart city, and ubiquitous computational environments. They ask, what is the place—the site—of the human in those visions? Rather than addressing human complexity and multifarious behavior as something chaotic that needs to be homogenized and "cleaned up" through socio-architectural planning, Steiner and Veel argue that we are dealing instead with "different epistemic paradigms, each of which have particular consequences for our way of understanding the world." Literary theorists would agree with Steiner and Veel in their suggestion that the novel—in their case the modernist novel *A Portrait of the Artist as a Young Man* by James Joyce—can function as a site for building potential worlds through narrative. Borrowing from possible worlds theory in philosophy, literary theorists propose that fictional texts can offer sites to construct, test out and simulate possible worlds and the socio-economic, natural, and technological processes that those worlds hold. Critics such as Thomas Pavel (1975, 1986) and Marie-Laure Ryan (1991) have proposed that fictional texts take part in constructions of possible worlds, as do other kinds of philosophical propositions, simulations, and, more recently, computer games. Possible worlds theories are grounded in the idea that "reality—conceived as the sum of the imaginable rather than as the sum of what exists physically—is a universe composed of a plurality of distinct worlds" (Ryan 2012).

Malcolm McCullough's contribution to this volume addresses one of the negative effects of our current ubiquitous computing culture—distraction. Tracking the analyses of overload, over-consumption, too much information, and superabundance of information, McCullough argues that one way to deal with this ontologically inescapable condition is to cultivate a different mindfulness. McCullough suggests that this mode of awareness would allow for, quite simply, human fascination. If people are invested and interested in what they do and where they are, they are not as easily distracted by information for entertainment. McCullough suggests that mastering this mindfulness is necessary to our continued "productivity and well-being." Not making a conscious choice among possible "attention practices" in the ever-present environment of demands for attention to networked machines (often our own mobile devices) would mean surrendering one's time to someone else's—something else's—discretion. Ubiquity, in McCullough's elegant phrasing, becomes then "experiential saturation" in "ambient information."

Sean Cubitt's chapter, "The Information Environment," also deals with information in his essay, not as knowledge but as "commodities, data, and [as] an environment." By way of analyses of radio spectra and telecommunications, Cubitt explores how information turns into environments that may or may not include its human subjects. He asks, provocatively, "what kind of humans the inhabitants of the information environment are becoming," and what violence unwitting or unwilling groups of people are being subjected to? Cubitt's essay is expansive in its treatment of the areas of human activity that are affected by the machinations of information as late capitalist, technoculturally driven environments, arguing that four environments in particular can be discerned: terrestrial, technological, informatics, and genetic. In changing the dynamics of how environments operate and their processes of inclusion and exclusion, Cubitt argues that we are better served by peer-to-peer networks that include both machines and humans. Such networks can ultimately change what we mean by ubiquity.

In their chapter, "Media Always and Everywhere," Sarah Kember and Joanna Zylinska flip the ubiquitous toward the cosmic, arguing that air is a better concept for ubiquitous media as they are "always and everywhere," like air. Kember and Zylinska suggest "cosmic media" as a mode of thinking against industry models that are human-centered. They propose instead thinking with the understanding that air is "a means of transport and communication," which not only humans but all living systems use. Although they do not mention Mark Weiser's vision for ubiquitous computing, we can recall the atmosphere of his all-encompassing environment in which computers seem to no longer be there but continuously serve human needs. However, unlike Weiser, Kember and Zylinska do not propose that media should aim to disappear—into thin air, if the reader would excuse the pun—rather, they have chosen air because of its "messy complexity."

The contributions in this section suggest different shifts and moves in the process of situating the discourse around ubiquitous computing and culture. They reveal the complexity of mapping what the territories and contexts are when speaking of the ubiquitous computing phenomenon broadly defined. These moves range from a geographic/cultural move from Western-centered, normative presuppositions of media arts' possibility to address networked technologies; a move toward inclusion in how we conceive of the participants and actors of networked media, the IoT and peer-to-peer networks; to addressing the effects of ubiquitous computing on our cognitive abilities, or how ubiquitous computational networks construct environments with deep and drastic repercussions for human life.

While Weiser's vision that "computer access [would] penetrate all groups in society" (Weiser 1991) seems to be near fulfillment, these contributions and others in this volume convincingly show the need for situating, contextualizing, and problematizing computing in all its myriad constructs and positions. We need to address the impact of ubiquity, not just technologically, but socially and individually as well. Implicitly arguing against Weiser's conviction that "the most profound technologies are those that disappear, [that] weave themselves into the fabric of everyday life until they are indistinguishable from it" (Weiser 1991), the essays in this section show how complex, complicated, and multifarious ubiquitous computing and ubiquitous media have become.

References

Auber, Olivier. 1986. *Poietic Generator.* http://poietic-generator.net/

Pavel, Thomas. 1975. "Possible Worlds in Literary Semantics." *Journal of Aesthetics and Art Criticism* 34, 165–76.

Pavel, Thomas. 1986. *Fictional Worlds.* Cambridge, MA: Harvard UP.

Ryan, Marie-Laure. 1991. *Possible Worlds, Artificial Intelligence and Narrative Theory.* Bloomington, IN: University of Indiana Press.

Ryan, Marie-Laure. 2012. "Possible Worlds." In Hühn, Peter et al. (Eds.). *The Living Handbook of Narratology.* Hamburg: Hamburg University. Accessed March 10, 2015. http://lhn.uni-hamburg.de/

Said, Edward. 1978. *Orientalism.* New York: Vintage Books.

Weiser, Mark. 1991. "The Computer for the Twenty-first Century." *Scientific American* Special Issue on Communications, Computers, and Networks. September. Accessed April 9, 2015. http://ubiq.com/hypertext/weiser/SciAmDraft3.html

THINKING IN NETWORKS: ARTISTIC–ARCHITECTURAL RESPONSES TO UBIQUITOUS INFORMATION

Yvonne Spielmann

Artistic Positioning

By focusing on artistic positions, I wish to raise awareness for creative practices that in aesthetic–technical ways reflect on digitally networked information and communication systems. As a starting point, it will be useful to identify the conceptual frameworks that determine theories, practices, and aesthetics as they intersect in media–cultural applications of current media technologies. They are, for the most part, associated with fluidity of constantly changeable media borders, the miniaturization of objects, and the increase of responsive environments. The main characteristics of the present situation are permanent flow, constant change, connection with everything, and endless continuation of processes. These characteristics also enter into building blocks with identifiable core parameters and are generally considered to be essential structures of contemporary global society. In this situation, I propose to take a closer look at conceptual frameworks that have fostered thinking in complexity and have promoted a high level of connectivity. This distinguishes media and cultural processes of the present and emerges with computation at large. The point of view that I discuss in the following considerations arises from a perspective of digitally informed humanities applied to examples of aesthetic–artistic practices. The focus lies on those practices that not only make use of digital technologies, but at the same time take a critical stance and pursue creative interventions into networked processes of the present.

I suggest pursuing methods of applied analysis and investigating creative practices that address questions of capacity regarding constantly changing and multiple interconnected technological forms. At the same time, there is a need to consider the specific cultural context that shapes and is shaped by the use of the presumably universal machine named computer. When we want to determine what a critical position of artists regarding these interwoven fields of influence can be, it will be worthwhile to observe points of interference where the aesthetic positioning suspends expectations and shifts perception. In this direction, creative practices will be able to employ tools, and experiment with the properties of devices differently. They can relocate ubiquitous appearances of more or less imperceptible, notably invisible, and unnoticeable processes that surround us in any given situation. As a premise for effective artistic responses towards a situation that is characterized by ubiquitous technological environments—discussed as the new paradigm of electronic and digital culture respectively—it seems necessary that these practices reflect on the state of the art of the present. A present that is characterized by ambient computing, smart devices, and omnipresent networks. At the same time, artistic expression needs to articulate a position of aesthetic intervention amidst a surrounding where everything can be traced, connected, surveilled, and controlled.

A shift of perspective in the arts manifests a position of inventive intervention. This means, for example, that existing devices are purposefully misused, remodeled, and changed in their functions in order to make us aware of the ways in which we have learnt to understand, accept, and also "communicatively" adapt to the properties of networked processing applications in many areas of everyday life. With regard to areas of digital cultures, smart technologies radically dissolve barriers between us and the machine world by diminishing the noticeable interfaces that were needed in most Virtual Reality applications. I would imagine that possibilities of creative intervention would consider the political–military implications of emerging technologies as well as the advancement of techniques in the commercial–industrial sectors. In this respect, I would think artistic practices bear an interesting potential for the articulation of a scientific–artistic model, a model that could rearticulate participatory and interactive features and express an imagination of other forms of the unseen and the unheard. In view of the growth of Virtual Reality applications in the commercial sectors or game industries on the one hand, and of the sophisticated overlay of real and virtual data in Augmented Reality applications on the other, the current strand of development in ubiquitous computing seems to foster properties such as smallness, fluidity, invisibility, sensor-based connectivity, and resultantly more and more interface-free encounters of human and machine code. In this situation of highly complex devices that enhance and challenge our intellectual capacity, a position of invention could be regarded not only as a representational reflection on the situation but also have value as an exemplary model to guide further practices.

Artistic intervention that takes position amidst the challenges and changes with which social and cultural relationships are confronted in networked societies—to borrow Manuel Castells' term in the broader understanding of art within global politics—necessarily needs to take into account media and also cultural connotations of thinking in networks (Castells 1996). By situating artistic–creative practices in networked environments, we can investigate how far the participatory idea of connectedness relates to governmental–political and military–industrial frameworks of controlled spaces that surround us in public and private sectors. Because of the reach of ubiquitous information across borders, there is an urgency to closer investigate the structural settings within the society that prefigure and shape the media cultural environment wherein novel technical applications are embedded. Clearly, they do not emerge in neutral spaces. Rather, they are configured and processed according to an existing order and rule with specific parameters of social acceptance and control, and they develop at a specific time and location.

As a result, thinking in networks does not liberate us from scrutiny and comprehension of the particularities of practical, economic, and—not to forget—cultural and aesthetic components and their interrelationships. For the discussion of artistic responses to the present situation of ubiquitous information processing in networks it will be important to link the creative world to larger parameters that are said to be structural factors of the present. These are: 1) surveillance and control and 2) supervision and monitoring. In this view, we can investigate how far the participatory idea of connectedness relates to governmental–political and military–industrial frameworks of controlled spaces that surround us in public and private sectors. The point is to set out alternatives and to critically respond to growing needs in the fields of social media activities. However, we shall not naively overlook that a large number of presumably uncontrolled, alternative activities may also work under the regime of surveillance and supervision of the master structure of the corporation or enterprise that provides the service for all. Therefore, critical awareness for critical positioning is also at stake. In view of our complex media culture, artistic thinking in networks is an important tool in reflecting on governmental and locational politics behind the technological drive into pervasive computing, as well as in raising discussions about the contextual attributes of the underlying conceptual framework.

Conceptual Frameworks

Conceptual frameworks have foregrounded and by and large driven the technological development of building blocks for programmable devices, tools, sensors, and further applications. One key tendency has been to miniaturize the tools and objects and to make their appearances more appealing to us. This is coupled with further efforts to smoothen our encounters with the machine world by predominantly dissolving the interface with its dual function of barrier and border and as bridge to connect to and embrace different worlds. In this respect, the use of networked devices follows a model of the machine that smoothly and not necessarily in anthropomorphic representation adapts to human behavior and environment. It "learns" from us by monitoring our customs and practice and not the other way round. Previously, the machine pattern of an electronic devices, let's say of an analogue image processor, required that we accommodate to a certain level of expert knowledge and learn the internal operational system, whereas with today's computational devices it is not required to take note of the interconnected processes. However, a dual concept exists since a long time, of machines that adapt to our environment and machines that force us to fit to their mechanism. Both directions contribute to conceptual ideas of complexity and connectivity.

In a critical view of the emergence of such concepts, we need to avoid a way of thinking in temporal progression and linear development of the kind "from–to." Enhancement means that we understand what it means to us today to be connected with the global world at all times and everywhere. It also means to decide on how we locate a present position in temporal and spatial terms to the overall translocal, transcultural, and transnational systems. How do we cope with an environment of multiple interconnected relationships? As it seems, local relationships have become more precious: cultural contexts in this respect matter as roots and by the same token as routes—to reframe James Clifford's observation that cultural and media concepts respectively exist in traveling relationships. In this direction the spatial relations of locational positions and differences should be included in a revision of a conceptual framework fostering "smart", "ambient," and "intelligent" environments (Clifford 1997). We may find points of synchronicity across different cultural and media contexts regarding the conceptual history of a framework that links people and computers. These foreground the building of tools and have instigated a wide range of experimental and mixed media practices in and with Virtual Reality and Augmented Reality.

A large part of the modern respectively post-modern imperative to think in networks has advanced after World War II along with new demands from the U.S. military–industrial complex in securing control in the Western world and to achieve faster and more complex information recording and processing. To remind us, as early as 1945, the U.S. government chief scientific advisor, Vannevar Bush, set the tone in his influential essay "As We May Think" by proposing the concept of "Memex," which was designed as a hypertextual machine to bring solution to the challenge of coping with increasingly information–saturated world (Bush 1945).

Bush advocated the emerging military–industrial complex in securing control in the Western world. In the following, conceptual thinking instigated Ted Nelson (Nelson 2001) to develop hypertext and hypermedia as a new cultural form. These influential concepts, "Memex" (Vannevar Bush) and "hypertext" (Ted Nelson), were meant to represent new structures to process and systematize complex and connected information. Further, in relation to the question of how we may link people and computers, Douglas Engelbart in the 1962 essay, "Augmenting Human Intellect: A Conceptual Framework," presents a machine vision to ameliorate the human capacity of intelligence by proposing higher levels of synergy and structure with support of personal computing. The objective to "augment human intellect" shall be realized by developing a "conceptual framework" that "must orient us toward the real possibilities and problems associated with using modern technology to give direct aid to an individual in comprehending complex situations, isolating the significant factors, and solving problems" (Engelbart 2001, 70).

In light of the development of new techniques, procedures, and systems that would better match these needs, Engelbart's proposal is far-reaching because it involves a two-way augmentation. The human capabilities have to be extended by training and new systems need to be improved. In summary, in the early 1960s Engelbart proposed a conceptual framework for "real-time interaction of collaborative computing," which, under the present paradigm of ubiquitous computing, foreshadows adaptions to virtual and augmented reality environments. In contrast to the framework of electronic culture that is based on television and video and follows the paradigm of plug-in tools, the novel experiences with computer-networked interaction follow the paradigm of structurally open-ended processes that can travel across time and space.

The cultural context of these systems in the Western post-war societies documents Engelbart's aim of mutual learning whereby the devices and the users would mutually adapt to each other by enhancing capacity and capability. The point has been made that the technological environment is in constant flow. One way of looking at the new environment is to regard the incorporation of devices as almost "natural" extensions of our daily actions and thought processes. In this respect, the augmentation that the devices manoeuver bring new affordances of complexity. Another way to look at the augmented computer tools is to regard their structural organization and how it is enhanced by "learning" step-by-step from previous steps. In this respect, the relational situation of omnipresent machine processes fosters connectivity. When we regard the communicative concepts behind the development of "thinking machines," "smart environments," "ambient intelligence," and so forth, I find that at least two components stand out as paradigmatic in order to sustain a ubiquitous level of computing. They are complexity and connectivity.

Interestingly, the idea of connectedness has its cultural roots not in the Western, but rather the Eastern philosophy. The notion of network thinking and related circular structures as a cultural form are more associated with Eastern thinking and differ from the Western cultural forms of polarities. Networking in Asian thinking does not, in philosophical terms, rely on subject–object relations, dualisms, and interrelationships that are of Western origin. In this, creative and cultural practices in the Asia-Pacific sphere manifest a seminal understanding of interconnectedness that characterizes a cultural specificity and is highlighted in the use of media technology: "The Far East thinks in networks. . . . The Far East has an almost natural connection to technical networking."[1] And in view of this, artistic–architectural responses to networked processing devices need to be regarded in how far cultural components and specific contexts play a role in achieving a new pattern in the overall conceptual framework of complexity and connectivity, since creative intervention cannot be invented in a neutral, abstract space.

In the following, I am especially interested in non-Western positions that in a different spatial setting revise subject-object positions, positions that connect to the centrality of Western central perspective (Bhabha 1994). Such structuring principles might now be remodeled so as to construct novel network options closer to a decentralizing connectivity. Japanese media artists Masaki Fujihata, Seiko Mikami, and the Japanese–European group doubleNegatives Architecture are core examples of a participatory connectedness that has such cultural locational, architectural, and technological implications. In a Western visual regime of modernity (Jay 1993), these examples appear to intervene by practicing another vision of mobile connectedness in mixed reality situations. These projects are not fixed and have effects on the environment and the location where they are performed, situations that do not stress end results but rather invite us to experience the fluid and changeable roots of making connections.

Mixed Realities

In a conceptual–historical view, the two machine visions of how to link people and computers, namely machines that adapt to us and machines that demand our adjustment to novel affordances, are intersected in the imaginary situations that are described in the science fiction novel *The Invention of Morel* by Adolfo Bioy Casares, written in 1940 (Bioy Casares 2003). In the novel, the narrator tries to discover the nature of the code of a ubiquitous machine that has been recording and retaining sensory perceptions and endlessly re-performs the actions of people who are no longer alive. There is no escape from the overall presence and routine of the machine and its performances which clearly dictate the rule for all times: They force us to fit to their mechanism. At the same time, the human figures who lived in the past and now reappear in the present almost seamless mix with the actual presence of the narrator so that the resultant mixed reality of overlaid time zones renders in the present the power of the device, invisible and unrecognizable. The convergence creates an almost seamlessly connected perceptual environment.

Predominantly, *The Invention of Morel* has been regarded as a founding myth of Virtual Reality, a situation where we adapt to and immerse into a virtually presented world. The idea of the construction is to diminish interfaces and provide possibilities to experience immersive encounters with simulated figurations of the virtual as if "real" and of the past as if "present." In addition, the novel's narrative also provides connecting points in direction of Augmented Reality when different actions of different time and space zones intersect in logically paradoxical situations. These mergers prefigure, for example, autonomous, self-reconfiguring machine processes that can result in the performance of multiple functions in dynamic and flexible environments. In Morel's novel, the perceptual environment meanders in-between time zones and has elastic spaces, because the locational data of the past and of the present are fused. One interesting point in the realization of paradoxical temporal–spatial situations lies in the dissolution of any central, hierarchical, or priority position: differences such as before and after and also inside–outside position dissolve. This conflation of spatial and temporal "data," which does not appear in linear progression, has been taken further in mixed reality applications where the paradoxical environments are technologically realized in artistic–architectural installations that foster increasingly complex connectivity.

In Masaki Fujihata's real–virtual installation modeled after Morel, *Morel's Panorama* (Fujihata 2006), two panoramas are interlaid and one is projected with the other. In re-inventing Morel's model on another technological level, Fujihata fuses two different levels of time and space at the real space of the exhibition site. On the one hand, there is a panorama presentation showing Fujihata reading out passages from the original novel. In Fujihata's case, the pattern for parallel reality is one of overlapping zones in cyberspace, and it originates in two incompatible virtualities. This past recording of himself reading from the novel, which Fujihata reproduces in image and sound in the space of the installation, is interlaced with a contemporary, site-specific recording produced by filming the viewers in the real spatial conditions where the virtual reality has been installed. A centrally positioned camera, equipped with a panorama lens, generates images of this second panorama, which is processed by a computer in real time, varied in form and size randomly, and overlaps with the other, previously shot panorama. Both cylindrical image forms integrate not only with each other but equally with the surrounding architectural space. In this real space, distorted by two virtual projections, the audience enters, as it were, as the third factor of the artistic work and is immediately an immersed component in the interwoven processes of recording and reproduction in the actual–virtual panorama.

In each performance that is a site-specific installation of *Morel's Panorama*, Fujihata's work demonstrates further fields of action that connect viewers/users in newly constructed networks and induct them into these open structures. The different localizations in time and space are a vital component of the interactive behavior of the audiovisual sequences that are displayed in the panoramas. Juxtaposing different kind of realities results in linkages that use computers and measuring and control instruments to develop the possibilities of physical activity with real people and places in an abstract–graphic depiction of subjective data that are captured at different time zones and from differing perspectives. The process testifies to Fujihata's intention of producing contacts and contexts beyond time and in in-between spaces—and not just in aesthetics but also in everyday, creative dealings with computers.

With *Morel's Panorama* (Plate 24), an inventive intervention into fictional science takes place because the fictional paradox becomes aesthetically–technically representable in a real–virtual way and demonstrates an expanded understanding of communicative interactions in the era of ubiquitous computing. In the gaining of new dimensions in and with "new" technologies, interactivity plays a key role. Fujihata, a pioneer of computer animation and interactive media and founder of the Graduate School of Film and New Media in the Tokyo University of the Arts, has described the cultural position of Japanese media culture as follows:

> I would like to think that media art was universal, but I don't think such a thing exists . . . It's true that Japanese artists are seen as important in Europe too, and they are often surprised by that. But I often think that means nothing but that they are misunderstood. To be extreme, those artworks are only acceptable because the artists are Japanese. The Europeans enjoy Japanese artists because Japanese take approaches which Europeans never would, and the Europeans take it as a kind of radical childishness. At first glance they are "new technology" and "fun." But when they are considered more seriously, they don't get the same attention. They see Japan as a country having crazy new technologies, which only they know how to manoeuver.

(Fujihata 2006)

Seiko Mikami and Sota Ichikawa in the group doubleNegatives Architecture work with a structurally comparable concept of interactivity in their installation. Seiko Mikami's large-scale three part spatial installation *Desire of Codes*[2] (Plate 25) addresses our perceptual encounters with networked systems. It poses the question of what sort of "inherent behavior" computer codes might have, particularly when their capacity to measure and move takes on an organic character.

In the first part, on the wall of the installation space, Mikami mounted ninety devices that are equipped with search arms that have small LED pointers and cameras and sensors to detect movement and sound of the visitors when they approach the wall. The whole structure is targeting us as if the technical apparatuses and the humans were different species entering into dialogue with each other. As the lights and the cameras follow the visitors' movements in space, the resulting effect is that the devices, which are driven by audible motors, move their arms "searching for" individual visitors like a buzzing swarm of mosquitoes. Various measuring data are combined to create the responsive effect: movements are captured by light sensors, distances, and movement measured by ultrasound sensors and temperature/body warmth measured by infrared sensors.

Of particular interest here is how the use of the sensors diverges from the norm, as Mikami has modified the individual instruments into a new type of multi-sensor capturing other data than what their original construction anticipated. Each of the combined sensors and the cameras do capture and measure independently, but they are networked together in a computer system and attuned to each other in a sort of "group behavior." Fine gradations result and enable this dynamic wall to act like a live participant. The audience for this "industrial invention" acts as an interface, with its difference from the machine and its similarity presented to its eyes and ears via miniaturized interfaces.

Because the devices resemble the size of toys, they become almost flattering interfaces, which appear harmless and handsome and not like control and surveillance apparatuses. One can note the cultural reference to miniaturized computers, electronic toys, and gadgets, which have spread like insects through the private and public sectors in Japan and South-East Asia. In her work, Mikami makes us aware of a close and personal relationship between the human perception in general and the individual senses and how they are affected, in particular. She also draws our attention to the humanoid behavior of increasingly small and smart robots and further machine devices that are equipped with sensory instruments to detect us, target our behavior, and go after us. It is precisely the kind of interface that is built by Mikami herself and not standardized mechanisms that evokes the experience of in-betweenness and makes us aware of our modes of perception in relation to the surrounding that is machine driven and operates by a chain of codes.

The other two parts of the installation further expand the artists' view of the desire of codes seen as a chain of behavior and response in correspondence to social behavior. Once we move away from the "Wriggling Wall" with its ninety units targeting us, we find ourselves surrounded and equally targeted by huge, six larger-than-life size robotic arms that hang from the ceiling and reach into the space. The robot arms follow the task to express desire of codes by way of following and recording movements of the visitors. The arms are equipped with cameras and projectors and simultaneously project the recorded footage onto the floor where we move. In the third part of the installation, "Compound Eye" Mikami further explores the anthropocentric effect of the miniature mechanical arms of the first part, "Wriggling Wall," where the LEDs are pointed on us like searchlights or an insect swarm.

If you enter this white room, 90 moving units of structures with built-in small sensitive cameras (0.0003lux) are placed across 15m long white wall. Each device senses with insect-like wriggling movements the positions and movements of visitors, and turns towards detected persons in order to observe their actions. Round-shaped screen (61 hexagonal parts) that looks like an insect's compound eye is installed in the back of the exhibition space. Visual data transmitted from each camera, along with footage recorded by surveillance cameras at various places around the world, are stored in a central database, and ultimately projected in complex images and sounds that are mixing elements of past and present onto the screen. This compound eye screen and the room's sound system express a new reality in which fragmentary aspects of space and time are recombined, while the visitor's position as a subject of expression and surveillance at once indicates the new appearance of human corporeality and desire.

(Mikami 2010)

The image structure of "Compund Eye" is imitating an insect's eye, wherein current and past recordings of viewers can interfere via computer programs with data information from search engines in the Internet, which have access, in real time, and permanently, to surveillance cameras in places all over the world. The model of the hexagon here becomes a permeable interface of global surveillance and multi-purpose connectivity: it makes us aware of how personal experience is caught up in worldwide data transfer and in reverse how we can reach out to all possible locations across time and space.

The philosophy of the installation is testing our experience of the behavior of machines as it is driven by codes. We are also invited to think about the appetite respectively the desire of the code to randomly grasp and process data from anywhere at any time and "produce" endless chains of information input and output. The installation demonstrates its own structural components such as repetition in the stream of data and thereby makes us aware of our own desire to create and produce something and at the same time shows our limits to influence and actually control the machine process with which we interact. Projecting data in a hexagonal form of presentation, together with the associations attached to a swarm of insects, points to the relative limitation of the human field of vision, but not just that. It also refers explicitly to seeing via apparatuses, which exemplarily creates translocal connections with surveillance cameras and enables us to observe simultaneously things that are not simultaneous and stand at a distance.

The work assumes difference, yet it reduces it to such an extent that an almost personal encounter does seem possible with multiple instruments functioning through sensors. This alerts us to the structural characteristics that exist in every hybrid interaction, yet which we are not meant perceive in most cases of immersive effects. By contrast, here a critical–sensual awareness of medially linked environments has become possible via rapprochement and distance. There is an interplay between recurring noises and lights trained on viewers, whereby participants experience the routines of permanent surveillance, and any of our actions that immediately become the object of surveillance and trigger an endless search for input data.

In a related approach, the Euro-Japanese art and architecture group doubleNegatives Architecture uses self-operating and self-modifying systems to engage us, the participants to closer investigate and rethink how handy technologies and complex military and political surveillance and control structures interact. This is evident, in particular when the group reinvestigates self-organizing mesh network devices that were initially designed for warfare purposes. Sota Ichikawa and the architectural group doubleNegatives Architecture extend the concept of the network as multilayered structures of interaction into a social–virtual sculpture. The makeup of the team is international, and it works on networks with comprehensive structures and components from military technology to give these latter different functions for concrete, architectural situations. As the concepts shift across in an exterior space constructed in real–virtual fashion, we can experience variables and constants from present-day transcultural stipulations in media technology. doubleNegatives Architecture consists of Sota Ichikawa, Max Rheiner (Switzerland), Ákos Maróy (Hungary), and Kaoru Kobata (Japan). With the installation *Corpora in Si(gh)te* (Japan 2007), they have constructed self-organizing systems in interior and exterior space and displayed the process of their development (Plate 26).

Therein lies an alternative aesthetic approach towards built environments (architecture) and dominant visual regimes (predominantly linear perspective). In the installation of *Corpora in Si(gh)te*, these parameters seem to be rather fluid and changeable. This raises questions of power and control: What instance is potentially responsible for reassembling the parameters? Can it be anyone? Does the system need us? Are there traces of emerging co-creativity between us and the system or is it immune to external communication? As a result, the work critically poses the question of how to organize communicative structures in a living environment where real spaces expand into mediascapes and changeability is rather formless, frameless, and fluid. The installation of *Corpora in Si(gh)te* mixes features of virtual and augmented reality in order to compose an almost living form of technologically enhanced and permeable architecture.

The group's philosophy is to use data input from nature/outside (wind, temperature, light), and to employ respectively misuse military technology (self-operating mesh networks) to build architectural environments with intelligent sensors that constantly adapt to the environmental data. In the architecture project *Corpora in Si(gh)te*, the concept is to decompose the parts and materials of real buildings and reassemble them as an autonomous structure with varying viewpoints, called super-eyes. The super-eyes are self-generating, self-assembling structures that exist in polar coordinates, not in Cartesian parameters. This indicates a multi-perspectival model departing from linear perspective that is incorporated in most computer graphics. Super-imposed architectural models are built from data measuring brightness, wind direction and speed, temperature, humidity, and sound. The generated 3D structure is constantly changing, demonstrating how the created corpora—which is constructed from the collected and connected data of multiple viewpoints—occupies and dominates the surrounding public space. The superstructure is interacting with the surrounding environment and it is also redesigning itself. It uses the technology of a mesh network for establishing decentered networks that restructure connections from scratch in all possible directions.

The mesh network in *Corpora in Si(gh)te* is realized in a real-time environment and has behavior like an organic structure or a nervous system. This fosters an understanding of virtual architecture growing like an organism and not like a concrete entity. Herein, a change of perspective goes hand in hand with interaction with surrounding environment. The project *Corpora in Si(gh)te* was installed onsite at Yamaguchi Center for Arts and Media, at the Venice Architecture Biennale, the Ars Electronica Center, and the Hungarian Cultural Institute in Berlin, each time creating from scratch a completely different intelligent structure, using sensors and wireless network functions that were placed in the respective real environment. The aim of this multi-site project is to demonstrate how we may change the function of, and challenge the ways in which we perceive and behave in relation to, disturbing, decentralized, unstable, constantly reassembling environments. The traveling concept of this project unfolds translocational specificity based on a fluid understanding of making connections.

As far as our living environment is more and more enriched with lesser noticeable computer processes, it is worthwhile to strongly consider the issue of connectivity in relation to space, environment and mediascape. It is for this reason that the artistic–architectural project of V Architecture realizes multiple activity with complex systems as a way of intervention and remodeling of environmental spaces: their proposal is to rethink architectural sites and cityscapes from a network position. Therein the mixed Japanese–European team gives the example of an effective approach to readdress such one-sided discourses that look from here to there, inside to outside. In contrast to these limited perspectives, the proposed architectural model suggests cross directions and networking practices that are relevant to the larger topic of intervention and extend mediascapes across different cultural contexts. As the work is meant to be translocational and changes in relation to the actual architectural structures that are revisited in a mixed reality installation, the traveling concept underlines the necessity to consider both media and cultural specificities in flexible hybrid contexts, wherein network communication can cope with ubiquitous technologies that spread out everywhere.

I wish to close my reflections on effective artistic responses to technological environments with another example from the Far East that is traveling across media and cultural zones and is radicalizing personally modified technologies in arbitrary models of *science-scapes* and achieves a new form of interaction. In this, Masaki Fujihata sets out to address in scientific experimentation the current state of development with ambient computing and omnipresent networks. The laboratory project *Orchisoid* tests out hybrid encounters as a new cultural form in the area of the contact almost made between orchids and us (Japan 2001–2007). The difficulty of synchronizing computers in networks, as is necessary for performing exact interactions between us and machines, forms the point of departure for this experimental arrangement with orchids.

With *Orchisoid*, the attempt is made to communicate between humans and machines without any sort of coding. The setup is equipped with measuring instruments, as in a scientific laboratory. The interactive distance between individual plants is measured, together with their behavior towards each other and their sensitivity to moisture, as when one of two plants standing close together is watered but the other is not. The plants are, in addition, tested for their sensitivity like biorobots, lifted onto a hydraulic platform and "driven" in all directions at high speed, while projected images of a botanical garden run past them and imitate a "real" environment for the plants. The project was developed in collaboration with the botanist Yuji Dogane, and Fujihata sees it as standing at the juncture of robotics and nature:

> In Botanical Ambulation Training footage filmed while walking through a botanical garden is being projected onto a wall. Orchids (mainly Cattleya) can see these projections from the baskets they are planted in. The aspects of tremor (acceleration, geomagnetism, inclination) in the images are being translated into impulses that shake the platform the flower baskets are sitting on, so that the flower baskets move perfectly in sync with the trembling of the images on the wall. Therefore, from the perspective of the orchids it must feel as if they were being carried in the hand (that actually holds the camera) around the garden . . . . What in the world could it be that the orchids are thinking while swaying gently on their metal pistons, watching pictures of a shaking greenhouse, and devoting themselves to "reproduction activities?"[3]

This new sort of experimental arrangement is not just a critique of technology; it also advocates maintaining difference and distance as the basic condition for a living interaction. That is because, when the sensory contact becomes too close and too strong, the vitality in dialog is put at risk. To that extent, this demonstration with plants sensitive to contact has a component criticizing the media by focusing on the ostensibly desirable removal of any distance and difference in all versions of touch media, something that here does not, however, appear as a goal or a way to more communication. On the contrary, Fujihata provokes dialog with difference and controlled interactivity, so that, in the in-between, something new and something different can arise.

FIGURE 18.1 Masaki Fujihata (2001–2007). Orchisoid. Japan
Image courtesy of the artist

As these examples demonstrate, artistic and aesthetic practices are not only contributing to the conceptual framework of thinking in complexity and connectivity, but at the same time take a critical stance and pursue creative interventions into contemporary networked processes. To further artistic–creative positions in computational development, it is important to mark the specific context of discourse and critique through the use of alternative models.

Notes

1. Han, Hyperkulturalität. Kultur und Globalisierung.
2. Exhibited at the Yamaguchi Center for Arts and Media in 2010, and also exhibited at InterCommunicationCenter, Tokyo in 2011.
3. Fujihata, "Botanical Ambulation Training."

References

Bhabha, Homi K. 1994. *The Location of Culture*. London and New York: Routledge.
Bioy Casares, Adolfo. 2003. *The Invention of Morel*. Trans. Ruth L. C. Simms. New York: New York Review of Books.

Bush, Vannevar. 2001. "As We May Think." In *Multimedia: From Wagner to Virtual Reality*, Eds. Randall Packer and Ken Jordan. New York: W. W. Norton, 141–159.

Castells, Manuel. 1996. *The Rise of the Network Society*. Oxford: Blackwell.

Clifford, James. 1997. *Routes. Travel and Translation in the Late Twentieth Century*. Cambridge, MA: Harvard University Press.

Engelbart, Douglas. 2001. "Augmenting Human Intellect: A Conceptual Framework." In *Multimedia. From Wagner to Virtual Reality*, Eds. Randall Packer and Ken Jordan. New York and London: Norton, 64–90.

Fujihata, Masaki. 2003. *Morel's Panorama*. Digital artwork.

Fujihata, Masaki. 2006. *The Conquest of Imperfection: New Realities Created with Images and Media*. Fukushima, Japan: Center for Contemporary Graphic Art and Tyler Graphics Archive Collection.

Fujihata, Masaki, and Dogane, Yuji. 2007. "Botanical Ambulation Training," In *Silent Dia-logue*, exhibition catalog. Tokyo, Japan: NTT/ICC, n.p.

Han, Byung-Chul. 2005. *Hyperkulturalität. Kultur und Globalisierung*. Berlin: Merve.

Jay, Martin. 1993. *Downcast Eyes: The Denigration of Vision in Twentieth-Century French Thought*. Berkeley, CA: University of California Press.

Mikami, Seiko. 2010. *Desire of Codes*. Unpublished manuscript, n.p.

A PORTRAIT OF THE ARTIST AS A SMART CITY: BODY, COMPLEXITY, AND URBAN LIFE

Henriette Steiner and Kristin Veel

In front of me an object towers. A sculpture. A body. But with flickering electrodes and fluorescent light. Terminator! I think of Renaissance automata and 1980s science fiction films. Body 01000010011011110110010001111001 (Plate 27) by the British artist Stanza is a life size piece in the form of the human body made out of horizontal layers of transparent Plexiglas on which little electrodes, lamps, and wires make up a complex pattern, like the veins and organs of the human body. The lights flicker, quietly. A red lamp is turned on here. A green one there. A large orange light suddenly appears. I see my own broken-up reflection in the transparent material of the sculpture. My left eye twitches. I suddenly feel a sharp pain in my right knee, as if my own body was mirroring the sculpture. The logic of the disharmonic rhythm of the flickering lights of the sculpture evades a clear explanation. The piece is a model of the artist's own body. But also an allegory or direct representation of the order of the contemporary city. Its movements and flows brought down to the human scale. Into the human body. It brings together body, city, and technology in a way that dissolves the boundaries between each, and in the flickering of the LED lights the complexity of the contemporary spaces we inhabit is given form.

In contemporary urban planning discourse, the concept of the *smart city* has been introduced as a strategic device. Its aim is to make use of self-reflexive information and communication technologies in large-scale infrastructural networks in order to analyze urban performance and make cities more competitive by allegedly allowing self-described "smart technologies" to make urban infrastructures more efficient. The discourse of the smart city can be seen as a contemporary attempt at articulating urban order in the face of the technological change of our present day. Smart city technologies also exemplify the increasing integration of self-reflective technologies and ubiquitous computing into urban everyday life. For smart city proponents, such technologies constitute a toolbox, which may be used to ease urban life to the benefit of us all. The aim is to create cities that are well structured, clean and free of vice. When replaced by *smart* ones, existing technologies on which contemporary urban infrastructures are based are represented as producing unnecessarily complex and inefficient conditions. As we have argued elsewhere, the smart city discourse can thus be seen as an attempt to provide a benign, ideal alternative to a perceived malign, inefficient, unsustainable, and humanly disempowering complexity in the contemporary city.[1] Insofar as this is the case, the smart city discourse may be seen as embedded in a long history of modern visions of urban reform, each allegedly saving the city from itself.[2] The smart city discourse addresses the city as a whole interconnected system whose complexity can be reduced by technological advances and, in this way, enable citizens to live a more harmonious life together.

Looking at the way in which *complexity* is approached in the *smart city* discourse, it becomes clear that this way of talking about cities approaches complexity as something we can *get rid of* or *add*, and the aim of the smart city is to make the world more manageable without *adding* further complexity (Steiner and Veel 2013). However, in this chapter, we shall argue that talking about complexity as something that can be cleaned up like chewing gum on the pavement, does not deal with the issue at hand. Our starting point is that rather than to assume that complexity is something that is possible to obliterate altogether, it, is instead a figure of speech or metaphor of thought for talking about phenomena that express a particular form of order which it is difficult for the individual to comprehend. Rather than being seen as simply *chaotic*, when a phenomenon or object such as a city is described as *complex*, its intrinsic structure and order is acknowledged and simultaneously held at bay conceptually. Insofar as we can talk about different *types* of complexity, as will be discussed in more detail later, these should be seen as corresponding to different epistemic paradigms, each of which have particular consequences for our way of understanding the world.

Paradoxically, the means for seeking to eliminate complexity in the smart city discourse are to embed additional technological layers in the urban fabric, using self-reflective technologies and ubiquitous computing. However, we shall argue that these technologies provoke a particular way of thinking about complexity, the cultural implications of which still need to be fully understood, this being the aim of the present book. The smart city discourse can thus be regarded as silently enfolding an inherent paradox. It entails a glossing over of the particular form of complexity, which the so-called *smart* technologies embody, while allowing for a naïvely optimistic discourse reminiscent of other modern attempts to improve the city by rendering it as a (complex) system.

IBM's website provides an example of the way in which the corporation explains "what is a smart city":

> Smarter cities drive sustainable economic growth and prosperity for their citizens. Their leaders have the tools to analyze data for better decisions, anticipate problems to resolve them proactively and coordinate resources to operate effectively.
>
> (IBM 2012)

As becomes evident here, the means to obtain the desired reduction of complexity are "collecting and analyzing the extensive data generated every second of every day" (IBM 2012). What is generally termed big data and regarded as one of today's information overload challenges by its proportions is thus used here as a means for reducing complexity (Mayer-Schönberger and Cukier 2013).

The aim of this contribution is to investigate the conceptualization of complexity, as located in the smart city discourse. Furthermore, by looking at critical engagement with smart city technologies from a contemporary art context, we aim to show that other instances of how we may grasp the complexity conceptions at work in a world permeated by self-reflective technologies and ubiquitous computing exist alongside that of the smart city discourse. We do this by pitching the discussion of complexity in the smart city discourse against its conceptual *other*, using Stanza's art work *Body 01000010011011110110010001111001* as a vehicle of our discussion. Focus is on the particular conception of complexity in relation to self-reflective technologies and ubiquitous computing on which this work relies. This arises from the way in which this artwork uses a form of smart technology in an urban context, but for the purpose of creating a work of art which reflects upon the increasing integration of self-reflective technologies and ubiquitous computing at work in contemporary urban life—rather than as a vehicle for improving urban infrastructure.

When used in cultural theoretic discourse, the notion of complexity reveals a long and complicated trajectory of shifting epistemic relations (Hillier 2007). The history of the use of the concept evinces slippages, which means that we need to take extra care whenever this concept is operationalized as is the case in the smart city discourse. If we can take as our starting point that ubiquitous computing and self-reflective technologies are a given in today's urban reality, we may say that the paradoxical glossing-over of complexity that we found in the smart city discourse, arises from the way in which this discourse is geared towards a particular understanding of technology. The question of interest to us here is: do we have at our disposal a more concise vocabulary that allows us to understand the ways in which these technologies impact our cities and the way in which the complexity at hand is understood and experienced? This leads us to the central issue: what means of interpretation can we put to use in order to begin to tackle these questions?

The method of this contribution is to consider how the smart city discourse stands in relation to two paradigmatic, cultural theoretic conceptualizations of complexity: *Romantic* and *Baroque*. These categories should be regarded as a necessary framework for approaching the issue at hand, not as a consolidation of the dichotomy that they instigate. Our aim is to illustrate the need for a less dichotomized conceptual apparatus in order to begin to grasp what self-reflective technologies may mean for the way we understand the workings of the contemporary city, and the role of self-reflective information technologies and ubiquitous computing in it. In doing so, we point towards how further research might look when trying to understand the way in which our own bodies engage with such an environment in the flickering, energy-saving light of the intermingling of technological data, harvesting and processing, and urban life.

(Un)bearable Complexity: Romantic and Baroque

In *Complexities: Social Studies of* Knowledge *Practices* (2002), science and technology scholar, Chunglin Kwa, introduces the distinction between *Romantic* and *Baroque* conceptions of complexity (Kwa 2002). It has since been taken up by a number of theorists such as John Law (2003), Joris Van Wezemael (2009), Paul Cillier (1998), and Jean Hillier (2007). This distinction allows us to take into account the degree to which speaking about complexity is embedded in historical and cultural paradigms, and how these influence our understanding of the matter at hand. The starting point for the present discussion is that the increasing omnipresence of self-reflective technologies and computing systems in our everyday lives means that they engender new experiences in ways that put pressure on our interpretive capabilities and challenge our conceptual vocabulary. As cultural theorists our task is, on the one hand, to develop a conceptual apparatus that allows adequate interpretations of these changes and the experiences they engender, and, on the other, to get to the bottom of discourses that try to operationalize such instances of cultural change for a specific purpose. The identification of Romantic and Baroque complexity paradigms is used here as a way of opening up this discussion.

According to Kwa, Romantic complexity refers to an epistemic paradigm that can be coupled to figures of thought that we know from nineteenth century Romanticism. Romantic, in this sense, should be regarded as a particular outlook on the modern world, and Romantic complexity as a way of trying to grasp aspects of the modern condition through a particular conceptual apparatus. To describe a given set of phenomena as complex, in this sense, may thus be seen as a way of coping with and understanding the changing realities of the modern world. Romantic complexity is characterized by the aim of describing complex and seemingly chaotic phenomena by uniting heterogeneous items into a functional whole. The emphasis is on fixed and natural laws. Being can be identified and described. As Joris Van Wezemael writes:

> The romantic metaphor implies the aim of grasping the "whole" as an emergent entity. It treats complexity as a phenomenon which is coupled to emergence. Although it displays a complexity of interior relations, it can be held as one whole. Its component parts are constituted by the very relations they have to other parts in the whole.
>
> (Van Wezemael 2009)

The individual parts stand in a causal relation to one another and are hierarchically ordered by the whole of which they are part. Society is regarded as an organism that is made available for the human mind through strategies of homogenization and abstraction, but also an irreducibility which follows its emergent properties. This is the centralized and controlled perspective of the planner, and this inclination to attempt to get an overview is an approach, which we also know as a response to the encounter with the modern metropolis of the nineteenth century and the notorious sensory overload this encounter may provoke.[3] According to Paul Cilliers, this is a mathematical and computational view which can also be associated with more contemporary theories such as cybernetics and chaos theory, which both aim to get an overview by *looking up*, that is, zooming out and abstracting until a whole can be identified (Cilliers 1998). In a discourse based on romantic complexity, there is a presumed fixed set of natural laws by which entities can be known and the patterns of a system can be modelled and predicted as emergent structures (Hillier 2007, 44–45).

If we now return to the question of complexity, technology, and the contemporary city with which we began, the rhetoric of the smart city purports to seek to reduce complexity— thus placing it in dialogue with age-old conceptualizations of urban planning (Van Wezemael 2009). This sense of complexity as a negative fact of the unordered city stands in contrast to notions of the city as a complex system but at the same time a smooth machine, one that is efficient and well organized through the insertion of particular forms of technologies. So what we are dealing with is in fact not a reduction of complexity (understood in its simplistic form as tending towards disorder), but a replacement of an argument around complexity as disorder with a different kind of understanding of complexity (which we here call Romantic). It is one that is based on the idea of the city as an infrastructural system that can be controlled and thus reshaped for the better, and it fantasizes the city as a closed container of which we can get an overview in the panoptic sense. It thus regards the city as an emergent, complex (implicitly global) whole that can and should be managed.

Identifying the smart city discourse as purporting a romantic notion of complexity points to a particular way of thinking about cities (as chaotic and disjointed) and a perception of technology as a tool that can be used to make cities and the world better and more whole. However, as already argued, the embedding of ubiquitous computing technologies in the urban lifeworld does not as such result in a well-ordered and systematized urbanity that can be viewed from above. Rather than following this line of interpretation, we may focus on the fact that the integration of these technologies into everyday life generates new forms of experiences. This means that we need to consider how we may describe and understand the city in the face of these technological changes.

In opposition to romantic complexity, Kwa positions what he terms *Baroque complexity*, and which, as a conceptual paradigm, Hillier aligns with post-structuralism. Significantly, Law conceptualizes the Baroque notion of complexity, following Deleuze's work on Leibniz. In this context, *Baroque* should thus be understood as a poststructuralist reading of the historical period of the Baroque (Law 2003, 2011). In such an interpretation of the world, we have no distinction between individuals and their environments (Hillier 2007, 46). The God's eye view has been replaced by the aim of managing flows. "Although there may well be some higher order level (such as a city), it is impossible to describe and explain it fully from a Baroque viewpoint" (Hillier 2007, 45). We have thus moved from Foucault's disciplined society to Deleuze's society of control. As an epistemic strategy, Baroque complexity is geared towards the specific and the concrete, where it discovers (material) heterogeneity (Van Wezemael 2009). Individuals act in multiple networks and patterns are rarely repeated. There are no natural pre-given boundaries, yet, connections are impossible to deconstruct. Van Wezemael writes that "[as] the Baroque discovers complexity in specificity, rather than in the emergence of higher-level order, we do not move off into the abstraction of an interrelated and emergent whole as the romantic approach does" (Van Wezemael 2009, 88). We therefore should not be surprised that Hillier describes Actor-Network Theory as a form of Baroque complexity thinking (Hillier 2007).

If the Romantic notion of complexity could be seen as a typical epistemic response to the experience of sensory bombardment that the modern metropolis engenders, this is borne out of the experience of a digitized network society. They both represent a response to a not dissimilar sensation of overload and therefore also attest to our contemporary incapacity to conceptualize environmental order. To think in flows, invisible but strong connections impossible to view from above, but where meaning resides in these relational points or where changes at one node in a network may inflict changes at other points of the network, seems a convincing way of conceiving of the world in a situation where our life worlds have been ubiquitously pervaded by network technologies—be it structures such as the World Wide Web or the integration of technology in everyday life situations. The vocabulary of Baroque complexity thus allows us to identify and describe characteristics of life in a smart city that are not possible to articulate when operating with only a Romantic notion of complexity.

Interestingly, the romantic notion of complexity when proposed at the discursive level seems to deflect our attention away from the consequences of the inherent complexity of form of the technologies in question. Understanding this form of complexity as Baroque has the advantage that it begins to grasp both the potential for a more distributed form of relating to the systematic aspects of urban life and the new regimes of control and micro-management that reach deeply, subtly and often unnoticeably into our everyday lives. Approaching complexity in the contemporary city as a Baroque complexity may therefore show us something about the consequences of the presence of self-reflective technologies and ubiquitous computing in our everyday life.

As presented here, the Romantic conception retains a somewhat nostalgic character, whereas the Baroque sounds more progressive. However, this lop-sided interpretation of the concepts is not quite fair when seen in a more general perspective. What is striking is the way in which both notions of complexity apply to a contemporary discourse concerning the integration of *smart* technologies into everyday urban life. However simplistic and dichotomized the two categories of Romantic versus Baroque might seem, they provide us with an interpretative framework that allows us to come closer to an understanding of the experience that self-reflective technologies and ubiquitous computing engender, and which we believe is embedded in the crossroads between these two conceptions of complexity.

One way of disentangling the discursive levels, and the capacity for knowledge about the world which they embody, is to see them both at work in the way in which the smart city implications are addressed and modulated in the sculpture *Body 0100001001101111011001 0001111001* by the British artist Stanza. Using the artwork as a way of reading the smart city against the grain may help us move beyond the smart city discourse as well as to tease out the complementarity of the Baroque and the Romantic constructions of complexity. This, in turn, may allow us to begin to delineate the limits of our current interpretative abilities when it comes to understanding the effects of the presence of self-reflective technologies and ubiquitous computing that to an ever greater extent are part of our everyday lives.

The Body, Ubiquitous Computing, and Urban Life

Body is a sculpture, 224 cm. in height, based on a 3D body scan of the artist, which through LED lights, motors, and wires visualizes the input it gets from a wireless sensor network in the city that collects data concerning temperature, light, pressure, and sound. This network is currently placed in South London, but nothing hinders its potential removal and installation in any other urban environment. The data sets it deploys are gathered from a sensor network and sent via a custom-made Java proxy server to the sculpture. However, the data, which is sent to the sculpture, exists both in real time and as a local archive data set. In this way, the sculpture always has a backup.

The description on Stanza's website reads: "This new sculpture captures the changes over time in the environment (city) and represents the changing life and complexity of space as an emergent artwork" (Stanza 2012). Here "city," "life," and "complexity" seem to be used synonymously, which makes it pertinent to explore how the notion of complexity is conceptualized. The account of the work goes on to describe how: "Body goes beyond simple single-user interaction to monitor and survey in real time the whole city and entirely represent the complexities of the real-time city as a shifting, morphing, and complex system." The artwork thus reveals an ambition that is no less romantic than that of the commercial smart city discourse. Its purposefulness is linked with an ambition of gaining overview—in an emergent form, of coming to see "the whole city" and "entirely represent the complexities," something that is demonstrated perhaps most explicitly by the fact that the work has a back-up, which would make the artwork function even if the live data-feed stopped. Yet, in the text the ambition of the overview is immediately qualified with the addition: "What you see as well as this body are hundreds of parts that come alive as the data changes and evolves. It's a hybrid work powered by live events." As soon as the view from above has been presented as an ambition, the possibility of such a perspective is thus drawn into question and replaced with a conception of *Body* as only a fragmented glimpse into a much larger network and an uncertainty as to which data are stored and which are live. This seems to correspond more to a view from below and accordingly bears the mark of a Baroque notion of complexity.

What we begin to see is thus a more multifaceted picture of what complexity entails in a concrete smart city environment. This oscillating dual set of connotations brings attention to the difficulty of talking about complexity without at the same time reducing complexity to something of which we can come to get an overview, and thus subscribing to a romantic view. This is what happens in the smart city discourse—where it also has its own moral and commercial logic in so far as there are significant marketing benefits involved in promising to be able to simplify accurately and productively, as well as to reduce a feeling of overload. However, the fact that this continued need for a systematization and an overview exists seems in itself to point to a sensation on a deeper level of the lifeworld we inhabit as being in fact difficult to grasp within such a romantic paradigm. Paradoxically, it seems to be the case here that the apparent simplicity of the smart city discourse and the aim of assuming the planner's view from above reveal an underlying recognition of the disorderliness of the view from below.

In order to further explore this dual set of complexity connotations, we shall now turn to look more closely at the conditions of representation in which this artwork inscribes itself. The issue of representation here is at the same time linked to current debates about data visualization involving abstraction as a representative mode, and to the situatedness of the human body, which calls for a more phenomenological approach. It is in this spectrum that the form of the sculpture becomes an articulation of the situatedness of the individual body in an urban environment permeated by self-reflective technologies and ubiquitous computing.

Data visualization is a field in rapid growth, which is only becoming more and more acutely necessary as our ability to gather and manage big datasets increases.[4] The take that Stanza has on this discussion is to insert an aesthetic paradigm into the discussion, by denying the viewer the ability to translate the data that in the piece takes the form of flickering LED lights back into the data it comes from. The experience is thus bound to be a confrontation with an illegible complexity denying the visitor the sense of overview as a cathartic moment of knowledge or understanding. Something (here, light) signifies a set of data, but we do not see the causal relations at work. We are merely told that they are there and forced to believe in their existence. However, at the same time, the sculpture's explicit exposure of its technological interior means that it refuses to black-box the technology. Rather, it titillates our curiosity and creates a wish to crack the underlying algorithm and understand the causal connections that turn the measurement of city conditions (which are already in themselves portrayed as a translation of city into data) into a flickering lightbulb.

Body thus poses the question: What *kind* of representation of the urban environment are we dealing with? And by attempting to answer this question, we invariably have to address the question of the *type* of complexity it enfolds. Although the piece—as the statement by Stanza emphasizes—aims to represent "the complexities of the real-time city as a shifting, morphing, and complex system" (Stanza 2012), we are confronted with a selection of parameters that allegedly stand in for the whole city. We must ask ourselves what types of measurements the artist has chosen as indicators for displaying what could be called the real time city? We are told these are temperature, light, pressure, and noise, which are all parameters that have to do with what may be called atmosphere or environment as it envelops us in the city and elicits a response from our different senses. This selection of parameters is, however, obliterated again insofar as it is not possible to directly trace which of them make which lamp turn on or off. In *Body*, it once again becomes a flow of data: a nervously flickering billboard pointing to an information overload that has not been made legible and smart, but that has been transposed into a different form; a visual representation that it is possible to take in in one glance. The piece thus presents a simplification which is necessary in order to make a complex environment intelligible; but by doing so, it in turn also exposes Baroque notions of complexity at work.

The notion of Baroque complexity, as it has been conceptualized by the theorists cited above, is closely linked to the vocabulary of Gilles Deleuze, and looking at Stanza's *Body*, it is difficult not to think of Deleuze's concept of the "Body without Organs" (*BwO*). This is a concept towards which he and Guattari return repeatedly throughout their writings, and which can be said to describe the virtual or potential body—a state of experimentation or aspiration that is presented polemically as a counterpoint to what they conceive of as the psychoanalytical search for selfhood:

A body without organs is not an empty body stripped of organs, but a body upon which that which serves as organs [. . .] is distributed according to crowd phenomena [. . .] in the form of molecular multiplicities.

(Deleuze and Guattari 1998, 30)

The *BwO* is a state of flow and continual becoming, and as such one might assume that any form of attempt to represent it will entail a simplification and a partial rendition.

This leads us to the striking appearance of this artwork, which so explicitly integrates the human form with technology. Indeed, it turns the body into a carrier, a projection screen, or perhaps more accurately an engine in which the fusion of data and human becomes an output of light, yet promising no easy interpretative framework. Insofar as the shape of the sculpture is based on the artist's body, it is connected to a specific individual with certain characteristics. Through the creation of the stratified data tower and the embedding of sensorial technology, however, this body as a representation of the artist himself becomes infused with data in a way that emphasizes its typology rather than its individuality. This is also emphasized by the title *Body 01000010011011110110010001111001*, which merges the corporal with data in a way that at the same time designates the specific and the general—the long number combination "01000010011011110110010001111001" and the human "body."

The statement on Stanza's website reads: "In 'Body 01000010011011110110010001111001' the urban environment provides a dynamic, flickering, and clicking sentience to the otherwise inert structure, reflecting the personal level of influence data has on an individual" (Stanza 2012). The interaction between the environment and the individual described here displays in a very concrete way the situatedness of the physical body in an external environment, which is both physical and virtual, a controlled yet independent structure. In a circuitous way, the artwork thus also comes to recreate a romantic notion of the artist as the creator that gives form with a godlike overview, isolated from the environment he portrays: In this rendition, the environment he portrays is implanted in his own body. He thus has to see his own translated body perforated by wires and light, and agency transferred to that of the surrounding environment that turns the lights in *Body* on or lets them die out. *Body*—as a representation of the individual as a whole, well-defined object—therefore also points to a more phenomenological breaking down of subject and object-world (the artwork as object out there with the world). Yet, if we consider the Deleuzian perspective that life in "the society of control" (Deleuze 1992) is characterized by a replacement of individuals by "dividuals" and the body not only as a physical body, but also as a portrait of corporeal potentiality as a vehicle of flows, we may begin to see how the artwork also represents the difficulty of dealing with a Baroque understanding of complexity. As we have seen, the Baroque notion of complexity implies that we are controlled on a level below the individual. Our bodies become part of the data flows. Stanza's *Body* embodies this merging of the body with technology. Yet, at the same time it struggles against this conception by having a concrete and clearly demarcated emergent form, which refers to none other than that of the artist. Eventually, the artist thus seems to indeed recognize the matter of fact of his own body to which he is intrinsically tied, and which provides him with his fundamental condition of being earthbound and thus with his humanity.

A Portrait of the Artist as a Smart City

He closed his eyes in the languor of sleep. His eyelids trembled as if they felt the vast cyclic movement of the earth and her watchers, trembled as if they felt the strange light of some new world. His soul was swooning into some new world, fantastic, dim, uncertain as under sea, traversed by cloudy shapes and beings. A world, a glimmer, or a flower? Glimmering and trembling, trembling and unfolding, a breaking light, an opening flower, it spread in endless succession to itself, breaking in full crimson and unfolding and fading to palest rose, leaf by leaf and wave of light by wave of light, flooding all the heavens with its soft flushes, every flush deeper than the other.

(Joyce 1992, 166)

Body's constant flicker between a Romantic and a Baroque understanding of complexity lies both in its articulation on the artist's website and in its physical presence. The Romantic and the Baroque can be regarded as different types of responses to the same overload challenge, which each have their limitations, and only perhaps in combination can they begin to help us interpret what is at stake when the city becomes infused with self-reflective technologies and ubiquitous computing and what forms of *experience* this engenders.

In the first part of this chapter we discussed the notion of complexity in relation to self-reflexive technologies and ubiquitous computing with respect to two typical conceptualizations of complexity. We have argued that self-reflective technologies and ubiquitous computing demand a conceptualization of complexity that is closer to the notion of Baroque complexity. This is so despite the fact that contemporary discourse, as we have seen with respect to the *smart city*, often talks about complexity in relation to these technologies as if it were closest to that of Romantic complexity—and that this may be seen as one of the problematic outcomes of the inherent paradox of the smart city discourse discussed here. We have then, in the second part of the chapter, turned to the artwork *Body 0100001001101111011001000111001* by the artist Stanza. With its inherent non-functionality, the artwork represents what may at first appear to promote the Baroque notion of complexity as an adequate vocabulary for understanding the complexity which these technologies embody. However, it also shows the impossibility of leaving behind the Romantic notion of complexity and points to the necessity of the complementarity of the two ideal typical conceptualizations of complexity as a hermeneutic predicament—as well as suggesting the necessity of their transgression.

What the analysis of Stanza's *Body* may thus tell us is that our conceptual apparatus with respect to providing us with adequate hermeneutic abilities for understanding the world around us in the face of the technological change of our present remains underdeveloped. We cannot simply argue for a leaving behind of the Romantic and an embracing of the Baroque when trying to understand the complexity before us. Both are too limited by their respective suggestions of providing a world view. With the reading of the artwork, however, we suggest a mediation of the two that uses them through transaction in praxis and thereby explores the two terms as interpretive devices, at the same time suggesting the possibility of their potential transgression. This suggestion compels us to turn to another intertextual reference that may take the reading in yet a different direction, a reference to which Stanza's *Body* seems to lend itself and which we have suggested in the title of this chapter: that of James Joyce's coming-of-age novel *A Portrait of the Artist as a Young Man* (Joyce 1916).

The novel is a canonical example of early modernist writing, which brings together the romantic notion of the omniscient, solitary artist with the experience of the world as a condition of flow between individual and environment represented by the narrative stream-of-consciousness technique which characterises this work. Stanza's *Body* is a portrait, implicitly of the artist, but it is also a portrait of a city, and it is precisely in this embeddedness of one within the other, facilitated by technology, that the qualities of the clear demarcating contours and irreducibility of the individual portrait (which the Romantic notion of complexity seeks) and the boundless and unruly flows of the network society (which the Baroque notion of complexity aims to capture) come together. A *Joycean complexity*, if we may suggest such a term, may thus be one which attempts to let that deep background of the urban order materialise through the texture of the writing, the representation, and only thus, rather than residing in preconceived categories and concepts.

Notes

1. We have dealt more extensively with smart city technologies as a discourse of urban reformation in a recent article entitled "For the Smarter Good of Cities? On the Smart City Discourse" (Steiner and Veel 2013). The present article departs from where that article ends, with the identification of a particular form of complexity potentially inherent in the smart city technologies, one that the marketing discourse surrounding smart city technologies glosses over, but which an artist such as David Rokeby brings out in his work.
2. The modernists talked about the city they were trying to rescue as infected with tuberculosis. For example, Le Corbusier writes: "the machine we live in is an old coach full of tuberculosis." (Corbusier, *Towards a New Architecture*, 277).
3. See for instance Georg Simmel on the sensuous sensory stimulation provided by life in the modern metropolis. (Simmel, "Metropolis and Mental Life")
4. See for instance http://datavis.ca/milestones/

References

Cilliers, Paul. 1998. *Complexity and Postmodernism: Understanding Complex Systems*. London: Routledge.

Corbusier, Le. 1986. *Towards a New Architecture*. New York: Dover.

Deleuze, Gilles. 1992. "Postscript on the Societies of Control." *October* 59 (Winter): 3–7.

Deleuze, Gilles, and Felix Guattari. 1988. *A Thousand Plateaus: Capitalism and Schizophrenia*. London: Athlone.

Hillier, Jean. 2007. *Stretching beyond the Horizon: A Multiplanar Theory of Spatial Planning and Governance*. Hampshire, UK: Ashgate.

IBM. 2012. "Smarter Planet Campaign." Accessed December 19, 2012. http://ibm.com/smarterplanet/uk/en/overview/ideas/

Joyce, James. (1992) 1916. *A Portrait of the Artist as a Young Man*. New York: Bantam Classic.

Kwa, Chunglin. 2002. "Romantic and Baroque Conceptions of Complex Wholes in the Sciences." In *Complexities: Social Studies of Knowledge Practices*, 23–52. Durham, NC: Duke University Press.

Law, John. 2003. "And if the Global Were Small and Non-Coherent? Method, Complexity and the Baroque." Accessed December 7, 2003. http://comp.lancs.ac.uk/sociology/papers/Law-And-if-the-Global-Were-Small.pdf.

Law, John. 2011. "Assembling the Baroque." CRESC, Open University. Accessed December 2011. http://cresc.ac.uk/sites/default/files/JohnLawAssemblingTheBaroqueWP109.pdf.

Mayer-Schönberger, Viktor, and Kenneth Cukier. 2013. *Big Data: A Revolution That Will Transform How We Live, Work and Think*. New York: Houghton Mifflin Harcourt.

Simmel, Georg. 1998. "The Metropolis and Mental Life." In *Simmel on Culture: Selected Writings*, 174–186. New York: Sage.

Stanza. 2012. "Body. By Stanza. Data Art." Accessed October 1, 2014. http://stanza.co.uk/body/

Steiner, Henriette, Kristin Veel, Panos Pardalos, and Stamatina Rassia. 2013. "For the Smarter Good of Cities? On the Smart City Discourse." In Stamatina Rassia and Panos Pardalos Eds., *Cities for Smart Environmental and Energy Futures*, 291–303. Vienna and New York: Springer.

Van Wezemael, Joris. 2009. "Housing Studies between Romantic and Baroque Complexity." *Housing, Theory and Society* 26 (2): 81–121.

PLATE 1 Rokeby, Taken
Image courtesy of David Rokeby

PLATE 2 Rokeby, Sorting Daemon

PLATE 3 Rafael Lozano-Hemmer, Under Scan
Image courtesy of Rafael Lozano-Hemmer

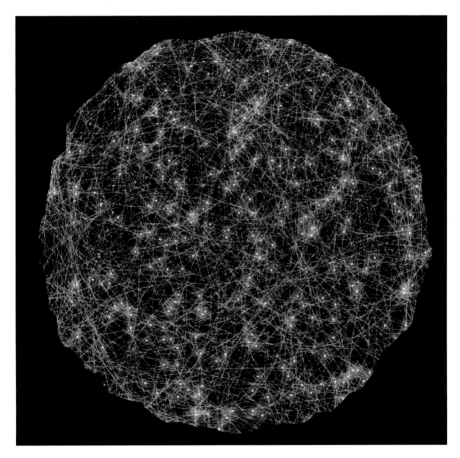

PLATE 4 Low orbit satellite trajectories

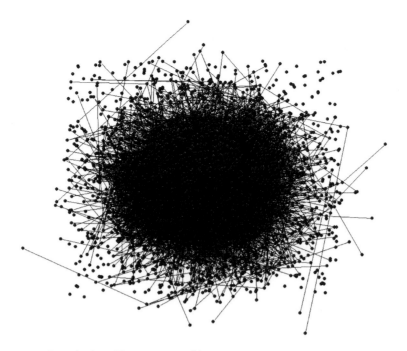

PLATE 5 Complexity of intense networking

PLATE 6 David Rokeby, Hand-Held
Image courtesy of David Rokeby

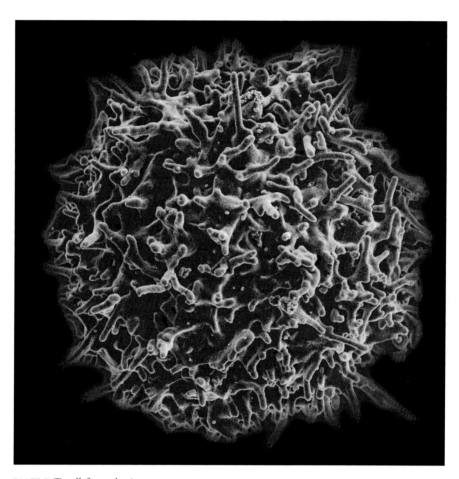

PLATE 7 T cell from the immune system

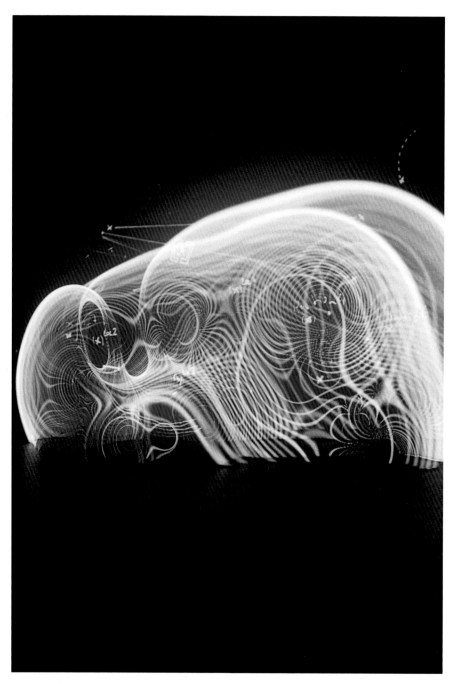

PLATE 8 Metadata-space visualization
Image courtesy of www.onformative.com

PLATE 9 David Rokeby, Plot Against Time
Image courtesy of David Rokeby

PLATE 10 Lenin's Predictions on the Revolutionary Storms in the East (Peking Foreign
Languages Press 1967) 2005, paper, silk, 1 strand 134 cm
Image courtesy of Simryn Gill. Photo by Jenni Carter

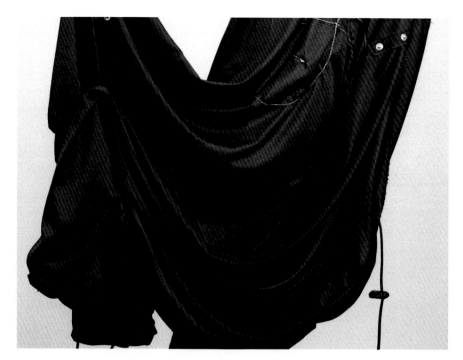

PLATE 11 Erin Manning, Volumetrics (2006–)

PLATE 12 Erin Manning, Stitching Time. Moscow Biennale (2013)

PLATE 13 Erin Manning, Volumetrics (2006–)

PLATE 14 Erin Manning, Volumetrics (2006–)

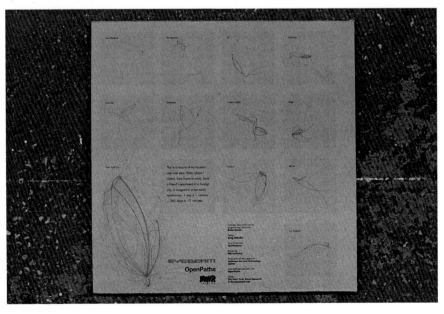

PLATE 15 Data visualization from Quotidian Record. Paths indicate the artist's movements and clusters of location as tracked during one year

Image courtesy of Brian House

PLATE 16 In Quotidian Record, artist Brian House transforms latitude and longitude
location data, into music melodies that can be played through a vinyl record

Image courtesy of Brian House

PLATE 17 IH+ feel the rumble of combustion engines

Image courtesy of Laila Nadir

PLATE 18 IH+ find a place to sit down. Ask the passersby if they have seen a rabbit in the area

Image courtesy of Laila Nadir

PLATE 19 IH+ in Copenhagen, DK. Photo by Morten Søndergaard

Image courtesy of the author

PLATE 20 Grimpant (2013). Teri Rueb and Alan Price. Dynamic mapping of Montpellier, France using regularly updated data from mobile app. Detail: Still image from animated responsive data projection, 30' × 10'

Image courtesy of the artists

PLATE 21 Grimpant (2013). Teri Rueb and Alan Price. Dynamic mapping of Montpellier, France using regularly updated data from mobile app. Detail: Participant using mobile app to record movement and geo-located sound

Image courtesy of the artists

PLATE 22 GPS-based sound walk (Spectacle Island) Set on Spectacle Island, Boston Harbor, MA. Detail: Participant walking on the island

Image courtesy of the artists

PLATE 23 Core Sample (2007). Teri Rueb. GPS-based sound walk and sound sculpture. Detail: Sound sculpture installed at Boston ICA Founders Gallery (created with Michelle Fornabai)

Image courtesy of the artist

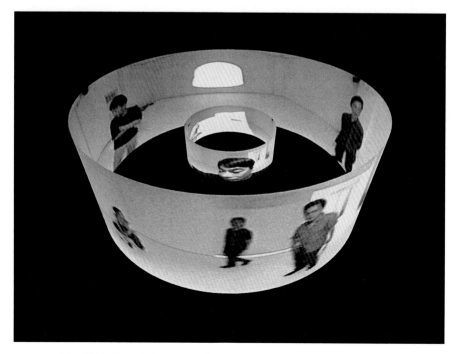

PLATE 24 Masaki Fujihata (2003). Morel's Panorama. Japan

Image courtesy of the artist

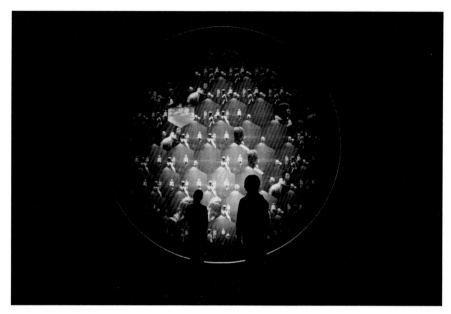

PLATE 25 Seiko Mikami. (2010). Desire of Codes. Yamaguchi: Yamaguchi Center for Arts and Media
Image courtesy of the artist

PLATE 26 doubleNegative Architecture (Sota Ichikawa, Max Rheiner, Akos Maroy, Kaoru Kobata, Satoru Higa, Hajime Narakuwa). (2007–2009). Corpora in Si(gh)te. Japan/Hungary/Switzerland, virtual architecture project
Image courtesy of the artist

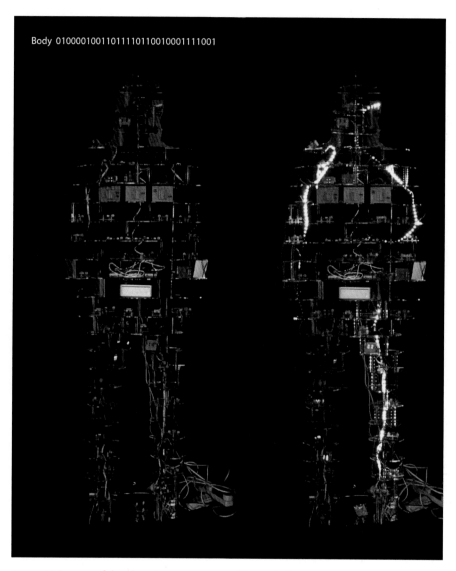

PLATE 27 Images of the changing appearance of Stanza's Body

Image courtesy of the artist

PLATE 28 Casual distraction, with complex support. Alex Gross. Dark Side (2010)
Image courtesy of the artist

PLATE 29 An example of urban distractions in the environmental history of information.
A London Street Scene (1835) watercolor by John Orlando Parry
(Wikimedia Commons)

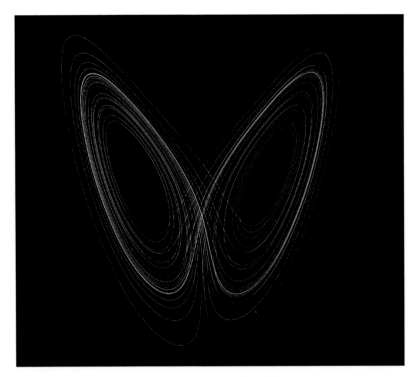

PLATE 30 The Lorenz, or strange attractor. Wikimedia Commons

PLATE 31 Ulrike And Eamon Compliant by Blast Theory, 53rd Venice Biennale, De La Warr Pavilion, Palazzo Zenobio, Venice (2009)

Photo by Anne Brassier

PLATE 32 Ulrike And Eamon Compliant by Blast Theory, TRUST: Media City, Seoul
(2010)
Photo by Seoul Museum of Art

PLATE 33 Ulrike And Eamon Compliant by Blast Theory, 53rd Venice Biennale,
De La Warr Pavilion, Palazzo Zenobio, Venice (2009)
Photo by Anne Brassier

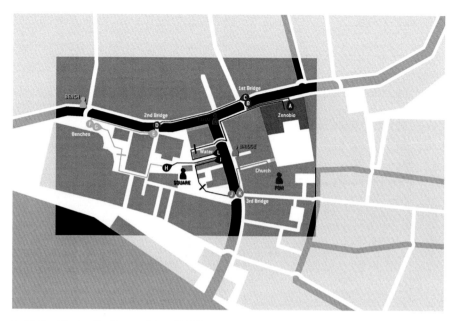

PLATE 34 Venice Performer Map (2009)
Image courtesy of the artist

PLATE 35 R–G–B mobile phone project by Electroland (2001)
Image courtesy of the artists

PLATE 36 Target Interactive Breezeway by Electroland (2006)
Image courtesy of the artists

PLATE 37 Target Interactive Breezeway by Electroland (2006)
Image courtesy of the artists

PLATE 38 College Faces (2013)
Image courtesy of the artists

PLATE 39 College Faces (2013)

PLATE 40 Crime Scene (2003) Mogens Jacobsen
Image courtesy of the artist

PLATE 41 POM/Power of Mind (2004, 2006) Mogens Jacobsen
Image courtesy of the artist

PLATE 42 Designing a TechnoSphere 2.0 creature. Using the Creature Create app, rotating and texturing in realtime 3D (2014) by Jane Prophet and Mark Hurry

Image courtesy of the artists

PLATE 43 Simulation of mixed reality scene with creature moving on table top (2014) by Jane Prophet and Mark Hurry

Image courtesy of the artists

PLATE 44 Composite simulation of the Walk in the Park app with sketch of tethered creature seen using AR (2014) by Jane Prophet and Mark Hurry
Image courtesy of the artists

PLATE 45 A diagnostic paper-chip by Diagnostics For All
Image courtesy of Whitesides Lab

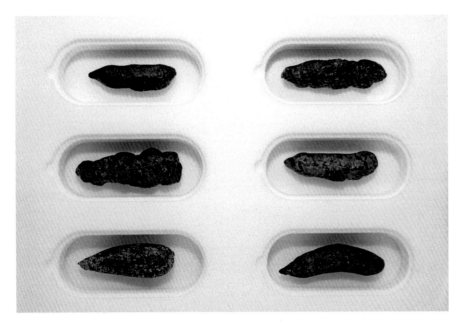

PLATE 46 Scatalog—a fictional catalog of human manure stained with genetically
engineered E. coli
Image courtesy of E. chromi project team

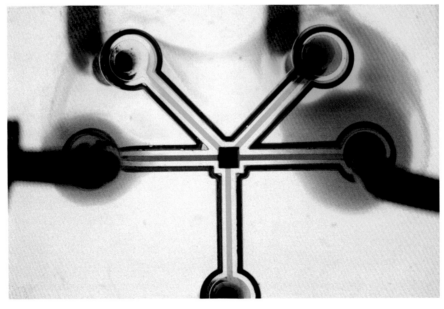

PLATE 47 Microfluidic system
Image courtesy of Folch Lab

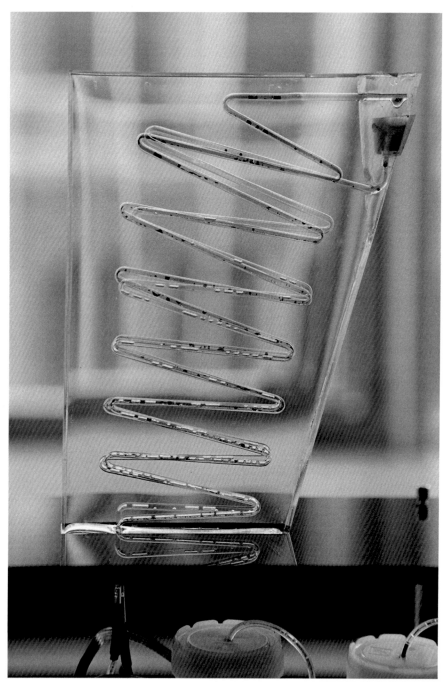

PLATE 48 The Oilwell. Prototype for a microbial perfumery that incorporates an indexical display

Image courtesy of Orkan Telhan

PLATE 49 Claire with her son at the beginning and at the end of Melancholia

PLATE 50 Claire with her son at the beginning and at the end of Melancholia

PLATE 51 The woman's writings

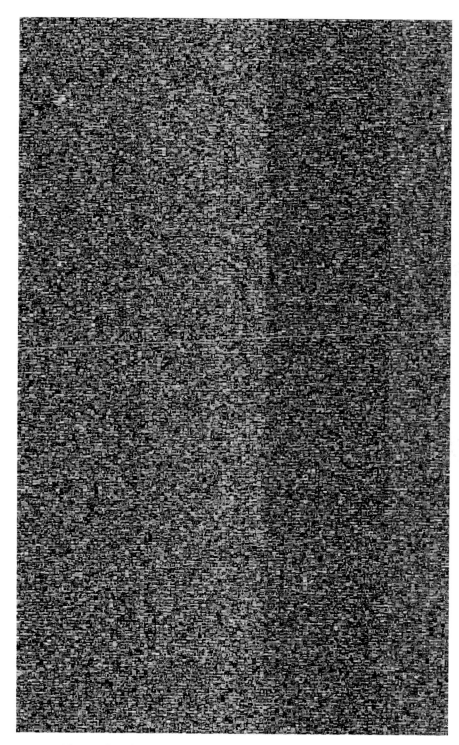

PLATE 52 Thousand Little Brothers (2014)
Image courtesy of the artist

PLATE 53 The "future TV" viewer is mostly leaning back and watching, possibly together with remote friends sharing an open audio channel for corner-of-the-mouth remarks and a subtle sense of presence. The interface is navigated with a standard remote control

PLATE 54 The menu on the TV screen shows the viewer's most recently active friends, with whom he stands in a reciprocal and actively initiated relationship, as well as a selection of the viewer's pathfinders (people he follows unilaterally)

DISTRACTION RECONSIDERED: ON THE CULTURAL STAKES OF THE AMBIENT

Malcolm McCullough

Distraction isn't what it used to be, in an age of ambient information. Notions of complexity help to explain why this is worth consideration. This chapter draws on the history of information, debates about overload, new paradigms in embodied cognition, and recent developments in urban computing to debate this claim. Generally, new patterns emerge when thresholds of enough complexity are reached: "more is different."[1] However, people of any era may have often felt distraction. Moreover, distraction has long been assumed to be the core trait of modern urban subjectivity. So more specifically to ambient information, never has quite so much of the perceptual field been quite so well cognitively engineered to appeal to the senses. Although nearly a century has passed since radio first made information truly ambient, today's conditions have become much more complex than broadcast; never was there quite such continuum of possibilities for shifting attention as exists today. This makes ubiquity something quite different from the industrial and media monocultural effects behind high modern sociological notions of distraction. And for an era of superabundant information, that makes surroundings more important.

Why Consider This Now?

The problem seems simple enough: too much information! The "ubiquity" of today seems quite different than the ubiquity of even just five or ten years ago. Who could deny the wondrous benefits of today's information superabundance? It has to count as one most salient aspects of these times. Yet few people seem able to manage this cornucopia very well; more and more complain of overload; some even admit to information overconsumption (Stone 2008). Recent developments in the ubiquity of media have pushed this problem to the cultural forefront. As shown in Plate 28, distraction has become frontpage news and an ongoing cultural debate.

Not only in its technological capacities but also in acceptable customs of its use, information media continue to diversify in formats, expand in reach, and increase its appeals to attention.

Yet overload has always existed. If you believe the old truism that you can keep only seven things in mind at once, then perhaps people began sensing overload as soon as there were eight! The unmediated world has always been overwhelming, all the more so whenever such basic needs as food or safety have not been met. Of course cognition is fairly well adapted to that; the mind filters the world well, and if it stopped doing so even briefly, the result would be madness. But cognition cannot fully adapt to accelerating technological change. Simply growing up with technology is not enough. Although quite adaptive, the brain cannot become just anything; attention-switching resources are still finite for instance (Pinker 2010). Meanwhile larger social constructs of attention and distraction seldom keep pace with technological change. Is there anything human beings do that has not been done while also texting?

"Is there anywhere on earth exempt from these swarms of new books?"[2] asked Erasmus, the first modern editor, in the sixteenth century (Blair 2003). Indeed, sensitive souls through the ages have complained of information overload, long before there were computer networks (Nunberg 1997). "The early modern experience of overload was different in many ways from today's," historian Ann Blair has observed. "For example, then only educated elite and a few areas of life were affected." Whereas today the Internet affects most people, nevertheless, according to Blair, "[w]hat we share with our ancestors, though, is the sense of excess." It seems a truism that anyone in any era might have felt excess wherever circumstances exceeded expectations (Levy 2008, 510–512). As historians often speculate, because even a single printed page or painted image might had much more impact in a world where those were rare, any change of format, context, or quantity may have seemed excessive. Thus a seventeenth-century Amsterdam merchant gathering news of ships arriving (in unprecedented numbers) might well have felt overwhelmed with information. It is unlikely that he would have used that word, however. According to its historians, the word "information" did not come into general use until the nineteenth century, when the rise of industrial technologies created massive amounts of printed matter to organize and store, and so led to libraries, catalogs, mass-produced newspapers, and disembodied telegraph signaling (Buckland 1991, 351–360). Nineteenth-century commentators ranted about the growing obsession with that antisocial new creation (but indeed centuries old successor to the shipping gazettes), the newspaper (Henkin 1998, 69–136).

Although environmental histories of information tend to be difficult to research, since few cultures preserved the casual ephemera of street-level communications for instance, it seems fair to say that the format, context, or quantity of those communications has increased overall. According to Ferguson, official signage for wayfinding, safety, and historic commemoration has steadily proliferated, for instance. As can be seen in Plate 29, color lithography brought advertising into the public sphere. Electrification extended the hours and range of civil street life. Neon signs were particularly controversial. A famous quip from Walter Benjamin invokes a mood of the ambient: "What, in the end, makes advertising so superior to criticism? Not what the moving red neon sign says, but the fiery pool reflecting it in the asphalt" (Benjamin 1996, 476).

From the rise of electronic media onward, cultural archives seem more ample; indeed to anyone who has grown up with these media, anything before them might seem from another age and less knowable. Modern media histories are presumably familiar enough to the readers of this volume. For of course cultural abuses of radio and television became a major cultural challenge of their age; indeed the very one which led to the rise of postmodern cultural studies, for whom broadcast media (including cinema) has remained the most important fare even until today in some circles. For present purposes, note how that period has left a bias that "media" mean remoteness of source and passivity of use. Broadcast media have been portals to and from someplace else, and their sources cannot anticipate the circumstances of their users.

This makes the rise of interaction design an important turn for cultural theory; at least some media can be local, two-way, and situated. Conversely, it makes an awareness of social constructs and critical positions increasingly important for technological design and practice.

These complex new disciplinary crossings suggest an important counterpoint to current obsessions with smartphones: there are situated technologies too!

"Just as fat has replaced starvation as the nation's number one dietary concern," sociologist David Shenk wrote in the 1997, "information overload has replaced information scarcity as an important new emotional, social, and political problem (Shenk, 29)." The term "information overload" itself was coined by *Future Shock* author Alvin Toffler in 1971. "Information anxiety" another similar term was coined by Richard Saul Wurman about twenty-five years ago, and "information obesity" appears to have been around for ten years or less. That food metaphor seems worth considering. When a formerly scarce resource becomes abundant, people instinctively consume it wherever and whenever they can, which naturally leads to overconsumption. Empty calories in the echo chambers of blogs and re-tweets instantly gratify the need to tell somebody whenever anything occurs to you. Much as with overconsumption of unprecedentedly available sugar and fat, today there is widespread overconsumption of information, especially when informational empty calories don't really satisfy (Grossman and Salam 2010).[3]

In what has to be a primary piece of inspirational scholarship for this volume, the cultural critic Mark C. Taylor has explained a complexity theory of how information and noise interrelate:

> If information is any difference that makes a difference, then the domain of information lies between too little and too much difference . . . Noise and information, in other words, are thoroughly relative; what is noise at one level or in one location is information in another moment or another location.
>
> (Taylor 2001, 110–123)

In short, not only can one person's noise be another person's signal, but even amid individual perceptions such shifts in frame of reference can inform. Information theory has much to say about chaos; cognitive science is very much a matter of swapping knowledge representations; art and design can be very good at triggering swaps; and emergence seems vital in all of these disciplines. In this cocktail-party example, note how words heard in the periphery affect not only how you move from group to group, but what the group talks about as it casually plays its language game from moment to moment. Yet if two people simultaneously speak into each of your ears, you cannot make sense of either of them. There do exist limits to cognition.

Cognition and Attention

As attention grows scarce in this age of superabundant information, now might be an excellent time to learn more about it (McCullough 2013).[4] Bought, sold, hoarded, and stolen, attention has become the coin of the realm. For of course attention becomes scarce as information becomes plentiful. Alas that's a truth that is easy to know but difficult to remember. Everywhere people handle ever more information as if that doesn't cost anything. So it is worth reciting the famous remark from information-science visionary Herb Simon:

> [In] an information-rich world, the wealth of information means a dearth of something else: a scarcity of whatever it is that information consumes. What information consumes is rather obvious: it consumes the attention of its recipients. Hence a wealth of information creates a poverty of attention.
>
> (Simon 1971, 40–41)

As in any amateur appreciation of the sciences, it is important not to jump to conclusions on how technology makes "us" think this way or that, as so much of the breezy neuro-babble this is so popular in the press seems to do. Attention remains a topic of enormous complexity, about which too little is known to express much at all with the kind of certainty that academics prefer. Even just the problem of multitasking, into which so many inquiries about attention quickly fall, is very much open to debate. For example, while adaptive learning is vital, and neuroplasticity definitely exists; nevertheless physiological limits definitely exist as well. Amid the process hierarchy by which the brain assembles cognition, switching costs and bottlenecks inevitably do occur, especially for executing tasks. Moreover, according to some famous studies, they may do so especially for people who take pleasure in switching (Ophir et al. 2009). In this regard, leading cognitive scientists contend that effective multitasking is just a myth; it just feels good (Rubinstein et al. 2001, 763–797).

Here instead of joining those debates, consider a larger, more consensual trend in the cognitive sciences. Over the last twenty years, there has been recognizable move beyond an emphasis on purely computational models of mind toward what is generally referred to as "embodied cognition." Naturally, as philosophers take up analogies from the technologies of their age, once upon a time there were steam metaphors of mind, where you could blow a gasket, or electrical, where you could get a charge out of something, and of course computational, where you could load an instruction set. While unlike steam, those computational metaphors do indeed describe many mental processes quite usefully, they cannot be everything.

Ever-increasing use of media has made vision seem more dominant, of course. Who first said that the look and feel of technology is almost all look and almost no feel? The jumpy nature of vision has made attention seem jumpy too. For example one of the oldest metaphors in cognition is of a spotlight. As vision keeps shifting, its selective focus does seem to illuminate. The gaze does usually indicate where deliberative attention has been directed. It does find things more quickly where it is expecting to find something. Because many such visual processes are relatively practical to study clinically, more so than situational awareness in the field at least, early cognition literature may have had a bias toward them. But of course embodied frames of reference also matter. Vision alone does not explain how attention gets assembled, nor attention's aspects of orientation and habit, nor the importance of context. More recent cognitive research thus goes beyond the spotlight metaphor, and beyond selective attention, to understand fuller roles of embodiment (Barsalou 2008, 617–645). For a first point to make about embodiment, easy to know but somehow difficult to remember: not all attention is visual. On how the mind is not just a disembodied linguistic processor, cognitive scientist and roboticist Andy Clark observed early on (in the 1990s):

> In general, evolved creatures will neither store nor process information in costly ways when they can use the structure of the environment and their operations upon it as a convenient stand-in for the information-processing operations concerned.
>
> (Clark 1989, 64)

On the nature of engagement, Clark and Chalmers summarized:

> memory as pattern re-creation instead of data retrieval; problem solving as pattern completion and transformation; the environment as an active resource, and not just a domain problem; and the body as part of the computational loop, and not just an input device.
>
> (Clark and Chalmers 1998, 59–74)

This use of props and structures assists with the processes of externalization and internalization, which activity theorists have shown is important to learning and tacit knowledge. Amid masterful, habitual, embodied actions, not only do technologies become more useable, but indeed attention may seem effortless (Dourish 2001).

Not all information is something sent. There are also immanent, natural, physical data, like tracks on a trail, traces of wear in a building, or configurations of tools in a workplace (Floridi 1997). Not all attention involves deliberation with symbols. There is also situational awareness. Many of the cues by which surroundings help individuals and organizations make sense of what they do are embodied in the objects, tools, props, and settings of those activities. Many of the affordances of situations, which are so important to masterful practices, interaction design, and the economics of attention, are implicit, undeclared, and emergent. To saturate life's situations with more explicit systems of procedures and names might thus be counterproductive.

The body has many operations of attention that do not rise to the level of consciously deliberative thought. The existence of tacit knowledge has long been recognized in the media arts, and not only for haptic orientation but also in the mastery of situated tasks, like craft. Contextual features so important to engagement may both exist and be recognized without ever having been named or placed as such. Many processes of attention may well very different pathways of the brain than those used for language-like symbolic processing (Goodale and Milne 1992, 20–25). For example, there are strong effects from holding or catching an object, in contrast to looking at it. Some of the most familiar forms of embodied cognition exist in the play of interpersonal distance—stand slightly closer or further from someone to try that one. Presence has strong effects not just in socialization but also in work, where physical props and configurations often matter, and where attention often emerges in the exercise of skills, amid internalized habits of engagement (Kaptelinin and Nardi 2006).

So for a quick summary on attention itself, several common misconceptions seem easy enough to identify. Not all attention is visual or selective like a spotlight. Not all debates on attention concern multitasking. Overload always existed, in one sense, and in another, overload isn't so much the problem as overconsumption. Superabundance is welcome, but it makes better attention practices more vital. Surroundings play a part in those practices. For as interaction designers know, affordances shape knowing. Not all attention is fragmented or paid; sometimes it just flows. Embodiment and orientation can be important components of attention. Not all attention involves thought. The human mind has always loved to wander, but it never had quite such exquisite means of doing so.

What Makes It Complex?

You do not have to be a cognitive scientist to see that distraction has become more complex. A designer, a cultural historian, an urban sociologist, or a technological entrepreneur might each have their own sense of this transformation. Of course distraction remains purely subjective and difficult to characterize in any general way (Jackson 2009). Of course it has always existed, often in very simple forms: to achieve distraction takes no more than a poor night of sleep, and to do so technologically takes no more than a pair of dice. Yet anyone can see that ever more mediated distractions have become ever more usual. Anyone who takes the trouble to learn more about the workings of attention might see the difference between industrial and informational eras for that.

It really is a question of ambient information. Again, never before did so much experiential saturation come from artifice, with such purposeful design of interface. What has changed is how much of the world offers appeal and not menace, novelty and not tedium, and immediacy and not heartbreaking distances. Never before has quite such a spectrum of the perceptual field been so deliberately placed, nor so deliberately engineered for cognition. Today as the format, context, and quantity of situated technologies diversify and increase, and as design for embodied cognition comes into its own, this too might be a moment of complexity.

This volume of essays is exploring the complexity of ubiquity from a great many scholarly perspectives. In general it asks whether formerly separate mediations of everyday life have begun to interoperate as systems. Context drives this transformation. Whether from a social, psychological, technological, architectural, or cultural-event perspective, the rise of tangible, social, and situated information technologies seems like a significant development of these times (Kahn et al.). Perhaps smartphones provide the most compelling elements of this scene, indeed some of the most sophisticated pieces of artifice ever devised, yet the situated elements give urban computing its social and cultural complexity.

Many of the scholarly inquiries here focus on particularly definitive traits of complexity, such as: the way small local changes can trigger larger, more systemic ones; how adaptation occurs more readily once feedback and micro-transactions have been introduced; how to move beyond conventional models of networking and usability to recognize that human actors are not always rational, and that particular combinations of technological actors may have emergent effects; and, especially, how systems can influence or be influenced by their environments.

Amid the many phenomena emerging amid this complexity and explored by the many experts in this volume, this essay reminds how one of the most fundamental emergent side effects of social and technological change is distraction. It is worth repeating that while a subjective state of mind, and one that could occur amid any era, culture, or technological circumstances, distraction has become culturally topical of late. For despite how human it has always been, today distraction is much more skillfully engineered. And despite how the social critics of modern broadcast culture made that process a central story in urban sociology, the increasing complexity of ubiquity has changed the conditions substantially. Even just the interface uses of gesture, facial expressions, physical location, or social proximity make it all more complex than sitting home alone, clicking on screens. This isn't a monoculture, nor just a competition for eyeballs, nor a centralized quest for control. Instead there is an explosion of possibilities and players, and a surge in the qualities of engagement, in an ever richer continuum of possibilities for shifting attention.

That early modern sociology thus seems worth another look. Many of the essays in this volume are doing that. First, recall how visual culture itself industrialized; and note how in the process, so did attention. What now seems a usual opposition of distraction and attention only took such form in the last third of the nineteenth century. That is when the pioneering psychologist William James began to explore it, for one. In particular, consider how usual it now is to assume that attention is something to pay. That was not always the case; only industrialization made it so, not only when attending factory machines, but also with respect to culture. As art historian Jonathan Crary observed:

> modern distraction was not a disruption of stable or 'natural' kinds of sustained, value-laden perception that had existed for centuries but was [instead] an effect, and in many cases a constituent element, of the many attempts to produce attentiveness in human subjects.

(Crary 1999, 49)

Through careful reading of both early texts of the then-formative discipline of psychology and selected paintings from the period, Crary was able to identify attention as a new idea. "Not until the 1870s does one find attention consistently being attributed a central and formative role . . . (Crary 1999, 13)"

Over a century later, scholars of a mindful, resistant urbanism still recite Georg Simmel's 1903 portrait of distraction, "The Metropolis and Mental Life," in which "there is perhaps no psychic phenomenon which is so unconditionally reserved to the city as the blasé outlook". (Simmel 1950, 4). In many ways this is because Simmel was among the first to express this new emphasis on attention. In a fittingly industrial metaphor, "blasé" means worn down through excess, not only from the labor or pollution that many sociologists protested, but also from unprecedented diversity of demands on attention, or as Simmel put it, "incapacity to react to new stimulations with the required amount of energy" (4). Although the word would have meant something less back then, this was clear statement of complexity. In what may be the most famous passage from "The Metropolis and Mental Life," the fatigue that dulls and blunts comes from "the intensification of nervous stimulation, resulting from the rapid telescoping of changing images, pronounced differences in what is grasped at a single glance, and the unexpectedness of violent stimuli" (Simmel 1950, 1–4). If any one cultural reference is familiar to the many writers and readers of this current volume, perhaps it is this one, perhaps because so many late twentieth century critics revived it. For as consumerism reached unprecedented levels in the 1980s, and as cultural theory reacted with an emphasis on privileging the reader, Simmel seemed far ahead of his time on the reader's experience of fragmented, decontextualized, desire-inducing media (Frisby 1984). Yet much has developed in a generation since then, and in a century since Simmel. In particular, the ability of media to distract, and their intentional placement for doing so, seem a world apart from the newly bright lights and noise of clanking industrial Berlin.

Furthermore, the stance of disengagement has reversed to where it has become the norm. There is no longer very much countercultural about tuning out. Whereas top someone displaced from traditional rustic life, to whom that tradition seems recent and memorable enough for constant comparison, urbanism amplifies the sense of displacement, or anomie, instead today, to someone who grew up in postindustrial sprawl, with disembodied friendships, nonstop media feeds, and informational empty calories, urbanism represents a prospect for relative sanity. When blasé is now the norm, instead tuning in becomes the countercultural position (Gallagher 2009). At the very least, urbanism provides a richer mix of perceptual options, and more rewards for mindfully managed attention. Tuning in is more complex, not only because civil society is far less strict and conventional, but also because the acts of tuning and tuning out are far more finely and frequently interspersed. The nature of the stimuli is more complex because instead of being accidental side effects of so many separate industrial elements, much more of it is a deliberate quest for a niche in the economics of attention. Overstimulation may be more subtle, widespread, and appealing than before, but blasé has become less of an option. Those who seek to tune out become only more vulnerable to thoughtless overconsumption, addictions to unsatisfying feeds, even attention theft (Hayes 2009). Instead, the best defense is to choose to tune in, to take interest, and to help your sensibilities slowly evolve.

The Role of Surroundings

Of course context matters more in an age of mobile, embedded, and tangible computing. Designers know in the abstract that surroundings alter intent. Many sites of life—kitchens, classrooms, boardrooms, laboratories, lobbies, sidewalk cafes, public plazas—are not only for particular activities but also about them. Sites put people into frames of mind, and often into particular spatial relationships as well, often at very carefully considered scale. So in a way, you could say that architecture and the city have always been technologies of attention.

Layers of technology accumulate in the sites of everyday life, which they seldom replace but often transform. So it is worth remembering that underneath all today's rush to augment the city, fixed forms do persist, and to notice and work with them can improve other sensibilities too. You might also say that cognitive role of surroundings is to serve as riverbanks for the flows of data and communications. The circumstances of engagement shape the flow of attention. Interaction designers understand this best about screens, especially individual graphical user interfaces. But the matter is more complex for aggregations of screens, or the relation of screens to other, more invisibly situated technologies, or the relation of technologies to the many other ways that context can inform. The ability to shift in an out of these important aspects of situational awareness depends on opportunities (and willingness) to put aside foreground attention to media and messages from and about someplace else. As Mitchell has noted, surroundings provide sites, objects, and physical resource interfaces for those electronic flows to be about. At the same time, surroundings provide habitual and specialized contexts by which to make sense of activities. And, where possible, surroundings furnish rich, persistent, attention-restoring detail in which to take occasional refuge from the rivers of data.

Consider the difference between fascination and entertainment. People who are fascinated with what they do or where they are, seem less dependent on entertainment, and less afflicted by overload (Gallagher 2009). It helps to remember that adaptive learning exists, and is necessary, but has its limits. Thus while there is no more such a thing as a natural state of cognition any more than there is such a thing as a digital native, it is possible to cultivate sensibilities. In better cases, fascination with less mediated conditions to which human cognition is better adapted has been shown to restore mental capacity for later, more mediated deliberative tasks. Thus to cultivate a more ambient situational awareness, outside of the furnished attentional frameworks of so many media, and attuned to a wider spectrum of space and time, may help mitigate information overconsumption. It may cultivate kinds of attention that you do not have to pay, and that flow without effort and that make other things seem to do so. This isn't just about stopping to smell the roses, although that sometimes helps. A new mindfulness to context becomes no mere luxury in an age of ubiquitous mediation. The kinds of sensibility that attention to surroundings helps to cultivate seem very necessary to productivity and well-being in an age of information superabundance and overconsumption.

This mindfulness may also be an important instance of complexity. In the economics of attention, amid an increasingly ambient, mediated, and hybrid continuum of possibilities to shift attention, is there some new kind of emergence? There is complexity both in this diversified world of media, and in the sensibilities that help with these new circumstances.

So to take away, here is a paradox to keep and share. Better sensibility to surroundings may reduce overload overall. This not a matter of paying attention, so much as cultivating the kinds of attention you do not have to pay.

Notes

1. While no expert on complexity, I have steeped in that field's works long enough, since, say reading Stuart Kauffman in the 1980s, that by now many of its truisms are second nature to me, and have become common parlance in enough academic culture, that it would be more difficult and less necessary to attribute all of them. "More is different" appears attributed to the physicist P. W. Anderson, but I surely learned of it elsewhere.
2. Erasmus, as quoted by Ann Blair.

3. A video discussion between Lev Grossman (Time) and Reihan Salam (Daily Beast).
4. To consider attention itself, and especially attention to surroundings, I have long been mining the literature, as an amateur but in a persistent and organized way, and with the benefit of excellent research library data databases that complement the open net. For more detail, see my *Ambient Commons–Attention in the Age of Embodied Information* (Cambridge: MIT Press, 2013).

References

Benjamin, Walter. 1996. "One Way Street: This Space for Rent" In *Selected Writings*, vol. 1 (1913–26), edited by M. Bullock and M. W. Jennings, trans. R. Livingstone, 476. Cambridge, MA: Harvard University Press.

Barsalou, Lawrence. 2008. "Grounded Cognition." *Annual Review of Psychology* 59: 617–645.

Blair, Ann. 2003. "Coping with Information Overload in Early Modern Europe." *Journal of the History of Ideas* 64: 11–28.

Buckland, Michael. 1991. "Information as Thing." *Journal of the American Society of Information Science* 42: 351–360.

Clark, Andy. 1989. *Microcognition: Philosophy, Cognitive Science, and Parallel Distributed Processing*. Cambridge, MA: MIT Press.

Clark, Andy, and David Chalmers. 1998. "The Extended Mind." *Analysis* 58 (1998): 7–19. Reprinted in *Philosopher's Annual* 21: 59–74.

Crary, Jonathan. 1999. *Suspensions of Perception: Attention, Spectacle, and Modern Culture*. Cambridge, MA: MIT Press.

Dourish, Paul. 2001. *Where the Action Is: The Foundations of Embodied Interaction*. Cambridge, MA: MIT Press.

Ferguson, Priscilla. 1994. *Paris as Revolution: Writing the nineteenth Century City*. Berkeley, CA: University of California Press.

Floridi, Luciano. 1997. "Semantic Conceptions of Information." *Stanford Encyclopedia of Philosophy*, edited by E. N. Zalta, http://plato.stanford.edu/archives/win2007/entries/information-semantic.

Frisby, David. 1984. *Georg Simmel*. London: Tavistock.

Gallagher, Winifred. 2009. *Rapt: Attention and the Focused Life*. New York: Penguin Press.

Goodale, Melvin and David Milne. 1992. "Separate Visual Pathways for Perception and Action." *Trends in Neuroscience* 15: 20–25.

Grossman, Lev and Reihan Salam. 2010. "Information Obesity." *Bloggingheads*, Accessed April 3, 2015, http://nytimes.com/video/opinion/1247468584580/bloggingheads-information-obesity.html.

Hayes, Tom. 2009. "Next Up for the Internet: The Attention Rights Movement." *TomBomb.Com*, January 22, 2009, Accessed April 05, 2015, http://tombomb.com/2009/01/next-up-for-the-internet-the-attention-rights-movement.html.

Henkin, David. 1998. *City Reading: Written Words and Public Spaces in Antebellum*. New York: Columbia University Press.

Jackson, Maggie. 2009. *Distracted: The Erosion of Attention and the Coming Dark Age*. Amherst, NY: Prometheus Books.

Kahn, Omar, Trevor Scholz, and Mark Shepard. *Situated Technologies* pamphlet series, Architecture League of New York, Accessed April 03, 2015, http://situatedtechnologies.net.

Kaptelinin, Victor, and Bonnie A. Nardi. 2006. *Acting with Technology: Activity Theory and Interaction Design*. Cambridge, MA: MIT Press.

Levy, David. 2008. "Information Overload." In *The Handbook of Information and Computer Ethics*, edited by K. E. Himma and H. T. Tavani, 497–514. New York: Wiley.

McCullough, Malcolm. 2013. "Peak Distraction." In *Ambient Commons, Attention in the Age of Embodied Information*, 275–284. Cambridge, MA: MIT Press.

Mitchell, William J. 2005. "In the First Place." In *Placing Words: Symbols, Space, and the City*, 1–20. Cambridge, MA: MIT Press.

Nunberg, Geoff. Ed. 1997 "Farewell to the Information Age." In *The Future of the Book*, 103–133. Berkeley, CA: University of California Press.

Ophir, Eyal, Clifford Nass, and Anthony D. Wagner. 2009. "Cognitive Control in Media Multitaskers." *Proceedings of the National Academy of Sciences* 106 (33): 15583–15587.

Pinker, Steven. 2010. "Mind over Mass Media." *The New York Times*, June 10, Accessed April 3, 2015, http://nytimes.com/2010/06/11/opinion/11Pinker.html?_r=0.

Rubinstein, Joshua S., David E. Meyer, and Jeffrey E. Evans. 2001. "Executive Control of Cognitive Processes in Task Switching." *Journal of Experimental Psychology, Human Perception, and Performance* 27: 763–797.

Shenk, David. 1997. *Data Smog: Surviving the Information Glut*. San Francisco, CA: Harper Collins.

Simmel, Georg. 1950. "The Metropolis and Mental Life." In *The Sociology of Georg Simmel*, Ed. and trans. Kurt Wolff, 409–424. New York: Free Press.

Simon, Herbert. 1971. "Designing Organizations for an Information-Rich World." In *Computers, Communication, and the Public Interest*, edited by Martin Greenberger, 40–41. Baltimore, MD: Johns Hopkins University Press.

Stone, Linda. 2008. "Continuous Partial Attention—Not the Same As Multi-Tasking." *Bloomberg Businessweek Online*, July 24, Accessed April 3, 2015, www.businessweek.com/business_at_work/time_management/archives/2008/07/continuous_part.html.

Taylor, Mark C. 2001. "Noise in Formation." In *The Moment of Complexity: Emerging Network Culture*, 99–124. Chicago, IL: University of Chicago Press.

Wurman, Richard Saul. 1989. *Information Anxiety*. New York: Doubleday.

THE INFORMATION ENVIRONMENT

Sean Cubitt

Information is no longer knowledge, held and produced by communities. It has become both a mass of commodities (data) and an environment that stands over and against communities and individuals. An environment environs. It does so because it has been excluded historically from the human that it environs. An environment is defined by this act of exclusion.

Exclusion occurs through a paradoxical process of enclosure and externalization. The first is an operation in the legal and political plane; the second in the economic. The apparent paradox derives from the division of political economy into two discrete practices and their associated professional and academic disciplines, politics, and economics (Mosco 2009), so that the contradiction at the heart of the process by which the commons becomes environment, appears as a difference in discourses rather than a real contradiction. In seeking to understand the nature of information understood as environment, this chapter begins by tracing the histories of enclosure and externalization that exclude environments from the human, thus changing the definition of what we mean by "human." It then looks at the two key media of the information environment, the radio spectrum and telecommunications, and at the data principles that have come to underpin their operation as environments in the early twenty-first century, and the contradiction inherent in the term "information economy." The final section analyses the relations of labor and consumption to the information economy, before concluding with a proposal on how a reintegrated political economy might make possible a new form of environmental politics.

Environments as Enclosures and Externalities

The history of the political-economic construction of environments is largely indistinguishable from the history of colonialism. The word "colonizing" describes very well the process of taking over a territory while at the same time excluding it from participation in the core business of the colonizing power. Thus if we say that capitalism has colonized the prison service, the term is partly metaphorical but also indicates a historical continuity—capital has always colonized new areas because it is compelled to expand by the law of the falling rate of profit—and the close parallels between colonialism as territorial expansion on the one hand and endocolonialism, the internal colonization of metropolitan nations and economies, on the other. The first great enclosure affected by nascent capital was the enclosure of common land.

For millennia, the poor had supplemented their crops and husbandry with grazing, hunting, and gathering in commonly held woods and waters. The enclosures of the fifteenth century and subsequently alienated the peasants from the land (Thirsk 1958), increasing their dependence on landowners and later on urban landlords and employers, while alienating the newly privatized commons, rendering it either legally protected domain or lawless wilderness. This process of enclosure expanded globally in the age of exploration, which threw colonized peoples off their common lands in favor of export-oriented agriculture. Driven to agriculturally marginal lands, the indigenous peoples of the colonized world retain ancestral links with land into the twenty-first century, when those territories too have become objects of avarice for mining and energy corporations: just one of the contradictions of colonial enclosure.

The second enclosure, immediate predecessor of the formation of the data environment, was the enclosure of skills traced by Marx in the *Grundrisse* under the concept of dead labor (Marx 1984). Skills that had been integral to common life, skills of weaving, sewing, knitting, cooking, smithing, and many more were enclosed, concretized in machines, and placed over against the poor, reconstituting them as workers subject to work discipline dictated by the factory environment. Similar activities occurred in the colonial era: skills associated with ceramics, dyes, horticulture, navigation, and many more were looted from the commons of their originators, industrialized, and the products sold back to the colonized. The enclosure of knowledge is in some respects only a further stage in the colonization of skills as dead labor, this time colonizing what Marx referred to as the general intellect: the shared and common knowledge, expressed in language, culture and design, on which the transmission of skills and the invention of new activities depends. By converting this knowledge into information, capital is able to enclose it in databases and databanks, commercialize through intellectual property laws, and sell the commodified form back to those from whom it was taken in the first place. Alienated from their own knowledge, the human subjects of the environmentalization of information become another kind of human being, as farmers became peasants, and artisans became workers. One task of this chapter is to ask what kind of humans the inhabitants of the information environment are becoming. An indication can be got from the revulsion of indigenous peoples against uninvited mapping of their territory, and unwanted DNA mining of their genetic patrimony (Smith 2012).

The enclosure of lands, skills, and knowledge has been accompanied by their externalization, the process of rendering something external (an "externality") to the economy. While colonial enclosure in one sense embraces the pre-existing commons in order to subsume it into increasingly global and universal capital, it is accompanied by a process of economic externalizing. In Kathryn Milun's account (Milun 2011), that which was legally *res communis*, held in common by everyone, becomes *res nullius*, belonging to no-one, and therefore available to be converted into property for division and exploitation. The description of both the Americas and Australia as *terra nullius*, no-man's land, opened them up to ownership by the colonists, and gave legal permission for ethnocide, since definitionally the indigenous were "uninhabitants,"[1] for all colonial intents and purposes not there. This ostensibly legal re-categorization of environments like the high seas and outer space is in effect an economization of the environment in question. The specific form taken by these enclosed commons, as they move from no-one's to someone's property, is that of economic externalities.

An externality is any consequence of economic action that is not accounted for in book-keeping. A positive externality might be, for example, the education of a workforce, which is paid for by local governments or churches, but which a firm benefits from; the commonest example of negative externality is pollution from a factory that is not factored into its profitability. Externalities are the unaccounted effects of economics, in the sense that they do not appear in the accounts. Externalized commons are of central importance to understanding the ubiquity of computing in two ways. First they indicate that the information economy inflects everyone's relationship to skills and knowledge, even those who have no access to computers or networks. And second they point ineluctably to the material infrastructure of the information economy: its dependence on physical places which, however, it excludes not only from its promotional materials but from its accounts. Thus for a mining corporation, there are costs of extracting, refining and transporting minerals, but the minerals in the ground come at either no cost whatever; or at the negligible cost of a government license, a fraction of which will be paid to the indigenous people whose lands will be desecrated in the extraction process. Hydroelectric and fossil-fuel energy for manufacture and use again affect indigenous peoples most (Auty 1993).

The old commons, now redefined as externalities, are also the key sites for dumping waste: the high seas and inner space crowded with dumped toxins, trash islands and space junk; old mine workings filled with radioactive waste from power plants; hazardous waste dumping in the global South. The problem is exacerbated because waste is no longer an unfortunate by-product of manufacture, distribution, and consumption but is integral to capital. The falling rate of profit that drives expansion also drives capital to over-production. That over-production can either be consumed (though the expansion of debt in particular) or wasted: these moments of destruction subsequent to the last economic action, that of purchase, no longer figure in accounts. The corporation has no means of accounting for the waste of energy and materials; in fact it requires wastage, as a way of destroying the fruits of over-production without incurring costs to itself. Thus the theory of environments as externalities is tied to the principle of integral waste at the core of neo-liberal consumerism. The function once served by conspicuous consumption is now served by conspicuous and inconspicuous waste. Those who make their livings in the vast waste tips of the global South *know* waste: from the point of view of the economy, it is mere information.

There are parallels to physical waste in the factory and information environments. While fixed capital tends to be protected against misuse and sabotage, the immense desolation of Detroit and other post-industrial landscapes indicates the degree to which machinery can be sacrificed on the altar of profit. The accounting principle of writing down and writing off machinery, the annual depreciation of the book value of the technologies it uses in manufacture, enshrines waste in the heart of industrial capital. Technological advances in automation are aimed at reducing the living labor required to produce goods, and the falling rate of profit drives it to surprising levels of invention, but as companies like General Motors began to earn more from debt financing than from manufacture, and when offshore manufacture of parts and ultimately assembly proved cheaper than paying taxes and respecting health, safety, and environmental protection laws in the global North, the only reserved elements of industrialization to remain human-dependent were design and marketing. Today both tasks are becoming automated in their turn.

Yet there is still over-production, to be destroyed through cycles of fashion and planned obsolescence, egregious in the computing and mobile media markets, requiring not only the waste of material goods, but the production, as cheaply as possible, of content to fill these devices. While prestige offerings generate significant profits, even greater ones are available to shopping channels, celebrity gossip, commercials, spam, and other time-fillers for Internet and broadcast. The ephemerality and the intellectual and emotional poverty of broadcast attracted much, often patrician criticism;[2] they have a core of value when least nostalgic for a literary,

DIY culture of an imagined past.[3] They point towards our acceptance of the second-rate, in content and in technologies. There is a practice of dumping waste content into broadcast schedules and Internet platforms that eventually diminish or stifle their productivity (Fuller 2001). Like the junk food dumped on the consumer market, junk media eventually require consumer pharmaceuticals to counteract their effects. The integration of waste extends to the enclosed commons of the information environment.

Environmentalization of the Radio Spectrum and Telecommunications

As Douglas Kahn announces in the opening lines of his work on communication arts, "Radio was heard before it was invented" (Kahn 2013). The radio spectrum is a critical resource for the information environment as infrastructure of broadcast, cellular network, satellite, and microwave components of the information environment. Since the first Radiotelegraph Service Regulations signed in Berlin in 190, allocation of wavebands has been carried out by nation-states, overlapping areas being handled by international treaty. In Europe and its colonies, the newly discovered radio spectrum was treated as *res nullius* (nobody's property) and deemed to form a public good; states therefore for the most part took over the whole spectrum for national purposes, including military and emergency use, and state or public service broadcasting. The United States opted to reserve one area of spectrum for state use, and to sell licenses for the remainder to commercial interests. Both approaches rapidly killed off citizen radio enthusiasts and their stations along with activist and common-interest activities (Douglas 1987), and for most of the twentieth century the use of the spectrum for two-way communication. The Radio Regulations now in force fall under the International Telecommunications Union (ITU), which has increasingly extended membership to corporations (McLean 2003).

At the same time, and in common with many other international treaties, while recognizing the status of corporations as legal "persons," the radio regulations do not recognize the claims of non-national groups, especially indigenous peoples. The nature of the radio spectrum as commons was brought to international attention by a claim brought by Rangiaho Everton to the Waitangi Tribunal, the body set up by the New Zealand Government to adjudicate on the terms of the Waitangi Treaty, which established the terms of settlement between Maori and colonizer's at the close of the Maori Wars in 1840 (King 2004). The Tribunal report notes:

> The claimant says that the Radiocommunications Act 1989 fails to acknowledge Maori rangatiratanga ["sovereignty"] over the radio spectrum and that, in assuming for itself the exclusive authority to manage the spectrum, the Crown is ignoring the Treaty principle of partnership and failing to establish, in consultation with Maori, adequate principles, policies, and legislative framework for Maori partnership in spectrum management. The claimant alleges that the Crown is continuing to develop and pursue spectrum management policy without Maori participation, and is creating a property right, and selling that right, without consultation with, or the agreement of, Maori.
>
> (Waitangi Tribunal 1999)

The terms of the Treaty give Maori rights over all forms of commons that pre-existed the European arrival in Aotearoa, New Zealand, including the right to contest the legal process of declaring a resource open to property rights. The Tribunal recognized among its key findings that:

1. nothing in the terms of the Treaty of Waitangi allows or foreshadows any authority on the part of the Crown to determine, define, or limit the properties of the universe which may be used by Maori in the exercise of their rangatiratanga over tikanga Maori [right ways of doing];
2. where any property or part of the universe has, or may have, value as an economic asset, the Crown has no authority under the Treaty to possess, alienate, or otherwise treat it as its own property without recognizing the prior claim of Maori rangatiratanga.

The Tribunal uses terms from Te Reo Maori because of the difficulty of translating between the cultures: Terms such as the common "treasure" for *tikanga* and "sovereignty" for *rangatiritanga* are loose and inaccurate, although *tikanga* includes for example traditional rights to fishing tidal waters. For current purposes, the significance of this case is that Maori understanding of the position of the spectrum is poles apart from its commodification under European property laws, even when the economic significance of the thing is allowed.

The space created by the construction of wired telecommunications networks is of a different order, in that it is a human construct. Established as a protocol for connecting a small number of computers used by U.S. defence contractors, the Internet spread slowly enough for its management to be undertaken as a public service by a small number of engineers throughout its early years. The mass expansion following the release of the Mosaic browser in 1993 led to complex negotiations, with an ambiguous relation between nationally established organizations and self-regulating discussion groups among engineers.[4] This unstable configuration, which had escaped the control of the ITU during the years of rapid deregulation of telephony, re-emerged as a topic of international significance when the UN devoted its annual summit conference to the topic of Internet governance in 2005. While there were important debates on technical issues, at the core of disagreement was the claim by a number of nations, led by China, that Internet governance, like radio and telephony, as a matter for states and international treaties, not for self-regulation and commerce, by then the major force in Internet content (Milton 2010). The internal self-regulation model, defended by most Internet activists, can nonetheless be criticized for an implicit elitism: anyone may join debates on engineering specifications, but only the highly trained will be recognized by their peers, quietly thus marginalizing the claims of indigenous, colonized and ex-colonized participants. The exclusion is not at all as powerful as it has proved in international arenas, and far less than in global governance structures like the World Trade Organization and the International Monetary Fund where corporate interests hold sway (deNardis 2009). Nonetheless, the absence of marginalized peoples from decision making is a critical weakness in the Internet Governance Forum established in the wake of the 2005 Tunis summit.

A number of technical topics are of significance to the nature of the information environment. Among them we might mention the principle of net neutrality, the principle that the Internet should carry materials regardless of the status of the message. This is contested by telcos who argue that having invested in the infrastructure, they are entitled to privilege their own paying customers over messages derived from rival corporations (Wu 2003). Where net neutrality is not observed, activities without the support of corporate players are disadvantaged—delayed, subject to data loss, and generally treated as second-class. This is particularly significant for developing nations, many of which cannot afford the membership fees demanded by important bodies, and can only implement standards but not help design them. This developing global class system applies to both telecommunications and spectrum where a single body adjudicates over common protocols and standards. Thus for instance, the

Motion Picture Experts Group (MPEG) has charge over the now near-universal compression-decompression algorithms used for both broadcast and wired communication of audiovisual signals, yet attendance at their conferences, and even access to key documents, shows very low levels of participation form the developing world, and virtually none from indigenous peoples (Cubitt 2014).

In both instances, the radio spectrum and telecommunications, the historical legacy of colonialism meets the new conditions of the information economy to form an infrastructure, now increasingly mingling the two. Spectrum auctions for direct broadcast by satellite, digital terrestrial television, and 4G mobile wavebands are undertaken as exercises in political economy from which the population are excluded, and only states and corporations have agency. The design and application of universal standards like the TCP/IP suite, the HTML language, and the MPEG codec occur without participation from end-users, and exclusively from the standpoint of a Northern, masculine, scientistic, and instrumentalist point of view. These qualities are, through their technical standardization and universality, increasing their embedded role in contemporary communication and cultural life. They are the principles of the information environment.

The Data Principle

Zizek observes that, reversing Marx's adage, today relationships between people no longer take on the fantastic form of relations between things. On the contrary, relationships between things increasingly present themselves as relationships between people (Zizek 2009). Such is the relation established by the misnamed social media platforms like Facebook, which encourage a performance of self as brand, while actively pursuing the task of rendering these personal performances as data to be mined for commercial and occasionally security functions. The information environment has in fact two functions. First, it encloses knowledge in the commodity form of countable and exchangeable units; and second, it extends the principles of datafication back over previous environments in the form of extractable information that can be deployed for the production of further commodities. Both processes apply to the datafication of interpersonal relationships, a process that extends to non-voluntary data systems such as the use of facial recognition in public surveillance systems (Kember 2013). Such systems can be traced back to time and motion studies of the factory worker (Smith 1993), to nineteenth-century laboratory experiments in pursuit of the elimination of fatigue (Rabinbach 1990), in attempts to structure communicative environments to minimize distraction (Crary 1999), and to the early beginnings of eugenics (Wegenstein 2011). These were nascent forms of the statistical management of populations that Foucault calls bio-politics (Foucault 2004), the characteristic form of rule that has evolved in parallel with the information environment. The datafication of environments concentrates the contradictions of enclosure and externalization by accounting the unaccounted, providing systematic models for measuring and regulating the activities of environments, in the interests of policing the boundary between human population and environment where, Foucault argues, contemporary politics is enacted: "Biopolitics' last domain is . . . control over relations between the human race, or human beings insofar as they are a species, insofar as they are living beings, and their environment, the milieu in which they live" (Foucault 2003).

The bio-politics of information can be seen in precisely these terms. As knowledge passes from population to environment, it changes the residual humanity against which it is defined. The production of symbols that drives the information economy can be treated as externality, an unpaid, free activity of creation undertaken by millions of Internet users (Fuchs 2008). At the same time, information capital also requires a paid class of skilled workers to design and build the interfaces through which unpaid labor can be gathered. The contradictory demands of innovation and standardization, of controlled creativity and universal technical norms, require a new kind of worker with a new kind of discipline. This in turn is reflected in the increasing instrumentalization of the university sector (Burawoy 2009), charged with producing this labor force at low or no cost to corporations, which however demand an increasing say in the education on offer. The term "creative industries" implies the proletarianization of the semiotic sector of information capital: the task of the education sector is increasingly to train this new class. This new "labor aristocracy" is rarely static, however. Constantly redeployed to new technical platforms and industries, populations of paid and unpaid content providers join the growing trend to precarization of information labor (Berardi 2009). Granted sufficient privileges to distinguish them from the harsher precarious status of migrant and underemployed workers, this new precariat is however equally exploited, and equally reduced to functionaries of the information economy.

If the conditions of labor under the bio-political regulation of the population-information relationship seem to clarify the significance of the division between them, other factors blur the boundary. There is in particular some merit in beginning to understand the free market of neo-liberalism as an environment itself, specifically an information environment. From a certain point of view, it is no longer the circulation of goods that matters as much as their symbolic status as brands, and their statistical presence as market shares and other performance indicators. To the extent that the market is no longer a matter of traded goods and physical money but of the exchange of electronic symbols increasingly handled by machines in automated or "algo" trading, the finance sector in particular has become indistinguishable from any other form of network mediation. Radio frequency identification (RFID) accompanies the flow of goods through increasingly automated container transport, while automated systems match sales to stocktaking and management in the retail sector, and both to the patterns of demand and other spending habits, Internet behaviors, geotagged mobile usage, banking, and loyalty card data collected from shoppers. Under such conditions, the distinction between population and environment begins to diffuse, while bio-political government becomes harder to identify with traditional actors in the political sphere.

Noted in passing above, the corporation now has the legal standing of a person. This gives a corporation legal properties of immense value, such as the right to claim to be the author of copyright materials (a right denied to tribes). But it also suggests that an important metaphor of postmodern and early cybercultural theories (Haraway 1985), the figure of the cyborg, needs to be rethought for the new century. The actually existing cyborg is not a Terminator-like creature, a human body with digital organs. On the contrary, the new cyborg is typically a very large technical network with human biochips implanted. The corporation as cyborg is such a distributed network of interconnected data storage and handling devices, in which human functionaries serve to provide sensory inputs, semantic content, and the degree of randomness which the machinic elements are unable to achieve on their own.[5] Lacking the sense of shame that ties humans to their obligations to their communities, the corporate cyborg has only one motivation: profit. It is because it is inhuman that the corporation can proceed with no care for externalities, to the point of risking species extinction. Seven of the top ten Fortune 500 companies are either in the automotive or oil businesses.[6] The pursuit of profit demands that they not only ignore evidence of anthropogenic climate change, but actively campaign against any measures to ameliorate it. This suicidal aspect of contemporary information capital marks it out as other than human, even anti-human, while at the same time the cyborg corporations have become the most powerful agents in contemporary democratic politics and global governance.

The shift of political agency to inhuman actors is a characteristic of information capital, and reopens the question of the person, not only as legal category but as economic and cultural. Deprived of land, skill, and knowledge in the successive enclosures of modernity, the human stands now at the brink of a fourth enclosure, that of the body. Increasingly treated as environment, both the individual body and the biomass of the human population are today seen as threatening and alien sources of disease, but also open to exploitation through bioscience, and commodification through dietary, pharmaceutical, and surgical body modification. The human body can therefore now function as exchange value, not only in the form of labor, as in the industrial phase of capital, but as a cost-free environmental res nullius open to commodification, and available as externality for dumping of excess production and waste. The residue is the human mind, but a mind whose function is either to provide unpaid creativity, or paid functions in corporate cyborgs. In this sense the environment has grown at the expense of the human, to the extent that the human person should also today be understood as a technical performance with biological organs as its functionaries.

Each enclosure excludes from the polity whatever has been rendered environmental. Land, skill, knowledge, and bodies had been integral to the polity of pre-modern formations, as they remain in extra-modern formations, especially those of indigenous peoples. Today they are excluded. Jacques Rancière argues that political life emerges from the struggle between an established polity and those which it governs, but who have no voice in their own governing (Rancière 1999). The implications of this are twofold. On the one hand, the ordinary conduct of political business in democracies is not in fact politics, in the sense that prefers rule by consensus to publicly debating the core question of politics: how are we to live and live well? (Mouffe 2005) On the other hand, it implies that the continuing and expanding exclusions of the environmentalizing process diminish the arena of the political, handing proper tasks of the polity, including the management of relations between populations and environments, over to a purely economic accounting.

Traditionally, Green Parties have addressed the politics of speaking on behalf of the organic environment. We have arrived at a condition in which environmental politics must embrace the exclusion of traditionally human affairs—skill, knowledge, and bodies—alongside the exclusion of land from a role in their own governance, even as they are governed, whether by the stern operations of the market, or the kindlier concept of stewardship. The present analysis suggests that speaking on behalf of the governed is in itself a continuation of colonialism, and that the excluded demand to speak on their own behalf. Such a renewed environmentalism needs to learn from the conceptual clash between colonial and international law and the challenges to it from indigenous cultures that do not accept the "zero-sign" of res nullius. In that act of challenging there begins, as Rancière suggests was the case with the demands of freemen and later of feminists, not only the inclusion of a new sector of the population into the polity, but a radical change to the nature of political life. Incorporating marginalized human populations—indigenous, migrant, nomadic, and imprisoned—not only enfranchises: it changes the meanings of central conceptual and legal tools like "citizen" and "nation." Writing of alternatives to the prison culture of the United States, Angela Y. Davis suggests that:

> Positing decarceration as our overarching strategy, we would try to envision a continuum of alternatives to imprisonment—demilitarization of schools, revitalization of education

at all levels, a health system that provides free physical and mental care to all, and a justice system based on reparation and reconciliation rather than retribution and vengeance.

(Davis 2003)

The lesson of this extension of citizenship to prisoners is that admitting a new cohort into the polity requires radical overhaul of many aspects of political life. Extending full citizenship to European Roma, for example, would require an extensive re-imagining of what we understand by both citizenship—when it is not governed territorially—and human rights—which at present are exclusively defined by the rights of citizens (Hunt 2008) (the sole exception, refugees, is a term almost never employed by metropolitan countries who do not wish to recognize the human rights of "asylum seekers"). Including excluded humans in national and global polities is already radical. Including the non-human would appear impossible, had we not already extended the franchise and legal provisions to include corporations.

Expanding the polity to include terrestrial, technological, informatics, and now genetic environments is in effect to reverse the enclosure and externalizing that has characterized capital to date. It is important to note the extent to which these environments are class-based. All four environments are experienced as arcadias by the Pompadours of the twenty-first century: The global elite, the one percent, inhabit them as those who enjoy legal right over them, and who therefore understand them as regulated and as disposed for their enjoyment. But all four are experienced as alien and destructive by those who have been dispossessed of their common fruits. The data-peasant who tends them is not bound to them by mutual benefit but by neo-feudal bonds of debt that not only tie them to working on machines, data, and bodies, but forecloses any possibility of an alternative future (Lazzarato 2012).

The inherent contradiction of enclosure and externalization is the Klein bottle of environmentalization. Like Agamben's state of exception that has become the rule, with the environmentalization of information, the excluded environments become foundational of the populations that inhabit them, and as ecological science has always argued, the species cannot be distinguished from the ecology that supports and is supported by it. The political aspect of this economic paradox is that it is not a stable binary but intrinsically contradictory and therefore unsustainable. There are no technological fixes for environmental catastrophe because the energy and materials for those technologies have to be found from a single, fixed planetary ecology. There is no informatic solution to technical problems because data does not exist in a vacuum but must be supported by storage and transmission technologies. The partition underlying contemporary rule is radically unstable.

Of the available tools for a new politics, one of the most promising is peer-to-peer (P2P) economies. Thus far, P2P has been imagined as a strictly human-to-human mode of exchange. Roberto Verzola of the Philippines Green Party is among the first to extend this analysis to non-human environments (Verzola 2010). Reasserting the commons as commonwealth from a purely human perspective is a fine first step. It already undermines the presumption of property rights and the externality of environments. Moving to re-establish ancestral skills and knowledge as common requires a greater leap of understanding. Even though the liberation of machines, as repositories of dead labor, from their servitude has a strong history, at least since Ted Nelson's *Computer Lib* (Nelson 1974), the ideology of unconstrained machines turning on their human masters has been the stuff of nightmares from Marx's vampiric vision of industrial capital (Derrida 1994) to the *Terminator* and *Matrix* film franchises. We have come equally to fear the revolt of the body (Creed 1993). The advance of peer-to-peer thinking into relations with the alienated forms of skills, knowledge, and bodies is the one way to change the meaning of ubiquity, from universal standardization to a commons, which includes all those aspects of humanity that have been severed from us, and which leave both us and them diminished and exploited. It seems only fair that the information environment, one of the last great enclosures, should contain in it the germs of the collapse of enclosure and externality.

Notes

1. The term derives from Solnit's account of indigenous Americans irradiated or displaced by nuclear testing in the southwestern United States: Solnit, Rebecca (2000). *Savage Dreams. A Journey into the Landscape Wars of the American West*. Berkeley, University of California Press.
2. For example Jerry Mander's (1978). *Four Arguments for the Elimination of Television*. New York: W. Morrow
3. For example Guattari, Félix (2000). *The Three Ecologies*, trans Ian Pindar and Paul Sutton. London: Athlone.
4. See for example Mueller, Milton L (2004). *Ruling the Root: Internet Governance and the Taming of Cyberspace*. Cambridge MA: MIT Press; Mueller, and Froomkin, A Michael (2003). "Habermas@ Discourse.net: Toward a Critical Theory of Cyberspace". *Harvard Law Review*, 116, January: 751–873.
5. See in this context Flusser's account of photographers as functionaries of the industrial-scale photographic apparatus in Flusser, Vilém (2000). *Towards a Philosophy of Photography*, trans Anthony Matthews, intro Hubertus Von Amelunxen. London: Reaktion Books.
6. Fortune's listing includes only U.S. corporations. The Financial Times' global FT500 has three oil companies, three technology companies, one food, one finance, and General Electric in its top ten.

References

Auty, Richard M. 1993. *Sustaining Development in Mineral Economies: The Resource Curse Thesis*. London: Routledge.

Berardi, Franco "Bifo". 2009. *Precarious Rhapsody: Semiocapitalism and the Pathologies of the Post-Alpha Generation*, trans Arianna Bove, Erik Empson, Michael Goddard, Giuseppina Mecchia, Antonella Schintu, and Steve Wright. London: Minor Compositions.

Burawoy, Michael. 2009. *Redefining the Public University: Developing an Analytical Framework*. New York: Social Science Research Council. http://publicsphere.ssrc.org/burawoy-redefining-the-public-university/

Crary, Jonathan. 1999. *Suspensions of Perception: Attention, Spectacle and Modern Culture*. Cambridge, MA: MIT Press.

Creed, Barbara. 1993. *The Monstrous-Feminine: Film, Feminism, Psychoanalysis*. London: Routledge.

Cubitt, Sean. 2014. *The Practice of Light: A Genealogy of Visual Technologies from Prints to Pixels*. Cambridge, MA: The MIT Press.

Davis, Angela Y. 2003. *Are Prisons Obsolete?* New York: Open Media/Seven Stories Press.

deNardis, Laura. 2009. *Protocol Politics: The Globalization of Internet Governance*. Cambrdige MA: MIT Press.

Derrida, Jacques. 1994. *Specters of Marx: The State of the Debt, the Work of Mourning and the New International*, trans Peggy Kamuf. New York: Routledge.

Douglas, Susan J. 1987. *Inventing American Broadcasting 1899–1922*. Baltimore, MD: Johns Hopkins University Press.

Flusser, Vilém. 2000. *Towards a Philosophy of Photography*. trans Anthony Matthews, intro Hubertus Von Amelunxen. London: Reaktion Books.

Foucault, Michel, Mauro Bertani, Alessandro Fontana, François Ewald, and David Macey. 2003. *"Society Must Be Defended:" Lectures at the Collège de France, 1975-1976*. Vol. 1. Macmillan: 244–245.

Foucault, Michel. 2004. *The Birth of Biopolitics: Lectures at Collège de France, 1978-1979*. St Martin's Press.

Fuchs, Christian. 2008. *Internet and Society: Social Theory and the Information Age*. London: Routledge: 157–189.

Fuller, Matt. 2001. "It Looks Like You're Writing a Letter: Microsoft Word." *Telepolis*. March 7, http://heise.de/tp/r4/artikel/7/7073/1.html

Guattari, Félix. 2000. *The Three Ecologies*, trans Ian Pindar and Paul Sutton. London: Athlone.

Haraway, Donna. 1985. "A Manifesto for Cyborgs: Science, Technology and Socialist Feminism in the 1980s." *Socialist Review* 80 (15:2): 65–107.

Hunt, Lynn. 2008. *Inventing Human Rights: A History*. New York: Norton.

Kahn, Douglas. 2013. *Earth Sound Earth Signal: Energies and Earth Magnitudes in the Arts*. Berkeley, CA: University of California Press.

Kember, Sarah. 2013. "Gender Estimation in Face Recognition Technology: How Smart Algorithms Learn to Discriminate." *Media Fields Journal: Critical Explorations in Media and Space* 7.

King, Michael. 2004. *The Penguin History of New Zealand*. Wellington, NZ: Penguin.

Lazzarato, Maurizio. 2012. *The Making of the Indebted Man: An Essay on the Neo-Liberal Condition*, trans Joshua David Jordan. New York: Semiotext(e).

MacLean, Don. 2003. "The Quest for Inclusive Governance of Global ICTs: Lessons from the ITU in the Limits of National Sovereignty." *Information Technologies and International Development* 1 (1): 1–18.

Marx, Karl. 1984. *Capital: A Critique of Political Economy*. London: Lawrence & Wishart.

Milun, Kathryn. 2011. *The Political Uncommons: The Cross-cultural Logic of the Global Commons*. London: Ashgate Publishing.

Mosco, Vincent. 2009. *The Political Economy of Communication: Rethinking and Renewal*, 2nd ed. London: Sage.

Mouffe, Chantal. 2005. *On the Political*. London: Routledge.

Mueller, Milton L. 2004. *Ruling the Root: Internet Governance and the Taming of Cyberspace*. Cambridge, MA: MIT Press. Mueller, Milton L. 2010. *Networks and States: The Global Politics of Internet Governance*. Cambridge, MA: MIT Press.

Nelson, Theodore H. 1974. *Computer Lib/Dream Machines*. Self-published.

Rabinbach, Anson. 1990. *The Human Motor: Energy, Fatigue and the Origins of Modernity*. New York and Berkeley, CA: Basic Books and University of California Press.

Rancière, Jacques. 1999. *Disagreement: Politics and Philosophy*, trans Julie Rose. Minneapolis, MN: University of Minnesota Press.

Smith, Linda Tuhiwai. 2012. *Decolonizing Methodologies: Research and Indigenous Peoples*, 2nd ed. London: Zed Books.

Smith, Terry. 1993. *Making the Modern: Industry, Art and Design in America*. Chicago, IL: University of Chicago Press.

Solnit, Rebecca. 2000. *Savage Dreams. A Journey into the Landscape Wars of the American West*. Berkeley, CA: University of California Press.

Thirsk, Joan. 1958. *Tudor Enclosures*. London: The Historical Association.

Verzola, Roberto. 2010. "Abundance and the Generative Logic of the Commons." Keynote speech for Stream III: The Generative Logic of the Commons, International Conference on the Commons, Berlin, Oct. 31—Nov. 2. P2P Foundation. http://p2pfoundation.net/Abundance_and_the_Generative_Logic_of_the_Commons

Waitangi Tribunal. 1999. *The Radio Spectrum Management and Development Final Report*. Wellington. NZ: Waitangi Tribunal.

Wegenstein, Bernadette. 2011. *The Cosmetic Gaze: Body Modification and the Construction of Beauty*. Cambridge MA: MIT Press.

Wu, Tim. 2003. "Network Neutrality, Broadband Discrimination." *Journal of Telecommunications and High Technology Law* 2: 141–178.

Zizek, Slavoj. 2009. *Violence: Six Sideways Reflections*. London: Profile Books.

MEDIA ALWAYS AND EVERYWHERE

A Cosmic Approach

Sarah Kember and Joanna Zylinska

From Ubiquitous Computing to Cosmic Media

Our piece starts from the key premise embraced by this book: namely, that the recently posited and widely proclaimed culture of ubiquitous computing needs to be subjected to an "unconditional critique." However, our aim here is to do more than that: rather than just mount a challenge to the notion of ubiquity with regard to computing and so-called ambient intelligence, we also want to raise questions for the promotion of the computational paradigm as supposedly the defining aspect of our lives in the early twenty-first century. Our reasons for this approach spring from the cognitive-affective doubt we share as to whether computation is truly the best framework for understanding the structuration of the global modern world and our wayfaring through it. Indeed, is computation the *most* ubiquitous thing there is? Isn't such a selection of an analytical pivot point just a retrograde reaction to the military-technocapitalist nexus, which has already decided the terms of the game and which then makes scholars and artists *respond* to it? Is such a choice of analytical optics not in danger of producing principally *paranoid scholarship* and *paranoid art* (even if we do know for sure now, courtesy of WikiLeaks and Edward Snowden, that they really *are* watching us)? If ubiquity is what is at stake here, why not focus on something truly pervasive and ubiquitous—such as, say, air? There are good reasons why we might want to shift from the metaphorical "atmosphere" or "ambience" of computational discourses to the messy complexity of actual air. To cite Polish philosopher, Monika Bakke, air is not only full of life but also,

> apart from being a means of transport and communication . . . is a habitat in its own right. The zoe of air comes in abundance and we—breathing organisms—are all in this together for better and for worse, dead or alive. We have finally come to realize that air is messy, being neither an empty space nor a void, but a space where species meet. And like any other life form, as Donna Haraway emphasizes, we find ourselves "in a knot of species coshaping one another in layers of reciprocating complexity all the way down."
>
> (2008, 42)

Such an attempt to expand or even "rebrand" ubiquity is more than an intellectual exercise. We see the notion of computational ubiquity (its uses and effects) as a conceptual and political challenge aimed at those of us who want to take techno-human relations and environments seriously, without just pandering to the financial and political interests of the techno-industry. Our proposition with this piece is therefore twofold: we want to take a careful look at ubiquity understood both as a discursive trope and a lived materiality while also extending the model of ubiquitous computing to what we are provisionally calling "cosmic media," with all the serious playfulness this latter concept involves. We could perhaps go so far as to say that *there is something in the air*—and this something is media . . . From this vantage point, ubiquitous computing becomes only a narrow spectrum of this mediating omnipresence, or should we rather say omni-becoming, of media.

"Cosmic media" is for us a figuration, one of the two we will use throughout this piece. Figurations are thought devices that play an important role in the work of Donna Haraway (1991) and Rosi Braidotti (1994) as a way of shaping a different political imaginary or performing an alternative image of the future. Well-known figurations proposed by those two feminist thinkers include "the cyborg," "nomadic subject," "modest witness," and "companion species." Such figurations "pose a radical challenge to the subject–object dualism that structures Western philosophy—which allows us to believe that humans and machines are separate entities that need to reintegrate and which centers on the sovereignty of the self versus the other" (Kember and Zylinska 2012, 125). What we are aiming to do with our "cosmic media" figuration is challenge the established industry definitions of computation (or, indeed, media) in order to look at the processes of communication across different scales, beyond the rubrics, measures, and (financial) values outlined by and for the human. This mode of thinking starts from the premise that it is not just us humans that communicate with one another and that all living systems—bacteria, plants, insects—exchange information. Air itself is a means of transport and communication. What we conventionally understand as media or computers are therefore just selected human-centric examples of communication and data swap. From this, rather expansive, vantage point, cosmic background radiation—which is a form of electromagnetic radiation in the universe supposedly left over from the Big Bang—can be seen as yet another medium, a form of communication that is literally larger than life. And if this is the case then we can perhaps say that the universe itself is a giant transmitter. Yet, just like with Haraway's cyborg, the conceptual expansion performed by "cosmic media" is devised as a critical intervention into various forms of Big Thinking, including Big History, Ubiquitous Computing, and Ambient Media—forms which, as we will demonstrate here, more often than not turn out to be just *not big enough* because they overlook too much in the process.

Arising out of our earlier experimental collaboration on *Life after New Media: Mediation as a Vital Process,* our intervention here thus proposes an alternative radical approach to the problems of complexity and ubiquity understood partly as problems of size. Challenging the instrumentalist logic of the all-encompassing "computational paradigm," it also suggests that seeing media first and foremost as ongoing and overlapping processes of mediation, rather than as a series of industry-produced objects, can help us open up the engineering mindset to some other forms of socio-political imagination. Mediation for us is "a key trope for understanding and articulating our being in, and becoming with, the technological world, our emergence and ways of intra-acting with it, as well as the acts and processes of temporarily stabilizing the world into media, agents, relations, and networks" (Kember and Zylinska 2012, xv). It literally points us "outside the box." We are partly inspired here by the North American communication theory (i.e., environmental theory of media, where media embrace both writing surfaces and travel networks) influenced by Harold Innis and Marshall McLuhan, as well as the European theory of "media ecologies," where media are understood in terms of complex dynamic systems.

Working with and across this eco-eco mix, we want to offer a feminist rejoinder to theories of ubiquity with an ironic yet nonetheless serious attempt to Think Really Big. The McLuhanian "all-at-onceness" perspective will allow us to see seemingly disconnected objects and events as related or even co-evolving, but also to raise critical questions for many upscaling and downscaling efforts performed by their "seers."

Ubiquity Effects and the Goldilocks Principle

The notion of mediation we proposed in *Life After New Media* aimed to challenge the claims and classifications of new, social, and now smart media; the false divisions between new and old that are increasingly expedient; and the limited and limiting preoccupations with technological, cultural, or economic convergence. Mediated existence is not reducible to the study of either technology or its use—to what Heidegger in his famous essay "The Question Concerning Technology" described as the instrumental and anthropological conceptualizations of technology (1977). Instead, life after new media is a facet of co-constitution and co-evolution. We humans as temporary stabilizations of mediations which always incur change are part of this ongoing living process (Kember and Zylinska 2012). We are also participants in what Mark Hansen, in this volume, terms "human technogenesis," that is, humans' emergence as technological beings, always already mediated. In this view of ubiquitous media—which we adopt here as a thought device, rather than an article of faith—concepts of space and time are extended, perhaps to infinity, with media history now reaching back all the way to geological "deep time." Media objects and histories as well as processes of technological mediation are increasingly regarded as ecological, biological, geological, and, ultimately, cosmological.

The distinction between media objects and processes of mediation, while by no means absolute, is useful heuristically (Kember and Zylinska 2012). It enables us to speak about the flows of mediation that encompass but exceed *things*. Mediation reconnects us to the McLuhanian "all-at-onceness" of the "world of electric information" (McLuhan 1964, 40), a mode of thinking that poses a challenge to many forms of conventional media analysis by presenting problems such as technology, use, organization, and production as mutually co-constitutive and co-dependent. Interstitial and infrastructural objects, the "gray media" of protocols, algorithms, and accounts, are arguably still *things* (Fuller and Goffey 2012). Mediation allows us to grasp how they relate to each other and to wider social and economic forces not *in time* but *as time*; how media objects are part of movement and hence, after Bergson, of life itself. Life here "is the double articulation of *bios* (politics and discourse) and *zoe* (nonhuman intensity), a continuous intensive creation that is also continuously articulated on a social level of power and knowledge that, increasingly during modernity, has been a level of technical media" (Parikka 2010, xxiv). As this statement suggests, there are two kinds of ubiquity effects, one pertaining to creative processes, the other to invented and marketized things. We are never fully relieved of our fetishization of media objects, be they shiny and new or obsolete and discarded, it seems. There is no refuge from instrumentalization, consumerism, and the operation of power as (new and old) media—black, white, or gray—stabilize, while environments of infomatter are turned into materials, such as glass, that are said to be smart.

Nevertheless, by attending to the multiple yet often invisible processes of mediation and taking time (and hence life and movement) seriously, we inevitably challenge our cherished mechanistic assumptions about cause-and-effect and about the representability of the media and technological world we have never merely inhabited. If it no longer makes sense to speak of humans being superseded by intelligent machines, it makes little more sense to imagine, the way many of the current discourses around ubiquitous computing and ambient media do, that we are being served and comforted by them. Companionship is more messy than that—it is more like air than like a network. It therefore resists being tidied into the ongoing fantasy of the master-slave relationship. Significantly, for Bergson, companionship and relations were never without limits and borders, but they could not be described in themselves. Relating as it is related, just as living as it is lived, can only be *intuited*. We can never actually see mediation, but we can intuit its unfolding—and our unfolding with and as part of it. (Equally, we can ignore its unfolding or even remain oblivious of its "itness".) However, what is gained through insight must then be conveyed, cut into familiar shapes and concepts made less familiar by the combination of, say, images with ideas, metaphors with maths, fiction with science—especially once we engage in scholarly pursuits and other human pastimes such as writing, discoursing and making sense. Alternative modes of communication, Bergson is clear (1992), might be more right in the sense of reaching toward a realism without representation, but they will always remain alternative and easy to dismiss.

One useful tool in such an effort, our second figuration, is the Goldilocks principle: a principle applied across disciplines as diverse as computing, engineering, biology, economics, and psychology, which postulates that something must fall within certain margins and avoid reaching extremes. Derived from a children's story "Goldilocks and the Three Bears" in which an unruly little girl visits a house inhabited by bears and trials their furniture and food for size and comfort, it is colloquially known as a "just right" principle. Having found the "just right" porridge, chair, and bed, the girl is eventually chased away by the bears, learning a valuable lesson, the way all young girls should, about the danger of wandering off and exploring unknown territory that is not truly hers. Yet, *from the Goldilocks perspective*, the dismissal of alternative modes of communication is a gendered habit, signaling as it does an operation of masculine scientism that is hardening in the face of that which should unstiffen it. It is as if intuition must still be regarded as a feminine trait, along with the unstiffening of language and communication. Must Goldilocks return to the question-accusation of phallogocentrism? If so, then she should never have left it.

When confronted with figures of speech, the will to science is strong. This tendency is particularly evident once the question of mediation has been temporarily forgotten or elided. This is when one ubiquity effect, the effect of process and relationality, and its attendant challenge to traditional forms of knowledge and communication, gives rise to another, the production of ubiquity as a series of media objects. The innovation of media and technological forms thus capitalizes and instrumentalizes our sense of life after new media, attaching it back to what we already know. The relatively new field of Ambient Intelligence (AmI) is a case in point. AmI means smart environments populated by networked, distributed things with the capacity to learn, adapt, sense, and predict. AmI is the love child of AI and the ongoing project of ubiquitous computing. It is interesting in as far is it stakes a direct claim to agency, intimacy, and relationality, appealing to and reinforcing the sovereign subject even as it converts that subject into a data object, like fattening cattle for the market. AmI plans to invade the environments, domestic and urban, of ordinary everyday life. It aspires to what Ulrik Ekman terms a "universalizing totality" that borders on the absurd, especially given the technological limitations of AmI systems such as face recognition technology (Kember 2013), the absence of a coherent infrastructure (Greenfield 2006; Ekman 2011), and no real public awareness of, or demand for it. Among the critics of this nascent technology, many are aware of the combination of hubris and abject technological failure but fewer point to the co-constituting science-fictional dissentions that write AmI into and out of existence. Does anyone really want to live with

Marvin the depressed robot or the door that demands cash for opening and closing, or, worse still, the universe's most obsequious lift (Adams 1981; Dick 2004)? Even as we chuckle at the thought, it is important to recognize that, just like its ancestors, AmI is adaptive, aware of its own limitations, self-mocking at times, and already in the process of figuring out where, in the public realm, it might make itself useful.

The central figure in AmI has changed from the butler to the nurse. The change coincides with the development of an adjacent field of Ambient Media or rather, its transfer from the context of advertising to that of assisted living and health-monitoring. Ambient Media is "the name given to a new breed of out-of-home products and services" (Pogorelc et al. 2012, 340). Research funded by the European Union aims to "enhance the quality of life of the elderly, release the burden on the supporting population, and strengthen the industrial base in Europe" (Pogorelc et al. 2012, 340). Funding is motivated and justified by "demographic changes, in particular the ageing of the European population, which implies not only challenges, but also opportunities for the citizens, the social and healthcare systems as well as industry and the European market" (Pogorelc et al. 2012, 340). Alongside social media and the wider field of Ambient Intelligence, Ambient Media articulate and disarticulate, avow and disavow the entanglement of life and capital. As new forms of profit accrue from our being, becoming, and behavior online and at home, our environments are increasingly naturalized by means of invisible, embedded computing and intimate, agential, emotional technologies personified once as butlers and now as nurses. The field of Ambient Media strives to define the media environment and determine the relations within it, moving from the promise of service to that of care in order to exploit a political opportunity and take itself seriously.

AmI and its offshoots remind us of the incommensurability as well as inseparability of ubiquity effects. The object of its focus is the techno-human that it services, cares for, and hands back to itself, courtesy of another, older era and an apparently cleaner, sterilized environment policed by domesticated matrons. Here, at home, in our homeland security, we are cleaned up, made human again, and put back to work, the elderly a synecdoche for the diseased, contaminated body made productive and subject to disciplinary reform—or converted to data and diffused within systems of control. If both ubiquity effects, that is, relationality and object-production, can be harnessed through ready frameworks of analysis such as process philosophy and bio-politics respectively, then what of the two combined? In as far as contemporary theories of mediation, media ecology, and media archaeology (which digs deeper, not to unearth lost histories but to look for new "conceptual cuts") all circle around a concept of ubiquity that is not only complimentary–contradictory, as indicated here, but also *complex*, then the new big–small history of media has, in a sense, already been told as big (small) history itself. To rephrase this as a question, to what extent is current thinking about media and mediation across different scales already anticipated in the discourse of Big History?

Simplifying Complexity: The Big History Approach

How can we think of ubiquity otherwise? How do we account for true media intensity and extensity, for media dispersal and diffusion across boundaries and scales? As mentioned earlier, media objects and histories as well as processes of technological mediation are increasingly regarded as ecological, biological, geological, and, ultimately, cosmological. The Big History model, a model that studies both human and nonhuman history, going back to the early days of the Earth and the universe, is one recent attempt to frame ubiquity and complexity. Our goal is to ask what is at stake in telling such stories of large historical cross-temporality and what their appearance at the current moment tells us about this very moment, both on an intellectual and political level. In other words, we want to examine "the potential complexity of ubiquity-effects" in our modes of understanding not just technologies and media but the universe as such.

As if it was responding to Carl Sagan's intimation that "We have grown distant from the Cosmos," Big History aims to be the discipline of all disciplines, a unified theory of human and natural history from the Big Bang to the Big Crunch (Sagan 2012, 12). Its principal unifying idea is complexity. It seeks to map the rise and fall of complexity as an emergent phenomenon (which, in a truly circular sense, gives rise to emergence) that centers on life—and on human life in particular. Humans, in Big History, are cosmically complex: "After almost 14 billion years of cosmic existence, the human species is arguably the most complex biological organism in the known universe" (Spier 2011, 24). The standpoint of Big History is the modern human in his technological milieu. It is from here that a truth is declared, namely that "there are phenomena that cross all scales" (Christian 2011, 7). Adopting the biological and ecological foundations of systems theory as a given, Big Historians naturalize the concept of complexity across scales of nature, life, and culture. Aside from a deference to physics (and the proposition that cities are the result of gravitational forces) and short of an agreed definition, what is on offer here is a familiar story of wholes exceeding the sum of their parts. The building blocks of nature, life, and culture (all the way from particles to planets, from cells to cities) matter less than their interactions, as if they were neurons in a cosmic brain. Complexity is what emerges from these interactions and interactions are what emerge from this complexity. Such circular (il)logic is an effect of the derangement of scale and the incredible, unabashed bigness of Big History that suddenly shrivels to a tight, defensive knot of self-interest. If humans are the heart and brain of complexity then, and here is the injunction, we must ensure, or retroactively shore up the conditions for its and our survival. There is a problem here, and it pertains to the endgame that is afoot. Big History defers to thermodynamics and hitches complexity to energy conservation, equilibrium, and entropy (or disorder) in a system. The universe, we are told, is at equilibrium and faces the inevitability of entropy as first our sun and then all others cool, implode, and die. Within the cosmic endgame we humans face another and that is literally the burning away of the available energy in our own ecosystem. If Big Historians have a philosophy of media and technology, it is an entropic one. They share with politicians and industrialists the belief that what damns us may also save us and so negentropy comes to be figured as sustainability. In the wake of thermodynamics, sustainability has its own three laws: population control, climate change control, and environmental equilibrium. This last law is what reconnects us to the cosmos and to Carl Sagan's promise that science (not just technology) is our salvation.

The scientism of Big History lies in its quest for an "underlying unity" (Christian 2011, xxiv) that may then become the answer to the question, the solution to the problem of life, the universe, and everything. Big History claims to cover all disciplines and offers what is, in fact, a whistle-stop tour of physics, astronomy, geology, and biology. Human history is cleansed of arts, humanities, social sciences, politics, philosophy, and economics (it's the ecology, stupid!). Interdisciplinarity as the heuristic model of complexity suffers from the same derangement of scale. What is at first expansive, collapses and contracts. The timelines do not add up to a theory of evolution and the tables of social organization made to look like star clusters never reveal the extent to which gravity, among cities and states, is material or metaphorical. As the timeline shrinks to the last 300 years, the social transformations described by sociologists are reduced to being events of planetary but not political significance (Christian 2011, 375). Power is elided by natural forces and enacted in their evocation by the Big Historians themselves. Their panoramic view from nowhere is only lightly masked by reference to Donna Haraway, who would not recognize, as a standpoint, the modern human. Or rather, she would recognize it as the normalized, masculine standpoint that remains allied, the way it always has, to science as the virile domination of the female body of nature (Jacobus et al. 1990). Complex systems are chaotic, that is, unpredictable, but out of chaos come order and predictability. The switch from thermodynamics to chaos theory is expedient. The injunction to control and conserve is tied to forecasting the next 100 years. This "is the scale we must consider if we want to pass the world on in good shape to our heirs" (Christian 2011, 471). Inheritance is not merely a vehicle for anthropocentrism here but also for paternalism. At the end of his TED talk, David Christian, author of the epic *Maps of Time*, brings his grandson onto the stage in order to underline his argument and indicate what Big History might really be about: Son, one day all this could still be yours.

Life after the Anthropocene, or the Derangements of Scale

What if we adopt the Goldilocks principle to think Big History—and an Ever Bigger Future? Would this ensure we do not expand—or contract—too much, and that whatever perspective we adopt still leaves us with the possibility of saying something meaningful and productive about processes and forces that far exceed our comprehension? Can there be "just enough" ubiquity? Is there a "beyond" to it? These questions are productively unanswerable, giving rise as they do to large-scale speculation about the fate of us humans as a species, the prospects for our planet and the future of the universe as a whole—the latter usually presented as a process of an ongoing expansion or catastrophic contraction. The Anthropocene is one rhetorical outcome of such speculation. Proposed by the Dutch chemist Paul Crutzen in 2000, the term Anthropocene describes a new geological epoch that is said to follow the Holocene. The need for recognizing this new epoch is justified by the level and degree of human influence upon the geo- and biosphere via processes such as farming, deforestation, and urbanization, urging us to respond to the challenges posed by that influence. The term has not been adopted by all geologists, but its use has significantly increased over the last decade. Yet even among its proponents there is disagreement at to when this epoch supposedly started: in the early days of agriculture some 8,000 years ago, with the Industrial Revolution, or during the last fifty years of excessive consumption. We could thus see the Anthropocene as a contested story of human–technological origins and evolution, a cut in the flow of space-time from the Big Bang to the Big Crunch. While it is inherently teleological and at least implicitly finalistic (there is an endgame afoot), the concept of the Anthropocene complicates mechanistic thoughts of causes and effects since it involves wholes as well as parts, and since we do not actually know what the endgame will be. Through this, it poses us humans (even those of a post-anthropocentric ilk) with the following question: How to think, describe, and represent an evolutionary–cosmological phenomenon of which "we" are but a constitutive part? Representations, as Karen Barad reminds us, rely on ontological gaps between themselves and that which they represent (Barad 2007). For Henri Bergson, representations as both images and forms of knowledge are necessary fictions, they are props to support the human. Yet, despite his investment in relational ontologies, Bergson himself had little difficulty cutting through such fictions (Bergson 1944).

The possibility of thinking and working through or perhaps across the boundary between the human and its constitutive other (machine, medium, animal, insect, particle, planet) is one difficulty that surfaces in the Anthropocene. The (often implicit) decision as to whether that boundary [and indeed *boundaryness itself*] is denied and dissolved, or affirmed and reinforced, has cosmic consequences, while also opening us up to the problem of scale.

Taking scale seriously involves following up on the etymology of the Latin word *scala*, which means "ladder," and thus climbing up and down various spatiotemporal dimensions in order to see things from different viewpoints. Scalar thinking is an inherently dynamic process. It requires us to become fully cognizant of time understood, after Bergson, as "duration," a continuous flow into which we as observers make insertions in order to carve out some "solids" from it, to temporarily stabilize matter into entities. In an attempt to grasp the passage of time, we make incisions in it with our proprioceptive and cognitive apparatuses, and then pass off the products of these incisions as images and representations of the world. This multi-scale mode of thinking may serve as a reminder for us that there is an excess to our acts of world-making and that it is perhaps imprudent or even irresponsible to forget about it in all kinds of discussions—those concerning politics, ethics, or even our everyday existence. Timothy Clark argues that considerations of scale end up challenging many ideas and common-sense beliefs about what we refer to as "our world," since any efforts to conduct environmental reform in one country, say, may be effectively negated by the lack of any such efforts in many other (frequently more powerful, wealthier, and more environmentally damaging) locations of the globe. This forgetting of scale results in what Clark calls "a derangement of linguistic and intellectual proportion," whereby filling the kettle with just enough water to make tea or buying a slightly less petrol-guzzling make of car are seen as ways of "saving the planet" (Clark 2012, 150). Yet it is not only many eco-activists and, more broadly, those who care about the environment and climate change that suffer from this kind of scalar derangement. The latter malady also affects many scholars in various disciplines, but perhaps first of all in the humanities, who simply *fail to think big enough*. Adopting a mechanistic approach to this presumed entity called "the world," they position this entity at a distance, and then try to *act on* it. This leads Clark to conclude that "dominant modes of literary and cultural criticism are blind to scale effects in ways that now need to be addressed" (Clark 2012, 150). The problem with this localized mode of thinking lies in the *apparent* grasping of complexity, which is nothing more than a form of reductionism, whereby "[r]eceived concepts of agency, rationality, and responsibility are being strained or even begin to fall apart into a bewildering generalizing of the political that can make even filling a kettle as public an act as voting" (Clark 2012, 151).

Yet such derangements of scale do not apply only to those unfortunate if well-meaning humanities scholars who seemingly cannot wrap their heads round the fact that agency and causality are more complex than their own human*ist* intimations might suggest. They apply in equal measure to those proponents of complexity who seem to forget that different stopping points on different scales have different affordances and effectivities. Indeed, the assumed shared materiality of the universe, or the fact that everything is made of the same stuff, frequently lacks an accompanying reflection that *not everything is made in the same way*. Stephen W. Hawking explains that "Despite the fact that the universe is so uniform and homogeneous on a large scale, it contains local irregularities, such as star and galaxies. These are thought to have developed from small differences in the density of the early universe from one region to another" (Hawking 1988, 122). A responsible, Goldilocks-driven thinking of complexity therefore requires the ability to theorize the significance of such local irregularities and—or, in other words, to reflect *on the difference of difference* across various scales.

A commendable attempt to think complexity and ubiquity across such various scales while simultaneously not losing sight of the singular differences that emerge has been proposed by Tom Cohen, editor of the groundbreaking book *Telemorphosis: Theory in the Era of Climate Change* and coeditor of the open access book series Critical Climate Change. Postulating a move beyond a self-defeating obsession with homeland security, in all its senses—political, environmental, epistemological, and ontological—Cohen counters Big History in its non-anthropocentric approach to the Anthropocene. It embraces extinction as an opportunity to condemn parochialism, paternalism, self-interest, and all forms of homeland security, not least the security of concepts, disciplines, and familial forms of knowledge and communication. The proposition is more than just a critique of what Bergson would call scientific and ordinary knowledge—it is a critique of philosophy as such, and of theory *as* the critique of scientific and ordinary knowledge. His Critical Climate Change proposes instead to rub everything out so that it (not "we" any more) has to start again. It remains invested in the entropy that Big Historians would save us from and damn narratives of salvation that prevent us from confronting our own ends. Theory is regarded as being complicit with such self-delusion, the humanities a protection racket for humans in its defense of "cultures, affects, bodies, and others" (Cohen 2012, 15). Preferring crisis to resolution, Critical Climate Change strives to open out the closed loops and reinforcing logics of the techno-*human* and to denaturalize it once and for all. In refusing the ontological, ethical, and epistemological *boundedness* of the human-machine-animal-other, Cohen also, perhaps inadvertently, spatializes "it" and in doing so, he himself perhaps forecloses on the political potential of *boundary-work* of the sort that is never done and never secure. The spatial register of Critical Climate Change makes it vulnerable to the scale effects of which it speaks, the big extinction and end-of-theory scenarios that collapse and make way for a new "domain of very small things" (Cohen 2012, 25).

Commendable in its attempt to move beyond our human narcissism in thinking about the world, Cohen's project risks a perspective that is *at once too big and too small*. Indeed, current thinking about the Anthropocene is oriented either towards the holy grail of science, the grand unified theory or theory of everything (as is the case with Big History), or towards an attempt to implode such a theory and reduce it to very small parts (as we see in the context of recent theories of human extinction). Between the master narrative and the partial, plural, incommensurate stories of human-technological relations there surely lies a "Goldilocks" approach that is not just right, but "just right," in the sense of being neither too big nor too small. From this perspective, the case for and against a theory of life (after new media), the universe and everything is seriously askew: it grows and/or shrinks out of all proportion on account of an all too familiar scientism allied to an all too familiar masculinism. *Who is telling us this story of human-technological evolution and from where?* From nowhere, it would seem. Both the big and small histories of the Anthropocene turn out to be his-stories that, from a Goldilocks perspective, could do with being retold.

This Is a Man's Universe: Re-telling the Story of Cosmic Media

It is worth critically reflecting on this return to scientism in contemporary critical discourses about media, technology, and computation. Why are we speaking of complexity and emergence, chaos and order—or rather, why are we speaking of them again? Twenty years ago, Katherine Hayles (1991), Vivian Sobchack (1990), and Isabelle Stengers (Prigogine and Stengers 1989) examined such phenomena within, and tied them to the culture and politics of postmodernism. Specifically, they marked a roundabout return to grand narratives and unified theories from within their own dissolution. Science, religion, and politics were dead, but not gone. For Sobchack, chaos as a route to order and control manifest not least through fractal geometry and self-similarity across scales could be regarded as being totalizing, even fascistic. At the same time, chaos theory romanticizes itself as the emergence of a new science (or the re-emergence of science). Chaos and complexity were always allied in their evocation of systems with magical, super-natural properties such as spontaneous self-organization. They pulled rabbits out of entropic hats and, through simple analogy, returned technological systems to their origins in nature. Every complex system, not just the weather, was subject to the butterfly effect of sensitive dependence on initial conditions. If these could not be predicted, quantified, and measured then what could be was the patterns they eventually gave rise to. It is interesting that what is not being evoked again is the strange attractor (Plate 30), the infinite, always drawn and never static figure of eight that depicted, rather than described, the boundary between objects in chaotic, complex systems.

From a Goldilocks perspective, the strange attractor is an icon of boundary work. A concept of boundary work as agential cutting is crucial to a retold her-story of life (after new media), the universe and everything—one that reverses and displaces the hierarchical dualisms of naturalized entities (Haraway 1991). The his-story version of history, on the other hand, some-times eschews this work in favor of an ontology of objects that might somehow spontaneously self-organize and effect change just by themselves. Inspired by Schopenhauer's treatise on sophistry in *The Art of Always Being Right*, Matthew Fuller and Andy Goffey argue that:

> Being sophisticated today is about operating with media forms, techniques, and technologies that are excessively, absurdly, finalized as to purpose and utility, but whose seductive faces of apparent, personalized seamlessness, whose coded and codified bureaucratic allure, when regarded from the right angle, present multiple occasions (kairos) for crafty—and well-crafted—exploitation.
>
> (Fuller and Goffey 2012, 18)

Such exploitation, it transpires, is founded on "strategematic" modes of writing that inhere within and emerge from the affordances of media and mediation themselves, from the "machinery" of things (feed receipt ticket book 16) that catch the correctly angled eye without being regarded as an artifact of it. Their "ethico-aesthetic" approach, oriented toward gray immanence for gray media (feed receipt ticket book 13), leaves no mark and takes no responsibility for it. The black and white divisions of Cartesian epistemology are set aside in favor of a "gray ontology" capable of declaring itself, but the question of "to whom" is never adjoined to that of purpose or ends. In as far as the desired endpoints include a repurposing or "reverse engineering" (feed receipt ticket book 9) of media and technology while the methods include an emphasis on writing and even writerliness, the potential for an alliance with feminist strategies of retelling stories about media big and small exists in that project. Yet it is arguably (self)hijacked by the significant elision of interventionism, propped by a sense that the systems, not the sisters, are doing it for themselves. Where Fuller and Goffey institute their own bifurcation of epistemology and ontology, the options, from a Goldilocks perspective, do not resolve themselves so simply. Goldilocks cannot choose between vitalism and instrumentalism as the ubiquity effects that affect her simultaneously in the co-constitutive unfolding in the technological world. Her judgment of what is too big and too small is predicated on her own discomfort and lack of entitlement within the homeland of the bear. If the just right bed exists, it is always, necessarily, in the eye of the beholder.

A retold story of cosmic media takes seriously, and responds to, the derangements of scale resulting from intensity and extensity. It might do so, however, by playing with them rather than falling prey to them. Irony and parody are the serious forms of play that help to make feminist, post-cyborgian boundary work work. They are the cornerstones of what is effective and attractive about the strange attractors termed figurations, to which we add our own: cosmic media and the Goldilocks principle. Like all figurations, Goldilocks is a myth turned inside out (Braidotti 1994). From the fairytale to the quest for inhabitable planets, Goldilocks offers to resolve the dialectic of hard and soft, hot and cold, big and small. We have put her to work within and against that dialectic which for us remains unresolved. "Just rightness" is a work in progress, a laboring on the boundary between, for example, two complimentary–contradictory ubiquity effects, or between eco-eco visions of life after new media that do not collapse, substitute, or resolve into each other. The strange attractor is not about harmony but tension. Goldilocks' quest is ongoing. What matters is her (sense of) perspective, her view from somewhere of a universe of cosmic media that exceeds and incorporates her—and within which she is only temporally at home.

References

Adams, Douglas. 1981. *The Hitch-Hiker's Guide to the Galaxy.* London: Pan Books Ltd.

Bakke, Monika. 2008. "Introduction." In *The Life of Air: Dwelling, Communicating, Manipulating,* edited by Monika Bakke. London: Open Humanities Press.

Barad, Karen. 2007. *Meeting the Universe Halfway.* Durham, NC: Duke University Press.

Bergson, Henri. (1911) 1944. *Creative Evolution,* trans. Arthur Mitchell. New York: Random House.

Bergson, Henri. 1992. *The Creative Mind: An Introduction to Metaphysics.* New York: Kensington Publishing.

Braidotti, Rosi. 1994. *Nomadic Subjects. Embodiment and Sexual Difference in Contemporary Feminist Theory.* New York: Columbia University Press.

Christian, David. 2011. *Maps of Time: An Introduction to Big History.* Berkeley, CA: University of California Press.

Clark, Timothy. 2012. "Derangements of Scale." In *Telemorphosis: Theory in the Era of Climate Change,* Vol. 1, edited by Tom Cohen, 148–166. Ann Arbor, MI: Open Humanities Press.

Cohen, Tom. 2012. "Introduction: Murmurations—'Climate Change' and the Defacement of Theory." In *Telemorphosis: Theory in the Era of Climate Change,* Vol. 1, edited by Tom Cohen. Ann Arbor, MI: Open Humanities Press.

Dick, Philip K. 2004. *UBIK.* London: Orion.

Ekman, Ulrik. 2011. "Ubicomp Cultures: Hyperbolic Vision, Factual Developments." *Fibreculture Journal* 19, http://nineteen.fibreculturejournal.org

Fuller, Matthew, and Andrew Goffey. 2012. *Evil Media.* Cambridge, MA: MIT Press.

Greenfield, Adam. 2006. *Everyware. The Dawning Age of Ubiquitous Computing.* Berkeley, CA: New Riders.

Haraway, Donna J. 1991. *Simians, Cyborgs and Women: The Reinvention of Nature.* London: Free Association Books.

Hayles, N. Katherine. 1991. *Chaos and Order. Complex Dynamics in Literature and Science.* Chicago, IL and London: University of Chicago Press.

Hawking, Steven. 1988. *A Brief History of Time.* New York: Bantam Dell.

Heidegger, Martin. 1977. "The Question Concerning Technology." In *Martin Heidegger, Basic Writings,* edited by David Farrell Krell, 287–317. New York: Harper & Row.

Jacobus, Mary, Evelyn Fox Keller, and Sally Suttleworth (Eds.). 1990. *Body/Politics. Women and the Discourses of Science.* New York and London: Routledge.

Kember, Sarah. 2013. "Ambient Intelligent Photography." In *The Photographic Image in Digital Culture,* edited by Martin Lister. Second edition. London and New York: Routledge.

Kember, Sarah, and Joanna Zylinska. 2012. *Life After New Media: Mediation as a Vital Process.* Cambridge, MA: MIT Press.

Parikka, Jussi. 2010. *Insect Media: An Archaeology of Animals and Technology.* Minneapolis, MN: University of Minnesota Press.

Pogorelc, Bogdan, Vatavu, Radu-Daniel, Lugmayr, Artur, Stockleben, Björn, Risse, Thomas, Kaario, Juha, Constanza, Estefania, Matjaž Gams, Lomonaco. 2012. "Semantic Ambient Media: From Ambient Advertising to Ambient-assisted Living". *Multimedia Tools and Applications* 58 (2): 399–425.

Prigogine, Ilya, and Isabelle Stengers. 1989. *Order Out of Chaos.* New York: Dell Publishing Group: Bantam Doubleday.

Sagan, Carl. 2012. *Cosmos.* London: Abacus.

Sobchack, Vivian. 1990. "A Theory of Everything: Meditations on Total Chaos." *Artforum* 29 (2): 148–155.

Spier, Fred. 2011. *Big History and the Future of Humanity.* West Sussex: Wiley-Blackwell.

MEDIA ART

Lily Díaz

Where is media art situated in the virtual and physical worlds? In the *Ars Electronica* (AE) 2015 online catalog, which should be one of its top exhibition venues, one needs to dig deeper to find that media art has not only been subsumed under the label of hybrid art but also that it exists in relation to other so-called "trans-disciplinary projects." Alongside "computer animation/film," "digital music and sound art," and "create your own world," this so-called hybrid art entry, which purports to transcend "boundaries between art and research, art and social/political activism, and pop culture," further includes so-called "autonomous sculptures," "media architectures," and "media-based interventions" in public spaces.

Media art is also conspicuously missing from the "art genres" place-holders in the Getty's Art and Architecture Thesaurus (AAT),[1] though the sample includes apocalyptic art, children's art, community art, court art, and dissident art. An initial search on "media arts" returns the following terms: "electronic art," "inter-media art concept," "multi-media art works," and finally "art, new media." In the AAT, the term "electronic art" is defined as a "collective term used to refer to all art works which employ electronic media or technology." The next term of "inter-media art" is described in AAT as a concept merging already known art forms that inaugurate a new type so that ". . . if the resulting art form gains currency and acquires a name, it becomes a new medium and is no longer intermedia." In turn, "multi-media art works" are defined as "contemporary works of art that employ several distinct art forms, such as sculpture and music or painting and light art." Finally, "art, new media" is described as "art that uses new means of mass communication, specifically electronic and digital technology, including video and other forms of motion and sound media." It could be argued that what all these labels share, apart from the lack of any obvious consensus, is a sense of hybridity, indeterminacy, and serendipity that also characterizes contemporary media art.

However, you might ask why, in a context of complexity, culture, and information technology, is this "situating" of importance to current discussions of media art? Earlier, the debate focused on "ways to build tribal allegiances" among nomadic media arts communities (ISEA 2004).[2] Thinking about today's situation can perhaps allow us to see how (and if) the different tribes have been codified. The names themselves might offer interesting hints clarifying the different currents and influential tendencies in contemporary art. Whether a label such as media art is used (or not) affords an opportunity to reflect on the existing coalitions of meaning-making that exert pressure regarding what the de facto media art projects constitute, how they are to be deciphered, and where they are to be situated. These coalitions include possible communities and groups as well as individuals who have a stake regarding the interpretation of facts, objects, or phenomena, and whose interests coalesce around the possible legitimization of an idea or concept. Names denote boundaries, what is included and what is to be left out. The names allow us to hypothesize and make historical comparisons about differences and similarities and moments in time when new ways doing and being in the world emerged and became situated as categories.

From an art historical perspective, there is the precedent of the so-called birth of the Art Object as a separate category with Marcel Duchamp's "readymades" at the beginning of the twentieth century. Donald Judd's "Specific Objects" in the 1960s also fits this trend that continued in the art world during the last two decades of the millennium with works such as Joseph Kosuth's ontological queries regarding the nature of art. This further solidified into conceptual interventions that now form a steady staple of works situated in high art fairs such as *Documenta*.[3]

During the first two decades of the twenty-first century, this tendency, whereby new art practices come to be, seems to be incrementing, mutating, and even abandoning the trappings of the art world. There are new genres and forms that use information communication technologies such as locative media art that employs mobile platforms to instantiate experiences situated in particular locations. In the contemporary art scene, terms such as these—that are not even yet listed in the AAT—refer to emerging practices that are event and process-oriented. By combining and blending multiple narratives and locations in time and space, as is the case with locative media art, they offer us less of an object and more of an experience. Furthermore, we find that these new ways of working are not strictly of art but many times refer to activities that are multidisciplinary, interdisciplinary, and even trans-disciplinary.

In the case of Blast Theory's *Ulrike and Eamon Compliant*, the work is based on events from recent European history and on the lives of two European political activists/terrorists. The script was created doing research and through interviews with people who knew the protagonists. The performance integrates and assimilates the landscape of each new location where it is staged "via the use of a mobile, location based platform that includes the communication devices themselves, as well as the space for interaction, defined through its multiple locations and routes" (Matt Adams in this volume). The audience who engages in the performance has the choice to assume one of these two roles. In this way, they play an active role in the "material realization and manifestation of spatiality" (Kwastec 2013, 104).

Terry Rueb's *Trace* and *Core Sample* installations are different because of the artist's emphasis on the landscape and the desire that the audience should experience the place where the artworks are situated in an embodied way. In *Core Sample*, layered sounds are used to evoke the material, geological, and cultural histories of the site as the audience explores the landscape (O' Rourke 2013, 151). As Rueb remarks in the interview in this volume, "I think that we are losing a certain kind of consciousness and connection to place. But then maybe more importantly, what does it mean to be lost in the digital age?"

In Chapter 27 in this book, Jane Prophet and Helen Pritchard present *TechnoSphere 2.0*, which makes use of mobile Android applications to enable people to create 3D creatures which they can take with them so as to explore both real world and virtual world locations. These beasties, made as part of the application, "individuate through entangled relations of GPS, hardware, software, the human, and the non-human in the city." In this manner, they anticipate and explore new relational couplings enabled by this type of locative media art.

Already in the 1990s, Debray emphasized how every art, regardless of genre or form, is related to a medium as a device or system of representation. Communications through media do not merely touch our eyeballs; rather, as Nathaniel Stern succinctly observed, they involve our entire body so that "[we] bring to vision all our present and past experiences of embodied sense-making to abstract and understand what we are looking at" (Stern 1996, 23). In media art as well as in situations more generally, information does not exist as an abstract entity but is something situated and situative in the system(s) or media that code, transmit, receive, and decode it.

Notes

1. AAT is a controlled vocabulary or "organized arrangement of words and phrases used to index content and/or to retrieve content through browsing or searching." Controlled vocabularies are important, since they can improve access to information.
2. ISEA 2004 conference cruise participants could "build tribal allegiances and reflect their own migration history."
3. *Documenta* is a yearly exhibition held in Kassel, Germany.

References

"Art and Architecture Thesaurus (AAT)." *The Getty Research Institute*. Accessed March 8, 2015. http://getty.edu/research/tools/vocabularies/aat/.

Debray, Régis. 1996. *Media Manifestos*. London: Verso.

"Inter-Society for Electronic Arts Newsletter # 97." *ISEA NEWS*. Published in May–July 2004, Accessed March 31, 2015. http://isea-web.org/_archives/newsletters/2004–2/097-may-july-2004/.

Kwastec, Katja. 2013. *Aesthetics of Interaction in Digital Art*. Cambridge, MA: MIT Press.

O'Rourke, Karen. 2013. *Walking and Mapping. Artists as Cartographers*. Cambridge, MA: MIT Press.

Stern, Nathaniel. 2013. *Interactive Art and Embodiment. The Implicit Body as Performance*. Canterbury, UK: Gylphi Books.

FROM SIMPLE RULES TO COMPLEX PERFORMANCES—INTERVIEW WITH BLAST THEORY'S MATT ADAMS

Lily Díaz

Introduction

Working together since 1991, Blast Theory is an internationally renowned artist group. Their work makes use of interactive media to create new, groundbreaking forms of performance and interactive art that mixes audiences and realities (virtual as well as augmented) across the Internet, with live performance, and digital broadcasting. The group, comprising artists Matt Adams, Ju Row Farr, and Nick Tandavanitj, has been honored with several prestigious awards including winning the Prix Ars Electronica for Interactive Art in 2003 and Winner in the Best Real World Game category at the International Mobile Gaming Awards in Barcelona (2010).

The present dialogue took place in the course of two interview(s) held with Matt Adams in the summer of 2014. During the interview(s), we discussed the theoretical and critical approaches used by Blast Theory in their work with interactive performance. Though the conversation focuses primarily on one specific artwork, namely *Ulrike and Eamon Compliant*, other works created by this well-known artist collective are also mentioned (Plates 31, 32, 33, and 34).

Ulrike and Eamon Compliant is a performance work developed for the 2009 Venice Biennale.[1] The work makes use of location-based technology and mobile devices to offer an array of hypothetical life experiences based on historical events. Visitors to the gallery who choose to participate are given the opportunity to choose between the roles of two renowned extremists and literally step into the shoes of West German left-wing militant Ulrike Meinhof, and co-founder of the Red Army Faction Eamon Collins, former Irish Republican Army (IRA) paramilitary and writer.

The choice made takes you in a journey where you are surreptitiously followed, through the use of a mobile device. At selected points, you are contacted via telephone calls and asked to follow instructions by an invisible observer who will also insert into the performance narratives and questions from events in Ulrike's and Eamon's lives. As you approach the end of the route, you will have an opportunity to express yourself as well as confront your own ideas and morals regarding political violence.

The discussion of *Ulrike and Eamon Compliant* in an interview for the present anthology about complexity is because of its structuralist approach to narrative development and because of its ability to expose the multiple contradictions and double binds present in issues related to the use of surveillance as a means of political control.

About Systems Thinking

Systems theory, which emerged during the twentieth century, has influenced every field of human activity, including art. Systems thinking points to a reorientation in the scientific way of thinking away from one-way causal paradigms and towards a perspective or approach that considers the interrelatedness of things. Bertalanffy described how, through the act of observation, we come to apprehend real as well as conceptual entities that are neither given data nor objects of direct perception. These latter conceptual systems are rather construed "by an enormity of 'mental' factors ranging from gestalt dynamics and learning processes to linguistic and cultural factors largely determining what we actually 'see' or perceive."[2] In systems thinking, the pursuit of knowledge is not seen as an approximation to reality or ultimate truth but rather as an understanding achieved from within a particular perspective. The emphasis is on holistic investigation with the objective of building bridges among the disciplines.

It is possible to conceive of art from a perspective of systems thinking. As Niklas Luhmann has stated: "Art is a kind of communication which in ways yet to be clarified makes use of perception,"[3] and "observing a work of art as art occurs when the beholder discerns from the work's structure the intentionality of the artist."[4] In the case of the current artwork discussed throughout this interview, the system components include the historical data about the lives of the characters represented, mixed with imaginative details created by the artists, and delivered to a distributed audience through an interactive performance.

One of the things that surveillance has in common with ubicomp is the decentralization of human agency (Bauman and Lyon 2013). This is also a key characteristic of *Ulrike and Eamon Compliant* and can be discerned precisely though this notion of distributed audience dispersed in the gallery, throughout the journey, or at the final destination point. The performance that features participation by the audience is triggered via the use of a mobile, location-based platform that includes the communication devices themselves, as well as the space for interaction defined through multiple locations and routes.

Systems Thinking in the Work of Blast Theory

Lily Diaz (LD): In what ways would you say that systems theory and thinking informs Blast Theory's creations?

Matt Adams (MA): The immediate association I have would be in two ways. The first would be in how a piece of interactive work would operate. The second would be in a theory about political and social systems and how our work is situated within that.

Anytime that we create an interactive experience, I think of it as a form of dialogue between us as artists and the members of the public participating in that work. So we are looking to establish some kind of grammar for that conversation. Sometimes we make works that are structured as games. *Can You See Me Now?*, one of Blast Theory's works, is of course an obvious example.[5] Without even going into game design and techniques and thinking about the mechanics, there is a system operating at the heart of the work.

How do you create a framework in which a player has direction about what they think that they are doing? Sometimes in our work that takes the form of a goal for the participant, but not always. Sometimes our works are games, sometimes not. A goal creates a simple initial motivation for any actions that the participant makes; it provides an overall arc for the whole experience and a way for them to appraise their actions beat by beat at a micro level. If that goal is absent, there is a new challenge for the participant: They have agency but how should they employ it?

Brian Eno describes interactive work as "unfinished" (Kelly). The system is always open. It tends towards chaos and entropy. Games tend to marshal this chaos via rules, goals, and a defined outcome but we are trying in more recent works to find different strategies. In their book *Performing Mixed Reality*, Steve Benford and Gabriella Giannachi talk about canonical trajectories versus participant trajectories.[6] The canonical trajectory is the "ideal" route through an interactive experience. The interactivity allows each participant to diverge from the canonical trajectory but ultimately there must be forces to guide or coerce the participant back towards the canonical trajectory.

One reason we began making games, such as *Desert Rain* in 1999, is because games are very accessible.[7] We all readily understand how to engage and how to measure our progress.

To move beyond that, we are drawing on the principles of dialogue. This is another interactive system that we are all familiar with. The "grammar"—both literal and metaphorical—is understood: We even have deep tacit knowledge about how to contest that grammar. This approach allows us to test and stretch the language of interactivity as far as possible.

During the research for *Ulrike and Eamon Compliant* I came across the work of Philippa Foot who is an English philosopher. In 1968, in her essay ("The Problems of Abortion and the Doctrine of the Double Effect"), she proposed for the first time the idea of The Trolley Dilemma, or the Trolley Problem as some people call it, which is a simple problem that can be answered in one or two ways. For example, a train trolley is running out of control down a railway track, and at the bottom of the railway track are five people who will surely be hit and killed if this trolley continues on its path. However, to one side there is a branch to this train track, and you can pull a switch that can switch the train to another track, and save those five people. Unfortunately there is one person on that track and this person will surely be killed if the train is switched. Would you pull the switch or not?

This is a profound concept because it has a number of important implications. One of those is that it suggests that you can test complex ethical and moral problems with members of the public. Rather than the age-old process of esoteric discussion between philosophers, suddenly complex decisions can be opened out to the public. By subtly shifting some aspects of the proposition it is possible to explore the nuances of moral problems. The whole field acquires an empirical aspect.

That really opened up a new door to us because it enabled us to think about the works that we create as having somehow the same properties as the Trolley Dilemma. That we could establish a situation where the decision that you are making might be binary, you'll make a simple "A" or "B" choice but it could, in doing so, embody a very complex set of concerns that might be moral, ethical, social, or political . . . it could take any number of forms.

As a performance, *Ulrike and Eamon Compliant* is structured around an incredibly simple system. These are the two choices (or the two roles to play), but it employs a complex set of rules that come with it, and the real issue is not which choice you make but rather: why *do* we choose one or the other? So we try to look as widely as we possibly can and be as heterogeneous as we can in our sources for what kinds of systems we might employ within our work.

Sometimes we try and vary those systems even within a piece of work—a good example is *Desert Rain*. In that work . . . [pause] . . . you begin that work with a briefing for the six members of the public. You put on a jacket that we give you, and you are told that you are going on a mission to find someone, so it's almost like a team-building exercise in the first few minutes. Then you are led through into a virtual environment, and you explore this virtual environment, and that has a framework. It is structured like a game, you have a goal, there are rules, and so on. At the end of that game, you come out of it and discover that some of the people that you were looking for within the game are in fact real people who were involved in the Gulf War of 1991, and so the work then becomes a documentary. A completely different system or framework is employed. It moves from team building through game play to documentary. At first, "Glen" is the name of a character in a game. By the end, Glen is a real person describing on video how he handled Iraqi casualties.

This is a kind of simplification of the work. But it just shows you how the work steps you through different kinds of systems for interaction, and as the work progresses the transition from one system to another forms a big part of how you understand that work to operate.

The Question of Agency

LD: How do you deal with the question of agency of the characters, as well as of the people who decide to participate in a work such as *Ulrike and Eamon Compliant*?

MA: In this particular work one of the key tensions is whether you accept the proposition that you are now Ulrike or Eamon, (each call treats you as if you are that person and talks to you as if you are a person). So then you may choose to accept that quite theatrical conceit and then frame your experience as: "I am now Ulrike Meinhof, famous West German terrorist." That, then, invites you to immerse yourself in a fictional world, and to play, and to imagine yourself as that person, to activate your imagination.

Or equally you may choose to reject that proposition. You may decide that it lacks credibility for you to pretend that you are now Ulrike as you walk through, for example, the streets of Venice. But then that resistance to the conceit of the work is also a driver for your experience.

You might reject the theatrical system, and you might reject the fictional framework and see the entire work as a representation of a third person. But each of those processes can be rich and productive. In a work about armed revolution and non-compliance with all social norms, your decision whether to accede to this intrusion is highly charged. You may revise your point of view as the work progresses, you may hold both ideas at once, or you may vacillate between the two.

At the culmination of the work, you arrive at the interview. You sit down and the interviewer says: "What would you fight for?" You now have to think about how to answer: "Am I Ulrike, or am I not Ulrike?" And that ambiguity, even if you rejected to be Ulrike for the whole previous thirty-five or forty minutes, you might think: "Ah, but this person now wants me to be Ulrike." Again, you are still negotiating an uncertain terrain, as to what is the system that is operating here: Is it theatrical? Is it fictional? Non-fictional?

Second-Order Observation

LD: Do you think that this might be a situation in which the work triggers some sort of second-order observation among those who choose to participate? That what really happens is that the work creates certain conditions that usher in this state in which they begin to observe themselves?

MA: That is indeed the larger question that *Ulrike and Eamon Compliant* poses . . . [pause] . . . the interview revolves around the question of political violence and it really seeks to establish and explore the impossibility of sustaining a pure position. It seeks to establish that all positions on the spectrum in relation to political action in general, and political violence specifically, involve compromise and hypocrisy. That even if you take, for example, the ultimate pacifist position in that interview, which some people do: "I would never fight anyone for anything." And then if you ask them then, "Well, what about if someone breaks into your house and is about to murder your child, would you commit violence then?" And they say: "No. I am a pacifist. I would resist passively. I would never engage in violence, even in that situation."

What you must accept, then, is that fascist or totalitarian regimes will take full advantage of that passivity. That those who claim violent power themselves, if they could choose anything for their opponents to be, it would be complete pacifists. This is what they would choose because this gives them complete and unlimited power, and because people who employ violence can always dominate those who under no circumstances will employ violence. This is where the kind of formal structure of *Ulrike and Eamon Compliant* is driving towards. It is trying to bring you to achieve a complex and very present consideration, or experience, regarding the moral questions around the issue of political violence.

In doing so, you are not only developing a critical awareness about the decision making of Eamon Collins or Ulrike Meinhof—you are also aware of your own decision-making processes, both within the work and outside the work.

LD: Now that we have talked about the "whole," I would be interested in going deeper into the work. How do you go about the creation of a "character" such as Ulrike? What sort of research do you engage in?

MA: Well, we work collaboratively, Ju (Ju Row Farr), Nick (Nick Tandavanitj), and I (Matt Adams). But usually one of us will take the lead on writing a piece of text. Not always. There are times when text . . . if you could track back how a text has been written, you will find that it is a palimpsest from all three of us, that all of us have put in different elements at different times, and different sentences are mingled and so on. But generally— especially in works that are more text-heavy, as *Ulrike and Eamon Compliant*—one of us will take the lead on writing.

I did most of the writing in that project, and it comes from a lot of research, using secondary sources. It is really about reading as much as possible about Ulrike's life. In Eamon's case, the main source that we had was his own memoir called *A Killing Rage*.[8] And then at one level, it is a traditional writing task, which is to imagine a character, to bring a character to life, to try and structure a narrative so that it is compelling and intriguing. That it is rich with strong detail.

But it also has a number of particular challenges, in terms of our work. One is that you listen on the phone, and the phone has its own affordances as a piece of technology. When a phone rings you find it difficult not to answer. It is a system of control. It allows crude forms of interaction through button pushes. The sound quality is poor and but it is private and directly in your ear. And in this work we were creating the telephone equivalent of an epistolary novel. There is a series of phone calls. Each call takes place in a different time and place, both in the narrative and for the participant. And then each call is mixing narrative with instructions. The work guides you precisely through the street step-by-step and this is one of the reasons it takes around ten days to adapt the work to each city.

The stories for Eamon and Ulrike are dealt with slightly differently. They both have internal inconsistencies. There is no pure logic that explains exactly what is going on. The voice of the calls could be their older selves reflecting on life, or making calls back to their younger selves or it could be a purely narrative device. This subjective instability runs throughout and there is no consistent logic.

And then, there is the interaction structure that is then set on top of that. First it deals with direction finding and way finding. There is a tremendous amount of work done in telling you where to walk and when to turn, and what to look for, and setting up landmarks for you. And there is a tension there between where the calls are set (in Germany in the 1960s or 1970s, or in Northern Ireland in the 1970s) and where the work is set (in Venice or in Seoul, for example).

This also involves a kind of performance style that is different because you need to talk slowly. You have to give room in which to understand every piece of information. Normally if you and I went to a reading in a bookshop or in a theatre, you can afford to miss a few sentences, and often you will drift off, either because you are distracted or because something unexpected in the text catches your interest and invites you to reflect for a moment about it, and by the time you come back in, you are a few sentences further on. In this work, we really cannot do that. We are giving highly relevant interaction information constantly that you need to process and be able to manage, otherwise you will get lost. So there is a tremendous amount of testing over and over to find a balance of all those different systems of language which are coexisting, and interlocking with one another.

LD: Would you say that these performances are in a way like open systems, since every time it is staged in a new location the setting and the people change?

MA: There is another way of looking at it, which would be to say that distinct from most of the work we have made, *Ulrike and Eamon Compliant* is very linear and the interactions it offers you are in general false . . . They lead to no substantive difference, with a couple of exceptions.

First, you are given the choice to avoid the interview room and finish the work without going to meet for the interview. Second, the interview itself is of course, a completely open discussion. We have a rough plan for the interview but it can unfold in a variety of very different ways depending on how people respond. So, there is one clear binary interaction and there is one strong, completely open interaction. But apart from that, the work is very didactic, very linear, and it goes out of its way to present you with choices that actually are false.

LD: As part of the research, did you interview people who knew Ulrike and Eamon?

MA: No. In this project it is all done through secondary sources. That is not always the case. In *Fixing Point*, for example, we interviewed the sister of Seamus Ruddy who had been in an unarmed Irish Republican group in the 1980s.[9] And there in *Desert Rain* we interview six participants in the First Gulf War, but in *Ulrike and Eamon Compliant* it is all secondary sources.

Authenticity, Uniqueness, and Complexity

LD: Do you research the characters, in order to construct them in a more authentic manner?

MA: Yes. A lot of the research is reading original texts written by both Eamon Collins and Ulrike Meinhof. And one of the reasons we chose those two is because there is a very extensive amount of writing by both of them. This not only gives access to their reasoning and their ideas but also to their particular way of expressing themselves

LD: So then you aim for a certain degree of authenticity?

MA: Authenticity is a very complex concept for me. There are many levels at which we could talk about authenticity, and clearly, at the broadest level, this work is inauthentic, it is entirely fictional, entirely constructed. You would never be fooled for one moment that this is not a construction. We are well aware that this work is a form of pretend.

On the other hand, we are definitely reaching for a kind of authenticity. We want you to believe in these characters. We want you to be interested in them as real people, in real political situations. And therefore, if you choose, you can bring your own knowledge of political violence, or of the era, the eras in which they were both active. That knowledge is relevant: It allows an active social and political engagement with the piece. That is another reason why we chose Ulrike Meinhof—even though she has been used over, and over, and over again by artists, writers, and theater makers.

And there is also an authenticity in terms of the political question. This work was made in 2009. It is in the immediate fallout of the financial crisis. It is a moment where the question of radical political change and a challenge to Western capitalism has emerged for the first time in a couple of decades. Even the most strident advocates of capitalism are forced to admit that there are some systemic problems, and the Occupy movement is emerging. And that is the key authenticity, which then leads all the way to the interview: "What would you fight for?"

When Ju, or I, or our associate artists do those interviews, we prepare very carefully for them. We work very hard to ensure an active and authentic conversation in the sense that when someone comes into the room they can engage with those questions, within their own vocabulary, thinking about those questions in their own way. We will at no point try and shut that down. It is a moment for that member of the public to have a conversation that is appropriate for them. That's why we say that it is a completely open discussion. There are elements that we are looking to achieve, ideas that we are trying to cover. But we are also trying to do it in a way that is as true as possible for each individual.

It is very important to us to create an interactive work. That enables each person to interact on their own terms as far as that is possible to do, within the constraints of each individual piece of work. We need to acknowledge and celebrate the fullest complexity possible within that exchange.

LD: What happens with the responses that people give to the interviews?

MA: Nothing. They are not recorded or saved. They are streamed live from the final interview room to the room at the start, but even then it is hard to hear what is being said from the final interview room.

Some of those discussions are amazing. People have confessed to attempted murder. People cry. People are very aggressive. People are very reflective. And clearly we could have made a film of those interviews and, at times, we have been tempted to do so. But ultimately what we want to do is to ensure that the capturing of those interviews is not constraining the types of conversations that we can have, and so, if we start to put a camera there, someone immediately thinks a second time about how they talk. They start to have another cycle in their brain running. "Who is filming?" "Why are they filming?" "What will happen with the film of this?" And there they are really jumping outside of this quite immersive and oppressive atmosphere—ultimately this is too great a risk for us to take.

Also, the structure is that once you have done your interview, you come out and walk around and stand behind the two-way mirror and then you watch as the next person comes in for their interview. So you then eavesdrop on that interview, and you also simultaneously become aware that someone eavesdropped on your interview: when you were talking someone else stood behind the glass. That realization throws a retrospective alarm back across your conversation: you were being covertly scrutinized.

But that does not diminish the sense during the conversation that this is a unique part of the work that you alone hold, and that this is something very special. It is a quality of live performance that is always present in our work. When live performance is at its best, every person's experience is different and no two performances are the same.

A Critical Approach

LD: What can you tell us about the ethico-political views of Blast Theory?

MA: I see the work that we make as political. But the form of that politics is in the fine details of how social, cultural, technological, and political systems interact. For me it is important that what we make affords all the complexity and ambiguities and contradictions that hold in relation to particular ideas—so we consciously avoid work that has an activist intent. We attempt to reflect [on] the politics of our work, by bringing audiences into close attention to political questions, but offering a tangential approach. For example, in Desert Rain—a virtual reality game about the relationship between reality, virtuality, the fictional, and the imaginary—we look at the Gulf War of 1999. Playing a war game that slides between those four modes of knowledge encourages reflection on the political ramifications of a collapse of the borders among them.

LD: What about the possible tensions between the critical views held by Blast Theory and the reality of working with corporate sponsors?

MA: There is a paradigm that is particularly common in visual art: the assumption that artists have total autonomy to stand outside of their social and economic structures, to comment on them. And I think that this is a very dangerous idea. Even the most well-established visual artist who essentially has an unlimited budget and unlimited time, and an ability to employ experts from a multitude of different disciplines, is deeply bounded by the structures in which they operate. My point of view is not that the work that we do is mired in compromise but that all artistic work exists in negotiation with the societies in which they operate. And then it is about how we conduct those negotiations, how transparent they are, and what kinds of effects they have on the work we make. I have a very clear idea about what those limits might be, and we have had no compunction in withdrawing from things, cancelling relationships when we felt that we were being requested to dilute our work unnecessarily. Some people see the fact that we work with large corporations as evidence of a lack of radicality. Other people see our work as politically engaged. It is not something on which I can make a definite claim. And I would say that we probably navigate it in some circumstances better than in others. Most European art makers that work in the same field as us are dependent to some degree on the State or the EU for funding. So, we are bounded by the social and political goals of our own culture. I do not see that as fundamentally flawed. It is a primary element of the context in which we operate. We seek to engage and to make change where and when we can.

Notes

1. "Ulrike and Eamon Compliant," Blast Theory, accessed March 29, 2015, http://blasttheory.co.uk/projects/ulrike-and-eamon-compliant/.
2. L. von Bertalanffy, General System Theory: Foundations, Development, Applications (New York, NY, Penguin University Books, 1968), 21.
3. N. Luhmann, Art as a Social System, (Stanford, CA: Stanford University Press), 13.
4. N. Luhmann, Art as a Social System, p. 39.
5. "Can You See Me Now?," Blast Theory, accessed March 29, 2015, http://blasttheory.co.uk/projects/can-you-see-me-now/.
6. Benford, Steve, Giannachi, Gabriella, Performing Virtual Reality, Cambridge, MA: The MIT Press, 2011.
7. "Desert Rain," Blast Theory, accessed 29 March, 2015, www.blasttheory.co.uk/projects/desert-rain/.
8. E. Collins, M. McGovern, Killing Rage, (London, UK: Granta, 1998).
9. "Fixing Point," Blast Theory, accessed 29 March, 2015, www.blasttheory.co.uk/projects/fixing-point/.

References

Bauman, Zygmunt, and David Lyon. 2013. *Liquid Surveillance, A Conversation*. Cambridge, UK: Polity Press.

Benford, Steve, and Gabriella Giannachi. 2011. *Performing Virtual Reality*. Cambridge, MA: The MIT Press.

Collins, Eamon, and Mick McGovern. 1998. *Killing Rage*. London, UK: Granta.

"Can You See Me Now?," *Blast Theory*, accessed March 29, 2015, http://blasttheory.co.uk/projects/can-you-see-me-now/.

"Desert Rain," *Blast Theory*, accessed March 29, 2015, http://blasttheory.co.uk/projects/desert-rain/.

"Fixing Point," *Blast Theory*, accessed March 29, 2015, http://blasttheory.co.uk/projects/fixing-point/.

Kelly, Kevin. "Gossip is Philosophy", *WIRED*, accessed March 29, 2015, http://archive.wired.com/wired/archive/3.05/eno_pr.html.

Luhmann, Niklas. 2000. *Art as a Social System*. Trans. Eva M. Knodt. Stanford, CA: Stanford University Press.

"Ulrike and Eamon Compliant," *Blast Theory*, accessed March 29, 2015, http://blasttheory.co.uk/projects/ulrike-and-eamon-compliant/.

von Bertalanffy, Ludwig. 1968. *General System Theory: Foundations, Development, Applications*. Revised ed. London: Penguin University Books.

COMPLEX HISTORICITY

An Interview with Electroland Principal Cameron McNall

Maria Engberg

The conversation with Electroland Principal, Cameron McNall, unfolded as an ongoing reflection on the reasons and original context of particular work, and how aspects of the work either anticipated technological advances or might be understood differently today as a result of the rapidly changing technology landscape. Electroland was formed in 2001 by Cameron McNall and partner Damon Seeley to create conceptual and experimental projects that often employ new technologies.

Maria Engberg (ME): Tell me about Electroland's earlier work and how you view it now.

Cameron McNall (CM): Let me start with a very early work, the R-G-B project from 2001 (Plate 35). Colored lights fill 81 windows at the Southern California Institute of Architecture (SCI-Arc) in Los Angeles. The lights are controlled by the touchpad of a mobile phone. Anyone with a mobile phone is empowered to call in and manipulate the lights. The technology is a combination of Arduino and old-school phreaking hardware. We had several intentions in the design of this work, and they mirrored or were inspired by developments in mobile tech, computing, and the Internet. We wanted to upset the relationship of public to private, of people to buildings, to demonstrate that any one person could interact with and manipulate an entity as large as a building. Inspired by game design, we contrived to allow gameplay at an urban scale. Another interest was the by-then ubiquity of the mobile phone. We thought, "this is interesting, everyone is carrying this device, we can do something to take advantage of this unprecedented situation."

Looking back, regarding the issue of public and private, the project makes visible the hidden electronic interconnectivity that binds us all, whether it be in mobile networks, the Internet, or in databases. The need to render visible the nature of interconnectivity is still an important role artists can and should play. The tension between the actions of a single user and the great effect they could have on the building face is still a unique aspect of the project and may remain unique to this project. The use of a mobile phone for something other than texting and voice of course anticipates the explosion of uses by what has now become known as a "smartphone"; it was an inevitable development, but R-G-B is among a few projects in the world that anticipated the development at this early date.

In all of our work we seek to create new and unusual experiences, and an aspect of technology may either inspire some aspect of the work, or might just be chosen as the appropriate tool or medium to enable the creation of something new and unexpected. In the case of R–G–B, while the central importance of the mobile phone might be mistaken as a novelty feature, the actual experience of the work is still powerful and enduring. The user experience follows the rules of interactivity, as we understood them at the time, which is to say that it is intuitive and easy to learn, and most definitely gives distinct real-time rewards for the user.

ME: Moving on to another early work, *Target Interactive Breezeway* from 2006 (Plates 36 and 37). An interactive light and sound installation for Target, located on the top-floor observation decks of Rockefeller Center in New York. Visitors who enter the space are sensed and tracked persistently by four 3D stereo-vision cameras (Electroland—Target Interactive Breezeway 2014). As each visitor moves around the space, individualized light patterns and sounds follow each person. What were some of the main lessons learned from this work?

CM: For the Interactive Breezeway, we sought to create a completely intuitive environmental experience that is shaped by lights and sound. It is important to know that the project exists in a public space, not a gallery, and the audience has absolutely no premonition that they will be walking through any kind of artwork. Several important insights were gained from this work. We quickly learned that people do not have eyes on the tops of their heads, and have no reason to look up to see the ceiling tracking lights unless we catch their attention first. Our solution was to introduce a flash of light accompanied by an appropriately quick and urgent sound when people first walk in the door. Deep body survival instincts are then engaged: "Whoa, what was that, it happened as I just walked in here, did I do that?" Visitors usually at this point momentarily stop and look around, and then begin to understand that they have entered the precinct of an unusual space over which they might have some control.

Another lesson is how important sound can be as an effective background to heighten and clarify the interactive experience. We know about the variable and emotive qualities of sound in cinema. Many of the same rules apply when artificial sounds are introduced to immersive interactive installations. It is not exactly "form follows function"; there is a lot of room to inform or to color an experience. This is an area in which we will see great growth and development in the years to come.

We learned that when we create interactive spaces, they often become social experiences. The overall experience invites, or you could say it "allows" strangers to interact with each other. They comment to each other, compare notes, take pictures. We also learned that social transactions become important for the apprehension and "gameplay" of the space, and it unfolds in a sequence. When you first enter, you are a spectator. You see people behaving strangely, and you observe them while learning more about what is going on. Then at some point your involvement becomes that of a participant, and this is the period when the social aspect becomes more prominent, interacting with others while exploring the experience. Finally, you transition to the role as a performer. You are aware that others just entering are curious about what you are doing, and you demonstrate aspects of what you have learned to others.

Another revelation from this project that was unfolding contemporaneously with the work is the importance of social media in shaping the perception of and interaction with the space. We were astonished that images and movies of the space were showing up on the Internet, and that we did not have to promote it at all! We began to understand that the value of the work for many visitors resided in its capacity to create sharable photos for Internet consumption. Once again, this is a phenomenon that is now so commonplace that it hardly seems remarkable, but we think it is critical to note how quickly the perceptual context of our work has been changed by social media. As a result, we now always consider the mindset and activity of the users and their preoccupation with sharing with a distant audience.

In the early days of our work, critics wanted to consider our work in the context of surveillance, while in fact this was not an interest or concern for us. Instead, we were interested in developing new relationships between people and spaces, and tracking is essential to accomplish this goal. It was surprising that on the one hand we had critics raising privacy and surveillance issues, and yet almost no actual users ever expressed any concerns or felt any sense of threat. It is perhaps scary that when tracking is clothed in a fun activity, people accept it with no reservation. But when you consider the quick adoption of the smartphone, and all of its attendant tracking applications, you see that people don't seem very concerned about the nefarious aspects.

ME: Since these earlier works, the Internet and our culture's reliance on ubiquitous mobile technologies have radically evolved. How does this affect your work as a whole?

CM: As previously discussed, mobile technologies, social media and the presence of the Internet create a very different context in which to create work. They also stratify our audience more; the younger they are, the quicker they adopt. What remains as a constant is that bodily apperception of a real space is a compelling experience that is very different from interaction with a hand-scaled or body-scaled screen.

The *College Faces* project was conceived in 2011 and realized in 2013 (Plates 38 and 39). We were not thinking specifically about Facebook even though the name might suggest that. We wanted to represent that the school was really about the people who occupied the school, and in the case of Gateway Community College, the faces of a community college are marvelously diversified in race and age. The use of big faces is also graphically interesting. We took something that was considered private, individuals' faces, and placed them at a very large urban scale. So by 2013, people were very used to having their faces represent them in the public forum of Facebook and the like; to be able to walk up to a giant face and touch it in a public space is a very different context and situation.

ME: Working with networked technologies in site-specific interactive installations over a number of years as Electroland has done, how do you think about the issue of complexity, for instance in terms of changing technologies, or audience appreciation and expectations?

CM: We focus on the present; what is interesting now, what can we do that challenges current perceptions, and how can we have fun. Fortunately, we are not burdened by practical applications; our projects must be successful only within their limited application and aspirations, which is to say art. In the course of our work we frequently stumble across phenomena that anticipate wider trends in ubiquitous technologies, and much of it hints at practical applications that could make a lot of money! But taking these things to market is very hard work and even deep-pocketed companies like Google fail more often than they succeed. Luckily, we get to be the guys who just get to goof-off all day; the future is probably unknowable and is at any rate not our problem. So long as we create satisfying experiences, the novelty of what we do does not diminish the experience.

References

Electroland—Target Interactive Breezeway. 2014. Accessed September 29, 2014. http://electroland.net/#/target-interactive-breezeway/

INTERVIEW WITH MOGENS JACOBSEN[1]

Morten Søndergaard

Morten Søndergaard (MS): I will begin by paraphrasing briefly the central notion of this book, which is aiming at addressing questions concerning "a third wave of computation"— and what this means in the practices of everyday life and art, among other things.

I would like to ask what your initial response to that notion is.

Mogens Jacobsen (MJ): First of all, I don't think of myself as working within ubiquitous computing—but if we think of Weiser's third wave (Weiser 1991), it seems like we in some situations are way past that (the omnipresence of high performing smartphones and cheap/small microprocessors) but at the same time returning to remote, centralized computing (I am writing this in a Google Document!).

But if we restrict us to the view of the computer as a box with its user sitting focused in front of the GUI [Graphical User Interface, ed.], then I see my own works in a different perspective.

MS: Before we go more into this, allow me to wheel back a little in your practice as an artist and, I guess, as a project developer or innovator within new media as well, to a presentation I heard you give at the Get Real conference in Roskilde in 2005 (Søndergaard 2005). Here, you stated that "you hate the word or concept of interaction." Could you perhaps, as a first move into establishing an idea of your artistic practice elaborate a little on that statement, seen from a 2005 perspective (what did you mean back then) and a 2015 perspective (what does it mean now)?

MJ: As I denounced interactivity back in 2005, I was mainly worried about three aspects: First, I was referring to the pure hype of interactivity. Second, I was objecting to the widespread use of the word—being used without any clear definition. At that time I used "reactive"—inspired by the works of John Maeda—to describe electronic artworks that responded to audience input in a local feedback loop. Coming from net.art, I missed the telematics, remote or networked elements in electronic art. And, lastly, I was trying to free digital art from being solemnly understood as a Windows, icon, menu, pointer (WIMP)/screen-/mouse-based thing, which was restricting the artspace to a desktop; and, to quote Mark Weiser, the world is not a desktop (Weiser 1991).

MS: Could you perhaps explain a little further your use of the word "reactive" in the light of the networked and Telematic elements in electronic artefacts you mention (and if you can give some examples from your own or other's production that would be great). First of all, what are the differences, if any, between the networked and the Telematic, in your definition—or perhaps you would prefer if I use the word experience here? Second, how does this difference (or similarity) feed into your notion of "freeing" art from the desktop?

MJ: I use the word "reactive" in want of any better word describing what happens in the local, short-term–real-time—loop between a person and a responding electronic art-piece. The feedback is immediate and one-to-one (between onlooker and system). This sort of reactiveness is almost expected. Go to any "digital" art show and observe a non-interactive/non-reactive work: you will see a lot of the guest start moving or waving in front of the piece, trying to figure out how to "operate" the art piece, and perhaps finally beginning to touch the piece and trying to "click" somewhere. The cliché of interactivity has grown us accustomed to this sort of experience—instant gratification within three (micro-) seconds.

Of course it was an important step, as computers became real-time tools: they moved from being "solvers" to become "explorer." In that sense the interactivity of real-time computation was a revolution. But lacking a mature "aesthetics of interaction," interactive art faces a danger of becoming purely a "populist art."

You will see a lot of great looking installations with large screens or projections filled with amazing imagery: particle systems, AR, 3D.

But I think there are more interesting things going on behind the screen—or perhaps between screens. One example is my work "Crime Scene" from 2003 (Plate 40). Here I deliberately choose to work within the dull aesthetics of office. The installation consists of two desktop-computers; beige plastic boxes with 17 inch CRT monitors on top. On the two screens only text was shown and there was no user interaction.

MS: When did you first get interested in computers as an artistic medium? And when did you move on to working "between" the screens—or did that happen gradually?

MJ: First of all: I was born in 1959, so I belong to a generation where access to computers during childhood was rare. But in the 1970s I went to a very experimental high school: the high school focused on music and computers. So besides having access to musical instruments, we had access so a shared computer: Huge blue thing, you programmed using punch card (now I sound really old!).

But my first cultural practices started when I studied film at the university in the start 1980s. There I met a lot of people experimenting with photography and music. At that point, I started a record/cassette label with some of my co-students. My personal interests were electronics—analogue synths and home build stuff—and the human voice. Later computers entered this practice—Commodore and Atari—and at that point I became interested in generative systems. Working with these machines, I started to expand my sound with visuals as well. Sadly, I don't have any of these programs today.

When the web started, I got a job working as a web designer. And as everybody else doing web design in the beginning of the 1990s, I learned a lot by looking at what other people were coding. Moreover, I soon got interested in the web as a platform for art. I met a few other Danish artists with the same interest and we formed a net.art group—and named it *Artnode* (www.artnode.org).

But after working for ten years with screen-based net.art, I felt a need to free myself of the GUI—I wanted to work with (different) materialities. One example of this kind of work would be *Power of Mind* (2004) where the electric power making the installation (and the website connected to it) work comes from the potatoes on display (Plate 41).

MS: Returning to the question of ubiquitous computing and Weiser's "third wave" which, to quote you, "we have moved way past"—what, then, have we moved into, in your opinion?

MJ: I think there is an important aesthetic riddle somewhere in this field. Talking about aesthetics in regards to the "old" visual (and auditive) User Interface (UI) was safe—we have the history—at least in general terms—of visual aesthetics. And of course the material gestalt of physical materials fits nicely within our aesthetic tradition of industrial design, handicrafts, and architecture. But I can't help feel there is more to it—more to the digital stuff. There is computation, communication, and interaction. Besides purely technical aspects—beauty in code as described by Donald Knuth —I feel we are only beginning to define aesthetics in these areas. Much work is still to be done (Knuth 1968).

Perhaps you could think on my surveillance related work in this way: as everybody else I am concerned about our privacy. But I am having a hard time trying to make this general concern fit with our willingness to use Facebook, Gmail, Bing, Google, Amazon, Netflix, and these "Big Data" warehouses. So, I hope people see my surveillance related works not as "naive" provocations. They are probably more investigations into mediated relational aesthetics or questions from a person who are just as confused as everybody else (or, should be).

Note

1. Conducted partly by email correspondence, September 2013–March 2014.

References

Knuth, D. 1968. *The Art of Computer Programming*. Boston, MA: Addison-Wesley.
Søndergaard, M., Ed. 2005. *Get Real—Real Time + Art + Theory + History + Practice*. New York: George Braziller Publishers.
Weiser, M. 1991. "The Computer for the Twenty-First Century." *Scientific American* 265 (3): 94–104.

UBIQUITOUS—ALIFE IN TECHNOSPHERE 2.0

The Design, Individuation, and Entanglement of Ubicomp Apps in Urban South East Asia

Jane Prophet and Helen Pritchard

Background

TechnoSphere 2.0 is a re-engineering of a 1990s networked artificial life (ALife) project that used a web interface to enable the design of ALife creatures, who were nicknamed "beasties." "Beasties" were then put into an ALife simulation housed on a PC. TechnoSphere was described at the time using the contemporaneously dominant discourse of interaction, "Most sites out there still only provide information to browse through, our aim with TechnoSphere was to offer a site where users did something (designed a creature) and where their interaction had an effect (each creature affects the digital ecology in the TechnoSphere virtual world" (Prophet 2002). The 1990s TechnoSphere was "launched" as a fully functioning ALife simulation that participants could not easily alter (Prophet, "Sublime Ecologies and Artistic Endeavors: Artificial Life and Interactivity in the Online Project" 1996). It was followed four years later by the production of a real-time 3D version (Prophet, "TechnoSphere: 'Real' Time, 'Artificial' Life" 2001).

TechnoSphere 2.0 takes contemporary ideas of making and ubiquitous computing much further than the previous version. It comprises a number of interconnected mobile Android applications (apps) allowing people to create creatures in 3D on their mobile devices, take them with them and intra-act with them as the creatures explore both artificial and real-world environments. The first app enables users to create their carnivore or herbivore creature by selecting a head, body, wheel, and eye design and then texturing it from a selection of patterns, seeing it from all angles as it spins in realtime 3D as each choice is made or altered (Plate 42). Once satisfied, they name the creature; any creature can then be added to a series of Augmented Reality (AR) apps (Plate 43).

The AR apps use mobile devices' built-in cameras to capture the live image and overlay it with computer-generated graphics. To achieve this, smartphones combine location via GPS data with orientation via compass information and movement via accelerometers and gyroscopes. Fiducial markers, which can be paper diagrams or objects, are used as points of reference that appear in the video image and are overlaid with a virtual object. In the first AR app, a creature can be seen moving around a table or other flat surface like the living room floor, and people can start to interact with it in a shared TechnoSphere world. Participants create the shared world by arranging pre-designed fiducial markers in their gaming environment. Users can make their own fiducial markers to register landmarks; these can be 2D printed paper and can be 3D objects or hand-drawn images. These landmarks tether static virtual 3D objects, each of which has specific properties. The virtual objects laid out as part of the navigable environment of the table top include trees, food caches with varying nutritional value, and a watering hole. Fiducial markers (colored graphic images printed out on paper) laid on the table are virtual meals; the image is data that causes AR foods to appear in the mobile device screen, displayed on top of the live video of the table top. If it is hungry, the creature can approach and eat the food cache it finds on the table. The next AR app adds obstacles and attractors to this table top environment and the virtual creature will be able to navigate around real life obstacles from the users' world. The virtual creature moves within the table top area that is partially controlled by the user, drinking at (or drowning in) the watering hole, eating at food sources, and following drawn pathways.

The AR environment can be further blended with the real world if users make 3D representations in real space of the virtual objects such as trees and watering hole. These 3D objects can be formed using everyday objects from the users' homes with fiducial markers added, or by users printing pre-designed slice forms on paper or card and assembling them. The creatures will interact with both virtual objects and with those virtual objects' real paper "twins." The paper versions of the ALife environment forms are then seen whether or not the AR app is in use, pushing the project further towards Mixed Reality (MR) where the ALife engine is impacted by the gameplay and the participants' design choices are meaningful (how a person designs their creature and how they design the landscape affects how a creatures grows and behaves).

The apparently human-defined graphic world is now tied to an ALife engine, the graphics and the creatures interact dynamically and in real time, and the shared world is entangled. Other AR apps use GPS to enable users to take their creatures around with them, tethered to the user via GPS. Humans can walk their creatures round their apartment, into their backyard, or to a public park, tethered via GPS so they scamper within a few feet of the user. This is one way to potentially meet other users and their creatures, if users choose to make themselves visible to others as they stroll.

The beasties made as part of TechnoSphere 2.0 individuate through entangled relations of GPS, hardware, software, human, and nonhumans in the city. The 1990s web-based version of TechnoSphere was populated by creatures that were autonomous, behaving according to rules embedded in algorithms of the ALife engine that defined each creature and its environment, but that did not enable human users and their interactions to permeate the ALife system. By contrast, TechnoSphere 2.0 takes that ALife engine as a starting point but then adds features that allow for human activity to become coupled to it. The inputs from human participants can then affect both the creatures and their environment, concretizing previously un-realized potentials of their ALife creature and their milieu. For example, by adding a watering hole or food sources on the AR table top app, a human user creates the conditions for a creature to carry out actions such as eating or drinking, creating navigable paths for the creature to follow or paths along which to race with another creature. Whether, or to what extent, a creature will take advantage of these human interventions will always depend on the creature's ALife engine.

Previous papers on ubiquitous computing research tend to focus on the exploration of future prototypes of technology and how such technology is part of everyday experience, or as Bell and Dourish state "on the future just around the corner" (Bell and Dourish 2007, 134). We investigate the tools of ALife and ubiquitous computing (ubicomp) as they develop together in the present-day, emerging, into previously undiscovered relationships and discuss what Ulrik Ekman has described as the potentialities of ubicomp "whose actualization we are not yet sure" (Ekman 2011, 1). We present our engagements with the project TechnoSphere 2.0 by analyzing the ongoing process of designing and developing a series of (apps) that form part of this ubiquitous ALife project. Jane McGonigal argues that ubicomp game design "formulates hypotheses about the value and feasibility of ubiquitous computing" (McGonigal 2007, 92), positioning prototype games as experiments to suggest that testing these prototypes via so-called playtests "provide citable proof of these hypotheses" (McGonigal 2007, 92), about ubicomp futures. We note that our project, like many in the ubicomp literature, is currently a prototype, developed as part of our method of using practice-based research to design processes for artificial life.

Our augmented reality mobile apps can be seen as experiments through which we test hypotheses that mixed reality opens up the possibilities for more affective experiences. Our use of the term mixed reality here recognizes a blending of the material and immaterial, as entanglements of humans and nonhumans. However, our methodology differs from many cited by McGonigal inasmuch as our goal is to produce a game that goes beyond prototype and playtest phase. The underlying premise of both the TechnoSphere 2.0 project and this chapter is that the process of making *matters*, that the materialization of an ubiquitous ALife project is a process of unveiling hidden potentials, what Albert Simondon refers to as moving from the abstract to the concrete (Simondon 1958, 16). This is a movement through which a "series of problems" is resolved (Simondon 1958, 14). Drawing on the work of Isabelle Stengers, we describe this process as one of *making*. Stengers outlines the figure of the "Maker" to express the creative process and assert that although the maker's values "pass into the world" (Stengers 2010, 295), the explanation of the values themselves does not fully explain what is made. For Stengers, makers themselves cannot fully explain what is made, even though they "explain themselves through the making process" (Stengers 2010, 295). Drawing on Simondon, Stengers also uses "making" to describe the process of "transduction." (Stengers 2010, 291). Transduction, in Simondon's theory of individuation, describes the process through which entities become individuated in a milieu/setting (Simondon 1992), a process that as Elizabeth Grosz notes is one in which "activity generates itself" and "objects and practices produce themselves" through their relations (Grosz 2012, 43). For both Stengers and Simondon, transduction describes the process through which entities emerge, importantly this is not an emergence *into* a context, environment or milieu that is then changed by them, rather entities emerge *with* their context, into an environment of individuation, what Stengers calls the "causality of coupling" (Stengers 2010, 259). Rather than conflating ideas of ubiquity and ALife with a sense of universality, we situate the practice of making TechnoSphere 2.0 in the environment of SE Asia to unveil the complexities of ALife entities in a particular ubicomp environment. The process of making a design or an app occurs in specific contexts and we note that the concept of ubiquity as a seamless technologically connected or universal, domain is flawed and that at present networks are not ubiquitous.

We position TechnoSphere 2.0 as a feminist technoscience project, a work that challenges critically any distinction or separation of "basic" and "applied" science. Writers on philosophy, science and technology studies (STS), and feminist technoscience studies, have variously argued that there is no pure science, rather it is "entangled in societal interests, and can be held as politically and ethically accountable, as the technological practices and interventions to which it may give rise" (Asberg and Lykke 2010, 299). A feminist approach to technoscience treats the tools of science, such as ALife, as socioculturally embedded and politically and ethically accountable. Historically, the discourses of feminist technoscience demand that we attend to material-discursive configurations (Suchman 2007a; Haraway 1997), building on the feminist science studies of the 1970s and 1980s and the ecofeminisms and cyborg studies of the 1990s (Hird 2009). These feminist technoscience engagements share a commitment to "processes of materialization and the entanglement of discourse and materiality" (Asberg 2010, 302).

The term "interaction" is commonly found in discussions of ALife. In those contexts, interaction assumes that there are separate individual agents, which in our case might be human and ALife creatures, and that separation between entities precedes and accompanies their interaction. Taking a feminist approach to the technoscience of ALife, we use Barad's term "intra-action" to suggest something different, that agency in ALife is a "matter of intra-acting; it is an enactment, not something that someone or something has" (Barad 2007, 178). As we have stated elsewhere, "Intra-action works as a counterpoint to the model of interaction, common within ALife and biological experiments, where it signifies the 'interaction' of separate individual 'bounded' agencies that exist apriori, and precede their interactions. For instance, interaction might signal a bounded human subject who is transformed through chemical interactions or produced through cultural relations. Instead intra-action signifies the materialization of agencies conventionally called 'subjects' and 'objects,' 'bodies' and 'environment' through relational intra-actions. Intra-action assumes that distinct bounded agencies do not precede this relating but that they emerge *through* their intra-actions" (Prophet and Pritchard 2015).

Another part of Barad's agential realism that has influenced our thinking about ubiquitous ALife is her theory that different entities interweave and entangle, in an ongoing process of intra-action, resulting in the production of new entities that in turn, entangle with others. These intra-acting entanglements differ from interacting components commonly described in theories of autopoiesis and autonomy that we will discuss later. Such entanglements are also distinct from a blended mass. "Entanglement does not mean that what are entangled cannot be differentiated, discussed or remedied, only that the different entangled strands cannot be adequately dealt with in isolation, as if they were unrelated to the others" (Hammarström 2012, 43). An intra-active understanding of entanglement also demands that individual strands are not understood as self-subsistent entities and therefore they differ from the separate and bounded agents common to ALife. In summary, entanglement proposes that individual entities are understood as continuously and co-constitutionally refigured in, and through, their mutual interdependence (Hammarström 2012).

The reconfiguring of boundaries in ALife through technological innovation, including ubicomp, stretches beyond modern practices of the twentieth and twenty-first century, and as Isabelle Stengers describes, the story of artifice and life is a "timeless story that transcends modern practices" (Stengers 2010, 207). Indeed, from the selective breeding of tulips, highlighted by the peak of tulip mania in 1637 (Schama 1987), to Vaucanson's defecating Duck of 1738, described by Jessica Riskin (Riskin 2003, 119), to Steve Grand's 1990's "Creatures" where Norns learnt language, ALife has repeatedly reconfigured our practices and caused us to reconsider the boundaries of the living and the artificial. However, despite the openness to engaging with the systems currently being designed (Aicardi 2010), ALife theories have remained bound to ontologies which privilege the opposition of life and artifice, inanimate and animate material, nature and culture. Writers on ALife and complex systems emphasize connection, interaction, and causality between anything that can be defined as a single agent, and in many cases between agents and their environment. As many artificial life researchers (Waldrop 1992; Langton 1999), and more recently literary theorists and philosophers (Hayles 2010; Stengers 2010) have stated,

ALife is a process of making that extends the idea that artifacts are made, bottom-up, through complex relations rather than in a top-down environment (Stengers 2010, 256). We suggest that ubicomp coupled with ALife is another instance of making where human and nonhuman agents intra-act, bottom-up, in complex environments. As we discuss later on in the chapter through the example of TechnoSphere 2.0, the coupling of ALife and ubicomp redefines practices that constitute ubicomp, unveiling previously un-realized potentials of the city. Our focus on making brings recognition to the ways in which ubiquitous-ALife is "bound up with practices" (Gabrys 2014). This shifts the focus from the users and devices to a practice-based approach that recognizes their entanglements. The making of software "stays with the trouble" (Potts and Haraway 2010, 322) of working on a project, from which we are not able to disentangle and that seems to always be in the process of becoming. As the TechnoSphere 2.0 beasties emerge, we cannot predict how they will concretize new relations with GPS, hardware, software, human, and nonhumans in the city of Hong Kong in South East (SE) Asia.

SE Asian Milieu or Setting

Ubiquity has also often been conflated with a sense of universality, as Dourish and Mainwaring note when they link ubicomp to colonial intellectual tradition, "[e]ven the name of the area identifies its universalizing scope" (Dourish and Mainwaring 2012, 133), though such universality has been countered by discussions of embodied experience coupled to specific social and cultural settings in the real environment (Bolter and Gromala 2003, 114–40). Our focus is on designing TechnoSphere 2.0 for a ubicomp that is already here, while acknowledging that this continues to be a shifting structure that is emerging with the technical, urban, and creative milieu of, in our case, Hong Kong. Given that the urban SE Asian location of Hong Kong has influenced our understanding of ubicomp and the way we design, as part of our team develop apps from there, it is perhaps especially important that we remain mindful of what Dourish and Mainwaring term the "third conception of colonialism: as a knowledge enterprise" in which they include ubicomp.

We will address, as far as space allows, the "central conundrum posed by the fact that Weiser's vision of the future is, by this point, not only an old one, but also a very American one" (Bell and Dourish 2007, 133). Our small team is spread from Europe to Australia, with a base in Hong Kong. As Eric Zimmerman has observed, "Games reflect cultural values . . . the internal structures of a game rules—forms of interaction, material forms" (Salen and Zimmerman 2004, 516). The designs for the TechnoSphere 2.0 game apps have been made "in dialogue with the larger cultural values of the community for which the game is designed" (516), and their materialities, emerging simultaneously with the milieu. Our practice-based research in Hong Kong revealed the propensity for socializing to take place outside the home in the city, public spaces like malls and parks being the place that people spend the majority of their non-work time. The practices of walking through public space in Hong Kong, while simultaneously "being online," are the modi operandi of most people, of almost all ages. As we move through Hong Kong by mass transit or on foot, we are streaming media, chatting via mobile text apps, and playing games, and this is one of the most dominant forms of experience in the city. Like Bell and Dourish who write about ubicomp in the SE Asian locations of Singapore and Korea, our location has prompted subtle but important shifts in our thinking about ubicomp and the design of our apps. It has been noted that "[t]he use of mobile phone in public places was particularly found to be impacted by cultural norms and tradition" (Chen et al. 2014, 2), and our focus on location-based experiences has been informed by close observations of how we use smartphones in

Hong Kong, "[u]nlike young people in developed countries who grew up using PCs, Asia's youth have grown up using mobile devices" (McGregor and Chan 2012, 10). China has three times as many mobile subscribers as the United States; 89 percent of these one billion consumers have a mobile device and two-thirds of Chinese mobile subscribers surveyed own a smartphone (ETC 2014, 17). Much research has used a comparative model to compare mobile phone use between North America and SE Asia including Hong Kong (such as Ji et al. 2010, Sia et al. 2009). Often these studies cite the key differences between North American, Australian, or other non-Asian groups and SE Asia groups as individual, knowledge seeking versus data gathering, collective connection and group conformity. These types of comparisons risk Chinese users being positioned as "others," re-inscribing a caricature of Chinese culture. In the design of TechnoSphere 2.0, we have been less interested in using the process to perpetuate a notion of a generalized "Chinese user" and instead we aimed to understand the specific practices of mobile phone use in Hong Kong. Through a nuanced approach to mobile phone use, we hoped to consider what "possibilities for new practices" (Gabrys 2014) it might offer. For example, we believe that mobile device practices in Hong Kong enable the significant extension of mobile leisure and gaming experiences into open and public spaces.

Earlier colonial ubicomp models assumed that what was then the present state of the art in centres of power would be models for the future of ubicomp in other regions. However, leapfrogging technologies—those technologies that accelerate development by skipping over what is currently considered inferior technologies and move directly to more advanced ones, (Brezis et al. 1983, 1216) in this case mobile phones that bypass the need for fixed lines—have disproved this colonial model. Hong Kong's ubicomp infrastructure in 2014 is notably different from that of the U.S. and Europe. Hong Kong's ubicomp infrastructure also differs significantly from the rest of China as Hong Kong's telecommunications industry is totally privately owned and faces no restriction on foreign investment. Unlike the U.S. and Europe, the fixed line technological infrastructure of Hong Kong is one that goes into condensed high rise apartment buildings, connecting large numbers of residents, and results in relatively rapid penetration of services as opposed to the rolling out of cable between single dwellings that are often far apart, which is common in many parts of the U.S. and Europe, and relatively expensive and slower to penetrate as a result. Of more significance is the way that smartphones have been taken up in Hong Kong. With 96 percent of residents using their smartphone to go online every day, Hong Kong has the highest mobile Internet usage rate in the Asia Pacific region. Hong Kong's subway system, the Mass Transit Railway (MTR), carries phone signals and smartphone use is almost universal. Authorities have been forced to use signs and constant audio warnings to passengers urging people to look up from their phones to avoid injury on escalators and Hong Kong is considering removing some seats from metro trains to create more room for commuters to interact with their devices (phys.org 2014).

The density of Hong Kong's population, resulting in crowded living conditions, results in a widespread lack of privacy at home and a concurrent use of air conditioned malls and busy street markets for socializing, doing homework, strolling, and, especially, eating out. This urban behavior is an intrinsic part of Hong Kong's ubicomp environment and the use of public parks in Hong Kong is also different from the United States with widespread use by people of all ages. Elders populate the parks in the early mornings doing tai chi and other exercises, on Sunday's most of Hong Kong's nearly 271,000 foreign domestic workers, almost all women, gather in parks and public places to socialize. Parks are very safe and in summer it is common for people to stroll and jog at night when the heat of the day has reduced. As public spaces in Hong Kong are largely seen as safe places for activity, day and night, a variety of ubicomp games and apps may be enabled. One of our app designs reflects the use of some of Hong Kong's parks as spaces where hundreds of dogs and their owners meet on Sundays and chat and play. In our design for TechnoSphere's "Walk In the Park," people go to the park to exercise their TechnoSphere 2.0 creature, rather than their canine companion, and as they walk through the park so does the creature. A TechnoSphere creature is tethered to its human by GPS and can share the human's fitness data from mobile apps such as MyFitness, which we connect to from the TechnoSphere 2.0 app. Through this linking the human's fitness impacts the activities and ALife of the creature. In addition, designing our "Walk In the Park" app to blend with the practices of humans and nonhuman animals has led us to design for visibility or privacy when walking with a TechnoSphere 2.0 creature (Plate 44). If visibility is selected, then your virtual creature will be visible to other people in the park, who are also using the app. TechnoSphere creatures (and humans) might meet and interact as a result.

It is important to discuss Hong Kong in relation to China, as any ubicomp app designed in this Special Administrative Region of China is likely to cross the border to Mainland China which has an estimated 618 million Internet users. China's Internet use in 2012 was still lower (44.1 percent) than Europe and America. While many regions in China, in contrast to Hong Kong, have restricted broadband infrastructure "the ubiquitous mobile phone and 3G/4G services have significantly altered access to the Internet. Pew Research (2014) reported that approximately 79 percent of China's Internet users now access the Web through a mobile device," (Pew 2014), which suggests that this is a "leapfrogging" ubicomp environment that is developing quickly. However, while many of Asia's youth use their mobile devices, there is a significant group with very different behavior that get online from home. These are known as the "Zhai", China's stay-at-home consumers, equivalent to Japan's Otaku. They "represent a large and growing consumer segment, [. . .] half of Chinese consumers. They prefer to pursue their interests—shopping, social networking, and surfing the Internet— from the comfort of their own homes" (McGregor and Chan 2012). The online activity of the Zhai depends on 90 percent coverage of broadband networks in so-called tier 1 and tier 2 cities. In China, it is estimated that by 2015, wireline broadband subscribers "will be outnumbered by wireless broadband subscribers" (McGregor and Chan 2012).

It is common to think of GPS and movement through urban spaces when designing and discussing ubicomp games, but our design of TechnoSphere 2.0's table top AR app, described in detail later, that allows people to create ALife creatures in their apartments, has been influenced by Zhai users and geared for play in smaller-scale domestic space. If calm technology is about the peripheries of attention (Weiser and Brown, 1997) and a greater sense of choice such as when to, if ever, focus on a game, then a calm ALife creature is one that does not make the attention-seeking demands of that older handheld pet, the Tamogotchi. At the same time many toys are literally in our peripheral vision, visible to us even when not in active play. The TechnoSphere 2.0 table top app can "disappear" but home users have the choice of making their own physical objects that can literally sit in the periphery for use by a TechnoSphere ALife creature that will autonomously live but that is enhanced through intra-action. Hong Kong and China both report significant increases in pet ownership, especially of small animals that are easier to accommodate in high-density living. We approach the TechnoSphere 2.0 creature as another nonhuman companion that traverses the city and resides in small domestic spaces with humans.

Our approach to the design of ubicomp apps is influenced by our local infrastructure, Hong Kong, which has its own particular characteristics. As Dourish and Bell note "an infrastructure is an infrastructure only from the perspective of specific peoples and technologies" (Dourish and Bell 2011, 37). As much research has demonstrated, cultural differences in mobile phone use have been reported in several studies (Ishii and Wu 2006, 97), for example, youth in different countries "differ culturally in their personal relationship patterns, creating different media trends" (Chen et al. 2014, 2) We would also argue that the new relations that these trends form lead to the invention of different ubicomp technics and the unveiling of its other potentials.

Entanglements of Ubiquitous-ALife: from Autopoiesis to Co-Making

TechnoSphere 2.0 can be seen as an example of the emergence of ubiquitous-ALife with the environment of Hong Kong. TechnoSphere 2.0 creatures do not just become through the intra-actions of the "TechnoSphere ALife engine" and the network (as they did in the 1990s version), but they also mutate and are contingent on the form, matter, and energy of urban technical environments. In TechnoSphere 2.0, the city's cellular structures, such as 4G data connections, mobile screens, and AR apps, allow TechnoSphere 2.0 participants to walk with their creature through the urban environment. The AR and MR of these walks demand that participants navigate relationally between physical and simulated spaces and objects. Rather than an ambient or pervasive vision of ubicomp, AR makes us aware of the technological structures, "AR art [. . .] wants to perform a reve(a)ling as part of its enactment. Neither the body nor the media disappear, but instead, they reappear as vectors for the expression and experience of art as both must be present in order to access AR art's invisible visualities" (Gould 2014, 26). The embodied experience of AR depends on physically moving the mobile screen to see objects within the live video image of the user's local physical environment, fed in through the mobile device's camera. As people alter their posture and movement, to better interact with their creature via AR, they configure public spaces differently which in turn configure the ALife creature differently. For example, the creature's need for food, exercise, or play may result in practices that configure different spaces in the city for different uses. Our design has been informed by the well documented practice of domestic workers who gather in their thousands on Sundays in Hong Kong. The workers (who are predominantly women) temporarily take over open (not necessarily public) spaces in significant ways. Subways and walls, designed to channel perpetual movement, become picnic areas as women gather and eat, talk and dance connecting with friends and family. These activities are often organized via mobile devices (Smales and Hsiao-Chun 2011). Open spaces in Hong Kong accommodate people using them in different ways, and are not policed in the ways that public spaces have been for gamers in North America. The TechnoSphere 2.0 design builds on the reappropriation of space that is already taking place in the city; this allows people, especially women, to engage with open spaces in ways we cannot fully predict, though we can be confident that the wider community will be accommodating.

In TechnoSphere 2.0, ALife and ubicomp are always already part of an entangled making that implicates humans and nonhumans. Like many working in the discipline of artificial life, modelling biological organisms and other systems using computing, both 1990s TechnoSphere and TechnoSphere 2.0 have been influenced by the work of Humberto Maturana and Francisco Varela who have written widely about the autonomy of biological systems. Their work, in particular their theory of autopoiesis, which preceded their writing on artificial life, has had significant impact on a wide range of disciplines that in turn influence current ubicomp thinking and practices. Autopoiesis describes the self-producing nature of bounded metabolic activity and one of their criteria for autopoiesis is that the system has an identifiable boundary. For Varela, autonomous systems that are also autopoietic, typically living systems, depend on those systems having organizational closure, "a topological boundary, and the processes that define them occur in a physical-like space, actual or simulated in a computer" (Varela 1981, 15). Varela goes on to argue that many systems that others have described as autopoietic are, instead, autonomous because they do not have topological boundaries, using as examples insect societies, human systems like institutions and animal societies. In each case, he notes that the unity's boundaries are not topological and/or that the interactions within these "wrongly categorized" autopoietic systems are not about the production of components, concluding "that these proposals are category mistakes: they confuse autopoiesis with autonomy. Instead, I suggest taking the lessons offered by the autonomy of living systems and convert them into an operational characterization of autonomy in general, living and otherwise. Autonomous systems, then, are mechanistic (dynamic) systems defined by their organization" (Varela 1981, 15). While drawing this important distinction between autopoiesis and autonomy, Varela nevertheless reaffirms the importance of organizational closure, stating once again "[w]hat is common to all autonomous systems is that they are organizationally closed" (Varela 1981, 15). Varela's perspective on autonomy has been criticized for this emphasis on closure and the secondary role that system-environment interactions play in his definition and constitution of autonomous systems. Artificial life researchers such as Barandiaran suggest "[i]ntroducing ideas from complexity theory and thermodynamics [. . .] [and a] more specific notion of autonomy as a recursively self-maintaining far-from-equilibrium and thermodynamically open system. The interactive side of autonomy is essential in the definition: Autonomous systems must interact continuously to assure the necessary flow of matter and energy for their self-maintenance" (Barandiaran 2004, 515). Specific concerns about the acceptance of organizational closure implied by a wider adoption of autopoiesis, outside of the biological sciences, have been raised by researchers from a wide range of disciplines (Hayles 2010, 174; Parisi 2013; Stengers 2010, 447). Therefore rather than use the term "autopoietic" to describe the TechnoSphere 2.0 ALife project, we use the term "autonomous" meaning that the process is not organizationally closed but is dynamic, including human agents, autonomous ALife and inhuman networks of data in keeping with its ubicomp entanglements. In TechnoSphere 2.0, the creature's ALife boundary is extended beyond the ALife software running on the app, to include feedback from the location of the mobile device running the app, such as GPS locations, walking routes, and movements. In this example of causal coupling, creatures behave and evolve *with* human practices in a partially bounded, autonomous system.

In TechnoSphere 2.0, the entanglement of humans, mobile phone networks, ALife creatures, and practice becomes apparent, for example, when eating at a restaurant. "Nothing in Hong Kong is more satisfying than flooding friends with photos of our food" (Chen 2012)—the practices of taking photographs of food are popular in Hong Kong and are part of a growing global trend that has prompted camera manufacturers like Nikon, Olympus, Sony, and Fuji to develop cameras with a "food" mode setting. When TechnoSphere 2.0 practices activate creatures during dinner, creatures appear on the dinner table visible through AR. Human users can feed their creatures by accessing data from the restaurant's menu, sharing an affective experience with them. Human users are probably eating dinner, listening to music, and watching other screens as well as the artificial creature that they can see on their real table top via AR, making intra-acting with TechnoSphere 2.0 an entangled or "polyaesthetic" experience. To engage with these creatures and their environment, humans need to use "multiple senses, and not only the senses of sight, hearing, and touch but proprioception as well" (Engberg and Bolter 2014, 6). Human participants, looking at the screen and maneuvering physical objects on the table top AR, or navigating as they walk Hong Kong's streets while watching their creature run alongside in AR, need to, as Jay Bolter and Maria Engberg say, "occupy two locations at once" (Ibid). Locations in which different potentialities are enabled through their relational couplings.

Ubiquitous Couplings

In TechnoSphere 2.0, public places, technical structures and ALife become configured relationally through a process of entanglement. Designing for ubiquitous-ALife as entangled is very different to a design of "interaction" as it engages with emergence through difference rather than opposition. As Lucy Suchman outlines, since Donna Haraway's eruption with the cyborg manifesto, feminist scholars have embraced "the inseparability of subjects and objects, 'natural' bodies and 'artificial' augmentations" (Suchman 2007b, 140). Coupled with this has been a focus on the importance of the emergent milieu or what we might call the mattering processes (Kavka 2008; cited in Blackman 2012, 173). Classical models of causality might describe the new configurations of public places, ubicomp and ALife as a series of linear deterministic relations, whereby objects designed and "used" by humans simply "do their thing" (Barad 2007, 130). However, the ontological commitments of Karen Barad, Isabelle Stengers, and Gilbert Simondon suggest that ALife allows us to see alternate forms of causality and individuation within ubicomp which are neither linear nor circular, but transductive, coupled, and entangled. This coupling takes place through the process of intra-action, the mutual constitution of entangled agencies (Barad 2007, 33). That is in contrast to the commonly held model of interaction which assumes that there are separate individual agencies that precede their interaction. We suggest that the ontology of entities emerges through what Stengers might term their relational couplings, including couplings with practices and apparatuses of production as exemplified by Barad. Barad's elaboration on the complexity of emergence is not dissimilar to Simondon's conception of individuation.

To expand a little on how these theories differ from the aforementioned autopoietic theory, in autopoiesis a unity is a network of discrete components that continuously regenerate the network devoid from any milieu. Here the operation of regeneration is distinct "from any relationship to a milieu, for there is no "milieu" (Stengers 2010, 259). Autopoietic theory is based on an analysis of ways that "living systems address and engage with the domains in which they operate" implying that that there is an easily determined boundary between living system and domain. This differs from the theories of Simondon, Stengers, and Barad, where the context emerges simultaneously with the individuation of the entity. Ideas of a "unity" and a "domain" in Varela's autopoietic theory might, at first glance, suggest that autopoiesis is not open, nor radically open, as previously discussed. As Whitaker has noted, this demonstrates "the difference between the open/closed dichotomy as it is employed in first-order cybernetics versus autopoietic theory" (Whitaker 1997, 6). However, writing about autopoiesis, Varela's mentor Maturana addresses his own use of the term "closure" and ties its use to the system's organization, he then emphasizes that, structurally, autopoietic systems "operate as materially and energetically open systems (in continuous material and energetic interchange with their medium)" (Maturana, "Autopoiesis: Reproduction, Heredity, and Evolution," 1980, 54). In contrast to Varela and Maturana's theories of interchange and regeneration with a medium, Simondon, Barad, and Stengers emphasize processes in which there is continual change and becoming for both entity and milieu. Diffractively viewed, Barad, Stengers, and Simondon's philosophy of ubiquitous-ALife does not exist in a continuous stable form but instead emerges into an already constituted field that alters both itself and other active elements in the field (Venn 2010, 139 cited in Blackman 2012, 173) albeit that for Barad the constituted field is itself always in a process of intra-actions. The important point is the recognition that the "milieu or setting operates as the technical actualizations of a potentiality" (Blackman 2012) within ubiquitous-ALife.

Conclusion

TechnoSphere 2.0 is constantly emerging as humans move around the city of Hong Kong with their mobile devices shadowed by any TechnoSphere 2.0 creature that lives on their device. Couplings of ALife and ubicomp become part of an entangled making between humans and nonhumans that extend the idea that artifacts are made through complex relations rather than in a top-down environment. TechnoSphere 2.0 is one example of what Stengers calls the new practical relationship between artifact and its maker. This is a relationship of making, of transduction, in which creativity and invention are unhinged from "humans." The making process is no longer "the logic of an inventor or a creator, but the logic of the invention of processes, objects and practices that produce themselves." A process of making enabled by the milieu that "generates the creative leap from the past and present of the pre-individual to the unknown future" (Grosz 2012, 43). The couplings of ALife and ubicomp in TechnoSphere 2.0 allow its participants to partially "see" an emergence in which they are entangled. As this ubicomp concretizes, adopting a particular structure, it "brings about the emergence of both individual and milieu" (Simondon 1992, 301). When TechnoSphere 2.0 becomes more widely available and we undertake playtests, one series of questions that we will ask is, not the "age old" question of how to prepare the conditions for artificial creatures to "await breath" (Stengers 2010, 207) but instead *what* do these new relational couplings enable?

References

Aicardi, Christine. 2010. "Harnessing Non-Modernity: A Case Study in Artificial Life." Thesis (Ph.D.), University College London (University of London).

Asberg, Cecilia, and Nina Lykke. 2010. "Feminist Technoscience Studies." *European Journal of Women's Studies* 4 (17): 299–305.

Barad, Karen. 2007. *Meeting the Universe Halfway: Quantum Physics and the Entanglement of Matter and Meaning.* Durham, NC: Duke University Press Books.

Barandiaran, Xabier. 2004. "Behavioral Adaptive Autonomy. A Milestone in the Alife Route to AI." *Proceedings of the 9th International Conference on Artificial Life*, 514–521. Cambridge, MA: MIT Press.

Bell, Genevieve, and Paul Dourish. 2007. "Yesterday's Tomorrows: Notes on Ubiquitous Computing's Dominant Vision." *Personal and Ubiquitous Computing* 11 (2): 133–143.

Blackman, Lisa. 2012. *Immaterial Bodies: Affect, Embodiment, Mediation.* Los Angeles, CA: Sage.

Bolter, J. David, and Diane Gromala. 2003. *Windows and Mirrors: Interaction Design, Digital Art, and the Myth of Transparency.* Cambridge, MA: MIT Press.

Brezis, Elise S., Paul R. Krugman, and Daniel Tsiddon. 1993. "Leapfrogging in International Competition: A Theory of Cycles in National Technological Leadership." *The American Economic Review* 83 (5): 1211–1219.

Chen, Yi-Ning, Ven-Hwei Lo, Ran Wei, Xiaoge Xu, and Guoliang Zhang. 2014. "A Comparative Study of the Relationship between Mobile Phone Use and Social Capital among College Students in Shanghai and Taipei." *International Journal of Journalism and Mass Communication* 105 (1).

Chen, John. 2012. *How to Be a Hong Kong Local: 10 tips on Faking It.* April 3. http://travel.cnn.com/hong-kong/life/how-be-local-10-tips-faking-it-316802

Dourish, Paul, and Scott Mainwaring. 2012. "Ubicomp's Colonial Impulse." *Proceedings of the 2012 ACM Conference on Ubiquitous Computing*, 133–142. New York: ACM.

Dourish, Paul, and Genevieve Bell. 2011. *Divining a Digital Future: Mess and Mythology in Ubiquitous Computing.* Cambridge, MA: MIT Press.

Ekman, Ulrik. 2011. "Editorial: Interaction Designs for Ubicomp Cultures." *Fibreculture* (19): 1–25.

Engberg, Maria, and Jay David Bolter. 2014. "Cultural Expression in Augmented and Mixed Reality." *Convergence: The International Journal of Research into New Media Technologies* 20 (1): 3–9.

ETC. 2014. "ETC Country Reports: China." European Travel Commision Portal. www.etc-digital.org.

Gould, Amanda Starling. 2014. "Invisible Visualities: Augmented Reality Art and the Contemporary Media Ecology." *Convergence: The International Journal of Research into New Media Technologies* 20 (1): 25–32.

Gabrys, Jennifer. 2014. "A Cosmopolitics of Energy: Diverging Materialities and Hesitating Practices." *Environment and Planning A* 46 (9): 2095–2109.

Grosz, Elizabeth. 2012. "Identity and Individuation." In *Gilbert Simondon: Being and Technology*, edited by Arne De Boever, 37–56. Edinburgh, UK: Edinburgh University Press.

Hammarström, Matz. 2012. "(Mis)understanding Intra-active Entanglement–Comments on René Rosfort's Criticism of Karen Barad's Agential Realism." *Kvinder, Køn og Forskning* 21 (4): 39–46.

Haraway, Donna Jeanne. 1997. *Modest_Witness@Second_Millennium.Femaleman(c)_Meets_Oncomouse: Feminism and Technoscience.* New York: Routledge.

Hayles, N. Katherine. 2010. *My Mother Was a Computer: Digital Subjects and Literary Texts.* Chicago, IL: University of Chicago Press.

Hird, Myra. 2009. "Feminist Engagements with Matter." *Feminist Times* 35 (2): 329–346.

Ishii, Kenichi, and Chyi-In Wu. 2006. "A Comparative Study of Media Cultures among Taiwanese and Japanese Youth." *Telematics and Informatics* 23 (2): 95–116.

Ji, Yong Gu, Hwan Hwangbo, Ji Soo Yi, PL Patrick Rau, Xiaowen Fang, and Chen Ling. 2010. "The Influence of Cultural Differences on the Use of Social Network Services and the Formation of Social Capital." *Intl. Journal of Human–Computer Interaction* 26 (11–12): 1100–1121.

Kavka, Misha. 2008. *Reality Television, Affect and Intimacy: Reality Matters.* London: Palgrave Macmillan.

Langton, Christopher G. 1999. "Artifical Life." In *Ars Electronica: Facing the Future*, edited by Timothy Druckrey, 261–268. Cambridge and London: MIT Press.

McGonigal, Jane. 2007. "Ubiquitous Gaming." In *Space Time Play: Computer Games, Architecture and Urbanism: The Next Level*, Eds., Friedrich von Borries, Steffen P. Walz, Matthias Bottger, Drew Davidson, Heather Kelley, and Julian Kücklich, 233–237. Basel, Germany: Birkhauser.

McGregor, David and Peter Chan. 2012. *Spotlight on China: Building a Roadmap for Success in Media and Entertainment.* Ernst and Young.

Maturana, Humberto R. 1980. *Autopoiesis and Cognition: The Realization of the Living.* Berlin: Springer.

Maturana, Humberto R. 1980. "Autopoiesis: Reproduction, Heredity and Evolution." In *Autopoiesis. Dissipative Structures and Spontaneous Social Orders*, edited by Milan Zeleny, 45–79. Boulder, CO: Westview Press.

Parisi, Luciana. 2013. *Contagious Architecture: Computation, Aesthetics, and Space, Kindle Edition.* Cambridge, MA: MIT Press.

Pew. 2014. http://pewinternet.org/fact-sheets/mobile-technology-fact-sheet/ (accessed June 1, 2014).

phys.org. 2014. *Hong Kong Metro Seats May Be Scrapped for Smartphone Space.* http://phys.org/news/2014–02-hong-kong-metro-seats-scrapped.html (accessed June 1, 2014).

Potts, Annie, and Donna Haraway. 2010. "Kiwi Chicken Advocate Talks with Californian Dog Companion." *Feminism & Psychology* 20 (3): 318–336.

Prophet, Jane. 1996. "Sublime Ecologies and Artistic Endeavors: Artificial Life and Interactivity in the Online Project." *Leonardo* 29 (5): 339–344.

Prophet, Jane. 2002. *Technosphere.* http://web.archive.org/web/20020625224810/www.heritageinterpretation. org.uk/journals/j2a-tech.html (accessed January 6, 2014).

Prophet, Jane. 2001. "TechnoSphere: 'Real' Time, 'Artificial' Life." *Leonardo* 34 (4): 309–312.

Prophet, Jane, and Helen Pritchard. 2015. "Performative Apparatus and Diffractive Practices: An Account of Artificial Life Art." In *Artificial Life,* (21) 3 Cambridge, MA: MIT Press.

Riskin, Jessica. 2003. "Eighteenth-Century Wetware." *Representations* 8: 97–125.

Salen, Katie, and Eric Zimmerman. 2004. *Rules of Play: Game Design Fundamentals.* Cambridge, MA: MIT Press.

Schama, Simon. 1987. *The Embarrassment of Riches: An Interpretation of Dutch Culture in the Golden Age.* New York: Alfred Knopf.

Sia, Choon Ling, Kai H. Lim, Kwok Leung, Matthew KO Lee, Wayne Wei Huang, and Izak Benbasat. 2009. "Web Strategies to Promote Internet Shopping: Is Cultural-Customization Needed?" *Management Information Systems Quarterly* 33 (3): 491–512.

Simondon, Gilbert S. 1958. *On the Mode of Existence of Technical Objects.* Translated from the French by Ninian Mellamphy. Paris: Aubier. Accessible at https://english.duke.edu/uploads/assets/Simondon_MEOT_part_1.pdf, Accessed September 06, 2015.

Simondon, Gilbert. 1992. "The Genesis of the Individual." In *Incorporations*, edited by Jonathan Crary and Sanford Kwinter, 296–319. New York: Zone.

Smales, Philippa, and Hsia Hsiao-Chun. 2011. "The Power to Organise and Engage: The Use of ICTs by Women Migrant Domestic Workers." Research Program Report, 2011.

Stengers, Isabelle. 2010. *Cosmopolitics II.* Minneapolis, MN: University of Minnesota Press.

Suchman, Lucy. 2005. "Agencies in Technology Design: Feminist Reconfigurations." http://lancaster.ac.uk/sociology/research/publications/papers/suchman-agenciestechnodesign.pdf.

Suchman, Lucy. 2007a. "Feminist STS and the Sciences of the Artificial." In *New Handbook of Science and Technology Studies*, edited by Edward J. Hackett, Olga Amsterdamska, Michael E. Lynch, and Judy Hackett Wajcman, 139. Cambridge, MA: MIT Press.

Suchman, Lucy. 2007b. *Human-Machine Reconfigurations: Plans and Situated Actions.* Cambridge, UK: Cambridge University Press.

Varela, Francisco J. 1981. "Autonomy and Autopoiesis." In *Self-Organizing Systems: An Interdisciplinary Approach*, edited by G. Roth and H. Schwegler, 14–24. Frankfurt, Germany: Campus Verlag.

Venn, Couze. 2010. "Individuation, Relationality, Affect: Rethinking the Human in Relation to the Living." *Body & Society* 16 (1): 129–161.

Waldrop, M. Mitchell. 1992. *Complexity: The Emerging Science at the Edge of Order and Chaos.* New York: Simon & Schuster.

Weiser, Mark, and John Seely Brown. 1997. "The Coming Age of Calm Technolgy." In *Beyond Calculation*, edited by J. Denning Peter and M. Metcalfe Robert, 75–85. Berlin: Springer.

Whitaker, Randall. 1997. "Exploring and Employing Autopoietic Theory: Issues and Tips." Paper presented for the opening plenary session in Biology, Cognition, Language, and Society: An international symposium on autopoiesis. Belo Horizonte (Brazil), November 18, 1997.

INTERACTION DESIGN

Maria Engberg

The notion of situating is central to interaction design. Interaction design is, as Jonas Löwgren notes, "about shaping digital things for people's use" (Löwgren 2014). In order to accomplish that task, one must understand "design as a process of creating new design practices that have a family resemblance (in Wittgenstein's sense) to the daily practices of both users and designers" (Löwgren and Stolterman 2004, 152). In the Scandinavian context, the notion of situating in interaction design really came to the fore with the emergence of participatory design in the 1970s and 1980s. Participatory design practices, as Pelle Ehn and others articulated them at the time, involved truly understanding "that every new design practice is a uniquely situated design experience" (Löwgren and Stolterman 2004, 152). The process of situating in these fields often involves employing ethnographic methods for gathering the information that is relevant for the design process as a whole. Field studies, as methodological tool, further point toward the importance of the site and of situating. Situating in participatory design, or in fields such as contextual design (Beyer and Holzblatt 1998) involves at first acknowledging that "those affected by a design should have a say in the design process" (Björgvinsson et al. 2012, 103). In a recent paper, Pelle Ehn together with collaborators at Malmö University revisited the history of participatory design, arguing that "a fundamental challenge for designers and the design community is to move from designing 'things' (objects) to designing Things (socio-material assemblies)" (Björgvinsson et al. 2012, 102). The move toward "socio-material assemblies" (echoing Latour) suggests that the shaping that Löwgren argued is central to interaction design can be understood as part of what Latour would call assembling the social (Latour 2005). This process must happen without predetermining what is and what is not social, what is and what is not a proper interaction, what is and what is not a suitable design.

Situating, site, assembling, and designing: these terms all indicate the importance of context, place, and user-engagement for the design process. In the related field of Human-Computer Interaction (as Bolter explains in "Interaction Design" in Part I of this volume), situatedness (for instance as explored and articulated by researchers such as Lucy Suchman in her seminal 1987 work *Plans and Situated Actions: The Problem of Human-Machine Communication*) became the nexus for realizing that human actions and interactions (with others and with objects) form part of our cognition. The action of situating and understanding situatedness require, too, an understanding of embodiment, as Paul Dourish articulated it in relation to human-computer interaction and interaction design (Dourish 2004; Dourish and Bell 2011).

The essays in this section rarely address the fields of interaction design or the act of situating explicitly. And yet, the insistence on understanding media from specific contexts involving social, cultural, and material complexities is clear. Ellis and Goggin address in their chapter the phenomenon of locative media in relation to disability. Locative media is "all about" situating the device and the user in relation to (a) place. Ellis and Goggin show how that process of situating is not neutral and involves complex understanding and decisions regarding that place and what kinds of lived experiences are allowed or foregrounded. Disability, then, can be understood as a "kind of cultural location." The situating of disability and the individual it concerns, is historically, culturally contingent as well as place-specific. In that regard, any media experiences, such as a locative media application, would involve a process of design. It follows from Ellis and Goggin's arguments that a designed interaction should take into consideration the complexity of a disability and its contingent contexts. Such a consideration exposes the normativity implicitly built into otherwise carefully designed user cases. Designing and situating interaction design within "Things" (in Björgvinsson et al.'s sense) as socio-material assemblies suggests a different construction of the social in which the particular design emerges and will live. A social that includes reflecting on the complex contingency of what the "natural" movements of interacting with, say, Google Glass, might actually mean.

Offenhuber and Telhan's chapter take us into situating of a different order. They take on disciplinary moves and acts of situating, in order to better address the meaning-making in contemporary visualizations. Inserting the Peircean semiotic indexical sign into the analysis of visualizations in computational designs allows Offenhuber and Telhan to elaborate on the trace. In addition to the symbolic and the iconic relationships between visuals and their intended meaning, there is the indexical sign that is visible through a trace caused by the phenomenon it seeks to represent. Offenhuber and Telhan's contribution to this volume thereby offers a complication of situatedness and the act of situating that occur in media once the phenomenon itself is no longer there. The index in visualizations, then, signals a presence that has moved beyond our vision, leaving a trace that suggests that the ability to situate is fleeting. Offenhuber and Telhan articulate the importance of semiotics in understanding how an object is framed and play into a particular context, leading them to suggest that the appearance of indexical signs will increase as our capability to design at, for example, the molecular level becomes more important. Their contribution points to current challenges that complex digital systems, beyond consumer grade digital devices, present to our systems of signs and semiosis. Offenhuber and Telhan remind us of areas that are not as frequently debated in interaction design, fields of hitherto highly specialized design processes.

The essays in this section, and others throughout the book, emphasize the centrality of site and situatedness for much of the current thinking about digital media and environments. Unlike the rhetoric of cyberspace in the 1990s—a connected but separate world to our own—the importance of context is clear and its complexities are taken into account as we articulate the impact of ubiquitous computing today. The lessons regarding co-production, collaboration, and participation from fields within interaction design and Human-Computer Interaction serve us well as the process of situating the phenomenon of ubiquitous computing in our contemporary cultural moment continues. On the other hand, the contributions by Ellis and Goggin, Offenhuber and Telhan also point towards weaknesses or moments of reductionism in current conceptual theories about design. Ulrik Ekman has noted that there exists an "undecidability," a gap between the actual developments in ubiquitous computing and the visions and concepts about it (Ekman 2011, 1). Whether such moments of unclarity or reductive models come from an overreliance on earlier concepts of understanding (visual) media, on differences between disciplinary concerns, or from models that have other goals than reflective ones, the essays show that the concepts of complexity and ubiquity need to be addressed so that heterogeneity and incompatibility also have a place in the discussion.

References

Beyer, Hugh, and Karen Holzblatt. 1998. *Contextual Design: Defining Customer-Centered Systems*. New York: Morgan Kaufmann.

Björgvinsson, Erling, Pelle Ehn, and Per Anders Hillgren. 2012. "Design Things and Design Thinking: Contemporary Participatory Design Challenges." *DesignIssues* 28.3 (Summer): 101–116.

Dourish, Paul. 2004. *Where the Action Is: The Foundations of Embodied Interaction*. Cambridge, MA: MIT Press.

Dourish, Paul, and Genevieve Bell. 2011. *Divining a Digital Future: Mess and Mythology in Ubiquitous Computing*. Cambridge, MA: MIT Press.

Ekman, Ulrik. 2011. "Ubiquity Editorial—Interaction Designs for Ubicomp Cultures." *The Fibreculture Journal* 19: 1–30. Accessed April 12, 2015. http://fibreculturejournal.org/wp-content/pdfs/FCJ-129Ulrik%20Ekman.pdf

Latour, Bruno. 2005. *Reassembling the Social: An Introduction to Actor-Network-Theory*. Oxford: Oxford University Press.

Löwgren, Jonas. 2014. "Interaction Design—Brief Intro." In *The Encyclopedia of Human-Computer Interaction*, 2nd edition, edited by Mads Soegaard and Rikke Dam. Aarhus: The Interaction Design Foundation. Available online at https://interaction-design.org/encyclopedia/interaction_design.html

Löwgren, Jonas, and Erik Stolterman. 2004. *Thoughtful Interaction Design: A Design Perspective on Information Technology*. Cambridge, MA: MIT Press.

Suchman, Lucy. 1987. *Plans and Situated Actions: The Problem of Human-Machine Communication*. Cambridge: Cambridge University Press.

DISABILITY, LOCATIVE MEDIA, AND COMPLEX UBIQUITY

Katie Ellis and Gerard Goggin

Disability is thus not just a health problem. It is a complex phenomenon, reflecting the interaction between features of a person's body and features of the society in which he or she lives.—World Health Organization (WHO)[1]

Google Glass has the potential to radically impact the lives of people with disabilities. Will you partner with us in making Google Glass more accessible? —Indiegogo crowdfunding platform campaign[2]

Introduction

As this volume outlines, the current phase of network societies has generated an intensification of pervasive, ubiquitous digital technologies and cultures of uses, with emergent, complex social functions, and politics. In this chapter, we explore a fascinating, instructive example of the actualization of such ubiquity-effects—the case of locative media technologies designed for and by people with disabilities.

With its roots in a range of developments in global positioning satellites, cellular mobile networks, ubiquitous computing, and place-making, locative media are important to the widespread diffusion of digital technology that rely upon location data. Mostly overlooked in the public discussion and scholarly research on locative media such as Foursquare, Facebook Places, apps, and so on, are the many locative media technologies designed for or used by different groups of users with disabilities. These technologies are often acclaimed for their potential to address the needs of people with disabilities, but there is little informed discussion, public debate, or critical analysis and research on their actual characteristics, potential, and implication. Notable here are the various mapping and way-finding applications taken up by blind users to meet a long-standing need for reliable, independent ways to navigate unfamiliar environments. Such locative media are following in the wake of previous online and mobile technologies, including first-generation cell phones, to construct a ubiquitous environment for disabled users, wishing, in the face of various prosaic and other events in their everyday lives, to situate themselves in relation to place. More recently, wearable-computing devices such as Google Glass have been explicitly designed, marketed, and promoted as a boon for those with impairments. Disability has also been a feature of the promotional discourses associated with the latest stage of autonomous vehicles—another area where Google is developing a well-publicized product in the form of its Google Driverless car.

So, we think there are important dimensions and dynamics of complex ubiquity effects that are structured around, and by, notions, power relations, and lived experiences associated with impairment and disability. As such, the first part of this chapter discusses the joining of two kinds of complexity at play in these ubiquity-effects centering on disability-inflected locative media. First, there is the complexity of the cultural shaping of the technology, and its materiality. Disability itself has been proposed as a kind of cultural location, the specificity and dynamics of which we need to understand (Snyder and Mitchell 2006). Second, there is the complexity of disability, as it is constituted in contemporary society. In its individuation, especially, disability is never just one isolated category, but always co-dependent on a diverse range of other instantiations of class, gender, race, ethnicity, locality, as well as historical and cultural specificity. In the meeting of the complexities of disability and locative media technology, we find an especially apposite, challenging example of the situation of ubiquity—what social practices emerge from it, what their cultural implications are, and how design makes sense of this. In the second part of the chapter, we discuss how these dynamics of complex ubiquity play in relation to disability through two case studies: way-finding locative media smartphones and apps, and Google Glass.

Assemblages of Locative Media

Locative media are an emergent, hybrid form of media (Farman 2012; de Souza e Silva and Firth 2012; Wilken and Goggin 2014). First and foremost, locative media are characterized by a range of technologies that gather information about a device, application, or user's location, and then process this in new ways (Gordon and de Souza e Silva 2011; Wilken 2014). An early such technology, developed initially for military purposes, Global Positioning Technologies used satellites to pinpoint the location of a device. These GPS devices are now widely dispersed across a range of technologies and applications: transportation, including planes; cars (satellite navigation, or satnavs); handheld or portable devices for wayfinding and navigation while walking, using a wheelchair, piloting a scooter, or riding a bike; mobile phones and tablet computers. GPS now qualifies, in many societies and wealthier groups in poorer societies, as a near ubiquitous technology that many of us now take for granted.

We have already alluded to a second major instance of locative media: the mobile phone. Rich Ling has developed a full and persuasive argument for the status of the mobile phone as a "social fact" (Émile Durkheim), a technology that, like the clock and car, is essential for belonging and participation in many societies (Ling 2012; Goggin 2006; Caron and Caronia 2007; Höflich et al. 2012). With the communicative mobility of the mobile phone, the social and cultural innovation and use that have shaped it, and its sheer, massive diffusion (according to the International Telecommunications Union beyond seven billion subscriptions in 2014, and counting), have not only meant that this technology is among the most pervasive. Rather, and significantly, with the advent of the mobile phone came a new emphasis on place and location. Because of its portability, at least from the 1980s onwards, when the mobile phone was available in lighter, less bulky designs, the handset could be used for communication in novel places; but, also, a key theme of this new mobile communication was actually about the place and location of the user and their proximate context, and environment (Wilken and Goggin 2012). Hence users specialized in phatic communication ("Where are you? I'm here. I've arrived"). With camera phones especially, not to mention text messaging, users commented upon, represented, and conveyed their places of mobile presence to absent and co-present others. A new phase of such place referencing and locational predication and conjuring was entered into once mobiles had the capability to triangulate themselves using their positioning via the cellular network transmitters, switches, and nodes. Add to this, the incorporation of GPS in mobile devices, and fully-fledged locative media was available for its domestication and reinvention in the defiles of everyday life (Richardson 2005 and 2007). At this point, roughly circa 2005–2008, we would argue that such locative, mobile media were increasingly ubiquitous (though still far from common among many users groups, cultural settings, and societies). Moreover, this incarnation of locative media was constituted by particular kinds of complexity, not previously encountered, whether in: earlier phases of media; precursors in telephony, telecommunications, and mobile communication; or the evolution of ubiquitous computing (ubicomp) (Ekman 2013; Dourish and Bell 2011; Galloway 2004; Weiser 1993) or pervasive computing. We'll return to this point, and chart the more recent dynamics of complexity in newer forms of locative media. Assemblage is a vogue term in current cultural and media theory (De Landa 2006; Goggin 2009; Acuto and Curtis 2013), but it really fits as a shorthand description of the socio-complexity of locative media (Wilken and Goggin 2014). For the present, we'd like to introduce the thought that at this smartphone stage of locative media, something else becomes a zone for much more intense visibility, design, and engagement: disability. As disability remains a murky topic generally, including in discussions of digital technology, culture, and media, let us briefly discuss and specify our argument about how the complexity of disability plays into the field of complex ubiquity effects.

The Politics of Complex Disability Effects

Thus far, we have outlined the emergence of locative media, and commenced an argument concerning its complexity. When disability meets locative media, it is important to formally note that we are encountering two major, distinct set of complexity dynamics—which of course, in actuality, are entwined. What are these two sets of complexity dynamics?

For much of the twentieth century, dominant ideas of disability were based on the medical and charity models—seeing disability as something that involved a bodily, mental, or sensory defect, or handicap, that made an individual an "invalid" (as it was once termed). As Colin Barnes notes:

> until very recently disability was viewed almost exclusively as an individual medical problem or personal tragedy in western culture. Yet there is a wealth of anthropological and sociological evidence to suggest that societal responses to people with impairments or long- term health conditions vary considerably across time, culture and location.
>
> (Barnes 2012)

The negative, "deficit" approach to disability was progressively challenged, in different ways, from the 1960s onwards. Most notably, such disablism was challenged by the "social media" of disability proposed by British scholars and activists (Oliver 2012; Shakespeare 2006), which has proven sufficiently influential to become something of an orthodoxy in recent WHO policy, and in the 2006 United Nations Convention on the Rights of Persons with Disability (Barnes 2012; Arnardóttir and Quinn 2009).[3]

For social model theorists, disability is constituted by the social and political arrangements that are applied to, and condition the lives of, people with impairments. An impairment—

vision impairment, hearing impairment, intellectual disability, deafness, chronic conditions, bodily or genetic difference from the "norm" (Davis 1995; Garland-Thomson 1996; Hamraie 2012)—does not necessarily result in a person being unable to participate in society, or to need "special treatment" or segregation and exclusion. Rather, societies and their environment often needlessly disable their members, by creating barriers to access, or not removing or modifying them, as well as relying upon narrow notions of ability (Campbell 2009). This occurs in technology and its systems, as much as other kinds of environments (Roulstone 1998; Goggin and Newell 2003; Ellis and Kent 2011). For instance, a smartphone or tablet computer can be used by a wide range of people with disabilities, if the device, interface, applications, and so on, are designed in an appropriate way. Indeed the smartphone and tablet computer, especially Apple's iPhone and iPad, are often credited with bringing about a "revolution" in accessible technology and social participation for people with disabilities (McNaughton and Light 2013; Gosnell et al. 2011).

A range of scholars, commentators, and activists have noted that the existing accounts of disability—the available, still hegemonic discourses as well as new discourses based on social approaches, cultural accounts, and human rights—fall well short of grasping the peculiar, constitutive complexity of disability. Much research on disability starts from the acknowledgement of the complexity of disability and impairment. However, disability theory is in a cul-de-sac when it comes to a breakthrough in specifying the contribution that disability, in particular, makes to the complexity of social life and cultural experience generally. There are various theories that seek to provide insights into the constitutive interaction of disability with gender, race, class, ethnicity, sexuality, socio-demographics, and other categories. In sociology, one of the best-known of these is intersectionality. However, there is little work available that brings together in dialogue general theories concerning complexity (Byrne 1988; Mason 2008),[4] and theories of disability (van Houten 2001; Almeida et al. 2010; Heylighen and Strickfaden 2012; Soldatic 2013).[5]

This is not the place for an extended discussion of this topic; however we do wish to emphasize the notion that disabilities have their own complexities that are woven into the complex ubiquity effects this volume seeks to elucidate. In addition, the complex ubiquity environment, with its intensive technological systems, now plays a formative role in the contemporary experience and shaping of disability and its social relations. An obstacle to discussions here is the relative lack of attention given to disability in critical literatures on technology, especially science and technology studies (STS), something that is slowly being remedied—although there remains little research as yet on disability and ubiquitous computing, media, and digital technologies (Seelman 2000; Moser 2006; Annable et al. 2007; Galis 2011; Blume 2012). In any case, let us now turn to a discussion of early locative media to concretely establish the dynamics concerning disability and ubiquity we see at play.

Disability and Early Locative Media

For many disabled users, the advent of the mobile phone offered an important new tool to tackle many of the issues of daily life centering on communication. Because of its portability, an important attribute of the mobile phone was its ability to provide new ways to address, negotiate, construct, and conjure with location. A 2000 study noted that for one of their research subjects, "the matter of safety was a real, everyday issue because of a physical disability" (Palen et al. 2000). Other studies noted the use and potential of mobile phones for independent navigation and wayfinding (Abascal and Civit 2000; Shaun et al. 2009). As well as so-called "extrinsic" or instrumental motivations for using mobile phones, there is good reason—if limited research—to suggest that, like young people, or older people (Conci et al. 2009), or indeed a range of socio-demographic categories, people with disabilities (which, of course, include all generations) adopted mobile phones for "intrinsic" motivations, including consumption, lifestyle, social rituals, cultural participation, gaining information and media, and so on (Goggins 2006).

Before mobile phones had location technology capability, other technologies, such as sensors, were available and used for navigation, as noted by Tom, a 46-year-old blind man, from Adelaide, South Australia, quoted in a 2000 study:

> Since being totally blind I feel much more traffic vulnerable, not so much getting lost or anything, just getting run over. And I have a secondary fear of actually causing injury to another pedestrian when I'm run down. So the mobility stuff [using an ultrasound sensor] is highly valued.
>
> (Lupton and Seymour 2000)

Yet, these emerging location and wayfinding sensor technologies also felt unwieldy and inappropriate for others. For instance, in the same study, Margie, a 24-year-old blind woman, emphasized the limitations of available locative technology—compared to the tried-and-trusted technology of a seeing-eye dog:

> A dog is far more suitable than using something like a mote sensor and a sonic pathfinder, for example, which are electronic aids that are either handheld, or one actually sits on your head, like a head band with ear plugs and a big thing across the forehead and stuff . . . [I]t's socially frightening to a lot of people . . . Whereas, for example, to walk around with a dog is completely and utterly socially acceptable. And I think with technologies, the more obtrusive it is, the more offensive it can become to some people.
>
> (Lupton and Seymour 2000)

As mobile phones developed to incorporate geolocalization through mobile phone networks and GPS (now standard in many phones), then to include sensors (such as in smartphones) and a wider range of interfaces (gestural, tactile and haptic, voice operated, text, and other methods), the kinds of technology development that were previously associated with a wide range of devices become focused on mobiles—precisely because the mobile phone had gained such wide user acceptance, and social taken-for-grantedness. Unlike a seeing-eye dog, the mobile phone did not in itself signify that it was a disability, or assistive technology.

Despite this potential, it took some years for mobile devices to emerge as a significant and ubiquitous locative media for users with disabilities. For instance, a 2005 paper by a key figure in accessible telecommunications and disability, John Gill, from the U.K. Royal National Institute, still presented a vision of location based information being mediated by a third party provider of information—rather than being delivered by mobile hardware, software, and databases, as we would expect now:

> In the event of service disruption [to public transportation], the disabled traveler needs information in an appropriate form about suitable alternative methods of reaching their destination . . . Mobile phones equipped with cameras can also be used to send visual

and location information to a service centre where an operator can then guide the user to their desired destination.

(Gill 2005)

Nonetheless, increasingly users expected mobile phones to offer the affordances of location-based technology. For instance, GPS navigation was on the high priority request list for users with vision impairment surveyed in a 2008 Japanese survey (Watanebe et al. 2008). Or, for example, a 2008 paper presented a proof of concept for a standard mobile phone with a built-in camera that used algorithms to ensure a blind or visually impaired pedestrian was guided to safely use a road crossing (Shen et al. 2008).

Emerging locative mobile media technology was also fashioned, and marshalled, for purposes of civic action and political activism concerning disability and accessibility. The best known case here is the decade-long art project *Megafone.net*, undertaken by the Barcelona-based artist Antoni Abad, in collaboration with marginalized communities around the world, in 2004–2014. The hallmark of *Megafone.net* is its pioneering use of mobile phones as a platform to give voice to these particular communities and their experience:

> Using mobile phones they create audio recordings, videos, text, and images that are immediately published on the Web. Participants transform these devices into digital megaphones, amplifying the voices of individuals and groups who are often overlooked or misrepresented in the mainstream media.

(Abad 2014)

In doing so, Abad pioneered the distribution and sharing of camera phones, and data, via mobile phones, before technological systems really supported doing this with the ease we now expect (Goggin 2014). In particular, Abad has worked with four disability communities: people with "limited mobility" in Barcelona (2006–2013), Geneva (2008), and Montréal (2012–2013); and blind people and people with visual impairments in Catalunya in the project *Punt de Vista Cec 2010*. A signature project was *GENÈVE★accessible 2008*, where wheelchairs users photographed obstacles in the Swiss city with GPS-equipped portable phones, and uploaded the images and data to the Internet to produce a map of the city's accessibility. The *GENÈVE★accessible* project attracted widespread international attention, not only for its disability accessibility achievement— but as one of the first such projects in user-generated, "crowd-sourced" data to provide evidence and momentum for social and institutional transformation. This kind of data-intensive participatory urbanism has now become relatively commonplace (Gabyrs 2014). For instance, IBM Sidewalks is another mobile application that has been designed to augment services such as Google Maps and Openstreetmap with disability specific information. This app relies on collaborative data collection. Citizens use the app to record and report accessibility issues around the city, labelling them as either regular, bad, or terrible. The information can then be used by city administrators to correct the problem or alert others to its existence. Where accessibility issues may be obscured by pre-existing street camera views of the city, this app relies on crowdsourcing information and the participation of users switched into ubiquitous computing (Shigeno et al. 2013).

Important as such design and technology experiments and developments were the breakthrough in locative media diffusion, and thus claim to ubiquity, came with the Apple and Google smartphone technology, operating systems, and apps ecosystems. For reasons of space here, as well as its illustrative nature, we will focus principally on Apple's iPhone. Apple had initially launched its iPhone with a relatively inaccessible operating systems—and received severe criticism as well as legal action from the U.S. disability movement, in particular. In 2009, Apple redesigned the iPhone for accessibility, receiving plaudits in the process. As Hollier explains "prior to the iPhone 3GS, it was largely believed that touchscreens and accessibility were mutually exclusive" (Hollier 2013). People with disability immediately saw the potential for accessibility information to become more widely available through crowd sourcing and locative media:

> I really hate it when we go into a restaurant and, after we've gotten settled in, I discover that I am going to need to negotiate stairs if I want to go to the restroom. Stairs are my nemesis at the moment and I would really like to know, before we go somewhere, that I won't be confronted by them. . . . an iPhone app [could be created] specifically for this kind of information. Like Yelp and its ilk, it would be powered by the social network, with people adding information about places that are wheelchair/cane friendly. (Sylvie 2009)

It is no exaggeration to say that beginning with the iPhone, the disability community began seeing the potential for ubiquitous computing. Two key priorities emerge through the insights quoted above and the broader motivations of the associated research: accessibility maps and accessible maps. First, the provision of accessibility maps, which offer information about inaccessible environments such as damaged footpaths or other physical obstructions, is identified as vital to the inclusion of people with disability in public space. Second, the available research identifies that much locative media is visually oriented and therefore inaccessible to people who are blind or vision impaired. There are moves also, therefore, to make these maps accessible.

A related development to locative media around wayfinding and navigation occurred in the web and Internet field—notably, in the World Wide Web Consortium (W3C) standards setting processes in 2013 where accessibility maps and accessible maps were discussed by the W4A (Web For All—the accessibility arm of the W3C; http://w4a). In line with the WHO definition of disability introduced in this chapter's epigraph, the W4A seeks to address the complex interaction between a person's body and the features of the society in which he or she lives. The growth and intensification of pervasive, ubiquitous digital technologies and associated cultures of use in the context of locative and wayfinding opportunities is therefore of particular interest to this standards setting group.

Consider, for instance, that people with disability are engaging in a constantly evolving technological system, sometimes while simultaneously experiencing degenerative (or changing) impairments. In her book *Claiming Disability*, disability scholar Simi Linton often writes of disability as "complex," as a complex "marker of identity," as well as the "web of social ideals, institutional structures, and government policies." This constitutive complexity of disability can also be explained by Alex Lubet's theory of social confluence, a notion to capture his argument that the experiences of disability and impairment changes depending on situations, technologies, and expectations. Social confluence as a subset of the social model of disability relates to the way different situations can be considered more and less disabling and the ways people with disabilities must constantly reappraise their identities and what they can do depending on the situation they find themselves in.

Identities are no longer fixed; we are always in the moment, re-defining and re-identifying. An unfamiliar environment, or unexpected change in that environment (whether a broken footpath or lack of Internet connectivity) is an example of social confluence. Ubiquitous locative media offers a new response to this fluidity of the lifeworld—potentially offering people with disabilities a form of prosthesis, an opportunity to re-define their stance. Locative media, like guidedogs and canes, helps users navigate an unfamiliar environment, as it intersects with the complexity of contemporary life and identify.

Broadly speaking, the importance of information technology to people's experience of disability has been approached from two distinct traditions. The first approach has emphasized the need for specialized, often expensive technology. The second (most recent) tradition has urged the need for disability technology to be designed as part of mainstream technological systems—with the key benefit of cheaper adoption and adaptation. For instance, David Calder, a representative of the first tradition, argues that navigation devices for people who are blind or visually impaired must be developed specifically for this group to avoid problems with individual configuration. By contrast, Scott Hollier, a leading proponent of the second approach, focuses on creating accessible apps for users with vision impairment by employing the mainstream features of smartphones and tablets:

> The majority of people want access to the same market-leading devices that the rest of the population use. They want to choose from the same library of apps and participate in the same activities online.
>
> (Hollier 2013)

Clearly, there are important interactions between the two traditions, as well as long-standing debates. What is notable is that the growing ubiquity of contemporary locative media is premised on mass market—but with a twist, allowing mass customization, through apps. What is especially interesting is how the contemporary experience of locative media for users with disability is leading to a re-imagining of their affordances and possibilities.

For instance, there are a range of critiques of how software design encodes particular kinds of perspectives and experiences, and excludes others. For instance, in her suggestive investigation of making locative media available "to all," Tierney argues that people who use public transport are often excluded from the benefits of locative media because they belong to socially disadvantaged groups such as the unemployed. Tierney argues that maps function as a representational system conceived from the point of view of a particular social group. Although she does not specifically mention disabled users, this kind of argument could be construed from a disability perspective. An obvious argument would draw attention to the visual bias in most maps, including locative media wayfinding apps—and the implications for the way that city is typically imagined, and mapped, in a visual mode and register. Such a narrow envisioning of space and maps is challenged by a range of approaches—not least those that note the importance of all senses to how our orientation in space, place, and time, especially sound and touch, but also smell (for instance, the emerging fields of sound studies, and sensory studies). In locative media, technology developers are grappling with these issues, to make cities better mappable, locable, and navigable by devices and their users. For instance, in 2014, Western Australian developer Voon-Li Chung released an android app to provide greater accessibility to people with vision impairment navigating the City of Perth public transport system:

> Stop Announcer (Perth) is designed to provide visually impaired users audio-based stop announcements for TransPerth services within Western Australia. Levels of detail and frequency of update announcements can be adjusted, and appears in the Status Bar to allow the user to access other apps (such as music players) while Stop Announcer is active. Destinations can be found either by entering the stop number (written on all TransPerth

stops), or by searching for nearby stops and routes. Commonly used routes can be saved for quick future access.

(Google play)

Such smartphone and tablet apps are increasingly being developed to replace guide dog or third person assistance in navigating public space. People who are blind or vision impaired are either unable to or experience significant difficulties accessing spatial information on the web such as maps because these applications are visually orientated. Innovations in locative media for users who are blind or vision impaired have shown that haptic technologies which offer non-visual means of access such as touch sense, vibration, force feedback mouse, and auditory channels can help to mitigate this (Poppinga et al. 2011; Pielot et al. 2010; Jacob et al. 2012; Rice et al. 2005; Wagner 2010; Giudice et al. 2012). Key to these innovations is the smartphone and tablet disability revolution we alluded to earlier. Smartphones and tablets are already designed to improve the visualization of web maps through features such as high definition displays, and touch screens. Given that they offer the opportunity for multimodal interactive capabilities including high definition displays and high quality touch screens, haptic technologies can theoretically be more easily introduced. However, the irony is that other like the *StopAnnounce* app discussed earlier, while representing important breakthroughs in accessibility restrict users to certain predefined areas of locative media possibility. Consider, instead, a recent development—Open Touch/Sound Maps—an android application that uses sonification, text to speech and vibration feedback to allow users a nonvisual way of accessing the publically available OpenStreetMap using a mainstream, mobile device, and the search functionality of Google Maps. Where previous innovations restrict users to "exploration of predefined map areas," Kaklanis et al. argue for more ubiquitous capabilities. Their app uses the GPS feature common in mobile phones to retrieve pertinent information and then present it using non-visual haptic measures including different frequency sounds, and touch screen technology.

To summarize our argument, thus far, we have discussed the way in which the development of locative media has offered new tools and possibilities for dealing with the complexity of disability in everyday life. As we have outlined, experiments in using locative media to respond to disability experience have been greatly strengthened, focused, and further catalyzed by the widespread distribution, consumption, and acceptance of the smartphone and tablet as techno-logical systems—but also platforms for socio-technical innovation. A consequence of the ubiquity-effects of such locative media has been that the dominant sensory modes of encoun-tering, representing, navigating, and negotiating everyday life have been contested, with new calls to acknowledge and design technology for the auditory, haptic, and other embodied aspects of contemporary life and environments.

Such a discussion can provide a context for our final case study in this chapter: Google Glass. Like the iPhone, Google Glass has been slowly launched—but already attracted intense interest. As a wearable device, and one of the oldest prostheses, a pair of eyeglasses, Glass represents a new social imaginary of ubiquitous media—in which disability is an explicit, leading aspect.

Google Glass

Google glass is a ubiquitous computing device in a pair of glasses that operates like a hands-free smartphone. Users can run apps, make voice or video calls, take photos, and play music.

The head-mounted wearable device was first introduced in April 2012, and popularized in a series of Google videos easily accessed on YouTube. An early demonstration video accompanying Google's product information features a hipster New Yorker navigating the city with the aid of his glasses, scheduling his social life via voice while on the go and receiving weather and transport updates through sight prompts. In its marketing inception, the technology was interpreted as beating Apple's mobile voice technology Siri at its own game and promising new directions in augmented reality. *Time* magazine included Google Glass in its list of the best inventions of 2012. While the Glass project is not the first example of this type of technology, it has received considerable media attention, in part due to the extensive field testing that has taken place since 2012. This careful approach to the innovation, user acceptance, and marketing is a notable feature of Glass. (Perhaps an approach informed by the design and marketing strategies Apple adopted in the remarkable success of the iPod, iPhone, and iPad.) Users applied to be part of the Glass Explorer program by responding to the twitter hashtag #ifihadglass.

Google has explicitly and prominently expressed its hopes that Glass would be beneficial for people with disabilities. For instance, Thad Starner, part of the Glass development team, describes Google Glass as reducing the time between intention and action, a mission he sees as directly benefitting people with disability (Popescu 2013). Google has encouraged developers to work with users with disability, to develop potential applications. It has also approached commentators, researchers, and experts with an interest in technology and disability to gain feedback and promote positive portrayal of Google for its efforts.[6] Such efforts have yielded fruit, with significant media reporting on aspects of disability and diversity, and also connecting Glass with other devices and platforms:

> Researchers at Georgia Tech, working with Google, have discovered that a smartphone app that teaches parents to use sign language with their deaf children is used more often when integrated with the headset. Other researchers have used similar technology to help visually impaired users to crowdsource everything from whether an outfit matches to whether a child's rash needs a doctor's attention. With Glass, they can take a picture of their outfit, for example, then post it to an Internet forum for feedback.
>
> (Tsukayama, 2013)

Elsewhere, prototypes apps developed with Google by Australian telco Telstra, for instance, offer new possibilities for blind users to gain information about their everyday environment. This is reported under the title "Google Glass and Telstra Come to the Help of the Disabled":

> OK Glass, what's this? With four short words, 31-year-old Kelly Schulz, 97 percent blind since birth, is given a glimpse of what's in front of her. Google's head-mounted computer snaps a photo and a reads a description into her right ear. "It is a male bathroom", a computerized voice tells her. Other times, "It is a $20 note," "a bottle of skim milk," or "a can of BBQ baked beans." Schulz trialed a prototype app on Glass for a day, and though she stresses that the best piece of technology has four legs, a wet nose, and responds to the name Gallia, she says Glass has massive potential.

In many ways, then, it has been very worthwhile for Google to make Glass available for users with disabilities and developers—using technology and software innovation ecologies to promote experimentation. Google also has a team in its Californian headquarters, who work in a more structured, systematic way on the accessibility of Glass.[7] How this dialectic between user and development experimentation, on the one hand, and Google's development of Google's product fundamentals, on the other hand, ultimately plays out is difficult to discern, at the time of writing. What is evident already, however, is a range of views among users, that at the least raise significant concerns.

One user who joined the Glass Explorer program was Lisa A. Goldstein, a journalist with profound deafness. Goldstein ultimately withdrew, writing one of the most scathing critiques of the technology describing it as "not for the hearing impaired" (Goldstein 2013). Her review for technology website Mashable chronicles her concerns the technology would not be hearing aid accessible or able to understand a deaf accent. She outlines the potential for communication issues on both sides given that "When Glass speaks, there's no captioning of what it says" (Goldstein 2013). By comparison, the technology has been positively reviewed by people with a range of other impairments, notably vision loss and spinal injury.

Four key themes emerge in the available disability reviews of Google Glass: first an increase in personal independence, or not having to rely on another person to do things such as take a picture or answer a text; second, the potential to participate in a more active social life, from attending bars to being treated better in public space when people are afraid their discriminatory behaviors are being filmed; third, the importance of access to a mainstream technology; and finally, the opportunity to gain information in real time, whether through crowdsourcing or available databases.

Tammie Van Sant, who is paralyzed from the neck down, was also part of the Explorer program. She describes an increase in independence since using Google Glass:

> Google Glass has given me a whole new world . . . For 18 years, I wasn't able to take pictures whenever I wanted. I can't even describe how amazing that is. I can answer the phone and actually hear the person on the other end and they can hear me. When I get a text, I can read what the text says on the little prism and answer it.
>
> (Popescu 2013)

Where Goldstein was critical of Google for not taking her concerns seriously and forcing her to communicate via telephone, a clearly inaccessible medium for someone with a hearing impairment, others, such as Greg Priest-Dorman, an advisor to the project have commended the mainstream market approach. He explains that previous wearable devices were developed by medical companies or amateur hobbyists who viewed technology as disability specific without taking into consideration the preferences of the wider consumer market. Priest-Dorman focuses on the potential wearable devices hold for the self-reliance of people with disability:

> We don't need them to live—they're not breathing machines. . . . But it's also an amazing feeling when you don't need to be dependent on someone.
>
> (Tsukuyama 2013)

Priest-Dorman's observations are a significant social comment on the social position of people with disability. Whereas disability is often thought of as a medical problem to be overcome or cured, Greg Priest-Dorman reveals the importance of devising inclusive technology as well as medical—to underpin participation in everyday life. AbilityNet's Head of Digital Inclusion, Robin Christopherson extends these ideas in his review of Glass. Like Priest-Dorman he comments on the way people with disability find ordinary, everyday activities more difficult than people without any kind of impairment:

Technology can really help overcome those difficulties—and the more mobile, aware, and intelligent that tech is the better . . . OK, so Google Glass only has one eye—but one eye's better than none believe me!

(Christopherson 2013)

In a way, the previous section also points to another type of complexity. To summarize, while still in development, Google Glass represents a fascinating yet conflicted development in disability and locative media. It has great potential, as testified by various users and developers quoted here. Yet, Glass is also presented in strikingly stereotypical ways, as yet another in a long line of technologies to bring us salvation from disability and impairment. It is unclear to us to what extent Google, with its evident good will in advancing accessibility and engaging with communities and users around disability, is tackling this burden of disability stereotypes and the implications for design and inclusion that follows. Here we would suggest it is much more useful to see Glass as a part of an evolution in ubiquitous technologies and their complex, culturally shaped co-ordinates. To place Glass in the socio-technical context of development of digital technology, via an account of locative media, but especially to see Glass through the lens of a critical disability approach to locative media is an important move in understanding the grounds and trajectories of such technology.

Conclusion

In this chapter, we have approached the question of complexity ubiquity-effects through an account of the intermingled evolution of disability and locative media technology. This discussion adds a number of important things to our understanding.

First, it is clear that locative media develops in fits and starts, especially when it comes to disability and accessibility. The potential of technologies that use locative information is evident for some years before systems articulate with each other, and produce efficient, near ubiquitous, and relatively easy-to-use affordances and applications. This occurs with the advent of smartphones and apps, yet even here there were many challenges and problems—something obscured in the celebration of the great strides in accessibility afforded by the iPhone and iPad.

Second, there is a recurrent tendency, in successive generations of digital technology, to represent disability as something soon to be overcome by technical innovation. Yet, even at the most basic level of impairment type, and technical feature and capability, locative media is a work in progress—and ubiquity is an achievement not yet realized. So while Google Glass— and its generation of wearable, networked computers and sensors—are impressive in their possibility, there is little acknowledgement still that the much vaunted *complexity* of these devices needed to be articulated with the matching *complexity* of the dynamic, evolving nature of disability in the social worlds and material environments in which the technology unfolds.

Acknowledgements

Katie acknowledges travel support provided by the WWW2017 Perth bid Committee and the support of the Australia Research Council for her Discovery Early Career Researcher award (DE130101712) in the research and writing of this paper. Gerard Goggin gratefully acknowledges the support of the Australian Research Council for his Future Fellowship project on *Disability and Digital Technology* (FT130100097) for the research and writing of this paper.

Notes

1. World Health Organization, "Disabilities," accessed March 12, 2014, http://who.int/topics/disabilities/en/.
2. "Make it Happen! Google Glass for People with Disabilities," December, 13, 2013, accessed March 12, 2014, http://indiegogo.com/projects/make-it-happen-google-glass-for-people-with-disabilities.
3. Barnes notes that: "Disability is now regarded in policy circles as not simply a medical issue but also a human rights concern. A major catalyst for this development has been the social model emphasis on the material and structural causes of disabled people's disadvantage."
4. Complexity theory is now a longstanding area of inquiry.
5. Complexity and disability is the subject of a forthcoming volume edited by Leanne Dowse and Gerard Goggin, and we are especially indebted to Leanne for the argument we put here.
6. One of us, Goggin, was approached by Google in this capacity, and received a demo of Glass in Google's Sydney office.
7. On Google's accessibility policies and initiative, see information on its website: "https://google.com.au/accessibility/research/. Broadly, Google characterizes its approach as follows: Google is committed to making the world's information accessible and usable to all users, including people with disabilities . . . We are devoted to making products that anyone can use and enjoy. We are committed to making accessibility a core consideration from the earliest stages of product design through release. We have formed a central accessibility team with a mandate to monitor the state of accessibility of Google products and coordinate accessibility training, testing, and consulting . . . We also strive to cultivate relationships with a variety of users and advocacy groups to solicit feedback. Alternative access modes will make our products more usable by everyone, not just people with disabilities . . . We hope to have a positive impact on the current state of accessibility on the Web, and to serve an ever-larger number of users."

References

Abad, Antoni. 2014. "Communities + Mobile Phones = Collaborative Visions," accessed April 28, 2014, http://megafone.net/message/index.

Abascal, Julio, and Antón Civit. 2000. "Mobile Communication for People with Disabilities and Older People: New Opportunities for Autonomous Life." In *6th ERCIM Workshop "User Interfaces for All,"* accessed March 19, 2014, http://ui4all.ics.forth.gr/UI4ALL-2000/files/Position_Papers/Abascal.pdf.

Acuto, Michele, and Simon Curtis, Ed. 2013. *Reassembling International Theory: Assemblage Thinking and International Relations.* Basingstoke, UK: Palgrave Macmillan.

de Souza e Silva, Adriana, and Jordan Frith. 2012. *Mobile Interfaces in Public Spaces: Locational Privacy, Control, and Urban Sociability.* New York: Routledge.

Almeida, Maruje, Angelino Alfonsina, Esteban Kipen, Aaron Lipschitz, Marcelo Marmet, Ana Rosato, and Betina Zuttión. 2010. "New Couple, Old Rhetorical Practices: Rethinking the Idea of Diversity and its Use in Understanding and Addressing Disability." *Política y Sociedad* 47(1): 27–44.

Annable, Gary, Gerard Goggin, and Deborah Stienstra. 2007. "Accessibility, Disability, and Inclusion in Information Technologies." *The Information Society* 23: 145–147.

Arnardóttir, Oddny Mjöll, and Gerard Quinn, Eds. 2009. *The UN Convention on the Rights of Persons with Disabilities: European and Scandinavian Perspectives.* Leiden and Boston, MA: Martinus Nijhoff.

Barnes, Colin. 2012. "Understanding the Social Model of Disability: Past, Present and Future." In *Routledge Handbook of Disability Studies*, edited by C. Thomas, A. Roulstone, and N. Watson, 1. New York: Routledge.

Blume, Stuart. 2012. "What Can the Study of Science and Technology Tell Us about Disability?" In *Routledge Handbook of Disability Studies,* edited by C. Thomas, A. Roulstone, and N. Watson. New York: Routledge.

Byrne, David. 1988. *Complexity Theory and the Social Sciences: An Introduction.* New York, NY: Routledge.

Campbell, Fiona Kumari. 2009. *Contours of Ableism: The Production of Disability and Abledness.* Basingstoke, UK: Palgrave Macmillan.

Caron, André H., and Letizia Caronia. 2007. *Moving Cultures: Mobile Communication in Everyday Life.* Montréal, Québec: McGill-Queen's University Press.

Christopherson, Robin. "Why Google Glass Is a Clear Winner for the Blind." *AbilityNet*, published April 18, 2013, accessed March 31, 2015, http://abilitynet.org.uk/blog/why-google-glass-is-clear-winner-blind

Conci, Mario, Fabio Pianesi, and Massimo Zancanaro. 2009. "Useful, Sociable, and Enjoyable: Mobile Phone Adoption by Older People." *Human-Computer Interaction — INTERACT 2009, Lecture Notes in Computer Sciences* 5726: 63–76.

Davis, Lennard J. 1995. *Enforcing Normalcy: Disability, Deafness, and the Body.* London and New York: Verso.

De Landa, Manuel. 2006. *A New Philosophy of Society: Assemblage Theory and Social Complexity.* New York and London: Continuum.

"Disabilities." *World Health Organization*, accessed March 12, 2014, http://who.int/topics/disabilities/en/.

Dourish, Paul and Genevieve Bell,. 2011. *Divining a Digital Future: Mess and Mythology in Ubiquitous Computing.* Cambridge, MA: The MIT Press.

Ekman, Ulrik, ed. 2013. *Throughout: Art and Culture Emerging with Ubiquitous Computing.* Cambridge, MA: The MIT Press.

Ellis, Katie, and Mike Kent. 2011. *Disability and New Media.* New York: Routledge.

Farman, Jason. 2012. *Mobile Interface Theory: Embodied Space and Locative Media.* New York: Routledge.

Gabyrs, Jennifer. 2014. "Programming Environments: Environmentality and Citizen Sensing in the Smart City." *Environment and Planning D: Society and Space* 32 (1): 30–48.

Galis, Vasilis. 2011. "Enacting Disability: How Can Science and Technology Studies Inform Disability Studies." *Disability & Society* 26 (7): 825–838.

Galloway, Anne. 2004. "Intimations of Everyday Life: Ubiquitous Computing and the City." *Cultural Studies* 18 (2/3): 384–408.

Garland-Thomson, Rosemary. 1996. *Extraordinary Bodies: Figuring Physical Disability in American Culture and Literature.* New York: Columbia University Press.

Gill, John. 2005. "Priorities for Technological Research for Visually Impaired People." *Visual Impairment Research* 7: 59–61.

Giudice, Nicholas A., Hari Prasath Palani, Eric Brenner, and Kevin M. Kramer. 2012. "Learning Non-Visual Graphical Information Using a Touch-Based Vibro-Audio Interface." In *Proceedings of the 14th International ACM SIGACCESS Conference on Computers and Accessibility (Assets'12) held on October 22–24, Boulder, Colorado.* New York: ACM Press.

Goggin, Gerard. 2014. "Smartphone Culture and Mobile Politics, *Avant La Lettre*: Antoni Abad's Megafone.net/2004–2014." In *Antoni Abad. Megafone.net/2004–2014*, edited by Turner Macba, and AC/E. Barcelona: Turner.

Goggin, Gerard. 2009. "Assembling Media Culture: The Case of Mobiles." *Journal of Cultural Economy* 2 (1–2): 151–167.

Goggin, Gerard. 2006. *Cell Phone Culture: Mobile Technology in Everyday Life.* London and New York: Routledge.

Goggin, Gerard, and Christopher Newell. 2003. *Digital Disability: The Social Construction of Disability in New Media.* Lanham, MD: Rowman & Littlefield.

"Google Glass and Telstra come to the help of the disabled." *News.com.au*, May 5, 2014, http://news.com.au/technology/gadgets/google-glass-and-telstra-come-to-the-help-of-the-disabled/story-fn6vihic-1226906066852.

Goldstein, Lisa. 2013. "Google Glass: Not for the Hearing Impaired," *Mashable*, published August 5, 2013 and accessed April 1, 2015, http://mashable.com/2013/08/05/google-glass-hearing-impaired/.

Google Glass, accessed March 31, 2015, https://plus.google.com/+GoogleGlass/posts.

Googleplay, accessed March 31, 2015, https://play.google.com/store/apps/details?id=au.com.picospace.transport.

Gordon, Eric, and Adriana de Souza e Silva. 2011. *Net Locality: Why Location Matters in a Networked World.* Malden, MA: Wiley-Blackwell.

Gosnell, Jessica, John Costello, and Howard Shane. 2011. "There Isn't always an App for That!" *Perspectives on Augmentative and Alternative Communication* 20 (1): 7–8.

Hamraie, Aimi. 2012. "Universal Design Research as a New Materialist Practice." *Disability Studies Quarterly* 32 (4). Available at http://dsq-sds.org/article/view/3246/3185.

Heylighen, Ann, and Megan Strickfaden. 2012. "{Im}materiality: Designing for More Sense/s." *Space and Culture* 15 (3): 180–185.

Höflich, Joachim R., Georg F. Kircher, Christine Linke, and Isabel Schlote, Eds. 2012. *Mobile Media and the Change of Everyday Life*. Frankfurt: Peter Lang.

Hollier, Scott. "10 Milestones in the Mainstreaming of Accessibility." *Net Mag*, July 15, 2013, accessed August 27, 2014, http://creativebloq.com/netmag/10-milestones-mainstreaming-accessibility-7135541.

Hollier, Scott. "Opinion: Do We Still Need Specialist Technology?" *Media Access*, June 13, 2013, accessed March 27, 2014. http://mediaaccess.org.au/latest_news/general/opinion-do-we-still-need-specialist-technology.

Jacob, Ricky, Peter Mooney, and Adam Winstanley. 2012. "What's Up That Street? Exploring Streets Using a Haptic GeoWand, Advances in Location-Based Services." In *Lecture Notes in Geoinformation and Cartography*, 91–105. Berlin: Springer.

Ling, Rich. 2012. *Taken for Grantedness: The Embedding of Mobile Communication into Society*. Cambridge, MA: MIT Press.

Lupton, Deborah, and Wendy Seymour. "Technology, Selfhood and Physical Disability." *Social Science & Medicine* 50 (2000): 1856.

"Make it Happen! Google Glass for People with Disabilities." *Indiegogo*, published December 13, 2013, accessed March 12, 2014, http://indiegogo.com/projects/make-it-happen-google-glass-for-people-with-disabilities.

Mason, Mark, Ed. 2008. *Complexity Theory and the Philosophy of Education*. Malden, MA: Wiley-Blackwell.

McNaughton, David and Janice Light. 2013. "The iPad and Mobile Technology Revolution: Benefits and Challenges for Individuals who require Augmentative and Alternative Communication." *Augmentative and Alternative Communication* 29(2): 107–116.

Moser, Ingunn. 2006. "Disability and the Promises of Technology: Technology, Subjectivity and Embodiment within an order of the Normal." *Information, Communication & Society* 9(3): 373–395.

Oliver, Michael. 2012. *The New Politics of Disablement*. 2nd edition. Basingstoke, UK: Palgrave Macmillan.

Palen, Leysia, Marilyn Salzman, and Ed Youngs. 2000. "Going Wireless: Behaviour & Practice of New Mobile Phone Users." In *CSCW '00 Proceedings of the 2000 ACM Conference on Computer Supported Cooperative Work*. New York: ACM. DOI: 10.1145/358916.358991.

Pielot, Martin, Benjamin Poppinga, and Susanne Boll. 2010. "PocketNavigator: Vibro-Tactile Waypoint Navigation for Everyday Mobile Devices." In *Proceedings of the 12th International Conference on Human Computer Interaction with Mobile Devices and Services*, 423–426. New York: ACM.

Popescu, Adam. "OK, Glass: I Can't Walk, So Help Me Explore." *Mashable*, accessed August 7, 2013, http://mashable.com/2013/08/07/google-glass-disabled/

Poppinga, Benjamin, Charlotte Magnusson, Martin Pielot, and Kirsten Rassmus-Gröhn. 2011. "Touch-Over Map: Audio-tactile Exploration of Interactive Maps." In *Proceedings of the 13th International Conference on Human Computer Interaction with Mobile Devices and Services*, 545–550. New York, ACM.

Rice, M., R.D. Jacobson, R.G. Golledge, and D. Jones, 2005. "Design Considerations for Haptic and Auditory Map Interfaces." *Cartography and Geographic Information Science*, 32 (4): 381–391.

Richardson, Ingrid. 2005. "Mobile Technosoma: Some Phenomenological Reflections on Itinerant Media Devices." *The Fibreculture Journal* 6, accessed March 31, 2015. http://six.fibreculturejournal.org/fcj-032-mobile-technosoma-some-phenomenological-reflections-on-itinerant-media-devices/.

Richardson, Ingrid. 2007. "Pocket Technospaces: The Bodily Incorporation of Mobile Media." *Continuum* 21 (2): 205–216.

Roulstone, Alan. 1998. *Enabling Technology: Disabled People, Work, and New Technology*. Buckingham, UK: Open University Press.

Rowan, Wilken, and Gerard Goggin, Eds. 2012. *Mobile Technology and Place*. New York: Routledge.

Seelman, Katherine D. 2000. "Science and Technology Policy: Is Disability a Missing Factor?" *Assistive Technology* 12 (2): 144–153.

Shakespeare, Tom. 2006. *Disability Rights and Wrongs*. London and New York: Routledge.

Shaun, Kane K., Chandrika Jayant, Jacob O. Wobbrock, and Richard E. Ladner. 2009. "Freedom to Roam: A Study of Mobile Device Adoption and Accessibility for People with Visual and Motor Disabilities."

In *Proceedings of the 11th international ACM SIGACCESS Conference on Computers and Accessibility, Assets '09*. New York: ACM.

Shen, Huiying, Kee-Yip Chan, James Coughlan, and John Braby. 2008. "A Mobile Phone System to Find Crosswalks for Visually Impaired Pedestrians." *Technology and Disability* 20 (3): 217–224.

Shigeno, Kelly, Borger, Sergio, Gallo, Diego, Herrmann, Ricardo, Molinaro, Mateus, Cardonha, Carlos, Koch, Fernando and Avegliano, Priscilla. 2013. "Citizen Sensing for Collaborative Construction of Accessibility Maps." In *W4A Proceedings of the 10th International Cross-disciplinary Conference on Web Accessibility in Rio de Janeiro, Brazil*. New York: ACM.

Soldatic, Karen. 2013. "Appointment Time: Disability and Neoliberal Workfare Temporalities." *Critical Sociology* 39 (3): 405–419.

Snyder, Sharon L., and David T. Mitchell. 2006. *Cultural Locations of Disability*. Chicago, IL: University of Chicago Press.

"Statistics." International Telecommunications Union (ITU), accessed March 12, 2014. http://itu.int/en/ITU-D/statistics/Pages/default.aspx.

Sylvie. "Disability and iPhone Apps. Population of One." 2009, accessed June 18, 2010. http://sylvienoel.ca/blog/?p=1195

Tsukayama, Hayley. "Google Glass, Other Wearables May Give the Disabled a New Measure of Independence." The Washington Post August 6, 2013, accessed March 31, 2015. http://washingtonpost.com/business/technology/with-wearable-technology-a-new-measure-of-independence-for-some-with-disabilities/2013/08/06/e258757e-fde4–11e2–96a8-d3b921c0924a_story.html.

van Houten, Douwe. 2001. "Complexity in a Varied Society: Diversity and Disability Management." *Emergence* 3 (2): 37–44.

"Une cartographie de l'accessibilité de la ville." GENÈVE★accessible 2008, accessed April 1, 2015. http://megafone.net/geneve/about.

Wagner, Armin. 2010. "Collaboratively Generated Content on the Audio-Tactile Map." In *ICCHP 2010, Part II. LNCS*, edited by K. Miesenberger, J. Klaus, W. Zagler, and A. Karshmer, 78–80. Heidelberg: Springer.

Watanabe, Tetsuya, Manabi Miyagi, Kazunori Minatani, and Hideji Nagaoka. 2008. "A Survey on the Use of Mobile Phones by Visually Impaired Persons in Japan." *Computers Helping People with Special Needs: Lecture Notes in Computer Science* (5105): 1081–1084.

Weiser, Mark. 1993. "Ubiquitous Computing." August 16, 1993, accessed March 5, 2014. http://ubiq.com/hypertext/weiser/UbiCompHotTopics.html.

Wilken, Rowan, and Gerard Goggin. 2014. "Locative Media: Definitions, Histories, Theories." In *Locative Media*, edited by R. Wilken and G. Goggin, 1–22. New York: Routledge.

Wilken, Rowan. 2014. "Mobile Media, Place, and Location." In *Routledge Companion to Mobile Media*, edited by G. Goggin and L. Hjorth. New York: Routledge.

World Health Organization, World report on disability. 2011. www.who.int/disabilities/world_report/2011/report.pdf, accessed September 5, 2015.

INDEXICAL VISUALIZATION—THE DATA-LESS INFORMATION DISPLAY

Dietmar Offenhuber and Orkan Telhan

Contemporary cultures of ubiquitous computing have given rise to new ways of interacting with digital information through embodied, ambient, contextual, performative means. Yet the way we visualize information still largely follows the logic of flat media. Data visualizations typically rely on symbolic languages found in charts, maps, or conceptual diagrams. Information graphics also frequently use abstractions of concrete objects, such as illustrations and assembly diagrams. In Charles Sanders Peirce's semiology, those two modes of representation would be referred to as symbolic and iconic signs. Information representations that transcend the established language of the flat display are rare and not always successful. We argue that the challenges of communicating embodied and ambient information call for utilizing a third category of signs from Peirce's semiology: the index—a sign that is linked to its object through a causal connection. In this chapter, we elaborate on the role of indexical signs in visualization and argue that indexical visualization deserves a vital place in today's computational design, visual communication, and rhetoric. Here, we present a series of examples to discuss the properties of indexicality and theorize it as a new design strategy that can inform the design process of today's material-based computation and synthetic biological design, which rely on the material organization of the sign and the conditions that encapsulate its meaning within its physical embodiment.

Introduction

Visual representations of abstract data are ubiquitous in contemporary culture. Infographics, data visualizations, or visual narratives are representations designed with the intention to clarify, persuade, or educate. Much has been written about the relationship between their visual languages and their underlying objective—how to distinguish a comprehensible visualization from an obscure or a truthful map from a misleading one. The resulting canonizations of visual languages (Few 2012; Ware 2010) establish guidelines for the mapping data sources to the appropriate visual variables (Bertin 1983), which again can be manipulated through a set of operations (Schneiderman 1996). Attempts to develop a corresponding visual language for information embedded in the physical world are not always successful. Ambient displays mapping information to light, sound, or movement remain incomprehensible if the object and mapping are not known (Wisneski et al. 1998). Contextual and location-referenced information is usually delivered within the narrow constraints of a smartphone display. In the domain of ubiquitous information, arbitrary symbolic languages are bound to fail without established visual conventions.

The disconnect between visual representations and the situation in which they are used also hint at the underlying issue of how data relate to the reality they supposedly describe. Instead of simply being a collection of given facts, a data set is the result of systematic observation and symbolic encoding. To account for this circumstance, Joanna Drucker proposes replacing the word "data" with the active form "capta" (taken) (Drucker 2011). If we understand "data" as a collection of symbolically encoded observations, could we think of a display that conveys information—without the symbolic encoding of data—though its object itself?

Charles Sanders Peirce's theory of semiology distinguishes between three categories of signs—symbols, icons, and indices. Within the narrow boundaries of Information Visualization, only two of these categories, icons and symbols, are primarily utilized—charts, graphs, or the underlying data artifacts themselves are examples of symbolic representations that use a visual language that is based on an arbitrary relationship between the sign and the object it stands for. Other than a shared convention, the number five and the symbol "5" have no direct relationship with each other. Architectural renderings, scientific illustrations, or assembly diagrams, on the other hand, are based on iconic signs. They can be decoded, because their representations resemble the objects they stand for.

Maps, diagrams, and most complex visual representations combine aspects of both resemblance and arbitrary conventions. However, this visual vocabulary has its limits, especially when we want to call attention to phenomena in the physical world around us—the realities of our living environment or the processes happening at the microscopic or molecular level. As a result, we treat most information as abstract, without considering the possibility that we could in fact observe their veracity directly with our senses. This requires that we take a step back from treating data as the literally "given" and consider the processes of how they were coded and aggregated as observations of a physical phenomenon. Before latent fingerprints can be captured in digital form, they have to be made visible through physical particles, chemical or biological processes. Before a fragment of DNA can be coded, it has to be amplified by several orders of magnitude through Polymerase chain reaction (PCR). The fragments then are physically stained with coloring agents to become visible to the bare eyes with a technique known as gel electrophoresis.

The link between data and object is often lost within in the digital domain; however, it is also intentionally obscured. The popular model-view-controller (MVC) design pattern in computer science, for example, demands a clear separation between code modules that model the information from data, the visual display of the data and tasks that allow the users to act on the data (Gamma et al.1995). This abstraction offers obvious advantages, since it boosts the capacity to aggregate and process information. However, it can also diminish the awareness of a causal link between data and object, which may get manifested as a lack of critical scrutiny of the origins and qualities of the data, or on the contrary, a mistrust and outright dismissal due to its generation process.

We believe that there is a third possibility beyond symbolic and iconic representation that can fill this gap in our current data-centric worldview—a strategy for visualization that can be best described with Peirce's third family of signs, the indices. As Peirce et al. note "The index is physically connected with its object; they make an organic pair, but the interpreting mind has nothing to do with this connection, except remarking it, after it is established" (Peirce et al. 1998, 9). A simple example would be the representation of fire, which is commonly found on fire extinguishers or vehicles carrying inflammable substances: an abstracted, but nevertheless iconic representation resembling a flame. The word "fire" would correspond to a purely symbolic representation, consisting of a series of arbitrary symbols. An indexical sign, on the other hand, would be the smoke that rises from an actual flame. While the interpretation of the sign may still be subject to cultural conventions, its appearance is strictly determined by the material basis of the object that signals the meaning.

The concept of indexical signs is by no means a novelty and has played an important role in industrial design history, visible for example in the aerodynamic forms of the streamline modern. However, in contemporary digital culture, data are often treated as a "raw material"—emphasizing their symbolic nature without considering their origin. Within information design and visualization, visual and numerical literacy call attention the internal validity of data sets, but cannot speak to the external connection with their objects. We think there are reasons why it might be worthwhile to explore the design space of indexical visualization. In the context of material-based computation, deep embedding of media into the environment, and design at the microscopic level, for example, the concept can be useful to call attention to the material basis of facts and hidden processes. They can turn us from being consumers of information to witnesses of an experiment. It can encourage careful observation and a critical curiosity for the ways information and knowledge can be linked to physical phenomena.

In this chapter, we discuss indexical visualization and design as an alternative approach to delivering information. In today's emerging design practices, living and non-living matter can be manipulated at the molecular level. The agency and autonomy of bacteria, for example, can be repurposed for different applications as if they are machines or computers. We find it increasingly important to discuss alternative paradigms that can represent the design affordances of such artifacts and look at new ways to design the role of information for communicating their functions and behavior. We will start with discussion of examples that employ indexical representations and show how information can be conveyed without symbolic encoding. We will then feature a number of design principles that can be utilized for different indexical design applications and illustrate them with hypothetical cases. We are interested in questions such as: What are the representational strategies that constitute indexical visualizations? What are their potentials and limits concerning expression, argumentation, and rhetoric?

Indexical visualizations have been with us for a long time. A broad range of artifacts—analog instruments, notations systems, and representations—from art, design, science, and engineering embodies different characteristics of indexicality. Often, the most common feature shared by these devices is the way they are designed to bear the effect that they are meant to communicate. Peirce gives a compelling example: ". . . an old-fashioned hygrometer is an index. For it is so contrived as to have a physical reaction with dryness and moisture in the air, so that the little man will come out if it is wet, and this would happen just the same if the use of the instrument should be entirely forgotten, so that it ceased actually to convey any information" (Peirce et al. 1998, 163). Indexical signs often incorporate iconic and symbolic aspects, as in the case of photographic paper or the charts drawn by a seismograph. Our concern however is not taxonomic—our aim is to distinguish and identify design strategies to emphasize indexical qualities that can help making legible the connection between an object and its context. Indexical displays address the central demand of ubiquitous computing for situatedness rather than abstract universality in its representations and practices. Instead of offering a fixed mapping between data and representation, indexical design offers a framework for guiding observation. The main point is not to endorse physical information displays over digital ones, but to emphasize the importance of causality in constructing meaning. To this end, the task is to choose and configure the material of the display so that it can isolate and constrain the phenomenon of interest such that the effect on the display apparatus becomes legible. In a way, it can be stated that indexical design is the framing of meaning through the choice of constraints.

Properties of Indexical Visualizations

Design choices for indexical visualizations can be illustrated through the mechanisms used in analog instruments for measurement. Using the example of a pressure gauge, Nelson Goodman describes the operations of semantic differentiation that are applied to translate the physical behavior of the device into a form of notation: from the analog signal into a visual trace (Goodman 1968, 157). While signal and trace are still causally linked, a semantic distance is introduced between gas pressure and the pen that produces the mark on paper. We are dealing with two different representations of gas pressure: first, the visual trace on paper produced by the pen moved by the pressure over multiple intermediary steps. But, second, one could argue that also the configuration of the instrument is a representation of the phenomenon, which it contains, embodies, constrains and reacts to. Based on these considerations, we can capture indexical visualization and design through a number of properties:

1. Indexical visualization represents an object through its own embodiment or its immediate impact on its environment.
2. Designing an indexical visualization means framing the underlying object in such a way that it becomes legible.
3. The framing happens by applying a set of constraints that act upon the object in such a way that only a specific aspect of the object is revealed and isolated from the object's other properties.
4. The indexical display remains linked with the underlying phenomenon through its visual or audible appearance. To some extent, its appearance is autonomous and not under the control of the designer.
5. Indexical visualization achieves its rhetorical strength by emphasizing this causal link, which allows it to achieve the status of evidence.
6. The specific configuration of constraints that act upon the object can be understood as the diagrammatic form of indexical visualization.

As an example, the physical configuration of the mercury thermometer (diagram) represents temperature (object) through the expansion of mercury (the object's material embodiment). This phenomenon is only legible because the mercury is constrained in a capillary glass tube, allowing it to expand only into one direction upon a change in temperature. Adding a corresponding spatial scale for comparison and quantification differentiates the amount of displacement further. At the same time, all other properties of the mercury are de-emphasized— its color, its weight, its unconstrained shape, and so forth. Compared to a digital thermometer with its multiple layers of sensing, abstraction, representation, and translation, the effect of temperature is rather directly observed.

It is necessary to distinguish between the physical response of the thermometer, which is inevitable, and the act of communication, which may or may not happen. While the representation of temperature is direct or explicit, the reading or contextualization of it is still a learned experience shaped by convention. Furthermore, indices are often difficult to recognize and interpret. Michael Polanyi describes the example of a student learning to read x-ray images of lungs—an ability, for him, that cannot be acquired only by following explicit instructions but rather learned over time in a master–apprentice like relationship. Although the information on the X-ray is immediate and physically explicit, the interpretation of the subtleties of the visual imprint is a slow process. Indexical visualization therefore aims to increase the legibility of the index through external constraints (Polanyi 1998, 106).

Indexical Design and its Display

The manifestations of indexical representations can be diverse, depending on their context and medium. Nevertheless, we think that it is possible to describe the design space of indexical representations using a few parameters. In our understanding, a main criterion is the causal distance between the object and its representation. Is the causal chain of events between object and representation short and direct, or the result of many intermediary events? In most cases, a shorter, more immediate connection would be preferable.

A second dimension is the semantic distance between the object and its representation. To what extent is the nature of the underlying phenomenon legible in the representation? Is the phenomenon translated into an arbitrary visual language or notation? While both dimensions, causal and semantic distance, are often linked, it does not necessarily have to be that way. The hygrometer in the shape of a weather house, with two figures that emerge from their respective doors because they are fixed on a disc that rotates with changing humidity, illustrates this difference. The chain of events is short and direct, yet the mechanism is hidden, and the representation allows no insight into this process, making it appear almost like a magical device. Again, a pure form of indexical visualization would involve a minimal amount of such symbolic mediation. These two parameters together span a space in which the indexical qualities of different examples can be compared. In this space, a representation with very short causal distance and a minimal amount of symbolic mediation would be indexical in the strong sense, a representation involving a long chain of causal events and a highly arbitrary representation will have very weak indexical qualities. The two parameters span up a two-dimensional space, in which the examples discussed in the following sections can be located.

Analog vs. Digital Representations

Most traditional analog instruments for measurement, recording, and displays are indexical to varying degrees; a sundial is arguably more than a mechanical clock. The installation *Meeting* by the artist James Turrell is probably one of the purest examples of an indexical display. The piece, originally installed in New York's PS1 institute, invites the visitors to observe the sky, framed by a square opening in the ceiling. This indirectly illuminated frame makes it possible to observe the subtle color changes of the sky in contrast to the matching illumination level of the surrounding ceiling (Adcock and Turrell 1990, 120). *Meeting* has the shortest possible causal distance between the object and its representation. At the same time, *Meeting* uses a short symbolic distance.

While digital representations that process input from the physical world can also produce deterministic and immediate outputs, as the causal link between input and output is obstructed through a mediation process, they can be considered indexical only in a weak sense. The separation of information from its original context, making information persistent and context interchangeable, offers a big advantage compared to analog technologies from a practical

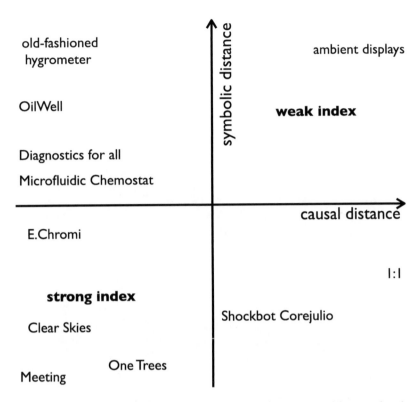

FIGURE 30.1 The location of the discussed examples in the space spanned by causal and symbolic distance

standpoint. However, this separation also means that the direct link to the original context will disappear or become arbitrary. Scholars studying the human factors of digital media, including Mark Weiser, John Seely Brown, and Hiroshi Ishii, have seen this arbitrariness as a disadvantage, and argued for emulating indexicality within the digital realm. Concepts such as *Calm Technology* and *Ambient Displays* are directly inspired by the indexical nature of analog instruments and the human capacity to constantly process a multitude of environmental cues without too much effort or with the background of attention (Brown and Weiser 1996; Wisneski et al. 2008). In most cases, this indexical nature is used as a metaphor rather as the actual driver of the display. Ishii's *Tangible Media Group*, for example, demonstrated that the amount of network activity can be mapped to the rotation speed of pinwheels or similarly the temperature of water from a faucet can be represented with colored light illuminating the water stream. While in these examples indexical mappings were created between digital and physical phenomena, the research focus is on simplifying symbolic relationships, rather than eliminating translation and mediation. Although the causal distance between the object and its representation is undiminished, these visualizations intend to create the appearance of a direct and immediate causal connection. On the other hand, in terms of symbolic abstraction, ambient displays operate with entirely arbitrary mappings between input and output, sense and response pairings, making them essentially symbolic or iconic signs.

FIGURE 30.2 Meeting (1986), James Turrell.
Photo courtesy of Jessica Sheridon

Other strategies in the digital realm try to minimize the level of symbolic abstraction rather than the causal distance between object and display. This can be achieved by establishing a clear structural correspondence between the object and its representation. The artist Lisa Jevbratt describes her project *1:1* from 1999 as an indexical visualization in which every single pixel of the display corresponds to a distinct entity—in this case a computer IP address (Jevbratt 2003). Unlike in most of our examples, here indexicality does not address the underlying physical substrate of computation, and remains in the symbolic realm by using an arbitrary mapping between a specific server on the network and a pixel on screen. However, by treating every pixel as a distinct marker with a direct correspondence to an object, the representation gains indexical qualities. In the same sense, treating a digital file as a raw stream of bytes and sending it directly to the sound device of a computer could be seen as an indexical representation within the digital realm.

If we go beyond the symbolic domain of computation, the experience of technical failures in the underlying electronic circuits are probably closest to our understanding of indexical representations. Failures can reveal underlying properties of systems that are normally hidden. *Glitch* artists, who exploit the unintended artifacts of digital media formats, sometimes directly manipulating and destroying the underlying electronic hardware, often exploit this aspect. The installation *Shockbot Corejulio* from the group 5voltcore is one such example, where a robotic device moves a steel brush over the circuits of the graphics board of the computer it is controlled by, triggering short circuits and occasional visual patterns created by the damaged electronics (Rebelo and Schroeder 2006).

In the natural sciences, especially in chemical and biological research, indexicality is the basis and necessary justification for almost all representation. The products of laboratories are discursive objects or *epistemic things*, as Rheinberger puts it, with the main purpose of providing material evidence for theoretical models (Rheinberger 1997, 9). In scientific publications, symbolic representations in form of graphs or scatterplots are typically augmented by photographs or similar records of evidence. Sound is also frequently used to represent activity over time. Based on its perceptual qualities, sonic displays are inherently indexical rather, since sound usually indicates events in the physical world and is a potent medium for communicating causal relationships (Hogg and Vickers 2006). In Hubel and Wiesel's classic neuroscience experiment, the researchers mapped visual neurons guided by the audible bursts created by an electrode, which was used to capture the activity of a single neuron in the visual cortex of a cat (Hubel 1959).

In diagnostic tests or chemical analysis, the symbolic distance is very short, since the representation follows the dictate of the material properties of the involved substances. However, with the emergence of new frontiers in biochemical design, such as synthetic biology, it becomes important to assess the ways the supposedly rigid, unmediated, and immediate connection between material and what it stands for can be manipulated purposefully. The design of the behavior of a chemical or biological marker—when engineered at the level of a single-cell organism—introduces new parameters to the design of indexical living matter. The organism, as a living design, has the ability to manipulate its own interpretation. It can grow, change, mutate, and eventually deviate from its designer's intentions. Bacteria, for example, exercise different preferences based on their environmental conditions. The availability of certain chemicals or the presence of other organisms around can influence their behavior. So when bacteria is designed to respond to a chemical marker, say produce a visual outcome in response to the presence of a particular molecule in its environment, the accuracy, precision, and repeatability of that chemical sign can show great variability based on the way organism exercises its agency throughout its life. Thus when the bacteria respond to the chemical phenomena and become their own indexical representation, the response can be immediate and direct and yet not entirely predictable. However, such index is inherently different from a simple analog design, as for example, the way the lead molecule in the thermometer responds to changes in temperature. The living organism can inherently exercise its own autonomy and introduce a level of indeterminacy to the overall design. On the other hand, the intent behind such indexical design can also be the actual manipulation and regulation of this autonomy so that it can turn into a legible source of information.

Examples

In the examples presented below, design operates at different resolutions: as pixels, genes, molecules, or atoms. In reference to Rheinberger's notion of epistemic things, we could refer to these units as *signthings*. As already noted, signthings can exercise different levels of agency and autonomy depending on their medium. Regardless of the scale on which signthings operate, it is important to note that the interpretation context—the framing of the meaning—always takes place at the macro level. Any state-, color-, or shape-transition at the microscopic level has to result in a visible effect that enables quantification, ordering, enumeration, and interpretation. Therefore, indexical displays are resolution-independent, making their intrinsic properties legible to an external observer.

In Natalie Jeremijenko's *One Trees* public art installation, a hundred trees, cloned from a single source, were planted across the Bay Area. The artist intended to emphasize the effect of spatial variations in air quality and microclimatic conditions on the genetically identical trees. Since the external conditions cause every tree to develop in a different way, *One Trees* is an indexical visualization, not only showing but also bearing the effects of changing environmental forces and interactions with urban life (Whitelaw 2006, 98). In the related project *Clear Skies*, Jeremijeno designs disposable dust protection masks to measure the particulate pollution Bay Area bikers are exposed to during their commute. To read the amount of dust that has accumulated in the mask, a grey color gradient is printed on the masks matching the different degrees of discoloration and hence pollution.

All of these signs, the state vegetation, the visible deposits of air pollution, are present in the environment and can be read as implicit cues by trained observers. The interventions by the designer emphasize these cues and provide a rubric for their interpretation, to translate them into explicit data points.

Beyond art projects, indexical displays can be found in research environment as well as in objects of everyday life. They rely on physical, biological, and chemical mechanism and combine biological, diagnostic, and therapeutic functions with information design. Personal pregnancy, HIV, and cholesterol tests use indexical representations designed to be understood by a broad population. By using synthetic or natural markers that respond to chemical or biological phenomena, such tests capture causality through material change—indicate presence of factors, change, quantity, or frequency through visual feedback.

Diagnostic For All, a non-profit enterprise, utilizes material-level interaction both for registering medical symptoms and for providing visual feedback for advanced diagnosis (Plate 45). In this design, biological reagents stored on traces or wells patterned onto chemically treated paper respond to the body fluids of the patients to detect liver complications. Upon contact with a patient, the paper device registers change by color and quantifies the phenomena through a scale printed onto the device. As the device primarily aims patients in developing countries with limited access to professional facilities, it is designed to register the embody the colorimetric output until it can be studied further by an expert in a remote location who can provide further diagnosis through a digital image of the paper.

The design of synthetic biomarkers for diagnostic purposes is also a research direction in synthetic biology, a field that is concerned with designing living systems with engineering methods (Endy 2005). Plate 46 shows *E.chromi*, a synthetic biology project in which bacteria are engineered to detect particular chemical signatures within the human gut flora. By incorporating color-making genes into the genome of Escherichia coli (E. coli), designers can turn the organism into a biosensor, which can respond to different disease patterns. As E. coli senses the chemicals, it can synthesize the proteins that will allow it induce a color-change in its physical embodiment. As E. coli with different color markings exit the body, they leave their traces on the human manure and provide the user with a visualization of their medical condition.

Synthetic biology is ultimately concerned with building living systems that function like biological circuits or computational hardware. It focuses on designing the biological equivalents of switches, logic gates, transistors, oscillators, and other kinds of devices, feedback, and decision-making systems that can execute complex computational instructions. Like the color-changing E.coli example, these designs exhibit indexical behavior and represent their functions or the outcomes of their functions visually in their material embodiment. Bacteria and other single-cell organisms can be synthesized with custom genomes, which can function like computational hardware that can sense, respond, and deliver not only information but also bio-molecular payload, compressing the difference between a sign and its material embodiment in the biological context.

Microfluidic systems—dealing with the control and manipulation of fluids at a micro-scale—are an important tool of synthetic biology (Plate 47). Like advanced thermometers, which provide both the biological context and the physical framing—and site—of the biological activity, microfluids can be implemented in different materials such as paper, glass, ceramics, or silicones, and can be designed to exhibit characteristics known from electro-mechanical and computational systems (Whitesides 2006). Microfluidic systems can be used to regulate the flow, mixing, and dissemination of chemicals—organic and inorganic fluidic matter—through micro channels. These "Lab-on-chips" are also highly informative systems, which can provide information regarding material-level interaction through visual patterning, measurement, and spatialization techniques embedded within the design of the system. 2D and 3D Bio-arrays, for example, are popular experiment design tools that allow the automatic study biomolecular differentiation through comparative analysis.

Micro or mili-capillary environments can also be designed as consumer artifacts that can expand their use beyond medical devices. *The Oilwell* by Orkan Telhan (Plate 48) is the prototype of a personal biosynthesis machine—a microbial perfumery—that incubates bacteria, which can exhibit different colors and smells based on the design of their genomes. The *Oilwell* features a clear silicon housing that functions as an indexical display. Here, the bacteria grown in a mix of nutritious media and mineral oil are pumped from an incubator towards a heating element through capillary channels. As bacteria go through their certain growth phase, they respond to the inhibiting compounds in the media: change color and indicate to the outside viewer that they are ready to emit smell. This process can be observed in real-time with plain sight like a thermometer. When bacteria is ready, the users can activate the pumps such that they can get pushed towards the end of the housing, where they get dropped onto a heating element and made to evaporate like a traditional oil lamp. While genetically modified bacteria are inevitably killed at the end of the process, the system provides a measure of safety for not letting the genetically modified organisms leave their confined environment. The *Oilwell* uses indexical design both as a functional and aesthetic element. Here, the bacteria can be made to grow a number of different smells—such as citrus, mint green, or banana odor—in a randomized fashion. Each smell can be visualized by a particular color marker—such as amber indicating banana, green citrus, and so on—and therefore be observed from outside before the bacteria is channeled to the pump. As bacteria go through different cycles of smell production, the users can determine when exactly to activate the smell based on its indicator color. Here, while the mapping of color to a particular smell could be left to a preference or an arbitrary mapping, the way bacteria signals the smell production to the audience is an indexical process. The integration of indexical designs to aesthetic and symbolic artifacts offer a new design space that can incorporate elements of biochemical design with the rich history of product design that is rooted in constructing meaningful experiences through the cultural and historical meaning of the artifacts. As a perfume bottle, *Oilwell* intends to combine the different design cultures of product design with biochemical design and pay close attention to different stages of creating a user experience from the form of the perfumery to the way its content can communicate its fabrication process to its user. Being currently a novel category, artifacts with living designs, require a different visual language that inevitably extend the ways we design experience and meaning without relying on information produced in symbolic or iconic ways.

For most applications of desktop and mobile computing, the symbolic domain is sufficient to represent and act on information. However, when computation is embedded in the physical world and carried through living organisms or chemical processes, we need to extend our understanding of computation beyond paradigms dominated by computational media and information design. Biochemical processes such as DNA assembly, protein synthesis, or bacterial transformation can be computationally modeled, viewed, and controlled inside a living organism without creating any symbols and information. As users, we can visually observe the process, give input, and act on the outcomes through markers that are physically coupled to the processes. Symbol-free computation allows us to act directly on the physical matter, avoid the intermediary representations, and minimize the distance between cause and effect.

While pure indexical displays offer a wide variety of affordances from biosynthesis to cellular or subcellular imaging and live visualizations, hybrid formats that integrate some form of symbolic abstraction (the second axis) into indexical design, offer another promising area of research. Hybrid visualization paradigms offer ways to map indexical information onto the symbolic domain and allow computation to take different roles in the symbolic or physical domain. A citizen-science project could, for example, use cameras to observe the change in the environment through a variety of organisms such moss, lichens, or algae which respond to PH, humidity, CO_2 levels, and so on by a physical change in their appearances. By digitally characterizing the effects of these bioindicators through cameras and sensors, it would be possible to device systems that can record changes over time and computationally monitor habitats through their own ecologies. In addition to designing feedback loops between indexical and symbolic systems, hybrid modalities can also be used to correlate calculated information and indexical observation to increase the reliability to symbolic processes. By registering the state of living phenomena (i.e. texture, color, etc.) through symbolic means, it becomes possible to observe phenomena beyond the life cycles of living systems or the limited durability of physical phenomena. The symbolic processes produce information that can be preserved indefinitely hence make hybrid systems really viable solutions.

As we present a multitude of approaches to extend information processing and visualization in ubiquitous computing to the indexical domain, advocate for hybrid models, it also becomes important to list the limits of indexicality.

The Limits of Staging Indices

The opportunities for indexical design, as illustrated by the examples above, are bound to certain limits. With its emphasis on causal relationships between material conditions, the difficulties in physically framing a phenomenon, and the challenges in making the phenomenon legible, the practice of indexical visualization operates in a tight space. It is applicable only to a small fraction of possible visualization tasks and problems. Beyond the challenges that have been already discussed in the earlier sections, we want to mention four other challenges to that pertain to the design of indexical visualizations.

Distortion

While the behavior of indexical displays is determined by the underlying physical processes, its appearance can nevertheless be distorted and exaggerated. In the thermometer, for example, the ratio between the dimensions of the capillary tube and the expansion rate of mercury would be an important criterion that will determine how much the element will spread in space. As the adjustment of this ratio will yield different amounts of spread along the axis, it will inherently determine how much visible difference can be indexed from temperature's effect onto the metal.

The interpretation of indexical displays relies on the context, which introduces a second possibility for manipulation. The marks on the scale placed next to the thermometer can be wrongly spaced, or not correspond to the actual behavior of the material, which might show linear or nonlinear characteristics. While many of these distortions could be resolved through repeated observation of the display under various conditions, it should not be ignored that the design of indexical displays includes a rhetoric element—of staging the object in the most effective way.

Ambiguity

The framing in indexical visualizations is a matter of explicating implicit and ambiguous information. Since the interpretation of physical traces and phenomena requires some level of expert knowledge, an effective representation for non-experts usually means a reduction of ambiguity. At the same time, this disambiguation can increase the causal distance between the phenomenon and the representation. To be convincing as "evidence," indexical visualizations require the presence of some amount of implicit information and ambiguity to be able to construct the basis of interpretation. Ambiguity is a necessary trade-off for the sake of minimizing the causal distance to the object. On the other hand, ambiguity can call attention to the physical properties of the object, offer additional cues, and therefore make the representation more believable—just as artifacts in analog media are an important means for verifying the authenticity of a document.

Ephemerality

Indexical displays change over time and often leave little trace of previous states. Either due to their physical characteristics or the way they are framed, it is often not possible to preserve their appearance over a longer time or create records of their previous states. If inscriptions are created, as in the case of a seismograph, the encoded information often does not have the same universally legible quality. The persuasive power of indexical displays is tightly coupled to their ephemerality. They are performative and show mechanisms and causalities rather than produce data. However, as visualizations, they do not afford the permanence characteristic of other representations: They require observation and interpretation, therefore the information they convey might not be the same for different observers. At the same time, the display is often locked into a specific context. As information displays, indexical visualizations do not offer the advantage of what Bruno Latour called "immutable mobiles": representations of information that are both stable and mobile and therefore allow operations that go beyond the representations immediate context (Latour 1987, 227).

Agency and Autonomy

A leather shoe can be bearer of the physical marks on its surface, and thus record the history of its users permanently, whereas the skin tissue of a cow will not be able to do this. As the live tissue will constantly renew itself, it may, on the other hand, show the effects of immediate causes—such as the change of color in an area when the tissue experienced a physical impact. Indexical visualizations that are designed from state-changing materials, biological or living materials introduce new kinds of opportunities and limits to representation. Agency is at the expense of ephemerality but introduces an ability to actively respond to change. Agency is also a source of active reframing, in which the design can change both its physical and material framing and the interpretation contexts at the same time.

The intent behind the manipulation, engineering, and programming of living matter also introduces different degrees and kinds of agency to indexical design. The autonomy exercised by single-cell organisms, for example, brings an inherent underspecificity to the overall design, subjecting it to operate at higher margins of uncertainty yet with the benefits of microbial intelligence. In a designed context, E. coli would be as a signthing, which would be expected to act, react, communicate, and live its own being. It will make decisions and bear the consequences of its own actions. However, in the meantime, it will be read as an index. Its responses to phenomena will be manifested as biological change and become legible under different interpretations that will frame it so.

Conclusion

Indexical strategies of visualization do not foreclose the act of interpretation. Instead of delivering quantifiable messages, they offer a framework for observation. In this chapter, we described a few principles for information design involving representations that highlight indexical properties, rather than employing iconic or symbolic visual languages. Since an indexical sign is a direct and necessary result of an underlying process, its appearance can only be indirectly manipulated by the designer. Design intervention therefore happens by applying a set of constraints that are aimed at making the underlying phenomenon legible. As long as the representation remains recognizable as a causal effect of the indicated phenomenon, the display becomes a persuasive demonstration of evidence. We intended to revise the place of the index among the palette available to the information designer, and identified and discussed a series of parameters—such as causal and symbolic distance—to assess different levels of indexicality. While the field of indexical design and visualization has not been thoroughly investigated, there have been individual attempts to capture indexical properties in visual designs. Our goal was to survey a series of examples that qualify as indexical visualizations as we describe them, and distill certain attributes and guidelines to design and interpret new kinds of indexical systems. While indexical representations currently occupy a somewhat marginal role in design, we expect that with the emergence of fields such as synthetic biology or microfluidic applications, they will become important in the near future. As we advance in our abilities to engineer molecular level responses to materials and use the agency of biological systems for specific design-making capabilities, we witness an increasing possibility to design visualizations that can compress the space between representation, translation, and mediation through the immediacy of cause-effect and input-output relationships.

Peirce's semiotic model provides a good backdrop to theorize new kinds of designs that can represent phenomena through themselves—exercise a different level of agency that lies outside the traditional visualization conventions that is built through icons and symbols. Under the category of the index, we described a new category of signs—signthings—that can utilize their physical embodiment—living and non-living nature—to exercise such agency. We believe that, as they find new places in the visual rhetoric, new types of indexical designs and visualizations will establish their own reading habits and interpretation conventions and fundamentally challenge our former experiences with signs and signifying systems.

Acknowledgements

We thank Gerhard Dirmoser for his insightful feedback and criticism.

References

Adcock, Craig E., and James Turrell. 1990. *The Art of Light and Space*. Berkeley, CA: University of California Press.

Bertin, Jacques. 1983. *Semiology of Graphics: Diagrams, Networks, Maps*. Madison, WI: University of Wisconsin Press.

Brown, John Seely, and Mark Weiser. 1996. "Designing Calm Technology." *PowerGrid Journal* 1 (1): 75–85.

Endy, Drew. 2005. "Foundations for Engineering Biology." *Nature* 438 (7067): 449–453.

Drucker, Johanna. 2011. "Humanities Approaches to Graphical Display." *Digital Humanities Quarterly* 5 (1). http://digitalhumanities.org/dhq/vol/5/1/000091/000091.html. (Accessed August 22, 2014).

Few, Stephen. 2012. *Show Me the Numbers: Designing Tables and Graphs to Enlighten*, Second edition. Burlingame, CA: Analytics Press.

Gamma, Erich, John Vlissides, Ralph Johnson, and Richard Helm. 1995. *Design Patterns: Elements of Reusable Object-Oriented Software*. Reading, MA: Addison-Wesley.

Goodman, Nelson. 1968. *Languages of Art: An Approach to a Theory of Symbols*. Indianapolis: Bobbs-Merrill.

Hogg, Bennett, and Paul Vickers. 2006. "Sonification Abstraite/Sonification Concrete: An 'Æsthetic Perspective Space' for Classifying Auditory Displays in the Ars Musica Domain." *International Conference on Auditory Display (ICAD2006), London, UK*.

Hubel, David H. 1959. "Single Unit Activity in Striate Cortex of Unrestrained Cats." *The Journal of Physiology* 147 (2): 226–238.

Jevbratt, Lisa. 2003. "Coding the Infome: Writing Abstract Reality." *Dichtung Digital* 29 (3).

Latour, Bruno. 1987. *Science in Action: How to Follow Scientists and Engineers through Society*. Cambridge, MA: Harvard University Press

Peirce, Charles Sanders, Nathan Houser, and Christian J. W. Kloesel. 1998. *The Essential Peirce: Selected Philosophical Writings, 1893–1913*. Indiana, IN: Indiana University Press.

Polanyi, Michael. 1998. *Personal Knowledge: Towards a Post-Critical Philosophy*. London: CRC Press.

Rebelo, Pedro, and Franziska Schroeder. 2006. "Performing the Order: The Messiness of Play." *Performance Research* 11 (1): 3–8.

Rheinberger, Hans-Jörg. 1997. *Toward a History of Epistemic Things: Synthesizing Proteins in the Test Tube*. Redwood City, CA: Stanford University Press.

Shneiderman, Ben. 1996. "The Eyes Have It: A Task by Data Type Taxonomy for Information Visualizations," In *Proceedings of the IEEE Symposium on Visual Languages*, 1996, 336–43, http://ieeexplore.ieee.org/xpls/abs_all.jsp?arnumber=545307.

Ware, Colin. 2010. *Visual Thinking: For Design*. San Francisco, CA: Morgan Kaufmann.

Whitelaw, Mitchell. 2006. *Metacreation: Art and Artificial Life*. Cambridge, MA: MIT Press

Whitesides, George M. 2006. "The Origins and the Future of Microfluidics." *Nature* 442 (7101) (July 27): 368–373

Wisneski, Craig, Ishii, Hiroshi, Dahley, Andrew, Gorbet, Matt, Brave, Scott, Ullmer, Brygg, and Yarin, Paul. 1998. "Ambient Displays: Turning Architectural Space into an Interface between People and Digital Information." *Proceedings of the First International Workshop on Cooperative Buildings, Integrating Information, Organization, and Architecture*: 22–32.

PART III

Eventualizing

EVENTS

Lily Díaz

Set against a gradated aquamarine background, an apple stands, a bit off-center towards the right, and hoisted on a thin brass tube. The fruit's stalk faces the audience who can clearly appreciate the seemingly simultaneous outward explosion in either side marking the entry and exit of the 0.30 caliber bullet. The photograph is labeled "Shooting the Apple, 1964" or "Bullet through the Apple 1964" (MIT Museum Collections—Objects). Created by engineer and inventor Harold E. Edgerton, it is a startling image now regarded as a canonic example of the technological advancement of twentieth century photography.

The shooting gun is an ironical reminder of the prevalence of militaristic ideologies in imaging and simulation technology research initiatives. It is also an early example of the transdisciplinarity advocated in this volume, since the image demonstrates the use of photography *as a method of research* that combines knowledge from different domains (Jussim and Kayafas 1987, 12–32). *Jammin' the Blues* (Open Culture), the 1944 Academy Award nominated movie directed by Gjon Mili, is but one early example of the art works resulting from these new partnerships between art and science.

Edgerton's innovation was emblematic because it could accurately record *within one frame multiple impressions* of an event as it occurred in time. This is a slight, but important, difference from Muybridge's "epistemological cinema" noted by Poulaki in her essay that captured individual instants of events into separate images. In Edgerton's work, time ceases to be the source event of individuation to become that which reduces complexity. As records of events, the work was understood by others as the mechanical manipulation of time in the same way as a "microscope or telescope manipulates space" (Canales 2011).

Edgerton's and Muybridge's works were not produced using digital media. However, they both intuit the new temporalities (see Patricia Pisters' essay in this volume) that would later surface in innovative time-based art and cinema of our time. Ridley Scott's *Gladiator* that blends blue screen image sequences with digital virtual sets to reconstruct entire historical eras from the past, James Cameron's *Avatar* that uses motion capture technology to explore the separation of being and seeing (Ng 2012) while empathically depicting non-human life beyond the Uncanny Valley (Cafaro et al. 2014, 1075),[1] and even real time virtual reality interactive simulations designed to provide museum visitors with dynamic, embodied experiences of vanished heritage sites (Bartley and Hancock 2008; Place-Hampi 2008; Reunanen et al. 2015)[2] are examples of new individuations emerging from Edgerton's and Muybridge's research. What all these projects have in common is the breakdown of the notion of event as a universal, continuous, and linear phenomenon into something to be captured into multiple layers for manipulation, re-composition, and individuation as a new form of experience.

To the extent that, as "fabulatory structures" (Pisters), these temporalities influence our individual psyche and our collective memory, they might have a significant effect and partly determine who we become. After all, for the Millenials[3] who grew up within the videogame culture, for example, it might be senseless to ask questions regarding the "realness" of online multiplayer games like *World of Warcraft* or *Habbo Hotel*. These *were* the places where friends were met and where playground battles were fought. Nowadays *hikikomori* is the term used to describe the estimated 500,000 to 1 million Japanese individuals who are documented as affected with societal withdrawal, some also suffering from Internet addiction (*The Atlantic*). This situation does highlight the need for critical perspectives on the reach and use of the new technologies, since it is not only the body but also the mind that can increasingly become entangled with the "toxic consumerism of hegemonic schemata" (Pisters). As Poulaki notes, though cinema was built upon the notion of the blind spot, or of the rendering of the gap between subsequent frames "invisible" to the audience, authors, and creators can choose to use the characteristics of media in critical way, as Lars von Trier does in the two films Pisters presents: *Melancholia* and *Antichrist*. Following this critical track, in an interview with Jay David Bolter in this volume, artist Elahi Hasan proposes to view the selfie as a form of political action. According to Hasan, the political dimension individuates not through the image—that instantly becomes one more among millions uploaded daily—but rather through the performance, in the taking of the selfie, and by virtue of "being there."

With the intensified co-development of cultural practices and "always on" computational devices our notion of time as a neatly organized continuum of events is perhaps replaced by heterogeneous and nonlinear fluctuations of becoming, somewhere between ordering of structures and dissipating into disorder (see Ekman's general introduction and his interim text on Individuation in this volume). Multiple events extend back into the past, or progress forwards toward some future, but they are always observed and experienced from the present. It is far from certain that existing reductionist approaches are capable of dealing with the complexity of such eventualizations.

Two concerns loom large. The first one relates to the erasure of the boundaries of the human and the machine. Such might be case in the recent turn towards what has been labeled "post-humanism" that insist on the bracketing (devaluing) of materiality and of embodiment (Hayles 1999, 48) of human life and culture.[4] The second relates to the role of memory as that which conserves the past and how it is through this preservation that we perceive difference (Bergson 1912). As Hasan remarks in his interview, one might ask: What happens with memory now that it is possible to save everything? Ubicomp intervenes in the negotiation of more complex understandings of temporal relations. But what happens then when we do not forget? Or when act of forgetting (or not) is denatured through technology into a commodity, as Pisters analysis of Omar Naim's *The Final Cut* shows us? An imminent danger, as Chun points out in her essay about memory in this volume, is the transformation of memory from an active process that involves the synergy of culture and biology into a passive state to be "provoked" by the plethora of devices in the environment. The loss of self-control caused by the reduction of human memory-specific complexity leads towards an ill-fated diminishing of inner life and human agency (see also Diaz' chapter elsewhere in this volume).

Notes

1   Cafaro et al. define the Uncanney Valley as a term coined by the Japanese roboticist Masahiro Mori to refer to the "counter-intuitive phenomenon where people may get suddenly uncomfortable with an artificial entity when it becomes very similar to humans."
2   In terms of financial scale, these installations are modest when compared to big budget Hollywood productions. Nevertheless they share the objective of developing time-based, totally immersive, and embodied, virtual experiences.
3   "Millenials" is a term used to refer to the generation born between the mid-1990s and early 2000s.
4   Hayles cautions us against "a systematic devaluation of materiality and embodiment."

References

Bartley, Elizabeth A., and John E. Hancock. 2008. "Virtual Reconstructions as Destination Tourism?" *International Journal of Digital Culture and Electronic Tourism* 1(2–3): 225–239.

Bergson, Henri. 1912. "Introduction to Metaphysics." Trans, T. E. Hulme. New York and London: G. P. Putnam's. Accessed on April 5, 2015. https://archive.org/details/anintroductiont00berggoog.

"Bullet through the Apple 1964." In *MIT Museum Collections—Objects*. Accessed April 31, 2015. http://webmuseum.mit.edu/detail.php?type=related&kv=96483&t=objects.

Cafaro, Francesco, Lyons, Leilah, Roberts, Jessica, and Radinsky, Josh. 2014. "The Uncanny Valley of Embodied Interaction Design." In *Performing Interactions, Proceeding of DIS 2014, 21–25, 2014 Vancouver, Canada*, 1075–1078. New York: ACM Press.

Canales, Jimena. 2011. "Harold E. Edgerton—'Doc' Edgerton and His Laboratory Notebooks." In *Aperture*. Accessed March 2, 2015. http://aperture.org/blog/harold-e-edgerton-doc-edgerton-and-his-laboratory-notebooks/.

"The Good and the Bad of Escaping to Virtual Reality." *The Atlantic* Feb 18, 2015. Accessed April 7, 2015. http://theatlantic.com/health/archive/2015/02/the-good-and-the-bad-of-escaping-to-virtual-reality/385134/.

Hayles, Katherine. 1999. *How We Became Post-Human, Virtual Bodies in Cybernetics, Literature, and Informatics*. Chicago: University of Chicago Press.

Jussim, Estelle, and Gus Kayafas, Ed. 1987. *Stopping Time: The Photographs of Harold Edgerton*. New York: Harry N. Abrams.

Mili, Gjon. 2011. "Jammin' the Blues." *Open Culture* October 21, 2011. Accessed April 3, 2015. http://openculture.com/2011/10/jammin_the_blues_by_gjon_mili.html.

Place-Hampi: Inhabiting the Cultural Imaginary. 2008. Retrieved April 7, 2015, from http://place-hampi.museum/contents/place-hampi.html.

Ng, Jenna. 2012. "Seeing Movement: On Motion Capture and James Cameron's Avatar." *Animation* 7(3): 273–286.

Reunanen, Markku, Lily Díaz, and Tommi Horttana. 2015. "A Holistic User-Centered Approach to Immersive Digital Cultural Heritage Installations: Case Vrouw Maria." *Journal on Computing and Cultural Heritage* 7(4): 1–11.

Ware, Colin. 2008. *Visual Thinking for Design*. Burlington, MA: Morgan Kaufman.

CULTURAL THEORY

Maria Engberg

For cultural theory (a very broad term encompassing theoretical writing from the historiography of Michel Foucault and the philosophy of Gilles Deleuze to the applied work of cultural studies and feminist theory), an event is never a simple or solitary entity. The relationship between or among events is never understood as cause and effect in the sense of nineteenth century positivism. For computer science, however, the concept of an event remains clear and simply defined. Events are at the heart of what computing is. In modern digital computers many processes run at once. Active processes are placed in arrays; an event *queue* or *heap* allocates cycles to running processes. To speak of "eventualizing" from the point of view of computer science would have to connect to the events that run to perform the tasks at hand, although the verb is not used in this manner in the field.

"Eventualizing" remains linked to Michel Foucault's term *événementialisation* (Foucault 1994) a neologism in French. The translation, or what Thomas R. Flynn calls a "barbarism in English" (Flynn 2010, 69), eventualizing is a process in Foucault's historiographic method in which the common sensical or given of a particular period or context is scrutinized by reversing the evidence. Thus, the conditions and practices of a particular time can be exposed and the historian can arrive at a different understanding.

The two chapter contributions in this section, by Maria Poulaki and Patricia Pisters, respectively, use film to describe how digital technology as a recording device and as an ontological condition of media impact how we understand cinema as a medium. While Poulaki and Pisters do not engage explicitly with the Foucauldian historiographic method, the insights their essays bring rely on an understanding of cinema's historical and socio-material conditions. Their chapters bring into focus different practices of seeing and looking, foregrounding aesthetic choices and material affordances alike, which allow us to see or to not see.

Poulaki focuses on invisibility and unawareness as part of cinema, in particular complex films, such as the work by Lars von Trier that she analyzes. Cinema is *the* medium that renders the invisible visible. Like Eadweard Muybridge's motion studies that captured that which the naked eye could not perceive, sequences of still photos can bring forth events that human vision cannot grasp while watching the moving image. Sequences and events come into clearer view as the flow is stopped and individual screens or shots can be interpreted.

Poulaki argues that the current technocultural conditions have profound consequences for film, and for its relationship with what we see. Provocatively, however, Poulaki starts with the premise that "many things in films stay under the threshold of visibility." In particular, she trains her eye on the editing techniques that allow von Trier to create complexity and self-reflexivity in his film. Shots and scene inserts become distinct units of meaning for the viewer to catch in order to understand or—even— see the system that lies beneath the individual moments. Eventualizing, then, happens through the well-known techniques of cinematography: repetition and variation, but with the distinctly contemporary media condition that digital technology affords. As Poulaki's analysis shows, repetition often occurs by having the same event, the same scene or object filmed from different angles, at different times. Other kinds of repetitions occur as the viewers have to gather clues in order to understand the sequence of events in von Trier's films. These complex events, Poulaki argues, make up a structural heterogeneity, enabling multiple relations between the individual units.

Patricia Pisters' contribution is also concerned with film and temporality. Not unlike Diaz and Chun's chapters elsewhere in this volume, Pisters explores the complexities of human memory as it is externalized and recorded by technology. In films such as *The Final Cut*, Pisters argues, we see a vision of how our processes of "impersonal individuation" can be controlled, manipulated, and recut by an increasingly prevalent and potent techno-industry. Pisters' essay asks us to consider what the ephemeral event is—as opposed to the recorded and possibly persisting event that become something else through technologies: a memory, a unit of history to be saved and shared.

There is, then, a conscious act—similar to the Foucauldian twist—in reexamining the evidence at hand to arrive at different interpretations of a particular condition. In the case of ubiquitous computing or the overall media condition in an age of computation, questions regarding what acts and agencies reside in the eventualizing come to mind. That events, flows, and procedures are foregrounded seems undisputable: the evidence for the predilection in contemporary technoculture for procedurality is overwhelming. Procedures imply events, processes, instances of computational algorithms that are acted upon by technologies. These mediatized procedures include or involve humans who echo in their own behavior the processes that are built into the machines. Imagine that you take your mobile phone with you on your daily run to track the path and speed with the help of an application, and you continuously use that application over time. Can you be sure that this tracking—a quantification and tracking of human behavior—does not eventually have an impact on the actions themselves? The recursive loop makes it increasingly uncertain who creates the process and who records it. As Pisters notes with respect to cinema, digital ubiquitous media form part of computational cultures in which technologies are "co-constitutive of our being."

In his book titled *Everyware*, Adam Greenfield argues that ubiquitous computing as a paradigm will come across to the average user as a single idea, what he calls "everyware." No matter how many companies, producers, programmers, or designers are involved in making our lived world rife with the potentialities of networked machines, everyware becomes then a unified phenomenon, a condition which means "information processing embedded in the objects and surfaces of everyday life" (Greenfield 2010, 18). The chapters in this section do not reflect directly on what that would mean, but by way of an earlier medium—cinema—they show how deeply and far-reaching the impact of any medium is. They also point toward how any conceptualization of ubiquity as everyware presents a vision that is, to put it bluntly, too neat. As Wendy Chun's contribution elsewhere in this volume reminds us, the classic vision of ubiquity of computers relied on an "everywhere yet nowhere visible." This runs counter to any serious exploration of film and film technologies' shaping and manipulations of our practices of looking. The individual events in a sequence of film or code need to be seized upon and scrutinized, Pisters and Poulaki would argue, rather than be allowed to cede into the background of a computationally enhanced environment.

References

Foucault, Michel. 1994. *Dits et écrits 1954–1988, tome 4 1980–1988*. Paris: Editions Gallimard.

Flynn, Thomas R. 2010. *Sartre, Foucault, and Historical Reason, Volume Two: A Poststructuralist Mapping of History*. Chicago, IL: University of Chicago Press.

Greenfield, Adam. 2010. *Everyware: The Dawning Age of Ubiquitous Computing*. New York: New Riders.

(IN)VISIBILITY, (UN)AWARENESS, AND A NEW WAY OF SEEING THROUGH COMPLEX CINEMA

Maria Poulaki

As cinema is considered a primarily visual art, it is a rather counterintuitive thought that many things in films stay under the threshold of visibility, and many others cannot be grasped in their entirety because of the never-ending movement of the film. Cinema itself was based on the—known at least for half-century before its emergence—phenomenon of the persistence of vision, according to which for a few milliseconds an afterimage persists on the human retina. This phenomenon is responsible for rendering the gaps between the subsequent film frames "invisible" to the viewers.

Cinema developed as a technology, as cinema critic and theorist André Bazin stressed (1967b), to render visible what was previously invisible, such as the galloping of a horse in the famous Muybridge experiment. Utilizing techniques of time manipulation, this early epistemological cinema captured with its "mechanical eye" what the human eye with its limited capacities could not discern.

However, even though cinema with its advent brought a new vision, it also created new conditions for invisibility, new blind spots. With the development of film, and as cinema became a language through the use of montage, the purely epistemic purpose of experimenting with and advancing visibility was set aside. Cinema becomes a medium for artistic expression rather than a scientific tool.

After the early years of non-narrative, or even "scientific," cinema, the issue of visibility becomes again pertinent in relation to cinema as language, and its precondition—montage, or the cut—the Hollywood narrative tradition, which prevailed since 1917 and to a large extent determined the trajectory of cinema as a medium, was based on the invisibility of the cut. As again Bazin writes in his essay "The Evolution of the Language of Cinema," "the use of montage can be "invisible" and this was generally the case of prewar classics of the American screen" (1967a, 24). He goes on to explain how the editing of scenes was following the "dramatic logic" of the depicted situation, without drawing attention to the cut itself, which, however, has an incredible power, as it seamlessly—in the case of classical Hollywood—controls our vision.

After the War, a different kind of cinema, present in movements such as the French New Wave (Nouvelle Vague), stood exactly at the opposite front, making its mission to make visible what was rendered invisible by Hollywood narrative and its editing techniques. Therefore, the cut acquires in films of Godard or Truffaut an increased visibility. With the employment of cinematographic techniques such as handheld camera shooting, scale shifts, blurred images, etc., films of Nouvelle Vague, or later Cinéma Verité, did not only have as their mission to enhance visibility; they aimed to expose the incapacity of the medium to do so; its power to conceal rather than to reveal. By drawing attention to techniques of cinematography and montage (such as the jump-cut), these movements exposed the language of cinema as distorting reality. Thus, a question of awareness rather than visibility becomes pertinent for the first time in the postwar period.

As with visibility, the relationship of cinema with awareness is dubious. Much more than visibility though, awareness is not considered to be a defining characteristic or effect of cinema; on the contrary, it is with unawareness that the cinematic situation has most often been associated, especially through the psychoanalytic tradition, and the relationship between cinema and dream (highlighted, among others, by Roland Barthes, Raymond Bellour, and Guy Rosolato).

At least conscious awareness and the Ego's defensive mechanisms are supposed to be partially suspended during film watching—as well as what is called disbelief—in order for the film to immerse the spectator into its story world. Perhaps more distinctively Jean-Louis Baudry (1986) and Christian Metz (1976) argued, the former drawing on Althusser, that the cinematic apparatus, creating dream-like conditions, puts the spectators in narcissistic isolation from the external real world. (Lewallen 2001)

This psycho-cognitive regression that the "dream factory" of cinema facilitates has been both theoretically and practically fought. In the 1970s, theories and techniques of self-reflexivity (under the influence of Brechtian theatre and Godard) were promoted both by art cinema and film criticism as necessary means for films to awaken the consciousness of viewers, and their critical thought. Self-reflexivity became a flag of self-conscious narration, requiring accordingly self-aware spectators. Elsaesser and Hagener (2010) comment on how, through techniques such as "nested narration (a film within a film), [. . .] pictorial framing which highlighted the constructedness of the *mise-en-scène*, or through an accentuated paraphrasing of traditional plot stereotypes, genre patterns and pastiche citations" (75), cinema developed its own "language of crisis" in order to express a self-critical stance towards itself as an illusion-generating technology (74–77). It also developed, through auteur films such as *Le Mépris* (Godard 1963), *8½* (Fellini 1963), *Blow Up* (Antonioni 1966), the metaphor of itself as mirror, where the spectator is supposed to face the image of him or herself in critical disillusionment (Elsaesser and Hagener 2010, 56).

The desire to know despite the inability to see lies at the core for cinematic epistemology. And quite counterintuitively, the act of seeing has been conceived in cinema theory as a way to challenge the medium's inherent invisibility and raise awareness of its techniques of manipulation.

Contemporary Complex Films and the Urge to Visualize

The way narrative films represent reality has fundamentally changed in the last decades. Whereas classical narration is still popular, other ways of complex narration, once considered avant-garde or experimental, have now made it to the mainstream. *Inception* is just an example of popularly complex cinematic narration. Nested narration, pictorial framing, and other self-reflexive techniques are characteristic of films that since the beginning of the last decade have been theoretically approached as "complex" (Steiger 2006; Simons 2008), "puzzle" (Bordwell 2006; Buckland 2009), and "modular" (Cameron 2008) narratives, or "mind-game" films

(Elsaesser 2009)—among other terms. Complex films flourished in indie cinema productions since the mid-1990s (and in diverse geopolitical regions, from the United States to Europe and Asia—see Buckland 2009) and now their modes are also encountered in Hollywood films (see Buckland 2014). Including from titles such as *Pulp Fiction* (1994) and *Fight Club* (1999) in the early days of this rising tendency, to blockbuster films such as *Inception* (2010) or *Source Code* (2011) lately, the corpus of complex films does by no means lend itself as a coherent object of analysis. However, most of them are characterized by their tendency to restructure the temporal sequence, to use stills and freeze frames, intense repetition, and other techniques that allow us to "look" during the process—and, by isolating either narrative or visual details, to defeat the medium's inherent invisibility.

These techniques are reminiscent of earlier avant-garde self-reflexive techniques, and various film theorists have found self-reflexivity (or self-reference) to be a central, if not the defining, characteristic of contemporary complex films (Mittell 2006; Lavik 2008). Although self-reference in arts has been considered a forced (and most of the times top-down) awareness of the medium or the "fiction," and the manipulation they exert upon viewers, the proliferation of self-reference in contemporary complex films goes further than the awareness created by meta-narration or meta-fiction; it becomes the skeleton of the film, its particular mode of organization. Self-reference organizes—instead of dismantles—the story world but also the communication between film and viewer, a communication that is aware of the "illusion" of the spectacle but also somehow stays indifferent towards illusionism altogether (Poulaki 2012).

In what follows, I will show how complexity creates and is created by the films' continuous self-reflexivity, which sets off the interplay of visibility and invisibility, awareness and unawareness in them, and negotiates the conditions of our cinematic visuality. I will particularly focus on the work of director Lars von Trier, one of the founders of the avant garde Dogme 95 movement. Apart from being known for his self-conscious and metafictional narration, "ensuring the viewer's distant observation" (Grodal 2004, 152; Ditzian 2008), Trier is also considered a master of complex films.

Complex films more and more explicitly challenge the objectivist epistemology on which Western subjectivity and cinema itself are founded. In classical narrative cinema perhaps we find an ideal incarnation of this epistemology, keeping the spectator immobile and distant from the spectacle, and allowing him to passively register reality from his vantage point. The stories of complex films balance between reality and illusion staying indifferent (or agnostic) towards the distinction of the two. The viewer needs to *look* for cues in the screen space to orientate him/herself in the diegesis.

Elsaesser named his "mind-game" films (a variety of complex films) after Lars von Trier's expression. The director used the term "mind-game" to describe how in his film *The Boss of It All* (2006), he set up a game with the viewers by planting "lookeys" (a combination of the words "look" and "keys") in the frames, that is, key-objects that hide in them and the viewer is challenged to discover them (Elsaesser 2009). As von Trier himself explains, "All Lookeys in a movie can be decoded by a system that is unique for the movie. To decipher the system is part of the challenge" (Mitchell 2006). I will use as examples the two films of the director *Antichrist* (2009) and *Melancholia* (2011), which are much more narrative films than *The Boss*, to argue that they set up the same game with the viewer but this time not only through hidden objects but also through shot inserts that we may see but not understand, till they match with one another, as soon as we decipher the system that binds them together.

Antichrist and *Melancholia*, apart from being narratively and stylistically complex, are aesthetically related to one another, and they repeat certain elements characteristic of von Trier's oeuvre as well as of complex films as a whole. From a narrative perspective, the two films are more conventional than previous works of the director, and that is so because they are more typical narratives, lacking the radically restricted narrative style of *Idioterne* (1998) or the Brechtian theatricality of *Dogville* (2003), for instance. *Antichrist* could nominate more easily as a puzzle or mind game film, in terms of its story and plot, *Melancholia* not as easily, although I would argue that from the perspective of the main protagonist Clair (Charlotte Gainsbourg) which we mostly share at least in the second part of the film, *Melancholia* also has mind-game characteristics.

In *Antichrist*, the protagonist (Willem Dafoe), a psychotherapist, thinks he has control over the difficult situation he finds himself in after the lethal accident of his young son, who, left unattended while his parents were making love, fell out of the window. He thinks he has the knowledge to cure his wife from the depression she suffers, but he soon discovers that she keeps a secret and manipulates him. In *Melancholia*, the marriage of Justine (Kirsten Dunst) is called off as she is hit by another depressive episode, while by coincidence this happens in the same period when a planet called Melancholia threatens to hit Earth. Justine's sister Claire (Charlotte Gainsbough) takes care of her during her depression, while she tries to fight her own fear in front of the possible catastrophe.

An overarching metaphor of blindness traverses both films. The vision and awareness of the main characters, the man in *Antichrist* and Claire in *Melancholia*, is restricted, despite both of them being very keen to see and discover the truth behind the events happening. Equally "blind" are the viewers, as they are not allowed any knowledge privilege on behalf of the films' narration. The characters need to somehow transcend common reason and believe in almost supernatural images and events through an enhanced and forced sight. The viewers' sight is on the other hand enhanced by visual inserts throughout both films, i.e. frames and shots which do not immediately serve any narrative purpose but repeat in different variations. This way our awareness of the film system is formed.

Repetition and variation of images is a common way through which films—each one to a different degree—construct their narrative and stylistic form (Bordwell and Thompson 2010). They are not unique features of the work of von Trier or, even less, of the two films I am discussing here. But still repetition and variation do have a specific function in complex films, and I will use these two films as cases of employment of these means to convey a particular systemic visuality. In both *Antichrist* and *Melancholia*, there are repetitions and variations of narrative and visual themes and patterns within each one of the two films, but also between them.

To start with visual themes, *Antichrist* abounds with repetitive rhizomatic graphic patterns. Many shots involve images of routes and earth—and the film gives a rather hostile portrait of the latter, through an obvious allegoric parallelism between mother and earth. Moving from the microscopic to the macroscopic, earth in *Melancholia* is imminently destroyed by the slow approach of a mysterious planet. Here round graphic patterns compete the rhizomatic ones, and harmonic lines are contrasted with perplexed shapes. Earth is still the main protagonist of both films, and in both cases it threatens a mother—two contrasting versions of which are played by the same actress, Gainsbourg, in the two films. The mother of *Antichrist* is unstable and dangerous, herself fearful of her connection to earth and nature, while the other of *Melancholia* grounded and protective, earthly in a comforting way, but at the same time anxiously awaiting the clash with an external force beyond her control; a smaller, bluer, "other earth" that is inescapably approaching.

Apart from graphic patterns repeated in each film and to some extent contrasted between the two films, a pictorial tendency characterizes both, through the shot composition and the emphasis on painting, writing (apart from images of books, the films themselves are structured as books and divided in chapters, something repeated in the last films of von Trier *Nymphomaniac I ans II*), and book illustrations. A parallelism between the two films can be drawn through certain oneiric frames aesthetically reminiscent of religious and fantastic iconography. For example, in *Antichrist*, such shot is the one depicting the advent of the main female character to Eden, the couple's cottage in the woods, where the previous summer the woman isolated with her son to work on her dissertation (on misogyny and Medieval witch-hunt). Other examples, at the ending of the same film, are the image of a tree surrounded by naked bodies—reminiscent of paintings of Hieronymus Bosch, as well as later in the Epilogue the shot of the inescapable embrace of the man with female figures. Lastly, in *Melancholia*, intensely pictorial compositions are most notably the 16 slow-motion shots of the opening sequence, some lasting for over 40 seconds, and occupying the first eight minutes of the film.

Besides graphic composition of shots and the pictorial attributes of the mise-en-scène, perhaps the most important (self-)reflexive and visualizing technique used in the two films is the repetition and variation of them, as well as of other shots and scenes. Many scenes are internally multiplied as they are compositions of similar shots of the same object taken from different angles and at different times—as it happens, for example, in the opening scene of the first part ("Justine") in *Melancholia*, and in several other scenes. This is characteristic technique of von Trier, the complexity of which has been discussed by media theorist Jan Simons (2007: 76). Moreover, in *Antichrist* there is a notable variation of one whole scene, at minute 34 and 56, respectively. In the first one we see the man walking in the woods when it suddenly gets windy and a strange sound is heard. As he turns he sees a deer standing still a few meters away from him, looking towards his direction. The deer starts galloping away (seen in slow motion), and the man realizes that it carries behind it a dead fawn, still hanging from the body of its mother.

Some twenty minutes later in the course of the film, the man is walking again in the trees when he notices some leaves moving. As he approaches and the wind starts again to blow, he puts aside the leaves to find something hiding behind them. When he reaches to touch it he realizes it is a fox, eating itself and the embryo it carries. These two scenes are almost identical in terms of mise en scène and theme, creating a time loop that disorients the viewer.

In *Melancholia*, all the shots of the slow motion opening sequence are repeated in one way or another later in the film. In one of the last scenes of the first chapter of the film, we see Justine at the library of the villa where her wedding ceremony takes place. She lays open some books with photographs of paintings, among which, Millais' *Ophelia* (a variation of which we saw in the opening sequence, with Justine herself in the place of Ophelia), and Karl Fredrik Hill's *Crying Deer*. The head and horns of the deer in this painting graphically match the composition of Justine's body in the opening shot of her walking through the garden with her wedding dress caught in weeds.

The opening sequence of *Melancholia*, a composition of pictorial shots, foregrounds the ending of the film. The shot at which Claire runs desperate carrying her son is repeated towards the end, only now the light and colors have changed; the shot is not anymore depicting a sunny day but gloomy atmosphere and hail, as the end of the world is approaching (Plates 49 and 50). Moreover, in the last scene, we see Justine wearing the same clothes she did in one of the shots of the opening sequence, where in turn the son of Claire was seen cutting sticks—foregrounding the construction of the "magic cave" by him and his aunt at the end of the film. Thus, the ending of the film *resonates* with the oneiric opening sequence of the beginning, creating a loop.

Just like *Melancholia*, *Antichrist* repeats towards the end a part of the opening black and white scene, showing it again in slow motion, but with a significant variation: In contrast with the opening, now we see a closer and not blurred shot of the mother's face, followed by a point-of-view shot to the child climbing out of the window—a revelation for the viewer who so far doesn't know that the woman watched the fall of her child (Figure 33.1). The scene is accompanied by the same music track—from Handel's *Rinaldo*. The recurrence of a musical theme is even more prominent in *Melancholia*, where Wagner's *Tristan und Isolde* creates a pattern throughout the film.

In both films the most important shot inserts are presented through slow motion or stop motion, like the passage of the woman to Eden in *Antichrist*, resonating with the walk of Justine through the garden in her wedding dress in *Melancholia*, or the man's encounters with animals in *Antichrist*. Such inserts evoke an enhanced visibility, which, however, resists rational interpretation, at the same time that they explicitly connect to the other visual inserts at other points in the films.

Apart from their reliance on repetition, variation, and contrast, the two films are pervasive of a hyperrealistic feeling and a deliberate factitiousness. The fantasy and the realistic elements in them have the same status, as if the films are taking an indifferent stance towards illusionism. The encounters of the man with the three animals in *Anti-Christ* (the "three beggars" as they're called, the deer, the fox, and the crow) are good examples of this stance—especially at the moment when the fox talks to him in human voice. The indifference or even mockery towards "the truth" is further demonstrated in *Melancholia*, where our attention is attracted to elements that are never entirely deciphered (like the golf hole with the number 19, or the bridge that for some reason cannot be crossed) and remain unexplained after the ending.

On the other hand, what the eyes see can be true even when it is blatantly unlikely. In *Antichrist* we already find the nascent theme of the impossible star constellation, which in *Melancholia* becomes the central theme of the film. An astronomic chart contained in the woman's

FIGURE 33.1 The revealing shot of the mother's look in Antichrist

dissertation includes star constellations in the shape of the three beggars—and named after them. Seeing the chart, the man doubts the validity of this depiction: "there's no such constellation", he murmurs. In *Melancholia* on the other hand, Justine immediately "believes" in the reality of the planet that has entered the Earth's solar system, even when the others are still unaware of it, and believe it is just a star among the others.

Vision is put under question in the two films, and especially the way we trust its technologies, from the most primitive (the metal circle that the husband of Claire constructs in order to measure the approach of the planet Melancholia), to the most sophisticated, like the telescope, the photographic camera (as explained below) and the film's camera itself (which can offer a misleading image, as in the starting scene of *Antichrist*, where it racks focus from the face of the mother, not allowing us to see her observing her child's fall) (Figure 33.2).

The relation of vision to awareness is problematized by the protagonists' reluctance to believe what they see (Dafoe in *Antichrist*, Gainsbourg in *Melancholia*). The way awareness emerges is through a ubiquity of dubious clues scattered throughout the films. The protagonist of *Antichrist* needs to scrutinize a series of similar polaroid pictures of his young boy in order to notice an irregularity in them, which confirms his suspicions. The image of the shoes of his son—a key to the unravelling of the mystery—has been already shown to us viewers at least twice: at the opening scene of the film, as well as in another scene where the man was staring at the same photograph without noticing its "error." Like him, we can't notice the errors in the film, which hide from us like lookeys that can only be discovered either through multiple viewings or through pausing and zooming. For instance, the variation of the animal encounter scene described above suggests such a double viewing that helps us decipher the pattern connecting the two scenes.

Among the lookeys hiding in this film, three miniature figures placed on the surface that the boy climbs to get to the window at the opening scene, have tiny labels on them, only visible by pausing the film and reading the image carefully: by doing this the viewer can notice that the figurines' labels foreground the three chapters of the film (pain, grief, despair) as well as the three beggars associated with each chapter (Figure 33.3).

Ironically, the duality of visibility-invisibility is explicitly highlighted in *Antichrist* through the woman's dissertation writings that the man discovers. One page of her manuscript refers to the Devil's marks on witches, which could be either visible as skin marks, or invisible. This meta-comment is however not entirely visible to us viewers, unless we again pause the flow of the film to read the page (Plate 51).

In the two films, as it happens in most mind-game films, there is no sovereign perspective or omniscient diegetic narrator—not even the camera. However, because of the themes they deal with (most of the times traversed with mystery) and through the use of self-reflexive techniques, narration constantly declares its power,[2] and reminds viewers to be alert and collect clues and lookeys, being ready to shift their perspective. As spectators we do look, but not from a sovereign position—we rather need to combine multiple clues or viewpoints, none of which offers a complete picture.

As already stated, self-reflexive techniques have been used in the history of film for the purpose of extended visibility ("spatializing time"), and also awareness. These techniques return in contemporary complex films, but here, it is not a shift from invisibility and unawareness to visibility and awareness that is pursued. Rather, a continuous interplay (or feedback) between the two is at hand. The complexity of *Antichrist* and *Melancholia*, like it happens with other complex films, is based on their piecemeal structure (which contains, as already discussed, aberrant

FIGURE 33.2 Lens focus hiding the mother's secret in Antichrist

FIGURE 33.3 The three figurines

"puzzle" pieces or visual inserts)—in *Antichrist* in a larger extent and scattered through the film, while in *Melancholia* less and more condensed in certain parts. The films invite a process of combination and recombination of these elements in order for the viewer to see the network they form. The interplay of awareness and unawareness in them takes place through the reflexive relationships of the film's units with one another, which makes the form of the film more complex and at the same time enables its systemic self-reference.

Complexity, Reflexivity, and Observation

Patterns are forms emerging when units like the shot inserts of puzzle films resonate forming a system. A theoretical framework of how systems are formed through self-reflexivity is given by the autopoietic social systems theory of Niklas Luhmann. Through the notions of observation and self-reference, Luhmann described how systems build their complexity and how they organize by re-structuring themselves.

In Luhmann's terms, self-reference is a form of systemic self-awareness. It is not related to visibility or contemplation; rather, it is an immanent systemic process. It emerges out of a system's multiple self-observation, and in turn helps its self-organization, the way that it chooses (selects) and (re-)arranges its elements.

Further on with Luhmann's conceptualization, systems are "blind" until the point when they draw a distinction between themselves and the environment. Visible in systems theory is only what acquires self-reference, and thus makes itself visible not only to external observers but also to itself. In other words, to be observed by an external observer, a system needs to make itself observable, and this happens by referring to itself. On the other hand, there is not really an external observer. As Luhmann writes, "Whoever observes participates in this system—or he does not observe" (1995, xxxiii).

Applying this theory to film, I would argue that as viewers we observe the film when the film observes itself. Moreover, that we see the film only when our "psychic system" (the third type of systems for Luhmann, apart from the social and the living/biological) is already structured by it, in other words when our cognitive and affective faculties have already been affected by the film's structure, to the point that viewer and film form parts of one system and the film exists in the mind of the viewer, as much as the viewer exists in the text of the film.

Borrowing Luhmann's framework and adopting a systemic view of films, we could argue that film systems observe themselves structurally, through instances that make their own formal constitution observable—to an external observer, the viewer. Luhmann distinguishes between different orders or levels of observation; basal self-reference, reflexivity, and self-reflection. At the level of *basal self-reference*, the system selects out of a multiplicity of elements those that can potentially be linked to others and are meaningful for the system. This can be said about the selection that the viewer makes out of the multiplicity of stimuli provided in a frame—although the film itself provides cues and directs (or not) attention to lookeys. At the level of *reflexivity*, relations are built between the elements and these relations become more complex with time as new elements enter the system and rearrange existing structures making new ones emerge. Lastly, at the level of *reflection* the system observes its own overall form, and makes itself observable to another system. Reflection makes a pattern visible. The three levels of observation are not succeeding one another in chronological sequence but they rather happen simultaneously and are connected in a continuous feedback loop. Self-reflection (observation of the system's overall form, which makes itself observable to another system) is triggered by the lower-order, reflexive, observation.

But how exactly does the film structure itself as a system, and how does reflexivity enable observation and organization? It does so through iteration and variation—which create resonance between its units—scenes, shots, frames, and objects. By means of referring to each other in a reflexive manner, the elements of the film produce a systemic form of self-reference.

An object, frame element, shot, or scene might be shown again but through a different perspective (for instance, that of a different character),[3] or it might be presented again but in a different way, as a variation or a distorted double, as it happens with the animal scenes in *Antichrist*, or the opening and closing shots in *Melancholia*. These instances of variation can be considered moments of reflexivity in the system of the film. As a type of self-reference and self-observation occurring by the reference of elements of the same level to one another, reflexivity generates—and is generated by—an overall organization; that of the system itself. Shots/scenes that refer back to previous or later ones (reflexivity), duplicate the present and introduce a different perspective—an observation from another point in time—upon the images shown/events narrated, and also upon the viewer's experience of them (reflection). By means of a continuous feedback, reflexivity is constantly interfering changing the existing patterns and delaying their completion, to the point that reflection (the formation of the system in the eyes of an observer) is never complete –therefore the films remain open-ended.

In complex film systems, the film's reflexive resonances mediate its overall self-reference, constituting a form of intricate and "blind" observation—a precondition for the film's communication with the viewer.

Luhmann's conception of observation and self-reference not only does not imply vision, but on the contrary, it is irrelevant to it. Observation emerges through an intricate reference of parts to one another, rather than comes from a sovereign center or from an external ideally located observer. Instances of systemic self-reference become instances of awareness, on behalf of the viewer/participant, that there is some kind of system s/he observes, and by observing it s/he participates in it.

As said previously, complex films, rather than simply creating awareness in a Brechtian fashion, they set up a constant interplay between awareness/visibility and unawareness/invisibility. It is only at the moment that a variated element is recognized as such that observation happens; and recognition presupposes a degree of previous blindness. And even at instances of observation, awareness is not definite or complete; rather, every observation introduces uncertainty at a different level, creating a mise-en-abyme structure in which the viewer constantly locates and loses herself. The moments of awareness contained in it do not close the film's system into a coherent whole, neither do they produce a definite meaning. Instead, these moments are always expanding the story world and strengthening the link between film and viewer, as well as the one between the film and other films or media—in an intertextual or transmedia fashion—rendering the film's organization more complex and ready to encompass further complexity at every point it observes itself. The viewer's own observation is never sovereign, and s/he is constantly reminded of this in the course of the viewing.

We spectators are far from being sovereign observers either, because the film is a dynamic flow rather than a static point. Thus, instead of seeing we rather "feel" the film as an entity acquiring its own agency through loops and resonances between its elements. Our "understanding" of the film happens in terms of a systemic communication between film and viewer and an emergent way of pattern-making.

In the end, knowledge or understanding are not so relevant categories through which we can approach the communication between film and viewer; it is awareness that would be more appropriate. The viewer gains cognitive and affective awareness of the constitution of a complex textual system (through patterns of heterogeneous points in time and space) in which there is no sovereign observing centre—internal or external, the viewer or the narrating agency—but many dispersed nodes, none of which is able to behold or reproduce "the whole picture." Through the arrangement of its elements, the film as system creates its own form of self-observation, which is intertwined with its complex organization.

Ubiquity of Observation

Although many puzzle or mind-game films have surveillance as a common narrative pattern (e.g., *The Usual Suspects*, *Fight Club*, *The Sixth Sense*, *The Jacket*, *Shutter Island*, *Inception*), I would argue that, beyond narrative surveillance (which implies a top-down and centralized Orwellian structure), it is more distributed observation that becomes a pervasive characteristic of the form of mind-game films. The sense of a ubiquitous surveillance/observation in them emerges from the bottom-up, out of the various units reflecting and observing one another. Observation is thus embedded in the structure of the film-systems, through the many instances of (and opportunities for) systemic reflexivity they contain. Through these instances the film organizes itself, observes itself, and at the same time makes itself observable to other systems (including the viewer).

Their feature of embedded self-observation brings contemporary complex films closer to complex systems, which organize through self-observation. Moreover, the same feature on the one hand reveals a tendency of films to reproduce in the structure of their plot their ontological transformation *vis à vis* digitization and computation (their composition out of units of meaning that need to be aggregated), and on the other hand points at the need to update our theoretical and methodological tools, so as to be able to address films as informational entities.

Narrative complexity is by no means a new phenomenon in cinema or other arts, nor does it confine itself to films that have recently been described as complex. However, as every art form might use the same or similar means in different eras to address different socially and culturally situated subjects, I would argue that through the employment of reflexive means, contemporary complex films are expressive of a culture of ubiquitous information and ubiquitous surveillance, which in turn places its subject in a position of dispersed observation.

Contemporary mind-game films perhaps "train" spectators (in line with Elsaesser's argument) to new systemic forms of meaning making, of perception and organization of story worlds that have to deal with unawareness and invisibility. Moreover, they require from spectators to adopt different forms of perception, rather than relying on their vision alone.

And how can these forms be useful? It depends on how complexity is treated. On the one hand, complex films might be more cognitively challenging than the average narrative film, in the sense of their structural heterogeneity, which enables a multiplication of relations between their units. The more their relations and links, the more is their complexity. On the other hand, by drawing attention on their complexity and making it observable, these films also set up a quest to reduce it through pattern formation. This process is important and useful not only for contemporary viewers but also contemporary social subjects. In the network society we inhabit, we witness a polarization between intricate and systemic self-organization, and attempts to render the complexity of systems observable and in the last instance manageable. Tagging and building block strategies are some of the most common mechanisms, used by various social structures and organisms, to track complexity, and render it manageable (Smith 2006). The fascination with complex systems visualization is a symptom of the desire to see and track the patterns that the resonances between a system's units form. And this kind of pattern visualization most of the times has nothing to do with the representational aspects of the objects/systems actually being visualized.

Contemporary technological and cultural conditions perhaps bring a qualitative shift in cinema's relation with visuality, i.e. the way we see. The way mind-game films attract our attention to individual elements (shots or scenes) through repetition and variation, not only creates complexity, but also temporarily manages it by making the system subject and object of observation. Hence by exposing complexity, films also render it manageable—and indeed train us spectators to different ways of engaging with distributed intelligence.

We get to see when links are formed between distributed and disconnected elements, and only then we become aware of the systems in the formation of which we participate, not as sovereign observers but as nodes, that will never hold or reproduce the whole picture.

Notes

1 See mainly Cameron 2008, but also Cubitt 2004 and Jenkins 2006.
2 The flash-forwards in *Melancholia* indeed create, as Bordwell and Thompson would have it, "a sense of narration with a powerful range of story knowledge" (2010, 233).
3 This different perspective might be the one of a different character. This is frequent in another kind of complex films, the multiple-protagonist films or "network" films (Bordwell 2006, 2007). These films distribute points of view among their multiple characters, who, kept isolated from each other for the most part of the film, represent different viewpoints upon the story world.

References

Bazin, André. 1967a. "The Evolution of the Language of Cinema." In *What is Cinema* 1, edited by Hugh Gray, 23–40. Berkeley, CA: University of California Press.

Bazin, André. 1967b. "The Myth of Total Cinema." In *What is Cinema* 2, edited by Hugh Gray, 23–27. Berkeley, CA: University of California Press.

Baudry, Jean-Louis. 1986. "The Apparatus: Metapsychological Approaches to the Impression of Reality in Cinema." In *Narrative, Apparatus, Ideology: A Film Theory Reader*, edited by Philip Rosen, 299–318. New York: Columbia University Press.

Bordwell, David, and Kristin Thompson. 2010. *Film Art: An Introduction*, 9th edition. New York: McGraw-Hill.

Bordwell, David. 2006. *The Way Hollywood Tells It: Story and Style in Modern Movies*. Berkeley and Los Angeles, CA: University of California Press.

Bordwell, David. 2007. *Poetics of Cinema*. New York: Routledge.

Buckland, Warren (ed). 2009. *Puzzle Films: Complex Storytelling in Contemporary Cinema*. Chichester: Wiley-Blackwell.

Buckland, Warren (Ed). 2014. *Hollywood Puzzle Films*. New York: Routledge.

Cameron, Allan. 2008. *Modular Narratives in Contemporary Cinema*. Basingstoke, UK: Palgrave Macmillan.

Cubitt, Sean. 2004. *The Cinema Effect*. Cambridge, MA: MIT Press.

Ditzian, Tamar. 2008. *Playing with Our Emotions: Genre, Realism and Reflexivity in the Films of Lars Von Trier*. Winnipeg, Canada: University of Manitoba.

Elsaesser, Thomas. 2009. "The Mind-Game Film." In *Puzzle Films: Complex Storytelling in Contemporary Cinema*, edited by Warren Buckland, 13–41. Chichester, UK: Blackwell.

Elsaesser, Thomas, and Malte Hagener. 2010. *Film Theory: An Introduction through the Senses*. New York: Routledge.

Grodal, Torben. 2004. "Frozen Flows in von Trier's Oeuvre". In *Visual Authorship. Creativity and Intentionality in Media*, edited by Torben Kragh Grodal, Bente Larson, and Iben Thorving Laursen, 129–167. Copenhagen, Denmark: Museum Tusculanum Press.

Jenkins, Henry. 2006. *Convergence Culture: Where Old and New Media Collide*. New York: New York University Press.

Lavik, Erlend. 2008. *Changing Narratives. Five Essays on Hollywood History*. The University of Bergen, Norway. https://bora.uib.no/handle/1956/3183?mode=full/.

Lewallen, Constance. 2001. *The Dream of the Audience: Theresa Hak Kyung Cha*. Berkeley and Los Angeles, CA: University of California Press.

Luhmann, Niklas. 1995. *Social Systems*. Translated by John Bednarz. Stanford, CA: Stanford University Press.

Metz, Christian. 1976. "The Fiction Film and its Spectator: A Metapsychological Study." Translated by Alfred Guzzetti. *New Literary History* 8 (1): 75–105.

Mitchell, Wendy. 2006. "Lars von Trier Unveils Lookey Concept." *Screen Daily*, December 6. Accessed November 15, 2013. http://screendaily.com/lars-von-trier-unveils-lookey-concept/4029856/.

Mittell, Jason. 2006. "Narrative Complexity in Contemporary American Television." *The Velvet Light Trap* 58: 29–40.

Simons, Jan. 2007. *Playing the Waves: Lars von Trier's Game Cinema*. Amsterdam, The Netherlands: Amsterdam University Press.

Simons, Jan. 2008. "Complex Narratives." *New Review of Film and Television Studies* 6 (2): 111–126.

Steiger, Janet. 2006. "Complex Narratives: An Introduction." *Film Criticism* 31 (1/2): 2.

Poulaki, Maria. 2012. "Self-Reflexivity, Description, And The Boundaries Of Narrative Cinema." *Cinéma & Cie* 12 (1): 45–55.

Smith, Edward. 2006. *Complexity, Networking, and Effects-based Approaches to Operations*. Washington, DC: CCRP (Command and Control Research Program) Publication Series.

CUTTING AND FOLDING THE BORGESIAN MAP

Film as Complex Temporal Object in the Industrialization of Memory

Patricia Pisters

"Memory fades. Even your most important moments slip away over time. And when you die, they will disappear forever. But not anymore. Surgically implanted into your child before birth, the Zoë Chip will record every moment, from birth to death, enabling their entire life to be enjoyed again and again by future generations."[1] This description of the film *The Final Cut* does not sound that much like science fiction in the age of ubiquitous computation. As Ulrik Ekman has shown in *Throughout*, contemporary life is permeated with a wide range of conspicuous and inconspicuous forms of technical mediation, ranging from micro-cameras to radio-frequency identification (RFID) chips, from pervasive surveillance grids to mobile and locative media to augmented realities, interactive cloths and ambient urban computing (Ekman 2013). In this chapter, I will focus on one particular aspect of the ways in which ubiquitous computing intervenes in our life, namely in negotiating a more complex understanding of temporal relations. *The Final Cut* may present a world were brain implanted cameras allow total recall of our lives, reproducing it like a Borgesian map (Borges 1999, 325). However, in order to sustain and make sense of life and death, we still need to select, cut, and edit. These memory processes are increasingly technologically mediated as well. As Niklas Luhman asserts, in our high tech society, memory and temporal relations have become increasingly complex processes that call for new ways of understanding temporal dynamics.[2] Films such as *The Final Cut* and contemporary cinema more generally provide us with images and stories that tell us something about these complex enfoldments of time mediated by ubiquitous computing. In an engagement with Gilles Deleuze's cinema books of the 1980s, I have described contemporary cinema as "the neuro-image" (Deleuze 1986; 1989; Pisters 2012). The thought of the neuro-image is indebted to Deleuze's philosophy of cinema and time but brings this to a digital epoch. In order to allow a more explicit technological, critical, and complex engagement with cinema as co-constitutive of complex temporalizations and eventualizations of life, this chapter stages an encounter, perhaps surprising, between Deleuze and Bernard Stiegler's *Technics and Time* (Stiegler 2009; 2011).

Tertiary Retention: Cinema as Temporal Object

Before zooming in on contemporary cinema of the digital age, it is important to establish the ways in which cinema as a media technology is not just a representation of what is going on in the real world, but a matter of a technology co-constitutive of our being. While Deleuze's cinema books are a rich conceptual source for understanding the immanent power of cinema, his engagement with media technology as such remains quite implicit. More explicit on this, Bernard Stiegler in his three volumes on *Technics and Time* proposes a reorientation (or "disorientation") of philosophy by conceiving technology and humanity as co-dependent, notably in the conjunction between technics and time. Stiegler defines technics as "a process of exteriorization [that] is the pursuit of life by means other than life" (Stiegler 1998, 17). He engages with industrially produced "analogico–numeric apparatuses," such as film, television, and computer networks, and demonstrates their profound influence and constitutive role for both individual and collective consciousness and temporality (Stiegler 2009, 111). To rethink time in relation to technology, Stiegler returns to Husserl who made an absolute distinction between primary retention, as the perception of time in the living present; secondary retention, defined as the imagined past as memory; and finally, recorded or mediated time, which Husserl called consciousness of image, a concept that Stiegler replaces with the concept of tertiary retention (Stiegler 2011, 16). Contrary to Husserl, however, Stiegler argues that primary and secondary retention are enfolded into one another by virtue of the fact that each primary perception is already colored by memory, and that this is a never-ending process. Moreover, he argues that tertiary retention, and any form of recorded or mediated memory ("objective memory" that is not necessarily lived on a personal level), does not come after primary and secondary retention but *precedes* other forms of memory: consciousness is fully entangled with and in large parts determined by mediated temporal objects. While the age of pervasive computing is heavily influenced by networks of digital objects, it is important to keep the temporal nature of cinema (analog or digital) in mind as fundamentally related to consciousness. As Stiegler explains in the third volume of *Technics and Time*:

> [C]onsciousness is *already cinematographic* in its principles of selection for primary memories, a selection that relies on criteria furnished by the play of secondary memory and associated tertiary elements, the combination forming a montage through which a unified flux is constructed (as "stream of consciousness"), but which is identical in form to the cinematic flux of an actual film, as a temporal object and as the result of a constructed montage.
>
> (Stiegler 2011, 17–18)

Selection, forgetting, and reduction are necessary for a present to pass and for a past to be selected from. This process is heavily mediated by a cinematographic apparatus. This is what Stiegler calls the "retentional finitude," that is, the "grounding condition of consciousness-as-temporal-flux" (Ibid. 20). Stiegler is not speaking in metaphorical terms here. He returns, for instance, to *Intervista* (1987) where Fellini himself, together with Marcello Mastroianni (and a crew from Japanese Television), visits Anita Ekberg at her house (Stiegler 2011, 22–24).[3] Together they watch again Mastroianni and Ekberg's performance as young actors in in *La Dolce Vita* (1960). Mastroianni, the actor in *Intervista* in the 1980s, talks to Sylvia on screen, the thirty years younger version of Ekberg in *La Dolce Vita*, while the now much older actress is sitting next to him. This properly cinematographic event, as Stiegler calls this scene, is very moving precisely because of the psychic and collective experience of time that it presents to us.

In his books on cinema, Deleuze also demonstrated how, in all Fellini's work there is a confusion of levels of the actual and the virtual, past and present, dream, memory, and the present, always already mediated by the cinematograph (or other media).[4] These "crystals of time," as Deleuze called them, demonstrate to us how deeply tertiary retention, as an impersonal principle, is indeed at the basis of our experience of time. I will return to these points but for now it is important to see that Deleuze's time-image is actually entangled with a technologically mediated form of time. Stiegler's concept of tertiary retention allows a more explicit acknowledgment of the constitutive role of technics in human consciousness: "consciousness functions just like cinema which enables cinema and television to take it over."[5]

Individuation and the Industrialization of Memory

Recognizing this power of the cinematographic object as a fundamental co-evolutionary aspect of the consciousness (mind) and media technology means that we have to ask what this exteriorization of our nervous system by a process of industrialization means for the understanding of who we are.[6] In this respect, Gilbert Simondon's theory of the individual as a meta-stable entity resulting from an ongoing process of individuation (rather than as a substance or stable category) is important for both Stiegler and Deleuze. Stiegler and Deleuze speak from very different traditions in philosophy (Stiegler departing from Husserl and Derrida; Deleuze following from Bergson, Spinoza, and Nietzsche). I do not intend to erase these differences between Stiegler and Deleuze, and I return to this further below. However, via this notion of a pre-personal field that is constitutive for us as individual as well as collective consciousness, an interesting encounter between Stiegler and Deleuze might be possible.[7] For Simondon, it is impossible to conceptualize the (human or non-human) "individual" as anything other than as an assemblage of dynamic relations that operate on a "pre-individual" level. Temperature, pressure, shock, and all kinds of other forces operate as information on organic and non-organic beings (such as technology, or rocks) that transform them by transduction. As Simondon explains:

> This term [transduction] denotes a process—be it physical, biological, mental, or social— in which an activity gradually sets itself in motion, propagating within a given area, through a structuration of the different zones of the area over which it operates. Each region of the structure that is constituted in this way than serves to constitute the next one to such an extent that at the very time this structuration is effected there is a progressive modification taking place in tandem with it. The simplest image of the transductive process is furnished if one thinks of a crystal, beginning as a tiny seed, which grows and extends itself in all directions in its mother-water. Each layer of molecules that has already been constituted serves as the structuring basis for the layer that is being formed next, and the result is an amplifying (sic) reticular structure. The transductive process is thus an individuation in progress.
>
> (Simondon 1992, 313)

Stiegler argues that the industrialization of memory functions as a pre-personal schematism that allows transindividual (and transindividuating) circuits of processes of individuation as "the adoption of both new lifestyles brought about by technical changes and retentions of a collective past that was never lived, made accessible by technical prostheses and allowing for transplants, migrations, assimilations, and fusions (. . .)" (Stiegler 2011, 60). As with the virtual in time-image described above, Deleuze does not explicitly refer to the pre-personal aspects of media technology *as technics*, but he does recognize the pre-individual and a-subjective field in any experience of perception and memory, which he refers to as the impersonal field of the virtual (Deleuze 2002). The actual (subjectivized) and the virtual (pre-personal) always form a continuously changing circuit: "The relationship of the actual and the virtual forms an acting individuation or a highly specific and remarkable singularization which needs to be determined case by case" (Deleuze 2002, 152). And the circuit between the actual and the virtual is a never-ending process of individuation as crystallization. In *The Movement-Image* and *The Time-Image*, Deleuze has demonstrated how the actual and the virtual translate in different ways in these two different modes of cinema. With Stiegler's techno-ontological insights in mind, we can say that by implication Deleuze shows how powerfully these technologically mediated images operate in processes of individual and collective memory, in psychic and collective individuations. While he acknowledges the existence of "bad cinema," Deleuze, however, focuses almost exclusively upon masterpieces of Western cinema (of both popular and art house cinema), sharing his profound insights into this dimension of collective audio-visual culture that continues to transduct our individuation processes.

Speaking from a more deconstructive and Derridean perspective, Stiegler is critical of the legacy of cinema and audio-visual culture (Derrida and Stiegler 2002). He is wary of the schematization of media formats and contents that also have the capacity to colonize and disindividuate the psyche with toxic consumerism and hegemonic schemata of a marketing solutionism that is as ubiquitous as our computational machines and comes to occupy the "pre-individual field" in a poisonous way. Stiegler calls this the malaise of our age that is triggering an "immense systemic stupidity" (Stiegler 2013, 131). Instead of allowing transindividual circuits of individuating *adoption*, he argues, the techno-logical system easily gives way to (slavish) *adaptation* to the norms of the business model. Based on the same pre-individual field, a being individuates (or disindividuates) as a metastable and transductive unity that changes and is transformed in the encounter with new potentialities that are capable of expressing both health and toxicity.

So how to find new criteria for evaluating the cinematographic mediations and the "industrialization of memory"(Stiegler 2009, 97–188)? Here we have another point where Deleuze and Stiegler might meet productively. While the pleasures of aesthetic appreciation and other more traditional criteria for valuing film remain significant, for both Deleuze and Stiegler it is more important to take to heart Fellini's insight about his invented memories and understand that the fabulatory structure and the performative quality of mediated stories have a (re)constitutive role in our (collective) memory, and hence in determining who we are and what we might become (Steigler 2011, 174–175). This is not inherently a bad thing; it merely asks us to think in new ways about what these mediated images or fabulations do. Looking at cinema in this way, one can see what Deleuze means by "the powers of the false": that, paradoxically, it can be both deadly and creatively productive (Deleuze 1989, 126–155). This also allows us to understand the problem with which Stiegler urges us to engage, namely, an "[a]nalysis of the critical condition of technoscience" so as to establish a criteriology for judging the quality of its fictions. According to Stiegler, a working through of the question of knowing what we want requires a re-examination of what/how the *technical life* (inventing, fabricating) actually is—something that "has always already shaken every axiomatic ontology at least since the appearance of the first stone tools four million years ago" (Steigler 2011, 205–206). Fabulation is not only at the core of cinema as Deleuze proposes in *The Time-Image*, but in its relation to technology it is also at the core of life. Deleuze argued (with Bergson) that "consciousness has become camera-consciousness" (Deleuze 1989, 23). In addition, Stiegler allows us to see that cinematographic consciousness is part of a fundamental technoscientific fabulatory flow that is yet again transformed in and by the digital era.

Even if it is not a masterpiece of cinema, *The Final Cut* could be considered as a meta-film that thematically addresses quite explicitly what happens with individuals in an age of ubiquitous computing, omnipresent cameras, and techno-flow. The film presents a world where "the problem of forgetting" has been overcome by unobtrusive and pervasive camera and computer technology, a "solution" offered by a multi-billion dollar company called EYE-Tech. Alan Hakman (Robin Williams) is a "cutter" whose job it is to edit footage taken from the brain implants of deceased people. In a way Alan Hakman could be seen as an embodiment of tertiary retention: he is the one who, after somebody's death, will select, cut, and compose a life into a 90 minute film that is shown to the deceased person's loved ones in a "Re-memory Ceremony." *The Final Cut* thus explicitly addresses the technoscientific aspect of memory and rememorization as part of an industrialization process. The Zoë implants are expensive and not everybody can afford such a memo-device for their new-born baby, while at the same time pervasive EYE-Tech publicity for the implant imposes it as the sociocultural norm. Throughout the film there are many references to the ethical concerns for psychic well-being that are implied in the implant (for instance, people committing suicide when they find out about the implant because of the unbearable thought that all of their life would be re-playable to others instead of remaining processed in the inner life, or survivors who become addicted to the Zoë footage of a loved one). These economic, social, and ethico-philosophical concerns are expressed by a resistance group that is fighting against the implant, organizing demonstrations, and providing tattoos that mess up the audio and video signal for recording and replaying. In this admittedly very explicit way, *The Final Cut* questions the toxic effects of industrialization on memory.

Hakman reconstructs the life-stories of his clients, choosing from the hundreds of thousands of life hours recorded directly on the brain-screen, classified in a huge audio-visual database categorized under tags such as "childhood," "sleep," "eating," "awkward face," "temptation," "personal hygiene," "career," "tragedy," etc. When at work behind his supercomputer, we see a human/non-human "analog-numeric apparatus" at work, searching, selecting, and editing that which becomes retroactively the story of a life. What is interesting is that the database categories that Hakman can search do refer to some sort of impersonal field.

Even if all the images contained in the database are of a specific individual, they are all related to something pre-personal: to sleep, to eat, to be tempted, etc. The complete exteriorization and objectification of these myriad events demonstrate, on the one hand, how natural (mental) processes of individuation is a selection and recombination of pre-personal events into the story of "a life." It is at the moment of death that this dimension reveals itself most clearly. Deleuze gives the famous example of the Dickens' story in which a rogue, held in contempt by everyone, is found as he lies dying: "Suddenly, those taking care of him manifest an eagerness, respect, and even love, for his slightest sign of life. (. . .) The life of the individual gives way to an impersonal yet singular life that releases a pure event freed from the accidents of internal and external life" (Deleuze 2001, 28). On the other hand, it is Hakman who has the selection of the eventualization and temporalization of "a life" in his hands, a life that he individuates into a story through the creation of a re-memory film. Obviously, this is a huge responsibility, and is portrayed as such in the film. However, what makes the film more interesting is that we can see Hakman not just as a character within a contemporary science-fiction story, but rather as an allegorical figure, a conceptual persona even, who shows us something about the way in which temporalization and eventualization work as complex forms of mediation in ubicomp culture today (Deleuze 1994, 64–66).

The Neuro-Image and the Third Synthesis of Time as a Complex System

The Final Cut does not problematize the externalization of memory as *opposed* to the materiality of human embodiment but presents it as a new problem that emerges from a "compositional co-existence," a co-development between the technical and the human. Stiegler refers to a co-individuation of human organs, technical organs, and social organs qua an "organology."[8] Since our technologies are entangled not just with our bodies as physical prosthesis, but also with our minds as cognitive prosthesis, it is important to rethink memory both as something cerebral and extra-cerebral. This connection between our image technologies and our brains provides another meeting point between Stiegler and Deleuze, albeit a more contemporized Deleuze. Already in the 1980s, Deleuze argued that cinema is a temporal object that is related to our consciousness, and even to the materiality of our brain screen. "The brain is the screen," he famously postulated in *Cahiers du Cinema* (Deleuze 2000). In a Bergsonian vein, Deleuze conceptualizes the cinematographic image as both material and immaterial facet of consciousness.[9] The movement-image and the time-image, the two different modes of cinematographic techno-aesthetics that Deleuze distinguishes, are each in their own way connected to a particular temporality. Movement-images (classical genre cinema) give us indirect temporal relations through a spatial logic of continuity montage. Time-images (modern post-war cinema emerging from Italian neo-realism) give us direct images of time without the spatial logic of linear continuity. In these modern post war images, it becomes hard to distinguish the actual (present) from the virtual (past) and time is already a more complex notion.[10] In our digital age, however, we should perhaps conceive of another dominant mode of cinematographic techno-aesthetics with an even more complex temporal architecture. Due to its profound entanglement with cognitive capitalism, ubiquitous computing, and a mental organology (man as "neuronal man"), I propose to call this "the neuro-image."[11] The most salient and obvious characteristic of the neuro-image is that we no longer just follow characters in their actions, nor do we look through their wondering and wandering eyes, but we experience directly the brain-worlds of its protagonists, sometimes indicated because characters are hooked up to some kind of brain machine, but very often without warning, for instance, entrapped in a schizoid delusionary world.[12] To be sure, the movement-image and time-image were also connected to the brain-screen. However, the entanglement of brain and consciousness with our contemporary media screens has intensified to a point where new temporalizations emerge.

Deleuze saw in cinema a particular mode of thinking that was close to both philosophy and to neuroscience. However, what might a new neuro-image mode of cinema bring to the discussion of ubiquitous computing culture and its inherent complexity? The neuro-image is part and parcel of a networked digital culture that operates with the logics of extended and complex narratives, networked software cultures, and database remixability. This is better understood by looking more closely at the specific and complex temporalization of the neuro-image. For this I have proposed to re-read Deleuze's cinema books in line with the philosophy of time that Deleuze develops in *Difference and Repetition*. Even if Deleuze does not explicitly refer to complexity theory, the thought system of difference and repetition developed in this book, and especially the conceptualization of time is a complex dynamic system that is marked by self-referentiality (feedback loops), emergent self-organization in serialized patterns, and radical contingency.[13]

As with Stiegler, Deleuze proposes time as a passive synthesis, in which the first synthesis is the living present that we embody in the here and now of our sensory-motor habitual behavior.

However, this foundation in the present of the first synthesis is grounded in the second synthesis of memory, the past in general that makes the present pass. In this ground of the pure past all layers of time co-exist. These notions of first and second syntheses are inspired by Bergson's thought of matter and memory (Bergson 1991). Each synthesis of time has its own relation to and conception of the past, present, and future, so we are already entering a complex temporal system. There is a third synthesis of time as well, which is time conceived from the future as such and this form of time is highly contingent and opens up to a growing complex temporal architecture. The third synthesis of time as developed by Deleuze is not the same as Stiegler's concept of tertiary retention. But before returning to Stiegler, let me develop the temporal complexity of the neuro-image.

In *The Neuro-Image* I suggest that Deleuze's cinema concepts can be seen in light of the syntheses of time developed in *Difference and Repetition*.[14] In this way, it is possible to argue that the movement-image has as its dominant temporal mode of expression, the first synthesis of time. The images have a firm foundation in the present; even flashbacks are anchored in a present that is stable and that we can always recognize as our spatial and temporal point of orientation. The time-image has the past, or the second synthesis of time, as its dominant temporal color. Here the co-existent layers of the past begin to speak for themselves. They pop up without warning, without firm anchors in the present, as in the confusion of both individual and collective pasts and present.[15] As already indicated, in the time-image, time, film aesthetics, and narration already become more complex, since the virtuality of the (traumatically) returning past is sometimes indistinguishable from the actual, as is clear in Fellini's films. However, it is the third synthesis of time, the futural, which is of primary import in the neuro-image as the cinematographic form cf the digital age.[16] As Deleuze explains in *Difference and Repetition*, the first synthesis and the second synthesis both have their own conceptions of the future (thinking the future either from the present as anticipation or from the past as cyclic or determined repetition).

It is in the third synthesis of time that the future *as* future presents itself as the temporal modality. In the third synthesis of time the future does not follow from what we know of the present or of the past, but it is the speculative and ungrounding dimension of time (Deleuze 1994, 90–91, 93–94). Here Nietzsche's ideas of death and eternal return are added to the Bergsonian ideas of matter and memory. Deleuze argues that while repetition in the eternal return excludes the repetition of the same, the third synthesis "cuts, assembles, and orders" to make possible the eternal return of pure difference (Williams 2003, 103). It is worthwhile noticing that Deleuze's third synthesis of time is a modern conception of the future, akin to that proposed by Niklas Luhmann as a modern temporal structure that only emerged, and had to emerge, in highly complex and highly technologically mediated modernity. Luhmann asserts that the future now becomes an open future: "Future itself . . . must now be conceived as possibility quite different from the past . . . It may contain, as a functional equivalent for the end of time, emergent properties and not-yet-realized possibilities" (Luhmann 1976, 131). Luhmann calls for a complex systems theory conception of time in which an open conception of the future allows "possible divergence of past states and future states" as well as "several mutually exclusive future presents" (Ibid., 136, 140). Even without completely unfolding Luhmann's complexity-in-time, one can see how this corresponds to Deleuze's open conception of the future in the third synthesis of time. This complex synthesis of time contains all other times (the past, present, and future of the first and second syntheses) *and* it opens up to all possible (not-yet-realized) past, presents, and futures that present themselves as serialized sequences. It is the third synthesis of time that encompasses "the totality of the series and the final end of time" (Deleuze 1994,

94). Luhmann and Deleuze seem to agree that society today has to "sequentialize predictions and actions into complex self-referential patterns" (Ibid., 145). Complexity has to be reduced in order to make sense, but, seen from various different points (or scenarios) in the possible future, things could have been different. Here we see the radical contingency of complex temporality conceived as third synthesis or open future.

Let's make this more concrete. The future is also dramatically and ontologically related to the event of death and even "the end of times." In *The Final Cut*, it is only at the moment when a person has died that the cutting and ordering is done as a "re-memory" from the point of view of what we want to remember for and from the future. However, since the future as such is always speculative and involves many options remixing can happen *ad infinitum*. It is always possible to imagine a different future scenario from which to fold back in time, re-order, and recut the events of a life into a different story, and end up with a remixed version of the past. Alan Hakman, at work on his computer with the database of all the events in a life of a deceased person, has to choose which story he will tell. Clearly, depending on the kind of future memory he (or his client) wants to retain, he cuts, re-orders, and reduces in different ways. Moreover, as Maria Poulaki has pointed out, *The Final Cut* presents reflexive feedback loops of complex narration where narrative closure is no longer possible:

> [F]ilms such as the *Final Cut* appear concerned not just with the technological incarnations of information, but also, and perhaps even more, with their own ability to communicate as potential information entities. Complex films are self-reflexive regarding their own cyborg nature—which has for long been underlying modern narratives—and "make explicit, to varying degrees, the technological underpinnings of narrative mechanism."[17]

And, as she further indicates, when Hakman by accident discovers that he himself has a Zoë implant, the feedback loops enfold even further and in ever more complex ways when he returns to his own "database of memories" where he discovers "a different past" than the one he was replaying in his traumatized memories.

This self-referential looping and modulating of time can be viewed as an allegory for our times of ubiquitous computing, where all the events of our lives, of world history even, can be captured and tagged with metadata only to become subject to re-assembly into new life stories and world histories. These stories become, more explicitly than ever before, parallel stories of the endless potential stories that could be told. To put it in cinematographic terms, we see here neither just a classic flashback that fits in an anchored present and continuity logic, nor just a crystalized time of post war cinema that brings the past as a direct layer of cyclic repetition into the present. Rather, the past now becomes like a feedback loop on parallel processors: From different points (of view) in the future, we can re-order the events of our life (or of history) into multiple stories. The tagline of *The Final Cut* "Would you live your life differently" points to the endless possibilities to rewrite history in a culture where so many audio-visual documents (fiction and non-fiction) have been stored in databases. This has important political implications, which are beyond the scope of this article. But clearly, trying another version of (individual or collective) history informs the choices that are constantly made in folding the Borgesian map in different ways in order to create a different version of the past always from a different future scenario.[18] The obsession with the future we also recognize in a different way: ubicomp, Big Data, and endless information have allowed that polling, profiling, prediction, prevention, and preemptiveness have entered our socio-political structures and increasingly determine politics and policing.[19] In this sense the neuro-image is part of, and perhaps even an aesthetic expression of, a much larger network of pervasive computing and the database logic of our age.[20] Without claiming that all knowledge and all data come together in one big networked system, the fact that it has become much easier to recognize patterns, sketch possible scenarios, and make new selections of the past based on these possible futures, is related to the privileging of the third synthesis of time characteristic of the neuro-image.

Although Deleuze does not explicitly treat of technology in *Difference and Repetition*, nor of the three syntheses of time in his cinema books, I think that the link between the neuro-image and the complexity of the third synthesis of time becomes tangible when considered as a form of tertiary retention which Stiegler posits. Here it is important to note another difference between Stiegler and Deleuze. Tertiary retention as defined by Stiegler is in fact strongly related to memory—it is a techno-premediation of memory, one might say. Deleuze's third synthesis of time, as we have seen, is related to the future as future, and does not necessarily relate to techno-mediation.[21] However, the scene in *Intervista* that Stiegler discusses in *Technics and Time 3*, for instance, is not just a premediated memory. It also prefigures a computational database logic of our epoch in which tertiary retention is colored by a future from which it speaks. As a sort of *YouTube* mash-up *avant-la-lettre*, Fellini has re-cut and re-edited the scenes from *La Dolce Vita*. In this way he comments upon the particular retentive significance the film has acquired in our collective memory, which, seen from the moment the original film was made, is a point in the future. Mastrioanni and Ekberg will live on as iconic lovers despite the fact that this is certainly not how they were presented in the original film. They have been recut from a point of view of the future.

Moreover, what makes this scene from *Intervista* very moving, is related to the fact that the mediated layers of time also anticipate another future, namely the future of old age and death, characteristic for the third synthesis of time. We see the actors as radiant adults, *and* when they are in the autumn of their lives. Implied in this is death: Mastrioanni has died in 1996, Ekberg passed away in 2015 at the time of this writing. Death in general is what lies ahead of us all. Stiegler refers to the categories of attention (present), retention (past), and protention (future) that can be synthesized in different ways. He argues that the resultant complex interplays of temporal dimensions are built on the anticipation of (our own) aging and eventual death (as "archi-protention" which is part of a deep unconscious core of our consciousness).[22] Both the archi-protention (our future death/death as an impersonal fact of the future) and the fact that tertiary retentions are related to forms of "objective memory" (cinematogram, photogram, phonogram, writing, painting, sculpting) that bear witness of a past not necessarily phenomenologically lived, bring Stiegler's techno-scientific argument respecting tertiary retention in contact with a Deleuzian conception of the third synthesis of time (Stiegler 2011, 28). Or, perhaps it is more correct to say that tertiary retention as archi-protention is related to the third synthesis of time of the neuro-image. Bringing Deleuze's cinema books and philosophy of time in contact with Stiegler's reflections on technics and time, provides a complex understanding of how our psychic and collective processes of "impersonal individuation" might be controlled as the techno-industry gets deeper under our skin and skull. Asking ourselves "who selects, and by what criteria" (Ibid., 223), and understanding that there actually never is a final cut, might keep us going, critically and creatively, recutting and refolding the Borgesian map for our rebirth and after-life in the eternal return of what has not-yet-been.

Notes

1 Press Information sheet *The Final Cut*, 35 mm Film, directed by Omar Naim (2004; Los Angeles and Berlin: Lions Gate Entertainment and Cinerenta Medienbeteiligungs KG, 2005), DVD.

2 Niklas Luhmann, "The Future Cannot Begin: Temporal Structures in Modern Society." Luhmann argues here for a complex understanding of time that matches the complexity of society: "Older societies did not produce such an elaborated framework, and they did not need it to understand themselves. They lived . . . within a less differentiated time" (149).

3 Stiegler also discusses films by Resnais, Antonioni, and Hitchcock.

4 Deleuze, *The Time-Image*, 68–97. Fellini had a vivid interest in the media. The Trevi Fountain scene, for instance, was a real event that had been covered in Roman newspapers in 1958 when Anita Ekberg spontaneously had jumped into the fountain. See Sam Stourdzé, Ed., *Fellini*, 124.

5 Stiegler, *Technics and Time*, 3, 77. Stiegler speaks of the "arche-cinema of consciousness" in "The Organology of Dreams," *Screening the Past*, June 2013, www.screeningthepast.com?2013?06?the-organology-of-dreams-and-arch-cinema.

6 Stiegler, *Technics and Time*, 2, 116. See also Ben Roberts, "Cinema as Mnemotechnics: Bernard Stiegler and the Industrialization of Memory."

7 In *Etats de Choc* Stiegler criticizes Derrida for not having understood the specific way in which Deleuze in *Difference and Repetition* departs from a Simondonian perspective of psycho-social individuations.

8 See for instance Stiegler's audio-visual lecture "General Organology, Digital Studies and the Neurosciences," *YouTube*, May 1, 2013, http://youtube.com/watch?v=0Hr2HYqE968

9 See "The Universe as Metacinema" and "Material Aspects of Subjectivity" in Pisters, *The Matrix of Visual Culture: Working with Deleuze in Film Theory*, 14–77.

10 For instance, Deleuze compares the temporal architecture of the time-images of Alain Resnais to the Baker's transformation in mathematics. *The Time-Image*, 119. Deleuze refers to Iliya Prigogine and Isabelle Stenger, *Order out of Chaos*, 267–280. The Baker's transformation is a complex transformation in conservative dynamical systems in that all values can be determined and are not contingent.

11 Pisters, *The Neuro-Image*. Deleuze was influenced by Jean-Pierre Changeux's book that appeared in the early 1980s and had a huge impact in France. Cf., Jean-Pierre Changeux, *Neuronal Man: The Biology of Mind*. See also Raymond Bellour, "Deleuze: The Thinking of the Brain." Stiegler refers to Changeux's work in *Technics and Time*, 2, 169–170.

12 In films such as *The Eternal Sunshine of the Spotless Mind* (Gondry, 2004) to *Divergent* (Burger, 2014), action literally takes place in the brain. For explicitly schizoid films are we can think of *Fight Club* (Fincher, 1999) and *Shutter Island* (Scorsese, 2010).

13 Gilles Deleuze, *Difference and Repetition*, 70–128. For a general theoretical introduction to complexity in social organizations and an interesting case study, see Donde Ashmos Plowman et al., "Radical Change Accidentally: The Emergence and Amplification of Small Change." While complexity theory presents many different positions that allow more or less determinism, hierarchical organization, or contingency, as demonstrated by the variety of the contributions in this book, I will suggest that Deleuze's philosophy of time resonates with Niklas Luhmann's social systems theory and his conceptions of (temporal) differentiation. See Niklas Luhmann, "The Future Cannot Begin." See also Niklas Luhmann, *Social Systems* and *Introduction to Systems Theory*.

14 Pisters, *The Neuro-Image*, 127–155. See also Pisters, "Synaptic Signals: Time-Traveling Through the Brain in the Neuro-Image," 261–274.

15 As for instance in *Hiroshima Mon Amour*, 35 mm Film, directed by Alain Resnais (1959; Paris and Tokyo: Argos Films, Como Films and Daiei Studios, 2003), DVD; See Patricia Pisters, "Flash-forward: The Future is Now."

16 There are countless ways in which the neuro-image expresses this obsession with the future. For instance, *Inception*, 35 mm Film, 65 mm Film, Digital, directed by Christopher Nolan (2010; Los Angeles: Warner Bros, Legendary Pictures and Syncopy, 2010, DVD) is told from a point of view of the future (old age or perhaps even death of the main characters). *Minority Report*, 35 mm Film, directed by Steven Spielberg (2002, Los Angeles: Twentieth Century Fox, Dreamworks, Cruise/Wagner Productions, 2002, DVD) shows us a world where crime is prevented via predictions from savants that can see the future on their brain-screens.

17 See Poulaki's chapter elsewhere in this volume. Here the reference is to Maria Poulaki, *Before or Beyond Narrative? Towards a Complex Systems Theory of Contemporary Films*, 29–30. Poulaki quotes Allan Cameron, *Modular Narratives in Contemporary Cinema*, 25. See also Warren Buckland, Ed., *Puzzle Films: Complex Storytelling in Contemporary Cinema*.

18 To give an example, the films of John Akomfrah deal explicitly with re-ordering and refolding the audio-visual archive of Britain's migration history, which changes our perception of that history as well as creates new images for the future archive. See for instance, *The Nine Muses*, Digital, directed by John Akomfrah (2010; London: Smoking Dogs Films, 2012), DVD.

19 For a popular account of the emergence of a "new and complex future" after 9/11, see James Canton, *The Extreme Future: The Top Trends that Will Reshape the World in the Next 20 Years*, x. For a report on the pervasiveness of ethnic profiling, see the report *Ethnic Profiling in the European Union*. As regards the use of ubiquitous computing for behavior profiling, consider Louis Atallah and Guang-Zhong Yang, "The Use of Pervasive Sensing for Behaviour Profiling – A Survey." One also recalls the pre-emptive war on Iraq that was based on the expectation of a future threat, not on a past assault.

20 See also Anna Munster, *An Aesthesia of Networks: Conjunctive Experience in Art and Technology*. Munster counters the pervasiveness (and flattening uniformity) of different data networks (which she calls "networked anesthesia") with aesthetic experience that engages with these networked databases.

21 Granted, a more nuanced position on this point is called for if one were to take into account the works that Deleuze has undertaken with Félix Guattari. *A Thousand Plateaus*, for instance, is full of machinic assemblages, war machines, abstract machines, the techno phylum, and the mecanosphere.

22 Stiegler, *Technics and Time*, 3, 27. On archi-protention, Ibid., 17, 30.

References

Atallah, Louis, and Guang-Zhong Yang. 2009. "The Use of Pervasive Sensing for Behaviour Profiling— A Survey." *Pervasive and Mobile Computing* 5 (5): 447–467. DOI: 10.1016/j.pmcj.2009.06.009.

Bellour, Raymond. 2012. "Deleuze: The Thinking of the Brain." *Cinema: Journal of Philosophy and the Moving Image* 1. http://cjpmi.ifl.pt/1-deleuze.

Bergson, Henri. 1991. *Matter and Memory*. Translated by Nancy M. Paul and W. Scott Palmer. New York: Zone Books.

Borges, Jorge Luis. 1999. "On Exactitude in Science." In *Collected Fictions*, 325. Translated by Andrew Hurley. New York: Penguin.

Buckland, Warren, Ed. 2009. *Puzzle Films: Complex Storytelling in Contemporary Cinema*. Malden and Oxford: Wiley-Blackwell.

Canton, James. 2007. *The Extreme Future: The Top Trends that will Reshape the World in the Next 20 Years*. New York: Plume.

Cameron, Allen. 2008. *Modular Narratives in Contemporary Cinema*. Basingstoke, UK: Palgrave Macmillan.

Changeux, Jean-Pierre. 1997. *Neuronal Man: The Biology of Mind*. Translated by Laurence Garey. Princeton, NJ: Princeton University Press.

Deleuze, Gilles. 2002. "The Actual and the Virtual." In Gilles Deleuze and Claire Parnet Eds., *Dialogues II*, 148–152. Translated by Hugh Tomlinson and Barbara Habberjam. New York: Columbia University Press.

Deleuze, Gilles. 2000. "The Brain is the Screen." In Gregory Flaxman Ed., *The Brain is the Screen: Deleuze and the Philosophy of Cinema*, 365–373. Translated by Marie Therese Guirgis. Minneapolis, MN: University of Minnesota Press.

Deleuze, Gilles. 1986. *Cinema 1: The Movement-Image*. Translated by Hugh Tomlinson and Barbara Habberjam. London: The Athlone Press.

Deleuze, Gilles. 1989. *Cinema 2: The Time-Image*. Translated by Hugh Tomlinson and Robert Galeta. London: The Athlone Press.

Deleuze, Gilles. 1994. *Difference and Repetition*. Translated by Paul Patton. London: The Athlone Press.

Deleuze, Gilles. 2001. *Pure Immanence: A Life*. Translated by Anne Boyman. Introduction by John Rajman. New York: Zone Books.

Deleuze, Gilles, and Félix Guattari. 1988. *A Thousand Plateaus: Capitalism and Schizophrenia*. Translated by Brian Massumi. London: The Athlone Press.

Deleuze, Gilles, and Félix Guattari. 1994. *What is Philosophy?* Translated by Graham Burchell and Hugh Tomlinson. New York: Verso.

Derrida, Jacques, and Bernard Stiegler. 2002. *Echographies of Television*. Translated by Jennifer Bajorek. Cambridge: Polity.

Ekman, Ulrik. 2013. "Introduction." In *Throughout: Art and Culture Emerging with Ubiquitous Computing*. Cambridge, MA: The MIT Press.

Ethnic Profiling: Pervasive, Ineffective, and Discriminatory. 2009. New York: Open Society Institute. http://opensocietyfoundations.org/reports/ethnic-profiling-european-union-pervasive-ineffective-and-discriminatory.

Hiroshima Mon Amour. 35 mm Film. Directed by Alain Resnais. 1959. Paris and Tokyo: Argos Films, Como Films and Daiei Studios, 2003. DVD.

Inception. 35 mm Film, 65 mm Film, Digital. Directed by Christopher Nolan. 2010. Los Angeles: Warner Bros, Legendary Pictures and Syncopy, 2010. DVD.

Intervista. 35 mm Film. Directed by Federico Fellini. 1987. Rome: Aljosha, Cinnecittà, RAI Radiotelevizione Italiana, 2005. DVD.

La Dolce Vita. 35 mm Film. Directed by Federico Fellini. 1960. Rome and Paris: Riama Film, Gray Film and Pathé Consortium Cinéma, 2004. DVD.

Luhmann, Niklas. 1976. "The Future Cannot Begin: Temporal Structures in Modern Society." *Social Research* 43 (1): 130–152.

Luhmann, Niklas. 1995. *Social Systems.* Translated by John Bednarz, Jr. with Dirck Baecker. Stanford, CA: Stanford University Press.

Luhmann, Niklas. 2012. *Introduction to Systems Theory.* Translated by Peter Gilgen. Cambridge: Polity Press.

Minority Report. 35 mm Film. Directed by Steven Spielberg. 2002. Los Angeles, CA: Twentieth Century Fox, Dreamworks, Cruise/Wagner Productions, 2002. DVD.

Munster, Anna. 2013. *An Aesthesia of Networks: Conjunctive Experience in Art and Technology.* Cambridge, MA: MIT Press.

Pisters, Patricia. 2011. "Flashforward: The Future is Now." *Deleuze Studies* 5, supplement: 98–115.

Pisters, Patricia. 2003. *The Matrix of Visual Culture: Working with Deleuze in Film Theory.* Stanford, CA: Stanford University Press.

Pisters, Patricia. 2011. "Synaptic Signals: Time Traveling through the Brain in the Neuro-Image." *Deleuze Studies* 5 (2): 261–274.

Pisters, Patricia. 2012. *The Neuro-Image: A Deleuzian Film-Philosophy of Digital Screen Culture.* Stanford, CA: Stanford University Press.

Plowman, Donde Ashmos, Lakami T. Baker, Tammy E. Beck, Mukta Kulkarni, Stephanie Thomas Solansky, and Deandra Villarreal Travis. 2007. "Radical Change Accidentally: The Emergence and Amplification of Small Change." *Academy of Management Journal* 50 (3): 515–543.

Poulaki, Maria. 2011. *Before or Beyond Narrative? Towards a Complex Systems Theory of Contemporary Films.* Dissertation, Amsterdam University. Amsterdam, The Netherlands: Rozenberg.

Prigogine, Ilya, and Isabelle Stenger. 1984. *Order out of Chaos: Man's New Dialogue with Nature.* London: Bantam Books.

Simondon, Gilbert. 1992. "The Genesis of the Individual." In Jonathan Crary and Sanford Kwinter, Eds., *Incorporations,* 297–319. Translated by Mark Cohen and Sanford Kwinter. New York: Zone Books.

Simondon, Gilbert. 2012. "On Techno-Aesthetics." Translated by Arne de Boever. *Parrhesia* 14: 1–8. http://parrhesiajournal.org/parrhesia14/parrhesia14_simondon.pdf

Stiegler, Bernard. 2012. *Etats de Choc: Bêtise et Savoir au XXIe Siècle.* Paris: Mille et une nuits.

Stiegler, Bernard. 2013. "The Organology of Dreams and Arche-Cinema." *Screening the Past.* www.screeningthepast.com/2013/06/the-organology-of-dreams-and-arch-cinema.

Stiegler, Bernard. 1998. *Technics and Time, 1: The Fault of Epimetheus.* Translated by Richard Beardsworth and George Collins. Stanford, CA: Stanford University Press.

Stiegler, Bernard. 2009. *Technics and Time, 2: Disorientation.* Translated by Stephen Barker. Stanford, CA: Stanford University Press.

Stiegler, Bernard. 2011. *Technics and Time, 3: Cinematic Time and the Question of Malaise.* Translated by Stephen Barker. Stanford, CA: Stanford University Press.

Stiegler, Bernard. 2013. *What Makes Life Worth Living. On Pharmacology.* Translated by Daniel Ross. Cambridge and Malden, UK: Polity Press.

Stourdzé, Sam, Ed. 2013. *Fellini.* Amsterdam, The Netherlands: Amsterdam University Press.

Roberts, Ben. 2006. "Cinema as Mnemotechnics: Bernard Stiegler and the 'Industrialization of Memory.'" *Angelaki: Journal of the Theoretical Humanities* 2 (1): 55–63.

The Final Cut. 35 mm Film. directed by Omar Naim, 2004. Los Angeles, CA and Berlin: Lions Gate Entertainment and Cinerenta Medienbeteiligungs KG, 2005. DVD.

The Nine Muses, Digital. Directed by John Akomfrah. 2010. London: Smoking Dogs Films, 2012. DVD.

Williams, James. 2003. *Gilles Deleuze's Difference and Repetition: A Critical Introduction and Guide.* Edinburgh, UK: Edinburgh University Press.

MEDIA ART

Ulrik Ekman

Media art always involved many creative and generative eventualizations whose dynamic unity and wholeness on plane of the artificial were very hard to grasp and articulate. In view of this, it is perhaps not altogether surprising that the encounters of media art with time and in time continued to unfold in interesting ways also after the hyperbolic discourses in the 1990s concerning the newness of new media and the allegedly disembodied, transcendental character of virtual reality. Even though the debates concerning electronic literature, the digital image, digital sound and music, digital film, video and animation, net art, early software art, immersive installations, gaming, AI, and artificial life have now departed from the announcements of revolutionarily new events, many of these lines of development are both in the museums and still alive and kicking. Both their offspring and the displacement in part by more and other recent kinds of media art projects such as mobile novels, social media applications and hacks, mixed reality gaming, surveillance art, urban media facades, relational and responsive architectures, and context-aware sites and environments demonstrate that questions concerning the media art event and the eventness of media art have not disappeared but have rather become even more difficult to answer.

In one sociocultural sense, the media art event becomes all the more sought after, more evanescent, but also less special and less of an event—insofar as it has become a general part of the experience economy in network societies. This tilt towards having installations of interactive media art projects come into presence as an event of a singular plural thus appears as a staying and appropriative trait in the first decades of the twenty-first century, something that happens more and more often and with more and more citizens in such societies. It accompanies multitudes of individuals' projects for a beautiful life and hence a gradually generalized aesthetic stylization of everyday cultural episodes. If Gerhard Schulze was right in his early diagnosis of the experience society, the media art event appears to have become everybody's business, and its eventness has become enrolled in a march towards one or more kinds of experience rationality (Schulze 1992). Over time, every such media art event externalizes and solidifies choices of action as routinized complexes of means to reach an experiential goal. Media art then makes explicit and testifies to the process in which everybody becomes an aesthetic event-manager and an artistic manipulator of subjectivity by instrumentalizing situations for desired experiential purposes. Perhaps the individual media art event cannot be said to have a predetermined direction here—it remains free, uncertain, and open to disappointment. However, Schulze's wager was that gradually and on the whole we see the emergence of a schematized experience rationality that is not a private affair but a matter of certain types of rationality we have in common and draw upon for orientation of choices and actions in our lives. If so, one might remark that this implies a linearization of the media art event, something that inscribes it under the heading of an experiential system time whose events can be numbered, measured, clocked, synchronized, and generally ordered as a linear sequence of instants.

A politically engaged media art project such as *Tracking Transience* by Hasan Elahi, who is interviewed in this section, might seem to resist the linear overcoding of individuals' time by surveillance by overdoing it, by overcoding the process of surveillance with self-surveillance that repeats and feeds back so as to make a difference that makes a difference. However, as Elahi remarks, this opening of another event-time at the limit of systemic surveillance is perhaps at best a short-lived and marginal phenomenon, seeing that selfies, self-documentation, and very willing self-surveillance is now very much the quasi-normative and widely practiced temporal order of the day. The selfie and the eventual process of self-documentation must then be rethought and redone as a political form of artistic expression, one perhaps capable of interrupting time-coding in the wake of the War on Terror.

This raises the question whether such a reduction of media art events to a Newtonian linear temporalization of experience is in fact what goes on and thus offers an adequate practico-theoretical approach, in spite of several discourses and theoretical traditions that would tend towards granting media art a critical potential, a creative surplus, an innovative priority, or a special status with respect to a more complex relation to time than linear schematization and organization of events. In particular, one might wish to engage with the question concerning the complexity or the reduction of complexity of eventualizations in societies whose networking logic has already intensified via massive and multitudinous correlations of cultural life forms and a third wave of computing known under such rubrics as ubiquitous computing, pervasive computing, ambient intelligence, and the IoT. As events, both media art projects and human lives are increasingly meshed with and co-develop with ubiquitous computing. It is far from easy to ascertain whether events bear witness to human temporalizations and media art temporalizations with technics in a co-development that stays with the relatively simple organization of a linear time, or whether something other and more complex is at stake, perhaps even so that the complexity of event-times is both emergent and irreducible.

Such a call for considering the complexity of media art eventualizations in a stronger sense may well appear as mere hyperbole. This is certainly the case insofar as one could be forced to accept the predominance still today of a Newtonian notion of time and a linear succession of event-instants, in the clocking of everyday culture but also in an entire array of sciences across the faculties. In cultural theory and studies of media art, for example, it is rare to see any departure from this paradigm, and in fact the challenges raised by such twentieth century contestants as the theory of relativity and quantum theory are not often taken into consideration, if at all. Moreover, the concern with structural systemic constraints, process control, and temporal exactitude in computer science in general means that hardware engineering, systems engineering, and software design are still very strongly inclined towards bringing about and maintaining a synchronized and linear system time.

However, several aspects of contemporary ubicomp culture conspire to problematize this, and so do related media art projects. Ubicomp culture is a sociocultural *and* technical thrust to integrate and/or embed computing pervasively, to have information processing thoroughly integrated with or embedded in everyday objects and ongoing practices, including those pertaining to human bodies and individual or social intentions in a given situation or context. Events in ubicomp culture problematize the Newtonian container of time and its line of instants partly because multiplicities of computational entities and multiplicities of human individuals and social groupings are involved, with differences in modes or *kinds* of temporalization (across the divide between an objectively realist and universal notion and subjective, social, anthropological, and biological notions of time and becoming). Partly, events in ubicomp culture raise questions of other notions of time because contingent ad hoc networking connectivity is at stake among at least some of its billions of computational units and its billions of human interactants. Both the synchronic dimension and the diachronic dynamics of such ad hoc networkings may concern emergence of non-linear organizations of event-time, including the events proper to self-organizing processes.

The media art projects engaging with the hardware, software, and interaction designs characterizing the unfolding of context-aware ubicomp in mixed realities obviously share the systemic operational and experiential encounter with such complexity of the event. However, for the most part, such contemporary media art projects and their interactants do not explicitly address and work with this question of the complexity of the event, and they typically reduce it by using a structural and synchronic frame which means that temporal processes are handled as linear series of events within a delimited and hierarchical organization. This mirrors quite well central parts of the predominant mode of operation in the fields of cultural theory and computer science during the last half century.

We have seen increasing research efforts and more interest in complexity theory, and today a "complexity turn" is quite a transdisciplinary buzzword. Already in 1948, Warren Weaver presented the key distinctions between simple problems with few variables, problems of disorganized complexity with numerous variables that call for probability statistics, and, in the middle, problems of organized complexity with a moderate number of variables and interrelationships which can neither be fully captured in probability statistics nor be reduced to a simple formula (Weaver 1948). He was particularly interested in organized complexity and proposed that these problems be solved via the co-operation of computers and cross disciplinary collaborations. One might well be tempted to argue that this is exactly what we have seen in a majority of efforts since then, also in media art—both a tendency to focus on synchronic complexity or order rather than the more demanding issue of diachronic complexity and emergence (novelty) *and* a tendency to parenthesize few-variable problems and disorganized complexity in favor of organized complexity. Although this certainly does not entail a brute reductionism, it still means that an array of disciplines and media art projects continue to demonstrate an inclination towards reducing the complexity of the event to what can me met in satisficing ways within an modularized architecture of temporal processes whose hierarchical organization safeguards linearization of time. Two influential examples in research would be Herbert Simon's work from 1962 on the architecture of complexity and Stephen Wolfram's work 25 years later on approaches to complexity engineering (Simon 1962; Wolfram 1986).

One wager in this book as a whole is that the coexistence of current ubicomp cultures and media art projects do not let themselves be reduced in that fashion. The events of ubicomp culture and media art actualize what Simon noted in passing—complex systems are not simply hierarchical and decomposable but operate with cross-cutting connections, and these may be more important than Simon wished to grant. These events may also concern what Wolfram observed—the evolution of many complex systems is probably irreducible, cannot be predicted by short-cut procedures, but can be found only by direct simulation. In that case, you might say that we are still awaiting media art events and approaches to these which admit of irreducible complexity and nonlinear events of emergence. It appears especially interesting to see whether the developments now ongoing in cultural theory, media art, and studies in science and technology will lead through cross-cutting or transversal events of emergence and approaches to these (Deleuze and Guattari 1987; Protevi 2006). This would give us a better appreciation of the ways in which a multiplicity of temporal processes in an individual co-organize something new (Whitehead 1929), how a multiplicity of social systems change the social system via cross-connections, or how a myriad of computational systems have a new ambient technical plane arrive. What is more, this would perhaps permit us a better simulation of events that cut across the way we still tend to layer time in disciplinary ways. We would be on lines of events that cut across the processes of individual time, social time, biological time, technical time to generate an event of heterogeneity from their co-evolution.

References

Deleuze, Gilles, and Félix Guattari. 1987. *A Thousand Plateaus*. Minneapolis, MN: University of Minnesota Press.

Protevi, John. 2006. "Deleuze, Guattari and Emergence." *Paragraph* 29 (2): 19–39.

Schulze, Gerhard. 1992. *Die Erlebnisgesellschaft: Kultursoziologie der Gegenwart*. New York: Campus.

Simon, Herbert A. 1962. "The Architecture of Complexity." *Proceedings of the American Philosophical Society* 106 (6): 467–82.

Weaver, Warren. 1948. "Science and Complexity." *Scientific American* 36: 536–44.

Whitehead, Alfred North. 1929. *Process and Reality: An Essay in Cosmology*. Cambridge, UK: Cambridge: University Press.

Wolfram, Stephen. 1986. "Approaches to Complexity Engineering." *Physica D* 2 (1–3): 385–99.

HIDING IN PLAIN SIGHT—
INTERVIEW WITH HASAN ELAHI

Jay David Bolter

Jay David Bolter (JDB):Your website offers a wealth of art projects organized by year from 2005 to 2013.[1] Perhaps we could start, then, with the overall trajectory of your work, including the work that predates your web presence.

Hasan Elahi (HE): I am frequently asked: What kind of work did you do before you were apprehended by the FBI and had this life changing event? Now that I have a twenty-year body of work, I am able to look back over it and see many similarities between the earlier work and Tracking Transience and my later work. Not only at the conceptual level dealing with citizenship, borders, and . . .

JDB: . . . surveillance?

HE: Surveillance was not necessarily in the vocabulary of my earlier work. But when I look back at the work even from the mid-1990s, I do find the concepts of citizenship, migration, and the individual within the context of the state. Those themes have been in my work for almost twenty years now. When the event took place with the FBI, when I had to spend half a year with them that really changed the way I think and the way I operate. If I compare my work before and after that watershed event, I see a kind of inverse relationship between my role as artist and my role as subject. The subject matter of the earlier work was impersonal, distant from me as an individual. The self-surveillance work that I am doing now is highly autobiographical, although it too is presented with a certain distance, as evidence. I am giving you highly personal information in an impersonal manner, whereas in the earlier work, I was providing impersonal information in a personalized manner.

JDB: That speaks to one of my concerns not only in your work, but in contemporary art in general—namely, the relationship and possible tension between the political dimension and the formal/aesthetic dimension. Your work is often thought of as essentially political. I wonder whether you think that is a fair evaluation of what you are doing. In other words, what is the relationship of the political to the formal in your work?

HE: My work is political, but I think there are multiple definitions of the political. What is the political dimension of resistance? What is self-identification? Historically artists have always been effective at holding a mirror up to their environment, given the current state that we are in, I think it only makes sense to reflect that condition. Whether it is read directly as political or not, that is the next level of my work. In some contexts, it is understood very much as a political statement, and I'm fine with that. But I am also fascinated by people who come to my work completely cold, not knowing the background. When you first look at *Tracking Transience* online, there is no preface, no description. All you get is this image and map, and this bombarding of image sequence after image sequence. You don't necessarily know what you are looking at . . . Let me backtrack a little bit. One of the aims of the project is to lead viewers to role-play as they experience the work—to replay the role of an FBI agent piecing together each bit of information. In that role, they may ask: Why am I looking at this toilet? Why am I looking at this plate of tacos? Why am I looking at an empty airport and a train station? Is there a thread there? This is something that intelligence agencies have to do all the time; they have to connect seemingly unrelated pieces of information that are actually very well threaded. I'm hoping that the viewer will go through that process in playing the role of the investigator. But then, as viewers become aware of the level of autobiographical detail, I'm hoping that a reversal will take place in their reading of the work, and that they realize: "This could very well be me; this could be my data." So even though the work lacks an explicit political preface, I believe it invites a political reading. I think it speaks very much of aspects of our social condition right now—both the continuous bombardment of images and also the self-documentation.

In this context, I would like to bring up a specific media practice that illustrates our condition: the *selfie*. When I first started this project a dozen years ago, the word "selfie" did not even exist. The big thing in media and culture at that moment was reality-TV shows. Such shows as *Big Brother* and *Survivor* had just started, and they were booming. I think *Big Brother* was a watershed moment in surveillance culture, because it was time in which the surveillance camera became a television star, a celebrity. These series foregrounded the idea of celebrity. You are watching people having a great time . . .

JDB: or a bad time . . .

HE: Or a bad time, yes. To turn a surveillance camera into a prime-time reality TV star, I think is a shift in our culture. We tend to think of the fascination with surveillance as a post-9/11 idea, but that is not so. Furthermore, when we think of surveillance cameras, we think of images that look pixelated and gritty. Some of my recent works involve videos that don't really look like videos or photographs; instead they resemble surveillance camera video. But if you think about the technology that's available today and remember the image quality even of popular camera phones, you see that there is no reason why surveillance video has to look pixelated. I'm convinced that the reason such video has to look that way is that if it looked too clear, too detailed, we would not accept it as surveillance. We would think of it as landscape. Let's remember the history of landscape photography in the United States, which is itself based on the earlier tradition of landscape painting . . . I'm thinking of the pioneering painters and photographers, doing the surveying of the western portion of the United States. Much of their work had its roots in the Northeast in the Hudson River School with its gorgeous vistas and its viewpoint representing the eye of God. Through this representational tradition, the eye of God constituted the original surveillance camera. Thus, although we tend of regard surveillance as a post-9/11 concept, I'm convinced that there is a direct link between the surveillance camera and selfie with which we document ourselves today on the one hand and the Hudson River School with its eye of God on the other. This representational technique invokes an ethical-aesthetic imperative that is deeply ingrained in Western culture: you behave because God is watching.

JDB: This argument recalls Foucault and the notion of the panopticon. We institutionalized the eye of God, as it were.

HE: Absolutely. Except that now the process takes place at arm's length, as we hold up our camera phones to take selfies. It is no longer that we are observed from God on high, in the abstract. Now the point of observation is just slightly above us, if you look at the angle of the selfie. This is the viewpoint from which we conduct our continual process of self-documentation . . .

JDB: . . . a process that is also self-reflexive. We don't have to depend on the NSA to document us because we document ourselves. With Facebook, Twitter, and selfies, we (at least millions of us) voluntarily enter into this process of documentation.

HE: Another thing that I find interesting—and this goes back to your question about the political dimension of my work— is this: I think that the selfie is a very political action, whether the participant is aware of it or not. But to appreciate its political significance, we need to think back for a moment, to the connection between war and artistic expression in the twentieth century. Before World War I, there were elaborate public monuments depicting traditionally heroic figures, such as generals. After the war, the monuments are different, more sedate. These monuments reflect an attempt to make sense of the world, because we had never before seen the carnage that World War I had brought. At the same time, there was a link between World War I and the birth of Dadaism. Likewise, following that trajectory, there was a link between World War II and the birth of abstract expressionism, at the time of the shift of world power from Europe to the United States. I am simplifying here, of course, and we can go into further detail. Once again, when you look at the Korean War and then the Vietnam War, those two are closely linked to the birth of minimalism and pop art, which were uniquely American movements because those two wars were uniquely American experiences, not European experiences. I am convinced that the form of artistic expression that is now linked to the War of Terror is the selfie and the process of continuous self-documentation. We've had cameras for many decades, and people have always been able to sit in front of a mirror and photograph themselves, but we have never done so to the extent that we do today with the cellphone camera. And the angle of the selfie, this arm's length, downward angle . . . how many photographs had that viewpoint before the War on Terror?

JDB: . . . because it is not the way you would set up a traditional camera for a self-portrait. Also, thinking historically as you do, it would perhaps be useful to consider the relationship of the self-portrait as an art genre to the selfie today.

HE: We don't give the selfie a lot of credit, but it is a very political practice. Another way to talk about it is in terms of political participation that is implied when people take selfies, whether they are aware of it or not. At the end of the day, it is not about the image, but about the act of making that image. I am convinced that in contemporary photography today—not necessarily in the high-art category of photography, but rather in the everyday and casual practice of photography—the political dimension lies in the act of taking the photograph rather than in the photograph as a document.

JDB: What you have said suggests a number of directions that we could now explore. Let me choose one or two. One difference between the selfie and the earlier practices that you have mentioned is, as you say, that those earlier practices often belonged to high or elite art (for example, in the case of the artist's self-portrait). The selfie is extremely important culturally in part because it is a widespread, popular practice. But there is the obvious analogy to family photography that was made possible by the invention of relatively inexpensive box cameras, of which the Kodak was the first example. The photography produced by the family for private consumption was generally regarded in the twentieth century as aesthetically trivial and political uninteresting. Such photography was thought of as evidence of the sentimentality and consumerism of American culture, not a political act. Does the selfie belong in that tradition?

HE: I'm not sure whether the selfie is in that tradition, but I think that those previous traditions can themselves be read in different ways. The Brownie, the classic box camera, and the idea of the vacation picture—we tend to dismiss such practices. But consider what the vacation picture meant for the idea of America as an expanding country. The Brownie or later the Polaroid gave expression to the significance of that vision of America through the road trip. The impact of that vision lay not necessarily in art or art photography. The impact was broader and more socially and economically varied, with implications for the transportation and the oil industry, for example. Consider the link between, say, the American road trip and American popular photography. We go on vacations in part to see things and to capture them in photographs that we bring home. In fact, the effect of popular photography is not that far removed from the effect of those gorgeous Ansel Adams photographs of many decades ago or the earlier Thomas Moran paintings of the West. . . . This might be the time to talk about how I stumbled into art. I had changed schools and majors many times and needed to finish a degree. My degree was actually in the arts, which is ironic because what I did in school has almost nothing to do with what I do now. I was able to use the platform of the arts to contain the many subjects I was interested in. Specifically, my degree was in printmaking, although for someone who hates the smell of ink, the career in printmaking is counterintuitive. What I was really interested in was not the techniques involved in making a print but rather the idea of the multiple, of replication itself. I was exploring the traditional media of prints, etchings, and lithographs not for their particular visual qualities; I was instead interested in the question: How does this single point a go to multiple point b's? This interest led naturally to working with digital media and the Internet, where replication is built into the technology. I look at the photograph in a similar way. When I take a photograph, I am still of course interested in the visual qualities, but the priority for me lies not with the one singular image, but rather with the broader collection of images and the perpetual documentation that the images provide. I treat photography and photographs from the perspective of the database, or as evidence, as a collection . . . and also as what I call the "alibi." I hardly ever show a single image. My photographs appear in large collections. Perhaps once in the last twenty years in which I have been showing photographs have I exhibited a single photo by itself. I have a show opening in a couple of weeks in which there are 32,000 photographs printed as one large image (Plate 52). The viewer is looking at a wall of information rather than a single photograph. Some of my colleagues who are photographers hold the single image in high regard. I feel a greater affinity to the notion of the collection. The idea is to look at the multiple, rather than the individual.

JDB: That has implications for the aesthetics of your work, particularly if one thinks of the individual image, the perfect image, as a modernist ideal. With Op Art and Pop Art, you see the beginnings of the aesthetic of the replication of the image, but Andy Warhol didn't have the technology available to him that you have today. You can work at a much larger scale. And when you mention the database, that prompts me to ask about

Lev Manovich's notion of the database as a fundamental aesthetic principle of the digital. Do you think Manovich is right?

HE: Absolutely. We can go even further with the idea of the perpetual database and the permanent database. In previous eras, artists were already concerned with the archive and the archival. On the other hand, when it comes to the question of permanence, of the work never going away, while institutions are certainly obsessed with that, some artists were not. When you look, for example, at a Rauschenberg, it may look like it's falling apart and that seemed to be ok. When some of the artists in the 1960s were creating these works, they did not intend them to survive for the next five hundred years. But the institutions want to preserve the work, to keep it locked in in that way. This is analogue preservation. Following up on Lev's idea of the database, the interesting thing is that now we have a permanent database. We have no motivation ever to delete anything. I don't even delete my spam. I don't know what Gmail does to it; I just leave it alone. I let it stay there because data storage is cheap. In the old days, we had two megabytes of hard drive space for email. Now five gigs or forty gigs—it doesn't matter. Data storage has become so ridiculously cheap that there is no longer a need to delete. Furthermore, there is a connection between deleting and the act of forgetting. We have all had the experience of doing an email search and having an old name pop up of a person we have completely forgotten about. All of a sudden you start thinking about this person and your previous connections and interactions with him or her. The practice of forgetting can be healthy. There are thousands of years of cultural significance in forgetting. In mourning, in memorials. But now we are in a situation where we don't have to forget, because everything is stored, everything can be called up. What happens to the database that never goes away? There are significant implications for us not just as individuals but as a society.

JDB: Does the understanding that we can preserve everything forever contribute to a sense of confidence or a sense of paranoia? For one thing, as so many have pointed out, all the data may be there, but the problem is finding the particular piece of data that one is looking for. Another issue is that if nothing is ever forgotten, then our transgressions are remembered along with our good deeds. Everything we have done or written is in the database somewhere and could emerge again with the least provocation.

HE: Can you imagine any teenager today eventually running for president, given the scrutiny to which we have subjected our candidates recently. They will face the accusation: "Back when you were 19 you did this and this and this." The record is complete. And if you do succeed in deleting something, the question will become, "Why did you delete this?" because there is now a noticeable gap in the record. There is a missing part, and that causes further suspicion. Maybe what we are really talking about is a shift toward transparency. Concerning your other point, we are currently in a situation in which it is hard to search the information, but I think that that is a temporary state. I think that we will eventually figure out how to search effectively. Google made 55 or 57 billion dollars last year in the search business. With those resources, it is only a matter of time before they (and we) figure out how to deal with these vast amounts of information. We are still in transition between the analogue and the digital. We have not fully stepped out of one and into the other. I'm hopeful that the search problem is something that we will address.

JDB: Your work is concerned with the ubiquity of information today and, as you say, its permanence, but does the work pass judgement on ubiquity? You spoke about a reversal that occurs for the viewer of *Tracking Transience*. Is that the moment when the viewer understands the enormity of what has happened to you and what could happen to all of us?

HE: Possibly. I think that reversal is a very important part not just of this work, but many of my works. For many decades now I have been fascinated by Magellan and his project of circumnavigation: if you go far enough in one direction, you come back in the other direction. This device of circumnavigation (or as I like to call it, Magellan's idea) is a key to my work. Circumnavigation and reversal have significant consequences in my work. Some of my work is frankly goofy, but if I don't present it in that way, the alternative is depressing and dark. In a way, I show you both sides: the crazy side and the dark side of our surveillance culture. The techniques of reversal and ambivalence in my work are representative of the condition of media today. How many photographs does each of us take in a year? There are more than 350 million photos uploaded to Facebook every day. An absurd number. But we are not spending as much time looking at the photos as the wealth of uploads suggests. The amount of time we devote to looking at photos is relatively unchanged. If we go back sixty or seventy years, they may have been one photograph in the house, on a wall, and you looked at it all the time. Now most of us take photographs all the time when we are out. We glance at the images we have taken and then may never look at them again. In viewing *Tracking Transience*, an image comes up: you might see a truck stop on Route 77 in Virginia, and you may never see that image again. It remains in the collection. We are all doing the same thing: amassing a database of images we may view only once—whether it happens in the context of political critique, in the way that *Tracking Transience* could be read, or in our everyday life. We take an image, glance at it, and then store it. The image does not recirculate.

JDB: Let me ask you one final question with regard to your database project. Given the amount of time it may take you to record your life in this way, how is it that you have time for other art work or for your duties as a professor? Does the act of self-documentation preclude other forms of action or art?

HE: It sounds daunting at first. However, it is really no different than many of us tweeting all day. How does one send out 20,000 tweets? For many of us, that activity has become part of our lives. How do we process thousands of text messages? I don't know what your email inbox looks like right now . . .

JDB: It is a disgrace. Thousands of messages . . .

HE: Exactly. Somehow we manage to get past these mountains of information that we produce and receive. In my case, it may seem as if all I do is document my life, but this task is not all demanding, because technology had changed so much that now the documentation is basically my phone. *Tracking Transience* is almost running on autopilot. As soon as I come to a new place, I take the photo and it's up online. I've just come into the office here. If you look on the website, you will see where I parked my car a few minutes ago before walking into the building. The ironic thing is that what I am doing is already obsolete in the sense that there are many solutions that you can now buy from the App store or Google Play that can track you more completely and accurately than my software ever could. I find it ironic that fewer than ten years ago people were saying: "This is a crazy idea. Why would you ever do this?" Now my project has been superseded in the sense that there are quite possibly a billion people doing this on Facebook every day.

JDB: The present ubiquity of this practice is in a certain sense part of the comment that your project makes.

HE: Is it still art if a billion people are doing it? We tend to be very particular in defining the role of art in our culture. We insist on these specializations, designating certain people to participate in certain aspects of culture. But if a billion people are doing this, . . . Facebook just surpassed the population of India and is only eighty million users away from surpassing the population of China. When you look at that number and compare it to the number of people who have access to clean water or health care or reliable electricity, it is amazing that one in seven people of the world's population is participating in the activity of self-documentation on Facebook. Has the world shut down, because these huge numbers of people have to update their status every few minutes? No, we've learned to adapt. We are incredibly adaptive beings. I find that exciting. Even the evolution of attitudes about my project indicates this adaptivity. In the beginning people asked why I would do this, but now my younger students ask: "What is the big deal?" That transition happened in a short period of time.

JDB: Your project changed from a unique artistic practice to a ready-made in that period of time.

HE: Absolutely. I think it is important that it is not just me: there are hundreds of millions doing this. The project is obsolete as technology, and perhaps for that very reason it functions as art again.

Notes

1. For Elahi's art pieces discussed in this interview, including *Tracking Transience*, see his website: http://elahi.umd.edu.

INTERACTION DESIGN

Morten Søndergaard

A definition of "interaction design" is hinging on how "interaction" is operationalized as part of the design vernacular. A number of assumptions immediately manifest themselves here, since this word alone invites a wide range of positions, often conflicting. Like philosophical positions on epistemology, they can be divided into camps: There are optimists as well as pessimists. Exemplifying the latter, Lev Manovich pointed out in "On Totalitarian Interactivity" that "interaction" is not representation but manipulation because it is focused on usability and thus limits the user's choices (and freedom) without making this obvious (Manovich 1996). Optimists, on the other hand, typically operate within the wider field of Human-Computer Interaction and, like Kees Overbeeke, see interaction primarily from the perspective of a user experience and an enabling affordance. Interaction is about perception, bringing affordances into a world. It "unfolds itself in possibilities for action" (Overbeeke and Wensveen 2003).

However, such views share a common ground: interaction design rests on a reductionist episteme; human action is reduced to a matter of codes and algorithms applied and the usability achieved; human context is reduced to the data utilized and tagged. But most importantly, perhaps, interaction design without a strategy to go beyond usability is a reduction of human perception and aesthetics to one, which does not encompass complexity.[1]

The various problems involved in such reductionism in interaction design, and the resulting naturalization emerging from the premise of usability and manipulation, as well as the questions of complexities arising from this, are addressed in this volume in various ways.

Since interaction is not in itself a medium of representation, but a functionalization of the possibilities data gives us, and since design, as the practice of the theory of usability and user experience which aims at functionalizing what is commonly and socially shared in a finalized product or situation (Krippendorff 1989),[2] then, "interaction design" cannot stand alone if the purpose is to arrive at "how to describe, analyze, synthesize, evaluate, reduce, or further the complexity of one or more of the current states and processes involving actualizations of ubiquity-effects" (Introduction, this volume).

Thus, in order to enter human experience, and be part of the possible actions of perception, interaction design has to be framed. On the one hand, it is always dependent on the codes and algorithms of the databases to which it is connected; on the other hand, the usability of these codes and algorithms has to be designed in order for the user to be able to access and use them. Interaction design, we are claiming in this volume, is more than the sum of its (largely) positivistic and product-aesthetic parts.

In the chapters in this section, interaction design is first of all presented as operational within creative and artistic experimentalism in ubicomp culture. The experimentalism is reflected, according to Löwgren's chapter in this volume, in "collaborative media," something that "is different from designing other forms of digital things." Experimentalism is also presented in artistic practices, such as performative and tangible interaction (Giulio Jacucci in this volume) or as "social feedback systems" (interview with David Rokeby in this volume).

With the replacement of mass consumption by mass production of cultural objects by users and the emergence of the "implied producer," interaction design might be seen as a way to appreciate and practice complexity. Henceforth, it is not only artists who create "art"; anyone may be an artist when finding ways of producing social reality through participation in social media. The manipulation of interaction is countered in the artistic "design" of interfaces of complexity. Elsewhere, David Rokeby terms it a "user interface for reality." As Rokeby further suggests, the interaction designer (or artist) "need to look at how our experience of the real world is constructed. In other words, what is our user interface for reality?" (Rokeby 1998).

This, in many ways, returns the exploration of interaction design to the question of manipulation/usability, and the dangers of naturalization. How can artistic creativity counter that? How can we implicate the user as producer of complex activities?

To slightly twist Rokeby's point above, it could be claimed that ubiquity *may/may not* create new ways of producing interaction designs that make it possible to investigate the user-interfaces that construct our reality. It may become a tool for critical introspection and magnification of real-life processes through real-time "artistic" scenarios (Norberg and Søndergaard 2005). The modalities involved in participation in real-time artistic scenarios, such as, but certainly not limited to, "installations" are both performative and experiential, which increases focus on the act of participation itself.

Interaction designs framing such investigations into complexity are collaborative practices "facilitating social and communicative processes" and navigating all the pitfalls inherent in the commercialization of the convergent media (Löwgren); it is "a performance" of complex actions (Jacucci); thus, "culture might be considered a complex artifact of social feedback" (Rokeby in this volume).

Through his practice, Rokeby is constructing both closed (postcybernetic) reality systems and ubiquitous "social reality" situations. However, whereas the "systems" are based on artefacts that break the rules of logic on which they rely, as in glitch or feed-back, Rokeby's "social realities" seem to rely on network-based "artefacts" operating between materiality and the performance of the "constituent human participant," which, according to Rokeby, is more complicated than "the behavior of a crowd."

As for the contributors to this volume, it is also our task as interactants in network societies to explore "how to talk about complexity, to appreciate complexity, and to practice complexity" (Law and Hassard 1999, 10), or risk losing "the capacity to apprehend" it (Law and Hassard 1999, 8–10). Through interaction design, we may achieve all of this or be manipulated to believe we have achieved it. It all depends on how we engage with interaction design: as tools of reduction aimed at usability for product design (and a ubiquitous techno-cultural industry), or as methodologically framing of acts of critically investigating complex cultural and social reality-constructs.

Notes

1. Dourish is advocating this theoretically (Dourish 2001), and "critical design" is doing it in practice.
2. "We are perceptually 'guided' by the visual appearance of the object in order to fetch the right 'cognitive model' for its use from long term memory" (Krippendorf 1989).

References

Dourish, Paul. 2001. *Where the Action Is*. Cambridge, MA: MIT Press.

Krippendorff, Klaus.1989. *On the Essential Contexts of Artefacts or on the Proposition That "Design Is Making Sense (Of Things)"*. Design Issues (5, 2), 9–39. Cambridge, MA: MIT Press.

Law, John, and John Hassard. 1999. *Actor Network Theory and After*. London: Wiley-Blackwell.

Norberg, Bjorn, and Morten Søndergaard. 1995. "Introduction." *Get Real. Real Time + Art + Theory + History + Practice*, edited by Morten Søndergaard. New York: George Braziller.

Manovich, Lev. 1996. "On Totalitarian Interactivity." Hanover, Germany: Heise Online. www.heise.de/tp/artikel/2/2062/1.html. Accessed April 15, 2015.

Manovich, Lev. 2009. "The Practice of Everyday (Media) Life." *Re-Action: The Digital Archive Experience: Renegotiating the Competences of the Archive and the (Art) Museum in the twenty-first Century*, edited by Mogens Jacobsen and Morten Søndergaard. Roskilde, Denmark: Museum of Contemporary Art.

Overbeeke, Kees C. J., and Stephan S. A. G. Wensveen. 2003. "From Perception to Experience, from Affordances to Irresistibles." *Proceedings of the 2003 International Conference on Designing Pleasurable Products and Interfaces*, 92–97. New York: ACM.

Rokeby, David. 1998. *The Construction of Experience*. http://homepage.mac.com/davidrokeby/experience.html. Accessed February 10, 2015.

INTERACTION AS PERFORMANCE

Performative Strategies in Designing Interactive Experiences

Giulio Jacucci

Introduction

Designing interactions within a ubiquitous computing rhetoric, we encounter established tenets originating from the visionary formulations (Weiser 1991) and updated scenarios (Abowd and Mynatt 2000). These have yet to be fully realized and include as main elements: multimodal interfaces, context-aware or adaptive computing, automated capture and access to live experiences, and connecting the physical and virtual worlds.

These themes can be related to important features of performances and theatrical practices, which are traditionally aimed through staging and performing at the design and interactive emergence of embodied experiences. This is the case for different performance forms ranging from improvisational theater, performance art to more traditional theater, which are related to ubiquitous computing tenets above as they are embodied, include techniques to improvise and adapt action following an underlying script and models, aim at the creation of a fictional space, and are concerned with expressing and experiencing action (Table 38.1). Tangible interaction includes opportunities for embodied expression and performance. Other features of ubiquitous computing such as adaptivity and context awareness are essentially reducible to agency of the system that needs to intervene following certain rules and improvise given certain situations. And as reminded above, the capture and access of experiences is a central ubiquitous computing concept that is related to how performative traditions practices are concerned with documenting and reenacting stories and experiences. Finally the combination of virtual and physical worlds opens a lot of opportunities to interpret, use, imagine, and consider the physical space in different ways.

The interaction as performance contribution to ubiquitous computing experiences is in the possibility to address the *complexity* of interaction that is otherwise to be considered at small fine-grained levels of small actions and details. Instead, interaction as performance for example gives some indications on how to consider the interaction overtime in phases that are experientially important, which features of the space are particularly relevant to collective interpretation of its meaning and narrative, and which interactions are to be considered important expressive acts in the co-experience.

TABLE 38.1 Relating ubicomp tenets to performative perspective aspects

Ubicomp Tenets	Related Performative Aspects
Tangible interaction	Embodied performance
Adaptivity, context awareness	Improvisation, interventions, creative constraints
Capturing, access to lived experience	Expressing action and experience
Connecting physical and virtual worlds	Staging a fictional space

Research Objectives

The aim of this work is to propose a conceptual framework infused in and derived from selected analysis of performance and theater that can help in describing and designing for ubiquitous interaction experiences. The objectives include: 1) selecting particular concepts from different works that investigate anthropology of performance, performance art, and theater anthropology relevant to ubiquitous interactive experiences; 2) exemplifying concepts with cases that include designing interactive experiences in a ubicomp context; and 3) summarizing the concepts in a framework to draw relationships and orient opportunities for their application.

In the next section, we summarize how design frameworks in human–computer interaction (HCI) oriented attentions from experiential to theatrical and performative perspectives. In Section 3, we introduce the foundations of an *Interaction as Performance* framework. In Sections 4 and 5, we introduce the framework composed of two interrelated views:

- Space and Constraints: Section 4 deals with the design of a fictional space in particular considering creative constraints that facilitated and guide interpretation and action.
- Time and Dramaturgy: Section 5 deals with the timing and role of interventions and dramaturgy that shape collective emergence of action.

The proposal is that these are views implicitly considered in design ubiquitous experiences and that an Interaction as Performance framework allows making these elements salient so that they can be considered more explicitly by designers.

From Experiential to Theatrical Design Perspectives in HCI

Theatrical and performance perspectives in HCI follow a broader development that has successfully impregnated HCI research with design perspectives and approaches that have valued experiential, affective, and pleasurable aspects neglected by cognitive frameworks. Traditional HCI approaches to evaluate the usability of products for people tend to see the person as a "user" and the product as a "tool," where the latter is used to accomplish a task.

Before the attention to experience design (McCarthy and Wright 2004), HCI researcher has been infused by frameworks that investigate the situated character of our actions and on how plans are used as resources (Suchman 1987), distributed character of cognition and action (Hollan et al 2002), the historical aspect of practice and to the mediating function of artefacts (Kuutti 1996). Phenomenological approaches have inspired different perspectives of action related to technology use, as the notion of involved unreflected activity and breakdown (Bødker et al. 1991). Ehn (1988) develops a different explanation of practices of design and use, using the language games approach of Wittgenstein and the notion of family resemblance. Ehn also discusses the consequences of considering computer artefacts as tools. Artefacts are objects made by human work. In designing computer artefacts, "the emphasis should be on concernful design of signs that make sense in the language game of use" (Ehn 1988, 164). According to Ehn, the computer should not be considered just a tool but designed artifacts recognizing the important of skills. Dourish (2001), drawing from ethnomethodology and phenomenology, proposes a new model of HCI based on the notion of embodied interaction that he defines as "the creation, manipulation, and sharing of meaning through engaged interaction with artefacts" (Dourish 2001, 126). Embodied technologies acquire meaning through the way in which users incorporate them into working practices. As a consequence, "the manipulation of meaning and coupling are primarily the responsibility of users not designers." Where coupling is the way, we build up relationships between entities during action, changing our focus and attention. In embodied interactions, the active nature of computers is important not as independent agents but "as augmentations and amplifications of our own activities." (Dourish 2001, 166). Design oriented frameworks have emerged like the one of Redström (2001) who proposes a design philosophy for everyday computational things, where meaningful presence is contrasted to previous imperatives from usability as, for example, efficient use. In this design approach, time is the central parameter as exemplified by Slow Technology (Hallnäs and Redström 2000) and aesthetics is the basis to design presence. Redström describes "the presence of an artefact in terms of how it expresses itself as we encounter it in our everyday life. Then we can think of artefacts as 'expressionals,' artefacts as bearers of expressions rather than functions" (Hallnäs and Redström 2000). Phenomenological approaches have also inspired design frameworks (Svanæs 1999). Deckers et al. (2012) propose a design framework for perceptual crossing between person and artifact that can be used to apply using design notions, such as Focus the Senses, Active Behavior Object, Subtleness, Reaction to External Event; these are relevant for designing perceptive activity in an artefact to reach involvement and reach a shared common space with the artifact.

All these contributions as well as attention from performative approaches as design techniques in creating and evaluating scenarios (Jacucci and Kuutti 2002; Macaulay et al. 2006; Binder et al. 2011) created the premise to explore performance and theatrical frameworks in HCI.

Laurel's work (1991) was the first to consider theatrical metaphors and drama in the context of HCI by applying the principles of Aristotelian poetics. Human computer experiences can be structured around the precepts of dramatic form and structure. Laurel's aim is to derive a poetics of interactive form. "Interactivity" here is understood as the ability of humans to participate in actions in a representational context.

Reeves et al. (2005) present a taxonomy with four broad design strategies for the performer's manipulations of an interface and their resulting effects on spectators: the "secretive," wherein manipulations and effects are largely hidden; the "expressive," in which they tend to be revealed, enabling the spectator to fully appreciate the performer's interaction; the "magical," where effects are revealed but the manipulations that caused them are hidden; and, finally, the "suspenseful," wherein manipulations are apparent but effects are revealed only as the spectator takes his or her turn. Benford et al. (2006) extend the above framework for designing spectator interfaces with the concept of performance frames, enabling one to distinguish audience from bystanders. They conclude that ambiguity to blur the frame can be a powerful design tactic, empowering players to willingly suspend their disbelief.

Dalsgaard and Hansen (2008) further extend the perspective of users as performers and audience. They not only observe how the user is simultaneously operator, performer, and spectator. Performing Perception is proposed to highlight how "her operations and thus her perception is heavily influenced by her knowledge of that her perception of the system is a performance for others." A central facet of the "aesthetics of interaction" is rooted in, as they put it, the user's experience of herself: "performing her perception." They argue that this three-in-one situation is always shaping the user's understanding and perception of the interaction, and they address the notion of the performative spectator and the spectating performer. This resonates with the concept of Spect-actor as proposed by Augusto Boal in the Theatre of the Oppressed tailored to situations of political or social oppression (Boal 1992).

Recent work also addressed temporal structures of interactive experiences with the concept of trajectories (Benford et al. 2009; Benford and Giannachi 2011; Gilroy et al. 2009). For Benford et al. (2009), trajectories are based on the fact that successful interactive experiences follow journeys that ensure a coherent and connected whole. These are shaped by the narratives of authors, influenced by orchestrators, but also steered by participants, in evolving spatial, temporal, and performative structures. They effectively draw from dramaturgy (Pfister 1998) proposing as key facets: space, time, roles, and interfaces. The framework presented is able to highlight important implications for designers by identifying transitions in trajectory in which continuity is at risk. Transitions include, for example, beginning and endings, transitions between roles, and traversals between physical and digital. Trajectories can be managed and interwoven enabling a coherent dramaturgy of experience. Recently, Spence et al. (2013), reviewing current perspectives, propose Performative Experience Design as potentially providing useful guidance among others on rules that sets the performance frame and guides actions such as turn-taking, mediating the expression of self to another, and attention to the unique aesthetics of performance. These could provide new "epistemological, theoretical, methodological, and practical approaches to understand people's interaction with an experience."

The Foundation of the Interaction as Performance Framework

The works above propose useful concepts however either use only a limited or remain limited in the extent of coverage the discussion is the framework of Interaction as Performance (Jacucci 2004; Jacucci and Wagner 2005; Jacucci et al. 2005). This framework is based on anthropological studies of performance that have roots in a pragmatic view of experience. The framework proposes a variety of principles that characterize performative interactions.

Processual Character and Accomplishment

One of the principles is that of accomplishment and intervention. Already the etymology of the term "performance" shows that it does not have the structuralist implication of manifesting form but, rather, a processual sense of bringing to completion or accomplishing. The concept of event and processual character is also key: performances are not generally amorphous or open-ended; they have diachronic structure, a beginning, a sequence of overlapping but isolable phases, and an end. Expression and experience is another element of importance. According to pragmatist views, an experience is never completed until it is expressed. Also, in an experience there is a structural relationship between doing and undergoing.

To formulate a performance perspective that is useful in furthering our understanding of how design is or can be accomplished, we will gather characteristics from the work of anthropologist Victor Turner and from the philosophy of John Dewey and Wilhelm Dilthey, on which Turner based his work. Moreover, other anthropological works, such as those of Eugenio Barba (theater anthropology) and Schieffelin (performance ethnography) will contribute additional traits. We have also found it useful to integrate these traits with views from performance art, such as the writings and works of Vito Acconci, a pioneer in this area. We will start in the following section by describing the core relationship between expression and experience as proposed by Turner. A more detailed articulation of characteristics will follow, along with an analysis of specific design episodes.

The Relationship between Experience and Expression

Victor Turner, one of the founding fathers of performance studies, provided an explanation of how a performance perspective includes relating expressions to experience (drawing from the philosophy of Dewey and Dilthey). This explanation serves to address how experience, expression, and perception form an intricate relationship.

Turner bases his approach on previous thinkers who addressed "experience:" John Dewey, who saw an intrinsic connection between experience and aesthetic qualities, and Wilhelm Dilthey, who argued that experience urges us towards expression and communication with others (Turner 1986).

Following Dilthey, Turner explains how meaning, which is sealed up and inaccessible in daily life, is "squeezed out" (from the German Ausdruck) through expressions such as perform-ances. In Turner's words, "an experience is itself a process which 'presses out' to an 'expression' which completes it" (Turner 1982, 13). According to this view, there is a processual structure of Erlebnis (experience or what is lived through); it has, first of all, a perceptual core. After perception, past experiences are then evoked, "but past events remain inert unless the feelings originally bound up with them can be fully revived" (Turner 1982, 14). Meaning is considered emergent and not predetermined in the event; it "is generated by 'feelingly' thinking about interconnections between past and present events" (Turner 1982, 14). Finally, it is not enough to achieve meaning for oneself, as an experience is never truly completed until it is communi-cated intelligibly to others or, in other words, it is expressed. As Turner puts it: "Culture itself is the ensemble of such expressions—the experience of individuals made available to society and accessible to the sympathetic penetration of other 'minds'"(Turner 1982, 14).

Energy and Consciousness as Opposed to Everyday Behavior

Unlike other kinds of behavior, performance requires more effort in terms of the energy, skill, and consciousness (thinking) of the acts. Eugenio Barba's approach contributes additional traits and features, such as the skills, energy, and consciousness (thinking) of the performer. For example, Barba and Savarese (1999) distinguish between daily and extra-daily "techniques" such as performances (Barba and Savarese 1999). We are less conscious of our daily techniques, where we apply also the principle of least effort, that is, obtaining the maximum result with the minimum expenditure of energy, but "extra-daily techniques are based, on the contrary, on wasting energy" (Barba 1995, 16). The principle might even be the opposite: "The principle of maximum commitment of energy for a minimal result" (Ibid.).

Event Character, Temporal and Narrative Structure

The etymology of the term "performance" shows that it "does not have the structuralist implication of manifesting form, but rather the processual sense of bringing to completion or accomplishing" (Turner 1982, 91). A performance is always something accomplished: it is an achievement or an intervention in the world (Schieffelin 1997). According to Turner, performances are not generally "amorphous or open-ended, they have diachronic structure, a beginning, a sequence of overlapping but isolable phases, and an end" (Turner 1986, 80). It includes an initiation and a consummation. "There was one way I loved to say the word 'performance,' one meaning of the word 'performance' that I was committed to: 'performance' in the sense of performing a contract—you promise you would do something, now you have to carry that promise out, bring that promise through to completion" (Acconci, in Acconci and Moore 2001).

Implications to Designing Interactive Experiences

These relations of Table 38.1 to ubicomp tenets become clearer if considered in a wider framework of how original HCI dominated by cognitive frameworks has been extended by experience design frameworks and performance perspectives (Table 38.2).

   While traditional HCI identifies a repetitive task with general validity to be targeted by the design, performance points to the organization of events that maintain a specificity given by the contingency of meaning and material. While, in general, HCI relies on recognition, accountability, and affordances at the interface, performance focuses on perception and experience. As Dewey teaches, recognition is interpreting something we already know, while perception occurs when we experience a thing that imposes surprising qualities that create new insights. Dominant tenets are usability, making an operation easy and efficient, for example, or exploiting affordances so that they can be carried out unthinkingly and making the tool disappear. On the other side of Table 38.1, a performance perspective aims at creating experiences where participants are more aware, think feelingly about the artefacts around them, and engage in the situation in reflection or perception in action. Moreover pervasive and context-aware scenarios propose sensing systems that measure and simulate space or recognize and sense situations. To this, "sensing humans" are contrasted with the idea that physical interfaces should make use of spatiality and materiality to enrich interaction using all senses. Moreover, space is configured and performed rather than measured, and situations are staged rather than recognized.

TABLE 38.2 Original HCI tenets and extensions from experience design and performance perspective

Original Human–Computer Interaction Foci	Extensions of Experience Design and Performance Perspective
Task, timeless, universal, replicable behavior	Event, ephemeral, unique, replicable experience
Usability, accountability, affordance	Expression, sense experience
Users, designers, administrators	Actors, spectators, directors, performers
Personalizing, computer artefact's view	Configuring, actor's view
Recognizing situations, sensing, simulating space	Staging situations, performing space
Eliminating secondary tasks	Amplifying action and communication

Space and Constraints: Designing a Fictional Space

When designing an interactive experience whether it's a desktop, mobile, or ubiquitous installation, the user interface provides context, language, and affordances to create a space of possibility sometime governed by a metaphor as for example the desktop one in personal computers. This is recognized by previous work such as Laurel (1992) in which computers are used as theater-stages and the concepts such as frames (Dalsgaard and Koefoed Hansen 2008, Benford et al. 2013) are operationalized in the search of a physical location, setting, or place that they do not interpret literally, but which will be used as a resource to create a "fictional" space. Performance has a lot to do with this process.

Spatial features may be functional, as in the case of the walls of a building, but they may also be symbolically charged, resulting in a specific perception of space during a performance. In a theatrical performance, for example, we are doing, "an essentially interpretative act, translating real bodies, words and movements into the objects of another, hypothetical world; . . . everything within the defined spatial compass of the stage is to be read differently from the objects seen elsewhere" (Counsell and Wolf 2001, 155).

Case: Bodily Interactions with Interactive Galaxy Installations

Galileo all' Inferno is a theatre show developed by Studio Azzurro, it has been performed daily between July 10 and 12, 2008 in the Teatro Arcimboldi of Milan, Italy. The show is composed of two parts, both different from an aesthetic and the technological–interactive point of view.

The first part of the show is a dance performance, during which the public attends the show in a classic way, sitting in the stalls. In the second part of the show, at the end of the performance, the audience can get on the stage and interact with two interactive installations "Ombra di stele." A projector transfers the image of a stellar field to a transparent vertical screen. Once passed through the screen, the beam of light is refracted and reflected, delineating stars on the stage, and some other stars on the opposite side of the entrance. When the visitor gets closer, (s)he is lighted by infrared rays, creating a shadow on the ground invisible to the visitor. A camera equipped with an IR filter detects this shadow. The signal is analyzed by a video-tracking algorithm that identifies the shapes of the shadows throughout a sequence of coordinates. The data are elaborated by a software that reacts in real time and generates the graphics. The image of the stellar field changes depending on the graphics and the stars concentrate around the shape of the infrared shadow based on two parameters: presence and persistence. As the visitor moves, the stars move with her/him with certain inertia. Looking at the ground (or at the backcloth), the visitor sees a constellation of stars surrounding his/her silhouette.

In this installation, the visitor as put forward in the section on foundation is both experiencing and expressing in the way that is at the same time a user and an actor in the act (cf. Dalsgaard and Hansen 2008). The design of the installation to be successful should bring the visitor to recognize the meaning attributed to the space in terms of the projection of the shadow into the star constellation and at the same time invite the visitor to approach and interact with the installation in the right position. The event and structured character of the interaction with the installation is concluded when the visitors discover that the stars gather around the shadow of their bodies.

"Galassie": In this installation, a projector throws a beam through a transparent screen positioned on the stage. It projects a geometry of a grate of coordinates, creating a visualization of stylized shapes similar to galaxies. The software is composed of two main components: the video tracking (Retina) and the generative/reactive algorithms programmed in Processing OpenGL. The video tracking defines the position and detects the outlines of the visitors with the help of an infrared lighting system. Every person who gets on the stage generates an expanding galaxy from his body. As the user moves, (s)he's followed by her/his own galaxy and by a grate that visualizes the persons, movement in a cyclic and generative way. Moreover, by using a set of directional microphones, a component analyzes acoustic features of voice based on a machine learning individualizes the emotional state of those present and influences the appearance of the galaxies. Three categories of emotions, neutral, positive, or negative are detected and they modify the color of the galaxies: a scale of grey corresponds to the neutral condition, a shade of light blue corresponds to the negative condition, and a shade of red corresponds to a positive condition. Thus three semantic categories are used to send status events and the galaxies will change the dominant color. As positive event is received, all the galaxies change to "warm colors"—yellow, orange, and red. If the status event is negative, the color ramp used by the galaxies changes to "cold colors"—blue, light blue, and violet. If the neutral event is received, the galaxies turn to a grey scale. This effect will reinforce the emotional climate with introspective colors (blue, light blue) in a "negative" condition or joyful colors (orange red) in a "positive" emotional condition. The grey scale suggests the need for change and is stimulating reactions from the group.

From a performance perspective, constraints can do much more than simply reduce complexity and add structure. In the traditions of such theater directors as, for example, Jacques Lecoq, Philippe Gaulier, Keith Johnstone, Peter Brook, Augusto Boal, or John Wright, the main concern of a director is to avoid telling performers what to do, while at the same time driving the creative process in order to make them work creatively and make things happen. The problem of avoiding dictating outcomes is common to design, which aims at the collective emergence of objects that provide new insights by encapsulating unexpected features.

The Creative Use of Constraints

The problem is well-known in most approaches to directing in the performing arts, where the major goal is to devise a performance by making it emerge with minimum control, and being ready to take advantage of the unexpected. As theater director John Wright says, "This is a shifting and mercurial world where anything is possible and everything has yet to be found. This means that as a director or facilitator you've got to find strategies that are likely to make something happen rather than strategies for getting people to analyze what they think they might do." A particularly relevant aspect for design activities is how the role of constraints can be developed within collective activities (Jacucci, Linde, and Wagner 2011, 24).

It has been noted that the relationship between creativity and constraints is mysterious and symbiotic (Laurel 1991). "Creativity arises out of the tension between spontaneity and limitations, the latter (like river banks) forcing the spontaneity into the various forms which are essential to the work of art" (May, quoted in Laurel 1991, 101). As remarked by Laurel (1991, 106), the "value of limitations in focusing creativity is recognized in the theory and practice of theatrical improvisation." In fact, her model of human–computer activity appreciates the role of improvisation within a matrix of constraints.

Similarly constraints can become resources in improvised performances following specific approaches, such as, for example, the practice of Keith Johnstone. So the designer or designers could be thought of as actors or directors utilizing constraints to make design happen.

Case: Analyzing Phases in Interactive Galaxies Installations

A study of the installation employed emotion questionnaires that indicated dominantly positive feelings, further described in the subjective verbalizations as gravitating around interest, ludic pleasure, and transport (Jacucci et al. 2009). However, through the video analysis, the contribution of multiuser participation in engagement was evident in exploration phases as they displayed similar features such as experience sharing and imitation, which were also found in the verbalizations.

The video analysis focused on two aspects of the installation, namely the interactivity and the co-presence with other visitors. The interaction analysis of people exploring the installations identified three recurrent phases: Circumspection, Testing, and Play. All of them are based on the exploration of the installation affordances, showing what visitors recognized as the possible way to interact with it.

Circumspection is the phase in which the visitor is entering the interactive area, observing the current setting and selecting a point to start from.

Testing is the phase in which the visitor starts to try to interact with the artwork by making a particular bodily movement such as "moving an arm" in order to find out which movements have a consequence on the configuration of the installation. In this phase, visitors usually remain within a portion of the installation, and appropriate it by exploring and testing.

Play is the phase in which the visitor interacts with the art installation in an aware, active, and involved way usually after having discovered the "working of a principle" behind the installation. In this phase, they do not just wait for the artwork reactions, but also try to provoke those reactions by using creatively the movements that were tested in the previous phase and new ones. Next, we will highlight two characteristics of these three phases emerged from the analysis, namely sharing the art experience and relying on imitation as a guiding principle for interaction.

The social component of the art experience is apparent from episodes that we called co-testing and co-playing. When visitors came on the stage with friends or family, they experienced the artworks by taking into account both the installation and the other people accompanying them. Entrance in the installation space, testing the artwork possibilities and finally playing with it developed as a common activity, where the users oriented both to the artwork and to their accompanying people. People in these groups tended to focus on a same portion of the installation, and to take turns into testing or playing with the artwork.

As we have seen, the event and processual character is demonstrated by different phases of circumspection, testing, and playing that make up the experience of the visitor in both installations. In both cases, the space is invested with different meaning and narrative that needs to be conveyed to the visitor along with constraints of how to act in it for a fictional space to emerge. Constraints are the features, rules, and parameters that govern how the elements are animated, what they respond to or conversely what the visitor should do to animate them (that stars gather around the shadow after some time, or how the galaxies follow the movement, and change their colors).

Dramaturgy in Collective Emergence and Interventions

Although the creation of a fictional space can be seen as an exercise for a reader of a book (involving therefore a writer and a reader), in this context we refer to fictional space as something that emerges out of the ongoing interaction between participants in design, be it a short session or through a project. In theater, we refer to fictional space, for example, as a representation of actions and human conflicts which participants create by performing and reacting to each other (Jacucci and Kuutti 2002). It is fictional because it is not a substitute for reality. It is created by images that are free from the rules of reality and conventions. It has a perspective, and it is a space because one can be in it or out of it. There can be rules of being and behaving that come into play as one "takes part" and becomes involved in a fiction. Furthermore, from the inside one can look outside, and vice versa. "In some cases with performances we aim at such a space because in order to set the imagination free, we need to change some of the rules of reality. Hence we inevitably fall into fiction" (Ibid 174).

However, not everything that is put forward by participants can be fruitful for the performance. The collective emergence of the fictional space can be affected if it is interpreted by other participants and, even more importantly, if other participants are able to produce a reaction from it.

The etymology of the verb to "intervene" is from the Latin verb intervenire, which means "to come between." This has evolved into the contemporary sense of occurring, coming in between two events also by way of hindrance or modification, entering as an extraneous feature or circumstance. Performance is there to emphasize the opportunity of exploiting the features of our involved action in the world and also in the way our accomplishments produce changes in it and therefore new insights for us. Performance is expression, and "like construction, signifies both an action and its result" (Dewey 1980/1934, 82). Performance approaches to knowing insist on immediacy and involvement (Denzin 2003) and favor an experiential, participative, and interventionist epistemology.

In improvisational performance, participants need to interpret performers' offerings (as actors and spectators do in theater) as they occur: actions, symbols, and props that are introduced into the scene are interpreted in the light of the unfolding action. This is necessary for the completion of the collective endeavor, which can lead to the construction of the fictional space. Other actors reacting to offerings achieve this completion. In other words, interpretations are not only the product of the imaginative activity of a single participant. Rather, what makes them valuable during group improvisations is their interactional character or their collective. This highly dynamic and interactive endeavor, which sustains a fictional representation, is what constitutes the imaginative ground on which participants contribute with their performance. Obviously, every contribution or reaction can potentially constitute an imaginative or creative achievement of some sort, and it can be produced by a variety of kinds of cognitive processes. Nevertheless, it is not free imagination. Every product of the participants' imagination that does not become part of the representation can be ignored or can constitute an obstacle to it.

From performance, we learn what kind of contributions from participants can foster the collective emergence of a fictional space (Jacucci and Kuutti 2002), for example, those that can be interpreted and "reacted to" by some other participant be this another user or the computer; those that can be part of the fictional space in which participants are performing (in that they can be interpreted as being part of it by other participants) as interpreted by some participant; and those that are inspired by the performance of physical actions, utterances, and significations by other participants.

Case: Spect-actors and Multimodal Synthetic Puppeting

Euclide is a virtual puppet that has an engaging role in the visit of a science museum in Naples, Italy. The system offers a multimodal interface to the puppeteer in order to animate a virtual puppet and entice the audience. A hidden animator controls the movements and mimicry of the virtual character through a multimodal interface including a data glove. The animator's hand movements "activate" the virtual character, controlling the mimicking, and digital effects alter the animator's voice.

The rendering of the character appears on a screen in a second space, the "stage." Five stages are scattered about the museum. The animator monitors the audience members via a microphone and a camera, and reacts to them. Therefore, the puppeteer can react and respond to people talking to the character.

The system offers 100 different features to the puppeteer for animating the character, among them jumping or having different costumes. To allow use of this great expressive power, with many elements sometimes utilized simultaneously, different modalities are proposed. The interface includes eleven screens, two computer keyboards, two mice, a data glove, a microphone, headphones, and a MIDI keyboard, all in the control room. Among these devices, three screens, one computer keyboard, one mouse, the MIDI keyboard, the microphone, and the glove are dedicated to real-time puppetry. The other devices are dedicated to system launch, switching between interactive areas or setting the puppet to inactive in order for the puppeteer to take a break.

After interviews with two different puppeteers and onsite observations different phases were identified in the interactive sessions. First in an approach phase, participants enter the interaction area, observing. Then they start trying to interact with the installation, by taking a particular action such as touching the screen in order to find out which actions have an effect on the installation. After this, participants interact with the installation in an aware, active, and involved way. This phase includes the climax or main action of the interaction session. Ending is the phase in which participants have their attention diverted from the installation before they leave. Table 38.3 shows that these phases are balanced in the sessions, with the exception of Approach, which could not always be recorded. In this regard, the structure of the sessions as explained by the puppeteer during the interview confirms this distribution: more actions are proposed during the playing phase.

The puppeteer uses the above plan as a resource for action and intervenes with different strategies to manage the emerging narrative. In this case, the spectators were mostly pupils and

TABLE 38.3 Phases in interaction sessions between visitors and puppeteer

Visitor	Puppet
Enter (one or several people, or only a voice)	Stops activity
Present themselves	Presents itself
Laugh	Skips happily
Asks what is funny	
Say bad words or abuse a bit	Repeats in a mechanical way
Cries, complains, and goes away	
Say a keyword	Changes costume
Tells a story	
Sings a song	
Ask questions	Answers normally
Answers as if crazy or slow	
Answers and asks the audience the same	
Greetings	Greetings

teenagers and sessions lasted more than two minutes, on average. It must be noted, however, that teachers interrupt some sessions and others are a continuation of a previous interaction. While improvised, sessions conform to a general structure, which is also reported in interviews with the puppeteers. This structure is similar to the ones discussed in the cases Ombre di Stelle and Galassie in the previous section. The groups of spectators generally are attentive to the installation (they did not talk to each other), actively interact with it, and show positive and growing interest as they interact. The puppeteer, therefore, is working with different resources, including a repertoire of gags, to be able to keep spectators engaged for several minutes. The narrative of the sessions emerges from the interaction and contribution of both the puppeteer and the spect-actors.

Conclusion

Designing for interactive experiences in ubiquitous computing requires considering embodiment, mixing virtual and physical, adaptivity, and social interaction. The coverage of interaction modalities in such systems can be broad encompassing different interface technologies, such as augmented reality (Morrison et al. 2009), multitouch and gestural interaction (Jacucci et al. 2005), and real time analysis of voice and speech coupled with position of users (as in the case of Galassie in this article; see also Jacucci et al. 2009) where galaxies that are generated and move according to motion of visitors changing color depending on their voices.

Studies indicate the decisive contribution of multiuser participation in engagement suggesting that a user's experience and ludic pleasure are rooted in the embodied, performative interaction with installations, and is negotiated with the other visitors in social interaction.

There are several contributions of an "Interaction as Performance" perspective to the design of interactive experiences in a ubiquitous computing paradigm:

Roles of users as performers and spectators, highlighting the embodied performance along with multiple roles of users simultaneously operator, performer, and spectator;

Fictional space, emphasizing the importance of a fictional space and its collective emergence;

Dramaturgical structures, foregrounding phases and the event character of experiences with dramatic structures.

The current frontier in engagement from a computational point of view is to develop adaptivity of interactive systems that take into account the more dynamic aspects of the points above. User Modeling in Adaptive interaction points to methods for changing a user model or the user interface in response to traces of interaction (Brusilovsky 2001; Jameson 2009; Glowacka et al. 2013). This has been addressed for example in persuasive technologies and feedback systems that monitor user interaction to analyze how far the user's state of behavior is from the desired one and accordingly issues a feedback to reach it (Gamberini et al. 2012). Other approaches like affective loop experiences monitor users, expression of emotions; the system responds by generating affective expressions, and this in turn affects users making them respond and, step-by-step, feeling more and more involved with the system (Gilroy et al 2009). This could be the next challenge for Interaction as Performance perspective in supporting computationally interactive experiences by directing adaptively the dramaturgy of interaction.

References

Abowd, G. D., and E. D. Mynatt. 2000. "Charting Past, Present, and Future Research in Ubiquitous Computing." *ACM Transactions on Computer-Human Interaction*, Special issue on HCI in the new Millenium 7 (1): 29–58.

Acconci, V., and T. Moore. 2006. *0 to 9 and Back Again*. Florence, MA: Ecstatic Peace.

Barba, E. 1995. *A Paper Canoe. A Guide to Theatre Anthropology*. London: Routledge.

Barba, E., and N. Saverese. 1999. *The Secret Art of the Performer*. London: Routledge.

Benford, S., A. Crabtree, S. Reeves, M. Flintham, A. Drozd, J. Sheridan, and A. Dix. 2011. "The Frame of the Game: Blurring the Boundary between Fiction and Reality in Mobile Experiences." *Proceedings CHI '06, ACM*.

Benford, S., C. Greenhalgh, G. Giannachi, B. Walker, J. Marshall, and T. Rodden. 2013. "Uncomfortable User Experience." *Communications of the ACM* 56 (9): 66–73.

Benford, S., and G. Gabriella. 2011. *Performing Mixed Reality*. Cambridge, MA: MIT Press.

Benford, S., G. Giannachi, B. Koleva, and T. Rodden. 2009. "From Interaction to Trajectories: Designing Coherent Journeys Through User Experiences". *Proceedings CHI '09, ACM*.

Binder, T., G. De Michelis, P. Ehn, G. Jacucci, P. Linde, and I. Wagner. 2011. *Design Things*. Cambridge, MA: MIT Press.

Boal, A. 1992. *Games for Actors and Non-Actors*. New York: Routledge.

Bødker, S., Breenbaum, J., and Kyng, M. 1991. "Setting the Stage for Design as Action." In *Design for Work: cooperative design of computer systems*, edited by J. Greenbaum and M. Kyng. Hillsdale, NJ: Lawrence Erlbaum Associaites.

Counsell, C., and L. Wolf. 2001. *Performance Analysis*. London: Taylor & Francis.

Brusilovsky, P. 2001. "Adaptive Hypermedia." *User Modeling and User-adapted Interaction* 11 (1–2): 87–110.

Dalsgaard, P., and L. K. Hansen. 2008. "Performing Perception—Staging Aesthetics of Interaction." *ACM Transactions on Computer-Human Interaction (TOCHI)* 15 (3): 13.

Deckers, E. J. L., P. D. Levy, S. A. G. Wensveen, R. Ahn, and C. J. Overbeeke. 2012. "Designing for Perceptual Crossing: Applying and Evaluating Design Notions." *International Journal of Design* 6 (3): 41–55.

Denzin, N. 2003. "The Call to Performance." *Symbolic Interaction* 26 (1): 187–207.

Dewey, J. 1980 (1934). *Art as Experience*. New York: Perigee Books.

Dourish, P. 2001. *Where The Action Is*. Cambridge, MA: MIT Press.

Ehn, P. 1988. *Work-oriented Design of Computer Artifacts*. Stockholm, Sweden: Arbetslivscentrum.

Gaberini, L., Spagnolli, A., Corradi, N., Jacucci, G., Tusa, G., Mikkola, T., Zamboni, L., and Hoggan, E. 2012. "Tailoring Feedback to Users' Actions in a Persuasive Game for Household Electricity Conservation." *Persuasive Lecture Notes in Computer Science*. 7284: 100–111, Springer-Verlag.

Gilroy, S., M. Cavazza, and M. Benayoun. 2009 "Using Affective Trajectories to Describe State of Flow in Interactive Art." *ACE'09*: 165–172.

Glowacka, D., T. Ruotsalo, K. Konuyshkova, K. Athukorala, S. Kaski and G. Jacucci. 2013. "Directing Exploratory Search: Reinforcement Learning from User Interactions with Keywords." *ACM IUI 2013 Proceedings of the 2012 ACM international conference on Intelligent User Interfaces*, March 19–22, Santa Monica, CA USA.

Hollan, J., E. Hutchins, and D. Kirsh. 2002. "Distributed Cognition: Toward a New Foundation for Human–Computer Interaction Research." *ACM Transactions on Computer-Human Interaction (TOCHI)* 7 (2): 174–196.

Hallnäs, L., & J. Redström. 2000. "Slow Technology; Designing for Reflection." *Journal of Personal and Ubiquitous*. Berlin: Springer-Verlag.

Jacucci, G., and K. Kuutti. 2002. "Everyday Life as a Stage in Creating and Performing Scenarios for Wireless Devices." *Personal and Ubiquitous Computing Journal* 6 (4): 299–306.

Jacucci, G. 2004. Interaction as Performance: Cases of Configuring Physical Interfaces in *Mixed Media*. University of Oulu, Department of Information Processing Science.

Jacucci, G., and I. Wagner. 2005. "Performative Uses of Space in Mixed Media Environments." In *Spaces, Spatiality and Technology*, 191–216. Dordrecht, The Netherlands: Springer.

Jacucci, C., G. Jacucci, I. Wagner, and T. Psik. 2005. "A Manifesto for the Performative Development of Ubiquitous Media." In *ACM Proceedings of the 4th Decennial Conference on Critical Computing: Between Sense and Sensibility*, 19–28. New York: ACM.

Jacucci, G., A. Spagnolli, A. Chalambalakis, A. Morrison, L. Liikkanen, S. Roveda and M. Bertoncini. 2009. "Bodily Explorations in Space: Social Experience of a Multimodal Art Installation." In *INTERACT 2009*, edited by T. Gross, J. Gulljksen, P. Kotzé, L. Oestreicher, P. Palanque, R. Oliveira Prates, and M. Winckler, 62–75. Uppsala, Sweden: Springer.

Jameson, A. 2009. "Adaptive Interfaces and Agents." In *Human-Computer Interaction: Design Issues, Solutions, and Applications*, 105. London: CRC Press.

Kuutti, K. 1996. "Activity Theory as a Potential Framework for Human–Computer Interaction Research." In *Context and Consciousness: Activity Theory and Human-Computer Interaction* edited by B. A. Nardi, 17–44. Cambridge, MA: MIT Press.

Laurel, B. 1991. *Computers as Theatre*. Boston, MA: Addison–Wesley Longman Publishing Co., Inc.

Macaulay, C., G. Jacucci, S. O'Neill, T. Kankaineen, and M. Simpson. 2006. "The Emerging Roles of Performance within HCI and Interaction Design." *Interacting with Computers* 18 (5): 942–955.

McCarthy, J., and P. Wright. 2004. *Technology as Experience*. Cambridge, MA: MIT Press.

Morrison, A., A. Oulasvirta, P. Peltonen, S. Lemmelä, G. Jacucci, G. Reitmayr, J. Näsänen, and A. Juustila. 2009. "Like Bees around the Hive: A Comparative Study of a Mobile Augmented Reality Map." In *Proceedings of CHI2009*, 1889–1898. New York: ACM Press.

Pfister, M. 1998. *The Theory and Analysis of Drama*. Cambridge: Cambridge University Press.

Reeves, S., S. Benford, C. O'Malley, and M. Fraser. 2005. "Designing the Spectator Experience." In *ACM Proceedings of the SIGCHI conference on Human factors in computing systems*, 741–750. New York: ACM.

Reeves, S. 2001. "A Framework for Designing Interfaces in Public Settings." In *Designing Interfaces in Public Settings*, 141–175. London: Springer.

Redström, J. 2001. *Designing Everyday Computational Things*. Gothenburg Studies in Informatics. May 20, 2001. Gothenburg University, Sweden: Dept. of Informatics.

Schieffelin, E. 1997. "Problematizing Performance." In *Ritual, Performance, Media*, edited by F. Hughes-Freeland, 194-207. London: Routledge.

Suchman, L. 1987. *Plans and Situated Actions: The Problem of Human-Machine Communication*. Cambridge, UK: Cambridge University Press.

Spence, J., D. Frohlich, and S. Andrews, S. 2013. "Performative Experience Design: Where Autobiographical Performance and Human–Computer Interaction Meet." *Digital Creativity* 24 (2): 96–110.

Svanæs, D. 1999. *Understanding Interactivity, Steps to a Phenomenology of Human-Computer Interaction*. Trondheim, Norway: Norwegian University of Science and Technology.

Turner, V. 1982. *From Ritual to Theater: The Human Seriousness of Play*. New York: PAJ Publications.

Turner, V. 1986. *On the Edge of the Bush: Anthropology as Experience*. Tucson, AZ: University of Arizona.

Weiser, Mark. 1991. "The Computer for the Twenty-first Century." *Scientific American* 265 (3).

THE COLLECTIVE NOVICE

A Designer's Reflections on Emergent Complexity in Collaborative Media

Jonas Löwgren

Introduction

When painting the broad-brush foundation appropriate to an introduction, the development of computing in society can be characterized in terms of three main epochs. In the first, computing took on the form of mainframe data storage and processing units supporting enterprises in handling organizational information. The second epoch consisted of the personal computing (PC) revolution where the power of information technology became available for individual domestic and leisurely use in the form of affordable and accessible desktop devices. Finally, the third epoch of ubiquitous computing has been predicted since the early 1990s (Weiser 1991) and is presently turning into the dominant computing paradigm in the wake of technological developments concerning the miniaturization of digital technology and the coverage of mobile Internet connectivity.

It is arguably accurate to characterize ubiquitous computing as a paradigm, also in the mindset-shifting sense of reversing many of the given assumptions from previous epochs. As ubiquitous computing infrastructures permeate our workaday and everyday lives, we find ourselves with round-the-clock access to all the information and computing power of the connected online realm. The potential consequences for the individual, in terms of empowerment as well as awe and confusion, can be considerable; however, my personal interest centers rather on the level of *sociality and ubiquitous, digitally mediated communication.*

For me, the crucial aspect of the ubiquitous digital infrastructure is the way it affords communication between people. Under the banner of convergence, it emulates or absorbs more or less all established media forms—text, images, voice, music, moving images, and so on. However, this is not a simple carrier upgrade; more significantly, the digital infrastructure also includes ubiquitous means for expression. Any connected citizen can communicate conveniently and efficiently in text in a multitude of ways, from the personal email to the broadcasted blog post. For images, there are digital cameras and web-based sharing. The list goes on; generally, the distinction between producers and consumers in established mass media that rested to some degree on access to means for production is increasingly blurred in the "new media," leading media scholars to characterize the practices of the new mediascape as presumption (Tapscott and Williams 2006) or produsage (Bruns 2008).

In our own work, we refer to the new cultural form of mediated communication as *collaborative media* and characterize it as follows (Löwgren and Reimer 2014).

- Collaborative media are *forms for practice*; they are oriented towards action and interaction and they inherently prioritize collaboration.
- Collaborative media offer a *framework of components* to combine and appropriate, where action is not limited to producing and consuming "content" but also extends to designing and redesigning the infrastructure.
- Collaborative media are *cross-medial and increasingly material*, cutting across established media structures and across the virtual/physical boundary.

My own expertise is that of interaction design, of shaping digital things for people's use. For the last fifteen years, I have devoted some of my efforts to the digital things that form the infrastructures for mediated communication. In other words, I have tried to be a designer of collaborative media. The main insight so far is that designing collaborative media is different from designing other forms of digital things, and the key differences appear to relate to notions of complexity and emergence. In this chapter, I will develop these notions further based on a design case in the area of tribal media navigation.

A Design Case: OurNewsOurWays

In 2007, I was involved in an international research project where scholars and professionals from the moving image industries worked together to explore the consequences of emerging new media platforms on the practices of audiovisual media production and consumption. The overall structure of the project took off from assumptions about relatively conventional media structures where specialist organizations would produce and distribute audiovisual media for subsequent consumption by audiences. The main challenge was to create "prototype production tools for the media industry that will allow the easy production of nonlinear media genres based on moving audiovisual images suitable for transmission over broadband networks" (Williams et al. 2004). One strand of work in the project focused on news and sports, creating a concept demonstrator of a "shape-shifting" news show called MyNewsMyWay where a broadcaster could create a content structure that would generate personalized news shows based on the viewer's preferences. Moreover, the demonstrator illustrated how the viewer could engage with the presented contents, drill down into background material, and change the playing time of the news show on the fly (Lindstedt et al. 2009).

My own involvement started from the observations that the MyNewsMyWay demonstrator relied on: 1) an edited media archive of professionally produced material, 2) complete and correct metadata for all available contents, and 3) professionally produced generative broadcasting data structures. All of these features are reasonable given the starting assumption of professional media production, but I found them to be limited in relation to the emergence of collaborative means for production. Moreover, the demonstrator required viewers to 4) actively formulate and maintain their interest profiles for personalization purposes—but it is rather well-known from related fields that this is unrealistic to expect in practical use (Light and Maybury 2002). To summarize, the challenge for myself and my colleague Amanda Bergknut became to design an alternative approach to the question of "What to watch on TV" in a near-future scenario in which the amount of available audiovisual media has increased by several magnitudes, the luxuries of complete metadata and professional curation cannot be counted with, and people cannot be expected to do a lot of self-profiling and similar efforts without immediate payoffs.

Briefly, the design process started with a broadly divergent phase of intertwined ideation and exploration, synthesized into six main directions for possible further development. These directions were assessed together with academic and professional partners of the MyNewsMyWay project, leading to further recombination and finally a proposed concept called OurNewsOurWays that was detailed as follows.

The OurNewsOurWays concept was based on social metadata collected from your tribe—a social structure of manageable size, characterized by a certain degree of common interest, mutual trust, and altruism (Maffesoli 1996). Social metadata formed the basis for collaborative navigation and viewing of professionally produced as well as "user-generated" TV material. The overall interface design was shaped to align with lean-backward modes of TV viewing in the living room rather than lean-forward activities of actively searching and browsing. Refer to Plates 53 and 54, and Figure 39.1.

More specifically, the design relies on the formation and active maintenance of a social structure that goes beyond existing notions of Facebook "friends" or Twitter followers. A viewer belongs to one or more *tribes*, each counting maybe a hundred people and formed through mutual agreement and active inclusion. Within the tribe, members share *social metadata* implicitly through their everyday actions of media consumption. In other words, the system keeps track of consumption actions such as which video clips a person watches and for how

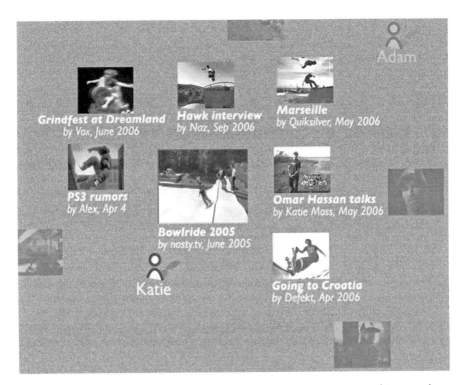

FIGURE 39.1 Social metadata are used to facilitate serendipitous discoveries. In this example, recent material is presented that has attracted the interest of two specific friends whose tastes and preferences the viewer is familiar with

long. Another source of social metadata is the existence of pathfinders, that is, people who are invited and agree to make parts of their consumption activities available for wider groups of viewers. Explicit curation actions such as active recommendations or zapping for a friend are also part of the social metadata, of course, and are weighted more heavily in the composite social recommender algorithm.

Technicalities aside, the key idea of the proposed design is that a tribe takes on the joint task of filtering and curating a potentially vast pool of audiovisual material in the sociocultural context of TV-watching practices. The main incentives include contributing to the shared benefit of the tribe members and experiencing the sense of sociality, common ground, and shared meaning that such joint engagement with the media offers.

When stated like this, OurNewsOurWays comes across as a fairly compelling concept for "future TV" in relation to the challenge it was created in response to: it seems to have some power to address the potential explosion of available audiovisual material, and it does address the shortcomings of self-profiling by drawing on implicit metadata generation. Specific design decisions concerning the interface are also validated in subsequent research and more recent market developments, such as the use of an open audio channel to create a low-key sense of presence (Harboe et al. 2008) or the grounding in lean-backward living room TV watching practices (Geerts and De Grooff 2009). However, with hindsight it is easy to see that the concept is based on a number of idealistic assumptions and includes an equal number of glaring omissions.

The six years gone by since 2007 have been marked by radical changes in the landscape of collaborative media, and particularly through the widespread dissemination and uptake of so-called "social media" where many millions of people are exposed for the first time to ubiquitous online communication and digitally mediated social structures. In terms of diffusion of innovation, collaborative media practices have spread from early adopters to the late majority, in fact approaching ubiquity in the strong sense of the word for some demographics. In this rapid development, there are certainly many examples of resilient tribal structures forming and thriving along the general ideas embodied in the OurNewsOurWays design. However, for every good example there is a bad one involving secterism, groupthink, deserted commitment, commercial exploitation, or simply the blandness of the least common denominator. It is obvious (and quite predictable!) that the big picture of the emerging collaborative mediascape is a complex one holding bright as well as dark sides, but this more nuanced perspective is essentially missing from our work on OurNewsOurWays.

The remainder of this chapter is devoted to unpacking some of these issues and considering their implications for designers and for our collective development in the collaborative mediascape.

The Big Picture: Bright Side, Dark Side

There are at least four apparent paradoxes to be identified in contemporary collaborative media practices, as follows:

Collaborative media are emancipatory—and confining. The broad distribution of means of production and the resulting many-to-many communicative structures of the collaborative media imply that the power to set communicative agendas is distributed outside established media institutions. For virtually any given topic, no matter how narrow or quaint, it is generally straightforward to find an online forum where a small tribe of geographically dispersed enthusiasts donate generously of their time and knowledge for the benefit of the other hundred or so enthusiasts worldwide.

However, it is equally clear that the freedom to find meaningful social contexts is also the freedom to abstain from alternate views and challenging perspectives. For virtually any topic, it is generally straightforward to find an online forum where the topic is single-sidedly elaborated, where criticism is banned, and where belonging is defined in terms of the few who are consistently misunderstood and maltreated by the surrounding hegemony.

Collaborative media provide freedom of expression—and media institutions capitalize on unpaid labor. In the arts and the entertainment industries, examples abound of grassroots productions that bypass the established quality assurance and distribution systems to address worldwide audiences directly, sometimes gaining massive attention and appreciation. People initiate and engage in debates on current affairs through blogs, microblogs, and online fora to an extent that significantly enriches the public sphere. Hobby-level creative expressions such as photography and craft can reach transformative levels when the creator is able to connect directly with worldwide audiences of peers having the time and the interest in engaging with the results. On a more serious note, collaborative media sometimes provide necessary outlets for grassroots movements in the context of repressive regimes controlling established media channels.

However, it is equally clear that media institutions capitalize on the unpaid labor manifested in the wealth of expression taking place in the collaborative media. Citizen journalism can be described as a win-win in terms of editorial quality assurance of source material that is unique based on opportunity or accessibility, but it might equally well be described as getting material for free that the newspaper would otherwise need to pay a journalist to produce. Individual subcultures such as the hacker and free software movements have systems in place such as copyleft, General Public License (GPL), and Creative Commons to ensure that material produced on an altruistic basis stays that way, but this is not true for the vast majority of so-called "user-generated content." A pertinent example is the recent debates concerning the rights to material posted on Facebook—it is worth remembering that Facebook as such is an empty shell, and all its commercial value ultimately derives from the contents that the users create and contribute without remuneration.

Collaborative media offer a wealth of material—and people waste time and effort on mediocre search and selection. It is commonly held that practically any information can be found online, through generic search engines or more specialized services. News on current affairs, for example, is available from around the globe in near real time from a variety of sources, including professional news producers as well as fellow online grassroots. The same holds for all manners of media contents, including growing archives of digitized pre-Internet material. In terms of consumer products, certain segments have been turned into profoundly global markets with the advent of online shopping.

However, it is equally clear that many people spend significant amounts of time and effort on searching for free and available online material as a demonstration of the liberating potential of collaborative media and their independence from established media institutions. What such strategies sometimes fail to recognize, however, is the meager quality of the results yielded in relation to the resources expended. The commoditization of editorial skills is a potential future scenario in relation to the increasing ratio of grassroots content production, and one that many media institutions are banking on in their survival strategies for the collaborative mediascape, but it cannot materialize as long as people are not asking for the editorial service.

Collaborative media offer freedom of choice—and foster mindless flock behavior. Related to the previous points, it is clear that the emerging many-to-many communication structures provide unprecedented levels of choice for the individual. No longer are we limited to what the media institutions choose to send our way, but we are able to choose between virtually every product of creative or expressive energy that the Internet offers. In popular culture as well as in current affairs and in highly specialized areas of interest, the supply of potentially interesting and relevant material is endless.

However, it is equally clear that the individual wavers under the sheer volumes of potentially interesting and relevant material. The paradox of choice (Schwartz 2004) leads to a certain degree of fatigue and a tendency to conform to the majority for easy satisfaction. A case in point is the phenomenon of Internet memes or viral memes, where a somewhat ordinary piece of online material is suddenly consumed by millions of people in an exponential dissemination process. What is happening here is media fatigue and a need for common ground, combined with a plethora of tools designed to facilitate easy sharing and distribution of something recently consumed.

To relate this back to the previous design case, it is straightforward to ask a number of questions.

- Could OurNewsOurWays accommodate biased and secteristic communicative practices around media consumption?
- Could commercial TV producers include tribally filtered selections in their pay-per-view offerings?
- Could OurNewsOurWays users spend hours seeking out material "for the benefit of their tribe" while lacking the skills to notice the sub-par quality or imbalance of the material?
- Could a tired and disinterested user choose the first recommendations without further reflection, thereby enforcing the top positions of those recommendations even more and contributing to flock behavior?

The answer to all these questions is obviously affirmative, and it is notable and troubling that the questions were not addressed when the project was executed.

A New Situation for Designers

At a somewhat simplified level of description, the traditional sense of design entails two intertwined strands: *Creating* concepts and ideas pertaining to desirable futures, and *assessing* those concepts and ideas with respect to their possible qualities if they were to be realized and deployed.

One of the main differences between experienced designers and relative novices is the ability to assess concepts and ideas based on a sense of quality (Löwgren and Stolterman 2004). That sense in turn represents years of synthesized experience, typically of the kind where the designer has contributed to placing an artifact in the world and then studied its outcomes and its qualities in actual use. Another constituent factor of the sense of quality consists in articulation of qualities in use—the development of a language through which expected outcomes could be named and discussed already in early stages of assessment.

As the previous section demonstrates, the OurNewsOurWays case shows quite clearly how this sense of quality was found wanting. What I did there—similar to many other examples of design and deployment of ubiquitous computing in the last two decades—was naïve and idealistic; it lacked a sense of quality that would have enabled me to assess the idea and its potential outcomes in a more well-rounded way. This could, of course, be a simple statement reflecting my incompetence, but I rather think it speaks to a larger set of phenomena.

First, designing collaborative media is inherently different from designing enterprise systems, personal tools, or consumer products due to the fact that the outcomes are emergent, ongoing, and contingent on dynamic and ever-changing social structures. For example, it makes only marginal sense to test a prototype of a collaborative media platform prior to its launch—because the relevant meanings of the designed artifact are created only in actual, social, communicative use. If there is no critical mass of users, and no real social structure inhabiting the prototype, then the results of the test are going to be irrelevant and possibly misleading. It is probably not a coincidence that all the major developers of "social media" artifacts abandon conventional development schemes with major releases in favor of perpetual-beta approaches of organic growth in the wild.

Another aspect of designing collaborative media is the changing nature of the design work, from shaping the digital material as such to facilitating social and communicative processes. As an example, consider our 2001–03 Avatopia project on designing a crossmedia platform for young social activists (Gislén et al. 2008). We found it necessary to structure the project as a participatory design process with some thirty participants distributed across southern Sweden, and upon completion we estimated that around forty percent of the granted project resources were spent on social and communicative interventions whereas only sixty percent went to what would traditionally be considered core interaction design activities. If we also factor in the value of the unsalaried participants' work, then the ratio would be closer to 80/20 with the larger number representing social and communicative interventions.

As pointed out elsewhere (Löwgren and Reimer 2014), this characteristic of collaborative media design processes mirrors recent developments in the general world of design and design theory. Current concepts like metadesign (Fischer et al. 2004), design thinking (Brown 2009), and design beyond the object[1] are all attempts to address the complexity of the contemporary artificial world and the changing role of the designer in society. Of particular relevance is the notion of infrastructuring, originally coined by Star and Ruhleder (1996) to refer to a new task for the designer to catalyze and facilitate a dynamic, Latourian network of human and non-human actants in constant movement. Björgvinsson and others summarize it thus:

> The [designer] role becomes one of infrastructuring agonistic public spaces mainly by facilitating the careful building of arenas consisting of heterogeneous participants, legitimizing those marginalized, maintaining network constellations, and leaving behind repertoires of how to organize socio-materially when conducting transformative innovations.
>
> (Björgvinsson et al. 2012)

The Avatopia example mentioned briefly above shared the aims of infrastructuring as expressed by Björgvinsson and others, albeit operationalized in a participatory design process that proved to be vulnerable to external forces when the partner responsible for running the activist platform suffered an unexpected budget cut and shut down the whole project a mere four months into steady-state operation. With hindsight, it is clear that even if we attempted to deal with some of the dynamic contingencies of designing collaborative media, we failed to leave behind a resilient pattern of socio-material organization. In the case of OurNewsOurWays, on the other hand, the design process was much more conventionally based on professional concept creation and concept assessment, and thus over-simplifying the task to the point where the work hardly can be seen as an authentic attempt to engage with the new public spheres of the collaborative media.

The Collective Novice

What the previous section suggests is that collaborative media represent a challenge to design, in terms of conceptual clarity as well as practical action. Tentative steps are being taken, but as a profession we are still a long way from the general competence and confidence that we exhibit when designing individual things for specified uses.

The second major constituency involved in collaborative media is production, and here the picture is similarly disturbing. Media production has had a long time to institutionalize into forms suitable for mass media production and distribution, and the last fifteen years since widespread Internet penetration started to become a reality have been marked by a certain degree of entrenchment of the established media institutions. In the news industries as well as music, film, and other forms of entertainment, the general stance towards the "new media" and the emerging collaborative media practices has been a strange mix of dismissal and fascination. This is not the place for a deeper study of recent media structure transformations— or, perhaps more accurately, the lack thereof—but it should be noted that the accumulated investments in "media assets" and distribution structures have added significant inertia to the necessary processes of finding new positions for professional producers in the rapidly changing mediascape.

If neither designers nor producers are adequately fit to deal with collaborative media, then one could imagine that the emphasis on distributed and collective action would lead us to look for answers among the people formerly known as the audience (Rosen 2006). However, it seems clear that the current uses and communicative practices of collaborative media leave a lot to be desired. Looking at what is happening in mainstream "social media" today, it is hard to avoid examples of people acting in ways that they would themselves consider unthinkable in other social settings.

The example in Figure 39.2 is admittedly an extreme one, but the general phenomenon of suppressing all critical faculties, failing to take the recipient's point of view, and disregarding the conventional norms of interpersonal conduct should be highly recognizable for anyone who has a Facebook account.

My argument is that designers, producers, and people at large are equally in the dark. In a sense, we are all *novices* when it comes to ubiquitous collaborative media: We lack the shared ability to assess potential outcomes of our actions. This collective novice is approaching a complicated and rapidly changing set of living conditions, and as could be expected the resulting sense is one of overwhelming *complexity*. What is more, this complexity is not predicted, certainly not planned, but rather *emerges* as a result of the properties of ubiquitous collaborative media. The more we engage—attracted by the bright sides and the potentially beneficial experiences and outcomes—the more we feed the dark sides as well.

It is somewhat ironic that one of the main overt aims of design has always been to reduce complexity (by means of making things more convenient, more accessible, more manageable, and so on). To return to the OurNewsOurWays case, there was a clear intention to reduce the complexity of a future explosion of available audiovisual media. One might even argue that the intention was fulfilled to some extent. Yet this well-meaning act of design work disregarded a whole new set of potential complications, related to the nature of tribal communicative structures.

As stated in the introduction, I see collaborative media as part of the mind-shifting paradigm of ubiquitous computing, permeating our everyday lives in rather irrevocable ways. Essentially, we are in the midst of changing some of the elementary conditions for social life, and what we see unfolding now is the emergent complexity of such a transformation.

FIGURE 39.2 "NN suggests that you like NN." Screenshot of an actual notification that was sent from Facebook to my mailbox some time ago. If I were to ask NN whether he would approach 500 remote acquaintances on the street, suggesting to each of them that they like him, I am convinced that he would shun the idea. One has to presume that he considers online sociality to be somehow qualitatively different from other kinds of sociality

In Conclusion

Generally speaking, the public debate on social and societal aspects of ubiquitous computing and collaborative media is marked by polarization into progressive and reactionary positions.[2] This situation, in which evangelists argue that the "Net Generation" grows different brain structures while luddites bemoan the loss of physical community's hegemony, indicates that we are at a relatively immature stage of collective conceptual development and we are coming to terms with our changing reality.

Speaking of the collective novice suggests an implied expectation of progress towards the collective intermediate and eventually the collective master. This is intentional; I think there is no turning back, and the present situation is rather intolerable. It is also an example of a designer's stance, where the essence is acting to turn current situations into preferred ones (Simon 1996). For me, a preferred situation is one where we collectively handle the ubiquitous collaborative media more maturely and proficiently, where we see them for what they are, and where we benefit from their bright sides while acknowledging and ameliorating their dark sides.

One step towards such a preferred situation is to pause, reflect, and articulate. When in a situation of collective emergent complexity, it seems wise to concentrate on the relations between local actions and overall outcomes. Putting words on those relations represents progress towards better understanding them. In academic terms, this is largely the realm of cultural studies and media and communication studies.

However, articulation and analysis are apparently not enough, simply because of the emergent nature of the complexity under scrutiny. In principle, there are an infinite number of local action possibilities in ubiquitous collaborative media, and in order to construct knowledge on relations between local actions and overall outcomes it becomes necessary to engage in experimentation and intervention. Understanding the potentials of collaborative media entails exploring the possibilities. As illustrated in the OurNewsOurWays case, and as argued earlier, such exploration must take place in the wild rather than in a lab in order for the outcomes to be meaningfully situated in emergent communicative practices and thus offer a glimpse of the bright-side as well as the dark-side nuances in play. Exploration in the wild amounts to interventions into heterogeneous settings, where agonistic processes of constructive friction between different agendas are sought and emphasis is placed on leaving repertoires for socio-material organization behind. The outcomes of such infrastructuring engagements are not limited to experience and analytical knowledge, but may include transformation of everyday practices— in short, they can lead to collective learning.

To conclude, it would appear that a reasonable way for a designer to contribute to building collective knowledge on ubiquitous collaborative media is to engage in transdisciplinary intervention and reflection.

Notes

1 The debate is current, but the concept was presciently coined by Thackara already in 1988 (Thackara, *Design After Modernism.*)
2 It is quite notable that the most comprehensive collection on the subject is entitled *The Digital Divide: Arguments For and Against Facebook, Google, Texting and the Age of Social Networking* (Bauerlein, *The Digital Divide.*)

References

Bauerlein, Mark, Ed. 2011. *The Digital Divide: Arguments For and Against Facebook, Google, Texting, and the Age of Social Networking.* New York: Jeremy P. Tarcher.

Björgvinsson, Erling, Pelle Ehn, and Per-Anders Hillgren. 2012. "Agonistic Participatory Design: Working with Marginalised Social Movements." *CoDesign* 8 (2–3): 127–144.

Brown, Tim. 2009. *Change by Design.* New York: HarperCollins.

Bruns, Axel. 2008. *Blogs, Wikipedia, Second Life and Beyond: From Production to Produsage.* New York: Peter Lang.

Fischer, Gerhard, Elisa Giaccardi, Yunwen Ye, Alistair G. Sutcliffe, and Nikolay Mehandjiev. 2004. "Meta-design: a Manifesto for End-user Development." *Communications of the ACM* 47 (9): 33–37.

Geerts, David, and Dirk De Grooff. 2009. "Supporting the Social Uses of Television: Sociability Heuristics for Social Tv." In *Proceedings of the SIGCHI Conference on Human Factors in Computing Systems,* 595–604. New York: ACM.

Gislén, Ylva, Jonas Löwgren, and Ulf Myrestam. 2008. "Avatopia: A Cross-media Community for Societal Action." *Personal & Ubiquitous Computing* 12 (4): 289–297.

Harboe, Gunnar, Noel Massey, Crysta Metcalf, David Wheatley, and Guy Romano. 2008. "The Uses of Social Television." *ACM Computers in Entertainment* 6 (1): 8:1–8:15.

Light, Marc, and Mark T. Maybury. 2002. "Personalized Multimedia Information Access." *Communications of the ACM* 45 (5): 54–59.

Lindstedt, Inger, Jonas Löwgren, Bo Reimer, and Richard Topgaard. 2009. "Nonlinear News Production and Consumption: A Collaborative Approach." *ACM Computers in Entertainment* 7 (3): 42:1–42:17.

Löwgren, Jonas, and Bo Reimer. 2014. *Collaborative Media: Production, Consumption and Design Interventions.* Cambridge, MA: MIT Press.

Löwgren, Jonas, and Bo Reimer. 2013. "The Computer Is a Medium, Not a Tool: Collaborative Media Challenging Interaction Design." *Challenges* 4 (1): 86–102.

Löwgren, Jonas, and Erik Stolterman. 2004. *Thoughtful Interaction Design: A Design Perspective on Information Technology.* Cambridge, MA: MIT Press.

Maffesoli, Michel. 1996. *The Time of the Tribes: The Decline of Individualization in Mass Society.* London: Sage.

Rosen, Jay. 2006. "The People Formerly Known as the Audience." *PressThink,* June 27, 2006. http://archive.pressthink.org/2006/06/27/ppl_frmr.html.

Schwartz, Barry. 2004. *The Paradox of Choice: Why More Is Less.* New York: Ecco.

Simon, Herbert Alexander. 1996. *The Sciences of the Artificial.* Third edition. Cambridge, MA: MIT Press.

Star, Susan Leigh, and Karen Ruhleder. 1996. "Steps Toward an Ecology of Infrastructure: Design and Access for Large Information Spaces." *Information Systems Research* 7 (1): 111–134.

Tapscott, Don, and Anthony D. Williams. 2006. *Wikinomics: How Mass Collaboration Changes Everything.* New York: Portfolio.

Thackara, John. 1988. *Design After Modernism: Beyond the Object.* London: Thames and Hudson.

Weiser, Mark. 1991. "The Computer for the Twenty-first Century." *Scientific American* 265 (3): 66–75.

Williams, Doug, Ian Kegel, Harald Mayer, Peter Stollenmayer, Maureen Thomas, and Marian Ursu. 2004. "NM2: New Media for a New Millennium." London: Queen Mary, University of London. http://nim.goldsmiths.ac.uk/papers/EWIMT%202004%20paper%20submitted%20for%20proceedings.pdf.

SOFTWARE STUDIES

Jay David Bolter

Any definition of the origins of the field of software studies is open to dispute. One could argue that software studies is simply a form of media studies because of its focus on the affordances of the digital as a material media technology. In *The Language of New Media* (2001), Lev Manovich was at pains to distinguish software studies from media studies. He claimed that the digital media constitutes a significant break in the history of media because it introduces into media culture the phenomenon of transcoding. Comparative media studies is not sufficient, because it does not take sufficient account of programmability, which has no historical precedent.

Media studies itself has taken and takes many forms. For many, it is closely related to cultural studies or communications studies, understanding media in terms of the economic and cultural conditions of their production and reception. For others, following McLuhan (1964), media studies begins by identifying the fundamental qualities of the each "medium," which proceed more or less explicitly from the technological platform. According to McLuhan, for example, television's impact and significance derived ultimately from the fact that the raster scanning of the cathode ray tube resulted in a relatively coarse visual image that the viewer had to work to assemble. The coarse image was what made television participatory, synesthetic, and "cool." McLuhan did not live to see digital media develop in the 1980s and 1990s, but digital media writers who looked back to McLuhan have found it attractive and relatively easy to define a set of essential qualities that made the digital medium unique. The impulse, by the way, to define a medium in terms of essential qualities derives from modernism in general and high modernist art theory in particular, as we can see in the classic essay on modernist painting by Clement Greenberg (1960). McLuhan was a popular modernist version of the elitist Greenberg, for McLuhan's theory was not limited to the artifacts and media of high art, but was applied equally to television, film, radio, and ultimately to all technologies that expanded the human sensorium. Digital media writers who follow McLuhan are essentialists and to this extent modernists themselves.

Software studies itself seems depend on an essentialist understanding of the digital because of its focus on the essential quality of procedurality. What makes the digital medium unique is that it executes an algorithm represented by programmed instructions, by code. This is a kind of eventualizing that seems to be reductive by definition: the events that result from the execution of a procedure all proceed from the previously written code. This does not mean, however, that the results are always predictable. Programmed systems or applications can produce novel results, or what many in software and games studies characterize as "emergent behavior," and one reason is expressed in a keyword for this volume: complexity. The programmed systems may be so complex that the programmer can no longer foresee the output, particularly when those systems interact with (are used by) human participants. It is procedurality that enables digital artifacts to be interactive or participatory. If there is a human user, then what she does (clicking with a mouse, making gestures that are tracked by a camera, and so on) constitutes input that is injected into the event loop of the program. The input is processed by the program and generates some sort of output (e.g., a change in what appears on the computer screen). In this way, the user effectively becomes part of the procedure, as her actions in turn prompt new responses by the computer to which she then reacts. (The fact that the user becomes part of the process, part therefore of the machine, is explored in the section of this volume entitled "Individuation.")

From the perspective of software studies, the digital artifact is realized (or eventualized) as the expression of a procedure. The realization takes place in the world, or at least before the eyes of a user or view, but the essence of the artifact remains the code that supports and produces the interface and its perceived output. For this reason, software studies has ironically much in common with an approach that would seem at first contradictory. In the 1990s, German media theorist Friedrich Kittler produced a famous essay "There is No Software (1992)," in which he denied the very notion of software in favor of the materiality of the digital and other writing technologies. The more recent platform studies represented by a series of volumes by MIT Press, edited by Nick Montfort and Ian Bogost, would also seem to affirm the idea that hardware underlies and therefore preempts software. But, both software and hardware studies are essentialist and therefore remnants of modernist aesthetics. Both insist on locating the essence of the digital medium in the technology itself: the distinction between hardware and software is a fungible one, as the notion of firmware indicates. Both approaches insist on a fundamental break between digital media and earlier media as forms of inscription and retrieval. This too is part of the modernist legacy, the notion that the medium is fundamentally new.

From a software studies perspective, then, how do we examine various forms of digital cultural production? How are they eventualized? The key is to look for the ways in which the digital artifact embodies a procedure and how that procedure comes to expression: in our case how ubiquity is expressed and how complexity develops as an emergent quality of the user's interaction with the artifact. Conversely, we may consider how media artists seek to avoid a reduction to procedurality and insist on the complexity of experience in our digital media culture. Hasan Elahi, one of the artists interviewed in this volume, has created a piece that seems both to resist and to succumb to the seduction of the procedural at the same time. His *Tracking Transcience* seeks to preempt government surveillance by acquiescing in it. The site provides a thorough, near real-time documentation of Elahi's daily activities and thereby spares the FBI the trouble: the agency can simply download his images and store them in their database. The irony is that Elahi's appears to renounce irony in becoming complicit in his own total surveillance. As he notes dryly in the interview, he offers the visitor to his website the opportunity to experience what it is like to be an FBI agent doing her job.

In this section too, interaction designer Jonas Löwgren outlines a different strategy for resisting the reduction of our complex media culture to procedure. He emphasizes the importance of interpersonal communication in and through today's ubiquitous computing environment. He studies and designs *collaborative media*, which are oriented to "action and interaction" and which are often cross-medial. Such platforms and designs do not seek to insert their human subjects into procedural event loops, but rather to do justice to the complexity inherent in human communication and intersubjectivity. In a similar spirit, Giulio Jacucci proposes strategies for experience design that derive from forms of theater and performance art: his emphasis on the performative quality of interaction design again aims to preserve the complexity of human interaction with digital systems. The whole outlook of his chapter is at odds with the perspective of software studies. In still another way, John Johnston points to the inadequacy of understanding the complexity of contemporary digital media culture in terms of coded procedures. His analysis of an *information event*—the singular "Flash crash" that resulted from the so-called "high frequency" computerized trading on Wall Street in 2010—proceeds from the undeniable fact that it was "both unprecedented and completely unpredictable."

The lesson, then, of many of the interviews and chapters in this section is that software studies, with its emphasis on the procedural and material essence of the digital, can provide at best only a partial explanation of digital culture today.

References

Greenberg, Clement. 1960. "Modernist Painting." *Forum Lectures*. www.sharecom.ca/greenberg/modernism.html, accessed September 7, 2015.

Kittler, Friedrich. 1992. "There Is No Software." *Stanford Literature Review* 9 (1): 81–90.

McLuhan, Marshall. 1964. *Understanding Media: The Extensions of Man*. New York: New American Library.

Manovich, Lev. 2001. *The Language of New Media*. Cambridge, MA: MIT Press.

INFORMATION EVENTS, BIG DATA, AND THE FLASH CRASH

John Johnston

I

On May 6, 2010, an unprecedented event occurred on Wall Street: without warning, from 2:42 to 2:47pm, the Dow fell 998.5 points, valued at about one trillion dollars. Equally astonishing, within minutes it began climbing back up and by closing stocks had almost regained their previous values. Investigations into what was dubbed "the Flash Crash" centered primarily on the extensive use of computer algorithms automated for "high frequency trading" (HFT). The general consensus was that the exchange of enormously large amounts of information in ultra-short bursts of time caused instability in the interactions among multiple systems, which included not only networked computers but also the human traders on the floor. The result was the sudden emergence or "bursting" of what I call an "information event."

Such events seem to occur typically in "frictionless systems" like the Internet, where the processing and exchange of vast quantities of information occur with minimal time and transaction costs.[1] The behavior of such systems is often nonlinear, and thus when graphed usually evinces power law distributions and highly anomalous behavior that make their long-term predictability extremely difficult. Not only Wall Street, but also contemporary financial markets are rife with such behavior, as Benoit Mandelbrot, Nicholas Taleb, and others have noted. Similar and analogous effects have been observed in social media, where information cascades, gnarls and epidemic or viral effects result from bursts of information moving through very large networks. In fact, information events may well be ubiquitous, occurring at all scales, and in any medium through which information is propagated when the volumes of exchange are high and the networks are densely concentrated.

To what degree are "information events" as such amenable to exact definition and scientific or at least more rigorous study? Taking the World Wide Web as the primary but not exclusive example, Albert-Laszlo Barabasi provided an early key source for understanding information diffusion and spread in relation to the dynamics of connectivity and network architecture (Barabasi 2002). The discovery of power law distributions in the Web's link–node structure led Barabasi and his team to the discovery that the Web is a scale-free, "small world" network, and that the existence of a number of large "hubs" is what "fundamentally define[s] the network's topology" (Barabasi 2002, 71). The presence of hubs, he finds, explains the particular "winner-take-all" dynamic observed in the network's growth, such that "those that have get more." To account for this dynamic, Barabasi postulates that there is a "preferential attachment" for new links to link to already-linked nodes, and that it is "an organizing principle acting at each stage of the network formation process" (Barabasi 2002, 91). In his chapter on "Viruses and Fads," Barabasi shows how hubs in scale-free networks vastly increase the diffusion or spread rate of infectious diseases and epidemics, computer viruses and malware, but he could have easily extended the range of his examples to include such events as the sudden and mushrooming mania for tulips in seventeenth century Holland and "herding" in contemporary stock market trading. This network topology, in any case, accounts for the many anomalies and the essential nonlinearity of information flow through complex networks.

More recent work of relevance here has been devoted to instances of ultra-fast information replication in viral videos such as the "Gangnam Style" video viewed over a billion times, and in digital meme complexes such as the ever-varying but always recognizable "LOLcats" meme. These two species of information events have been very usefully treated in two recently published studies: Karon Nahon and Jeff Hemsley's *Going Viral* and Limor Shifman's *Memes in Digital Culture* (Nahon and Hemsley 2013; Shifman 2014). Since precisely what makes a specific video go viral is difficult to determine, Nahon and Hemsley concentrate first on defining the signature of viral growth (slow initial climb, very steep increase, then leveling off, and decline), and then on the enabling technological and social conditions that produce "virality" on the Net, specifically the top-down control mechanisms versus the emerging patterns of behavior (bottom-up processes) that appear to govern social media platforms, particularly YouTube and Twitter. Perhaps the most interesting topic considered (but clearly requiring more research) is the "network gatekeeping" function (also called "filter forwarding"), in relation to which the authors consider only human agents, though of course information can be allowed to flow (or not) through linked networks without direct human intervention. In *Memes in Digital Culture*, Shifman points out that "many memetic videos started off as viral videos" (Shifman 2014, 58), which were then imitated or "remixed," as in the instance of the viral video "Leave Brittany Alone." Thus he distinguishes between "Internet memes and virals" according to the criterion of variability: "whereas the viral comprises *a single cultural unit* . . . that propagates in many copies, an Internet meme is *always a collection of texts*" (Shifman 2014, 56).

What makes a video go "viral," moreover, is not simply the number of times it is viewed but the time frame and duration of what we might call its "event status," according to which its specific content is less important than how it combines a peculiar eye-catching action with a relatively short duration (again, more research is necessary). Memes, on the other hand, possess referential and semantic components that assume and produce a recognition-participation effect. Shifman argues that "the Internet's unique features [which enable users to easily copy, vary, and re-launch memes] turned memes' diffusion into a ubiquitous and highly visible routine" (Shifman 2014, 17). While this seems generally correct, the "hypermemetic" logic that he claims "dominates" digital culture can hardly be said to exhaust or account for the multiplicities that the Internet sustains.

As valuable as these studies are, they do not account for the singularity of what I'm provisionally calling an "information event." The Flash Crash, for example, was not in any obvious sense either viral or hypermemetic, although the panic induced by the initial precipitous drop in market value did induce "herding" and other behavior associated with viral effects. One obvious difference is that both viral videos and Internet memes, as events, are endogenous to the Internet. Their significance follows from the fact that they reveal something important about the Internet and the participatory culture it has produced. Information events, in the sense I intend, while often originating online, have a much greater impact in their exogenous effects, not only carrying or propagating new information, but also re-contexualizing information itself in a way that noticeably changes its significance.

Consider the revelations of our ubiquitous surveillance, which seem to have come about in two distinguishable phases. The first phase of revelation was of low intensity and widely diffusive, and occurred just above the level of public perception. That is, it was generally known that there was a growing collection and tracking of our "personal data" for commercial use (primarily for the purpose of advertising, product development and sales). This form of surveillance was primarily documented and discussed by academics of contemporary media. (Greg Ulmer's *Profiling Machines* and Mark Andrejevic's *iSpy: Surveillance and Power in the Interactive Era* are two notable examples.) The general public accepted this form of surveillance, albeit with a low degree of assent, mainly because it had come about gradually and increased inevitably as credit agencies and advertising agencies began to adopt and rely more upon new digital technologies. The second phase of revelation follows from Edward Snowden's release of troves of documents revealing that our surveillance by the National Security Agency (NSA) and other spy agencies is much more extensive and comprehensive than anyone had previously suspected. Specifically, the collection and tracking of our data by the NSA entails and includes the continuous gathering and storage of all phone calls, text messages, and online searches of every American, as well as of every non-citizen in the United States. In contrast to the first phase, which can be said to consist of a cloud of micro-events whose consequences seem somewhat vague and not immediately threatening, Snowden's revelations occurred with the force of an information event, changing public perception of the scale and significance of surveillance qualitatively. Although mainstream media and government sources attempted to mollify the effect of the event by displacing attention to Snowden's theft of NSA documents and successful escape, the impact has been transformative.[2]

II

Something of the difference of the information event, in which an event produces new information about information itself, also seems to lurk in the new excitement surrounding the advent of Big Data. In their book, *Big Data*, Mayer-Schonberger and Cukier coin the term "datafication," which refers "to taking information about all things under the sun ... and transforming it into a data format to make it quantified" (Mayer-Schonberger and Cukier 2013, 15). The transformation of information into data enables us to use it in new ways, such as predictive analysis, and "to unlock the implicit, latent value of the information." As the authors assert, "[e]very single dataset is likely to have some intrinsic, hidden, not yet unearthed value." The word "data," of course, derives from the plural of the Latin word *datum*, which refers to "something given." A particular datum is recorded and stored because it is assumed to have value as information; but from massively large collections of data, or "Big Data," a completely new kind of information can be extracted, based on correlations. The authors offer a clear example in their first few pages. In 2009, the new flu virus labeled H1N1 was sweeping rapidly across the United States, but the Centers for Disease Control and Prevention (CDC) was unable to track its spread because of a two-week lag in reporting from public health agencies. However, engineers at Google quickly devised a method that could "predict" the virus' spread with great precision in specific regions and even states. Since Google collects all search queries made each day (roughly three billion at the time), it was simply a matter of correlating frequency of search term expressions like "medicine for cough and fever" entered in different regions of the United States over the previous few days. (Actually, combinations of forty-five search terms were used.) Tested against records of actual flu cases collected by the CDC in 2008 and 2009, Google's approach worked remarkably well, and could predict where the H1N1 virus was spreading almost in real-time.

In a provocatively-titled article, "The End of Theory: The Data Deluge Makes the Scientific Method Obsolete," Chris Anderson argues further that in the current "petabyte age" there is no longer any need for theory, specifically the tried and true "hypothesize, model, test" approach of traditional science (Anderson). In the latter's place, statistical methods applied to massive data sets—here Google is clearly the master—can provide unshakeable correlations that obviate the need for causal explanation. Following Gregory Bateson's oft-quoted definition, information is "a difference which makes a difference," it is tempting to suggest by analogy that correlations that make a difference produce or bring about a type of information event (Bateson 2000, 315).

Before the availability of massive data and the analytic tools that could reveal significant correlations within it, a basic model was necessary in order to connect the data sets. But a model, Anderson asserts, is only a "caricature of a more complex underlying reality." First the models of quantum physics proved to be too complex, unwieldy, and expensive for experimenters to test by falsifying the hypotheses. Inversely, the model of the gene has proven to be too simplistic in view of the discoveries of gene-protein interactions and a wide range of epigenetic influences. For Anderson, J. Craig Venter's model-free "shotgun gene sequencing" is the best new example of how data can be analyzed "without hypotheses about what it might show". By sequencing entire ecosystems rather than first sequencing the individual organisms assumed to be its constituents, Venter has discovered thousands of unknown species of bacteria and other life forms in volumes of ocean water and in the air. As Anderson describes it, Venter has thus accomplished what amounts to a methodological shift:

> If the words "discover a new species" call to mind Darwin and drawings of finches, you may be stuck in the old way of doing science. Venter can tell you almost nothing about the species he found. He doesn't know what they look like, how they live, or much of anything else about their morphology. He doesn't even have their entire genome. All he has is a statistical blip—a unique sequence that, being unlike any other sequence in the database, must represent a new species . . . This sequence may correlate with other sequences that resemble those of species we do know more about. In that case, Venter can make some guesses about the animals—that they convert sunlight into energy in a particular way, or that they descended from a common ancestor. But besides that, he has no better model of this species than Google has of your MySpace page. It's just data. By analyzing it with Google-quality computing resources, though, Venter has advanced biology more than anyone else of his generation.

Put another way, from correlations in Big Data Venter has extracted new configurations of information that "make sense" as the genomes of new species of organisms. In doing so he has produced an information event that increases scientific understanding while reducing our reliance upon or even doing away with the specific scientific models that previously organized observation and experimental hypotheses.

Yet in Venter's own autobiographical accounts of his research, models have hardly dropped away. In both *A Life Decoded: My Genome, My Life* and *Life at the Speed of Life,* the genome and other models of bio-molecular processes are evident in detail (Venter 2007, 2013).

However, in both books we do witness a strikingly new kind of model taking shape. In the first, it is the new model of the scientist as corporate entrepreneur, while in the second it is the computer model of hardware and software applied directly to the biology of life.[3] Venter, of course, first achieved fame (even notoriety) when his company Celera Genomics began to compete with the Human Genome Project (HGP), the U.S. government's attempt to sequence the entire human genome, the success of which was itself something of a spectacular, widely publicized "information event." Venter entered the race with the bold claim that Celera could do it faster and cheaper, and eventually, through President Clinton's intervention, the two efforts were melded into a cooperative venture. But closer inspection reveals that this was a very messy affair, which to some extent undermined confidence in public science and gave further impetus to science's corporate privatization (Mirowski 2011, 292–294).

Celera used the "WGS" method, which splinters the genome into very short fragments that can then be read and sequenced much faster than the alternative "hierarchical shotgun" method (also called "BAC walking"), which alternates between coarse-grained chromosome mapping and fine-grained sequencing. The latter method, preferred by the scientists already working on the HGP, is slower, more methodical and labor-intensive, but also far more accurate, especially for sequencing the large genomes found in mammals such as *homo sapiens*. In Philip Mirowski's account, "the WGS as practiced by Celera was quick and dirty just-in-time science, good enough for the undiscerning patent office, but not nearly of the quality that would underpin further genetic research" (Mirowski 2011, 293). Not surprisingly, the "cleanup work" had to be done by the HGP scientists, with many stretches of the human genome remaining in a draft state until fairly recently. Mirowski also notes that Venter's cheap and fast "just-in-time" approach was useful nonetheless—perhaps even critically necessary—for enticing "venture capitalist backers with a treasure chest of valuable intellectual property locked away in the human genome" (Mirowski 2011, 292). During the supposed collaboration, in fact, Celera "had access to the open archive of HGP sequence data in real time, while keeping its own findings proprietary and secret" (Mirowski 2011, 292).

However Celera's role in sequencing the human genome is ultimately judged, it is clear that Venter's practice of scientific research involves direct corporate sponsorship, the further development of faster and more productive computer technology, and privatized financial returns on investment capital. Venter's methods thus raise insistent questions about what kind of science he practices, specifically in his more recent efforts to synthesize genomes and to transplant them into existing species' cells and eventually to create synthetic life forms in which the "cells are completely controlled by a synthetic DNA chromosome" (Mirowski 2011, 127). The question here is not whether Venter's practice of synthetic biology reduces the inherent complexity of organic bio-molecular processes (a question also raised by the new "systems biology"). For Venter himself, genetic engineering has literally "evolved" into synthetic biology, and systems biology has "replaced" physiology (Mirowski 2011, 83). The question, rather, is whether what purports to be a scientific pursuit is not actually both a sophisticated return to and continuation of biotechnology, but now in a grand and attention-grabbing mode. In fact, at the outset of Venter's chapter (in his second book) on the "first synthetic Genome," he dwells briefly on that moment "in the 1970s when Paul Berg, Herbert Boyer, and Stanley Cohen began to cut and splice DNA" (Mirowski 2011, 83), and thus on the moment when Genentech, Big Pharma, and the biotech industries were born. The announcement of Venter's discoveries, as information event, thus reverberates with questions about the roles that Big Data and corporate funding will play in the development of science.

While Venter's corporate enterprise version of big data science may seem to have drawn us away from the information event, it actually points to the type of milieu necessary for information events to occur: The vast assemblage of computer technologies, heterogeneous institutions, and media practices in which huge information flows are produced and to some extent managed and directed, often by means of fairly simple "overcodings," as we see in the (self-promoting) importance of Venter himself as a titan of corporate science, which is extolled as model-free by the editor of *Wired Magazine*, itself a sleek advertising vehicle for the new Silicon Valley-style start-up capitalism. To be sure, popular memes and viral videos also assume and depend upon the same Internet assemblage and conglomerate of social media for their effects, just as much as the software viruses and malware intended to propagate exponentially to destructive or criminal effect. As information events, all are of interest because they reveal much about the Internet's structure and dynamics, as well as about the habits and practices of human users. But only rarely, it seems, do they produce singular and significant differences through new and unsuspected correlations of information.

Mandelbrot and Taleb's distinction between "mild and wild randomness" suggests one difference between types of information event (Mandelbrot and Taleb). Basically, viral videos and new Internet memes are rare but expected; however amusing or interesting, their short- and long-term effects are mainly significant in relation to the activities of a large, participatory Net culture, wherein these events not only visibly capture attention but also constitute a provocation to further participation through making and re-making. Consequently, we could say that we expect these events' generic recurrence. In this sense, a new viral video is a "mildly" random event. Venter's achievements are an interesting "in-between" example. With new access to Big Data and faster computational technology, we might expect the increased discovery and synthesis of new life forms, as well as a conceptual blurring of the difference. In contrast, the Flash Crash on Wall Street is an example *par excellence* of wild randomness. Like previous crashes, it was unanticipated, and like them, the direct consequences have been serious and long lasting.

III

Both unprecedented and unpredictable, the "Flash Crash" was a singular information event in the sense that it made new information available about the destabilizing effects of widespread high-frequency trading and how it dramatically increases an inherent instability already present in the current stock trading assemblage. The fact that this potentially destructive instability remains largely unaddressed further reveals something about financial capitalism's dominant role within the current configuration of political and economic power, both in the United States and globally. To appreciate the full significance of the Flash Crash, therefore, it must be situated within the context of a relatively recent shift in our understanding of the market economy and the ascendant role of finance capital more generally. This shift in turn points to new understandings of the vast information flows that unpredictably determine many of the essential features of ordinary life in the contemporary world. In the economy, generally speaking, the Internet and digital technology continue to provide widespread opportunities for innovation, but under current conditions it is uncertain whether they can function in ways other than according to the same "winner take all" logic that Barabasi demonstrates to be indigenous to the Internet's network structure.[4]

Investigations into "the Flash Crash" centered on the extensive use of computers for "HFT" and the risks of widespread "algorithmic trading." Algorithmic trading refers to the practice of using computers to buy and sell stocks automatically, according to sophisticated algorithms and without human intervention, though there is human monitoring. Basically these algorithms take data streams of recent market activity as input, and then, on the basis of complex probability functions, compute conditional actions—for example, if a specific price for a particular stock is found, buy or sell x shares. The simplest algorithms would search for the best price available within a specific time frame, but more complex algorithms incorporate time series analysis and machine learning for pattern recognition of price trends. The immediate effect of algorithmic trading was to greatly facilitate the process of buying and selling, which in turn considerably increased the volume of trading. HFT, a subset type of automated trading, seeks to take advantage of slight price differences by buying and selling in great volume in micro-bursts of activity lasting only a few milliseconds. Overall, a clear advantage of "algo-trading" is that it allows traders with the fastest and most efficient algorithms to trade in volumes and time intervals far beyond the capacity of human traders. Indeed, HFT traders make huge profits simply by constantly buying shares that drop slightly in price and selling those that rise slightly, over and over again. Though the profit on each exchange may only amount to a penny or less, when repeated thousands of times a day the result is often a significant monetary gain.

One acknowledged problem resulting from algo-trading (and especially HFT) is that during periods of intense trading the market can quickly lose liquidity—this happened in the Flash Crash—and the market has to be frozen temporarily in order to allow liquidity to re-enter and the markets to "re-normalize." More worrying is what appears to be the market's increased instability, and the greater likelihood of what in complex systems theory are called critical or "extreme events." These are events that occur unexpectedly in both natural and human systems that normally appear to be stable, or in a state of equilibrium. Sudden blackouts in the electrical power grid, hugely destructive earthquakes, landslides or tornados, or sudden stock market crashes are all examples of such extreme, often catastrophic events. Rather than assuming that the extreme event was triggered by some external and statistically unlikely constellation of events, a complex systems perspective shifts the focus to the internal dynamics of the system. No doubt it is rarely a question of simply one or the other, but complex systems, because they involve the interactions of multiple agents or sub-systems, are more easily pushed into chaotic, nonlinear regimes of behavior. The Flash Crash raised suspicions that it was precisely this kind of event, and thus indicative of a system instability. Indeed, inasmuch as it followed upon a series of market failures occurring over the past two decades—in 1987, 1998, and 2007–08—the likelihood that it symptomatically anticipated an impending major crash was widely felt. Despite these warnings of danger, however, almost no effective regulation has been imposed upon Wall Street. Presumably the markets are simply too lucrative for the rich and powerful, who have succeeded in systematically subverting legislative efforts to implement stabilizing measures.[5]

First introduced on the stock markets in 1999, High Frequency Trading had become a widespread practice by 2005. As an inevitable extension of computer technology to trading, it forms part of the larger history of how capitalism has been transformed by the new technologies it also develops. This history includes the formation of expanding markets and eventually an "integrated world capitalism" (as Félix Guattari called it in the 1980s), but most essential has been the creation of new forms of abstract value extracted from the flows of money itself.

A generally under-appreciated factor in capitalism's transformation was the large migration of highly trained physicists and mathematicians to Wall Street in the 1980s and 1990s. In *My Life as a Quant: Reflections on Physics and Finance*, Emanuel Derman suggests that this flow was spurred by the introduction of the Black-Scholes model of options pricing (a partial differential equation that involves complex computations). James Weatherall, in *The Physics of Wall Street: A Brief History of Predicting the Unpredictable*, narrates the stories of key physicists whose sophisticated modeling techniques have been applied to financial markets; however, though he touches on the parallel development of the complex financial products and instruments currently used in trading, he barely mentions algo-trading.[6]

The idea that computers could automate the buying and selling of stocks has probably been around since the first development of fast, stored-program computers. On the other hand, the evidence supports the assumption that profitable trading requires highly experienced and knowledgeable traders with an intuitive sense of the markets that may not be reducible to formal algorithms. Nevertheless, in the late 1980s, Doyne Farmer and Norman Packard, two physicists who had been among the first to explore nonlinear dynamical systems or "chaos theory", as it was popularly called, developed algorithms that learned to buy and sell effectively on the stock market. But to appreciate what they did, we must first consider the context of market theory.

For over a hundred years price fluctuations on the market have been considered a random variable; around 1900, in fact, the French mathematician Louis Bachelier showed that plotting market data as a time series of data points yielded the same results as a random walk, confirming the assumption that commodity prices rise and fall unpredictably. In the early 1960s, however, the mathematician Benoit Mandelbrot, who would soon become famous for his invention of fractal geometry and its mathematical applications, noticed that the fluctuations in cotton price and other commodities followed a power law distribution. In contrast to the re-assuring bell curve of traditional wisdom, which was assumed to reflect an overall balance or equilibrium around a specific range of values (the standard deviation), power law or fat-tailed distributions suggested a *sub rosa* "long memory" pattern in the markets. Such a pattern could not be explained by the increasingly influential Efficient Market Hypothesis (EMH), which gained ascendency in the 1960s.[7] In fact, the bell curve—or normal, Gaussian distribution—was a signature item in the assumptions of "the EMH," which basically reposes on the idea that the price of a market item or stock at a particular moment in time reflects all publicly available information as to its financial value. Essentially this means that the market is self-correcting (if stocks are underpriced or overpriced, for example), and that arbitrage and forms of risk-free trading are inherently limited to relatively short-term small gains or losses. In effect, the EMH supports a rational perspective and set of tools that can justify (and thus be used to sell) market investments on a large scale. Indeed, the core practice of building a large, diversified portfolio to insure against risk directly reflects the assumptions of the EMH.

In the 1990s, the supposed rationality of the EMH met with growing skepticism from several perspectives. First, the assumption that the human buyer or seller is always and everywhere a rational agent became impossible to maintain. (During the reign of the EMF those who did not appear to be knowledgeably rational were often referred to as "noise traders.") One solution would be to substitute the precise calculations of a machine for the trader's instincts and intuitions, and this is basically what we see with algo-trading. Second, growing evidence made it unlikely that the stock market can be adequately modeled as a system in equilibrium. There are, as Mandelbrot had discovered, not random but *systemic* deviations. Needless to add, this is something that trained physicists would not fail to notice, or at least would be on the lookout for. And third, the stock market itself was rapidly changing in both diversity and complexity, and therefore older models based on classic economic theory were increasingly viewed as probably inadequate. To cite a single example, from 1970 to 2004 the trading of financial derivatives such as "futures" grew from insignificant to over 270 trillion dollars outstanding in futures contracts worldwide.[8] Nevertheless, even when sharp-eyed economists and seasoned stock market experts saw inadequacies in the economic equilibrium model, they were understandably reluctant to give it up without a viable alternative, one with a conceptual clarity comparable to what modern economics had taken from nineteenth century physics. Inevitably, then, economists might have expected that physicists who had cut their teeth on chaos theory would one day come a-calling.

Founded in 1984 and explicitly devoted to the study of complex systems, the Santa Fe Institute was one place where the equilibrium model would fall under relentless critique and a complex systems theory alternative be proposed. In 1986, the Institute hosted a cross-disciplinary gathering of physicists and economists to discuss the proposition that the economy is best understood as a "complex evolving system." The model entailed features unfamiliar and even disturbing to classical (or neoclassical) economists: many complex variables, inherently incomplete information and essentially unpredictable, nonlinear effects. One invited economist, W. Brian Arthur, was already familiar with non-equilibrium models and proposed "spin glass [as] quite a good metaphor for the economy." Compared to an ordinary piece of ferromagnetic iron, spin glass is a confused or disordered magnet, with the spin orientations of its component atoms (and therefore their positive and negative feedback influences on each other) so variously distributed that its overall ground state was practically incalculable. Opposing the assumption of classical economic theory that the dynamic of supply and demand (which had seemed like common sense itself) always led to diminishing returns, Arthur argued for a perspective in which economic agents were always adapting new strategies that often led to positive feedback loops and hence "increasing returns." This meant that the market was necessarily a highly complex adaptive system with a multiplicity of equilibrium points that were always changing (Arthur).

Arthur illustrated his thesis with a familiar quandary: whether or not to go out to a popular bar or restaurant on a night when it might be too crowded. For Arthur, it was the El Faro Bar in Santa Fe, which on Thursday nights offered cheap drinks and Irish music. He had observed that unless attendance is below sixty percent of capacity, it will be too hot and noisy, and difficult to get a good table. Arthur then demonstrates that there is no deductively rational solution to the question: Shall I go this Thursday night? (On a given night, we should assume, N people will decide independently to go.) Expectational models are of no help, he reasoned, since if all potential attendees use the same approach, all will lose. For example, if all believe that *few* will go, *all* will go; if all believe *most* will go, *nobody* will go, and so on. So instead, Arthur considers a dynamic model that reflects how attendance might vary over time. Let's assume, he reasoned, that we have the exact attendance numbers for the past fourteen weeks, and based on them we make a collection of hypotheses or predictors about next week's number, such as: The same as last week's number, the inverse of last week's number, the average of the last four weeks, the trend based on the previous eight weeks, the same as two weeks ago (a two-period detector), or the same as five weeks ago (five-period detector), etc. Let's now assume that each agent possesses a set of such predictors that are checked and updated each week. The agent will decide to go or stay home according to the currently most accurate predictor in his or her set, which becomes the *active predictor*. It follows that the set of active hypotheses or predictors acted upon by the agents *will determine* the attendance; however, the attendance history *determines* the set of active hypotheses. Borrowing the term from John Holland, he calls the set of active predictors "an ecology."

Arthur then set up a computer simulation of his agent-modeling system. First, he created an "alphabet soup" of several dozen predictors, giving each agent (in a total of 100) a random selection. (Note that the agents will not continue to use predictors that don't work.) He then runs the simulation, tracking attendance for 100 nights on a simple graph. The results show that cycle-detector predictors are present but don't work, and are quickly "arbitraged" away. Mean attendance always converges to 60, and "on average 40 percent are forecasting above

60, 60 percent below 60." For Arthur, "this emergent ecology is almost organic in nature," for the simple reason that "while the population of active predictors splits into this 60/40 average ratio, it keeps changing its membership forever." The contours of the forest don't change that much, he analogizes, but the individual trees are changing all the time. Perhaps we can put it more clearly: in order to maintain variations within the 60/40 boundaries, the most effective set of predictors is always changing, precisely because all the other sets of predictors will change or evolve in relation to it in the next time step. That is, as soon as one hypothesis approaches highly predictive status, the others will mimic it and "herding" will occur. The very predictor that got you a perfect evening at the El Faro Bar will probably make it impossibly overcrowded next week. Overall, the simulation provides a better-than-most model for how the stock markets actually work, and why they are so hard "to beat" consistently.

This kind of computer simulation became a signature practice at the Santa Fe Institute. Both Farmer and Packer were residents during this formative period, and this is where they re-enter our story. As physicists experienced at tracking the behavior of "strange attractors" in nonlinear deterministic (i.e., "chaotic") systems, they believed that a pattern could be extracted from the time series of past market data that would allow them to predict, for a very short window of time, the likelihood that particular stock prices would rise or fall. Equally important, they were also familiar with new and creative approaches to computation. Consequently, rather than hand-coding algorithms that could detect "anomalies" or *systematic* deviations in the market they could then take advantage of, they invented a different approach: They evolved a set of genetic algorithms in a computer simulation in which traders are modeled as a population of software agents. Each agent deploys a particular strategy (instantiated in an algorithm) whose success is rewarded with replication and failure punished with death. Using this method, they evolved a highly adaptive, robustly competitive collection of agents that could actually mimic successful traders. Farmer and Packard found that if their evolved algorithms agreed on whether a particular price was about to rise or fall, the odds of a successful prediction fell within a reasonable margin of error, and could be used to make money on the markets, which they did.

Unfortunately, we lack a full critical history of computer-automated trading on the various world stock markets from the early 1990s (when Farmer and Packard founded The Prediction Company) to the dominating presence of HFT in the years leading up to the Flash Crash. Many of the technical details and specific trading practices are carefully guarded secrets, which is not surprising for an industry that has been able to avoid serious regulation. The accounts available are often written from narrow, hardly impartial points of view, by former traders with an agenda, or by hacks offering simplistic formulas for successful trading. One exception is Haim Bodek's *The Problem of HFT*, which pinpoints the most serious consequence of widespread HFT:

> HFT was all about manipulating the rules of the game. As HFT's dominated the electronic marketplace, the national market itself evolved into a low-latency traders' marketplace. [Here "low-latency" refers to the extremely short time interval of the actual trade.] This new marketplace was characterized by extreme asymmetries that adversely impacted the diversity of algorithmic trading strategies that could successfully operate in the marketplace. In the electronic marketplace meticulously designed to accommodate HFT strategies, HFT soon became the only game worth playing.
>
> (Bodek 2012, 6)

In ecosystem terms, where there used to be a diversity of markets and a variety of sustainable approaches to trading, there is now the domination of an HFT monoculture.[9]

Significant evidence for a fundamental instability in the stock exchange and financial markets began to emerge after the near financial meltdown of 2007–2008, and especially after the Flash Crash. The official Securities and Exchange Commission (SEC) investigations into the Flash Crash directly implicated algo-trading. A number of scientists thought that extensive algo-trading and the use of sophisticated algorithms on Wall Street had made the stock markets prone to turbulence and new instabilities. David Cliff, one of the U.K.'s most eminent computer scientists, notes in the *High Frequency Trading Review* that "global financial markets are now essentially a single, planetary-wide, ultra-large scale complex IT system," with "failure modes" that, like the butterfly effect, ". . . could ripple out over the entire system and cause big problems," adding that the Flash Crash "justified our concern." A team of computer scientists led by Neil Johnson, a physicist at the University of Miami, published the results of research analyzing "a set of 18,520 ultrafast black swan events that we have uncovered in stock-price movements between 2006 and 2011." These "ultrafast fractures," as Johnson describes them, indicate "the slow 'breaking' of the global financial system post-2006." While scientific evidence for such claims continues to accumulate, theoretically compelling accounts of this new instability in the stock markets also emerged. In particular, the French physicist Didier Sornette makes the case from a complex systems perspective in *Why Stock Markets Crash: Critical Events in Complex Financial Systems*, published before the Flash Crash in 2004. Subsequently, and most specifically in "Crashes and High Frequency Trading," Sornette extended his analysis to the Flash Crash, which he thinks confirms his argument that the stock market is a self-organizing critical system that cannot achieve equilibrium states: It is always subject to small perturbations that can easily cascade and ramify through the system, producing extreme events such as market crashes. "Re-normalization," he argues, is an impossible fiction. And yet, so too seems the prospect of serious regulation.

Unexpectedly, Sornette also discovered what may prove to be a means of detecting the imminence of an extreme event in complex systems, and thus in markets before another crash occurs. In 2009, he announced his discovery of what he calls "dragon-kings," which refer "to the existence of transient organization into extreme events that are statistically different from the rest of their smaller siblings" [specifically, they don't fall into the same power law distribution], ". . . and [thus] exhibit a degree of predictability." If the approach of a dragon-king can be detected, a crash can possibly be averted. To pursue this possibility, Sornette has joined efforts with several other physicists, building specifically on Hugo Cavalcante and Daniel Gauthier's work on coupled electronic oscillators whose alternating patterns of synchronicity and chaotic asynchrony suggest a possible way to steer the system away from a dragon-event.[10]

Meanwhile, HFT has been more widely deployed, with experts estimating that it now accounts for as much as half of the trading on U.S. markets.[11] HFT has also gotten much faster, with algorithms literally making "millions of moment-to-moment calls in the global markets", and making markets "wilder". During Wall Street trading on August 1, 2012, a piece of runaway code in Knight Capital's HFT software went out of control and could not be de-activated for 45 minutes, literally costing Knight $10 million dollars a minute. HFT has also become more opaque: "One set of signals the programs have to weigh are countless trade orders other algorithms send out and then quickly rescind." Are these signals strategic feints, market probes, the testing of new algorithms, or "fake trades . . . aimed purely at gobbling up bandwidth to slow down competitors?" All are possible, even simultaneously. One thing seems clear: the feasibility of effective regulation of HFT will depend upon the capacity to monitor market activity, but that too is a moving target. A first attempt by the SEC, a program called "Midas" that analyzes market data daily, turned out to be far too limited, offering no data on the "dark pools" and who is responsible for many trades; even the data it does record is not available for analysis until the following day.

IV

Thus far, the "Flash Crash" and the information events it has generated have been folded into a simple narrative: HFT machines and the secret algorithms that run on them have made the stock markets much more unstable, putting at higher risk the 401(k), retirement accounts, even the savings accounts of ordinary working people and ultimately the global financial system. Scientists who find these markets to be instantiations of fascinating complex systems are beginning to ring the alarm bells, and to seek ways to anticipate and thereby ward off impending financial catastrophe. Meanwhile, government regulation has proven to be politically impossible, with no reason to believe it will ever be adequate. In *Predator Nation*, Charles Ferguson argues that Wall Street and the big banks have effectively captured the relevant parts of the Federal government, thus insuring the continuation of their profitable practices and possibly another bailout if a crash should occur.

What makes this general narrative too simple, however, is the assumption that regulation or reform is a set of constraints that can and at some point will be imposed from outside the system, restraining the system to manageable, "safe" behavior. But it is possible that the contemporary market system—or at least stock market trading—is inherently not only risky but fundamentally resistant to stability and controllability. As Deleuze and Guattari argued decades ago, the logic of capitalism tends toward an absolute deterritorialization of flows by always displacing immanent or internal limits. In this perspective, HFT can be seen as constituting the leading edge of this deterritorialization, as ultra-fast trading and the algo-wars come to define a new machinic socius, and the site of an escalating arms race always pushing toward the limits of exchange and therefore toward its own self-destruction. Thus far, timely interventions by the State have been able to displace the costs to other sectors throughout the economy. In order to restore or shore up market liquidity, the Bush and Obama administrations have pumped trillions of dollars into the economy (including the AIG bailout). However, unlike the "cascade failure" that followed the collapse of Lehman Brothers in 2008, a similar catastrophe in the stock markets could be over in a matter of minutes and would be virtually impossible to reconstruct.

Given that HFT produces a torrent of flows that can't be "coded" by the algorithms that produce them or "overcoded" by the State, Deleuze and Guattari's analysis of capitalism in terms of flow, coding and the two forms of money may suggest a scaffolding for considering not only HFT but also the information events it produces. In conclusion I sketch the beginning steps of this analysis and suggest where it might go.

In lectures given at the Université de Paris at Vincennes in 1971, Deleuze defines the multiple flows on the "socius"—by which he means "a particular social instance which plays the role of a full body" for a particular society.[12] On this full body all kinds of flows flow and are interrupted, poles of entry and exit arise, and codes are developed that structure the various flows. Codes are not external to flows but the means by which they are inscribed or recorded on the socius. In so-called primitive societies, for example, rules of alliance provide codes that regulate the flows of women among them; thus "taboos represent a blockage of the flows of possible marriages." According to Deleuze, John Maynard Keynes developed the "first great theory of flows" and introduced desire into the theory of money.[13] But Deleuze's most essential point is that we cannot understand capitalism as an economy of exchange. Rather, there are series and different layers of coded flows that are differentiated according to their relative power. They operate by a calculus rather than simple addition and subtraction, a difference we see in the difference between compound interest returned on an investment and receiving a salary.

Let us consider a specific instance. Workers flow into a factory, where their labor transforms various materials into goods than then flow out of the factory, as do the workers at the end of the working day. The goods flow onto the market, where they are exchanged and monetary flows come back to the sellers and ultimately to the owner(s) of the factory, some of which is syphoned into the workers' salaries. A "coherent accounting system" (i.e., a coding) regulates these monetary flows. However, the structure and regulation of these flows cannot account for the existence of the factory itself, which involves another set of flows and a "differential apparatus" capable of producing "differentials of flow power." Here Deleuze refers specifically to the power of "financing" or financialization, the operations of which require that there are two kinds of money: the first form is simply money as the medium of revenue and payment in circuits of exchange; but the second is the money of the financing structure of capital itself. It is money as credit, and the power to create debt; ultimately it is the power of banks and financial institutions to create and destroy money itself, as was revealed in the finance debacle of 2007–2008.

Commenting on this aspect of Deleuze's theory, the Italian philosopher Maurizio Lazzarato notes that the "banking system, credit money, and finance are able to conceal this [difference in the two forms of money] by converting one flow into another" (Lazzarato 2012). The ways in which the flows of money as credit and finance "cover," control and regulate the flows of money as payment in advanced capitalism are indeed layered and complex. A crediting agency like a bank can "owe itself" the sum of a particular credit advanced, for example, but there are also many forms of leveraging available to it, with the State serving as the ultimate guarantee. In the terms of flow and code, a financial crisis is a deep rupture or break that suddenly opens up across monetary and credit flows, and threatens to stop the flows, in the specific sense that the code unravels and no one can determine the value of a particular stock, security or derivative at that moment. There were many such moments following the Lehman Brothers' failure and during the Flash Crash, moments when bankers and traders could not believe what their eyes were seeing. These moments of rupture must be sealed over and repaired by the State with an immediate infusion of capital and "guarantees" to prevent the entire economy from weakening and even collapsing. Needless to add, these instances are strongly marked or registered by information events, which can propagate both powerful affects and effects on the economy at large.[14]

Information flows, like monetary flows, are of course also coded in multiple ways and layers. Among the torrent of memes and videos always flowing on the Net, a catchy meme or viral video focuses attention on and greatly increases a segment of this flow. In each case, what defines an information event is the significant impact made on these flows by a particular new arrangement of the coding of images. At the molecular level, DNA also constantly flows from one organism to another, most obviously in sexual reproduction. In a specifically Deleuzian sense, Craig Venter has "cut" into this flow, diverting it through a machine that "reads" the DNA code and compares it to known segments; if it is a new or unknown configuration of code that can't be identified, it is assumed that it may be that of an unknown, newly discovered organism. This discovery and "flagging" of a new coding of DNA is the basis of the information event registered in the flows of scientific papers, news and commentary at higher layers. An information event thus marks a particular change in the coding of flows that has impacted the assumed regularity of flows on the socius. It operates as a differentiator of flows, a singularity in which the difference that makes a difference is signaled at higher, more generalized levels of flow, thus producing a duration of higher visibility within the general flow.

Notes

1. In *The Road Ahead* (1996), Bill Gates coined the phrase "frictionless capitalism," believing (correctly) that the new Internet would open new possibilities for capitalism. For critical discussion see Jens Schroter, "The Internet and 'Frictionless Capitalism,'" available at http://triple-c.at/index.php/tripleC/article/view/425/388.
2. For a thorough discussion of this transformation, see Bruce Schneier's *Data and Goliath*.
3. Venter writes: "This is now the era of digital biology, in which proteins and other interacting molecules in the cell can be viewed as its hardware and the information encoded in its DNA as its software . . ." (47)
4. Specifically, small innovative companies formed on the basis of a technological innovation are soon purchased and absorbed by giants of the industry. See Andrew Keen's *The Internet Is Not the Answer* for details.
5. In what seems to be the most recent of an ongoing series of examples, a secret provision in the 2015 Federal budget bill (written by Citicorp Bank and inserted by Republicans) stripped away certain provisions added to the Dodd-Frank Bill that prevented commercial banks from using the money in customer savings accounts for high risk trading. This is also a clear example of the now common practice of making ordinary citizens bear the financial risk of cavalier, irresponsible trading by large banks.
6. James Weatherall, *The Physics of Wall Street: A Brief History of Predicting the* Unpredictable. One of the most important and interesting stories is that of Edward Thorpe, a PhD in mathematics who was one of the first to use math to develop a strategy to win at gambling (specifically "Black Jack"). It is not incidental that his mentor was Claude Shannon, the inventor of information theory.
7. The Efficient Market Hypothesis is generally attributed to Eugene Fama, who "argued that 'sophisticated traders' . . . could be relied upon to attack any nonrandom patterns in the market and, in the process of making money off them, make them go away." Quoted by Justin Fox, *The Myth of the Rational Market*, 96–97.
8. Reported by Donald Mackenzie in *An Engine, Not a Camera: How Financial Models Shape Markets*.
9. *In Dark Pools: High-Speed Traders, AI Bandits, and the Threat to the Global Financial System*, the investigative journalist Scoot Patterson argues that in what started as "dark pools", or private markets operated mostly by big banks, the hottest HFT programmers soon so dominated with opaque, AI-influenced algorithms that HFT quickly spread and soon "the entire market had descended into one vast pool of darkness" (9).
10. See "Predictability and suppression of extreme events in a chaotic system," authored by Calvalcante, Sornette, Ott, and Gauthier, in *Physical Review Letters* (Nov. 8, 2013), https://physics.aps.org/featured-article-pdf/10.1103/PhysRevLett.111.198701. Sorentte's notion of "dragon-king" has been widely discussed.
11. All quotations in this paragraph are taken from Nick Bauman's article in *Mother Jones*,"Too Fast to Fail: Is High-Speed Trading the Next Wall Sreet Disaster?" (January/February 2013), available at www.motherjones.com/politics/2013/02/high-frequency-trading-danger-risk-wall-street
12. See in particular the lectures on 16/11/1971 and 14/12/1971, available in English translation at www.webdeleuze.com/php/texte.php?cle=116&groupe=Anti%20Oedipe%20et%20Mille%20Plateaux&langue=2 and www.webdeleuze.com/php/texte.php?cle=119&groupe=Anti%20Oedipe%20et%20Mille%20Plateaux&langue=2
13. See *Anti-Oedipus*, 230. In his lectures, Deleuze draws upon Daniel Antier's *L'Etude des flux et des stocks* to develop a more detailed analysis of flows in political economy and capitalism specifically.
14. In Robert Harris's techno-thriller *The Fear Index* (2012) we see an extraordinary example of how affects generated by public events can be data-mined and fed as input into a very advanced form of AI trading machine with autonomous learning capability.

References

Anderson, Chris. "The End of Theory: The Data Deluge Makes the Scientific Method Obsolete." *Wired Magazine:* 16:07, http://archive.wired.com/science/discoveries/magazine/16–07/pb_theory

Antier, Daniel. 1957. *L'étude Des Flux Et Des Stocks*. Observation Économique. Paris: SEDES.

Arthur, W. Brian. "Inductive Reasoning and Bounded Rationality (The El Farol Problem)." http://tuvalu. santafe.edu/~wbarthur/Papers/El_Farol.pdf

Barabási, Albert-László. 2002. *Linked: The New Science of Networks*. Cambridge, MA: Perseus Pub.

Bateson, Gregory. 2000. *Steps to an Ecology of Mind*. Chicago, IL: University of Chicago Press.

Bauman, Nick. 2013. "Too Fast to Fail: Is High-Speed Trading the Next Wall Street Disaster?" *Mother Jones* (January/February), http://motherjones.com/politics/2013/02/high-frequency-trading-danger-risk-wall-street

Bodek, Haim. 2012. *The Problem of HFT*. Lexington, KY: Decimus Capital Markets.

de S. Cavalcante, Hugo L. D., Marcos Oriá, Didier Sornette, Edward Ott, and Daniel J. Gauthier. 2013. "Predictability and Suppression of Extreme Events in a Chaotic System." *Physical Review Letters* 111 (19): 198701.

Deleuze, Gilles. "Capitalism, Flows, the Decoding of Flows, Capitalism and Schizophrenia, Psychoanalysis, Spinoza." http://webdeleuze.com/php/texte.php?cle=116&groupe=Anti%20Oedipe%20et%20Mille%20Plateaux&langue=2.Deleuze, Gilles. "Cours Vincennes: The Nature of Flows." http://webdeleuze.com/php/texte.php?cle=119&groupe=Anti%20Oedipe%20et%20Mille%20Plateaux&langue=2.

Deleuze, Gilles, and Félix Guattari. 1983. *Anti-Oedipus: Capitalism and Schizophrenia*. Minneapolis, MN: University of Minnesota Press.

Derman, Emanuel. 2004. *My Life as a Quant: Reflections on Physics and Finance*. Hoboken, NJ: Wiley.

Ferguson, Charles H. 2012. *Predator Nation: Corporate Criminals, Political Corruption, and the Hijacking of America*. 1st ed. New York: Crown Business.

Fox, Justin. 2009. *The Myth of the Rational Market: A History of Risk, Reward, and Delusion on Wall Street*. 1st ed. New York: Harper Business.

Gates, Bill, Nathan Myhrvold, and Peter Rinearson. 1996. *The Road Ahead*. New York: Penguin Books.

Keen, Andrew. 2015. *The Internet Is Not the Answer*. New York: Atlantic Monthly Press.

Lazzarato, Maurizio. 2012. *The Making of the Indebted Man: An Essay on the Neoliberal Condition*. Los Angeles, CA: Semiotext(e).

MacKenzie, Donald A. 2006. *An Engine, Not a Camera: How Financial Models Shape Markets*. Inside Technology. Cambridge, MA: MIT Press.

Mandelbrot, Benoit, and Nassim Nicholas Taleb. "Focusing on Exceptions that Prove the Rule," http://ft.com/cms/s/2/5372968a-ba82–11da-980d-0000779e2340.html.

Mayer-Schönberger, Viktor, and Kenneth Cukier. 2013. *Big Data: A Revolution That Will Transform How We Live, Work, and Think*. Boston, MA: Eamon Dolan/Houghton Mifflin Harcourt.

Mirowski, Philip. 2011. *Science-Mart: Privatizing American Science*. Cambridge, MA: Harvard University Press.

Nahon, Karine, and Jeff Hemsley. 2013. *Going Viral*. Cambridge, UK: Polity.

Patterson, Scott. 2012. *Dark Pools: High-Speed Traders, Ai Bandits, and the Threat to the Global Financial System*. 1st ed. New York: Crown Business.

Schneier, Bruce. 2015. *Data and Goliath: The Hidden Battles to Collect Your Data and Control Your World*. New York: W.W. Norton & Company.

Schroter, Jens. "The Internet and 'Frictionless Capitalism'" http://triple-c.at/index.php/tripleC/article/view/425/388.

Shifman, Limor. 2014. *Memes in Digital Culture*. Cambridge, MA: The MIT Press.

Sornette, Didier. 2003. *Why Stock Markets Crash: Critical Events in Complex Financial Systems*. Princeton, NJ: Princeton University Press.

Venter, J. Craig. 2007. *A Life Decoded: My Genome, My Life*. New York: Viking.

Venter, J. Craig. 2013. *Life at the Speed of Light: From the Double Helix to the Dawn of Digital Life*. New York, New York: Viking.

Weatherall, James Owen. 2013. *The Physics of Wall Street: A Brief History of Predicting the Unpredictable*. Boston, MA: Houghton Mifflin Harcourt.

INDEX